# TURKEY
# GUIDE

## YOUR PASSPORT TO GREAT TRAVEL!

### OPEN ROAD TRAVEL GUIDES SHOW YOU
### HOW TO BE A TRAVELER – NOT A TOURIST!

*Whether you're going abroad or planning a trip in the United States, take Open Road along on your journey. Our books have been praised by **Travel & Leisure, The Los Angeles Times, Newsday, Booklist, US News & World Report, Endless Vacation, American Bookseller, Coast to Coast,** and many other magazines and newspapers!*

*Don't just see the world – experience it with Open Road!*

## ABOUT THE AUTHORS

Adam Peck and Manja Sachet are American travel writers living in Istanbul, Turkey.

## BE A TRAVELER, NOT A TOURIST - WITH OPEN ROAD PUBLISHING!

Open Road Publishing has guide books to exciting, fun destinations on four continents. As veteran travelers, our goal is to bring you the best travel guides available anywhere!

No small task, but here's what we offer:

• All Open Road travel guides are written by authors with a distinct, opinionated point of view – not some sterile committee or team of writers. Our authors are experts in the areas covered and are polished writers.

• Our guides are geared to people who want to make their own travel choices. We'll show you how to discover the real destination – not just see some place from a tour bus window.

• We're strong on the basics, but we also provide terrific choices for those looking to get off the beaten path and *experience* the country or city – not just *see* it or pass through it.

• We give you the best, but we also tell you about the worst and what to avoid. Nobody should waste their time and money on their hard-earned vacation because of bad or inadequate travel advice.

• Our guides assume nothing. We tell you everything you need to know to have the trip of a lifetime – presented in a fun, literate, no-nonsense style.

• And, above all, we welcome your input, ideas, and suggestions to help us put out the best travel guides possible.

# TURKEY

# GUIDE

## YOUR PASSPORT TO GREAT TRAVEL!

### ADAM PECK & MANJA SACHET

# OPEN ROAD PUBLISHING

*1st Edition*

*To our parents, and to Penelope.*

Text Copyright ©1997 by Adam Peck & Manja Sachet
Maps Copyright ©1997 by Open Road Publishing
- All Rights Reserved -

Library of Congress Catalog Card No. 96-72602
ISBN 1-883323-48-7

Front and back cover photos by Atlas Magazine, Istanbul, Turkey. Maps by Rob Perry.

# TABLE OF CONTENTS

# CONTENTS

# CONTENTS

# CONTENTS

# CONTENTS

## SIDEBARS

# MAPS

# ACKNOWLEDGMENTS

We recall standing at the Pyramids years ago, a guide book in hand, and feeling helpless in the face of such a long and unfamiliar history. The guide book got us there all right, but did very little to put the Cheops and Chephren in context, did very little to say who the pharoahs were or why the pyramids were built. Open Road books hunt up excellent accommodations, restaurants, and background information as a matter of course; our personal inspiration for writing this book has been to give the visitor perspective on Turkey's ancient wonders, to make sense of a long and complicated history. To the extent we've succeeded it's a result of research and, more importantly, lots of help.

First and foremost we want to thank Alice Johnson, without whom none of this would have happened. The next link in our long chain of gratitude is our publisher, Jonathan Stein, who must not have called our references. Many thanks to Leyla Özhan at the New York consulate, who opened many doors for us, and to the staffs of the tourism information offices throughout the country - particularly Amasra, Ankara, Istanbul, and Trabzon.

Thanks to our deputy researchers Alice and Jean, Bill and Julie, Bob and Robin, Veronique and Ben, and Dustin Solberg. Thanks to Professor Christian Jeppeson (who in a single aside threw light on traveling in Turkey. When a truck began suddenly dumping a ton and a half of gravel at his archaeological dig site he groaned and rolled his eyes. "Is that bad?" we asked. "Not bad," he said, "Unexpected.") Thanks to Enver for letting us in on their respective projects. Special thanks to Istanbul's Kranzler Library, to Ertürk Zobi with Tursem, Aydın with Argeus in Ürgüp, and Ufuk Güven with Bougainvillea Travel in Kaş. Thanks go out to Savaş in Terme, Adem Tahtici in Sinop, Can Şengul in Kalkan and Istanbul, Süha Ersöz at the Esbelli Evi in Ürgüp, the incredibly kind and ridiculous Altan Karabelen in Bodrum, the Hotel Guide, and Doğan Senocak for helping Adam pass the Epstein Bar. Repeated thanks to Saim at Imperial Tourism in Istanbul.

Thanks to the many hotel and restaurant managers who made time to field our questions and showed us great hospitality. Thanks to Jessie for the software donation (we hope it was tax deductible), Martha for the research tools, Dominic for the camera replacement, SuperOnline for the use and abuse of facilities, and all the friends and family who wrote letters and email and sent or brought care packages.

Finally, thanks to Katie, Sinan and the Karate Kid, Sunaliza.

# 1. INTRODUCTION

People who choose to visit Turkey usually have three things in mind: the desire to witness firsthand a religion and a culture that are unfamiliar, to see one of the world's great legacies of ruins and natural wonders, and to relax at some of the planet's most breathtaking beaches.

This guide is dedicated to achieving these aims. We have sifted through the country's hotels and restaurants with a single criteria: *do we feel lucky to be there?* In most of the places we list the answer is an emphatic "yes." Dining in Turkey is a distinct and often unexpected pleasure wherever you go, but we have broken bread at lokantas and cafes from Trabzon to Marmaris to root out the best.

As for accommodations, Turkey has a collection of luxurious hotels and sophisticated bed and breakfasts that go for much less. In these pages you have your pick of bungalows in orange groves, rooms carved out of stone, restored Ottoman mansions, and squat, whitewashed houses crouched above the Aegean. Even within Istanbul you'll find artful, thoughtfully designed accommodations in many price ranges: you can get a decent double for $17 or, yes, $5,000 – we lead you there, too.

With gorgeous little inns as an incentive to keep the pace "yavaş, yavaş" (slow, slow), we guide you to the country's ruins, great and small, popular and remote. Ruins are interesting for their own sake, but we have plumbed myths and history to help you understand who lived here and what these stone ghost towns once were. We understand the temptation to speed through Turkey and visit the marquee ruins, but we firmly advise finding time to stay put awhile. You won't miss anything; to those who are aghast that you didn't see Troy, you'll be as aghast that they missed Arycanda, Artemesia, or the Island of the Amazons. Two extra days at Cappadoccia are worth much more than two hours at Pergamon.

This book, the result of thousands of years of research and scholarship, only scratches the surface. On your way between any great historic sites you can take a left, then a right and find a tomb or a fortress that no one has written about, that few people even know the name of. We've tried to distill the country's best, but with any luck you'll leave here in respectful disagreement. Turkey is a place to be explored.

# 2. EXCITING TURKEY!
# - OVERVIEW

If you are ever going to visit Turkey, do it now. There are a few heavily-touristed places where the golden age has already passed (Marmaris, Kusadasi, and Kemer, for instance), but the vast majority of the country is a delight. There are several reasons why.

**The people:** Turkey has a solid standard of living and a relatively robust economy. Turks tend to be cautious around travelers, but only out of politeness. If you smile or, better yet, attempt some small talk, most will open up in an eager gush of Turkish. Whether in cities or towns, people tend to be honest, friendly, and hard-working. There is a strong ethic of smothering the guest with kindness, and it can be unsettling to most of us. Throughout the country, your worst enemy will be your own conditioned wariness.

**The sites:** The most impressive ruins in ancient Greece aren't in Greece, they're in Turkey. And they're only a small part of the historic wealth scattered throughout the country. Lest you think it unfair that the Turks are in possession of Hellenistic ruins, consider that in the 10th century B.C. the Greeks seized lands that included the walled Hittite cities in the interior and the legendary site of Troy at the mouth of the Hellespont. The country is an improbable thicket of mountaintop fortresses from the Byzantine and Ottoman empires, of temples and citadels built by peoples and empires you've likely never heard of. The historic is intertwined with natural beauty, whether the striking blue-green water of the Mediterranean or the subterranean artistry of Cappadocia.

**The alternatives**: Cruise the Turkish coast in a twin-masted 60-foot gulet, scale mountainsides to investigate Lycian rock-cut tombs, discover churches carved out of the stone walls of Ihlara Valley, ski at Bolu, go rafting on the Köprüçay or Çoruh, copy out as-yet-undeciphered Lycian carvings, go birding, lay on the beach, pub crawl, study architecture, and visit the living flames of the Chimaera.

**The cost:** Turkey is inexpensive by American – let alone European – standards. Internal plane flights between any two points in western Turkey cost no more than $80. An overnight, no smoking bus from one side of the country to the other costs about $25. Many of the country's best hotels – even in notoriously expensive Istanbul – are in the $80 range.

---

### A WEALTH OF HISTORY

*Turkey's unique appeal is its historic wealth. Aristotle taught here. Alexander fought here. Julius Caesar left here saying "Veni, Vidi, Vici." Native sons Homer and Herodotus gave us accounts of the Trojan War and the Persian invasions of Greece. Turkey's history is thick, layer upon layer, a sticky, delectable, impossible thing, like a 70 foot tall baklava.*

---

## FOOD, DRINK, & VICES

Turkish cuisine is a delicious melange. Mediterranean staples such as tomatoes, garlic, onions and olive oil are combined with recipes that the Turks transported west in their migration. Turkish cooking has a vitality and richness that gives away its long history of borrowing and discarding. Successive empires and kingdoms have done away with the expendable and adopted the best of what had gone before; the result is a collection of insanely complicated dishes with rich, unexpected flavors.

A few of the staples of a Turkish kitchen that you will want to try are, of course, the *köfte* (meatballs) and *şiş kebaps*. Some of the more refined delicacies are *cacık* (cold soup with yogurt and cucumbers), *mantı* (yogurt and ravioli), *su börek* (a cheese pastry), and *güveç* (a succulent meat stew boiled in an earthenware pot and sealed with bread). Meals are taken slow, with great thick slices of fresh bread and an emphasis on *meze* – Turkish appetizers – often followed by more meze. In larger hotels, buffet half-board accommodations will confront you with a massive collection of mezes, challenging you to leave enough room for a token entree.

The Ottoman elite were great fans of these vices: Tobacco, Coffee, Wine, Opium, & Rakı. Although some holy men condemned coffee, opium, tobacco and wine as the "four pillars of the tent of debauchery," most enlightened Turks chose to take an alternative view; for them these were instead the "four cushions on the sofa of pleasure." Opium's popularity (within Turkey, anyway) has gone into serious decline, but *rakı*, a late bloomer, has stepped in manfully to take its place. Similar to Greek ouzo and other liquors in the Middle East, rakı is a licorice-flavored alcohol distilled from raisins, then distilled a second time with aniseed.

## TURKEY'S REGIONS

The bulk of Turkey is extremely safe and offers excellent traveling. That is not, unfortunately, the case in the southeast, as explained in Chapter 4, *Land & People*. As this guide goes to press there is no sign of relaxation of hostilities in the southeast and we echo the U.S. State Department's warning against traveling in that hazardous region. This guide offers a blueprint for the safest possible trip through the southeast, but only to keep you on the straight and narrow if you choose to throw caution to the wind.

This guide is broken down by regions. We start with the premise that you'll want to settle in for a few days at a time in various areas of the country and detail a route through the interior to Ankara and Cappadoccia, then joining a loop clockwise around the Mediterranean and Aegean to Troy. The Black Sea is covered from west to east, leaving you the options of a Black Sea ferry, plane, or bus back toward Istanbul, and even an extended trip into the interior.

### İstanbul

Turkey begins with İstanbul, a jarring and beautiful city where you're likely to disembark. İstanbul is epic, a historic place straddling Asia and Europe, Islam and Christianity, past and present. Reminders of Byzantine and Ottoman Empires that ruled here abound, mixed liberally with a brash, vital living city of 12 million. You can lose yourself in the warrens of the spice bazaar, take ferry cruises along the Bosphorous, see jazz shows in Taksim till dawn, and never even enter the magnificent museums, palaces, and mosques that have given the city its renown.

İstanbul is unmanageably large, with the irritating habit of wandering off the edge of your map. Fortunately, the visitor can concentrate on understanding a few fascinating areas such as **Sultanahmet** and **Taksim's Istiklal Caddesi**.

### The Interior

Turkey's interior is home to the oldest remnants of civilization, sites such as **Çatal Huyuk** near Konya, dating back to 7,500 B.C., and the sprawling city of **Hattuşas** northeast of Ankara – a relative youngster abandoned in 1200 B.C. These cities, and others in the interior such as **Gordion**, are mute testimony to surprisingly sophisticated cultures that thrived near the headwaters of the Euphrates in those dim years before Western Civ. lessons begin. Another of Turkey's most compelling places is **Cappadoccia**, a plain of soft, undulating stone that conceals rock-cut churches, houses, and even entire multi-level cities.

The interior is served by **Ankara**, Turkey's capital. This is a surprisingly pretty city on the Anatolian Plateau, convenient to the oldest ruins

in Turkey and a historic city in its own right. The city's fortress lends it a picturesque quality, while shrewd urban planning renders the town one of Turkey's most appealing. Other cities include the cluster at Cappadoccia, including **Ürgüp** and **Göreme**, and **Konya**, home of the whirling dervishes. Distances are long, but bus service is fairly comprehensive between most points, and roads are decent.

**The Mediterranean**

The Turkish coast is immense, wrapping entirely around the country and descending into four different seas: the Black, the Marmara, the Aegean, and the Mediterranean. You will find Hellenistic ruins at even the most remote locations along this huge coastline, but the character of the ruins and various towns vary widely (see Chapter 5, *Planning Your Trip*).

The Mediterranean Coast east of Antalya is interesting, but less alluring than the region from Antalya west. **Antalya**, one of Turkey's major cities, has a top-notch cluster of appealing hotels and pensions and serves as a base for visits to several of Turkey's great Hellenistic ruins. A batch of holiday villages are located just west of Antalya, but beyond them the coast relaxes into a set of lazy, beautiful coastal towns. This region, the **Lycian Coast**, is famed for its forbidding mountains and beautiful valleys, most of which feed down toward beaches and ruins such as **Olympos** and **Patara**. In weeks of traveling you would only scratch the surface of the beaches and ancient cities area between Antalya and **Fethiye** – probably our favorite region.

The coast retains its remote character until **Marmaris,** although the Dalaman airport has led to the establishment of several large hotels. **Dalyan,** a city that hugs a beautiful, winding river below ancient **Caunos,** is of particular note.

## The Aegean

The coast gets busier north of Marmaris, but there are still hundreds of isolated coves and bays. One of the great ways to visit this section of coast is by *gulet,* traditional wooden ships that cruise between Bodrum and Antalya between April and October. The ruins of **Cnidos** and a collection of smaller ancient cities pepper the coast near here, winding up toward **Bodrum.** Bodrum, former site of one of the Seven Wonders of the World, is a pleasant mix of cosmopolitan and relaxed, and many small, attractive towns are located on the peninsula nearby.

The most famed of Turkey's ruins is near Kuşadası, **Ephesus.** An estimated 250,000 people lived in this metropolis in Roman times, and the scale and grandeur of the city is almost shocking. There are good accommodations nearby, and Ephesus is in fact just one of many great ruins in the area. **Priene** and the tumbled **Oracle at Didyma** to the south are both compelling, as are **Pamukkale** and **Aphrodisias** inland, two of Turkey's most magnetic sites.

Continuing north, Turkey's second-largest city, **Izmir,** stands on the site of the former **Smyrna.** Izmir is a beautiful bay city, but it offers few beaches or ruins of its own and is mostly useful as a base. **Sardis,** capital of Lydia and home to King Croesus in the sixth century B.C., is inland of Izmir. **Pergamon** and **Troy** are the greatest ancient ruins in the northern Aegean, although the former, of which few have ever heard, is much more dramatic than the latter, of which we all have heard. Troy's fame is derived from Homer's *The Iliad,* not from the jumble of ruins. The jumble of ruins at Troy, however unremarkable, is a worthy stop for anyone who recalls *The Iliad.* Near Troy is **Assos,** once home to Aristotle, and now home to an excellent set of waterfront pensions and hotels.

Between Troy and İstanbul are the **Gallipolli battlefields** and, south of the sea of Marmara, the city of **Bursa.** Bursa was one of the first Ottoman capitals in the years before they stormed onto the global scene, sacking and subduing swaths of Europe and Asia and seizing the Mediterranean as their own. Bursa, now a spawling city, still preserves reminders of its Ottoman past in excellent mosques and burial sites of early sultans. The city is also blessed with the curative geothermal waters welling up from the foothills of **Mt. Olympos,** now **Uludağ** ski area.

**The Black Sea**

   Passing İstanbul and continuing along the Black Sea coast, you will find yourself off the beaten track. Pensions and hotels are still available, but the Black Sea is altogether quieter until you arrive at the eastern reaches, such as **Trabzon**. There are beautiful beaches at **Amasra** and **Ünye**, picturesque ruins just inland of Samsun at **Amasya**, and even at the **Island of the Amazons**, now a free camping site just off the coast at Giresun.

   Trabzon, once the capital of the Empire of Trebizond, is still decorated with the fallen walls of its palaces and several old churches and mosques. Inland of Trabzon, and in the interior stretching toward the Georgian and Iranian border, are monasteries (such as the famous **Sumela Monastery**) and alpine meadows where travelers often choose to backpack or even whitewater raft down to the Black Sea.

---

### DISCO TURKEY & QUIET TURKEY

*If you're looking for a wild time, most large coastal towns have their share of large hotels and throbbing nightlife – but **Marmaris** on the Aegean coast must be considered (after İstanbul) the capital. Marmaris is packed with tourists in search of a good loud time all day and night, a perpetual Fort Lauderdale Spring Break. The hotels of **Kemer** on the Mediterranean coast west of Antalya offer loud aggressive fun, but it is less concentrated than Marmaris. **Bodrum** is like Marmaris to some extent, but quieter and leavened with a good bit of history. Truth to tell, most big hotels come with built-in nightlife, and whereever you go along Turkey's coast in season you'll find bars and dance places open until at least midnight.*

*If you're looking for a quiet time, **Olympos**, **Kekova**, and **Patara** on the Lycian coast are fine, sedate spots in gorgeous settings. The Black Sea is home to several quiet spots such as **Ünye** and **Amasra**, and many small towns along the Aegean offer calm coastal beauty. Good choices here include **Bozcaada Island** and the towns on the **Bodrum peninsula**. Of course, the interior is extremely quiet, probably more quiet than you want outside of the heavily visited areas such as Cappadoccia and Ankara. Even **Ürgüp** in Cappadoccia, however, offers several intensely peaceful, idyllic places to retreat.*

# 3. SUGGESTED ITINERARIES

If you have six weeks, you can do a whirlwind tour of Turkey. But you don't have six weeks, so accept that you have to make some decisions. We have some ideas about what you should see, but we won't presume to dictate a route (other than our perfect little Blue Cruise route below). Instead, use our suggestions as a guide for seeing what you want to see.

Here's what we suggest. First, decide why you're interested in Turkey. Then take a look at the following list of **"four day"** destinations and select one or two places. You can see just as many astounding things if you stay in one place for four days as you can by moving to a new hotel every night. It's a better way to become acquainted with the people who live in Turkey, and, besides, it's much more relaxing.

Of course, you don't want four days everywhere. Some places, Pamukkale, for example, probably suffer from prolonged exposure. So, next, pick a few places you'll want to stay for a night. Spend a night near Aphrodisias, one at Pamukkale, one at Hattuşas, one in Bursa – you get the idea. Weave this pattern of "four day" destinations and overnight stops together, and you have a good itinerary.

If you just have time for İstanbul no problem: we offer a variety of options below to have a fun and rich experience in Turkey's always fascinating capital city.

## TRANSPORTATION

While you're deciding how to get from place to place, consider all of the options. Rental cars are expensive, but handy along the coasts where many of the best ruins are slightly out of the way. Flights within Turkey are inexpensive, and a good idea if you're short on time and covering large distances: Cappadoccia to İstanbul or Bodrum, for instance.

Another option, probably the most popular, is bus travel. Buses are good and cheap, and western Turkey is magically arranged to have the diameter of an overnight bus ride. From any city on one side of the map to any city on the far side is about 12 hours. A fourth, often overlooked option is the train, which has a reputation for being slow and uncomfortable. The reputation is richly deserved, but there are exceptions; consider the slightly expensive sleeper trains between İstanbul and Pamukkale, İstanbul and Izmir, and İstanbul and Ankara.

## THE PERFECT ISTANBUL HOLIDAY

İstanbul offers too much, a staggering array of things to do and see. Here are some suggested itineraries for vacations of between three days and one week. If you have longer, don't worry; you'll never run out of things to see.

The finest museums and attractions in İstanbul are conveniently clustered at the head of the peninsula in the old city. This district, called **Sultanahmet**, is the city's must-see: the 1,500 year old Haghia Sophia, Topkapı Palace, the Basilica Cistern, the Blue Mosque, the Archaeological Museum and the grounds of the Hippodrome are all bunched together within one square mile. Just inland are the Grand Bazaar, the Egyptian Spice Market, and the Süleymaniye Mosque – one of the masterpieces of the Ottoman master architect Sinan.

Conveniently, too, many of our favorite hotels are located here. You can spend one exhausting day in the area or several days poking around in a more leisurely fashion. Keep in mind that even the seven day itinerary is, by necessity, dramatically abridged. Tempting alternatives include: attending late spring musical performances at St. Eirene, shopping for a carpet or kilim, hitting the nightclubs, catching a movie (most films are subtitled in Turkish and retain their original sound), making a weekday visit to the Princes Islands or Kilios for a swim, playing a round at the Klassis Golf Club, gambling at one of the luxury hotel's casinos, taking a break from the urban clamor at Yıldız Park, and even taking a side trip to Edirne or Yalova.

We give the Four Seasons our highest recommendation among the luxury hotels, while several excellent, more affordable hotels are tucked away in the same neighborhood including the Empress Zoe, the Armada, the Yeşil Ev, and the Ayasofya Pansiyonlar. The Yucelt International Youth Hostel, directly alongside the Haghia Sophia, is the best of the budget hotels. These itineraries begin on the morning after you arrive.

## THE PERFECT THREE DAYS IN ISTANBUL

This agenda assumes you're moving fast and not suffering unduly from jet lag. Most people can't (not to mention don't want to) see so much so fast. For that reason we recommend not adhering strictly to this agenda; when the mood strikes buy a Herald Tribune and take a nap at the hotel. Also note that our dining options, while simply perfect, of course, are expensive; dinners especially. Consult the *Where to Eat* section of our İstanbul chapter for further information.

## Day 1 – Sultanahmet

Tour Topkapı Palace
Lunch at Topkapı's Konyalı restaurant
Visit the Haghia Sophia
Visit the Baths of Haseki Hürrem directly across from the Haghia Sophia,
    now a government carpet/kilim shop with fair, standard prices that
    give you a good idea what you should spend if you plan to make any
    purchases. You may even find what you're looking for here.
Stroll along the Hippodrome
Visit the Islamic Art Museum
Coffee at the Islamic Art Museum
See the Blue Mosque
Visit the Mosaic Museum
Visit the Carpet and Kilim Museum
Dinner at Sarnıç Restaurant in Sultanahmet, located in a beautifully
    restored Roman cistern

## Day 2 – Greater Sultanahmet

Follow Divan Yolu up to the entrance of the Grand Bazaar
Work your way along the upper side of the Bazaar to the Süleymaniye
  Mosque. Grab a bite at Darüzziyafe if you're hungry.
Wind your way down towads the Spice Bazaar
Lunch at Pandeli in the Spice Bazaar, or pide or kebap on the street.
Visit the Yeni Cami, just outside the doors, then follow the course of the
  rail tracks back up past the Sirkeci railway station into Sultanahmet
Visit the Archaeological Museum complex on the Topkapı grounds, just
  inside the gate from Gülhane train stop.
Visit the Basilica Cistern
Taxi or train up the Marmara shore to Florya (near the Yeşilköy stop) for
  dinner at Beyti.

## Day 3 – The Bosphorous

Early start down to Eminönü for a Bosphorous ferry
Cruise the Bosphorous to either Sariyer or Anadolu Kavağı
At Anadolu Kavağı visit the fortress and have lunch at the waterfront.
  The ferry crosses to Sariyer upon departure; get off here unless you'd
  rather cruise back to Eminönü
At Sariyer visit the Sadberk Hanım museum. If you've come directly
  here dine at one of the waterfront fish restaurants or taxi up to Rumeli
  Kavağı and lunch at Yedi Gün.
Return down the Bosphorous by taxi or (Eminönü) bus as far as Rumeli
  Hisar and visit the Ottoman fortress.
Call Körfez Restaurant for a launch to pick you up and ferry you across
  for dinner.

## THE PERFECT SEVEN DAYS IN ISTANBUL
## Day 1 – Sultanahmet

Tour Topkapı Palace
Lunch at Topkapı's Konyalı restaurant
Stroll along the Hippodrome
Visit the Islamic Art Museum
Coffee at the Islamic Art Museum
See the Blue Mosque
Visit the Mosaic Museum
Visit the Carpet and Kilim Museum
Dinner at Sarniç Restaurant in Sultanahmet, located in a beautifully
  restored Roman cistern

## Day 2 – Greater Sultanahmet

Follow Divan Yolu up to the entrance of the Grand Bazaar
Work your way along the upper side of the Bazaar to the Süleymaniye
    Mosque. Grab a bite at Darüzziyafe if you're hungry.
Wind your way down towads the Spice Bazaar
Lunch at Pandeli in the Spice Bazaar, or pide or kebap on the street.
Visit the Yeni Cami, just outside the doors, then follow the course of the
    rail tracks back up past the Sirkeci railway station into Sultanahmet
Visit the Haghia Sophia
Visit the Basilica Cistern
Visit the Baths of Haseki Hürrem directly across from the Haghia Sophia,
    now a government carpet shop with fair, standard prices that give
    you a good idea what you should spend if you plan to make any
    purchases.
Taxi or train up the Marmara shore to Florya (near the Yeşilköy stop) for
    dinner at Beyti.

## Day 3 – The Bosphorous

Early start down to Eminönü for a Bosphorous ferry
Cruise the Bosphorous to either Sariyer or Anadolu Kavağı
At Anadolu Kavağı visit the fortress and have lunch at the waterfront.
    The ferry crosses to Sariyer upon departure; get off here unless you'd
    rather cruise back to Eminönü
At Sariyer visit the Sadberk Hanım museum. If you've come directly
    here, dine at one of the waterfront fish restaurants or taxi up to
    Rumeli Kavağı and lunch at Yedi Gün.
Return down the Bosphorous by taxi or (Eminönü) bus as far as Rumeli
    Hisar and visit the Ottoman fortress.
Call Körfez Restaurant for a launch to pick you up and ferry you across
    for dinner.

## Day 4 – The Land Walls

Cab or train to Yedikule
Walk outside the walls to Balıklı Church
Cab or dolmuş north along walls to Edirnekapı
Church of Chora (Kariye Cami)
Lunch at Kariye Hotel's Asitane Restaurant
Continue along the walls to Tekfur Saray
Cab or walk to Eyüp Cami
Stroll through the cemetery to Pierre Loti's Cafe for coffee
Cab, bus, or a long walk back to Sultanahmet via Eminönü
Back to the Sultanahmet for some rest
Dinner at the Tuğra Restaurant in the Çirağan Palace

## Day 5 – İstiklal

Walk across the Galata Bridge, take Tünel train to Galata
Stop in at Galata Tower for a cup of coffee
Stroll along İstiklal Caddesi, checking in at the bookstores and antique
shops at the lower end of the street
Lunch at one of the many cafes along İstiklal
From Taksim Square taxi to Askeri Müze (Military Museum)
Visit shops just uphill in Nişantaşı
Return to Taksim, return down İstiklal
Dinner at Rejans Russian Restaurant

## Day 6 – The Museums

Get a big breakfast and walk up to the Archaeological Museum Complex
on the Topkapı grounds
Visit the Museum of the Ancient Orient, the Archaeological Museum and
the Çinli Kösk
Have lunch on the grounds, or wait until you are through and get lunch
at one of the small gözleme and döner restaurants in Gülhane
After leaving the museums, stroll through Gülhane Park, which continues out to the tip of the peninsula and the Column of the Goths.
Dinner at Siam (Thai), Tandoori (Indian), or Osteria da Mario (Italian) for
something different.

## Day 7 – The Lower Bosphorous

Arrive early at Dolmabahçe Palace for a morning visit
Have coffee outside the Dolmabahçe Seraglio
Continue up the Bosphorous on foot to Beşiktaş for a bite of lunch
Visit the Deniz Müzesi (Naval Museum) on the Beşiktaş waterfront
Walk up the Bosphorous, turning in at the Çirağan Palace for a walk
along the palace grounds. Stop in at the patio bar for a drink
Continue walking to Ortaköy for an afternoon of shopping for evil eye
bracelets and sitting in a waterfront cafÈ writing postcards
Dinner at Vito in Ortaköy

## OTHER PLACES TO SPEND FOUR DAYS

We suggest that you pick a spot and stay there for a little while. This
isn't something you need a car to do (although it helps). We recommend
the following locations on the quality of their accommodations and the
number of incredible ruins, beaches, or natural wonders nearby.

## Ürgüp or Üçhisar, Cappadoccia

You could spend a week and never see the same thing twice. An endless maze of rock cut churches, underground cities and eerie land-scapes. They even make wine.

## Dalyan

An excellent beach, a gargantuan Classical ruin, rock cut tombs, hot springs, great fish restaurants and lots of puttering along the main avenue, Dalyan River, in a boat.

## Antalya

The Kaleiçi area has a stylish collection of bed and breakfasts, and Antalya is surrounded by some of the greatest cities of antiquity.

## Kalkan

Kalkan is a beautiful little fishing (and tourism) town perched above the Mediterranean. Its pretty old houses are the perfect place to return to after spending your days at Patara, Xanthos, Letoon, Pınara, Tlos and Saklikent in the west and a whole lot more in the east. Unfortunately, many visitors get sucked in by Patara Beach, one half hour west, and never go anywhere else: try to avoid this grim fate.

## A Blue Cruise Boat

You stay in one place while sunken ruins, hilltop castles, swimming, beaches, and delicious food deliver themselves to you.

The route below assumes you have one week to cover the ground between İstanbul and Bodrum. This accomplishes that in reasonable, enjoyable chunks, keeping the distances short, the sites stellar, and the accommodations at a premium.

1. Sunday – İstanbul. Overnight sleeper train to Pamukkale.
2. Monday – Hieropolis, baths. Overnight Pamukkale Motel.
3. Tuesday – Aphrodisias. Overnight Chez Mestan.
4. Wednesday – Continue to Kuşadası. Visit Kuşadası. Overnight Kismet Hotel.
5. Thursday – Ephesus/Selçuk. Overnight Kismet Hotel.
6. Friday – Miletus, Priene, and Didyma. Overnight, Didim Pansiyon.
7. Saturday – Ferry to Torba/Bodrum. Meet Blue Cruise.

---

### ITINERARY TIPS

*Can you afford a boat trip? Then do the Blue Cruise. Fit it in at the end of your vacation so that you go home as well rested (and tan) as possible.*

*Do not rent a car in İstanbul, but along the Mediterranean and Aegean coasts they can be a big help.*

*Spend more time in İstanbul than you think you need.*

# 4. LAND & PEOPLE

## LAND

Turkey straddles Europe and Asia, with İstanbul and a small section of the country jutting into Europe. The bulk of the country is in Asia, a giant rectangular peninsula that emerges from the east: Turkey has a convenient resemblance to your right hand. This "peninsula" is bounded by four separate seas: the **Black Sea** in the north, the small **Sea of Marmara** between the Bosphorous and Dardanelle straits, the **Aegean** in the west, and the **Mediterranean** in the south. All told Turkey is 780,500 square kilometers, a little larger than Texas or any of the European nations.

Turkey's great size and key location mean it has a lot of neighbors, which is not to say they are all a particularly close-knit community. Relations with Georgia, Azerbaijan, and Bulgaria are quite good, but relations between Turkey and her other neighbors (Armenia, Iran, Iraq, and Syria) are always a little dicey. Turkey's hydroelectric projects in the southwest have both Syria and Iraq stewing over the seeming threat to their water supply.

Turkey's relationship with its final neighbor, Greece, is another story altogether. The land border with Greece is only 206 kilometers long, but this is hugely deceptive since the heavily patrolled border between the Turkish Republic of Northern Cyprus and Greek Cyprus is a de facto Turkish border, and Turkey is ringed with Greek islands along almost the full extent of her Aegean and western Mediterranean coasts. The two countries exchange slights and diplomatic insults at the slightest provocation, and have on several occasions – including the Kardak Rocks crisis in 1996 – come surprisingly close to war.

Turkey's interior is dominated by several great mountain ranges, with its breadbasket on the fertile **Anatolian plateau**. The Mediterranean, Aegean, and Black Sea coasts are likewise fertile areas for olives, fruit, and forestry. Turkey is one of only ten nations with a net food surplus.

## PEOPLE

Turkey's population is approaching 70 million – and approaching it rapidly. The fertility rate in 1994 was 3.2 children per woman, a huge figure by modern standards. A considerable minority of this population, probably 14 million people, live in the İstanbul area, with others concentrated in Bursa, Izmir, Antalya, and Ankara. The population is heavily Muslim, but the republic is strictly secular. Estimates of the Muslim population run between 95 percent and 99 percent. Recent estimates put the **Kurdish** population at 20 percent, and the rest are primarily ethnic Turks.

### Islam

The first questions you begin to form on arrival in Turkey will probably have to do with its minarets and mosques, the covered women and pious-looking men. Turkey is a secular nation, but its population is overwhelmingly Muslim. Most North Americans will find this religion and its trappings alien and maybe even a little disconcerting.

Islam is a vital religion, a cousin of Christianity and Judaism. The core beliefs are remarkably similar, the central cast of characters is virtually identical – Noah, Moses, Abraham, and even Jesus.

---

### MUCH ADO ABOUT NOTHING

*The ugly hand of Islamic terrorism appeared to show itself in the winter of 1994 when two Americans went missing during a ski trip to Bursa. Newpapers in the U.S. kicked up a frenzy, until the two men turned up safe and sound in a snow cave, caught by a storm, not Hamas. There is simply no reason for you to be concerned about becoming a victim of Islamic terrorism while visiting. For one thing, terrorist groups are usually associated with Arabs, and Turks are, as they will take pains to clarify, not Arab. Turks are simply Muslim – probably 95 percent or more. As in North America, that simply means that they are good, God-fearing folk who may try to suffocate you with pastries and cake.*

---

### The Koran

**Mohammed** was born in Mecca around 570 A.D. He was a trader's son, and grew to be a trader himself. He was more than 40 years old when he received his first visitation from the Angel Gabriel, and Gabriel returned over the course of several years to give him the word of God. Mohammed committed much of what Gabriel told him to writing, forming the core of the **Koran**. Some final chapters were passed down by word of mouth and finally incorporated into the Koran under the third Caliph, Uthman (644-656).

The Muslim God, **Allah**, remains very similar to the God of the Jews and Christians. In fact, Sura 5:83 of the Koran says "You will surely find that the nearest in affection to believers are those who say "We are Christians," and this is amplified and expanded in 2:63: "Believers – Jews, Christians, and Sabians [a splinter Christian sect] – whosoever believes in God and the Last Day and does what is right, they shall have their reward with the Lord." This inclusive note has been echoed by such luminaries as the Sufi-inspired Celaddin Rumi, or Mevlana, he of the whirling dervishes. Unfortunately, this apparently clear line is muddied by 3:79, which warns that anyone who fails to select Islam will be "lost."

Within Islam there are two major sects, **Shi'ite** and **Sunni**. Turkey's Muslims are Sunni, and they worship the Koran together with a second text, the **Sunna**. The Sunna is a compilation of laws and guidelines derived from the lives of the Prophet Mohammed and his wife. The combined codes of the Koran and Sunna form the **Shariat**, or law. The Sunni caliph is a supreme judge, and he was for many years closely allied to the Ottomans. The Shiites, too, adhere to the Sunna, but they have their own caliph. Among the Shi'ites the caliph is more than the supreme judge, he is a leader, the voice of Allah, and a ruler in his own right. As a result, Shi'ites always remained aloof of the Ottoman sultan, who could never be their ultimate leader without also being the Shi'ite caliph. This schism has had bloody repercussions since ancient times, and under the Ottomans the rift was widened by Sultan Selim I's (1512-1520) bloody anti-Shi'ite campaigns in Persia.

---

### THE CALL TO PRAYER

*"Allah is most great. I testify that there in no god but Allah. I testify that Mohammed is Allah's apostle. Come to prayer, come to security. God is most great."*

*Morning prayers have an additional verse reminding the listener that it is "better to pray than sleep." All verses repeat.*

---

Like the rest of the Islamic world, Turkey celebrates **Ramazan** (you may know it as Ramadan). From sun up until sundown most practicing Muslims forgo eating, drinking and even smoking. There are special dispensations for military personnel and foreigners, but you shouldn't make a big point of eating when you find an open restaurant, and it is in poor taste to eat on the street during daylight. The day-long fast is elaborately broken at sunset, when huge meals appear and families gather together.

Ramazan's dates change from year to year; it is based on the lunar cycle. Ramazan is currently going through its winter period, meaning that the days are short and the fasting is fairly painless. Summer poses a sterner test. The end of Ramazan is marked by **Şeker Bayram**, an exchanges of gifts and a great celebration. Another holiday, **Kurban Bayram**, commemorates Abraham's willingness to sacrifice Ishmael. Families throughout the country slaughter sheep and other livestock, and it is an occasion for most offices to shut down for a full week.

### Turkish Mannerisms

You're likely to meet few people more friendly than the glowering Turkish man watching you from in front of his shop. Turkish men have a habit of appearing to be somewhere between impassive and ferocious, but they're almost always amiable and helpful.

Moreover, for all of the histrionics you're going to see in traffic jams and marketplaces, Turks are slow to anger and remarkably self-disciplined. In what may be a testament to the importance of extended family and neighborhood community, they are unusually sane, reasonable people.

A few local habits are likely to arouse some curiosity, even resentment in most North Americans. The big one is *Yok*. When the bus is gone, the small change is exhausted, the rooms are full and the shop is closed, you will be met with Yok, and its accompanying upthrust chin. In our culture this gesture is dismissive and rude; not so here. It simply means no, a firm and final no.

---

### WINTER IN ANATOLIA

*"As in the yards of houses in Ürgüp, so across the high country of Anatolia I had watched people preparing for winter. Gathering and storing fuel as well as food is an obsession with the inhabitants of those high, wild, unforested plains. I sympathized with the man I saw standing before his hoard of wood, heedless to the heat of the sun on his back as he reckoned up the long bitter weeks of January against the stock of logs in his yard. Was it enough? I knew how he felt – it is never enough, there isn't enough firewood in the world to quench the craving for plenty which gnaws at the wintry heart of the lover of fires."*

Philip Glazebrook, ***Journey to Kars: A Modern Traveler in the Ottoman Lands***, London: Penguin, 1984.

---

The *tsk tsk* noises (often with the aforementioned upthrust chin) are one of the Turks' great socialization tools. You'll hear it when someone is showing too much flesh, doing something unsafe, or otherwise getting out of line. North Americans accustomed to a live-and-let-live ethic are usually ill-prepared for this very judgmental chastening, usually performed by women. If someone is going way over the line you'll hear the tsk tsk in conjunction with an *Allah allah*. (Sounds like *Allah hallah*.) This phrase, meaning, more or less, "how come?" or "what's up with that?," can also simply be an expression of wonderment.

There are scores of other peculiarities, but none so important as the fact that if you go to the trouble to mime a conversation with someone, or send them a copy of a photograph, or help get their car out of a ditch, you'll have a friend for always.

## The Kurds

The Kurds' story is not unique; they are a distinct people without a distinct homeland. They have unique language, culture, and traditions, and the majority of them live in southeast Turkey or just across the border in Iraq or Iran. The most famous incidents involving the Kurds were Saddam Hussein's attacks on their villages with poison gas in the late 1980s, but nowhere have the Kurds met with a great welcome. Iraq, Iran, and Turkey have spent years trying to hustle the mujjahdin-like Kurdish fighters back and forth into one another's countries, but never with much apparent success.

The NATO no-fly zone over northern Iraq has given the Kurds a de facto homeland, but in the absence of a marauding enemy air force the Kurds fight among themselves (which resulted in Saddam Hussein's intervention in September 1996). Turkey's role in all of this is intentionally vague. News coverage of southeastern Turkey is heavily discouraged, but everyone knows that the area is occupied by Turkish soldiers. Reports trickle in about skirmishes and occasional major battles between the Turkish military and Kurdish rebels. As happened in America's Vietnam, differentiating between civilians and fighters has grown more and more difficult, and not even the de facto media blackout conceals that it is a nasty little war.

As an adjunct to the fighting in the southeast, Kurds have taken to bombing Turkish sites in both Turkey and Germany. The attacks are rare, motivated by a desire for publicity. As recently as 1994, tourists were targeted in bombings – including incidents at the Haghia Sophia and the Grand Bazaar in İstanbul. In 1996, Sivas in central Anatolia was rocked repeatedly by Kurdish suicide bombings, but attacks targeting tourists seemed to tail off. A name you will often hear associated with the Kurdish problem is the Kurdistan Workers' Party, or PKK. The party formed to give the nation's approximately 10 million Kurds a voice in Turkish politics – laws passed in 1924 had denied them even the right to speak Kurdish. The Turkish government leveled terrorism charges at the leadership of the party and packed them off to jail, thereafter banning the party. Predictably, given no legitimate outlet, the Kurds have continued their campaign violently.

Travel in eastern Turkey is dangerous. Americans and Germans have been kidnapped. We strongly recommend against excursions south of Artvin or east of Cappadoccia, although we include an itinerary of what has become a fairly well-traveled route in The East.

## Tobacco

Tobacco, what any visitor will soon conclude is the nation's pet vice, has been a part of Turkish culture for hundreds of years. A 1612 treaty with England opened the door to the imports of English tobacco traders, and the door that the tobacco traders opened the Marlboro man has since barged right through, offering cigarettes instead of narghile tobacco. Turks are big smokers, big even by European standards. Non-smoking North Americans, spoiled by successful anti-smoking campaigns at home, may be unprepared for smoke in buses, taxis, restaurants, and most other public areas. Rare indeed is the public area without cigarette smoke, although anti-smoking campaigns have made some headway, and municipal buses, some private dolmuş, upscale restaurants, and good theaters now offer respite from smoking (look for *Sigarasiz* or *Sigara İçmisiz* signs). Note also that the Muslim holy men, some of the earliest anti-smoking campaigners, prohibited smoking in mosques and other holy areas hundreds of years ago.

**Narghile**s were once a common sight in Turkey as in many Arab countries, and narghile tobacco is still produced on the Black Sea. However, these classic pipes are decidedly rare these days. If you're interested in smoking a narghile you'll have to go looking for it. In İstanbul, try the Nargileci on Çorlulu Pasaj in the Grand Bazaar near Divan Yolu – ask someone selling narghiles where it is (*narghileci nerede?*) go left or right, ask again, and continue until you're there or back where you started. Sit down when you take a draw off of one of these monsters.

## Opium

Of the four pillars, opium enjoys the least popularity today. Turkey continues to export one-third of the world's legal opium, but its success as a vice has tailed off. The government has taken serious steps to regulate the production of narcotic opium, which is a product of mature plants, by harvesting the plants while young. Legal opium has uses in pharmaceuticals. Although Turkey is not a source of heroin, the western world alleges that it is a major smuggling route for heroin from Afghanistan and elsewhere in Central Asia.

# TURKISH LANGUAGE

Turkish gives the new arrival virtually no familiar benchmarks. Sentence structure is the reverse of English, and Turkish has incorporated precious few English words. As someone is bound to point out, Turkish is very systematic and logical, but then so is the computer language C++. A fat lot of good that does you on a two week visit.

Thanks to Kemal Atatürk's reforms, Turkey now uses Latin, not Arabic, characters. These correspond roughly with English, with several notable exceptions:

| Letter | Sound | Example | Pronunciation | English Meaning |
|---|---|---|---|---|
| c | j | Cami | (jah-mee) | Mosque |
| ç | ch | Çatal | (cha-tall) | Fork |
| (i) | ee | Bin | (been) | Thousand |
| ı | uh | Topkapı | (top kap uh) | Topkapı Palace |
| ş | sh | Teşekkürler | (tey shey kyur ler) | Thanks |
| ö | oohr | Göz | (goohrz) | Eye |
| ü | ehw | Yüz | (yehwz) | Hundred |
| ğ | extends sound | Sağol | (sa-ohl) | Thanks |

## The Basics

| English | Turkish | Pronunciation |
|---|---|---|
| Yes | Evet | ay-veht |
| No | Hayır | higher |
| Thank you | Teşekkürler | tey-shey-kyur-lehr |
| Thanks | Sağol | sa-ohl |
| Please | Lütfen | lewt-fen |
| Good day | İyi Günler | ee-yee goon-lehr |
| Good night | İyi Akşamlar | ee-yee ak-sham-lar |
| No, none,nothing | Yok | yoke |
| Many, much | Çok | choke |
| Good | İyi | ee-yee |
| Bad | Kötü | koohr-tehw |

## Traveling

| Today | Bugün | boo-gehwn |
|---|---|---|
| Yesterday | Dün | dewhn |
| Tomorrow | Yarın | yahr-uhn |
| I will go | Gideceğim | git-eh-jeh-em |
| I will stay | Kaleceğim | kal-eh-jeh-em |
| We will go | Gideceğız | git-eh-juhz |
| We will not go | Gitmeceğız | git-meh-juhz |

| Hour | Saat | sa-aht |
|---|---|---|
| Minute | Dakika | da-key-ka |
| Depart | Kalkar | kahl-kar |
| Airport | Havaalanı | hav-a-alahn-uh |
| Bus station | Otogar | oto-gahr |
| Train station | Tren istasiyon | tren is-tas-ee-yohn |
| Port | Liman | lee-mahn |
| When | Ne zaman | ney-zah-mahn |

## Days

| Monday | Pazartesi | pah-zahr-tey-see |
|---|---|---|
| Tuesday | Salı | sahl-uh |
| Wednesday | Çarşamba | char-sham-ba |
| Thursday | Perşembe | pear-shem-bay |
| Friday | Cuma | joo-mah |
| Saturday | Cumartesi | joo-mahr-tey-see |
| Sunday | Pazar | pah-zahr |

## Phrases

I want a room
  *Bir oda istiyorum*        beer oda ist-ee-yorum
How much is this?
  *Bu ne kadar*          boo nay kadar
Is breakfast included?
  *Kahvaltı dahil mı?*        kahvaltuh da-yeel muh?
Where is the bus station?
  *Otogar nerede?*        oto-gahr nair-duh?
I like it.
  *O seviyorum*         oh sev-ee-or-um
I don't like it.
  *O sevmiyorum*         oh sev-mee-or-um
I want it.
  *O istiyorum*          oh ist-ee-or-um
We don't want it.
  *O istemiyoruz*         oh ist-em-ee-or-um
Help me.
  *Yardım edim*         yahr-duhm a-deem
Shame! strong term
  *Ayıp*            ay-yuhp

# Numbers

| | | |
|---|---|---|
| 10,000,000 | On milyon | on milyon |
| 1,000,000 | Milyon | milyon |
| 100,000 | Yüz bin | yehwz been |
| 10,000 | On bin | on been |
| 1,000 | Bin | been |
| 100 | Yüz | yehwz |
| 90 | Doksan | dohk-sahn |
| 80 | Seksen | sehks-sen |
| 70 | Yetmiş | yet-mish |
| 60 | Altmiş | alt-mish |
| 50 | Elli | el-lee |
| 40 | Kirk | keerk |
| 30 | Otuz | oh-tooz |
| 20 | Yirmi | yeer-mee |
| 10 | On | on |
| 9 | dokuz | doh-kewz |
| 8 | sekiz | sek-eez |
| 7 | yedi | yeh-dee |
| 6 | altı | al-tuh |
| 5 | beş | besh |
| 4 | dört | doohrt |
| 3 | üç | yewch |
| 2 | iki | ee-key |
| 1 | bir | beer |
| 0 | sifir | see-feer |

| | |
|---|---|
| 450,000 TL. | Dortyüz elli bin Turkish Lira |
| 23,945,000 TL. | Yirmi üc dokuzyüz kirkbeş bin Turkish Lira |

# 5. A SHORT HISTORY

Many people come to Turkey with no intention of buying a carpet or kilim and wind up hauling three or four onto the flight home. The same may be said of the local history, which can get under your skin just as quickly (if not as expensively).

## EARLY HISTORY

The history of civilization in Turkey is as old as that in Egypt and Persia, with considerable overlap. Evidence of civilized human occupation in Turkey dates back to the Anatolian settlement of Çatal Hüyük in 7500 B.C. This cluster of earthen dwellings was located earlier this century near Beyşehir Lake, west of modern Konya, and evokes the pueblos of the American southwest. Çatal Hüyük was settled at the same time that people began producing specialized tools for harvesting, and, indeed, the settlement was built atop fields of obsidian, one of the first stones used to fashion simple tools.

Even at this early stage humans were, ever so slowly, beginning to gain technological momentum. Ever bright and imitative, no sooner had an idea proved a success than others were attempting to duplicate it.

The ability to harvest allowed people to settle in one area, which in turn provided traders with a center for distribution. What some wanted to trade for, others wanted to take; defensive walls appeared over the course of the next 2000 years, and by 5000 B.C. there was a network of small fortified towns throughout modern Turkey, stretching down into Egypt and out through Iran and India on into China.

The **Bronze Age**, dating from 3200 B.C., is a time marker because it represents a dawning ability to combine two naturally occurring metals, copper and tin, to produce bronze, a tougher material. Archaeologists have identified about one dozen settlements in Asia Minor near natural metal deposits, and communities bent on mining ore further enforced the need for trade – where once there was food, now there was food, metal, metalworking technology, and, of course, the weapons and art produced with metal. Humans were beginning to specialize, in a process that has been gaining momentum ever since.

There was a technological advance on two fronts: war and art. Tribes began building up their power through alliances and conquest. Meantime, artisans were giving them things to fight for; they began developing their metalworking skills and mastering new metal alloys to create small statues, diadems, bracelets, and necklaces. The intricate pieces in the **Treasure of Priam** discovered by Heinrich Schliemann at **Troy** date from 2500 B.C. This Troy, Troy II, seems to have been among the pioneers of a new sort of industry; instead of mining ore or producing textiles, the Trojans built a fortified city on a hill overlooking the mouth of the Hellespont.

Merchants, unable or unwilling to battle the great north wind that blows down the Hellespont nine months of the year, stopped at the mouth of the strait and did business in the marketplaces of Troy. The Trojans encouraged this with a naval force that could close the strait or demand payment for safe passage. Thus Troy profited from all the trade between east and west and became the marketplace of interior Asia and Europe. Centuries of such commerce made the city prosperous.

## THE HITTITES

The history of the region really begins taking shape in about 2000 BC, when **Assyrian** traders from the south appear in Anatolia with great stores of tin, which, combined with native stores of copper (probably secured through trading elsewhere), allowed large-scale production of bronze. Better yet, for historians, the Assyrians were in the habit keeping records of their business in cuneiform script on slabs of clay. Knowledge of earlier kingdoms is largely a matter of guesswork – the Sumerians, for instance, left a large, shadowy footprint. With the Assyrians' help, historians have been able to reconstruct details of one of the greatest Anatolian empires, the **Hittites**.

The Hittites, like so many cultures to appear later, entered Anatolia from the east and soon were masters of the native Anatolian population. The new arrivals, however, were no cultural imperialists; they adopted the religion and much of the language of the indigenous people, largely Hurrians. In the 20th Century B.C., these people built their first major city, Kanesh (near Kültepe, from which they began to dominate the rest of central Anatolia). In the 18th Century B.C., the capital was shifted back to Hattuşas (Boğazkale), and soon the Hittite Kingdom was in full flower, encompassing Babylon and the entire Anatolian plain.

The Hittites suffered some difficult years, but for the bulk of its existence, so powerful was the Hittite Kingdom (later the Hittite Empire) that in the 14th Century B.C. the widow of **King Tutankhaman** sought a Hittite prince to be her new husband. Her hopes were not realized; the son of the Hittite King Suppiluliuma I was killed on the journey to Egypt. The two empires continued in the habit of cross-pollinating their nobility, but there were some bumps along the way. Under Muwatalli II (1306-1282 B.C.) the Hittites took the field against an Egyptian invasion by Ramses II, the irrepressibly successful pharoah immortalized in Percy Byshe Shelley's *Ozymandias*. On this one occasion Ramses II was stopped dead, beaten at the **Battle of Qadesh** (1286 B.C.) and forced to withdraw through Palestine. Upon his arrival home, the pharoah put a positive spin on the battle of Qadesh – hieroglyphs at Karnak speak only of a great victory.

After the death of Muwatalli II, the Hittite Kingdom began an abrupt decline; Greek and Mycenaean colonists and traders had at last appeared to the west.

## THE TROJAN WAR

Troy's relationship with the Hittite Kingdom is unclear. Their roots were similar, their architecture much the same, but the two kingdoms were operating in different spheres. If Homer's account of the Trojan War is to be believed almost the whole of the mainland to the south and east supported Troy, and this might have included the Hittites and certainly included the **Paphlagonians**, or Kaşka, from the eastern Black Sea.

The Trojans never had the enduring martial success of the Hittites, but they were a thorn in the Greeks' side. An allied force of Trojans and Mysians conquered the region around the Sea of Marmara in the 14th Century B.C. and extended their territory into Thrace as far as Macedonia. Having moved so far west, the Trojans were preying on Greek settlements and colonies as well as barring entry to the Hellespont, and may well have constituted the most dangerous of the kingdoms scattered along the coast. At roughly the time of the Hittite King Muwatalli II's death and civil war among the Hittites, the **Greeks** united, and, perhaps seeking to take advantage of the strife in Anatolia, descended on Troy.

Homer's *Iliad* offers a dramatic and glorified account of the struggle between the Greeks and the Trojans, but, in short, the Greeks stripped Troy of its lands and burned it to the ground around 1250 B.C., clearing the way for colonization throughout the Aegean and up into the Sea of Marmara and the Black Sea. Within a century the Hittite capital was also sacked and burned, probably by the Paphlagonians. Even the Mycenaeans, by all accounts the great victors in the Trojan War, collapsed. An era was at an end, and a new one was not yet under way.

## THE ANCIENT DARK AGE

The next several centuries were chaotic. The people of the fallen Hittite Empire staked out new kingdoms, the peoples of the northern Aegean were scattered after the Greek victory at Troy, and all the while colonists from the Greek islands continued to seek footholds along the coast of Asia Minor. The **Sea Peoples**, a combination of Greeks, islanders, and displaced Anatolians, began a wave of determined piracy that threatened even the Egyptian pharoahs. Settlers occupied the whole of the Mediterranean basin in this time.

Amid this upheaval, several small kingdoms succeeded in establishing themselves. The **Phrygians** descended on Asia Minor from Thrace, establishing their capital near Gordium. The Phrygians ranged far and wide, even forming an alliance with the Paphlagonians along the Black Sea coast and going to war against the Babylonians in the east. Having settled into the capital of their budding new empire, the Phrygians were distressed to see the **Cimmerians** (of Conan fame) swarm down from the Russian steppes, cross the Caucasus Mountains, **upset the apple cart**, then eat the apples.

The Cimmerians destroyed Gordion in 714 B.C., and spent the next two decades belligerently sacking and looting the cities of Asia Minor as far south as Ephesus. Historians tell us that the Cimmerians were driven south by invaders in their own homeland, which suggests that the Russian steppes had an advanced level of brutality. The Cimmerians were outstanding warriors but uninspired administrators, and at the end of their rampage they dispersed and settled into the kingdoms they had conquered, melting into the local population within a few generations.

In the east, refugees from the Hittite Empire and the native populations established kingdoms on the shores of Lake Van, eventually cementing a coalition under Sarduri I (840-830 B.C.). This became the **Urartian Kingdom**, founded to fend off the increasingly aggressive Assyrians, and it grew powerful enough to command the bulk of Anatolia. The capital city from 810 B.C. was Tuşpa, on Lake Van, and Urartu's borders were at one time the Caucasus in the north, Syria in the south, the Tigris River in the west and its eastern frontier penetrated deep into modern Iran. The Urartians were able to beat back the Assyrians, and under Sarduri II (753-735 B.C.) they even campaigned to the doorstep of the Assyrian capital at Ninevah. The Assyrians soon resumed their attacks, however, forcing the Urartians on two occasions to take refuge in their impregnable fortresses at the Rock of Van and suffer the destruction of their homes and crops.

The Urartians outlasted the Assyrians in the end. The Assyrians fell to the growing might of **Persia** in 612 B.C., and the Urartians were incorporated into the **Lydian** Empire in 590 B.C.

## PERSIA

King Croesus became King of Lydia in 560 B.C., and immediately began a campaign along the coast of Asia Minor. His irrepressible armies had pacified all of western Turkey within seven years, and the wealth of his capital at Sardis gained great renown – the term "rich as Croesus" has survived (albeit barely) to this day. Croesus put great stock in oracles, and the Oracle at Delphi was the most uncannily accurate of these oracles. Thus Croesus, on the verge of testing his might against his greatest remaining foe, asked the oracle whether he should cross the river Halys and attack the Persians. "Make war on the Persians and you will destroy a great empire," said the sly oracle.

Croesus heard in these words what he wanted to hear, crossing the river and verily getting his clock cleaned at the Battle of Pteria in Cappadoccia in 550 B.C. Croesus retreated in disarray to Sardis, where the Persian King Cyrus' surprisingly rapid pursuit left Croesus no time to assemble a new army. The Persians seized and sacked Sardis and Croesus' empire was ruined, fulfilling the oracle.

Now the Persians assumed control of Asia Minor, replacing the Lydian yoke with their own. The Greek settlements, foreshadowing centuries of conflict, did not take well to Persian administration. In the northern cities entire populations were slain or enslaved. In 540 B.C., the Persian General Harpagus marched on the cities of Lycia along the southwest coast. The collection of Anatolian and Greek peoples along that remote coast fled or fought; in the epic case of Xanthos – and perhaps Caunos as well – the men of the city massacred their own women and children and threw themselves hopelessly into battle against the over-whelming Persian army, dying to the last man.

Persian rule was complete on land, but the islands of the Mediterra-nean remained largely under Greek control, and it was from here that a major revolt by all of the Ionian cities – roughly between modern Çeşme and Bodrum – erupted in 498 B.C. Led by the greatest city of the coast at the time, Miletus, and assisted by fleets from Athens and troops from the Peloponnese, the Ionian cities scattered the Persians. Darius, the Persian King, soon mounted an overwhelming counterattack, seizing back all of what he had lost and carrying the war back to Miletus, which he sacked and destroyed in 494 B.C.

Even so, the Persian victory was incomplete. Athens remained free to conspire against Persia, and it was against this threat that Darius now moved. Seeking to root out the problem at its distant source, Darius launched a great armada in 490 B.C. The fleet of 600 ships sailed directly for Greece, where cavalry and footsoldiers sacked several towns, pro-gressing toward Athens. The Greeks made their stand just west of Athens at Marathon, scoring a dramatic and unexpected victory that left 6,400 Persians dead to 192 of their own. The Persians fled back to their ships and sailed for Asia, and an enraged Darius was forced to begin assembling another army.

Darius did not live to see the next invasion, which was launched by his son **Xerxes** in 480. Xerxes amassed a colossal army – Herodotus exaggerated its size at seven million – and personally marched into Europe, relying on the land approaches to Athens. At the approach of this force most enemies fled or opened their gates. Only upon arrival in Greece did the Persians meet fierce resistance, but the most valiant Greek opposition could do little more than delay a Persian army whose thirst, Herodotus reports, emptied rivers. The Greeks once again sought to make their stand at Athens, but they soon realized the futility of fighting the overwhelming Persians and retired to the sea. Xerxes sacked Athens, winning his hoped-for victory, but the victory was hollow – no sooner had the Persians torched Athens' acropolis than the Athenians led the Greek navies in a rout of the Persian fleet just offshore.

Later that year, Xerxes retreated with a large part of his army to Asia Minor, where he received the worst news yet: in the second year of the invasion the remaining occupation army was routed by the united Greeks at the **Battle of Plataea**. This victory was commemorated by a statue of intertwined serpents cast from the shields of fallen Persians, a trophy that now stands in the **Hippodrome** in İstanbul. Few of the fleeing Persians survived the long journey home.

Athens now sailed forth into Asia Minor, freely sacking Persian-held cities and putting the Persian army and navy to rout near Aspendos. The Persians might have been defeated once and for all, had not dissension erupted within the Greek ranks. In 432, the Spartans and Athenians became embroiled in what was essentially a Greek civil war, the **Peloponnesian War**, during which the Persians reasserted themselves in Asia Minor and provoked continued warfare between their Greek enemies.

The Peloponnesian War ended with Spartan victory in 406, returning the focus to Asia Minor. Here, a battle of succession dragged in a great army from the west, as a young Persian prince, Cyrus, coerced the Greeks to help him win the Persian throne from his brother. After penetrating deep into Persia, the Greek force defeated the Persian army, but in the course of the battle lost the Persian prince. Without him, they had no claim to the throne, and no friends in Persia; they were stranded in hostile territory thousands of miles from home. **Xenophon**, their general, gives an account of the retreat of these 10,000 soldiers in the *Anabasis*, The March Up-Country.

## ALEXANDER THE GREAT

In the ensuing years the Persians strengthened their hold on Asia Minor. They were represented by fairly autonomous satraps, including Mausolus (377-353) who constucted the **Mausoleum at Helicarnassus**, one of the Seven Wonders of the World. The Persians continued fighting the Lycians along the Mediterranean coast, while in the north they came into conflict with King Philip of Macedon. The animosity kindled in the latter of these border skirmishes was fateful. Philip's son, **Alexander** (355-323), crossed the Hellespont in 334 B.C. and systematically defeated every Persian army that confronted him. After scouring almost the whole of modern Turkey for Persian allies, he met Persian King Darius at the Battle of Issus (near Antakya-Hatay) in 333 B.C. and routed him for a final time. Alexander went on to destroy the Persian Empire and led armies past the boundaries of the known world into India and Central Asia.

### ALEXANDER'S PROPHESY

*Alexander's youth was filled with omens that he would grow up to be a great conqueror, but before he set out on his invasion of Persia he wanted to make sure he hadn't misread the signs. Alexander visited the Oracle at Delphi in the hopes of confirming his destiny, but was met by the priestess, who told him that, for now, the Oracle was silent. Alexander ignored this and forced his way toward the Temple, dragging her along. She tried to resist, but, failing, said "You can't be stopped!" At this Alexander wheeled around and left Delphi. He had his prophesy.*

Alexander's military genius was overwhelming, but he failed to attend to his own succession. After altering the face of the world, Alexander died in 323 B.C. and his empire began to disintegrate. His son was just an infant, hardly fit to rule, and Alexander's many brilliant generals were soon at each other's throats. Alexander's son was assassinated, and the rivals for power, or **Diadochoi**, began a long, costly campaign. This is one of the most confusing chapters in history, with Alexander's generals all staking a claim to pieces of the empire. Many pretenders to the throne were defeated or assassinated, and others settled for small provinces.

The most successful of Alexander's former generals were **Antigonus** in Asia Minor; **Seleucus** the One Eyed, who founded a southern empire out of Syria; **Ptolemy**, who established a kingdom in Egypt; and **Lysimachos**, whose Aegean claims later formed the heart of the Kingdom of Pergamon. Even these relatively successful generals suffered grim fates; Lysimachos defeated and killed Antigonus in 301, Seleucus overwhelmed Lysimachos at the Battle of Corupedium in 281, and Seleucus was poisoned the next year by his own son.

## THE ROMANS

Historians invariably paint the **Romans** as bustling, driven, and vulgar, but they were clever, too. They deserved their reputation for military acumen, but the truly astonishing thing was the Romans' administrative ability and their foreign policy cunning. This was evident in their patient and ultimately successful policy in Asia Minor.

Two of Asia Minor's most powerful kingdoms forged alliances with the emergent Romans. The **Kingdom of Pergamon** sided with the Romans against the Seleucids at the Battle of Magnesia in 190 B.C., and maintained friendly relations. The **Kingdom of Pontus**, on the Black Sea, contributed to the Roman force that finally defeated Rome's great maritime rival, Carthage, in 149. During this time Rome's presence seemed limited in Asia Minor despite its clear influence in many coastal cities.

The appearance began to fade in 133 B.C., when Attalus III of Pergamon died and left his kingdom to the Romans. This peculiar inheritance reeked of Roman intrigue, but the citizens of Pergamon had only the slightest opportunity to protest; the Romans entrenched themselves quickly. Thereafter, Rome's escalating role in the affairs of Asia Minor began to worry and anger some of its autonomous neighbors. This unease exploded under **Mithradites VI** (120-63), King of Pontus, who fanned uprisings and waged a series of wars against Rome.

Mithradites' first Pontic Wars resulted in great massacres of Romans and ended in stalemates, but Mithradites' luck against the Romans finally ran out. The final Pontic War began in 72 B.C. and led to complete victory for the Roman generals **Lucullus** and **Pompey**, who broke and scattered the Pontic armies and pursued them to Armenia, where Mithradites ended his life. In the dying convulsions of the Kingdom of Pontus, Pharnaces II was crushed by three Roman divisions under **Julius Caesar**, who afterward reported simply *"Veni, Vidi, Vici" – I came, I saw, I conquered.*

Cities in Asia Minor had been wary of Roman rule, but it proved an almost universally prosperous period. Secure behind Rome's distant borders and enjoying the advantages of safe commerce, most of the world blossomed. Monuments, fortresses, and cities sprang up during the Roman Peace, many of them decorated by statues and stonework displaying the artistry of a wealthy age. The Romans borrowed their aesthetic from the Greeks, but seem to have been naturally deft administrators. Rome placed lands under the control of regional governors, and, excepting unusual periods of vicious taxation, populations were often better off than they had been under local rulers. At its height Rome's reach extended from England to the Arabian desert, and the Mediterranean was the Empire's private lake.

## THE BYZANTINE EMPIRE

Roman rule was enduring, but it eventually eroded. The excesses of various emperors are renowned, but the less glamorous stories of heavy taxation truly laid the groundwork for the collapse of Roman power in most of the world. In one famous case heavily taxed farmers were deserting the fields in such great numbers that the **Emperor Diocletian** (285-305) decreed that men must assume their fathers' careers.

Diocletian's heavy taxation and zealous attempts to make the lower classes contribute revenue to the imperial coffers had another face as well. Diocletian was responsible for one of the empire's last, greatest spasms of Christian genocide. During the final years of his reign, Diocletian ordered the imprisonment and execution of untold thousands of Christians, probably including **St. Nicholas**. Economics and religion had always been closely connected, and such was the case now. Under the Roman empire, Christianity had blossomed among the poor and the powerless and turned into a religion of resistance. Rome understood the threat from an early date, crucifying Jesus and executing Christians for sport in Roman circuses. Diocletian understood this, too; the masses were listening to the dangerous words of Christian clerics, not their governors and their Roman emperors.

However, Diocletian was one of the last emperors to persecute Christians. His efforts did not eliminate Christianity; it only seemed to drive it deeper. His successor, **Constantine**, continued many of Diocletian's reforms, but on the issue of Christianity he took a dramatically different course. After assuming the throne in 306 he was famously accommodating to the religion, eventually embracing it as his own. In this Constantine was less pious than populist: the masses in the east were largely Christian, and after uniting the divided empire and shifting the capital to **Byzantium** (later **Constantinople**), Constantine sought their support. The new Roman Empire (which always considered itself the Roman, not Byzantine, Empire) became, by fits and starts, a Christian empire.

Rome fell to **Alaric** and the Goths in 410 A.D. This was not, incidentally, a mere onslaught of barbarians, but a studied campaign under Alaric, a Roman general with command of the western theater. The Byzantines, secure behind the then-indomitable walls of Constantinople, became the Roman standard bearers. The Roman Empire was to dramatically evolve in its new captial. Christianity, once a threat, was established as the state religion by Theodosius I (379-395). Under the **Emperor Justinian** (527-565), this left one of its indelible marks in the form of the **Haghia Sophia**, an enormous cathedral that remained the largest free standing structure in the world for 1,000 years, and stands today. Constantinople became a repository for objects of value and beauty, and the empire renewed itself time and again after repelling invaders from the very walls.

The Byzantines were masters of intrigue, with a legacy as old as Rome itself of dividing and suborning its enemies. Some emperors were masters of this, some were masters of warfare, and some, like **Heraclius** (610-641) and **Basil I** (867-886), were masters of both. The latter is best known for his long campaign against the Bulgars, and the cruelty of his final victory; after capturing 10,000 Bulgars Basil ordered all of them blinded, with the exception of one man per 100, who was left a single eye to lead the others home. In the midst of the dark ages, this cruelty hardly dimmed the Byzantine's precious light. With Europe turned barbarous, Constantinople was the last western refuge of culture and civilization.

## THE TURKS

**Mohammed** began his teaching around 612, and the Arabs were quick to heed his call. Taxation had almost invited revolt, and Mohammed's Muslim teaching came of age while the Byzantine Empire was badly weakened. Soon after his death, the Arabs coursed into the west under the flag of *Jihad* (holy war), sacking Alexandria, ravaging Asia Minor, and investing Constantinople itself. This new threat was ended by a decisive Byzantine victory in 718, but foreshadowed events yet to come.

Muslims prospered in the deserts of Arabia, eventually spilling into the Holy Land to take Jerusalem in the tenth century. At the same time, a new group of tribal warriors were emerging from the northeast and taking up the Muslim mantle. These were **Turks**, akin to the Bulgars and various other peoples that had challenged Byzantium in earlier years. Turkic tribes, warrior opportunists and refugees from central Asia, began establishing themselves along the eastern borders and creating turmoil along the frontier. The short-lived Kingdom of Armenia, centered on Ani near Kars, was an early victim of the Turks. The Byzantines were slow to react, and when, at last, the young, promising emperor Romanus IV Diogenes marched east to pacify the newcomers, his efforts were hamstrung by administrative errors and treachery.

In 1071, Romanus' large Byzantine army was soundly defeated at the **Battle of Manzikert** (modern Malazgirt, north of Lake Van) by Alp Arslan, leader of the Selçuk Turks. Romanus IV was captured and ransomed at a great cost in treasure and prestige, and the Selçuks won land concessions from the Byzantines.

The Byzantines were badly shaken by the loss of power in Anatolia. In the best Byzantine tradition, out of this hardship emerged a strong, able leader. Alexius I Comneni (1081-1118) checked the Selçuks, broke a siege of Constantinople, and appeared ready for a campaign to restore control of Anatolia. However, Alexius' plans were completely undone by a most unwelcome helping hand. Anger over the loss of the Holy Lands had been percolating in the west, and in 1097 the **First Crusade** erupted out of Europe. The Crusaders marched through Byzantine lands en route to the Holy Land, and the benefit of their victories over Arab armies there were almost offset by the damage they did to their Byzantine allies. Alexius I did his best to take advantage of the Crusaders, but bitterness developed on both sides.

The hard feelings came to a head in the **Fourth Crusade** in 1204, when the Crusaders turned on their Orthodox Christian brethren and sacked, burned, and looted Constantinople itself. The Byzantines regrouped in Asian kingdoms, where the Selçuks were now facing troubles of their own; Mongols had emerged from the east, crushing their armies and seizing possession of most of their cities. Turkish tribes, too, continued to appear, among these the followers of Ertuğrul whose son Osman would found the Ottoman dynasty.

## THE OTTOMANS

The Byzantines recaptured Constantinople in 1263, but the turmoil in Asia Minor ensured that they would not reestablish their mastery of Anatolia. Without that, they were a shadow of their former empire, vulnerable to the warlike **Ottomans** that settled on their frontier at Eskişehir, south of the Sea of Marmara. The Ottomans were warlike, the product of a hardscrabble nomadic background, but the first Ottoman sultans were much more than warlords.

**Osman**, **Orhan**, and **Murat I** ruled from 1288 to 1389, and each proved a far-sighted administrator as well as a formidable soldier. While other Turkic settlements flared up and quickly faded, the Ottomans were patient and shrewd, marshalling their strength and avoiding confrontation except on their own terms. The Ottomans insinuated themselves ever closer to the Sea of Marmara, taking Yenişehir, then Bursa. By 1360, they were in possession of a broad expanse of land between the Dardanelles and Eskişehir, and by 1370 they had shifted their capital to Edirne north of Constantinople.

The Byzantines watched the Ottoman conquests with increasing alarm, but were no longer strong enough to risk confrontation. Without military power, the Byzantine reliance on diplomacy was futile. The

Byzantines had nothing left to bargain with; Europe regarded the Ortho-dox Greeks as enemies worse than the infidel Turks, and Constantinople's coffers were empty. **Sultan Beyazid I Yildirim "Thunderbolt"** began relentlessly choking off the city in 1398. Three years later, on the verge of Constantinople's capitulation, the Tatar conqueror **Tamurlane** appeared in Asia Minor. Beyazid abandoned the siege and assembled an army to meet the threat. The armies met at Ankara in 1402, each force with a mystique of invincibility. Tamurlane orchestrated a masterful battle, and Beyazid was defeated and captured.

In the aftermath, Tamurlane's armies sacked most of the principal cities of Asia Minor. Had Tamurlane sought control of the region it would have been his, but the western campaign was simply a diversion. Tamurlane left Asia Minor in 1403, marching back into Central Asia en route to a planned conquest of China. He died en route to China and his possessions evaporated.

After Tamurlane's departure, Beyazid's sons fought one another for the broken empire. **Mehmet I** emerged victorious in 1413, and his work and the work of his son completely restored the Ottoman Empire.

Meanwhile the Byzantines had done nothing to help themselve after their reprieve from Beyazid's siege, and by 1451 it was too late. **Mehmet II** (1451-1481) assumed the throne with the immediate intention of taking Constantinople. For this purpose he ordered the construction of ships, fortresses, and special artillery pieces. He cut the city off as his great-grandfather Beyazid had done, then in 1453 laid siege to the massive land walls.

After two months of bloody fighting, the Ottomans seized Constantinople, at last accomplishing what Muslim armies had been striving to do for 700 years. The Ottoman conquest was traumatic, but the new rulers revitalized the city. Sultan Mehmet II forced subjects to resettle in the underpopulated city, and soon restored it to a bustling, vibrant metropolis. Within three generations the Ottoman Empire matched the Byzantines at their zenith, controlling the eastern Mediter-ranean, Egypt, eastern Europe and the Balkans, the Black Sea, and Iran. During the empire's high water mark under **Süleyman the Magnificent** Europe echoed with the peals of "Turk Bells," church bells lamenting another Turkish victory. During this period the Ottomans represented a terrifying mystery to the westerners, a practically invincible military that advanced into battle to the terrifying crash of a military band, bringing superior tactics and an alien religion.

The mystique began to fade under Süleyman the Magnificent's successor, Selim II. Süleyman himself was partly to blame for the decline, having instituted short-sighted economic reforms and killing his well-loved eldest son Mustafa as a result of harem intrigue. Selim could chug wine, but was otherwise a feckless dolt; Selim's dithering led to a great naval defeat at the **Battle of Lepanto** in 1571. For the Europeans this success was an inspiration and a turning point, after which they gradually began recapturing their lost lands. It was just one battle among many, but Lepanto signaled an end to the Ottoman's dominance in open warfare. Even so, the empire was to remain mighty for another century, and it would stay intact for more than three more centuries.

The credit for the Turks' continued success had little to do with its later sultans, who were generally as bad as the first ten had been good. In the absence of leadership from the sultan, several **Grand Viziers** emerged from the Palace Schools to lead the empire wisely. Preeminent among these were the **Köprülüs**, three generations of Albanians who guided the empire in the absence of an effective sultan.

By the 19th century, the Ottoman Empire had lost its vitality and was called **the sick man of Europe** by Russian Czar Nicholas. In a peculiar twist, neighbors endeavored to prop up the floundering empire for fear that its collapse would open the door to Russsian expansion. From Peter the Great onward the Russians had stalked their southern neighbor, coveting its ports and its access to the Mediterranean. A series of wars brought the Russians ever closer to their goal – and as early as 1804 Napoleon judged that the Ottoman Empire was certain to "fall in our time." Despite the best efforts of some of the late Ottoman sultans to bankrupt the empire and antagonize its powerful neighbors, the Ottomans hung on into the 20th century.

But only just. Ottoman citizens had become aware of Western reforms and began demanding a say in the rule of the country. This was provisionally granted in 1908, but proved a failure. In the midst of the struggle for a relaxation of the sultan's autocratic powers, the Turks found their former vassals in the Mediterranean and the Balkans rising up and defeating their foreign garrisons. Most humiliating were a series of defeats at the hands of the Romanians, Greeks, and Bulgarians beginning in 1910.

Just as Turkey was recovering from this, it was dragged onto the global stage; **World War I** had begun. The Turks weighed in on the side of Germany and the Central Powers against France and England. The Ottomans scored an unexpected early victory at **Gallipoli** under Mustafa Kemal, later known as Atatürk, but this promise was followed by dramatic defeats in Arabia. With the war's end, the Turks and their German allies shared defeat, and the **Treaty of Sevres** was designed to finally dissolve the Ottoman Empire. Most of the victorious allies were ceded tracts of the former empire. İstanbul became a neutral territory, and the Turkish nation was squeezed into the interior between Sivas and Eskişehir.

## KEMAL ATATÜRK

At first it seemed that the exhausted and demoralized Turks were resigned to the partition, with the exception of some hotheads in the interior. The British now turned to **Mustafa Kemal**, (who later became **Kemal Atatürk**) the most highly respected military man in Turkey after his leadership at Gallipoli and on the Syrian frontier, to take a post in Anatolia and pacify the people there. Kemal accepted the appointment, but upon arrival in the interior immediately turned on the allies and what had now become a pet Ottoman government. Kemal sought out nationalist leaders, helped convene a congress, established a nationalist army, and renounced the government in İstanbul.

To the government, Kemal was a traitor, and to Kemal the government that signed onto the disgraceful Treaty of Sevres was the traitor. The rebel nationalist government condemned the treaty, which concerned the European negotiators. The matter came to a head with Greece's 1920 invasion. This forceful occupation of their Sevres Treaty lands on the Aegean was encouraged by Britain, but proved a grave mistake. The Turks' apathy exploded into anger at the violence of this invasion by their former vassals; Mustafa Kemal's nationalists marched against the invading army.

After stalemating the Greeks in the interior, Kemal began a push for the Aegean, which he reached in September 1922. The **War of Independence** ended with the Greeks sailing away from a burning Izmir, and the allies realizing that the genuine Turkish government was now Kemal's nationalist body at Ankara.

World War I left Western Europe with little stomach for continued fighting, and some of the allies (Italy and France, for instance) were not pleased that the original partition had left Britain in command of the Mosul oil fields. Kemal's nationalists left the divided allies no choice other than to fight or draft a new peace. The allies chose the latter, and in the **Treaty of Lausanne** Turkey's borders were extended to their current size (the Hatay/Antakya area was a later addition). The treaty also approved an exchange of populations, shifting Greeks in Turkey to Greece and Turks in Greece back to Turkey.

Kemal's series of dangerous gambles had paid off, and he now set about establishing a strong, western-looking nation. He set the tone immediately, making Ankara the permanent capital and turning his back on the intrigues of İstanbul. He steered a careful, peaceful course with his neighbors as only a military man could do, and carried out a raft of remarkable reforms. He abolished the fez, put women on equal footing with men, changed the alphabet from Arab to Latin letters, eliminated "Arab" words in the Turkish language, created a secular government, and instituted a tradition of last names, choosing Atatürk, or "Father Türk" for himself. Kemal Atatürk proved one of the most charismatic and visionary men in history, with a rare strength of will that made him both a great revolutionary and a great nation-builder.

According to a popular story, British Prime Minister Lloyd George, surveying the wreckage of the Treaty of Sevres, shook his head and said "A man like this comes along once a century; how could we have known?"

## THE TURKISH REPUBLIC

Atatürk was the first president of the Republic, and remained so until his death in 1938. Atatürk's successor was one of his close friends and top generals, **Ismet Inönü**. Inönü continued Atatürk's secular vision, and was careful to heed Atatürk's advice against entering World War II. Turkey succeeded in maintaining its neutrality despite the entreaties of various allies. Only in 1945, with the allies marching toward Berlin, did Turkey cast its lot with the winners. In the aftermath of the war the Soviet Union began making claims on Turkey's eastern cities on behalf of their Armenian citizens. These claims resulted in almost immediate American support for Turkey, in accordance with the Truman doctrine of discouraging Communist expansion, and in reprisals against Turkey's long-persecuted Armenian minority.

Turkey was embraced by the North Atlantic Treaty Organization (NATO) in 1952. Turkey was that organization's stable southern anchor throughout the Cold War, and remains so today with NATO's largest standing army. That stability, however, was not a reflection of internal politics. During the last years of Ismet Inönü's presidency, the first major popular elections were held and the country seemed ready to settle into western-style democracy. It was an abortive attempt; the military staged a coup in 1960, charging the sitting Democratic Party with bungling the economy and, ironically, undermining democracy. The principals of the deposed government were ousted and some of them, including Prime Minister **Adnan Menderes**, were executed. A new constitution was drawn up and new elections were held in 1961.

This process was to repeat itself at ten year intervals. The 1971 coup came in the wake of a deteriorating economy and leftist uprisings. The military seized power and called for new elections, and a particularly troubled period began. The Greek island of **Cyprus** had been a trouble spot ever since the United Nations was forced to step in to separate Greek and Turkish Cypriots in 1963. Pressure increased, fed by the old rivalries between Greeks and Turks, until a Greek patriot staged a coup on the island with the intention of uniting with Greece. The clumsy coup attempt was the invitation the Turks had hoped for, and within 48 hours Turkish troops were ashore and seizing key towns and mountains under the (authentic) pretense that the Turkish population was in danger.

UN negotiators, NATO, and America moved quickly before Greece and Turkey had a chance to go to war. The issue was not – and is not – resolved. UN peacekeepers were posted along the border (known as the Green Line), and remain there today. The northern section of the island declared its independence in 1983, establishing the Turkish Republic of Northern Cyprus. "Greek" Cyprus enjoys international recognition, while Northern Cyprus is recognized only by Turkey.

The Greeks weren't the only former subjects creating headaches for Turkey in the 1970s. Kurdish and Armenian minorities began agitating violently against what they considered a legacy of oppression. In this they received at least tacit support from Russia, seeking what it had always sought, to weaken Turkey. Perhaps as a reaction against the chaos, Islamic fundamentalists began calling for a return to religious government. This only served to compound the problem, and, like clockwork, the military staged another coup in 1980.

Turkey's exercise in democracy seemed to have failed again. Bülent Ecevit, Süleyman Demirel, and Neçmettin Erbakan, all major players in today's Turkey, were arrested and imprisoned, as were thousands of others throughout the country. Amnesty International charged Turkey with 250,000 political arrests between 1980 and 1988. The restrictions and human rights violations, however, seemed to bring a degree of peace. A military general, Kenan Evren, assumed the presidency and, once again, called for elections.

The 1990s were ushered in, remarkably, *without* a coup. The country was on a relatively even keel at last. Iraq's invasion of Kuwait and the Gulf War turned attention away from internal problems. Turkish President **Turgut Özal** provided the allies with military support and initiated economic sanctions against Iraq, and Turkey's airfields were critical to the war. Iraq's demonization for its treatment of its Kurdish minority, however, drew attention to Turkey's own Kurds. Turkey moved to loosen restrictions on the Kurds, legalizing the language that had been declared illegal in one of the Republic's first acts. The reforms seem to have come too late, though; an internal war has erupted in Turkey's southeast, fomented and supported by Iraq, Iran, and Syria. As always, Turkey can be certain where its neighbors stand.

Europe remains stuffy toward the Turks. Over the din of objecting Greeks, the European Economic Community welcomed Turkey as a member in 1995, but there seems little chance that Turkey will be invited to join the European Union despite its membership in NATO. Not all Turks are sure that EU membership would be to Turkey's advantage

## HUMAN RIGHTS

*Turkish officials often simmer over Turkey's lousy human rights record. They intimate that Amnesty International and US-financed human rights investigators are making it all up. Sadly, they're not. The greatest problems have been in the southeast of the country, where martial law is in effect and the jittery Turks are heavy handed with the local population. Abuses are not, however, confined to the southeast. In the not too-distant past people with unpopular views would simply vanish, as was the case in Argentina and elsewhere in the world. Police have abused Turkish journalists so often that the Society for the Protection of Journalists lists Turkey with the likes of North Korea and China as one of the most dangerous places in the world for reporters. For further information, write to Amnesty International.*

*That said, internal and external pressure has long been mounting against Turkey to curb its abuses, with good effect. Turkey's economic pact with the European Union is contingent upon progress in human rights, and the United States and Canada are among the countries encouraging Turkey's progress. More importantly, however, courageous Turks have become accustomed to speaking out against political imprisonment and other crimes through the rapidly-growing and outspoken media. Local journalists, a courageous bunch who have seen their peers killed for their opinions, deserve particular recognition for publicizing incidents of brutality at great risk to themselves. The attention and concern of people within and without the nation have left their mark, and today the press enjoys increased freedom and human rights abuses appear to be subsiding. But concerns remain, particularly about torture in prisons against political prisoners and treatment of Kurds.*

anyway. Some push for stronger ties with Central Asia and the Middle East. The 1995 elections gave a hint of that sentiment, when the fundamentalist **Islamic Refah Party** led by **Neçmettin Erbakan** won the largest share of the votes. Two conservative parties, led by former Prime Minister Tansu Çiller and Meşut Yilmaz, proved unable to form a viable coalition government, forcing Çiller together with Erbakan in the summer of 1996.

The rise of an Islamic party was a stunning event in the Republic's steadfastly secular history, but Erbakan's populist stump speeches have been tempered since his election. Moreover, he has ventured to neighboring Islamic countries and often found them as cool to Turkey as Europe often seems to be. Turkey is vital to Europe, Central Asia, and the Middle East, but, in the end, Turkey stands alone.

## PRESIDENTS OF THE TURKISH REPUBLIC

| | |
|---|---|
| Kemal Atatürk | 1923-1938 |
| Ismet Inönü | 1938-1950 |
| Celal Bayar | 1950-1959 |
| Cemal Gürsel | 1959-1966 |
| Cevdet Sunay | 1966-1973 |
| Fahri Korutürk | 1973-1980 |
| Kenan Evren | 1980-1989 |
| Turgut Özal | 1989-1993 |
| Süleyman Demirel | 1993- |

# 6. PLANNING YOUR TRIP

## BEFORE YOU GO

### WHEN TO VISIT - CLIMATE & WEATHER

Turkey bills itself as the "world's largest open air museum," so it comes as no surprise that weather is important. You will want to write postcards home to the effect that "Using some fallen columns as a bench, we rested in the shadow of the Temple of Apollo," rather than "Hands numb. Slipped in mud going up to $%#& Temple of Apollo and broke camera. Knee hurts." Generally, it is important to stick to the spring, summer, and early fall to avoid rain and cold temperatures.

The tourism season proper runs from late May through early September, and, fortunately, the tourism weather usually runs from April through mid-October. Along the southern coast you can even milk a few extra weeks of comfortable swimming weather, but in the interior – including İstanbul – you cannot fudge these dates much without risking arctic conditions. When winter storms hit, they can be long and patient, blowing bitter cold down past the Russian steppe and over the Black Sea toward the Aegean. The interior becomes muddy, frozen, and windswept, and sights like Cappadoccia lose a lot of their charm. Even İstanbul, a city at sea level on the same latitude as Redding, California, can become dark and (speaking of Redding) joyless in the winter.

Note that during the the truly cold spells, the Bosphorous actually freezes over, an event that is said to happen only once a century. The coastal areas usually remain mild in the winter months – the beaches of Antalya average 50° F, but do not count on getting your mid-winter tan.

As the thermometer goes, so go airfares and room rates. So, too, go crowds. It is not uncommon to have a good part of a marquee attraction like Ephesus to yourself in April and May, but come August tour buses disgorge thousands of tourists – if the bay hadn't silted up and forced the Ephesians to abandon the city, the tourists certainly would have driven them out. Book ahead in the high season – Turkey is absolutely wonder-

## TEMPERATURE CHART IN °F

|  | JAN | FEB | MAR | APR | MAY | JUN | JUL | AUG | SEPT | OCT | NOV | DEC |
|---|---|---|---|---|---|---|---|---|---|---|---|---|
| Antalya | 50 | 52 | 55 | 61 | 68 | 77 | 82 | 82 | 77 | 68 | 58 | 54 |
| Aegean (Izmir) | 48 | 50 | 52 | 61 | 68 | 77 | 82 | 80 | 73 | 65 | 58 | 50 |
| İstanbul | 41 | 43 | 45 | 54 | 61 | 70 | 73 | 73 | 68 | 61 | 54 | 47 |
| (Black Sea) Trabzon | 43 | 43 | 45 | 52 | 58 | 68 | 71 | 71 | 66 | 58 | 54 | 48 |
| (Interior) Ankara | 32 | 34 | 41 | 52 | 61 | 68 | 73 | 73 | 65 | 55 | 47 | 36 |

ful in the summer, and that has not been a secret for 4,000 years. If you do brave the inclement weather and venture to Turkey in the off season, you will be rewarded with plentiful vacancies, low rates, and friendlier, less frayed people.

## WHAT TO PACK

You know what you'll want to bring along, but here are a few tips. Winter in Turkey – especially the interior and, to a lesser extent, İstanbul – is cold. Forget about the Mediterranean, most of Turkey is downright wintry.

A few things you might not think of: a black crayon and large pieces of sturdy paper for making rubbings of inscriptions in stone; a good flashlight, particularly handy in the caves and warrens of Cappadoccia; a flat plastic sink stopper for emergencies; converters for 220 volts, which will burn out most 110 volt North American electrical appliances; two prong adapters for the electrical outlets; a Turkish phrasebook; watercolors or charcoal, even if you don't think you can draw or paint; a pocket calculator; and earplugs to muffle the 4 a.m. call to prayer. Also, if you're bringing a laptop computer, check our computer section for accessories you may want.

As far as dress, you can probably leave the tie at home, but Turkey is fairly conservative and so should you be. Once off the beach try to avoid anything too revealing. Skin may not draw a second glance in İstanbul or at the beaches, but it will in most of the rest of the country. Women should bring along a shawl – or count on buying one in Turkey – for use in mosques and holy sites. Most coastal cities are used to seeing skin, but in some smaller towns the moment you leave the beach parking lot you are in a conservative village; try to respect the local sensibilities.

## WHAT TO READ

Some people have been working their way through books on the area since childhood and they're still missing important pieces. If this were a class, the most fun damned class you ever had, required reading would include:

Kinross, Lord Patrick, *Atatürk, The Birth of a Nation*, London, 1964

Kinross, Lord Patrick, *The Ottoman Centuries, The Rise and Fall of the Turkish Empire*, New York, 1977

Norwich, John Julius, *Byzantium: The Early Centuries*, London, 1988; *Byzantium: The Apogee*, London, 1991; *Byzantium: The Decline and Fall*, London 1995

Herodotus, *The History* (trans. David Grene), Chicago, 1987

Homer, *The Iliad*, (trans. Richard Lattimore), Chicago, 1951

Xenophon, *The Persian Expedition* (trans. Rex Warner), Middlesex, 1949

**Special Interest Guides**

Blake, Everett C. and Edmonds, Anna G., *Biblical Sites in Turkey*, İstanbul, 1977. Discusses the Seven Churches of Revelation, and addresses the religions that Christianity supplanted.

Bean, George, *Aegean Turkey, An Archeological Guide*, London, 1966; *Turkey's Southern Shore, An Archaeological Guide*, London, 1968; *Turkey Beyond the Maeander, An Archeological Guide*, London, 1971; *Lycian Turkey, An Archeological Guide*, London, 1978. Bean's books are the finest written on Turkey's ruins.

Ceram, C.W. *Gods, Graves, and Scholars*, London, 1961. A wonderfully written account of modern archaeology and its major players.

Abidine, Zeynep et al. *İstanbul and Northwest Turkey*, Knopf, New York, 1993. A beautiful guide book dedicated to İstanbul.

Dubin, Marc and Lucas, Enver, *Trekking in Turkey*, Hawthorne, Australia, 1993. The only English book of its kind for Turkey.

Misc. Ed., *İstanbul: The Halı Rug Guide*, London, 1996. What to know and where to buy in İstanbul.

Glassie, Henry, *Turkish Traditional Arts Today*. Excellent background resource for kilims and carpets.

**Recommended Literature**

Pamuk, Orhan, *The White Castle*, London, 1990; *The Black Book*, Boston, 1994.

Kemal, Yasar, *Mehmed, My Hawk*, Harper Collins, New York, 1993; *Anatolian Tales*, Writers & Readers Publishing, 1983.

Twain, Mark, *The Innocents Abroad*. An American icon's dim view of Turkey.

## PASSPORTS & VISAS

Residents of the United States and Canada will have no problems getting a three month **tourist visa** upon arrival. Getting a visa can be somewhat stressful if you happen to be coming overland – the Turks seem to post their second string immigration officers in Edirne and Antakya – but don't let their histrionics faze you. Most Americans, Europeans, and Asians get their visas at the point of entry. Immigration officers at airports and seaports are usually professional and quick.

The easiest way for residents of the Canada or the United States to apply for a **passport** is to call the main branch of the local post office and follow their instructions. They have the forms you need, or they can tell you who does. Canadians can call for further information at *Tel. 800/567-6868* or (Quebec) *283-2152*, and the U.S. Passport Information office has 24-hour service at *Tel. 202/647-0518*.

Keep a photocopy of your passport with you – or exchange with your traveling partner – as a hedge against thievery. A lost passport will bring your good times to an end, so keep some other identification with you to help the nearest U.S. consulate or embassy get you set up with a new one.

Note: Technically, yes, you are supposed to keep your passport with you at all times. If you want to shed the passport in big cities, however, the worst that will happen is an overanxious police officer will make you return to your room and show it. You will want to make sure that you have your passport along while you are in transit, and bear in mind that police often set up automobile checkpoints along roads within İstanbul and other cities. A minor hassle can graduate to a real problem if you do not have your passport while in transit.

### CUSTOMS

As discussed in the İstanbul chapter, since you're almost sure to arrive there, you're unlikely to be pulled aside at customs. If you are, the sorts of things you aren't supposed to have you're not likely to have; more than 400 cigarettes, for instance, or five liters of liquor. Notebook computers, once illegal with a hard disk greater than, uhm, 128K, are now welcome. Some of the stranger restrictions are universally ignored, but you never know; five rolls of film is technically the limit, as is 2.2 pounds of chocolate and 3.3 pounds of coffee. You needn't worry about any of these unless it looks like you're going to start up your own business.

Customs on departing was once a hassle, with lots of cross referencing between receipts and numbers in your passport. Now it's as effortless as entry. If you have purchased an antique carpet you were given a receipt and a certificate; you'll want to have these handy. Export of antiquities of any kind is forbidden, although old carpets can be exported with the proper paperwork.

You were once able to recoup 15 percent of large purchases with a refund of Turkish value added tax, and technically you still should be able to. If you depart the country within three months of your purchase, make your purchases at authorized hotels and shops, and live outside of Turkey, you are eligible. The reality now is that this money will not be refunded. Most expensive items you're likely to have purchased – carpets and kilims, for example – are sold without VAT added. If you ask for an invoice the shop will tack on the 15 percent charge, and they'll give you some paperwork to try to get the 15 percent back. It's sort of ridiculous, so few people abide by it. Hotels have to charge you the tax, but for the time being there is no hope of getting it back.

**Returning Home**
Fresh food is forbidden, as are Cuban cigars, cigarettes in excess of 200, and alcohol in excess of one liter, although this last item is rarely observed. More worrying, if you indulged in lots of carpets and kilims, is tax. You are allowed $400 worth of purchases tax-free, but the next $1,000 is taxed at a 10 percent rate, and thereafter matters become confusing based on the sort of item and the specific tax rate. Sure, you can fudge a little – not that we would recommend it – but the customs guys are pretty shrewd. Tax is payable immediately. Most major international airports take credit cards. For more information contact the United States customs office, *Tel. 703/318-5900.*

## ACCOMMODATIONS

We have put a premium on finding spots with peace and quiet, places where bougainvillea climb the rails and the view is good. Sometimes we recommend pensions, sometimes three star hotels and inns, and even, occasionally, giant beachfront hotels. The common denominators among our finds include attention to detail, friendly management, and the aforementioned peace. As a result, we tend to neglect destination resorts such as Marmaris, Kemer, and Ölüdeniz in favor of the smaller, friendlier places nearby .

Make no mistake, this hardly sentences you to being a placid bookworm on your vacation. We recommend bars, night clubs, and belly dancing restaurants – not to mention paragliding, rafting, canyoning, cycling, diving and scaling sheer cliffs to poke around in cave tombs. But at the end of the day it does your heart good to have a pretty terrace, a tidy room, and a helpful staff. Unfortunately, the best of the hotels we have selected are so nice that you won't ever want to leave the premises and actually see Turkey.

## RESERVATIONS

If you are planning your own trip and booking ahead, it is always wise to inquire about the best available rates from the sales office at the hotel you are interested in. If, for instance, you would like to stay at the Sheraton in Ankara, their sales office will be much more flexible than the toll free reservation office; the cost of faxing Turkey will be more than offset by your savings. If you're staying  more than one night, on business, or use nice stationery you should get a discount. If it's the off season in the region (which is August and September in Ankara, by the way), the sales personnel will be particularly keen to cut your rate.

American Express, Council Travel, Wagon Lit, and other companies have travel management offices that can be of service. They are often able to secure discounts of 30 percent or more.

We have provided fax numbers for those hotels that have them; most do. If you're dealing directly with a hotel they should send you a list of half board rates and other options if they have them. **The prices given in this book are for the high season;** you may be pleasantly surprised by the rate you get. If you learn that the hotel you are interested in is booked, ask the hotel directly which travel agents they work with. There's a strong likelihood they have rented a cluster of rooms to one of the British agencies, and the agency will have rooms.

**Finally,** we have accepted no money or inducements in exchange for favorable reviews.

**Booking Agencies**

Booking agencies specializing in Turkey can arrange accommodations and even transfers in areas of particular interest. These are not, strictly speaking, tour group companies, although several of them offer excursions. The advantage of these companies is that they arrange accommodations at many of the nicer hotels in heavily trafficked areas at a bulk discount, and can often offer a much better deal than you will get independently. If you're looking for a resort hotel along the Mediterranean or Aegean, inquire about their hotel selections.

You'll notice the following companies are based in the UK, since our former imperial rulers are far more used to dealing with Turkey than North American companies. Besides, you can find American agencies on the Internet; www.turkey.org has a good listing of American companies, though none we know of are as practiced in Turkey as the following:

**Tapestry Holidays,** *286 Chiswick High Rd., London W41PA UK, Tel. 44 081 742 0077.* For the moderate price range, a strong selection of hotels on the Mediterranean. One of the best of the lot.

**Anatolian Sky,** *Imex House, 52 Blucher St. Birmingham B11QU UK, Tel. 44 021 633 4018.* Specializing in classic hotels in İstanbul and north of Marmaris on the Gulf of Gökova.

**Authentic Turkey,** *20 Notting Hill Gate, London, W113JE UK, Tel. 44 071 221 3878.* Authentic has a collection of affordable accommodations on the mediterranean.

**Mosaic Holidays,** *Patman House, George Lane, London W45LY UK, Tel. 44 081 532 9050.* Mosaic has a good collection of fancy, large resorts.

**Sunquest**, *9 Grand Parade, Green Lanes, London N41JX UK, Tel. 44 081 742 0077.* Turkish Maritime Lines uses Sunquest as its English sales office, and the company has a good catalog of hotels throughout the country.

## GETTING TO TURKEY

### BY AIR

A few flights serve Ankara directly, but virtually everyone arrives in İstanbul (see İstanbul chapter, Arrivals and Departures, for more information). İstanbul's **Atatürk Airport** is served by a host of major airlines, including Air France, British Air, Lufthansa, and Delta. The national carrier, **Turkish Airlines**, is a well-run organization and is worth considering for its direct New York-İstanbul flights. With a direct flight you won't arrive fresh, but you'll be in much better shape than if you fly via Helsinki, London, or Frankfurt. Plus, you won't miss your connection in Europe or have to wander around an extra airport jet-lagged, and Turkish Airlines sometimes throws in a free transfer to Kayseri or Antalya.

No matter who you fly, fares to İstanbul aren't cheap – but there are good fares lurking out there. A good travel agent can save you hundreds of dollars. The cheapest low season return fares from New York to İstanbul begin at $700, but these prices erupt in the summer, when a return fare increases to $1,150.

A few of the best place to go hunting for fare information in North America are:

- **Turkish Air Travel Bureau**, *20 East 49th St., New York, NY 10017, Tel. 212/888-1180*
- **Travel CUTS**, *187 College St., Toronto, Canada M5T 1P7, Tel. 416/979-2406*
- **STA Travel**, *273 Newbury St., Boston, MA 02116, Tel. 617/266-6014; 920 Westwood Blvd., Los Angeles, CA 90024, Tel. 213/824-1574; 17 East 45th St., New York, NY 10017, 212/986-9470; 166 Geary St., Ste. 702, San Francisco, CA 94108, 415/391-8407*

The UK has an excellent collection of shops with cheap airfares – the only trick is you have to get to Britain. The enduring champion among London's bucket shops is **Trailfinders**, *46 Earls Court Rd., London, W8 6EJ, Tel. 44 171 937 5400.* You can also consult the backpacker's rag, London-based *TNT Magazine* (free issue at http://www.tntmag.co.uk).

---

### THE JET LAG-MATHEMATICS TRAP

*Turkey is 11 time zones away from the U.S., which means you can be prey to awful jet-lag if you aren't careful. A surprisingly effective trick to simply not to do the math. As you fly across the Atlantic, set your watch when the pilot tells you the local time. Do not start calculating how long you've been awake or what time it should be. You will exhaust yourself if you begin thinking. Take a look at the sky: is the sun setting? Then it's evening. It's just evening.*

---

## BY BOAT

If you're fortunate enough to be leaving for Turkey from Italy, there are Turkish Maritime Lines ferries weekly, one from Brindisi, several from Venice. As detailed below you should contact **Turkish Maritime Lines**: *information in Turkey, Tel. 212 244 2502, Reservations Tel. 212 249 9222, Fax 212 251 9025.*

A wiser course may be to make reservations through an English broker, **Sunquest London Holiday Ltd.**, *23 Princes St., London, WIR 7RG UK, Tel. 44 171 499 9992, Fax 44 171 499 9995.*

### • Antalya/Marmaris/Izmir/İstanbul-Venice, Italy

Ferries leave Marmaris and Antalya at noon on Wednesday, arriving in Venice on Saturday at 10 a.m. Departures from Venice are scheduled at 4 p.m. Saturday. In the off season, the cost for cabins with windows starts at $350 per person, one way, increasing to $450 in the high season. Interior cabins with four beds begin at $250 in the off-season, increasing to $310 in the high season. Pullman seats cost $210 in the low season. Meals are included on the three day trip. Ferrying a car is $240 in the high season, plus port tax.

Izmir and İstanbul departures are at 4 p.m. Wednesday, arriving Venice at 11 a.m. Saturday. Prices are the same for the Antalya and Marmaris ferries.

### • Çeşme-Brindisi, Italy

Ferries depart Çeşme, west of Izmir, at 11 a.m. Tuesday and noon Friday. The trip takes 31 hours, arriving Brindisi at 6 p.m. Wednesday and 7 p.m. Saturday. Ferries return to Çeşme from Brindisi after a five hour wait. Ferries do not run in the winter. One way high season fare ranges between $400 for a deluxe cabin and $180 for a four bed, internal cabin. Pullman armchair rates are $160 in the high season, and car ferrying costs $200, plus $30 port tax. Full board is included.

For information about sailing your own ship into a Turkish port, contact Istanbul's **Chamber of Maritime Commerce**, *Meclisi Mebusan Caddesi No. 22, Salıpazar, İstanbul, Tel. 212 252 0131, Fax 212 293 7935.*

## GETTING AROUND TURKEY

### BY AIR

**Turkish Airlines**, the national carrier, and the smaller, cheaper **İstanbul Airlines** are the two options for flights within Turkey. Virtually every major city in Turkey has air service, but connections are either through İstanbul or Ankara. Air fares are fairly uniform from İstanbul; $75 one way, $125 return.

İstanbul Air has much less frequent flights and serves only the prime airports – Trabzon, Antalya, Dalaman, Ankara, and Izmir – but their fares average about $60 one way, $100 round trip. Istanbul's domestic airport has a terminal apart from the international section.

For information within Turkey, do yourself a favor and contact **Imperial Turizm**, *Divan Yolu Caddesi No. 31, Sultanahmet, İstanbul, 212 513 9430, Fax 212 512 3291.* The address and phone number for **Turkish Airlines** is: *Atatürk Hava Limanı, Yesilköy, İstanbul, Tel. 212 663 6300, Fax 212 663 4744.*

### BY BUS

Bus travel in Turkey is cheap, popular, and efficient. The top bus lines have spacious, comfortable coaches, coffee, comfortable seats and – on the main İstanbul routes – fresh copies of the *Turkish Daily News*. Bus connections are easy in the west and along the Black Sea; faster, nicer, and often cheaper than train service.

In 1997, Turkey put an end to smoking on inter-city buses. It remains to be seen how well the regulation is observed. You should still stick to the major carriers when possible and continue asking for "Sigarasiz" (no smoking) buses if smoke is an irritant.

**Varan** is the finest bus line, followed by **Ulusoy**. In the next echelon, Kamil Koç and Metro do a good job. The prices are outstanding: Varan's relatively expensive service from İstanbul to Antalya – 12 hours, overnight – runs $30, and the 19 hour trip from İstanbul to Trabzon is $35.

You should also be familiar with the **dolmuş**, a term we use throughout the book. A dolmuş is a public transport minibus, a little more expensive than normal buses but usually more comfortable. They're privately run, with rates based on the distance they take you.

In many cities the **otogar**, or bus station, is located outside of town. In such cases, there will almost certainly be ticket offices in the center of town, and you can get a shuttle out to the main otogar. Such is the case in İstanbul, where ticket offices are ranged around Taksim and Sultanahmet.

One final note: try to avoid the front seats – one through four – on overnight trips. The drivers often maintain a long dialogue with their friends, and should you want to sleep through a stop you'll be bothered by noise, smoke, and cold from the open door.

---

### BUS TRAVEL WITH STYLE & PANACHE

*"People on Turkish buses are either going home or leaving home. I never met anyone who admitted to traveling on business or state duty... This was a swift, strong Ulusoy bus, from the long-distance road fleet which binds the Turkish continent together. Every hour or so, the conductor came down the aisle with a glass carboy of cologne. Cupped hands were held out and filled; faces and necks were laved and massaged. The conversations fell away, and the passengers slept."*

Neal Ascherson, **Black Sea: The Birthplace of Civilisation and Barbarism**, London: Vintage, 1995.

---

## BY CAR

Driving in Turkey is not a decision to be taken lightly. Turks have a remarkably more ... improvisational driving style than what you are accustomed to. Anyone can pull out in front of you at any time, and Turkish drivers expect it. You have to be prepared for it, too. The traffic laws seem to correspond almost exactly with physical laws – if your car is moving at 50 kilometers an hour and a truck wants to pull out 250 meters ahead, can the truck pull out in front of you if it assumes you will begin braking rapidly? If the answer is yes, the truck will pull out. You'll soon learn that to get anywhere, you have to do as they do.

Turkey's big cities don't require a car, and in İstanbul in particular you don't really want a car. Roads are laid out on a "maze" pattern, and they're subject to frequent gridlock. Turkish drivers tend to be good, but in İstanbul the combination of an alien driving style and congested, confusing roads makes the cheap local taxis an immensely better and more efficient option.

For all its peculiarities, driving seems remarkably more civil than it is in America. If you pull out ahead of someone, they may not like it but it won't bother them. Everyone is used to being cut off or jumped in line, and there is a nice flexibility to Turkish driving when you get used to it. If you're short on time, you probably won't get used to it. Take cabs.

Many of the main highways in Turkey are toll roads, so try to have smaller denomination currency available.

| DRIVING PHRASES | | |
|---|---|---|
| Caution | Dikkat | dee-kat |
| Stop | Dur | dyoor |
| Slow | Yavaş | yah-vash |
| Do not enter | Gırılmez | guh-rul-mez |
| One way | Tek Istıkamet | tek es-te-kahm-et |

**Car Rental**

Make rental car arrangements from home. Your local Avis, Budget, and Hertz representatives can be of great help. Once here you lose most of your bargaining power, and you're likely to be tagged with a few extra fees and charges. Renting cars in Turkey is expensive enough without compounding the problem.

Standard rates are slowly coming down, but they remain unusually high. This has something to do with incidence of accidents, but more to do with the local financial arrangements with the main rental car offices.

Sample rates are $300 per week for a very small Fiat Uno from April to June, and $366 per week in high season. A Suzuki Jeep costs $430 per week between April and June, $590 in the peak season.

Another advantage enjoyed by the large American-based agencies is the ability to deal with one-way rentals between different offices, which allows you, for instance, to set out from Kayseri near Cappadoccia and wind up in Selçuk on the Aegean.

## BY FERRY

Ferries within, and around Turkey are very popular in the high season, and reservations are necessary. **Turkish Maritime Lines** books directly, and ordinarily has an English speaker on hand *(Information: Tel. 212 244 2502, Reservations: Tel. 212 249 9222, Fax 212 251 9025)*. You can also make reservations through the English broker, **Sunquest London Holiday Ltd.**, *23 Princes St., London, WIR 7RG, Tel. 44 171 499 9992, Fax 44 171 499 9995*.

Once in Turkey you can make international reservations through **Karavan Travel Agency**, *Tel. 212 247 5044, Fax 212 241 5178*.

There are either four or five cabin classes on Turkish ferries. Deluxe and "A" cabins have sea views and are the most expensive. "B" and "C" cabins are cheaper, but offer no views. Hususi, or private, cabins are available on some routes, offering semi-deluxe accommodations. Pullman chairs are also available, as is space on deck in the summer season.

Teachers, students, people 65 years and older, and children 7-12 years old receive a 30 percent discount.

### Internal Ferries
#### • İstanbul-Izmir
*Depart İstanbul 6:30 p.m. Friday, arrive Izmir 12:45 p.m. Saturday. Depart Izmir 2 p.m. Sunday, arrive İstanbul 9 a.m. Monday.*

Double cabin fares range between $75 per person for a deluxe cabin and $30 per person for a "C" class cabin, with three levels in between. In addition, you can book a round trip from İstanbul ("Hafta Sonu Tur"), using the ferry as your hotel in Izmir on Saturday night: this increases the fare two and one-half times. Ferries run throughout the year. Meals are served three times daily, breakfast $3, lunch and dinner $10. Car transport costs $50.

A second option is the quicker İstanbul-Bandirma ferry, which connects with the Bandirma-Izmir train. This journey costs only $10 per person, departing İstanbul four times weekly with the Bandirma ferry. Departures are at 9 a.m. on Tuesday, Thursday, Friday and Saturday, with arrival in Bandirma five hours later. Contact the main ticket office in İstanbul at *Tel. 212 249 9222*, where English speakers are usually available to help you.

#### • İstanbul-Trabzon
Ferry service operates between late May and September, leaving İstanbul at 2 p.m. Monday, arriving at Trabzon about 9:30 a.m. Wednesday. The ferry continues on to Rize, then returns to İstanbul, departing Trabzon at 7:30 p.m. Wednesday. Arrival in İstanbul is at 3 p.m. Friday. Intermediate stops can include Zonguldak, Sinop, Samsun, and Giresun. Prices range between $30 for a Pullman seat and $80 for a "Lüks" cabin. Its worth the extra $30 expense to get an exterior cabin with a window.

Turkish Maritime Lines charges $55 for car transport between İstanbul and Trabzon. You may want to bring food along, as the food on board is relatively expensive ($10 for fixed menu lunch or dinner, $3 for breakfast). For a reservation from ports within Turkey, your best bet is to contact the local tourism information office and ask an English speaking staffer to make a reservation for you – the Trabzon information office is particularly accustomed to this. In İstanbul you can call the Maritime Lines offices direct, *Tel. 212 244 2502*.

### Regional Ferries
#### • Mersin-Turkish Republic of Northern Cyprus
Mersin is the most popular departure point for ferries to Northern Cyprus, with three ferries per week. Monday, Wednesday and Friday ferries depart Mersin in the late evening, arriving at Gazimagusta by 8

a.m. For information and to make reservations, check with the tourism information office on the waterfront (*Yeni Mah., İnönü Bulvarı, Tel. 324 231 2710*). Prices are expensive for the ten hour trip – $80 for a lüks cabin and $30 for a pullman seat. The ferry rates are little better than the airline prices from İstanbul, which run $60 to $80 per person. Ferries for Northern Cyprus also depart from Alanya and Taşucu near Silifke – the latter with two hour service to Girne, Cyprus – for $29.

• **Trabzon-Batum, Georgia**
Prices and times fluctuate, and it is necessary to complete a visa application at the Georgian consulate in Trabzon or in İstanbul. The tourism information office can be of help, as can local travel agencies such as Afacan Turizm in Trabzon.

• **Sinop-Odessa, Ukraine**
Ferries operate sporadically between Turkey's nothernmost point and Odessa in the Crimea. As with Georgian ferries, visas should be secured prior to departure. Contact the main Turkish Maritime Lines reservation office for more information, or the Sinop tourism information office.

### Greek Islands

There are many small ferries serving the Greek islands offshore of Turkey, with routes including the following: Ayvalık-Lesbos; Çeşme-Chios; Kuşadası-Samos; Bodrum-Kos; Marmaris-Rhodes; Kaş-Meis. Day visits are ordinarily not penalized with heavy border fees, but overnight stays are. Rates vary according to Turkish-Greek relations.

## BY TRAIN

Train service in Turkey is generally slow and uncomfortable, but most lines are extremely cheap. You can travel from İstanbul to Van in the far southeast, a 43 hour trip, for about $20.

As interesting as the train/ferry route above is, it doesn't fit into many schedules. Two far more popular and practical trains are the **Ankara Ekspress** and the **Pamukkale Ekspress**, departing Istanbul's Haydarpaşa Station. Both feature sleeper cars, departing in the evening and pulling into their destination in the early morning. Information is provided in the İstanbul chapter.

## SEEING TURKEY ON YOUR OWN

We strongly advise seeing Turkey independently, and if you bought this book that's what you believe, too. However we have to concede that group tours are an excellent option if you want to see everything on a budget (See *The Tour*, below). If you have three weeks, you might consider taking full advantage of a two week tour and the discount airfare and see Turkey with the group, then take the third week off by yourself in the place you like best.

Otherwise, Turkey is a place to be explored at your leisure. Good guides can make your experience much richer in some ways, but your best memories will always be of finding a cave by yourself, or having a quiet picnic atop an ancient acropolis.

## The Tour

Many American travelers, having made the long journey, feel compelled to see everything. The compulsion is understandable, and it can be rewarding, but consider Turkey's size and the distances involved. Seeing Troy, Pergamon, Ephesus, Bodrum, Antalya, Cappadoccia, and İstanbul, each deserving of achaeologists' entire lifetimes, requires great energy and resolve. If you intend do the grand tour, following in the footsteps of Alexander, consider a tour package. Two-week tours, airfare from New York included, can cost between $1300 in the spring and fall and $1700 per person in the summer. That price includes flight, meals, guides, transfers, entry fees, perfectly decent four star hotels, and no smoking coaches. The group tour companies secure rooms at a huge volume discount – hotels that cost $110 walking in the front door may go for as little as $15 in some seasons. You simply cannot see Turkey as cheaply and effortlessly any other way.

For cheap, thorough Turkey vacations in good quality accommodations we recommend **Tursem Tourism International** (*US Tel. 800 223-9169, 212 935 9210, Fax 212 935 9215*). Tursem offers tours at the rates mentioned above and has a deservedly good reputation and knowledgeable guides – our recommendation is confirmed by no less an authority than our own parents, who took a two week tour with Tursem. A huge listing of other tour companies with US or Canadian offices can be found on the Internet at *www.turkey.org*.

In addition to the whirlwind tours, you can find several niche tour companies. Among those with good reputations and interesting angles are **Inter-Church Travel**, *Middleburg Square, Kent CT201AZ,UK, Tel. 44 030 371 1535*, which features religious tours to the Seven Churches of Revelation; and **Art Tours**, *Valıkonağı Cad. No. 77/3, Polat Apt., Nişantaşı, İstanbul, Turkey, Tel. 212 231 0487, Fax 212 240 4945*. Art Tours focuses on city tours, specialty painting, and art tours.

## The Blue Cruise

You may not know about Blue Cruises, and before you make any plans you should. Blue Cruises, as sailing trips along the Turkish coast have become known, have become a staple of the perfect Turkish vacation; it was good enough for JFK Jr. and his wife on their honeymoon. Fortunately it requires neither blue blood nor old money to sign onto a week-long cruise along the Turkish coast, stopping at ruins and white sand beaches. Weekly rates begin at $250 per person in the off season – a remarkably good price for a week of ruins, sun, meals and a bed. Not everyone can fit time for a cruise into their schedule, but we highly recommend it. Just because you're relaxing on a boat doesn't mean your trip is historically bankrupt; you'll stop in at gorgeous sunken ruins and old citadels.

**Gulets** have small launches for running back and forth to shore, and most gülets have some fishing tackle on board, so you can sink a lure into the sea and make yourself feel more productive while you spawl in the sun. Food is usually filling, although this is one of the glaring weaknesses with the cheaper companies. As you'll realize the moment you set foot in Bodrum or Marmaris, there are dozens, even hundreds of companies that offer cruises. They are all competent, but there is obviously some variation. Most companies send you out in a classic twin-masted wooden sloop, called a **gulet**, that sleeps between 6 and 10 people. Some large ships are beginning to turn up now, the equivalent of cruising tour buses that can sleep upwards of 30. **Tirhandils**, smaller sailing vessels, are also available.

There are two basic ways to hire a gület. The least expensive way is to take a berth. Gulet companies that hire out this way charge at least $250 per person per week in April, May, and October, and $375 per person per week in August and September. This usually excludes food and drinks (arranged beforehand) but includes the rest, including captain, cook, and deckhand. For meals you can buy and cook the food you want at a savings, shopping in small ports of call, or arrange for the company to send a cook along. These trips are almost always enjoyable, but as anyone who has lived on a boat knows, your trip can be made or ruined by your bunkmates.

The alternative is to rent an entire boat and make up your own group. This is obviously more expensive, although you can spread the cost out over the number of people you bring along. The standard expense for renting a boat (with captain, cook, and deckhand) is between $2,500 and $5,000 for one week.

May and October are usually the best times to go, offering a combination of good weather, small crowds (even the most remote cove is usually packed in August), and low prices. As discussed, there are hundreds of companies offering their blue cruise services. For more information, contact the **Bodrum Chamber of Maritime Commerce**, *Fırkateyn Sok. 19, Bodrum, Tel. 252 316 2398, Fax 252 316 1601.*

We have selected a few of the most reliable and specialized companies below. Note that whatever their home port, many boats serve the entire coast between Antalya and Bodrum, and you can occasionally make arrangements to meet a boat elsewhere.

**WESTMINSTER CLASSIC TOURS**, *Colquhoun House, 5 Richbell Place, London WC1N 3LA, U.K., Tel. 44 171 404 3738, Fax 44 171 404 3638.*

A London-based company specializing in particularly English gulet cruises focusing on painting or the classics. Westminster's trips are among the very best available, with high quality food, boats, and guides that keep your mind enjoyably agitated. Westminster's inclusive prices from London, including all meals and transfers for an eight day trip, vary between $1,500 per person in low season and $2,200 in July and August. Prices are cheaper if you hook up with the company directly in Turkey, and Westminster also can handle reservations from North America.

**BITEZ TOURS**, *Cumhuriet Cad. No. 65, Bodrum, Tel. 252 316 2454, Fax 252 316 3101.*

Bitez has a small fleet of good ships and its captains actually raise the sail on occasion. Each of its boats has three cabins (six berths), with the exception of the Merhaba, a single cabin uncrewed 26 footer. Bitez' boats sail out of Bodrum harbor and even the three cabin vessels sail with only one or two crewmembers. Rates are $2,500 per week in the high season for a one-crewmember boat and $3,000 per week for a slightly larger ship. The 26 footer, a bareboat charter, is $900 per week with assurances of your ability to operate a boat.

**SAVILE ROW TOURS & TRAVEL**, *6 Blenham Terrace, St. Johns Wood, London, NW8 OEB, Tel. 44 171 625 3001, Fax 44 171 625 8852.*

Savile Row, a company that specializes in arranging Turkey vacations for sophisticates, offers a "luxury mini-cruise" for three days. Savile's biggest selling points are reliablity, their new 88 foot gulet *Levante*, free wine and air conditioned rooms. The price you pay for three days of such luxury is $275. Boats depart from Kalkan.

**ADAM VOYAGES**, *Kumbahçe, İmren Sokak No. 6, Bodrum, Tel. 252 316 3764, Fax 252 316 4986.*

Adam rents whole boats, which may pose problems for people traveling solo or as couples. If you can find others to split the cost with you, however, this is an excellent company with eight beautiful ships. This is one of the more standard yachting companies, with prices at or near the average but particularly good service. Rates for eight-berth boats are $2,200 per week in April and November, $2,600 in May and October, $3,350 in June and September, and $4,200 per week in July and August. Meals cost $20 per person per day.

**AEGEAN YACHT SERVICES**, *Paşatarlası Cad. No. 21, Bodrum, Tel. 252 316 1517, Fax 252 316 5749.*

A major yacht building company that now offers one of the area's largest fleets. Very professional company with boats between four and ten cabins (plus an 18 cabin leviathan). A crewed, five cabin boat costs $2,500 per week in April and November, $5,000 in August. The "deluxe" eight cabin boats cost $3,500 per week in April and November, $7,100 in August. Food is extra.

**CANER YATCILIK,** *Demre, Antalya. Tel. 242 871 5085, Fax 242 871 5594.*

Caner Yatcılık is a small operation with a single boat, the Mutlu Kaptan. This business is run by two brothers, Mustafa and Mutlu, who are friendly, knowledgeable, and excellent hosts. The Mutlu Kaptan is a 16-berth yacht available for a better price than many smaller boats run by big companies. We're hesitant to recommend companies that aren't well-established, but we make an exception for the Caner brothers. Rates for the full boat are about $700 per day in season, making the company quite economical when the boat is well-booked.

**Trekking, Rafting, & Kayaking Trips**
One of the favorite trekking sites in Turkey is **Mt. Ararat,** but the Kurdish conflict has rendered that region dangerous. A group of Germans were kidnapped there in 1994, and most people steer clear of Ararat now. Ararat was never considered the most beautiful places to trek anyway, but the place that was considered the most beautiful is in an even more dangerous place in the far southeast corner of the country.

Enough bad news. Treks are available throughout the rest of Turkey, with particularly excellent long distance hiking in the **Toros Mountains** of the south and the **Kaçkar/Altıparmak** range in the north. We have included information on hiking in the Kaçkars, but you will want a local contact for maps and further information. In some cases you are best served by locating maps in North America.

Turkey's **Çoruh, Dalaman,** and **Köprüçay** rivers offer some fun, challenging whitewater – Çoruh particularly. Kayaking is another option, although don't expect to find anything fancy. Sea kayaking has also started to appear, and high time, too. Turkey's long, magnificent coast is perfectly suited for kayak trekking.

The following companies will be able to help you arrange all of the above:
• **Alternatif Turizm,** *Bağdat Cad. No. 36/8, Kızıltoprak, İstanbul, Tel. 216 345 6650, Fax 216 348 1053.*
• **Bougainvillea Travel,** *Çukurbağlı Cad. No. 10, Kaş, Tel. 242 836 3142, Fax 242 836 1605.*
• **Parkur Tourism,** *Atatürk Cad. No. 18/6, 07980, Kemer, Antalya, Tel. 242 814 4823, Fax 242 814 4824.*

## TAKING THE KIDS

*Turks love children. Turkish children generally rule the roost, going to bed much later than customary in the US and throwing habitual tantrums. Parents often sit by with deaf ears as their children run and scream all over a restaurant or even a theater.*

*If you bring a young child with you on your trip to Turkey, she or he will be the center of attention, subject to cheek squeezing, gifts of candy and other treats, smiling, and much commentary. However, one friend characterizes the cheek squeezing in particular as "verging on violent;" the first thing her daughter learned to say was "Don't touch me." If your child is not comfortable with being touched by strangers, then Turkey is perhaps not the place to take him or her on vacation. In addition, there is not really much in the way of child-specific activities aside from going to a playground, swimming pool, or beach. Istanbul's sidewalks and crowds are also difficult to navigate with a baby stroller.*

*Of course, many visitors bring their children, especially adolescents and teenagers. Older children are likely to be interested in the historical sites and the stories that go along with them, the sheer "oldness" of it all. The seaside resorts are quite accustomed to Turkish families arriving en masse with children when school is out for the summer, and consequently offer daycare and childrens' activities.*

*Although there is some jarred baby food available in supermarkets, and pasteurized milk is widely available, many Turkish restaurants are accustomed to preparing special dishes for their customers' babies. Another friend's 9-month old daughter is especially fond of köfte (meatballs), and they have no problems getting meatballs made for her without the spices (baharatsız).*

# 7. BASIC INFORMATION

## BUSINESS HOURS
The opening hours of tourism sites and museums varies greatly, but in general museums remain open 9-5 or 9-6 in summer, occasionally with a one hour break at lunch. Most museums are closed one or two days a week, with Monday a standard off-day. Ruins are usually open in daylight hours.

Standard government office hours are 9-6, Monday-Friday, with an hour break at lunch. The government offices you'll really need, like the Visa office at the airport and the police, are always open, and some post offices (PTTs) remain open 24 hours, providing telephones and telephone cards. Standard businesses maintain 9-6 hours, open Monday-Saturday. Many urban shops remain open until late, usually well beyond nightfall.

## COMPUTERS & INTERNET SERVICE
**Computers**

Most hotels have fax machines you can use for a fee, but if you need to send a fax from your own notebook computer you may run into problems. Few hotels in Turkey have snap-in jacks (what we like to call RJ-11 telephone connectors) for their phones, so you can't count on simply plugging in your computer and firing off faxes or e-mail. The best hotels offer the proper jacks, and major hotels in both Ankara and İstanbul have business centers that can be of use. Otherwise, you have the following options:

First, determine if the hotel line is digital or analog. Most phone lines are analog, but the newer digital lines can zap your modem-card because of excessive voltage. Warning signs for a digital line include LCD displays on the face of the phone and sophisticated features. Otherwise, to determine if the line is digital you can check with reception, although they're not going to have the faintest idea. You can also resort to IBM's Modem Saver.

Acoustic couplers are available at some computer stores, allowing you to use lines that are sheathed in plastic and buried in the wall in one end and the phone at the other. You simply attach the coupler to the telephone headset and do what you normally do, but this method can markedly slow down communication. We are told that the maximum speed with couplers is 1200 baud.

A screwdriver, wire cutters, electrical tape and a length of cord ending in a standard RJ-11 connector of the sort that fits into your PCMCIA slot can do the same job, especially if you have a James Bond bent. Unscrew the phone bottom and fish out the line ends (or chop it in the middle, if need be). Splice the end of your own connector cord to the live line coming from the wall, plug it in and go to work. Please put the phone line back together again.

Turkey's phone noises are comprehensible to computers accustomed to North American rings and tones.

For further information consult *http://www.cris.com/~kropla/phones.htm* or TeleAdapt Ltd.'s site at *http://www.teleadapt.com.*

## The Internet

Internet access has been available in Turkey for several years via the universities, but only in 1996 did it become commercially available. There are a number of small ISPs in Turkey, as well as at least one large-scale online operation. At press time (this could all change), no hotels in Turkey offered Internet access in their business centers. Nor did any ISPs offer temporary accounts for travelers.

**SuperOnline** offers temporary Internet access accounts for travelers with an 800-like number so you can dial into their POPs from anywhere in Turkey. You can register from home by calling or faxing their customer support center, or you can purchase access kits at many bookstores, hotels, and retail software shops once you get there. The temporary package includes Web access, file transfer, and chat; for email they offer optional email accounts if you can't access your home email address via telnet or by entering your DNS number into your email program. See SuperOnline's English home pages for pricing and further details: *http://www.superonline.net.*

If you are a CompuServe or America Online member, however, you may connect at speeds up to 28.8 bps and log into your account by dialling İstanbul and Ankara numbers. The 64 kbps leased line connection is via a network used by an international association of airlines. By the time of publication it may have been upgraded to 256 kbps. Be aware that there is a surcharge for this service, on the order of $6/hour for America Online and $12/hour for Compuserve.

Call your provider's customer service to find out for sure. The phone numbers are *212 234 5168* in İstanbul and *312 468 8042* in Ankara.

For Internet resources on planning your trip to Turkey, you need do no more than a simple search on your favorite search engine. There are plenty of Turks living abroad, and they enthusiastically broadcast information about their country and culture on their home pages. One Internet and online service provider in Turkey, SuperOnline, will have online content in English available free on the Web, including tourism information. From their SuperSite you will be able to make plane and hotel bookings, as well as find out concert dates and other calendar information: *www.superonline.net, www.superonline.com*. These services should be available in the first half of 1997.

One of the best sites comes from the Turkish Embassy in Washington, D.C. Their Web pages include a listing of American tour operators who specialize in Turkey: *www.turkey.org*.

To whet your appetite for the aesthetics of travel in Turkey, have a look at the photography-rich pages of Turknet, home to the online editions of Atlas Travel Magazine and books about Turkish architecture from the French Editions Didier Millet (both in English): *www.turknet.com*.

## ELECTRICITY

The current in Turkey runs at 220 volts (compared to 110 at home) and the plugs are shaped differently, two round prongs like those used in Germany. Just because you have a plug adapter doesn't mean the current will slow down on its way to your favorite traveling appliance: 220 volts burns out electical motors intended for use with 110 electricity. Post-1994 notebook computers usually have an internal adapter, but most other devices (including printers, hair dryers, and battery chargers) do not, and require a current converter.

Even with a current converter you may subject your electical device to undue wear and tear, although notebook computers' internal mechanisms are built for the task. Hairdryers are not; bring a cheap one.

## ENGLISH LANGUAGE READING MATERIAL

The *Turkish Daily News*, based out of Ankara, is the country's only English-language newspaper. The News has suspect editing and peculiar news judgment, but certainly offers insight into the country's affairs. For sheer news and analysis, the weekly *Probe* magazine distills the most interesting stories and is staple reading among those who are expected to know what's going on, reporters and diplomats and the like.

*Cornucopia Magazine* is a beautiful, glossy full-size magazine focusing on Turkey. Cornucopia concentrates on literature, art, and the refined aspects of travel. The magazine is not especially practical, but it will inspire you to want to return again and again. To subscribe from North America, contact *Cornucopia Subscriptions, P.O. Box 269, West Islip, New York 11795-0269, US* (one year, three issues, $30).

*The Guide*, based in İstanbul with occasional Ankara editions, offers the best calendar of Istanbul's current events available in English, together with articles on things to see and do within the city.

You will find copies of *The International Herald Tribune, Newsweek,* and *Time* in most large or frequently visited cities. Financial junkies can get the *European Wall Street Journal,* sports junkies can pick up *USA Today,* and you always have the option of London's *Financial Times* or the excellent news magazine, *The Economist.* These periodicals arrive first at the airport, second at Taksim Square in İstanbul, and on down the line until two days later, when some few *Newsweeks* are delivered in Kaş or Trabzon.

## HEALTH SERVICES & CONCERNS

Before setting out for Turkey be sure your insurance plan will cover you. Some plans neglect overseas countries or even include Europe but exclude Asia, a tricky proposition for a visit to Turkey. Turkey has socialized medicine, but that service doesn't ordinarily extend to you. Private hospitals expect immediate payment. Costs are reasonable – $55 for a check-up in İstanbul and $50 for a set of X-rays, for instance.

Top notch urban medical care in Turkey is right at the Western standard, if lacking the equipment you would find in American hospitals. Many doctors are western-trained, and many, too, are English-speaking. Outside of İstanbul and Ankara medical care is predictably less sophisticated, but doctors are usually quite competent.

For an up to date list of recommended hospitals and specialists in your area, contact the Canadian or U.S. consulates and embassies in İstanbul, Izmir, Adana and Ankara. **The emergency medical service phone number is 112**.

Pharmacies (Eczane) occupy a more important place than they typically do in North America, and if you can explain your ailment the pharmacist will often have just the thing. If you're looking for a particular medicine you may have to sift through lots of boxes, since the brand name you are familiar with will be different here. The active ingredients and the manufacturer will usually be the same.

### Vaccinations & Shots

There are no special vaccinations or shots recommended for visitors to Turkey. Malaria, historically a great problem along the Mediterranean coast, is no longer an issue. The eastern end of the Mediterranean, near

Adana, still generates occasional cases, but the rest of the country is free from anopheles. This is not to say there aren't mosquitoes. Incense coils (spiral tütsü) are an effective defense, as are small devices that plug into electrical outlets and agitate a small tablet of pyrethrin. This burns an odorless chemical and tends to keep mosquitoes at bay. Most hotels will offer one of the above, or, better yet, a fan.

## HOLIDAYS

Turkey has several fixed holidays every year, in addition to the major religious celebrations that are are based on the moon cycles and change from year to year. The secular holidays can put a little crimp in your travel plans, but **Ramazan** and the main religious celebrations (**bayrams**) can wreak havoc (see Chapter 4, *Land & People*). The celebations are an excellent time to visit in some respects, but there's no denying they can be a hassle. This is not a great concern for most travelers, since the holiday cycle is in the middle of winter right now.

Secular holidays are:
- **January 1**     New Years Day
- **April 23**     Independence Day and Children's Day
- **May 19**     Atatürk Day and Youth and Sports Day
- **August 30**     Victory Day
- **October 29**     Republic Day

In 1997, Kurban Bayram, a national holiday, occurs between April 30 and May 2. In 1998, Ramazan begins around December 30 and continues until February 27. Şeker Bayram begins at the conclusion of Ramazan and lasts three days. Kurban Bayram occurs between April 19 and April 23.

## MONEY & BANKING

ATM exchanges have become the best way of obtaining foreign currency overseas, and ATM machines with international access are available throughout Turkey – **Yapı Kredi** and **AkBank** are two popular Turkish banks that support most ATM exchanges. Be sure you know your credit card PIN number, not just your savings account withdrawal number. Virtually all bank machines will recognize a standard Visa or Mastercard PIN (and often, disconcertingly, welcome you by name), but people report trouble with other codes.

The advantage to ATM foreign currency withdrawals is that although you incur a fee from your home bank, that fee is typically more than offset by a favorable exchange rate. If you intend to use an ATM card, it is wise to check with your local bank and ensure that the card is approved for international withdrawals – some aren't.

Although ATM cards are an excellent new option for travelers, you should still bring along a modest supply of cash and travelers checks. If your Visa card fails you, you'll have cash on hand for exchanges. Your Visa card will still be of help if you can pantomime your dilemma at a bank, where they can usually get clearance to debit your account.

Note: every year more than $70 million in foreign currency is taken home as a memento and stuck in a desk drawer. Granted, foreign cash has some souvenir value, but you have an alternative to letting your Turkish Lira devaluate into colored paper: **UNICEF's Change for the Good** program collects foreign currency and turns the proceeds over to charity. For information on donations, call their New York office, *Tel. 212/ 503-6437.*

## Changing Money

The Turkish Lira is fully convertible, and there is no black market to speak of. Money changing offices (**Dovız**) can be found throughout the country. We haven't listed them in these pages because they are everywhere. They are particularly popular near heavily-touristed sites, but not exclusively so: Turks buy dollars or German Marks as a hedge against inflation. Cash exchange rates are typically posted outside each office, and can be double-checked against the daily exchange rate published on the cover of Turkey's English language paper, the *Turkish Daily News.* Passports are not required unless you go to the bank, and the process is ordinarily quick and painless. Travelers' Checks fetch about 90 percent of the cash exchange rate and can be a hassle.

---

### DOLLAR-LIRA EXCHANGE RATE
*The May 1997 exchange rate was US$1 = 135,000 Turkish Lira.*

---

Do not exhange money at hotels. There is no advantage to it except convenience, and you're going to be walking past a Dovız within five minutes of leaving the front door anyway. Hotel exchange rates lag about one month behind the real rate, which in Turkey is pretty substantial – 5-10 percent.

## POST OFFICES

Turkey's post offices are marked by large yellow and black **PTT** signs, and they have branches near the heart of every city. You will usually find telephones (see Telephone section below) and telephone cards here, as well as the postal services you'd expect.

Stamps (**pül**) for standard letters to the United States or Canada cost about one dollar, with postcards only slightly cheaper. You can buy postcard stamps, but you will want to turn your unstamped regular mail over to someone at the PTT. They will weigh it, perhaps punch some numbers into a calculator, look at the numbers, punch a couple more in and voila, that much money will get your letters to their destination. Mail service is generally quite reliable.

If you are shipping something like a carpet home, your dealer should explain in great detail how the system works, and will often take the responsibility upon him or herself (if in doubt, however, ship it yourself to ensure that you get what you paid for). At the post office you will be expected to display the contents of your parcel, after which you can complete your wrapping job and send it along. Send the package registered mail.

Note: to ensure your postcard or letter gets where it's going, include the proper Turkish for its destination: ABD for US, Kanada for Canada, Ingilitere for England.

## RELIEVING YOURSELF

In what is probably an extension of the public buildings that are associated with mosques, Turkey's cities have a surprisingly generous number of public restrooms. These are often located down a flight of stairs from the street level, sometimes marked "WC." **Bay** is man, **Bayan** is woman. In extremis, ask *"Tuvalet nerede?"* (where is the toilet) and someone will point you in the right direction. You are charged on exiting, usually 15¢ or so, and you get what you pay for. Occasionally you will be given a splash of lemon cologne, but this won't happen in the city. Service stations are another option, and, finally, since you may very well have a Gore-tex coat or Tevas or a big blond head of hair you also have the option of using hotel restrooms. Just barge in like you own the place.

Most hotels have standard sit toilets, but at some point you're likely to find yourself confronted by a floor toilet. If you've never used one, there's nothing to it. The traction pads to each side are, duh, for your feet. This system is more sanitary than the sit toilet, since you aren't in contact with anything, but it can be a little hard on the knees. Don't even think about bringing a newspaper, unless it's in lieu of toilet paper. You flush with a small bucket or hose located to the side. Keep a stash of toilet paper with you; you are unlikely to find any within. If you find yourself without toilet paper, try, ahem, irrigating yourself.

## SAFETY & AVOIDING TROUBLE

Travelers from abroad are a precious commodity. Turkey's tourism industry has been growing at an 18 percent clip for almost 15 years, reaching a rate of 6.6 million visitors and $4 billion in revenues annually.

## TRICKERY & DECEIT WARNINGS

*If you're a single man out walking along Istiklal Caddesi late at night, be wary of anyone who approaches you and works vigorously to steer you to a bar. Episodes are occasionally reported of foreigners being taken off by themselves under the pretext of seedy Red Light business and winding up forcibly relieved of their wallets.*

*People have been slipping travelers a mickey on buses and trains for decades now, and Turkey is no exception. It goes like this: someone offers you a tainted drink or snack, knocking you out. While you're blacked out they rifle your pockets and leave with your valuables. This is especially insidious because you'll be offered so many things out of genuine hospitality. All you can do is have faith in your own judgment of people and a willingness to risk impoliteness. When in doubt, say you have a cold sore.*

*Be wary of people who find out where you're going and happen to be going the same way themselves. An Australian acquaintance traveled from Cappadoccia (Nevşehir's bus station is often involved) to Antalya with a non-Turk, booked into a hotel with him, and went down to the marina to get a boat for some fishing. Once in the boat, the hanger-on remembered something he'd left in the hotel, and ran off to retrieve it. In the process he retrieved the Australian's room key, then his belongings. The story had a sort of happy ending; the Australian found his backpack one week later being fenced in a Selçuk leather shop, his name still emblazoned on the outside. The leather shop owners, eager to get in on this happy coincidence, sold it back to him for $150.*

*One ploy you're unlikely to expect is pickpocketing by a crowd of older women. They will jostle against you, using all of the normal ploys that pickpockets use, and rely on their appearance of pious fundamentalism to disarm you. This can blindside even the most paranoid veteran traveler.*

Turkish police officers and other officials receive extensive warnings about the importance of tourists, and the Tourism Ministry knows that a single well-publicized case of tourist mistreatment could easily put a 10 percent dent – that's $400 million – in its revenues.

After 1994's wave of terrorism against tourists the Tourism Ministry, the police, and the military set about posting guards at the country's popular tourist sites to ensure visitors' safety. In the absence of that danger there is little left to worry about. Standard crime like mugging and assault is negligible by American standards, even in big cities like İstanbul. And better still, at least from a selfish perspective, violent crime is rarely directed against outsiders; it usually boils up in domestic family disputes. Don't misunderstand: pickpocketing, purse snatching, and mugging do occur, they are simply very rare. The bottom line is to keep your wallet securely hidden.

Most of Turkey's streets are bewilderingly safe at all hours. Also note that while Turkish police may become slightly impatient with you, they will not – and should not – ever be hostile.

## Defamation

Several years back in Çanakkale, an angry Australian was cursing at a pension owner and made a mistake: he said "You $&#*@Turks!" As the pension owner told me, so long as the Australian confined himself to heaping abuse on the pension owner himself he was fine; the moment he generalized to the Turkish people he had defamed the nation. The Australian sat in jail for a night mulling this over.

Defamation of Mustafa Kemal Atatürk, the founder of the nation, is also off limits. The North American penchant for irreverence could get you in surprisingly serious trouble, so be on good behavior.

## Women Travelers in Turkey

In the last several years, Turkish women in urban areas have been wearing increasingly form-revealing clothing such as leggings, mini-skirts, and tight T-shirts, jeans, and sweaters. Many Turkish women are also favoring skimpy bikinis on beaches and at pools, but only when with other female or male companions, or with children. Despite this cosmopolitanism, there are some realities for women traveling in the country (and especially in less-touristed areas) that you ought to know.

In general, you should have few or no problems in the touristed and urban areas of western Turkey. However, it's best to stay on the conservative side, and wear long, loose pants or skirts and sleeves that cover the arms to the elbows, just for the sake of politeness. Then again, if you're obviously a foreigner, sometimes it doesn't seem to matter what you're wearing. I have gotten as much unwanted attention while wearing formless, bulky winter clothing as I have in skimpy summer clothes.

Perhaps incongruously, I have never felt physically threatened in Turkey. Even in cases where I have been groped on a bus, I have not felt threatened – merely angry. I fear for my physical safety significantly less on a day-to-day basis in Turkey than I do in the U.S.

Here are a few things to keep in mind:

You will get stared at if you don't look Turkish (whether because of clothing or other factors). Both men and women do the staring however, and before getting offended, it's helpful to remember that staring does not have the same negative associations attached to it as it does in North America. It's largely a sign of curiosity, of noticing someone unusual.

This is best understood if you keep an open look on your face, and perhaps a smile (although it is best to avoid eye contact with men). In most cases you'll get sincere, friendly smiles right back. It's not to say, however, that men will not stare at you in ways you find uncomfortable.

If a man makes unwanted comments to you, the best reaction is no reaction. A response is often considered license to speak further. A noise you may hear is "Shht! Shht!" which is generally used to get anyone's attention – not only womens'. But it's used for getting womens' attention, as well, and it's best to just ignore it.

If you are on crowded public transportation and you suspect that you are being felt up, chances are you're right. Generally Turks do not touch one another on public transportation, unless they know each other, even when it's very crowded. And foreign women aren't the only targets. A couple of years ago there was a feminist "lavender ribbon" campaign which distributed sharp pins attached to lavender ribbons, for women to use as anti-groping devices. If you have become certain that you are being touched, you have several options:

A) Move away if possible.

B) Say loudly, *"Çok ayıp!"* (much shame) or *"Ne yapıyorsun?"* (What are you doing?).

This latter option does not always have the desired effect, as the man you are accusing is likely to become angry and defensive in an attempt to save face. But with any luck he will be embarassed and get off the bus at the next possible opportunity.

Along the Black Sea and in some parts of İstanbul, you may be mistaken for a prostitute (aka a "Natasha") by some men if you are blonde and Eastern European-looking. There has been an influx of Russian and Romanian young women into Turkey, and the unfortunate reality is that they often turn to prostitution to support themselves. Prostitution and brothels are legal in Turkey.

Bring a scarf with you (or buy one in Turkey) for covering your head in mosques and tombs.

If you're traveling alone, make it clear to the front desk manager that you want a room near other women or families. In the hotels we have recommended, there should be no need to do this. Ask for the **aile salonu** (family room) in restaurants if you don't see any women in the main seating area. If the restaurant doesn't have one, the proprietor should send you to one that does. Don't go into places to be social where you see only men. Your sociability will give the "wrong message."

If traveling between cities by bus, the ticket seller will seat you next to another woman traveling alone.

For advice on Turkish baths, see Chapter 9, *Shopping & Other Pleasures.*

## TELEPHONES

Turkey's phone system is in good shape. Most urban Turkish lines are sleek and digital, and reaching home on a clear line is relatively easy. There are two types of phones. The older phones take **jeton**, grooved tokens that come in small (küçük), medium (orta), and big (büyük) sizes. The larger the token the greater the credit, but they are worth only 15¢, 25¢ and 50¢ apiece. Older phones occasionally let you dial into your international operator and make an international call, but you'll have to deposit more tokens every few minutes. If your token isn't being taken, stubbornly keep feeding it back in until the phone accepts it.

The new phones, well-established in urban areas and finally appearing in the hinterland (try nice hotel lobbies and the PTT office), take **phone cards**, not coins. These cards are available in denominations of 30 ($1.50), 60 ($3), and 100 ($5) credits. The new phones offer English language prompts and are a pleasure to operate. If you get 100 credits, this should be adequate for two weeks worth of local and domestic calls, but be forewarned that the credits burn off in about 3 minutes if you're calling North America. Even the new phones can be reluctant to put you through to the international operators (listed below), meaning that you may have to buy up a few phone cards and change them in the course of your conversation.

Hotel lines are predictably expensive, so remember to dial up your international operator from your room even if you're phoning city-to-city in Turkey, let alone calling home. Remember the time differences (see below under Time).

Calling card international operator numbers are: **ATT**, *Tel. 00800 12277*; **MCI**, *Tel. 00800 11177*; **Sprint**, *Tel. 00800 14477*.

Turkey's phone code is **90**: from North America dial 011 + 90 + three digit area code + seven digit number.

## TIME

The time difference between Turkey and the US east coast is seven hours (occasionally eight when North America shifts into daylight savings). The time difference between Turkey and the west coast is 10 hours (occasionally 11).

To put it simply, if it's 9 a.m. on Tuesday morning in Turkey, it's 2 a.m. Tuesday morning on the east coast and 11 p.m. Monday on the west coast. America is 7 to 10 hours in the past.

## TIPPING

Tipping is not an institution in Turkey. Places with a large population of foreigners are accustomed to the tipping phenomenon, but workers at small local restaurants are often pleasantly taken aback by money left on the table. The better the restaurant, the more likely it is that a tip is expected, but – the corollary – the more likely it is that the gratuity is included. Check your bill. When in doubt, 10 percent tips are fine.

Pay taxi drivers what you owe them, rounding up to a convenient amount. Even this isn't expected outside of tourist districts. You can reward barbers (kuafor) and masseurs in Turkish baths with a small tip, although, again, in lightly touristed places they'll probably be surprised.

## TOURISM OFFICES

Tourism offices – marked with a big, fat white dotted "i" on a blue background – can be of great assistance throughout Turkey. The staff will usually speak some English and will certainly have some maps and brochures. They are not supposed to recommend hotels, but they can direct you to hotels and restaurants that fit your description. They're happy to help you find particular hotels. Note that in some towns, Antalya for instance, travel agencies set up shop behind a big counterfeit information sign. This is pretty clear once you're inside; if they try to sell you on a particular trip, don't give them your business.

Hours vary, but most tourism offices keep normal office hours – 9 a.m to 6 p.m. with a break a lunch. We have provided the addresses and numbers of tourism offices throughout Turkey in the appropriate sections.

You can get tourism information from the **Turkish Embassy** in the US, *1717 Massachusetts Ave. N.W. Ste. 306, Washington D.C., 20036, 202/429-9844, Fax 202/429-5649* and from the **Turkish Consulate** in New York, *821 United Nations Plaza, New York, NY, 10017, 212/687-2194, Fax 212/599-7568.* You can also check out the official home page at *http://www.turkey.org/turkey.*

## WATER

Bottled water is not a vanity in Turkey, it's the way that most people drink. The only difference is the small blue plastic bottles you buy cost 80¢, and the 15 gallon jugs that the Turk buys also costs 80¢. If you want to fill your water bottles up at a water shop (*"Su istasiyon"*) that's fine, too; this way you can get in on the better prices. In İstanbul the water is heavily chlorinated, and although it's unlikely to hurt you, it tastes awful.

# 8. SHOPPING & OTHER PLEASURES

## SHOPPING

## SHOPPING FOR TURKISH GOODS

Turkey is traditionally renowned for a wealth of goods that include kilims and carpets, ceramics, gold and silver, copper, leather, and cotton goods. You'll have no trouble being tempted – there are things to buy at every turn. The one trouble you may have is in making decisions amidst the sensory overload and jumble of options that characterizes Turkish bazaars and street life in general. But once you get your rug or bowl away from the hubbub, its individual beauty will stand out.

**Haggling Primer**

During the bargaining process, naivete or lack of finesse can actually work to your advantage. An American friend of ours swears by her bargaining technique, which basically strips away all the layers of pretense: she stands with the object she wants while an excited shopkeeper punches out amounts on his calculator and shows them to her. When, as usual, the price is high, she reacts as if the price is too high, shaking her head. "I just stand there looking dumb," she says, "and the price keeps dropping." Although all merchants have calculators at the ready, you may want to bring your own pocket calculator along to make price conversion faster and easier. It's also handy for quick checks of restaurant and bar tabs.

**Tip 1:** In the Grand Bazaar, resolve only to ask prices in the first five stores you enter – not to buy.

**Tip 2:** Don't start bargaining unless you're willing to purchase the item. If the merchant meets your price, you're supposed to buy it. It's not particularly rude to change your mind unless you've been haggling for an hour or more. Even then, you may send the price still lower.

**Tip 3:** For items that are not rugs or jewelry, you can offer a fraction of the shopkeeper's first price. The shopkeeper will invariably refuse this offer, but at least it gets the bidding closer to the item's wholesale cost. And, depending on the item, your final price could get that low anyway.

**Tip 4:** Shops in Istanbul's Grand Bazaar are prime real estate, in the $1 million range. They do good business. Hang around and look at their wares all you want, and do not feel a sense of obligation to buy out of concern for the shopkeeper's time.

**Tip 5:** Do not expect to be able to bargain down the prices of gold and silver by much more than 10 percent of the asking price (although it never hurts to try); Turkish friends say that the profit margins are not as high on jewelry as they are on other items.

**Tip 6:** Hitting some of the coastal resort towns in late October when most establishments start shutting down for the winter will ensure you some bargains. (Although this tactic could also backfire if you are going to those resort towns for the famed nightlife, or to soak up sun on a beach.)

**Tip 7:** Many sellers of big-ticket items such as rugs or antiques now take credit cards. Some merchants may charge you the fee (usually 2-3 percent of purchase price) that the credit card company charges them; make sure you ask about this before striking your final deal.

## SHOPPING FOR A FEZ

*"Come with me," he said, placing a disproportionately large hand in mine and leading me along a chilly corridor. He stopped in front of a door and turned a key in the lock. We stepped inside. As my eyes adjusted to the weak light, I could see that it was a fez repository. I had never seen so many fezzes in my life. They stood in wobbly stacks against the walls, fez stalagmites rising to the ceiling among lesser formations that strove for space at my feet. They lay horizontal along shelves, tubes of fezzes wrapped in brown paper which in some cases had split open and spilled to the floor."*

Jeremey Seal, **A Fez of the Heart: Travels Around Turkey in Search of a Hat.** London: Picador, 1995.

## BUYING KILIMS & CARPETS

Expect to be beguiled by the many beautiful rugs sold in Turkey. Well-crafted Turkish rugs are a treasure that will outlast you, the perfect keepsake from a trip to Asia Minor. They come in a dazzling array of colors and patterns, woven, knotted, and embroidered with silk, wool, cotton, and even goat hair. There are rugs to fit every budget, from a $30 simple wool kilim to magnificent Hereke silk carpets that run well into the thousands of dollars.

There is no shortage of places to buy kilims and carpets, no matter where in Turkey you go. One of the best places is, of course, Istanbul's **Grand Bazaar**, simply because of the sheer number of dealers and variety of stock. And the rugs come from all over the Balkans, the Caucusus, the Middle East, and Central Asia – not just Turkey. Some Turkish friends tell us to avoid buying rugs in İstanbul if you'll be going elsewhere in Turkey, because prices can drop in less touristed areas. But the likelihood that you'll find anything significantly cheaper outside İstanbul is fairly low, unless you've got the time and inclination to hunt. In some towns like Kuşadası, in fact, you're sure to run into outrageously inflated prices because of the cruise ships that dock there and unload loaded visitors.

There are terrific and fortuitous stories about visitors innocently walking down a street in the interior and spotting a local fellow biking an oversized kilim up a long hill to his distributor. He sells you the carpet for a song, delighted to cut out the middleman, and everyone goes home happy.

It happens. Usually, however, the carpets get to their distributor and into the hands of the shrewd carpet salesmen. You will find the cheapest prices in the interior – the **Konya Bazaar** west of Nevşehir is a particularly good spot. İstanbul has a mountain of carpets, but steady tourist traffic keeps the prices higher.

Turks have been weaving kilim, a flat-weave style of rug, for almost 1,000 years. What began as a floor covering among nomadic Selçuks has become a work of art appreciated the world over. Traditionally the patterns in carpets and kilims will mean something; common motifs include symbols for male and female fertility. For all the tradition, rugs sometimes reflect an individual weaver's humor – in some sumak pieces you can find a small car in among all the animals. Different regions produce their own distinctive designs and, commerce being what it is, rug-makers also churn out the designs that people seem to like.

Rug sellers may tell you that a rug's high price is justified by the fact that it was made by the weaver for use in the home, not for sale. Which does not explain why the rug is now for sale. Unfortunately, carpet and kilim salesmen have also passed along their wily advice for almost 1,000 years, and today's breed of Grand Bazaar rug hawker is the end product of nine centuries of rug selling guile.

### Types of Rugs

The **kilim** (kee-leem), or flat weave rug, is made by weaving yarn horizontally on the vertical "warp." (The warp consists of the loose threads that are like tassles at the end of the rug.) On many kilims the front and the back are virtually identical. The most common Anatolian patterns are geometric, with many triangles.

The **cicim** (jee-jeem) is an embroidered kilim, and is not usually reversible.

The **halı** (hall-uh), or carpet, is made by knotting yarns horizontally along the lengthwise warp. The yarns are then cut to a uniform height, to form the fuzzy "top" of the carpet. Anatolian carpets frequently have a distinctive double-knot on the underside, whereas carpets from other regions may have single knots. One of the more common carpet patterns is the slightly steepled rectangle, representing the mihrab, or prayer niche. Such devices indicate a prayer rug, and these can range in size from the small rugs designed for use by individuals at prayer time to the giant rugs covering the floors of mosques.

The **sumak** (soo-mak) is another flat weave rug. The threads are wrapped around the warp, not woven.

**Materials**

In woolen rugs, the quality of the wool is important. Machine spun wool can be more oily than hand spun wool, with the result that dyes do no hold as fast. In turn, the rug's color deteriorates more rapidly. Furthermore, machine spun wool is looser and yields less precise patterns. To distinguish machine-spun from hand-spun wool check the tails, or the warp, at the end of the rug. Hand spun wool is very tight and irregular, while machine spun wool is very regular, but loose. Hand spun wool is also more "dry" (i.e. not as oily to the touch), while machine spun wool smells of lanolin and may feel oily. A further frustration to the average North American carpet buyer is that the wool of live sheep is superior to the wool of dead sheep. How do you tell the difference? You don't.

Many rugs, both kilims and carpets, utilize cotton for their warps. Again, check the tails at the end of the rug – if you can't tell the difference by feel, cotton is usually a bright, bleached white. You can also ask – cotton in Turkish is "pamuk." While a cotton warp is not inherently bad, and cotton warps actually make for a tighter weave and yield wonderfully detailed and intricate patterns, they are not as forgiving as a wool warps. Cotton looks dirtier faster and breaks down more quickly than wool. Cotton is also more susceptible to mildew in damp climates.

The most expensive rugs are made with silk, and often with a silk/wool combination. The silk has a sheen to it that wool does not achieve, and feels, well, silky underfoot.

Synthetics are also used in rug-making. Nylon fibers can be found in beautiful rugs and carpets, but their presence means it should cost you significantly less than a natural fiber rug. You should be particularly wary of synthetics around Kayseri. The only way to tell whether the yarns contain synthetics is to pull a small piece of the fiber out of the rug and burn it. If it melts, rather than burns, don't pay a natural-fiber price.

## Dyes

Sometime between 1865 and 1879, German aniline dyes were introduced in the Ottoman Empire, and by 1920 natural dyes were effectively dead. Chemical dyes created a single, consistent color and were easier and cheaper to produce than natural dyes. The poorer of these artificial dyes would bleed, but the better dyes yielded perfectly decent products. They fade more quickly, dulling rather than curing, but artificial dyes were used, and continue to be used, in some of the finest carpets and kilims.

In 1975, efforts were begun to recreate the natural dyes, and after years of dredging up old dye recipes and experimenting, experts have recreated most of the natural colors. Camomile, for instance, yields an excellent yellow; maddar produces red; sumac and maddar combine to make purples; indigo and camomile combine for greens. The list goes on.

Natural dye production remains a niche activity (dyes from the Konya region are especially lovely), and its advantages are usually so subtle that only customers with deep pockets or exacting standards are interested in the greater expense. Natural dyes age extremely well. The colors become deeper and richer over time. Finally, natural dyes produce kilims with subtle gradations in color – a large field of yellow, for instance, will be a slightly uneven combination of beautiful yellows.

## Age

When shopping for rugs, it's useful to keep in mind the distinction between "previously owned" and "antique." Antiques bring in more money, and therefore some shady characters want to pass rugs off as older than they are. Antique rugs are out there, but they're very expensive and you usually have to go looking for them. Reproduction pieces are readily available, so if you're interested in a traditional pattern, you don't necessarily have to buy an antique to get it.

There are sneaky ways of falsifying a rug's age. Sometimes they're left out in the elements, sometimes they're washed in a bleach solution. Sometimes they have dirt rubbed into them to give the appearance of having been used on the Anatolian plains. Dealers who specialize in antique rugs will have the pieces professionally cleaned and repaired – and repairs should not look like the person just learned how to darn socks. Be duly suspicious, but don't let it ruin your shopping fun.

Genuinely antique rugs will be expensive because, well, they're antiques; they're hard to come by. Antique rugs have seen a couple lifetimes' use; this means that they can be more delicate than new rugs, which is something to keep in mind if you plan on stepping on yours.

### Rug Shopping Tips

Measure the prospective floor or wall space in your home before you leave and convert it into centimeters. Also shop around a little to get the prices of rugs you like.

Find a shop on your own instead of allowing yourself to be led to one. If you buy something, 10 percent (sometimes far more) goes into the pocket of your guide.

Select a few that you are interested in and ask about them all. Don't let on if you have a particular favorite, even though it means lavishing attention on rugs you aren't serious about. If the world of bargaining is not at all to your liking, there are also shops with fixed prices. For a few suggestions, see our İstanbul chapter shopping section.

Smell the rugs. If you smell gasoline, the material was probably treated with gasoline to hold it together. It is prone to fraying and, not surprising, it will smell like gas. If you smell chlorine, the rug has been bleached to give it a slightly aged appearance. Not only is it not as aged as the vendor may claim, after a bleaching the carpet is sure to wear relatively quickly – an heirloom for generations becomes an heirloom for 10 years or less.

If you're looking at carpets, spread the fibers and look at their roots. The best carpets made with natural dyes will have a fairly uniform color at both the end of the fiber and at its root. Less choice carpets, if not new, will be faded on the surface.

Rub a few spots with a damp handkerchief. The handkerchief should come away clean. If it does not, one of the following is amiss: a good rug has been inexpertly retouched (i.e. shoe polish, watercolors, or even felt tip markers) or the rug in question was made with second rate chemical dyes and is going to bleed a little and fade a lot. It may be a good idea to ask the dealer before doing this. If he's selling good stuff, he shouldn't mind.

You're often advised to enquire about the density of the knots in carpets, which is usually expressed in "knots per centimeter." You'll get answers like 32 and 42, and sometimes 72 or 116. The theory is the more knots per centimeter, the better the carpet, but it's a fundamentally irrelevant question. The dealer probably doesn't know, you don't understand what the numbers mean anyway, so our advice is don't ask about the density of the knots. Instead, look at a few different carpets and see for yourself which are tight and dense and which are loose.

If you have been sold a carpet or kilim that the dealer
he must send you on your way with export papers cer
purchase is not a national treasure. Otherwise you are violating ı u.
antiquities laws.

To ship or not to ship? Although most dealers who offer you the
option of shipping your rug home for you are perfectly honest in their
intentions, it is probably worth your while to pay the airline's extra
baggage fee if necessary than to risk your valuable new purchase.

It's understandable to feel stupid going through all of these circum-
locutions, but it's a good idea to go through them nonetheless if you want
to buy a rug you will enjoy for years to come. It is also understandable to
fail a rug on each of the above points and still love it so much you must
have it – just don't pay too much.

How do you know if you're getting a good deal? The short answer
is, you don't. Ultimately, you're getting a good deal if you like the rug and
you've paid an amount of money for it that you're willing to part with.
One final note: Unless you're a collector, it's probably a bad idea to take
the rug to a dealer when you're back in North America to ask what it's
"worth" because you may not like the answer. The worth is in your daily
enjoyment of the rug and in the memories of your visit to Turkey.

## CERAMICS

Everyone knows about the rugs, but Turkey's bazaars will tempt you
in other ways as well. Another essential element of Turkish art emerged
from the kilns of İznik, where ceramics took hold in the 1400s. The İznik
patterns, typically in gorgeous blues and turquoises (and sometimes
reds), decorate many of Istanbul's greatest landmarks. They have been
faithfully recreated on plates and bowls by contemporary artists and
fetch $20 to $150 prices in big city bazaars. If you have the luxury of time,
do not make any purchases on your first shopping excursion, in the heat
of the moment. Look around first.

During your spin through the bazaars, ceramics merchants will often
try to convince you of a piece's quality by dinging it on the edge with a
finger and letting it ring, nodding gravely and saying *"Kalite"* (quality).
Try to ignore this senseless exercise, find what you like, get a price, gently
knock the price down – even if this particular shop has "fixed wholesale
prices because we are the distributor for blah blah..." – then go back to the
hotel. While there talk to other travelers or anyone you can trust about
what they would pay, and sleep on it. If you continue feeling you must
have those bowls and like the deal you're getting, then buy. You can have
your purchases wrapped in bubble wrap and cardboard for safer traveling.

## İznik Ware

The Selçuk dynasty introduced tile making to Anatolia, and nowhere did it come to fuller flower than in İznik tile workshops in the 16th and 17th centuries. İznik's ascendance corresponded almost exactly with the Ottoman Empire's own rise, reaching its peak during the reign of Süleyman the Magnificent and his chief architect, Mimar Sinan. In Sinan's hands, the beautiful tiles were put to appropriately magnificent use throughout the empire, including Süleymaniye Mosque and the private chambers at Topkapı Palace.

Tiles, dishes, bowls and other porcelain-like goods were made with white clay and originally decorated with blues and turquoises. It is a trademark of the İznik workshops – in İznik, Diyarbekir, and İstanbul – that decorations are in the form of flowers or patterns. Tulips, carnations, and the Tree of Life are traditional motifs. Owing to the strict interpretation of the Koran's admonishment against idolatry, decorators were barred from making likenesses of people or creatures. If that seems odd, consider how the Muslims felt about the Christian penchant for decorating churches and homes with pictures of a Muslim prophet, Jesus Christ, after he was mutilated and nailed to a cross.

Cut off from such vivid western avenues of artistic expression, Muslim artists poured their energies into calligraphy, geometric patterns and other decorative devices (birds are often represented, an exception to the idolatry stricture). The resulting ceramic work, particularly in the case of İznik ceramics in their heyday, is beautifully artful and timeless.

As time went on, the tile makers began introducing a greater palette of colors, including reds and purples, and the patterns grow busier. By the late 1500s, the increasingly muddled designs were accompanied by poorer glazes. By 1700, the İznik workshops had closed. Magnificent artwork thrives in a healthy, affluent society, and İznik's decline corresponded to mounting decadence and decay in the Ottoman Empire.

The **Kütahya** ceramic shops were peers of the İznik shops, and outlasted İznik without ever achieving the same success. Like the İznik shops, Kütahya began producing tile in the 1400s, but when İznik fell into its decline Kütahya attracted some of its artists and carried on. Some of Kütahya's business, unlike its rival, was in ecclesiastical tiles, pendants, and icons for the Christian church. Kütahya thrived into the 1700s, thereafter beginning its own slow decline. Kütahya shops finally closed their doors early in this century, and are now enjoying a tourism-generated revival. Many of the ceramics you see today are made in Kütahya.

## GOLD & SILVER

Gold, or **altın**, holds a special place in Turkish culture. Its significance is not only as a hedge against rampant modern inflation; there is also a long history of giving gifts of gold to commemorate weddings, circumcisions, births and engagements. At wedding receptions, brides are decorated with gifts of thick gold chains and coins pinned to their chest. In rural Turkey, savings accounts often take the form of 22 karat bangles on womens' arms. Turkish savings banks with depositors would fork over the cash equivalent of just some of the estimated 4,000 to 6,000 tons of gold they are hoarding. That's about 80 grams per person.

Turkey's position as the world's seventh largest fabricator of gold jewelry is in evidence everywhere – most main streets have their own gold shops. About 30 percent of all retail gold shops in Turkey are around the **Grand Bazaar**, along with about 4,000 manufacturers. The mass producers lurk on the outskirts of İstanbul, and threaten the small-time jewelers around the Bazaar. Businesses that work only 30 kg of gold per year cannot compete with the 8 tons of jewelry produced by the seven largest firms.

There is some risk of not getting what you paid for. Jewelry manufacturers in Turkey are not obliged to have their products certified unless intended for export. However, some jewelers use serial numbers that can be traced through the İstanbul Chamber of Goldsmiths. If you stick with numbered pieces, you should be fine. Gold should also be stamped with its karat. Ask the shopkeeper to show you the daily price of unworked gold at the caratage you are interested in. The shopkeeper should have daily prices. Watch the weighing, then calculate the value of the gold and the charge for labor.

---

### BAZAAR JEWELERS

*"Many of the jewelers (in the Grand Bazaar) are still working in Dickensian conditions, crammed into poorly lit, unventilated rooms...yet when the final product has been finished and is held up to the light, there is a communal pride in the creation. Artisans often enter the trade as a tea-boy – it is an industry staffed exclusively by men – and make their way slowly up the ladder, for as long as they can keep their eyesight."*

*From* **Gold in Turkey**, *İstanbul: Turk Ekonomi Bankası and IBS Research & Consultancy, 1996.*

---

For silver, or **gümüş**, you can browse through the bazaars in many cities and towns, including Istanbul's **Old Bedestan** in the Grand Bazaar. You will find new, used, and antique silver items; bracelets in varying widths and necklaces that are woven from fine silver wires and have decorated clasps. The latter are traditionally from the **Trabzon** area on the Black Sea. Silver jewelry is also generally sold by weight. Just make certain that the stamp is 925 or higher, or else you're getting an inferior alloy instead of sterling.

## LEATHER

If you are interested in purchasing leather goods like jackets or accessories, Turkey is the place to do it. The annual sacrifice of cows and sheep for Kurban Bayramı keeps stores of leather high and a long tradition of leatherworking for export generally keeps the prices lower here than in western countries.

In İstanbul, a good place to start looking is the **Covered Bazaar**, but, as with everything else there, you must be discriminating. Be sure to check stitching, buttonholes, and zippers. If you are uncertain about your ability to assess quality, or if you can't find exactly what you're looking for, you can either have something made – many shops offer 24-hour delivery of made-to-order leather clothing (but make sure you're under no obligation to buy) – or you can head to some of the retail shops on **Istiklal Caddesi** near Taksim. You probably won't find any great bargains at the retail shops unless you locate the old-season rack, but at least you can be sure that the stitching won't come undone anytime soon. Many leather goods shops are in a neighborhood called **Zeytinburnu** (outside the city walls, just south of the E5 freeway) – the factories used to be here as well, but have since moved further out in order to improve the scent-quality of the area.

---

### THE EVIL EYE

*This ubiquitous round blue symbol is, of course, steeped in superstition, but it can be taken quite seriously by otherwise non-superstitious and secular folks. You'll find blue eyes dangling from car exhaust pipes, from rear-view mirrors, backpacks, necklaces and bracelets, pinned to the sweaters of small children, and hanging above doors in restaurants, hotels, stores, and apartments. These blue eyes, like the real thing, are said to protect one from the evil eye. The evil eye can be cast unwittingly; even an admiring compliment not followed by "Maşallah" (may Allah protect) can cast the eye. This has a lot to do with covetousness and acknowledging the role Allah has in creating wonderful things. Not only do blue eyes act as proof against the evil eye, they are able to cast the evil eye more readily than brown-eyes.*

## TEXTILES

Cotton towels are said to have gotten their start in **Bursa** for use at the mineral baths, and cotton still figures prominently in the bazaars there. The more dramatic tale is that of silk, another longtime Bursa specialty. In Byzantine times the Emperor Justinian sent a mission to China. The mission's ostensible purpose was diplomatic and religious; the real reason was Justinian's desire to cultivate silk-manufacturing in the Byzantine Empire. Several years later, the missionaries returned with the secret: hollowed-out cavities in their walking sticks hid silkworms. The Chinese secret was out, and Justinian's sturdy little silkworms helped break the Chinese silk monopoly.

Today, not much is left of actual silk cultivation in Turkey. In the mid-19th century, western silk worms were virtually wiped out by a bacterial disease. Turkish textile factories once again use imported Chinese raw silk for the production of their wares, with a single exception. As for cotton, you will have a hard time beating the standard made-in-the-US cotton towels hanging in your bathroom at home. There are, however, places to find beautiful Made-in-Turkey textiles (see the İstanbul chapter's shopping section).

## OTHER PLEASURES

## TURKISH BATHS - HAMAMS

Communal baths were used in Roman times, but, as the very name "Turkish bath" suggests, they are significant to Ottoman culture. In an age when western Europeans went without bathing, the Ottomans were very conscientious about staying clean, perhaps stemming from the cleansing rituals of Islam. Perhaps, too, the Ottomans inherited their fondness for baths from the Byzantines, who had continued the Roman tradition while it collapsed in the chaos of medieval Europe. Communal baths have been an integral part of life in Turkey for two thousand years, but with better living standards the **hamam** is slowly fading from daily life. Don't worry, though; you'll still find plenty of hamams, but your best bets are tourist spots or small towns.

The Turkish bath of the western imagination is an erotically charged place, an impression fueled by the works of various European painters. Hamams are, however, primarily places to get clean, relax, and socialize. The classical hamam design includes both mens' and womens' quarters. If there are no separate quarters, then men and women go on separate days, or during separate hours. The mens' area is typically larger and more luxurious than the womens', and mens' hours are invariably longer.

Hamams were historically (and in rural areas still are) one of the only public places outside the home that women could socialize. A contemporary Turkish pop singer, Sibel Tüzün, stages one of her videos in a hamam, in which the women are entertaining one another with dancing and singing. This apparently still happens, although we have not witnessed it.

In recent years, some hamams in the more touristed areas have gone co-ed. Various stories circulate about travelers who go alone to co-ed hamams being subject to unwanted sexual touching by the masseur. The only way to avoid this possibility is to go to the hamam with a male companion, or, not to get scrubbed. We would hazard to guess that most Turkish women would not allow themselves to be scrubbed by a man, and you will find neither female Turkish bathers nor female Turkish attendants/masseuses in co-ed hamams. So, when in Byzantium ...

Many Turks actually wrinkle their noses at the idea of a going to a hamam, claiming that hamams are "dirty." This is only true to a point. If you're sensitive about germs, have a strong allergic reaction to mildew, or have problems with chronic sinusitis, then perhaps you should avoid them. Otherwise there's no evidence that they are unsafe. To hedge your bets you can always try a watered down version of a hamam at one of the major hotels. In places like Bursa, you'll have the hamam to yourself.

The prices in touristy, historic hamams hover in the $15-$25 range. This price should include a scrubbing and massage, but when you compare that with the $5 price paid in neighborhood hamams for the same, if not better, service, you might feel gouged. You're paying for convenience, the workers' English skills, and, often, a beautiful, historic setting.

You'll find hamams fed by natural springs at **Yalova/Termal, Bursa**, and **Pamukkale**. (See İstanbul, Pamukkale, and Bursa for details.)

**Visiting the Hamam**

You will enter a reception area, the **camekan**, which in some hamams is also used for changing. Some hamams have private changing rooms where you may lock up your clothes and valuables, and others have common changing areas and small valuables lockers at the desk. Typically you pay when you enter, and pay extra for rubbing ("*keselemek*") and/or massage ("*masaj*") in neighborhood hamams. You may get tokens to give to the masseur or masseuse. You will receive a linen **peştemal** with which to wrap yourself.

If you see any wooden or plastic slippers lying around, you should wear them. Not only is this for traditions' sake (the hygeine factor is negligible, especially with the wooden ones), but it may also be to protect your feet from unbearably hot marble if the heat is coming from below.

The only hard and fast rule for men is to never show your genitalia, regardless of whether you're in a co-ed or sex-segregated hamam. This is considered highly improper. Men should wear the peştemal at all times (although in some hamams, wearing a bathing suit is acceptable). Although rules for women on this may be more relaxed in some hamams, it is better to wear your underwear under the peştemal and then disrobe further depending on what you see others doing than it is to offend the other bathers and go back to the changing room to put your underwear back on (this from personal experience). Some Turkish women even wear their bras into the hamam. Use your best judgment.

You will pass through the **soğukluk** – an antechamber or passage-way of intermediate temperature – on your way to the **havlet**, the room where you perspire. Lie down on the **göbek taşı**, the hot stone slab heated from below.

Once you've started sweating and perhaps have doused yourself with water a few times (taking care not to splash other bathers), get rubbed down by the **tellak** (attendant) with the abrasive **kese**, which loosens your dead skin. You'll be surprised at how much comes off an otherwise "clean" body.

Afterwards, get soaped up and rinsed, and then massaged. This process, although unlike deep tissue massage, is nonetheless vigorous and remarkably relaxing in combination with the heat and steam of the bath.

If you've had enough, you can proceed from here back to the camekan, where you may wrap yourself in a dry towel, recline on lawn-chairs, and sip a beverage. When you're good and ready, go back to your chamber to dress.

---

## TURKISH BATH SUGGESTIONS

*Tip 1: you may want to make a point of drinking some water before going to the hamam. Often there is bottled drinking water available for sale during your cool-down period (in addition to tea, Coke, beer, etc.), but the heat may be more difficult to bear if you're feeling dehydrated in the first place.*

*Tip 2: Take your shampoo and soap with you in a plastic bag, and tip money for the masseur or masseuse. Try to see how other people deal with tipping. About 20 percent of the fees charged, distributed among the attendants, is appropriate.*

## MANLY PLEASURES - SHAVE & A HAIRCUT!

Everyone knows about the Turkish baths, but something that most male visitors find far more rewarding is a shave and a haircut. Barbers in most parts of North America do some snipping and call it good. Not so here. The haircut is followed by a shave, a long, marvelous process with a straight razor that leaves your face perfectly clean. In the likely event you've never had a shave at the barber, be sure to do it here.

With the completion of the shave the show is not over; next you will usually be fussed over with lemon cologne, flaming things, balms, and even a shoulder rub. The cost? Usually about $5 in İstanbul.

## ALTERNATIVE LIFESTYLES

The 1995 Turkish film *İstanbul Beneath My Wings* stirred great controversy and was even banned in some municipalities for its depiction of an Ottoman sultan's homosexual activity. That the film was based in fact was beside the point. In the Turkish mainstream, charges of homosexuality are considered a grave insult.

There is no specific reference in Turkish law to homosexuality, but there are references to public morals and public order – community standards by another name. This makes it legal for police to take anyone "suspicious-looking" in for interrogation. There is no organized queerbashing per se, but gays have not been allowed by the government to openly organize, stage Pride Festivals, protests, etc. Gays and transvestites/transgendereds (lesbians are not as targeted because they are less visible) are routinely roughed up by police.

That's the bad news, but it isn't that simple. In 1996, an entertainer named Zeki Muren died during the taping of a television program. Hundreds of mourners were shown on television, weeping at his casket and his face adorned the covers of every daily newspaper. All of this public grief was, ironically, for one of Turkey's most beloved and flamboyant female impersonators, and a homosexual.

İstanbul in particular has a lively, if necessarily underground, gay and lesbian (mostly gay) culture. Other cities with homosexual-friendly establishments include Ankara, Izmir, Bodrum, and Kaş. Most of the places listed under Istanbul's Nightlife section are homosexual-friendly; none are exclusively gay. Note: It's safest finding places on your own where you feel comfortable, rather than accepting invitations you receive on the street.

For further information and listings contact: **Lambda İstanbul**, *Email: turkiye@qrd.org, Web: www.qrd.org/qrd/* – this is the Web address for the Queer Resources Directory. You'll find Turkey under the Europe heading in Worldwide Queer Info.

# 9. FOOD & DRINK

## FOOD

Americans asked to name a Turkish dish would, sad to say, probably venture a guess of "Uh, Turkey?" Well, surprise: Turkey has a rich culinary tradition and your meals here will be highlights of your visit. True Turkish cuisine is rare; it was a product of a time when women spent their days at home preparing complicated, time consuming dishes. Precious few places prepare Turkish food the way mother used to make it; mother's liberated now and holding down a job. What passes for Turkish food in many places is no less authentic, it's just simpler recipes. To taste Turkish cuisine at its exquisite height you need to try one of the handul of places that take the time to make dishes properly; **Washington Restaurant** in Ankara and **Haci Abdullah** and the **Tuğra** in İstanbul are a few good examples.

But the staples of Turkish cooking are available everywhere, and cheaply. Stroll through a market and you'll see why Turkish food can do no wrong. Tomatoes, onions, eggplants, cucumbers, garlic, artichokes and peppers grow in great abundance, while recipes borrow from Mediterranean, Arab, and Turkish traditions. With this legacy, and these raw materials, it's almost unfair.

Turkish food emerged slowly, a product of cross-fertilization like the Turks themselves. The Turkic peoples migrated from Mongolia, bringing far eastern nomadic cuisine on the long journey west. A few of the original Turkish dishes appear to be **mantı** (ravioli in yogurt sauce), **börek** (pastry with meat and cheese filling), and meat cooked on a skewer – **kebabs**. To this the Arabs contributed spices and breads, while coastal areas near the Mediterrean and Black Sea offered a great collection of fish, fresh vegetables, and fruit. The Selçuk Turks picked up a habit of baking their meat in clay ovens evocative of India. The Ottomans, with their domination of the entire Mediterranean basin, began experimenting with the classic olive oil/tomato/garlic/onion combinations so popular in Italy. The result of these many influences is a distinctive and mouthwatering local cuisine, varying by region.

## Mezes

The one thing you must know about Turkish dining is the wonderful institution of **mezes**, or appetizers, which is probably an imperfect translation, since it is common for friends to gather and consume mezes alone with bottles of rakı. Excellent examples are **kalamar**, fried calamari; **patlican salata**, eggplant puree; and **yaprak dolma**, stuffed grape leaves, all of which go very well with a blue summer sky and a sea view. The meze is more than just a precursor to the meal, it is an integral part of the dining ritual.

## Kahvaltı

One exception to this culture of complex food is **kahvaltı**, breakfast. North Americans accustomed to scrambled eggs, potatoes, and thick slices of bacon are in for an often disappointing shock. First of all, pork products are not a part of the Muslim diet and will only appear at breakfast in the best of the five star hotels. Second, Turks take their breakfast simple and light; bread, cheese, tomatoes, honey, and hard boiled eggs. Again, unless you're at a first class hotel you're going to have to become accustomed to this European menu. Turks are sensible people, so you can generally expect coffee.

### KEY FOOD WORDS

| | |
|---|---|
| *Afiyet Olsun* | *Eat well* |
| *Şerefe* | *To your health* |
| *Izgara* | *Grilled* |
| *Fırın* | *Baked* |
| *Et* | *Meat* |
| *Balık* | *Fish* |
| *Sebze* | *Vegetable* |
| *Meyve* | *Fruit* |
| *Su* | *Water* |
| *Sut* | *Milk* |
| *Ekmek* | *Bread* |
| *Kuru fasulye ve pilav* | *White beans and rice* |
| *Pide* | *Bread with toppings* |
| *Lahmacun* | *Thin crust pizza* |
| *Köfte* | *Meatballs* |

# DRINK

## Coffee

When the Sultan Selim I (The Grim) conquered Yemen in the early 1500s, he installed a local governor who, stuck in Yemen for more than

20 years, turned all of his attention to the local coffee pla.. the governor was recalled to İstanbul he brought coffee with hin., sultan at that time, once again Süleyman the Magnificent, was a.. impressed. Süleyman, in addition to his other contributions to the empire, introduced a **Kahvecebası**, a coffee brew master at the palace. Once established at the palace, it was just a matter of time before coffee was popular throughout İstanbul.

Skeptical Venetian traders had a taste of this hot bean liquid, and chose to import a few cases on a flier. It is at this point that coffee passed a crucial test. According to sheerly apocryphal stories, a Pope, Pius perhaps, took a speculative sip of the heathen drink and, on the spot, blessed it and pronounced it a proper drink for Christians, too. London, Paris, and the major cities of Europe were soon importing coffee. Completing the dramatic tale of coffee's appearance on the world stage, when a great Ottoman invading force was defeated at the gates of Vienna in 1683, an Austrian general discovered crates of coffee in the abandoned imperial tents and brought it within the city walls. He used the coffee to open Vienna's first coffee house. (Had the Turks purposefully retired from the battlefield and left men secreted in massive boxes of coffee...) Other nations, notably Britain, began cultivating coffee in their own possessions, but İstanbul was firmly established as antiquity's Seattle.

For North Americans, Turkish coffee is thick and silty; unfamiliar, but not bad. Avid coffee drinkers may not like it, not on account of its potency but because its taste is mildly bitter. It comes already sugared, unless you ask for it without: *sade*, plain; *az*, a little; *orta*, middling; *çok*, a lot. Most people take it orta. Pouring in milk will disturb the grounds at the bottom of the cup, and is not done.

If you want regular coffee, you'll find mostly Nescafe, although some cafes and restaurants offer *filterkahve* (filtered coffee) and espresso drinks. If you would like milk in your Nescafe, ask for *sütlü kahve*.

## Wine

At a latitude similar to California's Napa Valley, Italy, and France's Loire Valley, wine connoisseurs can expect to locate some delicious wines in Turkey. The country does produce some good wines, but if wine touring is a critical part of your agenda Turkey is probably the wrong place.

Anatolia had an ancient wine making tradition, probably the world's oldest. The first hard evidence appears in engravings dating to the Hittite Empire. The spirit was seized upon by the Greeks, who honored Dionysius during the grape harvest, and amphoras used for wine storage have been found in the holds of sunken ships departing Asia Minor in early Hellenistic times.

After the arrival of the Muslims and their proscriptions against alchohol the ancient industry faltered and died. The Ottoman's contribution to the world of wine is nicely summed up by **Selim II** ("the Sot"), who, as his name suggests, was not afraid to have a snort or two, whatever the religious misgivings of his subjects. In 1569, Selim rerouted an invasion force intended to challenge Spain in the western Mediterranean and instead invested his Venetian allies on Cyprus. The reason? Selim wanted better wine, and a powerful adviser with a dislike for Venice lured him with the promise of tasty Cypriot wines.

Selim II needn't have gone to such lengths to secure good wine – there is plenty of suitable terrain on the Turkish mainland, and beginning in the 1920s grapes have been cultivated for wine making. If you enjoy wine, you will be trying some of the local labels since wine imports are allowed only to a select few top-end restaurants. The **Kavaklıdere** and **Doluca** labels are especially dependable, and the islands offshore, such as **Bozcaada**, continue to produce nice wines as well.

The wine here is quite cheap, ranging up to six dollars for a nice red or white. A bottle of **Buzbağ red** (*kırmızı şarap*) from the government alcohol producer Tekel costs $1.30 and is, believe it or not, just fine, while Doluca's somewhat elite **Villa Doluca** whites and reds cost $4. You can take "wine tours" of a primitive kind by visiting wine manufacturers, **şarap fabrikası**, on Bozcaada, Ürgüp, and elsewhere. **Göreme**, near Ürgüp, hosts an annual wine festival in early September. There are other, smaller wine producers that make fine products, but their labels are difficult to find.

### Rakı

Similar to Greek ouzo and other liquors in the Middle East, rakı is a licorice-flavored alcohol distilled from raisins, then distilled a second time with aniseed. **Yeni Rakı**, the common and readily available brand distributed by the government monopoly, is 90 proof and quite cheap; a liter bottle costs about $4.

There is a tradition and a culture to rakı drinking, an almost ceremonial protocol. The perfect rakı setting is a summer evening, at a table with good friends and a wide selection of Turkish **mezes**, or appetizers, and grilled fish to follow. Clear rakı is poured into a tall, slender glass, and topped off with an equal or slightly greater amount of water. The water turns the rakı a cloudy white, and several glasses later all the world becomes fairly hazy. Rakı drinkers become pleasantly inebriated, a state referred to as *sarhoş*. Rakı is known as lion's milk, owing more to its color than to the belligerence of its drinkers.

## TIPS FOR DINING OUT IN TURKEY

•You want something to go? "To go" is *paket*.

•İşkembe is intestines (tripe), and tripe soup is supposedly curative for hangovers. There are lots of small İşkembeci in big cities, some with the diced up tripe on a big grill out front where you can get a sandwich.

•In smaller restaurants you won't find a menu. They aren't hiding it from you, it's just that 90 percent annual inflation makes printing menus an exercise in futility. Go ahead and, proferring a pen and paper, ask how much for particular items: *"Bu ne kadar?"*

•**Döner** shops have the hunks of revolving meat, which are shaved down and stuffed into half-loaves of bread with tomato, onion, and salt. for about 80¢.

•In heavily touristed places, keep a crystal clear record of your bill as you order (and expect an additional 20 percent in tax and service charge). Nothing can sour the memory of a night out like the feeling you've been ripped off.

•**Köfte** sandwiches are sold out of carts throughout many cities. At a word from you the man will begin grilling up a handful of small meatballs, which he then packs into a half loaf of bread with some onion and tomato sauce. Delicious.

•If stomach ailments are a concern, down lots of yogurt to keep your stomach in good fighting shape. The food and germs here are different, so you may be afflicted with Atatürk's Revenge, but most people have no problems. Note that Ayran, a traditional drink of water and yogurt, isn't as lousy as it sounds, but it is often made with tap water – a bad idea.

•You're bound to see baked potato carts (**Patates Fırın**). Which toppings do you nod your head yes to? We honestly can't be of any help in this matter. There are pickles, lentils, potato salad, butter, cheese, something like cranberries, several other large colorful mounds of food, and, of course, a long squirt of mayonnaise. You can watch from a distance and try to sort out what you want and what you don't – better, probably, to walk right up, nod your head saying *"her şey"* (everything), and mutter an *"Allah Korusun"* (God protect).

•Turkish pizza, **Lahmacun**, has a thin crust and a layer of spicy ground lamb and tomato sauce. It often comes with a side of lettuce, onion, and lemon. It's so thin it's almost a cross between a burrito and a pizza; we love it.

•While dining at restaurants, consider ordering little bits at a time, keeping an eye on your neighbor's table for things you like the look of.

•You can tell what sort of restaurant you're dealing with fairly intuitively. If you see a huge hunk of lamb or chicken rotating on a spit outside you're eating for less than $10, usually less than $5. If there is no

..., it may well climb upwards. Rotating meat is generally a sign of oily, filling food cooked by men for men. Turks keep late hours, and restaurants open accordingly.

- When in doubt, order **kuru fasulye** and **pilav** – white beans and rice. This comes with bread. Another personal, ubiquitous favorite is **patlican salata**, or eggplant salad. Anything with eggplant is good, whatever your prejudices against the vegetable.
- Sauces are notably absent from most Turkish dishes, including fish.
- The greatest testament to the importance of food in Turkish culture was the hierarchy of the Ottoman Janissary Corps. These elite soldiers were organized by kitchen titles; the Chief Cooks, the Bakers, the Soup Makers, and even the much dreaded Pancake Makers. To express their dissatisfaction or anger with a sultan, the Janissaries would overturn the giant pilaf cauldron.

## DINING PHRASES

| | | |
|---|---|---|
| Breakfast | Kahvaltı | kah-vall-tuh |
| Lunch | Öğle yemek | oyluh yem-eck |
| Dinner | Akşam yemek | ak-sham yem-eck |
| Bakery/pastry shop | Pastanesi | pas-ta-nay-see |
| Restaurant | Lokanta | lo kan ta |
| Grill restaurant | Ocakbaşı | ojak-bash-uh |
| Bill, please | Hesap, lütfen | hes-ahp, loot-fen |
| Service Charge | | |
| Included | Servis ücreti dahil | ser-vees ooch-reh-tee da-heel |
| Keep the change | Ustu kalsın | oos-too kal-suhn |
| How much is this? | Bu ne kadar? | boo nay kadar |

## SAMPLE MENU

The following list of Turkish food is on the menu at **Haci Abdullah Restaurant** in Beyoğlu, İstanbul. Haci Abdullah enjoys an unrivalled reputation for serving good, authentic Turkish food. Believe it or not, this is just the abbreviated version of the real menu. If you can't find it on their menu, it probably ain't Turkish.

### Soups (Çorbalar)

| | |
|---|---|
| Domatesli pirinç çorbası | Tomato and rice soup |
| Düğün çorbası | Yogurt and veal soup |
| Erenler çorbası | Semolina soup |
| Et suyu çorbası | Veal bouillon with vegetables |

| | |
|---|---|
| Ezogelin çorbası | Lentil and red pepper soup |
| Güvec | Stew |
| İşkembe çorbası | Tripe soup |
| Ispinak Kök çorbası | Spinach-root soup |
| Kremalı Domates çorbası | Cream of tomato soup |
| Mantar çorbası | Mushroom soup |
| Mengen çorbası | Vegetable soup |
| Mercimek çorbası | Lentil soup |
| Sebzeli pirinç çorbası | Vegetable and rice soup |
| Tavuk suyu şehriye çorbası | Chicken and vermicelli soup |
| Yoğurtlu yayla çorbası | Yogurt and mint soup |

**Meat dishes (Et)**

| | |
|---|---|
| Beğendil kebap | Veal with eggplant puree |
| Beyin tava | Fried lamb's brains |
| Bıldırcin pilavlı | Quail with rice |
| Bonfile sote mantarlı | Sauteed beef with mushrooms |
| Çerkez tavuğu | Circassian chicken |
| Çomlek kebabı | Lamb and vegetable stew |
| Çulluk yahnisi | Woodcock stew |
| Dalyan köftesi | Lamb and veal meatloaf |
| Dana böbrek tava | Fried veal kidneys |
| Dana külbastı | Grilled veal |
| Dana rosto | Roast veal |
| Dana taskebabı | Veal and vegetable stew |
| Fırında kuzu budu sebzeli | Roast leg of lamb with vegetables |
| Güvecte pilavlı Pilic | Chicken and rice stew |
| Hindi kestaneli | Roast turkey with chestnuts |
| Hindi firin | Roast turkey |
| İspinaklı Püreli kebap | Veal with spinach puree |
| İzmir firin köftesi | Meatballs with potatoes |
| Kadınbudu köfte | Fried lamb and veal meatballs |
| Kağit kebabı | Lamb papillote |
| Kagıtta piliç | Chicken papillote |
| Kuzu ciğer sarma | Roulade of lamb's liver |
| Kuzu dolması | Lamb pilaf |
| Kuzu Elbasan tava | Lamb baked in bechamel sauce |
| Kuzu firin | Roast lamb |
| Kuzu haşlama | Boiled lamb |
| Kuzu incik | Roast leg of lamb |
| Kuzu incik soğan yahnisi | Lamb and onion stew |
| Kuzu kapama | Lamb baked with vegetables |
| Kuzu kavurma | Braised lamb |

| | |
|---|---|
| Kuzu sarma | Lamb roulade |
| Kuzu tandir | Tandoori lamb |
| Manisa kebabı | Meat filled crepe |
| Ördek fırın | Roast duck |
| Patlıcanlı kebap | Lamb with eggplant |
| Piliç dolması | Chicken pilaf |
| Tavşan yahnisis | Rabbit stew |
| Terbiyeli köfte | Meatballs in lemon and egg sauce |

### Grilled Meats (Et Izgara)

| | |
|---|---|
| Biftek ızgara | Grilled thin beefsteak |
| Bonfile ızgara | Grilled filet of beef |
| Ciğer ızgara | Grilled lamb's liver |
| Dana böbrek ızgara | Grilled veal kidneys |
| Dana pirzola | Grilled veal chops |
| Karişik ızgara | Mixed grill |
| Köfte ızgara | Grilled meatballs |
| Kuzu pirzola | Grilled lamb chops |
| Kuzu şiş kebap | Lamb shish kebab |
| Tavuk fileto ızgara | Grilled boneless chicken breast |
| Tavuk şiş | Chicken shish kebab |

### Cold Hors D'Oeuvres (Mezes)

| | |
|---|---|
| Bakla ezine | Bean curd |
| Barbunya pilaki | Pinto beans |
| Beyin salatası | Boiled lamb's brains |
| Biber dolması | Stuffed bell pepper |
| Enginar | Artichoke |
| İmam bayıldı | Stuffed eggplant |
| Kereviz | Celeriac |
| Lahana dolması | Stuffed cabbage leaves |
| Piyaz | White beans |
| Taze fasulye | Green beans |
| Yaprak dolması | Stuffed vine leaves |
| Yoğurtlu bakla | Fresh broad beans with yogurt |

### Hot Vegetables (Sicak Sebzeler)

| | |
|---|---|
| Bamya | Okra and tomatoes |
| Biber dolması | Stuffed bell pepper |
| Domates dolması | Stuffed tomato |
| Ispinak püresi | Pureed spinach |
| Kabak dolması | Stuffed zucchini |
| Karnıyarık | Meat-filled eggplant |

| | |
|---|---|
| Patates püresi | Mashed potatoes |
| Patlican silkme | Stewed eggplant |
| Sebze sote | Sauteed mixed vegetables |
| Türlü firin | Mixed vegetables and lamb |
| Yaprak dolması | Stuffed vine leaves |

### Rice and Pasta (Pirinç ve Makarna)

| | |
|---|---|
| Asya pilavı | Garbanzo pilaf |
| Buhara pilavı | Lamb pilaf |
| Bulgar pilavı | Cracked wheat pilaf |
| Fırında makarna | Macaroni and cheese |
| İç pilav | Lamb's liver pilaf |

### Flaky pastries (Böreği)

| | |
|---|---|
| Ispanaklı tepsi böreği | Spinach baked in philodough |
| Kıymalı börek | Chopped meat baked in philodough |
| Kol boreği | Chopped lamb baked in philodough |
| Mantı/Tatar böreği | Ravioli with yogurt |
| Peynirli börek | Feta baked in philodough |
| Su böreği | Feta pastry |
| Tavuklu börek | Minced chicken in philodough |

### Fish (Balık)

| | |
|---|---|
| Alabalık ızgara | Grilled rainbow trout |
| Barbunya ızgara | Grilled red mullet |
| Çinekop ızgara | Grilled young bluefish |
| Hamsi buğulama | Anchovy stew |
| Kalkan fileto ızgara | Grilled turbot filet |
| Kefal haşlama | Boiled striped mullet |
| Kılıç şiş ızgara | Swordfish shish kebab |
| Levrek buğulama | Sea bass stew |
| Lüfer ızgara | Grilled bluefish |
| Mersin buğulama | Sturgeon stew |
| Palamut ızgara | Grilled bonito |
| Sardalya fırın | Baked sardines |
| Sinarit fileto izgara | Grilled sea bream filet |
| Somon ızgara | Grilled salmon |
| Tekir ızgara | Grilled surmullet |

### Salads (Salatalar)

| | |
|---|---|
| Çoban salatası | Chopped tomatoes, onions, peppers |
| Çeşitli turşular | Assorted pickles |
| Domate hıyar söğüş | Sliced tomatoes and cucumbers |

| | |
|---|---|
| Hindiba salatası | Chicory leaves |
| Karışık salata | Tossed salad |
| Karnabahar salatası | Boiled cauliflower |
| Pancar salatası | Boiled beets |
| Roka salatası | Rocket leaves |
| Satilik salatası | Minced cucumbers and tomatoes |
| Turp salatası | Radishes |

# 10. THE BEST PLACES TO STAY

## SMALL HOTELS

**ANTIK THEATRE HOTEL,** *Kıbrıs Sehitleri Caddesi, 243, Bodrum, Tel. 252 316 6053, Fax 252 316 0825. Rooms: 20. Double: $110, Half board $148.*

Once a hotel is given the smart title "best small hotel in Turkey" by *The New York Times*, it can't really be considered a secret anymore. Despite the enthusiastic recommendation, however, the Antik Palace remains a quiet, comfortable place, and doesn't feel like its been the least bit spoiled.

The hotel's architect, Cengiz Bektaş, built the terraced hotel into the side of the hill just below the ancient Helicarnassus theater, with every room looking out on the picturesque Castle of St. Peter through its shuttered door and windows. Every level has its own small patio with a deliberate jumble of gravel and stepping stones and greenery sprouting by the rail, with bougainvillea crawling up wooden frames and old terracotta pots tucked in corners. On the bottom tier is a deep swimming pool, and guests gather here on summer nights, toasting the magnificent castle and bay below.

The decoration is simple whites and marble, with spare wood furnishings. You'll find a candle and an old framed nautical chart or boat diagram for decoration. The suite room, with its long couches, private terrace, fireplace and steepled skylight, is simply one of the finest rooms available in the country. The aesthetics are helped along generously by a good staff that, far from aloof, is engaging and friendly; in this the tone is set by the manager, Altan Karabelen.

The Antik Theatre Hotel is directly across Kıbrıs Sehitleri Caddesi from the Bodrum theater, and the hotel patios are ideal for late evening dining, the castle illuminated and the harbor alive with lights. The hotel has an excellent chef, and at $38 extra half board accommodations should be considered. At least spend an evening at the Sunset Bar.

**ESBELLI EVI**, *Turban Girişi, Çeşme Karşısı, PK 2, Ürgüp, Cappadoccia, Tel. 384 341 3395, Fax 384 341 8848. Rooms: 7. Double: $64.*

In Cappadocia's Zelve valley, monks spent 800 years poring over the Bible, living simply, and slowly chipping away at the soft tuff to create churches, living areas, and bedrooms. Being monks, they were busy, but rarely rushed. They could take their time deciding where to carve a window out of a cliff face, where to connect two spaces with a tunnel, where to build a shelf.

Travelers today come from thousands of miles to wind through the labyrinthine corridors, entering unlikely looking holes at ground level and emerging hundreds of feet above. But lost in 700 years of abandonment and erosion is the careful attention to detail of monks with a lifetime to contemplate the stone and the greenery of the valley below.

The Esbelli Ev in Ürgüp probably comes close to capturing the sense of precision and detail that would have once been found here. The Esbelli is not the product of many lifetimes; in fact in some ways it has been put up in a terrible hurry. After purchasing property in the hills above Ürgüp village in 1979, Esbelli Ev owner and host Süha Ersöz mulled over the site and set to work in 1987. He cleaned and recarved three rooms from the living rock, rehabilitating the stone houses above. Four years later he began inviting guests. In the following years he purchased some adjoining land and completed a few more rooms. "Seven rooms in seven years is not the way most people do business," says Süha Bey.

And seven rooms is all the Esbelli will ever be. Seven sets of guests are probably too many, the owner laments. He enjoys best of all getting to know the people who pass through his hotel, cultivates an almost familial relationship with them. Repeat guests arrive with gifts of CDs and photographs, and send photographs and postcards throughout the year.

The only affront that seems to register with Süha Bey is when guests rush off in the morning and stagger in at night. Ersöz is not in the business of processing customers, he wants people to visit and enjoy his hotel. In 1995 he was forced to scuttle an arrangement with a tour company; the guests were up at 8 a.m. and limping in ten hours later. He'd much rather you lingered over your excellent breakfast on the patio, then read a paper for a little while until it is seemly to mix yourself a gin and tonic (in the refrigerator with all the other beverages, no charge). Ersöz has created a halfway house in the old style, a place to relax and catch your breath. Monks spent lifetimes here just sitting and looking, and they weren't as crazy as they sound. If you're going to see where they lived, you might as well see why they lived here.

# BEST PLACES TO STAY

**EMPRESS ZOE,** *Akbıyık Cad. Adliye Sok. No. 10, Sultanahmet, İstanbul, Tel. 212 518 2504, Fax 212 518 5699. Double: $70. Rooms: 28.*
The Empress Zoe will not do at all for those uneasy around art. This small gem in the Sultanahmet district is painted in muted yellows, with appealing woodwork on the walls and bedsteads, fine metal rails and fixtures, a heavy dose of antique stone peeking from the walls, and thick slabs of rock underfoot. The decor is traditional Turkish in an environment of artistic licentiousness, with kilim and other textiles played off against dramatic full-wall renderings of Ottoman sipahis (cavalrymen) and Byzantine emperors. Every room has a bathroom finished in marble, with shower. Satellite television is available in some rooms, as it is in the public areas. Note: avoid room 33.

The lobby and terrace highlight the entire hotel. Both are dramatic and appealing, the lobby slightly off-kilter with its angles and arches; the terrace offering a generous view of the Sea of Marmara, with a cozy interior for after the weather turns. Staff is helpful and English-speaking (the hotel is owned by an American), and the three year old hotel is the best value for money in İstanbul. The Ibrahim Pasa Hotel, just off of Istanbul's Hippodrome, is in the same mold.

**LES MAISONS DE CAPPADOCE,** *Semiramis A.Ş., Belediye Meydanı No. 24, BP 28, Uçhisar, Tel. 384 219 2813, Fax 384 219 2782. Houses: 7 (12). House/6: $1,300 per week. Studio/2: $400 per week.*
French architect Jacques Avizou came to Cappadoccia as a tourist in 1987, returning home with some photographs, tourist chotchkes, and some inspiration. Since then he has returned annually, often flying back to Orly Airport with more substantial souvenirs, such as title deeds. Through his Turkish company, Semiramis, Avizou has renovated a clutch of houses and studios in Uçhisar, doting over them and mending them in exacting fashion. There are five houses and two studios currently available, with a further seven houses probably available in 1997. Each is faithful to the peculiar architectural legacy of the area, with arches, stairs, and rooms carved out of the valley wall, finished with blocks of stone. Each house and suite is equipped with a kitchen, and you should solicit advice on some Turkish recipes while here. Patios command Pigeon Valley below and you are free to use the pool at the nearby Kaya Hotel. Unfortunately you may never make it that far from the house, let alone all the way to Göreme and Zelve.

Houses and studios, accommodations for anywhere from two to six people, are available for weekly rental. Contact Semiramis for information about shorter stays. Open April through October.

**ASPEN HOTEL**, *Kaleiçi Mermerli Sok. Turizm Müdürlüğü Yani 16-18, Kaleiçi, Antalya, Tel. 242 247 0590, Fax 242 241 3364. Rooms: 40. Double: $105.*

Antalya's old town is thick with small, pretty hotels, and the Aspen is the best of the lot. The Aspen perches a short distance above Antalya's old harbor, a compound of restored buildings with a pleasant garden. The attractive rooms have landscaped patios decked with flowers and littered with odds and ends of marble. The view from most rooms is excellent, particularly from rooms 106-110. All rooms have satellite television, minibar, and air conditioning.

**SULTAN PALAS HOTEL**, *Dalyan, Tel. 252 284 2103, Fax 252 284 2106. Rooms: 26. Double: $550 per week, high season;$450 per week, mid-season. Half board. Closed October 30 to April 1.*

The Sultan Palas is a charming retreat tucked away on the "other side" of the Dalyan River, alone in a small valley at the base of the sprawling Caunos ruins. The hotel's centerpiece is the stone tower that serves as a late evening bar, although some might claim that the generously sized pool is the crucial bit. Rooms are practical and have their own balconies, but the real fun is in lounging at the poolside or joining in on one of the many day trips.

The Sultan Palas caters to vacationers who are in the area for several days or a week – and hosts Taifun and his English wife Linda excel at keeping you as busy as you care to be. The hotel has its own boat service between the hotel dock and town. The hotel offers cheap, interesting day excursions around the Dalyan area.

**OLYMPOS LODGE MOTEL**, *P.O. Box 38, Kemer/Çıralı Olympos, Tel. 242 825 7171, Fax 242 825 7173. Rooms: 8. Double: $100.*

The Olympos Lodge is one of the most beautiful little hotels in the whole of Turkey, admirably blending into the landscape behind a screen of orange trees and a large landscaped garden. Çıralı is one of our favorite places in its own right, with a collection of rough, pleasant lodging, but the Olympos Lodge is a quantum level above the other hotels in the area in craftsmanship and location (a quantum level in price, as well). The Olympos Lodge's handful of cottages are scattered along the course of a stream, beyond which the beach trails off toward the Olympos ruins. Down the beach and inland in the opposite direction is the strange living fire of the Chimera. The shaded lawn just above the beach is ideal for retreating in the heat of the day, and dinner in the evenings is the best in the area.

The small collection of rooms helps establish a sense of community among the visitors, and most people who visit seem determined to return. Finally, the owner was reticent about being written up, a classic sign that his hotel deserves to be.

**KALKAN HAN**, *Kalkan, Tel. 242 844 3151, Fax 242 844 2048. Rooms: 16. Double: $65.*

High on the slope above the Kalkan harbor, the Kalkan Han embodies the tasteful, whitewashed ideal of the classic Mediterranean town. The hotel was designed by Haydar Karabey, who helped the municipal government establish its far-sighted zoning standards and locked Kalkan into its charming shape before giant hotels could move in and sweep away what makes Kalkan so appealing. The design mirrors the Greek/ Turkish architecture native to the area, but there's really nothing tricky about it; wood and stone construction on clean, simple lines. Rooms are good-sized and spartan, with ceiling fans, well-appointed bathrooms, and balconies along the upper floor.

Amid all of this simplicity, however, the Kalkan Han has a remarkable way with the complex, whether serving the finest dinners in the area or helping you make arrangements. The Kalkan Han is smartly managed, with a courteous and likable staff. The Han is located at the upper end of town just uphill from Kalkan's single entry road.

## LARGE HOTELS

**KISMET HOTEL**, *Akyar Mevkii, Kuşadası, Tel. 256 614 2005, Fax 256 614 4914. Rooms: 102. Double: $110. Half board available. Restaurant.*

The 31 year-old Kismet is the grand old institution of Kuşadası, a sparkling relic of old world calm and decorum that has seen guest such as Jimmy Carter and Queen Elizabeth II (separately). In a region where three-year-old hotels appear tattered, the Kismet is natty, with marvelously manicured grounds and a charm like San Simeon. In fact, the Kismet's lineage is far more distinguished than San Simeon's: it was built not by a newspaper publishing magnate, but by descendants of the last Ottoman Sultan.

For all of its Ottoman roots, the Kismet is very English colonial, the perfect location for an afternoon gin and tonic under the trees. The rooms are attractive and peaceful, with shutters that open and allow the sea breezes to blow through. The tennis court is one of the most beautiful anywhere, but a mishit backhand will float to Egypt. The great appeal of the Kismet, beyond its own relaxed atmosphere, is its proximity to Ephesus, just twenty minutes north by car, and the other ruins in the area. Open April-October.

**FOUR SEASONS HOTEL İSTANBUL,** *Tevkifhane Sok. No. 1, Sultanahmet, İstanbul, Tel. 212 638 8529, Fax 212 638 8530 (North American Reservations: Tel. 800/332-3442). Rooms: 65. Double: $225.*

This hotel opened in 1996 and immediately won praise for its luxury and location. The Four Seasons is far and away the most ambitious hotel in a city filled with excellent hotels, and it's exclusive fellows are all bunched far from Sultanahmet and cater mostly to business. The Four Seasons expects that you're here for pleasure, and sets about making everything right. Four Seasons İstanbul is precise and lovely, with a constant shower of tiny flourishes and amenities. The genius of the hotel is in the details of each room, the great basins, attractive interior shutters, the bags of potpourri hung in the closet; bathrooms offer separate showers and baths. There is a distinct Turkish quality as well; kilim, tilework, small Ottoman prints and portraits, all thoughtfully conceived.

The refined atmosphere of the hotel belies a grim past. This building was a notorious Turkish prison into the 1960s, and although the interior design scheme has come a long way, small traces of the old building remain (the red and blue floor tiles in some of the stairwells beside the hotel elevators, for instance). The project has been greeted warmly by most İstanbullus, but some find the idea of sleeping in an old prison less interesting than morbid. Mindful of the grim history on the site, some of the building's touches seem to have a certain evil-Christo element: designers dressed up an old wall-top guard tower in bright pastel hues and pretty trim, for instance.

If you are unnerved by the notion of sleeping in a former prison, you might be comforted by the fact that long before becoming a Turkish prison (in the late 1800s) the same real estate was on the grounds of the Byzantine Royal Palace: there are pampered, well-fed ghosts here to keep the prisoners' wretched souls company. Walls and arches belonging to former palace buildings are visible skirting the Four Seasons.

The former prison day-yard now houses the Four Seasons' restaurant, run by a Venetian chef who specializes in California and Mediterranean cuisine, now, evidently, mentioned in the same breath. Make reservations at both the hotel and the restaurant far in advance.

**ÇIRAĞAN PALACE KEMPINSKI,** *Çırağan Caddesi No. 84, Beşiktaş, Tel. 212 258 3377, Fax: 212 259 6687 (North American Reservations: Tel. 800/ 426-3135). Rooms: 322. Double: $195-$5,000.*

This is where John F. Kennedy Jr. and his wife stayed on their honeymoon, as did a vacationing Hillary Clinton. President Bush stayed in 1991. The Çırağan has certainly arrived, and by a very circuitous route.

Sultan Abdül Aziz originally intended the Çırağan Palace to replace the Dolmabahçe Palace, finding Dolmabahçe too confining. Workers put the finishing touches on the Çırağan Palace – very much like the Dolmabahçe both in terms of its layout and baroque aesthetic – in 1874, but its Kismet seemed bad from the beginning. Abdül Aziz was deposed in 1876 and imprisoned here. He slashed his own wrists with a pair of scissors just a few days later, which sent his successor, Sultan Murat V, spiralling into madness. Murat was then deposed in favor of Abdül Hamit II, still in 1876, but Abdül Hamit was too paranoid to live exposed on the water and commissioned a new palace at Yıldız Park. The Çırağan Palace became the prison of Murat V and the Sultan's other rivals and potential heirs, for which it became known as "The Cage."

The palace's prospects seemed to brighten in 1908, when nationalist Turks succeeded in forming a parliament and chose to house it here. The parliament, however, was a resounding failure, and the Çırağan Palace burned to the ground in 1910. The ruins still lay there 75 years later, when a group of investors began laboriously restoring the blackened ruin. Their work was completed earlier this decade, and the Çırağan has flourished.

This is one of the Leading Hotels of the World and a standard selection on the top 100 hotels list, but we have to attach some caveats. The interiors are surprisingly gaudy, sometimes even downright ugly. The Çırağan is not far from Sultanahmet and the bulk of İstanbul's sights – except on mornings, evenings and weekends, when the sea road gets choked with traffic. Then the three mile drive can take a half hour or far longer. Finally, the world's handsomest and most important people stay here, but they stay in the suites, housed in the actual palace building. The suites are stunning, with fine views out over the Bosphorous and attractive, ornate detailing. The standard rooms are just that, standard, and they not in the authentic palace, but in a new wing that was built as a hotel.

Still, with one-half mile of Bosphorous shoreline, an excellent standard of service, and a worldwide reputation, the Çırağan is a luxury hotel in the finest sense. Seriously, who wouldn't want to stay in a genuine Ottoman Palace?

**IBEROTEL SARIGERME PARK**, *Ortaca Postanesi PK 1, Ortaca, Tel. 252 286 8031, Fax 252 286 8043. Rooms: 372. Double: $160, Half board.*

A short drive – or a one hour pair of dolmuş – east of Dalyan is one of Turkey's finest holiday villages.

In a land filled with hotels that are less than the sum of their parts, the Sarigerme Park is a bewitching exception. The Sarigerme Park is precisely what most of the large beachfront hotels intend to be, a full-service retreat with archery, soccer, horse riding, volleyball, and a whole range of beachside diversions. Nighttime even brings the noisy "animations,"

Turkey's ubiquitous and typically unsuccessful humor and dance numbers, and here they work. Here everything works.

The Iberotel benefits from its great size – it is more than 140,000 square meters – and from the happy coincidence that the property is on the grounds of ancient Pisilus. The bulk of the ruins are off the path to the beach to the right. Here you can clamber up a hill and poke around the acropolis, trampling through the thick undergrowth to investigate tumbled Roman structures and the large ring of 6 foot wide city walls. The necropolis is built on the buttress just above the beach, with other ruins scattered around the hotel grounds. Amateur archaeologist Heinz-Otto Lamprecht has identified many of the Pisilus ruins, and hotel staff leads occasional tours of what amounts to its own ruins.

Just as the hotel takes care of the big things, it is mindful of the small things as well. You get a pot of coffee in the morning, not a tiny cup; you get good potatoes and eggs if the standard bread, jam, cheese and tomato diet is wearing thin. Getting a dolmuş to the local transit hub of Ortaca is easy since the route is partially funded by the hotel. Most rooms have a balcony bedecked with flowers, and air-conditioning and CNN/NBC is standard. The beauty salon even offers a six-day regimen of massage and every other form of relaxation and beautification.

The grounds are nicely tended, with paths down to a long sand beach that offers beach lounging furniture and umbrellas. Europeans love these things. The hotel buildings are low and unassuming, and many rooms are located in smaller two story bungalows. The hotel's largest building is set back into a hillside hardly visible from the beach, with flowers tumbling from the balconies. As you would expect from such a well-run hotel, the staff is helpful and professional.

Note: the Pisilus ruins are open to the public, and the Sarigerme beach is also public, accessed from the main road to the west.

# 11. ISTANBUL

The Roman Empire continued uninterrupted for more than 1,500 years, and for 900 of those years **Constantinople** was the capital. Behind its great walls were a collection of soaring palaces and towers, columns and arcades to commemorate hundreds of victorious battles, a stadium that seated 100,000, and the world's greatest cathedral, the **Haghia Sophia**. Byzantine Roman conquests further adorned the city with treasures from Persia and Egypt, creating a repository of art and architecture that, during the medeival ages, had no peer. Constantinople was the world's envy.

The city enjoyed every advantage. It was protected by the world's greatest set of fortifications and bordered on three sides by the sea. Its natural harbor provided the perfect anchorage for controlling passage through the **Bosphorous**, and merchants seeking to pass overland from Europe to Asia were forced to cross here. When the city finally fell to the Crusaders in 1204, it was as much due to weakness within as the forces arrayed against it. So long as the city was governed by a strong ruler it was indomitable, and, accordingly, it flourished under the Ottomans until the 17th century, and remained untouched by the Ottomans' enemies until the 20th century.

Constantinople, later **İstanbul**, is filled with reminders of its magnificent history. The Bosphorous still flows past the tip of the old city, the **Golden Horn** cuts into the European shore. City walls, towers, great mosques and cathedrals, cisterns, and palaces are a permanent part of the background. In the foreground is a crowded, bustling city whose people seem to have one foot planted firmly in Europe, one in Asia.

The muezzin awaken you with the call to prayer at the first hint of light, and you roll out of bed into streets filled with people hawking hats, watches, fake Levis, underwear, hammers, fresh eggplants, condoms, shoeshines, and spare parts. The city is loud and disconcerting, with salesmen bickering and wheedilng, tinkers and vegetable sellers wailing, gas trucks blaring their competing jingles, and always a few merchants directing tempting yells of "Hello my friend!" or *"Yessss"* in your direction. Cars roar past, squeezing between you and the gaping holes torn in the pavement, dirty shoeshine boys elbow each other aside to importune likely-looking gentlemen, and a dissonant honking fills the air.

İstanbul is chaos, but within the chaos, order. İstanbul is a big city; New York City is half the size of İstanbul. The people of İstanbul are civil and kind. On first sight, İstanbullus may seem a taciturn bunch, but they're almost always good hearted and helpful. The least agreeable people in town will be the ones looking for you in Sultanahmet, but usually they, too, are charming, friendly, and surprisingly helpful. Especially if you want a carpet.

Unless you go looking for trouble, say in the back streets off of İstiklal Caddesi late at night, you're unlikely to find it. This is especially true outside of the heavily touristed districts, whether in İstanbul or elsewhere in the country. The Turk's kindness is liable to surprise you, but, sadly, the greater the influx of foreigners, the more it wears away. In Sultanahmet and crowded areas you're well-advised to keep a hand on your wallet; in the inimitable words of Artemis Ward, "Trust everybody, but cut the cards."

---

### WHAT TO EXPECT IN ISTANBUL

*İstanbul can appear a huge, daunting maze. You probably have some preconceptions when you set down in Paris, London, and even Hong Kong, but few people arriving directly from North America know what to expect of İstanbul. Expect lots of people – the population is approaching 15 million, and the city sprawls for 100 miles. Expect lots of smoking and moustaches. Expect honking cars. Expect to see chunks of the gigantic walls and towers that kept the city safe during more than 30 sieges. Expect a beautiful skyline, perhaps the most beautiful in the world. Expect to see gaudy palaces and lofty cathedrals. Expect people in Sultanahmet to have a brother who owns a carpet shop. Expect to be awakened by muezzin calls. Expect tea. Expect spending a lot of time on your feet, and a lot of money on a carpet. Expect to enjoy yourself, because İstanbul may be alien and chaotic, but it's an exciting, benign sort of alien and chaotic.*

---

### Byzantium

No one knows how long people have settled at the tip of the peninsula that is the heart of historic Byzantium. The first evidence of small settlements at the tip of İstanbul's peninsula – near modern-day Topkapı Palace – dates to the 13th Century BC, but these minor fishing villages were only satellites of a major trading center at Chalcedon across the Bosphorous on the Asian shore.

Tacitus wrote that when an expedition of Greeks under Byzas set out to found a new city in the 8th Century B.C., the Pythian Apollo advised them to settle opposite the land of the blind. When the expedition arrived in the area they concluded that the Chalcedonians must have been blind not to see the defensive and commercial advantages of the spit of land directly across the water on the European shore. The peninsula was protected on three sides by the Golden Horn, the Bosphorous, and the Sea of Marmara, and Byzas' colonists erected walls to seal off the tip of the peninsula and hold enemies at bay.

The oracle was right: Byzantium proved a secure and thriving town. Fishermen prospered and Byzantium's small fleet could lay at anchor in the Golden Horn, emerging to challenge ships as they sailed through the Bosphorous, particularly ships fighting their way north against the current. Byzantium quickly eclipsed Chalcedon's power, and by the second century BC it had complete command of the straits.

An interesting cast of characters passed through Byzantium during the 1,100 years before Constantine the Great's arrival. **Alexander**, peculiarly, did not conquer Byzantium. His father Phillip II mounted a siege in 340-339 BC, but never entered the city in force. The siege is notable as the occasion that the Byzantines' credited the Goddess Hecate with saving the city and thereafter adopted her symbol of the star and the crescent moon that was, in turn, taken by the Ottomans upon their seizure of the city 1,800 years later. By the time of Alexander's famous campaign in 334, Byzantium was an ally, providing ships to the young conqueror.

Byzantium was less helpful to the Roman general **Septimius Severus** (193-211 AD). Byzantium sided with Pescinnius Niger against Severus during a Roman civil war of the late second century AD, and after defeating his rival in Asia Minor, Severus continued to bear the Byzantines a grudge. In 196 he leveled Byzantium, tearing down its walls and massacring its citizens and soldiery. Two years later he relented and commissioned the rebuilding of a city on the site. Severus was successful both in destroying Byzantium and in rebuilding it; he expanded the ring of city walls and established the great **Hippodrome** and other fixtures of the later city.

Curiously, the next great figure in the city's history also involved an enemy. **Constantine**, Emperor of the West, marched against Licinius, Emperor of the East, in 324, attempting to consolidate the power of the Roman Empire. The pivotal battle in the campaign took place on the Asian shore of the Bosphorous within sight of Byzantium, which at the time was subject to Licinius' rule. Perhaps recalling the ire of Severus several generations before, Byzantium threw its gates open to the victorious Constantine immediately after the battle. This gambit worked;

Constantine forgave the Byzantines their support of his rival and accepted the city's welcome. Several years later, Constantine sought to relocate the Roman capital in the stable eastern empire and away from the tumult of Rome. After narrowing his choices, Constantine chose ... Troy. Work began at the small Roman city before the emperor reconsidered, halted work, and finally selected the more defensible Byzantium.

Byzantium was still quite humble to be the imperial seat of Rome, and in 326 Constantine began an ambitious building program to render Byzantium an appropriate capital for his empire. He completed work on the **Hippodrome**, erected palaces and arcaded roads, built new land walls in a circuit that would today enclose the ruins of the **Valens Aqueduct**, beautified and repaired churches, and imported appropriate imperial chotchkes such as the 5th Century BC Bronze **Serpent Column** commemorating the Greek victory over Persia at Plataea.

Byzantium was founded anew in 330 AD after four years of renovation, and the city, soon called Constantinople, proved a resounding success.

**Constantinople**

The city was such a success, in fact, that one century later **Constantinople** was undergoing growth pains as its population bumped up against the land walls. Theodosius II's engineers endeavored to remedy this in 413 BC, but their efforts were undone by a quake 34 years later. Never have so many moved so quickly; by nasty coincidence Atila the Hun was riding roughshod over Europe at that very time, and he had a covetous eye on the Roman capital. Constantinople's citizens worked round the clock, restoring the walls and even adding outer fortifications to the long circuit. A disappointed Atila took his rampage elsewhere, and the citizens of the city breathed a sigh of relief.

In the fifth century, the division between the eastern and western empire became complete, with the west spinning into chaos, punctuated with repeated sacks of Rome. Constantinople was now the greatest outpost of Roman imperial rule. In the sixth century, the ambitious Emperor **Justinian** sought to suitably decorate the city, commissioning the construction of the **Haghia Sophia** in 532, a massive cathedral that still stands today. The fame and rumor of this huge cathedral – for one thousand years it remained the largest in the world – helped establish Constantinople as the world's greatest city.

Constantinople prospered during the frequent periods of Byzantine expansion, and panicked during its equally frequent contractions. No matter how grave the empire's position, however, its enemies were always frustrated by the city's soaring walls. At various times the Arabs, Goths, Avars, Persians, and Bulgars laid siege to Constantinople, and in the darkest moments different armies would approach the city simultaneously, as in the Avar and Persian campaigns of 619.

Century after century Constantinople held out against its external foes, but soon after the millenium the situation for the empire, and its capital, became particularly grim. Turkic tribes appeared in the east, and, spearheaded by the Selcuk Turk **Alp Arslan**, humiliated Byzantine armies and seized large tracts of Asia Minor. The **Selcuks** rolled through the Armenian buffer area, seized Ani, captured Caesera (Kayseri), and destroyed a grand Byzantine army at Manzikert in 1071. The former Byzantine resolve to reclaim lost territory was gone; Imperial armies stood by while the Selcuks continued their campaign, seizing Jerusalem in 1077 and establishing themselves all along the Mediterranean and Aegean coasts as far as Smyrna (Izmir).

In 1090, Constantinople was on the ropes; the emir of Smyrna allied with Patzinak armies from the Russian steppes to lay the city siege by land and sea, but a shrewd alliance with Turkic peoples in the north broke the siege. The Empire seemed to have endured the worst of it, and now Emperor Alexius had an opportunity to regain Asia Minor.

In the midst of his planning, "help" came from an unexpected quarter. The first wave of Crusades began in 1097, the beginning of the empire's decline that ended in the temporary loss of Contantinople itself (See Crusades section in Chapter 5, *A Short History*). Following the end of the Crusade period (1261), the Byzantine Empire had lost influence in most of its traditional Asian lands and had been shorn of its wealth. Moreover, while the Crusaders and Byzantines had dithered over Constantinople, the Turks had dug in along the frontier, with grave consequences for the Byzantines.

### The Ottomans

One of the most precocious Turkish tribes arose along the northern Aegean coast, established by a march lord named **Ertuğrul**. Most of the Turkish tribes were ferocious warriors and awful administrators; not so the budding kingdom of Ertuğrul and his son, **Osman**. These Turks, who took the name Osmanoğlu, or Ottoman, exhibited military acumen, evenhanded governance, and intelligent diplomacy. They gradually established a bustling state on the fringes of the Byzantine Empire, confronting and defeating a Byzantine army near Bursa in 1336.

This early success won the Ottomans renown, but they remained careful not to overreach their grasp, preferring treaties and accords to outright conflict. At this they were a remarkably quick study, matching the crafty Byzantines move for move: the Ottomans soon became hatchetmen for the Byzantines, but the hatchetmen used every opportunity to seize new territory. By 1366, the Ottomans had conquered Thrace and Bulgaria in addition to their Asian lands, virtually encircling Constantinople.

The rulers in Constantinople were initially unwilling – and soon unable – to arrest the growing threat. Arranged marriages and diplomatic manipulation, two important tools of Byzantine statecraft, had lost their effectiveness in the hands of weakening emperors. By 1396, the land approaches to the city were blockaded and the Ottomans were harassing the shipping lanes. **Beyazid I**, the great grandson of Osman, was slowly choking off the city, and his armies camped outside the walls, waiting for the inevitable capitulation.

The surrender never came. Beyazid's armies, triumphant throughout Europe and Asia, were drawn off to meet a sudden threat in the east: the advance of **Tamurlane**. There, in the **Battle of Ankara** (1402), Tamurlane shattered the Ottoman forces and captured Beyazid. Tamurlane's armies took the whole of Asia Minor in the same year, leaving great piles of human heads to mark their passing, but for Tamurlane this was a mere diversion before his long-considered campaign against China. Constantinople's residents, fearing they had gone from the frying pan to the fire, breathed a great sigh of relief at his departure into the east.

Alas, the Byzantines failed to take advantage of the vacuum created by Tamurlane's passing, and the Ottomans demonstrated great resilience. After struggling through a ten year interregnum, the Ottomans emerged in 1413 with much of their former territory returned. For Constantinople, the defeat of Beyazid was only a delay, not a reprieve.

### Constantinople Becomes İstanbul

Sultan **Mehmet II** ascended the throne in 1451, inheriting an empire that had been put in excellent order by his father, Murat II. Mehmet immediately set to work on plans to capture Constantinople, erecting fortresses along the Bosphorous and Dardanelles to cut off support by sea and tending to other details, such as commissioning a metal-caster to create an arsenal of heavy cannon. He also devised an audacious scheme to dislodge the Byzantine navy from behind the heavy chain stretched across the mouth of the Golden Horn: his men created a long path of rollers and hauled his ships overland to the Golden Horn from the area near Dolmabahçe Palace. The city thus cut off, Mehmet and an army of 250,000 accomplished what none had succeeded in doing for 1,000 years: breaching and storming the land walls. Ottoman soldiers enjoyed three days of plunder, and all of Islam celebrated the long-sought fall of the city.

Mehmet II proved as thorough and tireless in planning the rebirth of Constantinople as he had been in planning its downfall. He imported people from conquered territories to repopulate the city and carried out ambitious construction projects, including countless public buildings and **Topkapı Palace**. Rid of the suffocating external pressures that the Ottomans themselves had contributed to, Constantinople – or **İstanbul**, as it came to be known – was a thriving metropolis within Mehmet II's own lifetime.

---

### THAT'S NOBODY'S BUSINESS BUT THE TURKS

*The name "İstanbul" is not, as often reported, a perversion of "Islampolis." The name derives from the Greek "Eis ten polin," or "to the city," a phrase that was commonly used by the Turks in reference to Constantinople, and was formalized under Atatürk.*

---

Ottoman rule brought a period of unprecedented security to İstanbul. Mehmet II rebuilt the city walls and added new fortifications such as **Yedikule,** but there were no direct threats to the city for centuries. İstanbul enjoyed great prosperity as the seat of Ottoman imperial power, and the Ottomans, like the Byzantines before them, decorated the capital with plunder from their territories and engineered great new public buildings. İstanbul owes a great debt to **Sinan**, chief architect during the heyday of the empire. Many of the mosques and **türbe** (tombs) scattered around the city were designed by Sinan, and he was also responsible for shoring up the Haghia Sophia and executing civil engineering projects throughout the empire.

At the height of the Ottoman Empire, which saw its greatest successes under **Süleyman the Magnificent** (1520-1566), İstanbul was once again the world's great city. At its greatest extent, the Ottoman Empire controlled almost the entire Mediterranean and Black Sea, the Caucasus, Eastern Europe, and the Holy Land, and many of the revenues returned to coffers in İstanbul. Like Constantinople before it, İstanbul benefited from a long peace, a time during which palaces and mosques appeared to beautify the city and inspire its visitors.

### The Republic

As the Ottoman Empire faded, its capital remained secure. On those occasions in the nineteenth century when even İstanbul came under threat, whether by the Egyptian Mehmet Ali in 1832 or the Russians in 1878, the world's other powers would act in defense of "the Sick Man of Europe." It suited the purposes of the European nations, Russia included, to stand in the way of anyone else defeating and occupying Turkey. This policy was of no help in World War I, however, and it is then that İstanbul faced its most serious threat.

According to a plan advanced by Winston Churchill, Britain and France sought to force the Dardanelle Strait with warships and threaten İstanbul. If the Ottoman Empire refused to end its alliance with Germany, the British were prepared to pound İstanbul with their guns, destroying the vulnerable seaside palaces and kindling a firestorm among the city's wooden houses.

The plan failed, bogging down in Gallipolli because of the young Mustafa Kemal's (Atatürk's) tenacious leadership. The Ottomans remained in the war, cutting off shipping to Russia and prompting the collapse of the Czar, but eventually shared the defeat of their German allies. The war cost the Ottomans all of their possessions south of Iskendrun (formerly Alexandretta), but the peace was truly devastating. According to the **Treaty of Sevres**, the Ottoman Empire was partitioned to Italy, France, England, Russia, Armenia, and Greece, and the Marmara sea corridor, including İstanbul, became part of an occupied "control zone" whose fate was uncertain. The Ottoman Sultan was welcome to stay in İstanbul, where Allied gunships could keep an eye on him, but the only truly Turkish state remaining bordered the Black Sea and extended only partway across the Anatolian plateau.

Enter, once again, **Atatürk**. The charismatic leader galvanized his people – rallying them against an ambitious invasion by the hated Greeks – and mounted a successful War of Independence. After driving the Greek armies literally into the sea at Izmir, diplomats of the new Turkish state, refusing to abide by the Treaty of Sevres, forced a war-weary Europe to end its plans for partition and return Turkey in its present form. Dissension among the allies, some of whom were unhappy at their share of the partition, contributed to the Turks' success. According to the final accord, İstanbul and the chunk of Thrace south of Edirne were restored to Turkey as well, sparing the great city from falling into foreign hands.

Atatürk, for all his love of Turkey, was not especially fond of İstanbul. It was, to his mind, a city of intrigues, grown too large to be trusted. The nationalist capital, originally Ankara by necessity, became Ankara by choice. Thus İstanbul, a capital for almost 1,700 years prior, became Turkey's second city (at least politically). The change hasn't hurt the city's popularity; İstanbul's population has exploded, and an estimated 14 million people line the shores of the Bosphorous.

## ARRIVALS & DEPARTURES
### By Air
**Atatürk Airport** (Atatürk Havaalamanı) is the hub of both national and international air travel in Turkey. Most international carriers have offices here, as do the airlines responsible for Turkey's internal air travel.

İstanbul serves most of Turkey's major cities, indeed most flights between towns take you via İstanbul. **Turkish Airlines**, *Tel. 212 663 6363*, is the nation's government subsidized leader, with reliable service and reasonable prices – $160 will get you a round trip to any airport in the country and to Northern Cyprus. Cheaper still, for a small sacrifice in promptness and number of towns covered, is **İstanbul Air**, *Tel. 212 509 2122.*

For reservations while in İstanbul, consult **Imperial Turizm**, *Divan Yolu Caddesi No. 31, Sultanahmet, İstanbul, 212 513 9430, Fax 212 512 3291..*

## Arriving By Air

If you're like most travelers, İstanbul's Atatürk Airport will be your first contact with Turkey. Your initial jet-lagged view of İstanbul is likely to be a muddle. In the interest of smoothing those rough edges, here's what to expect:

You get off the plane and board a small bus. The bus fills with passengers and carries you to the international terminal, where you get off the bus and stand in line at the visa desk (on the far side of the room as you enter) or go straight to one of the several passport control lines if you already have a Turkish visa. After paying $20 for a glue-on stamp in your passport, you return to the passport control lines. There the date is stamped in your passport and you continue on to the baggage claim area. Pick up your baggage and, probably, walk right past the customs tables. If they do decide to have a look through your bags you're unlikely to have something you shouldn't. They don't care about cameras or laptop computers, if that's a concern. Fifty feet later you are through the swinging doors and in the arrivals area, exposed to the public.

If you are part of a tour this is where you will be met by your tour company. Otherwise, you can pick up a telephone card upstairs at the PTT office (100 units, $5) and make calls or, alternately, head directly to a hotel. The easiest way to do this is to take a taxi from directly in front of the arrivals area – a 20 minute ride along the Sea of Marmara to the old city, Sultanahmet, should be only $10. Fresh off the plane, jet-lagged, boggled by the exchange rate, lugging all your bags and knowing how to say Yes (*Evet*), Thank You (*Mersi*), and Nothing (*Yok*), don't fuss over any other means of transportation.

If you're determined to get into town cheaply, however, grab one of the Havaş buses ($2), which leave hourly or half-hourly from 5 a.m. to 11 p.m. These buses can drop you between Laleli and Aksaray on the tram route to Sultanahmet (40¢), or take you up to Taksim Square. From Taksim you can catch buses for most places in the city, or grab a cab – the area is teeming with them. Don't bother searching for municipal İETT buses at the airport – their appearances are downright unusual.

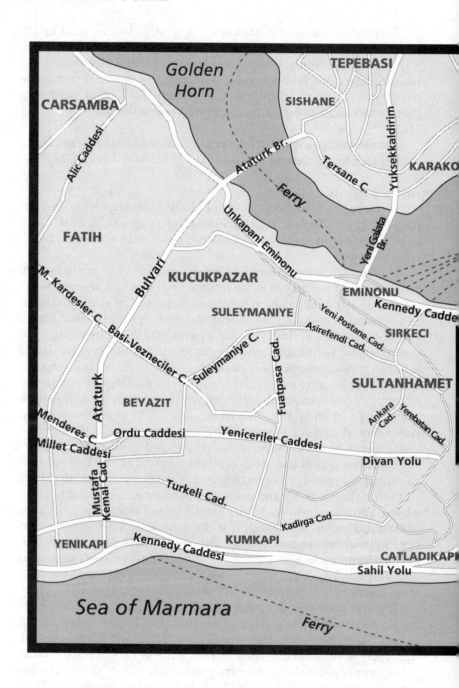

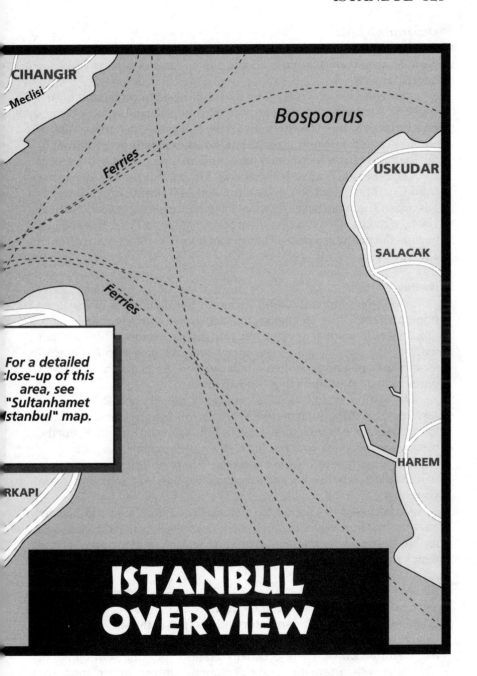

CIHANGIR

Meclisi

Bosporus

Ferries

USKUDAR

SALACAK

Ferries

For a detailed
close-up of this
area, see
"Sultanhamet
Istanbul" map.

HAREM

RKAPI

# ISTANBUL OVERVIEW

## Departing By Air

The airport clogs easily so plan to actually be there a solid two hours prior to departure for international flights, and one hour early for internal flights.

As mentioned above, taxis are the simplest and most reliable means of getting back and forth to the airport until one of the rail or subway lines puts through a stop. The alternative is the Havaş bus, departing Taksim Square across from the Marmara Hotel hourly and half-hourly throughout the day, with the half-hourly departures in the morning and evening.

The other alternative is the **Havaş Airport Bus** service, departing from Cumhuriet Caddesi, which runs off of Taksim Square towards Nişantaşı. The buses wait by a white kiosk with a green, yellow, and blue Havaş sign just 100 feet downhill of McDonalds and Pizza Hut and just beyond the public bus stops. They depart hourly and half-hourly from 5 a.m. to 11 p.m.

## By Bus

Sinan, the Ottoman master architect, is rolling over in his türbe (tomb). The new Esenler Otogar is a litter-strewn concrete abomination, much more functional than the old mud pit bus station at Topkapı, but without the appeal. All of the many bus routes servicing İstanbul terminate here, and it is often a maelstrom of touts and honking and buses locked into automotive Gordian knots.

The station is several miles outside of the city walls. The metro services the station, but it inexplicably fails to serve anywhere you want to go. Buses serve Esenler (departing from Taksim and Eminönü), but the best option is to book your bus through a travel agent or one of the small regional bus offices at Taksim or Beşiktaş. The price is the same, but they will shuttle you to Esenler and spare you the hassle of getting there on your own.

As discussed in Chapter 6, *Planning Your Trip*, **Varan** and **Ulusoy** offer the best bus service in the country. See the sidebar on the next page for bus distances, travel times, costs, and which bus companies service which route.

## By Boat

Cruise ships dock at **Karaköy**, just across the Galata Bridge from Eminönü. There is a Tourism Information office at the site.

For international ferry connections (Venice, Brindisi), contact **Turkish Maritime Lines**. There is usually English speaking staff on hand. They offer both information and reservation numbers: Information, *Tel. 244 2502*, Reservations, *Tel. 249 9222*, or **Karavan Travel Agency**, *Tel. 247 5066, Fax 241 5178*.

# BUS ROUTES FROM ISTANBUL

Distances given in kilometers (km) and prices from İstanbul for the top-end bus companies are as follows:

| Place | Distance | Travel Time | Cost | Bus Company |
|---|---|---|---|---|
| Adana | 938 km | 15 hours | $30 | Varan |
| Amasra | 490 km | 8 hours | $15 | Özemniyet |
| Ankara | 454 km | 6 hours | $25 | Varan, Ulusoy |
| Antakya (Hatay) | 1120 km | 20 hours | $35 | Kamil Koç |
| Antalya | 724 km | 12 hours | $30 | Varan, Ulusoy |
| Artvin | 1360 km | 24 hours | $40 | Ulusoy |
| Ayvalik | 570 km | 9 hours | $15 | Kamil Koç |
| Bodrum | 815 km | 14 hours | $25 | Varan, Ulusoy |
| Bursa | 234 km | 4 hours | $8 | Ulusoy |
| Çanakkale | 340 km | 6 hours | $15 | Kamil Koç |
| Dalyan (Ortaca) | 895 km | 15 hours | $24 | Kamil Koç |
| Edirne | 240 km | 3 hours | $5 | Çağlar Turizm |
| Erzurum | 1229 km | 20 hours | $25 | Ulusoy |
| Fethiye | 1000 km | 17 hours | $25 | Kamil Koç |
| Izmir | 565 km | 9 hours | $22 | Varan, Ulusoy |
| Kas/Kalkan | 870 km | 16 hours | $30 | Kamil Koç |
| Kemer | 800 km | 14 hours | $30 | Varan, Ulusoy |
| Kuşadası | 666 km | 10 hours | $25 | Varan Ulusoy |
| Marmaris | 850 km | 14 hours | $32 | Varan, Ulusoy |
| Mersin | 932 km | 16 hours | $32 | Varan, Kamil Koc |
| Ürgüp (Nevşehir) | 730 km | 10 hours | $20 | NevTur |
| Patara (Kınık) | 950 km | 17 hours | $30 | Kamil Koç |
| Ünye | 825 km | 14 hours | $25 | Ulusoy |
| Side | 815 km | 14 hours | $32 | Ulusoy |
| Trabzon | 1135 km | 20 hours | $30 | Ulusoy |

For ferries along the Black Sea Coast and to Izmir, contact Turkish Maritime Lines directly. Ferries depart for the Black Sea on Saturdays at 14:00, and for Izmir on Friday evenings, 18:30.

For more information on all these cruise options, see the Getting Around Turkey section of Chapter 6, *Planning Your Trip,*

Bosphorous Cruises and trips to local destinations such as the Princes Islands are covered in Getting Around Town, below.

## By Train

Trains leave İstanbul regularly for destinations throughout Turkey. **Sirkeci Station** (the Sirkeci stop on the tram line, just east of Eminönü) serves the European shore, including other European countries. **Haydarpaşa Station** serves the Asian shore.

For travel into Turkey, you may book a train from Sirkeci and depart from Haydarpaşa, book directly from the Haydarpaşa station, or leave it in the hands of a travel agent like Tur-İsta, *Tel. 212 513 7119*. The hub for these trains is Haydarpaşa Station, *Tel. 216 336 0475*, on the Asian shore of the Bosphorous. Note that when you're looking at schedules İstanbul is usually listed "H'pasa," for the name of the railway station, just as Izmir is listed as "Basmane." To reach Haydarpaşa, go to the Eminönü waterfront – the Üsküdar Iskele building – and board a Haydarpaşa-bound ferry, leaving every 20 minutes. The Haydarpaşa ferry stop is at the train station, and ticket booths and train boarding areas are clear.

Trains depart daily for Ankara and Pamukkale (Denizli). Train travel is slower and more expensive than bus travel, but we recommend the İstanbul-Ankara route, in particular. It offers shades of the Orient Express charm, a dining car, and room to roam if you're claustrophobic on buses. The **Ankara Express** has sleepers and departs İstanbul's Haydarpaşa Station at 10:30 p.m., arriving in Ankara at 7:30 the next morning. The cost for a berth in a sleeper car is $28, while seats are less than half that.

The other train of interest is the **Pamukkale Express**, departing Haydarpaşa at 6 p.m. and arriving in Pamukkale 14 hours later. The Pamukkale Express is a bit more weathered than the Ankara Express, but it also offers sleeping berths and costs $35 for a double sleeper.

Most other trains do not offer sleeping berths, but various train lines serve most of the country. The **Eastern Express** serves Kars near Armenia, rumbling along slowly and cheaply ($20, arriving almost 60 hours later). Other trains include the **Fatih Express**, with an 11:30 p.m. departure to Ankara, and the **Başkent Express**, with a 10:30 departure to Ankara. Note that the ferry-train service to Izmir is covered in the ferry section.

## ORIENTATION

İstanbul has three distinct sections. The first is on a peninsula jutting into the mouth of the Bosphorous from the west. This is now known as **Saray Burnu**, and was the original site of Byzantium. At the tip of this peninsula are most of the city's great landmarks – including Topkapı Palace and the Haghia Sophia – relics of the two empires that have ruled from here. The barrier of 1,300 year old land walls that once protected the peninsula still stands four miles inland, a five-mile circuit of towers and multiple walls fallen in some places and pierced by highways in others. These walls enclose seven hills, as at Rome. The greatest mosques and museums are located here, but İstanbul's population has long since leapfrogged the old city walls and pushed its way deeper inland

The population pressure has other outlets as well. A series of bridges join the Byzantine peninsula with the other European shore opposite the Golden Horn. This area, known as **Pera**, was a walled adjunct to Constantinople populated by foreign businessmen, and is best identified by the round, cone-roofed Galata Tower. The area has undergone dramatic growth for a full century, sprawling further and further north toward the Black Sea. Areas that were lush suburbs just 20 years ago are the concrete jungles of today, and there is no sign of the sprawl letting up. The greatest development has taken place in a corridor along the ridge behind Galata Tower, from İstiklal Caddesi past Nişantaşı and on toward Mecidiyekoy. The communities along the European shore of the Bosphorous – Beşiktaş, Ortaköy, Bebek, İstinye, Sariyer – have also grown drastically, threatening to overdevelop the length of the Bosphorous' northwestern shore.

Finally, the third section of town is across the Bosphorous Strait in **Asia**. Modern development of the Asian shore began in earnest after the completion of the Boğazaçi (Bosphorous) Bridge in 1973, and was accelerated with the addition of the Mehmet Fatih Bridge. The Asian shore remains slightly more sedate than the European shore, with more room and better municipal planning, but it, too, is sprawling. As a drive south will make glaringly evident, İstanbul's borders are marching relentlessly along the Marmara shore. Urban planners claim the city measures 100 miles across, and statisticians say the population is between 12 and 15 million.

### Detailed Advice – in English

While in town, pick up a copy of the English-language bimonthly magazine, *The Guide*. *The Guide* offers the best calendar of İstanbul's current events available in English, together with articles on things to see and do within the city. This magazine is most useful once you arrive, but if you're anxious you can get an expensive subscription (roughly $80 for six issues) by writing The Guide, *Medya Pazarlama San. ve Tic., Ali Kaya Sok. No. 7, Levent, İstanbul, Tel. 283 2061, Fax 280 8275*. Also look for a website on SuperOnline.

If you plan to spend significant time in İstanbul, you should pick up a guide to the city. The finest guide to İstanbul's historical sites is, far and away, *Strolling Through İstanbul* by Hilary Sumner-Boyd and John Freely. This guide is a staple of expat libraries, and is often accompanied by Freely's *The Bosphorous*, which details İstanbul's famous strait.

---

### GETTING THE MOST OUT OF ISTANBUL

*Arriving in İstanbul is a bewildering experience. The language and culture are in many ways unrecognizable; unlike Paris and Berlin, for instance, most new arrivals have little conception of how İstanbul will sound and feel. It's easy to be mildly paralyzed by the sheer size of the city, the scale of its ancient walls and its great domed mosques. Compounding this, you probably don't know where to begin.*

*This guide is designed to address that, dividing the city into reasonable, enjoyable days. We recommend you treat our recommendations as a sort of menu, selecting a day you want to spend and following it from beginning to end.*

*A guidebook can only get you so far, however. One of the best things you can do is abandon yourself to the Grand Bazaar or to İstiklal Caddesi near Taksim. It takes a little time to adjust to the novelty of İstanbul and become comfortable, and one of the best ways is by immersing yourself in the city. You'll want to know a few friendly words (plus "Gerek Yok" – I want nothing) for the persistent shoe shine boys), but a wander through the city's bustling streets is an education in more ways than language practice. Only this way will you begin to relax and understand that İstanbul is a safe, unthreatening place to travel. Women traveling alone, particularly, may find aspects of the city a nuisance, but the city is not dangerous by western standards.*

*İstanbul is packed with jazz clubs, bazaars, vegetable sellers, tea houses, Turkish baths, and boats plying the Bosphorous. Most people arrive here determined to see the grand old palaces, museums, and monuments, and find themselves delightfully distracted by the fascinating place İstanbul has become. We hope you do, too.*

---

## GETTING AROUND TOWN

**Maps**

The Tourism Information office distributes a serviceable map of İstanbul, although it is imprecise. If you plan on spending any substantial time in the city, it will be worth your while to spend $10 for a copy of *İstanbul A-Z*, a handy 400 page atlas that shows even the tiniest roads.

## By Bus

İstanbul's municipal bus system, İETT, is thorough, but crowded and unpredictable. Route schedules are so useless they are not printed; buses generally leave the initial station on time, but İstanbul's traffic snarls are certain to delay their progress. Prices vary with inflation, but are usually between 25¢ and 50¢.

There are two distinct kinds of buses, each with a separate payment scheme. The real municipal buses, marked İETT, take small tickets (**bilet**) available at kiosks and from private vendors near many bus stops. Buy a ticket, squeeze on board, and slip it into the ticket box at the front of the bus – don't be alarmed if the metal ticket box is belching flames, they just do that sometimes.

When İstanbul upgraded its municipal buses it wisely chose to keep the older ones in circulation. The older buses, most of them a faded cream and orange, are now privately run. They do not take bus tickets, instead accepting cash once you are on board. The fare is identical to the municipal buses.

The bus terminal most useful to travelers is typically that at **Eminönü**, next to the Egyptian Spice Market and the end of the tram line. This terminus is within walking distance of Sultanahmet (or you can take the tram to Sultanahmet if you prefer). At Eminönü, buses on the inland side of the highway travel over the Galata Bridge and out along the Bosphorous, including such places as Taksim Square, Ortaköy, Bebek, Rumeli Hisar, Dolmabahçe, and Sariyer at the upper end of the Bosphorous. Buses on the Golden Horn side of the highway travel into the interior of the peninsula, including such sites as Yedikule, Edirnekapi, and Eyüp.

Recently, new green "environmentally friendly" buses have appeared on the streets of İstanbul. The old red buses are being slowly replaced. On the old red municipal buses there are new electronic devices at the front door that look like they will eventually be used for some kind of swipe card system rather than the "stuff the paper ticket into the metal box" system. Nothing is changing with the private orange buses that take cash (they run on the same routes as the municipal buses).

## By Car

We tried to warn you. Driving in İstanbul is going to send your blood pressure off the scale and probably take more time than hailing taxis would. Alas. If you've taken the plunge, remember not to take getting cut off or squeezed personally; it's a different conception of traffic law, but it generally works pretty well.

People park every which way in İstanbul and don't get towed – but there is the remote possiblity it could happen to you. If you are unfortunate enough to be towed, you can find your vehicle at the nearest parking/impound lot. In the Sultanahmet area, the Bayraktar Otupark is the designated impound area. For other areas, check with your hotel.

## By Ferry From Eminönü

İstanbul has always been a maritime city, and that tradition is one you should endeavor to continue. Ferries and sea buses from İstanbul serve all of the nearby coastal communities, even such outlying spots as the Princes Islands and Yalova on the Sea of Marmara.

The ferry line from Eminönü offers an inexpensive and enjoyable **Bosphorous cruise**. İstanbul's antiquated – but seaworthy – ferries depart the Boğaz Hatti ferry terminal (building 3) at Eminönü every morning, leaving at 10:35 and 13:35, arriving at the north end of the Bosphorous one hour later. The ferry is rarely crowded, and the cruise does wonders for helping get oriented after arriving. Highlights along the cruise north are the Dolmabahçe and Çırağan Palaces on the European (left) shore, followed by the pretty Mecidiye Camii in Ortaköy poking out into the strait just before you pass beneath the Bosphorous Bridge.

Just past the bridge on the Asian waterfront is the Beylerbeyi Palace, a summer lodging of the sultans and their guests. Further along the Asian shore you pass the small, ornate Küçüksu Palace in an indent on the Asian shore, followed immediately by the small fortress at Anadolu Hisar. Sultan Bayazid I built Anadolu Hisar here at the narrowest point along the Bosphorous to choke off shipping, but his great-grandson Sultan Mehmet II was responsible for the massive, beautiful fortress on the European shore, Rumeli Hisar.

Note Rumeli Hisar's unique shape, which led many observers to mistakenly believe it was built to resemble Sultan Mehmet II's tuğra, or signature. After passing beneath the second Bosphorous bridge – this one named for Sultan Mehmet II – you chug past a collection of pretty communities, finally arriving at Anadolu Kavağı on the Asian shore. You have two and one-half hours at Anadolu Kavağı to sightsee and sit out by one of the waterfront cafes, after which you make a leisurely return to Eminönü, pausing at Sariyer for one half hour. The trip takes about five hours and costs less than $5. Information is available at *Tel. 522 0045*, but be prepared to hand the phone off to a Turk willing to translate.

As an alternative to cruising on the municipal lines, you can arrange a private trip, complete with cocktails and meals. Contact **She Tourism**, *Tel. 212 233 3670*.

Other ferry trips of interest include those departing for Üsküdar (6 a.m. to midnight), and Haydarpaşa Railway Station (7 a.m.-8 p.m.) from Eminönü's Üsküdar ıskele (building 2), with constant service throughout the day. Ferries also leave Eminönü bound for the Princes Islands, but we recommend the slightly more expensive – and much quicker – Flying Dolphin sea bus (Deniz Otobusleri) service from Kabataş (see below).

**By Ferry From Kabataş**
Sea buses (**Deniz Otubusleri**) depart from Kabataş near Dolmabahçe, offering rapid service to the beaches of the Princes Islands and the thermal baths near Yalova. Look for the dolphin logo.
**Schedule 1**: Leaving Kabataş, İstanbul to the Heybeliada, Princes Islands. The cost is $2.50.

| Weekdays | Weekends |
|----------|----------|
| 8:40 | 10:15 |
| 9:25 | 11:45 |
| 10:55 | 13:45 |
| 13:40 | 15:45 |
| 15:40 | 18:50 |
| 17:15 | 20:20 |
| 18:50 | |
| 19:30 | |
| 20:15 | |

Final departure from Princes Islands is 19:30 on weekdays, 19:00 on weekends.

**Schedule 2**: Leaving Kabataş, İstanbul to Yalova (Termal, Bursa). The cost is $5.

| Weekdays | Weekends |
|----------|----------|
| 8:30 | 9:15 |
| 11:00 | 11:35 |
| 13:45 | 14:45 |
| 16:10 | 17:45 |
| 18:25 | |

Final departure from Yalova is at 19:30 on weekdays, 19:00 on weekends.

**By Foot**

İstanbul may seem intimidating to the less urban among us, but the truth is the city is a big pussycat. Below are some of the best places to go well-shod, with estimated times (where appropriate) for the entire walk, loitering and dining included.

•**Sultanahmet** clearly recommends itself for those who enjoy walking. Seeing Topkapı Palace alone requires a hike, and clustered around the open area of the former Hippodrome you can visit the voluminous Haghia Sophia, the Blue Mosque, and two underground cisterns. From here the Grand Bazaar is a ten minute walk, directly up Divan Yolu Caddesi and right just beyond Çemberlitaş, the iron-ringed column that dates back to Constantinople's founding. *Duration*: two days.

•The roiling, endless area behind the **Grand Bazaar** may seem daunting, but it's harmless and fascinating. Touts whistle, sales carts clatter, and all manner of textiles, furniture, appliances, bronze and plasticware are piled along the narrow lanes. Enter at any point, take a left, a right, and another right and you become marvelously lost amid the chaos, finding tea shops, curio sellers, and any number of spots you would like to file away and return to later. Chances are, even if you try, you never will.

Amid the bustling there is almost never any ill will, and once you leave the heavily touristed Grand and Spice Bazaars you're unlikely to be accosted by touts. So long as you're resourceful enough to hail a cab or regain your bearings when you become disoriented, it is a wonderful experience. *Duration*: until you are sick of hearing "Hello my friend" (see shopping section of this chapter).

• A walk along the city's defensive walls, beginning at **Yedikule** and heading north, can be grueling, but the former outskirts of the city are peppered with curiosities. Yedikule is enjoyable to look around, but continuing along the walls requires some intrepidity. You can easily spend about six hours walking along the walls and exploring some of their nooks and crannies. *Duration*: six hours (see Seeing the Sights, City Walls section).

• A walk from Eminönü to **Taksim Square** passes through some of the most beautiful of the city's 19th century districts, along a long, busy pedestrian street lined with boutique shops and markets. From Sultanahmet, follow the tram tracks downhill to Eminönü. From there, cross Galata Bridge, turn left and, almost immediately, duck into the nondescript "Tünel" station. A 15¢ token will take you on a brief and historic subway ride to the top of the hill, from whence you turn right, then immediately left along the main avenue. This avenue is serviced by a trolley, but you want to walk, right? *Duration*: three hours to Taksim Square (see Seeing the Sights, İstiklal section).

• A cruise and a hike to the fortress at Anadolu Kavağıcan fill a day. At the end of the Bosphorous ferry line originating in Eminönü on the Asian side (Anadolu Kavağı), you can hike up a hill to Yoros Tepesi, a giant medieval fortress. You should have three hours at Anadolu Kavağı, which is ample time to climb to the citadel and have a leisurely look around. *Duration*: One and one-half hours (see Seeing the Sights, Anadolu Kavağı section).

## By Train

İstanbul's only genuine local train service runs from **Sirkeci station**, *Tel.* 212 527 0051, near Eminönü, around the tip of the peninsula and out along the Sea of Marmara past the city walls to Halkalı. This service covers only the European shore of the Sea of Marmara and the eastern shore of Küçük Çekmece Lake, but is ideal for reaching Yedikule and the City Walls or for an afternoon diversion.

To board the train at Sirkeci enter the main station and stay to the right. Buy tokens at the booth, use one at the turnstile, and wait at the landing for the next departure. Trains depart every 15 minutes, and run throughout the day until 10 p.m. Fare is only 25¢.

The train is also a cheap, quick means of getting to the city center from the outlying areas – including the airport-area hotels (use the Yeşilyurt or Yeşilköy stations).

The train stops at stations in each of the following neighborhoods, in order: Sirkeci, Cankurtaran, Kumkapı, Yenikapı, Kara Mustafa Paşa, Yedikule, Kazlıçesme, Zeytinburnu, Yeni Mahalle, Bakirköy, Yeşilyurt, Florya, Menekşe, Küçükcesme, Soğuksu, Kanarya, and Halkalı.

İstanbul also has a **trolley car** running along İstiklal Caddesi between Galata Tower and Taksim Square. If you're in a hurry, take it (the conductor takes standard İETT bus tickets). Otherwise, İstiklal is a great place for a stroll.

## By Subway

İstanbul has the third oldest subway system in the world, the **Tünel**. The city's antique subway route runs from the northern shore of the Golden Horn, directly behind the Galata Bridge, to the top of the hill near the Galata Tower. In a great victory for the preservation of antiquity, the route, decor, and machinery haven't changed much since service opened in 1877, although the cars have been updated.

The two minute ride costs 25¢, and spares the long walk up the hill. From the Galata Bridge, turn left at the big intersection and look for the unpresupposing entrance on the inland side. At the first, and only, stop, leave the building and turn right, then take a left onto the main pedestrian street, İstiklal Caddesi. (see Seeing the Sights, İstiklal section)

İstanbul's **Metro** line is more up to date. This slick subway system serves the outlying areas, including the main bus station at Esenler. The only problem is it terminates in Aksaray, far from the end of the peninula and thus shy of anywhere you would want to go. From the Aksaray station you can hump your belongings to the tram line, further along Adnan Menderes Bulvarı, or get a cab. Purchase tickets (25¢) at a ticket booths before entering, and if you are departing from Aksaray be careful to take the line specifying Esenler or Otogar – one of the lines deviates into a different suburb.

A new subway line is under construction from Taksim Square to Gayrettepe and Mecidiyekoy. The opening date is unknown.

**By Tram**

İstanbul's blue and gold-trimmed **tram** line runs from Eminönü past Sultanahmet and out through Topkapı Gate (not to be confused with Topkapı Palace) toward the suburbs. The tram lines run every 15 minutes on a simple, direct route into and out of town. The tram requires its own specific ticket (**Bilet**), available at a kiosk near each of the stops for the 30¢ price of a bus ticket. You use the ticket to mount the landing before being whisked away in sleek comfort. Avoid rush hours.

**By Taxi**

Taxi service is subsidized in İstanbul, and is thus cheaper here than in most parts of the country. Service from the airport to the Sultanahmet area – a 20 minute ride without traffic – costs about $15. Fares within the city are likewise cheap, provided the driver uses the meter properly and doesn't take advantage of the dazzling size of Turkish currency and add a zero to the fare. The other trick is, of course, driving you to your

**TAXI LANGUAGE**

| Turkish | Pronunciation | English |
|---|---|---|
| (name of place)' ye gidiyorum. | ye gid-eeyore-um | I am going to (name of place) |
| Sol | (soul) | Left |
| Sağa | (sah) | Right |
| Dogru | (dohroo) | Straight |
| Dur | (duwr) | Stop |
| Ineceğim | (in a ji im) | I will get out. |
| Şurada | (shoor-ada) | There |
| Lütfen | (LOOT-fen) | Please |

destination by the most circuitous route: however we recommend waiting a few days before you begin accusing your driver of this, since you'll find that most normal routes are fairly circuitous.

Day rates (**Gündüz**) are in effect from 6 a.m. to midnight. The after hours rates (**Gece**) are roughly double the daytime rate. Taxi drivers are accustomed to small tips. İstanbullus round up to the nearest convenient figure; 1.85 million TL becomes 2 million TL, and if the fare is an even 2 million they won't expect more.

## WHERE TO STAY

In town for just three days? It's probably worth your while to stay in the **Sultanahmet** area. Most of what you came to see is here, together with a wonderful variety of hotels, ranging from the elite (Four Seasons), to the charming (Armada and Empress Zoe), to the youth hostels (Yücelt Youth Hostel and the Orient House). Business and conventions take place on the outskirts of the convention valley, near Taksim.

### NEGOTIATING FOR ROOMS IN ISTANBUL'S MAJOR HOTELS

*If you're making reservations, you're negotiating from strength. Individual bookings are icing on the cake, always much more profitable than group rates averaging half the rack rate or, sometimes much less. The hotel's sales/reservations staff should be eager to get you booked. For more information see Chapter 6, Planning Your Trip.*

*Be sure of what you're getting. Do you have the Bosphorous view or the cheaper "city (or, ah, garden) view?" Is the 15 percent VAT included? Is breakfast included?*

*Are you on business? Are you staying three days? Are you making reservations ahead of time? Are you booking in the winter? These are all bona-fide reasons for a substantial discount.*

*Discounts are difficult to gauge. Some hotels (and those charging less than $80) genuinely may not budge more than 20 percent. Even if you're making reservations for the high season, you should get at least a 20 percent discount. At most big hotels you can lop 40 percent off of the high season price.*

*If you ask what discounts are available and are told there are none, what they really mean is none until you aren't willing to pay the full rate.*

*Maybe we've been spending too much time in bazaars, but here's the proper way to negotiate. First, ask about the high season price. Inquire about three-night stays, fully intending to stay, for instance, for five. Get the discounted price for three nights, then give a counteroffer and say you'll stay for five nights.*

Prices in İstanbul are less seasonal than in some areas, but they are quite negotiable in the off-season. You will often be able to secure a 20 percent discount without trying and a 40 percent discount if you demonstrate an extended stay, business travel, or a bit of bargaining ability.

## Sultanahmet

If you're in İstanbul primarily to see the sights, Sultanahmet is the place to stay. This district is in the heart of the old city, within walking distance of the wonders that brought you to İstanbul in the first place. The district was a run-down prison borough in the middle of the century, but some far-sighted individuals at the Turkish Touring and Automobile Association began renovating the area, culminating in the opening of the Yeşil Ev in 1984. This restored hotel set the tone for many of those to come, and today Sultanahmet is host to a range of hotels that include backpacking hostelries and a Four Seasons. The tourist influx has resulted in a hodgepodge of carpet shops, curio sellers and travel agencies in the area.

**FOUR SEASONS HOTEL İSTANBUL**, *Tevkifhane Sok. No. 1, Sultanahmet. Tel. 212 638 8529, Fax 212 638 8530 (North American Reservations: Tel. 800/332-3442). Rooms: 65. Double: $225.*

This hotel opened in 1996 and immediately won praise for its charm and location. The Four Seasons is far and away the most ambitious hotel in a city filled with excellent hotels, and its exclusive fellows are all bunched far from Sultanahmet and cater mostly to business. The Four Seasons expects that you're here for pleasure, and sets about making everything right. In Four Seasons tradition, the İstanbul hotel is precise and lovely, with a constant shower of tiny flourishes and amenities. The genius of the hotel is in the details of each room, the great basins, attractive interior shutters, the bags of potpourri hung in the closet; bathrooms offer separate showers and baths. There is a distinct Turkish quality as well; kilim, tilework, small Ottoman prints and portraits, all thoughtfully conceived.

The refined atmosphere of the hotel belies a grim past. This building was a notorious Turkish prison into the 1960s, and although the interior design scheme has come a long way, small traces of the old building remain (the red and blue floor tiles in some of the stairwells beside the hotel elevators, for instance). The project has been greeted warmly by most İstanbullus, but some find the idea of sleeping in an old prison less interesting than morbid. Mindful of that, some of the building's touches seem to have a certain evil-Christo element: designers dressed up an old wall-top guard tower in bright pastel hues and pretty trim, for instance. If you are unnerved by the notion of sleeping in a former prison, you might be comforted by the fact that long before becoming a Turkish prison (in the late 1800s) the hotel was on the grounds of the Byzantine Royal Palace: there are pampered, well-fed ghosts here to keep the prisoners' wretched souls company. Walls and arches belonging to former palace buildings are visible skirting the Four Seasons.

The former prison day-yard presently houses the Four Seasons' restaurant, run by a Venetian chef who specializes in California and Mediterranean cuisine, now, evidently, mentioned in the same breath. Make reservations at the hotel far in advance.

Selected as one of our best places to stay – see Chapter 10.

**HOTEL ARMADA,** *Ahırkapı. Tel. 212 638 1370, Fax 518 5060. Double: $115. Rooms: 110.*

The Armada is built on the grounds of the naval barracks of Heyrettin Paşa, known in the west as Barbarrossa or Red Beard. Barbarrossa made the Ottomans the scourge of the seas, but little is left of the old quarters other than some ruined foundations beneath this excellent hotel. The owners of the Armada – one of whom owns the small Kalkan Han on the southern coast – have created a relaxed and elegant hotel with large, uncluttered lobbies and fine rooms. The hotel's three floors sprawl parallel to the sea, and careful consideration has been taken to create comfortable public spaces to complement the well-equipped rooms. Rooms offer satellite TV, baths, air conditioning, mini bar, and a view of either the Sea of Marmara or the minarets of the Haghia Sophia just up the hill. The hotel uses environmentally-friendly products and olive oil soap, the pioneer of this effort among local hotels.

The staff is courteous and friendly, and the hotel is located just a five minute walk from the Haghia Sophia or the gates of the Topkapı Palace. The Armada is a well-designed modern hotel reflecting the tradition of the area. The Armada even has a 1954 Mercedes Benz 032 H-L bus for transfers to and from the airport.

**YEŞIL EV HOTEL,** *Kabasakal Cad. No. 5, Sultanahmet, 34400. Tel. 517 6786, Fax 517 6780. Rooms: 25. Double: $125.*

The Yeşil Ev is the Grand Dame of Sultanahmet's stylish hotels. The Turkish Touring and Automobile Association undertook the rehabilitation of a ruined nineteenth century mansion on the site in the early 1980s, a relatively daring venture at a time when Sultanahmet was a ragged, disreputable district. The hotel opened in 1984, and this extremely convenient and atmospheric old-world hotel was an immediate success. In the decade following, Sultanahmet has been scoured and rebuilt with the Yeşil Ev serving as a model for many enterprising hoteliers.

The Yeşil Ev is designed on the lines of a winter mansion, with a conservatory downstairs and heavy carpets and drapes in the rooms. The bedsteads are brass, and the trimmed ceilings are hung with chandeliers. Be warned that the Ottoman style is ornate, occasionally bordering on the gaudy. Brisk, simple lines were not a telltale feature of late Ottoman

---

**ISTANBUL HOTEL FINDS & FAVORITES**

*These are the best of Istanbul's smaller hotels, places that will charm you without driving you to bankruptcy.*

*AYASOFYA PANSIYONLAR, Soğuçeşme Sok., Sultanahmet, 34400, Tel. 513 3663, Fax 513 3669. Double: $100. Rooms: 70.*

*EMPRESS ZOE, Akbıyık Cad. Adliye Sok. No. 10, Sultanahmet, Tel. 518 2504, Fax 518 5699. Double: $70. Rooms: 28.*

*HOTEL ARMADA, Ahırkapı, 212 638 1370, Fax 518 5060. Double: $115. Rooms: 110.*

*SPLENDID PALAS, 23 Nisan Cad. No. 71, Büyükada, Tel. 216 382 6950, Fax 216 382 6775. Double: $110. Rooms: 60.*

*VARDAR PALACE, Sıraselviler Caddesi No. 54/56, Taksim, Tel. 212 252 2888, Fax 212 252 1527. Double: $90.*

*YEŞİL EV HOTEL, Kabasakal Cad. No. 5, Sultanahmet, 34400, Tel. 517 6786, Fax 517 6780. Rooms: 25. Double: $125.*

---

interior decorating, but the style is wholly appropriate in this old building, in this historic neighborhood. Weighing in on the side of the Yeşil Ev's decorating sensibilities was former French president François Mitterand; he stayed here in 1993.

The hotel's backyard offers a spacious garden, itself worth the price of admission in congested Sultanahmet. Meals are served here in the warm months, while guests retreat to the restaurant in the winter.

**AYASOFYA PANSIYONLAR,** *Soğuçeşme Sok., Sultanahmet, 34400. Tel. 513 3663, Fax 513 3669. Double: $100. Rooms: 70.*

The Ayasofya Pansiyon is a row of remodeled Ottoman-era houses squeezed between the walls of Topkapı Palace and the Haghia Sofya. Rebuilt by the same organization responsible for the Yeşil Ev, the Ayasofya has nine houses built up against the walls of Topkapı and a tenth, with a large garden, just across the cobbled lane. The charming old houses are quite popular, although their popularity has left evidence of wear and tear in some of the rooms. The caveat offered at the Yeşil Ev applies here as well; late Ottoman decor is gold-framed, bright, and a bit gaudy. If that's not a concern, the back rooms, abutting the walls, are predictably dark and slightly discounted, and the front rooms are worth the extra ten dollars.

Because the rooms have been carved out of existing houses, they vary dramatically. Some of the best rooms in the establishment are located in the third house, rooms 301-304, the former residence of Fahri Korutürk, the sixth president of the Republic. Also excellent are the 12 rooms in the Konuk Evi, the newest addition (1994) to the Ayasofya Pansiyonlar. The

Konuk Evi stands on the grounds of the Ayasofya's patio garden behind its own gate. The Konuk Evi is yet another building that has been dramatically remodeled by the Turkish Touring and Automobile Association, which also tidied up the garden area for meals in the summer. One of the secret highlights of a visit here is the old Roman Ayazma, or holy spring, entered from the lower garden level. The ayazma, with its vaulted roof and tall columns, has been converted into a bar, offering spirits, if no longer the Spirit.

On weekdays, inquire about the Çelik Gülersoy İstanbul Kitaplığı, a library housed in one of the buildings built against the wall; the prints and photographs inside depict İstanbul through the course of the Ottoman reign, in many ways a city unrecognizable today.

**EMPRESS ZOE**, *Akbıyık Cad. Adliye Sok. No. 10, Sultanahmet. Tel. 518 2504, Fax 518 5699. Double: $70. Rooms: 28.*

The Empress Zoe will not do at all for those uneasy around art. This small gem in the Sultanahmet district is painted in muted yellows, with appealing woodwork on the walls and bedsteads, fine metal rails and fixtures, a heavy dose of antique stone peeking from the walls, and thick slabs of rock underfoot. The decor is traditional Turkish in an environment of artistic licentiousness, with kilim and other textiles played off against dramatic full-wall renderings of Ottoman sipahis (cavalrymen) and Byzantine emperors. Every room has a bathroom finished in marble, with shower. Satellite television is available in some rooms, as it is in the public areas. Note: avoid room 33.

The lobby and terrace highlight the entire hotel. Both are dramatic and appealing, the lobby slightly off-kilter with its angles and arches; the terrace offering a generous view of the Sea of Marmara, with a cozy interior for after the weather turns. Staff is helpful and English-speaking (the hotel is owned by an American), and the three year old hotel is the best value for money in İstanbul.

Selected as one of our best places to stay – see Chapter 10.

**HOTEL ALZER**, *At Meydanı No. 72, Sultanahmet. Tel. 212 516 6262, Fax 212 516 0000. Rooms: 24. Double: $85.*

The Alzer is located at the southern end of the Hippodrome, across from the Blue Mosque. The hotel has an excellent location overlooking the Hippodrome, and is housed in a charming old Ottoman-era building. The Alzer's interiors are busy Turkish, with lots of knick knacks, carpets, and kilims. Several rooms have large bay windows and all have dark wood interiors and impressive detailing. The front rooms, with views of the Hippodrome, are the most interesting, but several of the back rooms are nicer. Open all year, though it gets a bit drafty in mid-winter.

**HOTEL TURKOMAN**, *Asmalı Çeşme Sok. No. 2, Sultanahmet. Tel. 212 516 2956, Fax 212 516 2957. Rooms: 25. Double: $70.*

The Turkoman is another of the distinctly Turkish bed and breakfasts in the area. Several rooms have brass bedstands, and all of the rooms have antique furnishings. Like the Alzer, located nearby, the Turkoman is on the Hippodrome, just around the corner from the Turkish Islamic Art Museum. The Turkoman has an excellent terrace and a very helpful staff.

**İBRAHİM PAŞA HOTEL**, *Terzihane Sok. No. 5, Sultanahmet. Tel. 212 518 0394, Fax 212 518 4457. Rooms: 19. Double: $95.*

The Ibrahim Pasa Hotel is housed in an old Ottoman mansion, just across the street from the real İbrahim Paşa's palatial mansion. The hotel has a relaxed, comfortable feel, but is at the same time one of the most sophisticated of the restored mansions, with room service and satellite television in rooms. The lobby is an excellent place to cool off after a day's exploring, or to warm up in the winter. Reception is helpful and English-fluent. The İbrahim Paşa is another of the hotels at the southern end of the Hippodrome, and has a lovely terrace.

**HOTEL VALİDE SULTAN KONAĞI**, *Cankurtaran Mah., İshakpaşa Cad., Kutlugün Sok. No. 1, Sultanahmet. Tel. 212 638 0600, Fax 212 638 1460. Rooms: 17. Double: $75.*

An ambitious corner lot hotel just below the gates to Topkapı Palace. The Tourism Ministry has an edict against spoiling the neighborhood's aesthetic, and the Valide Sultan is, technically, restored, although it was in reality gutted and put together anew. As a result, the hotel has more dependable plumbing and other not-so-minor features than its genuinely restored neighbors, but perhaps lacks some of their authentic cachet. Like many hotels in the area, the Valide Sultan has an excellent terrace, with the great dome of the Haghia Sophia above, the Topkapı walls to the side, and ships laying at anchor in the Sea of Marmara below.

**AYASOFYA HOTEL**, *Küçükayasofya Cad. Demirci Reşit Sok. No. 28, Sultanahmet. Tel. 212 516 9446, Fax 212 518 0700. Rooms: 21. Double: $60.*

The Ayasofya Hotel is a restored Ottoman-era house a short walk from Sultanahmet's major sights. Rooms have showers, toilets, and fans, and the television room has satellite TV. The Ayasofya Hotel offers a good, personal standard of service, and is an excellent place to return to after a day of hoofing it around town.

**YUÇELT YOUTH HOSTEL**, *Caferiye Sok. No. 6, Sultanahmet. Tel. 212 513 6150, Fax 212 512 7628. Double Rooms: 16. Double: $14.*

Budget hotel fads come and go, but the Yuçelt's ground zero location and International Youth Hostel reliability make it a consistently good choice. The Yuçelt has both dorm rooms and double rooms, a Turkish bath, terrace, clothes washing options, and small cafe with a television. The Haghia Sophia is directly across the street, as are the Haghia Sophia's dramatically loud minarets.

**ORIENT YOUTH HOSTEL,** *Akbıyık Caddesi No. 32, Sultanahmet. Tel. 212 517 9439, Fax 212 518 3994. Double Rooms: 10. Double: $11.*

The Orient is down the slope from the Haghia Sophia, and has earned a reputation for budget excellence. The hotel is always packed with the flower of Australian, British and American youth, who are willing to swap stories and share the latest traveling gossip. It gets noisy, but stays clean. Dorm beds go for just $4 apiece, so, mathematically, if you spend four nights here instead of at the Çırağan Palace or Four Seasons you'll have saved enough money for a free round trip to Asia on your next vacation.

---

### ISTANBUL'S HOTEL ELITE

*If you're on an expense account or can afford to treat yourself to the best Istanbul has to offer, try one of the following.*

*CEYLAN INTERCONTINENTAL, Askerocağı Cad. No. 1, Taksim, Tel. 212 231 2121, Fax 212 231 2180. Rooms: 395. Double: $235.*

*ÇIRAĞAN PALACE KEMPINSKI, Çırağan Caddesi No. 84, Beşiktaş, Tel. 212 258 3377, Fax 212 259 6687 (North American Reservations: 800 426 3135). Rooms: 322. Double: $195-$5,000. Tuğra Restaurant.*

*FOUR SEASONS HOTEL İSTANBUL, Tevkifhane Sok. No. 1, Sultanahmet, Tel. 212 638 8529, Fax 212 638 8530 (North American Reservations: 800 332 3442). Rooms: 65. Double: $225.*

*İSTANBUL HILTON, Cumhuriet Cad., Harbiye, Tel. 212 231 4650, Fax 212 240 4165. Rooms: 500. Double: $280. Chinese Restaurant.*

*PERA PALAS HOTEL, Meşrutiyet Cad. No. 98/100, Tepebaşı, Tel. 251 4560, Fax 251 4089. Rooms: 139. Double: $180.*

*SWISSÔTEL THE BOSPHOROUS, Bayıldım Caddesi No. 2, Maçka, Beşiktaş, Tel. 212 259 0101, Fax 212 259 0105. Rooms: 600. Double: $200-$1800. Chinese, Japanese Restaurants.*

---

**Taksim**

Probably the most central location in a city filled with central locations. There's little of historical interest to see in the immediate vicinity, but it's convenient for business and an extended stay. Taksim is at the entrance to İstiklal Caddesi, a wide pedestrian avenue filled with restaurants, bars, and shops.

**VARDAR PALACE,** *Sıraselviler Caddesi No. 54/56, Taksim. Tel. 212 252 2888, Fax 212 252 1527. Double: $90.*

A shocking find in the mile-a-minute Taksim area. The Vardar Palace is classy, clean, well-managed, and a bargain at $90 for a double per night in the high season. There's not much of a view and no satellite TV, but that's a small price to pay for such fine attention to detail and such a choice location. The building was erected in the 1800s and is evocative of both Selcuk architecture and the Levantine style popular at the time. The interior is attractive and open, providing a respite from the chaos outside. Rooms are well designed, with full baths and solid craftsmanship. As always, a helpful, intelligent staff is a key to enjoying your stay; the Vardar's staff is responsive and responsible. If you stay here have a look at the nasty and expensive "four star" establishments down the street towards Taksim Square.

**PERA PALAS HOTEL**, *Meşrutiyet Cad. No. 98/100, Tepebaşı. Tel. 251 4560, Fax 251 4089. Double: $180. Rooms: 139.*

After passengers disembarked from the Orient Express, they were shuttled here. This classic hotel opened in 1892 and has been visited by a slew of famous and powerful people, ranging from Kemal Atatürk and French President Valerie Giscard d'Estaing to Greta Garbo and Jacqueline Kennedy Onassis. The Orient Express no longer operates, but the Pera Palas clings to its grand old reputation. There's old world charm to burn here, but you must pay to burn it. Rooms are ostentatious but comfortable. The Pera Palas is not especially convenient to Taksim Square – its almost a full mile south – but you'll never want for a taxi here. The pedestrian avenue, İstiklal Caddesi, is just up the street, and the U.S. Consulate is two blocks away. If you're a great Agatha Christie fan, there's some senseless anecdote about how she wrote *Murder on the Orient Express* while here, somehow losing ten days and a mysterious key. Like we said, if you're an Agatha Christie fan you'll love it.

**THE MARMARA**, *Taksim Square, Taksim. Tel. 212 251 4696, Fax 212 244 0509. Rooms: 432. Double: $270.*

The Marmara is an İstanbul fixture, towering above Taksim Square. It remains as convenient as ever, with marvelous views and a good, attentive staff, but its interiors have fallen off the pace set by the city's best hotels. The Marmara is convenient to Conference Valley just to the north. Reservations personnel are happy to cut a deal.

**HOTEL PLAZA**, *Siraselviler Cad. Aslanyatağı Sok. No. 19-21, Cihangir. Tel. 212 245 3273, Fax 212 293 7040. Rooms: 24. Double (Suite): $55.*

The Hotel Plaza – not to be confused with the Plaza Hotel in Gayrettepe – effectively has six rooms, its seaview suites. The other rooms, including the six sea-view standard rooms, are plain and uninteresting. The suites, however, offer some of the city's best Bosphorous views, with enclosed sun decks and an excellent, airy feel. The view is irresistible. The Plaza opened in 1955, and was once one of the city's premier hotels. Time has taken a toll, but the Plaza remains a peaceful eddy just off of Taksim Square. If you can't get one of the suite rooms (401, 405, 301, 305, 201, or 205) the accommodations are not especially enticing.

**Conference Valley**

İstanbul's Conference Valley is, as the name suggests, the site of many conferences and conventions. The United Nations held its Habitat for Humanity intenational conference here. The valley is less than one mile north of Taksim Square, and has a huge collection of elite hotels.

**HYATT REGENCY İSTANBUL,** *Taşkışla Cad., Taksim. Tel. 212 225 7000, Fax 212 225 7007. Rooms: 360. Double: $280 plus VAT. Italian restaurant.*

You know Hyatt Regency and you know what you can expect. All of the hotel's opulence and glittering grandeur is mildly squandered on one of the city's less prime pieces of real estate above the Conference Valley. You still get Bosphorous views from the proper side, but this isn't one of İstanbul's great locations. It is, certainly, one of İstanbul's great hotels, and very convenient for those on business.

**İSTANBUL HILTON,** *Cumhuriet Cad., Harbiye. Tel. 212 231 4650, Fax 212 240 4165. Rooms: 500. Double: $280. Chinese Restaurant.*

The Hilton is aging remarkably well, helped along by a top notch staff that is largely responsible for the hotel's inclusion in various Top 100 lists. There are no less than four junior Hiltons in İstanbul, but this is the eldest, and the best. Between the service, the spacious grounds, the facilities, and the precise, careful decor the Hilton is an excellent choice for business. The İstanbul Hilton is located in the Conference Valley, and its facilities are often used during large conventions or conferences. There is no more central location if you are attending a conference in Harbiye. As a tourism hotel the Hilton gets lower marks, suffering because of its distance from Sultanahmet, but the Military Museum is just up the street. Plus, with the right room, you have a pretty good view of İnönü Stadium and can catch a game with İstanbul's Beşiktaş side.

**CEYLAN INTERCONTINENTAL,** *Askerocağı Cad. No. 1, Taksim. Tel. 212 231 2121, Fax 212 231 2180. Rooms: 395. Double: $235.*

The Intercontinental was designed as if the architect's mission was to create a massive building that looks like a hotel. Exterior architectural misgivings aside, the Intercontinental, opened in 1996, has challenged the Swissôtel and the other five star goliaths as the best in the city. The Intercontinental is a very impressive establishment, with elaborate and appropriate local flavor. Management has assembled a friendly, helpful staff to guide you through the hotel's full A-list of amenities. The Intercontinental is deservedly one of the most expensive hotels in the city: $235 sticker price plus 15 percent tax and $22 breakfast.

**Along the Bosphorous**

Most of the Taksim and Conference Valley hotels overlook the Bosphorous, but there are also some excellent hotels further north.

Several of these hotels are convenient to the Conference Valley, and all of them are popular for business or short stays. These hotels are generally inconvenient to the bulk of the city's historical sites in Sultanahmet.

**SWISSÔTEL THE BOSPHOROUS**, *Bayıldım Caddesi No. 2, Maçka, Beşiktaş. Tel. 212 259 0101, Fax 212 259 0105. Rooms: 600. Double: $200-$1800. Chinese, Japanese Restaurants.*

The Swissôtel is one of the city's premier luxury hotels, solid, tasteful and expensive. The hotel's view commands the Bosphorous, as well as the mosques, churches and palaces of the old city. It is one of the premier vantage points in the city, and the beauty of the site is combined with a generous set of amenities – including one of the city's best gyms, tennis courts, and a rare thing indeed, a running track. Other services are similarly good.

**CONRAD INTERNATIONAL İSTANBUL**, *Yıldız Cad., Beşiktaş. Tel. 212 227 3000, Fax 212 259 6667. Rooms: 620. Double: $185 plus VAT.*

A gently curving, good looking building, as huge hotels go. The Conrad, a Hilton by-product, is one of the city's undeniably five star establishments, but with competition as stiff as it is the Conrad doesn't have the cachet of some of its peers: Pearl Jam stayed across town, but their roadies stayed here. The rooms and facilities are very good, and the Conrad is – compared to the Çiragan, Intercontinental, or Swissotel – priced to move. Service is fine.

**ÇIRAĞAN PALACE KEMPINSKI**, *Çırağan Caddesi No. 84, Beşiktaş. Tel. 212 258 3377, Fax 212 259 6687 (North American Reservations: Tel. 800/ 426-3135). Rooms: 322. Double: $195-$5,000.*

This is where John F. Kennedy Jr. and his wife stayed on their honeymoon, as did a vacationing Hillary Clinton. President Bush stayed in 1991. The Çırağan has certainly arrived, and by a very circuitous route.

Sultan Abdül Aziz originally intended the Çırağan Palace to replace the Dolmabahçe Palace, finding Dolmabahçe too confining. Workers put the finishing touches on the Çırağan Palace – very much like the Dolmabahçe both in terms of its layout and baroque aesthetic – in 1874, but its kismet seemed bad from the beginning. Abdül Aziz was deposed in 1876 and imprisoned here. He slashed his own wrists with a pair of scissors just a few days later, which sent his successor, Sultan Murat V, spiralling into madness. Murat was then deposed in favor of Abdül Hamit II, still in 1876, but Abdül Hamit was too paranoid to live exposed on the water and commissioned a new palace at Yıldız Park. The Çırağan Palace became the prison of Murat V and the Sultan's other rivals and potential heirs, for which it became known as "The Cage."

The palace's prospects seemed to brighten in 1908, when nationalist Turks succeeded in forming a parliament and chose to house it here. The parliament, however, was a resounding failure, and the Çırağan Palace burned to the ground in 1910. The ruins still lay there 75 years later, when a group of investors began laboriously restoring the blackened ruin. Their work was completed earlier this decade, and the Çırağan has flourished.

This is one of the Leading Hotels of the World and a standard selection on the top 100 hotels list, but we have to attach some caveats. The interiors are surprisingly gaudy, sometimes even downright ugly. The Çırağan is not far from Sultanahmet and the bulk of İstanbul's sights – except on mornings, evenings, and weekends, when the sea road gets choked with traffic. Then the three mile drive can take a half hour or far longer. Finally, the world's handsomest and most important people stay here, but they stay in the suites, housed in the actual palace building. The suites are stunning, with fine views out over the Bosphorous and attractive, ornate detailing. The standard rooms are just that, standard, and they not in the authentic palace, but in a new wing that was built as a hotel. Still, with one-half mile of Bosphorous shoreline, an excellent standard of service and a worldwide reputation, the Çırağan is a luxury hotel in the finest sense. Seriously, who wouldn't want to stay in a genuine Ottoman Palace?

Selected as one of our best places to stay – see Chapter 10.

**HOTEL PRINCESS ORTAKÖY**, *Dere Boyu Cad. No. 36-38, Ortaköy. Tel. 212 227 6010, Fax 212 260 2148. Rooms: 76. Double: $120.*

An ambitious new hotel in one of İstanbul's most popular Bosphorous night-spots. Young, swinging types collect here in the evening, attracted by Ortaköy's beautiful waterfront and a selection of nightclubs that includes the Princess' own Hard Rock Cafe knockoff, the Rock House. The Princess offers good value for the money, and an unusual location. Like the Çırağan Palace, the Princess is choked off from the Sultanahmet area during heavy traffic, and is not especially convenient for sightseeing.

**HOTEL BEBEK**, *Cevdet Paşa Cad. No. 113-115, Bebek. Tel. 212 263 3000, Fax 212 263 2636. Rooms: 47. Double: $100.*

The Hotel Bebek, perenially due for restoration, will get that restoration someday and be a beautiful place indeed. Meantime it gets by on its unbeatable location directly above the Bosphorous (only one hotel south of Bebek has such a prime location, and that's the $180-$5,000 per night Çırağan Palace. And, believe it or not, the Hotel Bebek is right on the water, not set back like the Çırağan.)

Location aside, the Hotel Bebek has been allowed to slide precipitously. Its waterfront rooms are clean and serviceable, but they're also stained and worn. At the $100 price you can do better in Sultanahmet, but if you want to be able to sleep just above the Bosphorous this is the cheapest option. If you're not in a waterfront room, forget it. Bebek is an interesting little borough with a cosmopolitan feel. This owes to nearby

Bosphorous University, İstanbul's finest institution of higher learning, and explains the many international book and magazine shops, plus the small, excellent Bebek Kahve, a great place to stop in for a bite in the morning. The Hotel Bebek's own Les Ambassadeurs restaurant is popular among the local B.U. students and grads, as is its waterfront bar. Bear in mind that where there is a waterfront bar there is noise.

### Princes Islands & Elsewhere

**SPLENDID PALAS**, *23 Nisan Cad. No. 71, Büyükada. Tel. 216 382 6950, Fax 216 382 6775. Double: $110. Rooms: 60.*

A fixture in İstanbul, the Splendid Palas has long been the hotel chosen by İstanbullus themselves. The reason? It's tucked away from the bustle of İstanbul on Büyükada, one of the Princes Islands just three miles and three hundred years offshore of the city. There are no cars on Büyükada, just beaches, restaurants and horse-drawn carriages. There is frequent ferry service from both Kabataş on the Bosphorous and from the docks at Eminönü. Büyükada is the only island served by the high speed sea buses, nine times daily on weekdays, five times daily on weekends. This service is occasionally disrupted by high seas, but such events are extremely rare in the months this hotel is open; the hotel closes between November and late April, and in the spring and fall months room prices are halved.

There's a certain English Imperial flavor to the hotel, owing to its old association with a pre-WW I English yacht club. There's a certain English Imperial tiredness to the hotel, as well, whose spacious lobbies and pleasant furnishings are all slightly worn. The hotel has an enjoyable garden and a cooperative staff – although English is not a priority.

**HALKI PALAS**, *Refah Şehitleri Cad. No. 88, Heybeliada. Tel. 216 351 9550, Fax 216 351 8483. Double: $90. Rooms: 45.*

Another Princes' Islands option, this one on a slightly less convenient island than the Splendid Palas. The Halki Palas has beautiful small rooms, spacious, open sitting area, and feels like what it is, a retreat from the city. Life on Heybeliada is slow, but hardly comatose; there are lots of small shops and restaurants where you can while away your time when you aren't in İstanbul proper. From Heybeliada you can catch normal ferries throughout the day, or the faster sea buses from Büyükada one ferry stop away. Transportation between islands is free. Closed between November and April.

**KARIYE HOTEL**, *Kariye Camii Sok. No. 18, Edirnekapı. Tel. 212 534 8414, Fax 212 521 6631. Double: $115. Rooms: 27.*

The Kariye is well off the beaten path but conveniently near several marvelous Byzantine and Ottoman sights. Named for Kariye Camii, which is, in turn, named for The Church of St. Savior at Chora it replaced, the Kariye Hotel is a former mansion directly beside the famous church. The mansion has been divided into 27 rooms, and the broad patio outside is used for restaurant seating in the summer. The decor is Ottoman-style, with gilt framed pictures, carpets, and elaborate light fixtures. The rooms are nice, if slightly expensive considering the unusual location. Staying at the Kariye yields a completely different view of the city than the Sultanahmet, Bosphorous, or Taksim hotels, and affords opportunities to dwell on the frescoes at St. Saviour, the site of Mehmet II's triumphant entry to Constantinople at Edirnekapı, and the ruined old Byzantine palaces at Tekfur Saray and Blachernae, near Ivaz Efendi Camii.

**KLASSIS**, *Silivri, İstanbul. Tel. 212 727 4050, Fax 212 727 4049. Rooms: 303. Double: $180.*

Do you golf? That's probably the best reason to check in at the Klassis while on holiday. Lots of people visiting the Klassis are escaping İstanbul, but it makes sense to do it the other way around if you want to put in some time on the links and see İstanbul. The hotel is 65 kilometers from town, which creates some hassles getting into and out of the city, but this can be finessed easily enough. You'll even get to visit the city center by rail entering from this direction. The Klassis Golf and Country Club has an 18 hole championship course and a nine hole three-par (greens fees, clubs, and a cart cost $102, less in winter). Other of this imaginatively designed hotel's amenies are tennis courts, bowling, three swimming pools, squash courts and fully-outfitted rooms. Finally, if you want to exercise the part of your brain where PIN numbers are stored, hit the casinos.

**KLASSIS PARK**, *Londra Asfaltı, Otel Sokak No. 1, Küçükcekmece. Tel. 212 524 2337, Fax 212 598 9611. Rooms: 110. Double: $140.*

Do you want to be near the airport? The Klassis Park is the newest and best of a cluster of hotels in the vicinity of the airport. Although somewhat distant from the core of the old city, İstanbul's venerable train line runs nearby, and can whisk you along the Marmara shore to the Sultanahmet area in less than one-half hour. The hotel is clean and organized as only a new hotel can be, and the interiors are pleasant. The Klassis Park has all of the amenities you would expect from a new luxury hotel – pool, satellite television, and restaurants.

## WHERE TO EAT

İstanbul's best restaurants are widely scattered, and to take advantage of the city's fine dining you'll need to log a few miles in a taxi each evening. That's a small price to pay. İstanbul's dining options are becoming ever more diverse, which is fitting for a city of 14 million. American cuisine is among the most successful transplant: there are dozens of McDonalds, several Wendys and Burger Kings, two Kentucky Fried Chickens, a Subway Sandwich Shop and even (one of the signs of the Apocalypse) a Domino's Pizza. You can always inquire about these restaurants at your hotel, although they're everywhere and easy to spot. If you plan on an extended stay, pick up a copy of *Dining & Wining in İstanbul* at one of the English language bookshops.

We used the following guidelines to determine the price of a meal in our ratings below: less than $4 per person, inexpensive; $4 to $10, moderate; $10 to 25, expensive; more than $25, very expensive.

### Sultanahmet

Sultanahmet has dozens, probably hundreds of small restaurants, and they are all fairly dependable. Don't shy away from the food offered by street vendors; we recommend it, and you'll soon see why. For Sultanahmet's best dining, however, try the following.

**SARNIÇ**, *Soğukçeşme Sok., Sultanahmet. Tel. 212 513 3660, Fax 212 513 3669. Moderate-Expensive.*

The Sarniç is expensive, and the Sarniç is worth the money. Where else can you dine deep inside a stone chamber that was once a Roman cistern? The Turkish Touring and Automobile Association has lovingly restored this cistern – that was once, believe it or not, an auto repair shop. To make the structure suitable they began digging out the floor and carefully scrubbed and mended thousands of years of dirt and damage. The present floor, still some 10 feet above the old cistern floor, is deep enough. The interior of the cistern is now light and open, decorated with cast iron dividers and candlabras, wooden tables and chairs and simple, elegant place settings. The six great single-piece columns are lit by hundreds of candles and, on occasion, a roaring fire in the giant hearth. The Sarniç restoration is just one of many executed by Çelik Gülersoy and the Touring and Automobile Association.

Which brings us to the food, which is why you'd be interested in coming in the first place. The Sarniç kitchen is one of the best in İstanbul, and the meal will help complete what is probably İstanbul's most fascinating dining experience. The Sarniç offers both Turkish and international dishes, ranging from the best Turkish mezes to thick cuts of red meat and baked chicken. The Sarniç is located just down the cobbled lane from the Ayasofya Pansiyonlar, against the outer wall of Topkapı. Sarniç, sensibly enough, means "cistern."

**KONYALI**, *Topkapı Palace, Sultanahmet. Tel. 212 513 9696. Moderate.*

The Konyalı, the only restaurant within the grounds of Topkapı, has been serving captive audiences surprisingly good – if overpriced – lunches for many years. You can survey the offerings and make your choice accordingly. Kebaps and other grills are always good; if you're a

hungry carnivore opt for the karışık izgara, or mixed grill. If yo
in the mood for a real meal, stop by the cafe in the same court.
**KATHİSMA RESTAURANT**, *Yeni Akbıyık Cad. No. 26, Sultanahmet.
Tel. 212 518 9710, Fax 212 516 2588. Moderate.*
The Kathisma is a sparkling find in the Sultanahmet area. The
restaurant was remodeled in 1996, and has a hole-in-the wall feel, with
brick walls and good wood furniture. More importantly, the food is
delicious, particularly the roast lamb and "Sultan Chicken." The Kathisma
used to have jazz musicians play in the evenings, and they still turn up
on occasion. "Kathisma" refers to the Imperial box at the Hippodrome,
once located nearby.
**TÜRKISTAN AŞEVİ**, *Tavukhane Sok. No. 36, Sultanahmet. Tel. 212
518 1344. Moderate-Expensive.*
If Turkish dishes are not Turkish enough for you, the Türkistan
Aşevi has food from Central Asia. The restaurant is near the İbrahim Paşa
Palace in a restored mansion with beautiful flat weave rugs from this
region. Friendly service with pleasant little quirks: you wear slippers
while dining and the ayran, a drink made with soda water, is likely to suit
your taste buds better than the standard kind. Try the chicken mincemeat
or mixed kebap, with a big side of Turkistan rice.
**PANDELI**, *Mısır Pazar (Spice Bazaar), Eminönü. Tel. 212 527 3909.
Moderate.*
This is one of İstanbul's landmark restaurants, housed in the space
above the entrance to the Spice Market. Pandeli makes the most of its
historic atmosphere with beautiful sky blue faience on the walls and
well-prepared traditional dishes. You pay for the atmosphere, but not an
excruciating amount; lunch here costs $15 or less. This is the place to
forever alter your opinion of a vegetable: order the beğendil kebap, lamb
with a sauce of pureed eggplant.
**PUDDING SHOP**, *Divan Yolu No. 6, Sultanahmet. Tel. 212 522 2970.
Moderate.*
We feel compelled to mention the Pudding Shop, because it is a
Sultanahmet institution and you're likely to hear about it. Once upon a
time this was a meeting point on the classic backpacking trail between
Europe and the Far East. People heading in both directions would meet
here, those just in from the east dispensing advice and the pudding shop
dispensing its fine pudding. At the time Sultanahmet was a neglected
backwater, and the pudding shop stood forth as the best of the lot.
Enough history: Sultanahmet has changed and so has the Pudding
Shop. It still has pudding, it still has perfectly fine dinners, but it also has
high prices and snooty waiters. There's nothing wrong with getting a
meal here, but you'd probably enjoy yourself more just up the street at the
Vitamin Restaurant.

**CENNET**, *Divanyolu Cad. No. 90, Çemberlitaş. Tel. 212 513 1416. Inexpensive-Moderate.*

Okay, this is where half of the city's tourists go, but it's a good break from a day in the bazaar. Cennet specializes in gözleme, made in front of you and filled with your choice of potatoes, cheese, spinach, etc. The restaurant serves other dishes as well, but gözleme is the restaurant's big selling point. Meantime, while you await your sputtering gözleme you have the option of sitting around low tables on cushions and putting on a fez while musicians stroll around and play music until you pay them to leave. Cennet is a riotous good time or a living hell.

**BACKPACKER'S UNDERGROUND CAFE**, *Akbıyık Cad. No. 14/1, Sultanahmet. Inexpensive.*

This is just what it seems, a cozy little bar with cheap beer and cheap information about wherever you're going.

**West of Sultanahmet**

**METSOU-YAN,** *Hotel Merit Antique İstanbul, Laleli. Tel. 212 513 9300. Kosher. Moderate-Expensive.*

İstanbul's sole Kosher food restaurant, open from 7 p.m. to 11 p.m. Closed Fridays.

**DARÜZZİYAFE**, *Şifahane Cad. No. 6, Süleymaniye Mosque. Tel. 212 511 8415. Moderate.*

When important Ottomans commissioned the construction of a mosque, they built much more than the domed structures we marvel at today. Mosques were always joined by a set of public buildings ranging from schools to soup kitchens, and the Süleymaniye, built for the most powerful Ottoman sultan, had one of the most extensive sets of public buildings. The Darüzzıyafe was the Süleymaniye's soup kitchen, and it continues to dish out food to this very day.

These days the clientele is deeper in the pockets, the menu has gone upscale, and the food is probably better. A mixed grill, always one of the better and more expensive items on a menu for meat-eaters, is $6, and it's very good. The Darüzzıyafe kitchen continues to create top-quality Turkish dishes, and the setting is excellent, whether in the stone interior or the courtyard. The only jarring note, here in the mosque complex, are the occasional belly-dancing displays staged by tour groups. The restaurant is to the left as you look at the main entrance (the one you can't use) of the Süleymaniye, through a gate, and across a narrow road.

**Taksim**

**GALATA TOWER**, *8th floor, Galata Tower, Tünel. Tel. 212 245 1160, Fax 212 245 2133. Daytime: moderate; dinner: very expensive.*

Galata Tower's cafe is open through the day serving coffee and some snack food. As night falls, however, things go rapidly upscale: A potent single price ($70) includes dinner, drinks and a musical bellydancing extravaganza, keeping you in food and drinks from 9 p.m. until midnight. The food is fine, the entertainment is fine, the drinks are fine, the view is marvelous,and the building is genuinely fascinating. Note the plaque on the inner wall on your way up; sure enough, long before Orville and Wilber were a glimmer in Mrs. Wright's eye, a scientist strapped on a pair of wings and leapt from the top of Galata tower, soaring about one mile across the Bosphorous. He came along at the wrong time, however; the Ottomans were past their prime, and all he did was stir up fear in the sultan's heart. The flier was exiled.

**GALATA RESTAURANT & BAR,** *İstiklal Cad, Orhan Adlı Apaydın Sok. No. 11, Beyoğlu. Tel. 212 293 1139. Moderate-Expensive..*

Many visitors find their way to Galata Tower, but only the smart few locate this "meyhane" just uphill off of İstiklal Caddesi. Like Galata Tower, Galata Restaurant has food and entertainment, but the similarities end there. The cozy Galata Restaurant is a favorite among Turks and some expatriates, all of whom gather here many evenings to sing Turkish folk songs. The Galata is a lot of fun, even if all you can do is hum along, drink, and eat excellent Turkish/Greek food and top notch mezes. The music lasts from 9 p.m. to midnight. Galata is closed on Sundays. As you ascend İstiklal Caddesi from the Tünel and Galata Tower the Galata Restaurant is just off to your left at the narrow lane by the Cafe Marti.

**REJANS,** *Emir Nevruz Sok. No. 17, Galatasaray. Tel. 244 1610. Expensive.*

Excellent Russian food, a staple in this neighborhood since three White Russian women fled the budding Bolshevik state with most of the old country's best recipes. If you've ever been curious about borscht and real beef stroganof, this is your chance. The lemon vodka is comely and dangerous. The restaurant is located four blocks downhill of the bend in İstiklal. Atatürk himself is reported to have loved this spot. The service is as helpful and friendly as their distant peers at Ed Debeviks in Chicago.

**NATURE & PEACE,** *İstiklal Caddesi, Büyükparmakkapı Caddesi No. 21, Beyoğlu. Tel. 212 252 8609. Moderate-Expensive.*

One of İstanbul's only dedicated health food restaurants (also see Zencefil below). Pretty building and interesting health/vegetarian menu. A bit hard to find; walking down İstiklal Caddesi with Taksim Square at your back, take a left past the cinemas on Büyükparmakkapı, the street with Pandora book store. The restaurant is on your left one block along.

**BILSAK,** *Soğancı Sok. No. 7, Cihangir. Tel. 212 293 3774. Moderate.*

A bland looking building disguises one of the area's most popular bars and a great little restaurant. The menu is diverse and excellent, with curried chicken, lentil mantı, seafood pasta, and mushroom linguini. It has a slouchy, chic feel to it, with old movie posters, a great paint job, and definite appeal among trendy expatriates. The first puzzle is getting in – enter the nondescript lobby and take the elevator to five. Down from Taksim Square on Siraselviler Caddesi, then left past the Almanya Hastanesi (German Hospital).

**SUSAM RESTAURANT AND BAR,** *Susam Sok. No. 6., Cihangir. Tel. 212 251 5935. Expensive.*

The Susam is difficult to find, and you begin wondering what the big deal is until you set foot inside and witness the beautiful view out over the Golden Horn to the old city. Heavily untouristed, this is about as secret as they get. English will be a mild hassle, but everything will work out with the Susam's very professional service. The menu has a number of seafood dishes, including grilled sea bass. Open all year, but if you come in winter you'll miss the opportunity to sit outside on the deck and marvel. Follow Siraselviler from Taksim Square taking a left on Yeni Yuva Sokak opposite the Spar Supermarket. Susam is at the end of Yeni Yuva on Susam Sokak. Look for the Mediterranean blue wall.

**HACI ABDULLAH,** *Ağa Canii Yanı Sakızağacı Caddesi No. 17, Beyoğlu. Tel. 212 293 8561. Moderate.*

The Hacı Abdullah is an İstanbul institution, and has become a gathering spot for some of the city's sharpest minds. The appeal here is that often advertised but seldom found commodity, "traditional" Turkish cooking. The menu is vast, and includes dishes for the adventurous such as grilled veal kidneys and fried lamb's brains. Fortunately, there is a menu in English.

We would encourage the duck, the dolmas, and anything including eggplant. A generous dinner for two will run to $15. Alcohol is pointedly not served. A short walk down İstiklal from Taksim Square and right one block.

**ÇIN LOKANTASI,** *Lamartin Cad. No. 17/1, Taksim. Tel. 212 250 6263. Closed Sundays. Moderate.*

The Çin Lokantasi (Chinese Restaurant) is generally thought to have the best Chinese food in town. The restaurant is run by a Chinese expatriate and has almost everything you would expect; sweet and sour chicken, spring rolls, and chow mein included. Some of the dishes won't taste quite like you'd expect; American Chinese food makes concessions to its audience, and Turkish Chinese food does the same. Just down the street from Taksim Square on Lamartin Caddesi.

**ZENCEFİL,** *Kurabiye Sokak No. 3, Taksim. Tel. 212/244-4082 Moderate.*

Zencefil's vegetarian menu changes daily and includes specialties from different parts of the world. Only natural, locally grown ingredients are used, and they offer homemade bread, wine, and herbal teas. Open noon-10 p.m, closed on Sundays. From Taksim, go down Istiklal and turn right after the French Consulate. Go down the hill one block and take the first left onto Kurabiye Sokak. Zencefil is on the left.

**FIVE STAR RESTAURANT**, *İstiklal Caddesi, Taksim. Tel. 212 250 2440. Inexpensive-Moderate.*

If you want a quick, cheap hassle-free dinner in the Taksim area, this may be the place. The restaurant just a few doors in from Taksim Square with the huge rack of chickens in the window offers an excellent alternative to the standard sit down restaurants. You select your food from a buffet line and pay for it, requesting roasted chicken (tavuk) at the register ($2.50). In a separate line the chicken server gives you the chicken in question and a helping of rice or gruel. Ask for rice "pee rinj, loot fen" or he will default to the gruel.

The big advantage to this restaurant is that, having paid in advance, there is no nastiness with an inflated bill. The food is greasy and good, but it's nothing special.

**TAKSIM TAŞ FIRIN**, *Siraselviler Cad. No. 30, Taksim. Tel. 212 243 4810. Inexpensive.*

The green and white livery of this nice place can get lost amid the cluster of restaurants opposite the Dilson Hotel one block from Taksim Square, but if you want a quick bite to eat we recommend finding it. There are lahmacun (Turkish pizza) places all over the city, lots of them cheaper, but we had our first lahmacun here and never found any better. The prices are as good as you'll find on İstanbul's beaten track ($.60). The Iskender Kebap is also good ($2.25). If you like, pick up a few lahmacun to go: "Paket Istiyorum."

## Conference Valley

We recommend getting out to hotels along the Bosphorous and in the Etiler area, but if you're staying near here and want to find some good food, try the following:

**DİVAN LOKANTA**, *Divan Hotel, Elmadag. Tel. 212 231 4100. Expensive-Very Expensive.*

The best of the hotel restaurants in the conference borough. Excellent Turkish cuisine in a very nice setting on the hill above the Bosphorous. The Divan Hotel has been leapfrogged by some of its competitors, but the restaurant has maintained its standard of excellence.

**SPASSO**, *Hyatt Regency İstanbul, Taksim. Tel. 212 225 7000. Expensive-Very Expensive.*

Italian food in an open, unusual setting. Spasso is a cross between a bistro and an art project, and it mostly works. Food is prepared in the open and service is top notch. Specialties seem to be the pastas and sauce, and if you're looking for Italian wine this is one of the places to get it.

**RISTORANTE ITALIANO**, *Cumhuriet Caddesi No. 6B, Elmadağ. Tel. 212 247 8640. Italian. Moderate-Expensive.*

A small restaurant that we might term exquisite if it cost more. Instead it's surprisingly affordable, and one of the best Italian restaurants in the city. Owner Emrullah Gümüştaş is likely to personally welcome you upon arrival. Italian and Turkish spoken, with English necessities.

**ŞEHZADE RESTAURANT**, *Taşkişla Caddesi, Harbiye. Moderate-Expensive.*

The Şehzade is decorated like an old Ottoman street, with each wooden house a different room. Very interesting design and good, country-style Turkish food.

### Along the Bosphorous

**TUĞRA**, *Çırağan Palace Hotel, Beşiktaş. Tel. 212 258 3377. International. Very Expensive.*

Only the finest Ottoman recipes have made their way onto the Tuğra menu. This restaurant, located in the wing of the Çırağan Palace Hotel that once was part of the palace itself, is a baffling and precious treat. The setting on the Bosphorous is marvelous, the dining area spacious and ornate, and the menu exotically unfamiliar to new arrivals. Don't let this deter you; nothing on the menu will disappoint, and the waiters are not too snooty to help; they understand your problem. If you want to splurge on the finest Ottoman cuisine, the Tuğra is your place.

**RISTORANTE VITO**, *Osmanzade Sok. No. 13, Ortaköy. Tel. 212 227 6598. Italian. Expensive.*

A painfully pretty small restaurant serving Italian food. The decor is part subterranean, part art nouveau. Service is attentive and food is well-prepared. Particularly delicious is the tortellini and chicken with a heavy spinach sauce, and the gnocchi, although the latter can be hit or miss.

**SEFARAD**, *Muvakkit Sokak 33, Ortaköy. Tel: 212 261 2983. Sokak, Ortaköy. Inexpensive-Moderate.*

This tiny vine-covered restaurant, one half block from the Ortaköy Princess Hotel, may fool you. If you judge books by their covers you'll pass right by; the downstairs dining area is usually empty. If you venture up the stairs, however, you'll enter a vaulted, wood-panelled "attic" space. This cozy area is usually crowded with an interesting mix of people. The menu is standard Turkish fare, with seasonal fresh fish. Try the patlican salatası (eggplant "salad" – more like eggplant spread).

**MYOTT**, *Iskele Sok. No.14, Ortaköy. Tel. 212 258 9317. Cafe. Moderate.*

İstanbul's slickest coffee shop, serving Italian coffees instead of Nescafe. Crowds gather here, very hip crowds, but if you can slip in this is a nice, overpriced spot for pastries and coffee. Myott also serves Muesli for breakfast on weekends.

**KÖRFEZ**, *Körfez Cad. No. 78, Kanlıca (Asia). Tel. 212 332 0108. Fish. Expensive-Very Expensive.*

A romantic fish restaurant on the Asian shore. Phone ahead and ask to be met at Rumeli Hisar – the Ottoman fortress on the European shore of the Bosphorous – and the Körfez will happily send a small boat across the strait to collect you. İstanbullus agree that the fish here is the finest in the city, reserving special praise for the sea bass (levrek) leached with rock salt and baked. Dinner and drinks for two can climb quickly toward $80, but there's no denying the Körfez is a marvelous experience. Closed Mondays.

**YEDI GÜN**, *Rumelikavağı. Tel. 212 242 3798. Fish. Moderate.*

The Bosphorous is lined with fish restaurants, and it would be an awful conceit for any one of them to claim it was the best. Yedi Gün could probably make a pretty could case, however. Excellent seasonal fish, and a shrimp stew (güveç) that will bring tears to your eyes. The restaurant is located in Rumelikavağı at the very upper end of the Bosphorous, thus not at all convenient unless you're in Sariyer anyway. It's definitely worth a taxi ride from there.

## Etiler

İstanbul's Etiler area is home to the city's best collection of restaurants. Etiler restaurants cater to İstanbullus, but are all well-acquainted with travelers and expatriates. You may have problems getting here from Sultanahmet between 3 and 7:30 p.m., when traffic can lock up.

**OSTERIA DA MARIO**, *Dilhayat Sokak No. 7, Etiler. Tel. 212 265 5186. Italian. Expensive.*

İstanbul has several Italian restaurants, but the Osteria Da Mario has the best food of the lot. Classic Italian atmosphere and classic imported Italian ingredients.

**SAI THAI**, *Aytar Caddesi, Levent Işhanı No. 3/6, Birinci Levent. Tel. 212 283 5346. Thai. Moderate-Expensive.*

Come on, a two week vacation can't be enough time to have Thai food withdrawal. Still, if it should happen to you, Sai Thai is on hand with emergency doses of chicken satay. Sai Thai is an exactingly detailed restaurant down to its low tables and liveried food servers – although there are standard tables also available. The curry chicken and Thom Ka Ghai soup are mind benders. Open for lunch from noon to 3 p.m. Located just beyond the Zincirkuyu stop.

**TANDOORI**, *Alkent, Tepecik Yolu, Etiler. Tel. 212 257 8479. Indian. Moderate-Expensive.*

İstanbul's cuisine is becoming increasingly international, and Tandoori has arrived to fill the gap in Indian food. Surprisingly good food considering it has no local competition; excellent curries, of course, and Indian vegetarian dishes. Service can be slow. The restaurant is located in Alkent, a gated community near Etiler.

**YİRMİDOKUZ ULUS** (29 Ulus), *Adnan Saygun Caddesi, Kireçhane Sok. No. 1, Ulus. Tel. 212 265 6181. French. Very Expensive.*

Some believe this is the best restaurant in the city, and pound for pound it might be, but featherweight portions can be a problem if you have a cruiserweight appetite. French cuisine in a beautiful setting overlooking the Bosphorous – excellent in the summer. Reservations are necessary.

**SUNSET GRILL & BAR**, *Adman Saygun Cad. Kireçhane Sok., Ulus Parkı No. 2, Ulus. Tel. 212 287 0357. Californian. Expensive-Very Expensive.*

Sunset Grill & Bar has one of the finest Bosphorous views in the city. Sunset serves slightly overpriced California-style cuisine, but in this setting the price isn't going to spoil your mood. In good weather you should make reservations for a table outside under one of the pavilion tents. Try the grilled prawns or the salads. The drinks are excellent, but you're here for the setting. The restaurant is located just below Ulus Park on the road between Ortaköy and Akmerkez.

### Kumkapi and Along the Sea of Marmara

Our main recommendation for Kumkapi is to avoid it. If you want a blaring, boisterous time, it's all right, but its former charm is long gone. On your way into cobbled pedestrian waterfront area you are besieged by wheedling restaurant hustlers, and the experience deteriorates from there. Many of the restaurants tamper with your bill, the food is of uneven quality, prices are high, and most of the people are tourists. Kumkapı thrives, and it will continue to thrive, but it doesn't need your business. Other places have food every bit as delicious, and are more enjoyable (Ortaköy, Bebek). If you must go we recommend against the Caretta Restaurant.

**YENGEÇ BALIK LOKANTASI**, *Telli Odalar Sokak No. 6 Kumkapı. Tel. 212 516 3227. Moderate-Expensive.*

The shrimp (karides) and the kalamari (kalamar) are outstanding. The local specialty, grilled bluefish (lüfer izgara) is usually dry enough that you'll want some wine or rakı.

**BEYTİ**, *Orman Sokak No. 8, Florya. Tel. 212 663 2990. Moderate.*

Far out along the Sea of Marmara, you have to want to get here. And well you should. Nairobi has the Carnivore, İstanbul has Beyti. The restaurant has carefully maintained its excellent reputation as a meat restaurant, and The Beyti Kebap is the house specialty, a "karışık," or mixed grill, of great proportions and delicacy. Although the meat dishes are good, you can stick to vegetarian options such as the patlican salatasi.

## SEEING THE SIGHTS

Whatever your interests you will want to spend at least one or two days in the **Sultanahmet** area. After that you can take a cruise on the Bosphorous, shop in the Grand Bazaar, walk along the city walls, or visit one of the myriad museums scattered around town. We have tried to keep the sights arranged in a way that makes them convenient to one another. Follow the itineraries suggested in Chapter 3 or follow our descriptions from beginning to end and you'll see the best the city has to offer. And you'll be really tired.

The reasons the Sultanahmet area is so compelling are about this many: The Topkapı Palace, the Haghia Sophia, the Blue Mosque, the Basilica Cistern, and the Archaeological Museum, plus a handful of other museums. This was the site of the ancient settlement and has always been the center of İstanbul. Once you've had spent some time here you'll want to begin straying farther away, first up the **Bosphorous** to the fortresses there, then to some of the city's excellent musuems and districts, such as **İstiklal Caddesi**, the grand pedestrian lane above Galata Tower and **Ortaköy**, a charming little neighborhood.

# Sultanahmet Region

Sultanahmet, named for **Sultan Ahmet I**, the builder of the Blue Mosque, has a critical mass of historic sights. If you have a day, this is where you spend it. If you have a few days, you could easily spend them all here. The area is fairly open and pretty, and aside from some hustlers who want you to buy their wares, it's pleasant.

## Topkapı Saray

**Topkapı Palace** is the greatest Ottoman museum in the world and a fascinating relic of the Empire's lost glory. Visitors can spend the day in the gardens where Sultans spent their time, look through their most private rooms and the rooms of their entourage, and reanimate the might and mystery of the palace. An immense collection of weapons, jewelry, and treasure adds color, and, finally, some of the holiest artifacts in the Muslim world are here to remind you that the Sultan ruled in spirit as well as flesh. In addition to the museums within the palace itself, there are three excellent museums located in Topkapı's outer court, including the Archaeological Museum (see below).

An entrance fee of $5 is exacted at the inner Topkapı Gate, with an additional fee for the harem inside. Topkapı Palace, *Tel. 212 512 0480,* is at the head of the peninsula in Sultanahmet, within a circuit of walls behind the Haghia Sophia. Signs direct you to Topkapı.

## INSTANBUL SIGHTS INFORMATION AT A GLANCE/1

| Location | Price | Hours | Closed |
|---|---|---|---|
| TopkapıPalace | $4, $7 | 9:00-17:00 | Tuesday |
| Archaeology Museum | $2 | 9:30-16:30 | Monday |
| Cinli Kösk @ Arch. Mus. | | 9:30-16:30 | Monday |
| Museum of the Ancient Orient @ Arch. Mus. | | 9:30-16:30 | Monday (some afternoons) |
| Aya Sofya (Haghia Sophia) | $3 | 9:30-17:00 | Monday |
| Yerebatan Cistern | $2 | 9:00-17:00 | |
| Museum of Turkish and Islamic Art | $2 | 10:00-17:00 | Monday |
| Binbirdirek Cistern | $1 | 9:00-17:00 | Saturday, Sunday |
| Mosaic Museum | $1 | 9:30-17:00 | Tuesday |
| Halı/Kilim Museum | $1 | 9:00-16:00 | Monday |
| Yıldız Saray Şale Köşkü (Yıldız Palace Chalet) | $1 | 9:00-18:00 | Monday, Thursday |

## History

Sultan Mehmet II captured Constantinople in 1453, but by that time the city was a mere shadow of its former self. Many of the city's treasures had been plundered just 200 years earlier by fellow Christians in the Fourth Crusade, and the subsequent governments suffered under severe economic strain largely at the hands of the Ottomans themselves. By the time the Ottomans claimed the city, parts of the vast metropolis were deserted and broken down and the Imperial Palace itself was a shambles. Sultan Mehmet II was nonetheless proud of his prize and, ever industrious, Fatih set about restoring the city. He imported people from conquered territories to swell the population, commissioned a covered bazaar, and invested in other neglected infrastructure to jump-start the city's commerce.

Finally, in 1460 he ordered an ambitious new palace complex on the hill at the tip of the peninsula, replacing the temporary administrative complex near today's Grand Bazaar. The result was Topkapı Palace, a sprawling creation that covers most of ancient Byzantium, and a capital that satisfied Mehmet II and his successors for 400 years. Topkapı benefits not only from its location at the crest of İstanbul's First Hill, but from its proximity to Byzantine-era landmarks such as the Haghia Sophia.

Topkapı Palace became the soul of the Ottoman Empire, the place that nurtured its administration, education, military supremacy, and spiritual leadership. As the Ottoman Empire expanded, its armies won a fearsome reputation. The Empire expanded deeper and deeper into Europe, accompanied by the knell of "Turk Bells" in cities throughout Europe to signal that yet another city had fallen to the Muslim armies. To a cowed western world, Topkapı Palace was the mysterious and frightening center of this relentless power. Behind Topkapı's impossibly distant walls, Ottoman sultans lived in a world of magnificent rumor and luxury, issuing forth only to march at the head of another victorious Ottoman army. European embassies were ignored or treated with contempt, while Ottoman armies stormed ever westward to the booming march of the Mehter.

Even in decline, Topkapı was a mystery. Within its walls the Imperial guard and high officials conspired with women of the harem or the chief eunuchs, creating an often deadly climate. Princes were assassinated as women tried to position their sons to become sultan, the military advanced the prospects of one prince over the other, or even revolted against the Sultan. If the strengths of the Empire were manifest at Topkapı Palace, so, too, were its insular weaknesses. The haughty superiority of the early sultans deteriorated into a stubborn closed-mindedness that helped grease the Ottoman's long slide from power.

## INSTANBUL SIGHTS INFORMATION
## AT A GLANCE/2

| Location | Price | Hours | Closed |
|---|---|---|---|
| Beylerbeyi Saray (Palace) | $1.50 | 9:00-17:00 | Monday, Thursday |
| Galata Tower | $1.50 | cafe 8:00-21:00 | |
| Yedikule | $1 | 9:30-5:00 | Monday |
| Tekfur Saray Byzantine Palace | $1 | 9:00-17:00 | Wednesday, Thursday, Sunday |
| Kariye Camii (St. Savior at Chora) | $4 | 9:30-16:30 | Tuesday |
| Rumeli Hisar | $1.50 | 9:30-16:30 | Monday |
| Dolmabahçe Palace | $4, $7 | 9:00-16:00 | Monday, Thursday |
| Naval Museum | $1 | 9:30-17:00 | Monday, Tuesday |
| Military Museum | $1.50 | 9:00-17:00 | Monday, Tuesday |

**SULTANAHMET ISTANBUL**

### Sultanahmet Sights Key

1 Topkapi Palace
2 Archaeological Museum
3 Haghia Sophia
4 Yereban (Underground Cistern)
5 Hippodrome
6 Fountain of Wilhelm
7 Obelisk
8 Serpent Column
9 Colossus
10 Turkish & Islamic Arts Museum
11 Binbirderek Cistern
12 The Blue Mosque
13 Mosaic Museum
14 Grand Bazaar
15 Cemberlitas
16 Ferry Terminals
17 Spice Bazaar
18 Sirkeci Train Station

## The First Court

The Palace was built on a sprawling plan in four distinct courts. The first, outer court is immense, incorporating the entire head of the peninsula. With the contemporary addition of a road for tour buses you may not realize you are in a court at all. The main entrance is the Imperial Gate behind the Haghia Sophia. Note the row of niches to each side as you enter; these spaces were once kept stocked with the heads of enemies of the Empire.

Much of the hewing of human heads was done by the resident Imperial guard, the **Janissaries**, for whom the huge first court was once named. The Janissaries were the elite fighting corps at the heart of the Ottoman military, and one of the cornerstones of Ottoman martial success for 300 years. As the Ottoman Empire began bringing more and more lands under its control, Sultan Orhan initiated a shrewd policy with his Christian subjects. Rather than persecuting minority religions, Orhan chose to offer religious freedom to Christians and other non-Muslims, which secured their reluctant allegiance.

At the same time, he conscripted many of their sons to convert to Islam and serve in the Janissary Corps. Strange as the practice sounds it was quite successful, elevating the young Christian males to an educated, martially respected status and giving the Sultan a crop of young men that became full time soldiers, administrators, and military engineers in an age when warfare was a seasonal occupation. Furthermore, the Padishah's much-feared personal army served as a counterweight against whatever peasant armies Ottoman great houses could muster, thereby heading off internal challenges to the throne.

Breakthroughs in military technology usually presage periods of conquest, and the Ottoman's standing army of Janissaries proved to be just such an advancement. As a third arm of the military, together with peasant infantry and the sipahi (cavalry) supplied by the great houses, the ably-led Janissaries were used late in battles to shatter enemy lines. Opposing armies of part-time soldiers could rarely match the Janissaries, for whom warfare was a way of life. Their commanders, Janissaries themselves, were posted to captured fortresses on the frontier to ensure loyalty to the sultan. The garishly dressed soldiers were the only Christian Ottoman subjects whose conversion to Islam was compelled, but this occurred at such a young age that no significant problems ever came of it.

As the empire eroded, so did the Janissary Corps – recruitment changed so that the sons of administrators and nobles could send their sons to the corps and the body became highly political. By 1700, they no longer intimidated enemies of the empire, just the Sultans themselves. Several ill-fated attempts were made to eliminate the corps, but in 1826

Sultan Mahmud II succeeded in defeating and dismantling the corrupt Janissaries.

The first court is often overlooked by people who make the intuitive beeline for the central palace grounds behind the Gate of Salutations, but the buildings down the slope to the left are worth your time. The first building, near the outer wall, is the **Haghia Irene**, a much senior church to the upstart Haghia Sophia. The Haghia Irene dates back to Byzantium, and in 330 A.D. was rebuilt as Constantinople's central church. Like the Haghia Sophia, it was repeatedly damaged and restored, although Justinian's magnificent restoration of the Haghia Sophia eventually relegated the Haghia Irene to virtual anonymity. After the Ottoman capture of Constantinople the Haghia Irene became an armory and a storehouse, but under the Republic it was cleaned up and is used today for concerts in the late spring and early summer. Chamber music, particularly, benefits from the excellent acoustics of the Haghia Irene. For concert schedules contact the Tourism Information office.

### Elsewhere in the First Court

Below and behind the Haghia Irene are the extensive grounds of the **Archaeological Museum** and its outbuildings. A small road lined with sarcophagi and statuary runs downhill alongside the Haghia Irene to the museums. After exiting the lower gate you are in **Gulhane**, at the lower end of Divan Yolu Cad. and just down the street from the Yerebatan (Basilica) Cistern. This lower entrance is also almost directly opposite an elaborately roofed gate outside the Topkapı walls. The gate is the **Sublime Porte**, the entrance to the residence of Grand Viziers from Süleyman the Magnificent's time. Most official business was done here, not in the palace itself, and "Sublime Porte" soon became synonymous with Ottoman power.

Today the Sublime Porte enters into a police station. If you enter the palace grounds at Gulhane, the upper path takes you to the museums and beyond, while the lower path, to the left, passes into a municipal fairground frequented by the parents of howling, cotton-candy decorated children. Choose wisely.

Through the fairground, at the tip of the peninsula, is the 50 foot tall **Goths Column**. This column dates to a third century siege by the Goths, who were reportedly turned away with the help of a small fee: the inscription reads *"To Fortune, who helped us gain our victory over the Goths."*

### The Second Court

To enter the true interior of the palace you must pay at the ticket kiosk along the right side of the road. This second gate is the **Gate of Salutations** (Babüsselam), decorated with the Tuğra of Mehmet II, builder of the palace. For those who missed the point at the Imperial Gate, two large stones for displaying more human heads. Salutations, indeed.

Upon entering you find yourself not in a palace at all, but in yet another park. To orient yourself, take a look at the diagram on the wall inside the gate, or at the scale model.

Behind a wall to your right are the palace kitchens, an original feature of the palace that was enlarged and modified – partially by the master architect Sinan in the late 16th century. The kitchens are often overlooked in the face of so much wealth and beauty, but they add a wonderful human element. More than 4,000 people are estimated to have lived here, many of whom expected to eat very well. Truth is, it's easier – if less fun – to identify with the harried palace cooks laboring over their massive pots and preparing exotic meats and pastries than it is to identify with the sultans.

In addition to standard cooking items, the Topkapı kitchens are now filled with display cases bearing porcelains from around the world – including Süleyman's pet collection of Chinese celadon. Other rooms have glassware and appropriately oversized kitchen utensils. Note, too, the superbly functional design of the kitchens, all the handiwork of the architect Sinan.

On the other side of the park along the back wall is the **Imperial Treasury**, now used as a museum of weapons. If you have a teen-age boy along, make a beeline for this place. The Janissaries once assembled in the second court to receive their quarterly wages from this hall, and it was often arranged that payday would coincide with important state visits. In the Empire's heyday, outsiders would witness thousands of the intricately dressed imperial guard waiting in eerie, disciplined silence to receive their gold and pay allegiance to their sultan. It is said to have made quite an impression. Today the treasury is full of standards, maces, swords, armor, spears, rifles, and other wicked-looking paraphenalia from the 7th century onward. Most of the weapons are Ottoman era, including the extremely accurate Turkish war bows (tirkeş). Take a look at the impressive swords carried by Mehmet the Conqueror and Süleyman the Magnificent.

The **Imperial Council** chambers are further toward the west wall. Renovation of the Imperial Council rooms were completed in 1996, and you can see parts of the original reliefs that decorated the interiors and exteriors, together with painted recreations. It was in this council chamber that the Sultan's top advisors deliberated literally under the watchful eye of the sultan, who eavesdropped on meetings of the **Divan** (Council) from an grilled area high in the wall. On Mondays and Thursdays the main Topkapı tower looming above the council chambers is open from 11 a.m. to 2 p.m., but there is a $1.50 charge next to the harem tour booth.

The **Quarters of the Halberdiers with Tresses** are beyond the harem and tower ticket booths along the west wall. The Halberdiers were simply porters and guards charged with caring for the harem, and their exposure to the beautiful residents therein compelled them to grow their hair long and wear high-collared uniforms that obscured their view (and, presumably, vice versa).

### The Harem
Against the wall is the ticket booth for half-hourly harem tours – activity comes to a halt at lunch. If you want to see the harem, you have to go with a tour – unfortunately the tight corridors and the large size of tour groups can render the guides unintelligible even when you manage to cram into the same room. If you are with a small group of your own, ask for a private tour ($15). In either case, make arrangements soon after arriving at Topkapı, otherwise the tours may fill up. The 300-room harem is a fascinating place whether you are interested in architecture, history, or simple carnality.

The Harem was supervised by the **Black Eunuchs**, a tradition that began when hundreds of gelded Sudanese men were brought back to İstanbul as an oddity. The Chief Black Eunuch could rise to great power within the palace, and became a pivotal player in the conspiracies of the crown princes and their mothers.

The women of the harem were invariably slaves and prisoners of war, selected for their beauty at a young age and educated within the harem. The Koran forbids such treatment of people of the Book – Muslims, Christians and Jews – but a lawyerly interpretation allowed particularly toothsome Christian and Jewish girls to be conscripted to the harem.

Yes, the Sultan could have his way with the women of the harem, but everything was subject to strict protocol with selection and grooming and preparation all part of the package. It was like a big, very promising date. The rigid, awkward-sounding structure of the harem is summed up by the fact that the **Valide Sultan** – the sultan's mother – was often charged with selecting the women for her son, and was always quite aware of what he was getting up to.

Some historians trace the decline of the Ottoman Empire to 1558, when Süleyman the Magnificent was manipulated by his wife, Roxelana – a member of the harem – to have his son Mustafa assassinated. Mustafa was at the time governor of northern Anatolia, a favorite of the Janissaries, and a robust, intelligent leader. His death, combined with that of another son, Beyazid, left the path clear for Roxelana's own son, Selim II, to become sultan. He proved a very poor one. Roxelana is famous for her influence on Süleyman, and was the first sultan's wife to live within

Topkapı Palace. After Roxelana, wives and harem members continued living at the palace, and became heavily embroiled in palace intrigues. Roxelana's conspiracy against her son's stepbrothers was the first time the mother of a prince helped arrange the murders of her son's rivals, but certainly not the last.

---

### HAREM HEARSAY

*Eunuchs were reportedly selected for their ugliness.*

*Not all of the eunuchs, reports say, were as gelded as they seemed.*

*Cucumbers were sliced before distribution to the women of the harem.*

*Women in the private harems of young heirs and rivals to the throne were forbidden to bear any children. Visible pregnancy among the princes' or rivals women was punishable by death.*

*Execution of harem women – sometimes done by the hundreds with the ascendance of a new sultan – was by drowning in the Bosphorous.*

*Circassian women, from the Caucasus in the northeast, were usually considered the most beautiful and formed the core of the harem population.*

---

**The Third Court**

The harem tour empties out at a corner of the third court, not far from the main gate, the **Gate of Felicity**. The interior of this court was given over to, of all things, lots of teenage boys. These were the non-Muslim youths collected from throughout Ottoman lands to fuel the Janissary Corps, administering and protecting the empire. Many of the younger boys attended school in the long buildings to either side of the gate, thereafter graduating to the military, administrative, and finance schools, or, in the case of the most promising, the sultan's personal staff. The **White Eunuchs** were charged with teaching and administering the boys, and they ruled in this court as the Black Eunuchs ruled within the harem.

Directly inside the gate is the **Audience Hall**. This building has oriental understatement considering its importance, but it was magnificently appointed. The hall was an original feature of the palace, and the current structure is the result of subsequent rebuilding and modification as late at 1860. The throne within dates to the 16th century, and was decorated with rich, jewel-bedecked hangings. Foreign embassies were occasionally received here, although appearances by the Grand Vizier and Ottoman nobles were far more common.

Behind the Audience Hall is the small, locked **Library of Sultan Ahmet III**. If you peer through the windows, you can see books inside. The White Eunuch's mosque just to the side is now an adjunct to that library. Unless you have the key, these are clearly the two least interesting features of the third court.

Farther along the west wall past the old mosque building, are the **Privy Chambers**. Until the Republic few but the Sultan and the Grand Mufti could look at the religious artifacts in this room. Once every year, in the middle of Ramazan, the two men would enter the sacred room and pay respects to Mohammed. The items here were not publicly displayed until the 1960s. Many of the items here were collected under Selim I (the Grim), whose successful campaigns added Mecca, Medina, Jerusalem, and Cairo to the Ottoman Empire. In the large front room is the Door of the Great Mosque in Mecca, a scale model of Jerusalem's Dome of the Rock, several Kaaba keys, meticulous copies of the Koran, and other Islamic artifacts.

Even on the busiest summer day you will notice a hushed, respectful atmosphere here, and it intensifies in the smaller room to the side. In this room are some of the most prized possessions in the Islamic world, Mohammed's swords and bow, his footprint, his seal, and soil from his tomb. Also here, a mixture of the holy and the macabre, are hairs from Mohammed's beard and one of his teeth, raising the question that if cloning technology ever really takes off ... Even holier still are the items in the closed area to the side of this room, Mohammed's robe (the Holy Mantle) and the Holy Standard. This final relic was displayed by the Ottoman army when it went to war with the infidels in the west.

Leaving the Privy Chambers, the next room in our clockwise path contains a variety of calligraphic inscriptions. Further along are the three adjoining rooms of the **Hazine**, or Treasury. These rooms are stocked with a splendid array of Imperial wealth – thrones, weapons, and jewelry. There is also a huge collection of precious stones, including the **Spoonmaker's Diamond**, an 86 carat stone found in the ruins of the old Byzantine Palace by a spoon maker, who sold it for a pittance. If that fails to impress, have a look at the emerald that weighs in at almost seven pounds.

Another curiosity is the forearm of St. John the Baptist, a desiccated old piece of bone partially gilt in gold. Creepy. Together with the armory and the holy relics, the treasury highlights the visit to Topkapı. The final room in this court, in the southeast corner, has a collection of imperial robes and clothing.

### The Fourth Court
The deepest interior of Topkapı is not dark and mysterious, rather it is a terraced garden overlooking the sea. Sultans would retire here during the day with chosen friends, relaxing in the pavilions that dot the court. The Sultan's personal physician maintained an office here, in the **Hekimbaşı Odası**, or Physician's Room, and there were various kiosks were built to commemorate military victories.

The lower gardens had their moment of glory during the "Reign of the Tulip" under Ahmet III in the 1720s. More than a frenzy of aesthetics, this was one of the first times the empire looked beyond its borders and acknowledged the value of other western institutions such as the printing press and heavy industry. Tulips, having made their way from Persia to Holland years before, became a concrete expression of the new interest. The Ottoman elite gamely followed their Sultan's lead and pitched themselves headfirst into arts in general and the cultivation of tulips in particular. The gardens were filled with rare and valuable tulips, which would be illuminated at night by turtles bearing candles. Another jewel in the court is the beautifully-tiled **Circumcision Hall**, built by Sultan Ibrahim in the 1640s.

On the east side of the court the **Mecidiye Köskü** is raised up on a marble terrace. This was the last addition to the palace, and its architecture presages the Dolmabahçe Palace built several years later by the same Sultan, Abdül Mecit I. Today this building contains Topkapı's restaurant, Konyalı.

## Archaeological Museum, Ancient Orient Museum, & Çinli Kösk

A single fee ($2) gives entrance to all of the buildings within the museum complex, *Tel. 212 520 7740* – although the Cinli Kösk and the Ancient Orient Museums are often closed in the off season. The entrance is just within and uphill of Gühane tram stop inside the outer Topkapı Palace walls. The entrance is also accessible from Topkapı's First Court, below and behind the Haghia Eirene Church.

Often overlooked because of the vast Archaeological Museum, the entrance to the **Museum of the Ancient Orient** is immediately to the left as you enter, flanked by massive Hittite Lions. The collection here helps clarify the history in Asia Minor. Among its most significant relics is the Treaty of Qadesh, a peace accord between the Hittite King Muwatallis and the Egyptian Pharoah Ramses II dating to the 13th century B.C. It is the oldest known peace agreement. A recreation of the avenue leading to the gates at Babylon is also on hand, an impressive entry to a city that Herodotus reported as having walls the height of a football field (he phrased it differently.)

**The Archaeological Museum** (the columned building stretched along the right side of the court) is the finest museum of antiquities in Turkey, and contains one of the most complete collection of pieces from Asia Minor in the world. Suffice it to say that upon entering the museum you are met by a giant statue of **Beş**, "Half God of Inexhaustible Power and Strength and Protection against Evil." Beş was certainly tough looking, anyway; he was the legendary equivalent of Hercules for natives of the eastern Mediterranean. For most visitors the Archaeological Museum's highlight is the **Alexander Sarcophagus**, so called not because it was Alexander's sarcophagus – an artifact that remains unfound – but because of the elaborate decoration of Alexander's exploits on the exterior. The sarcophagus belonged to Abdalonymous, a King of Sidon in modern Lebanon, who was clearly quite impressed by the young Macedonian conqueror.

The other attractions in the Archaeological Museum are many and extremely varied; curators have collected 50,000 artifacts here over the last century, since ancient people were like absentminded dogs, forever burying things and losing track. The displays are orderly and well-captioned, particularly the new section concerning the history of İstanbul. This section is arranged in chronological order and offers relics from every one of the city's many ages. There is also a full scale reproduction of the Doric temple at Assos and innumerable pieces of jewelry and pottery.

Within the Archaeological Museum is a room devoted to **Hamdi Bey**, the founder of the museum. This remarkable man pioneered Turkish archaeology as it is practiced today. He was the first scientist to study Nemrut Dağı and was responsible for the dig at Sidon that turned up the Alexander Sarcophagus. Colorful stories surround the crusty old archaeologist who so fiercely protected the empire's ancient heritage; worried that the delicate Alexander Sarcophagus would be damaged in transit, Hamdi Bey lashed himself to the massive stone object. The lesson hit home; the sailors obviously transported the sarcophagus with great care.

The **Çinli Köşkü**, housed in the elaborate building opposite the Archaeological Museum, serves today as a museum of tile and ceramics. The building dates back to Mehmet II Fatih, who, like those after him, was prone to retire here during the day. Stories tell of Mehmet II whiling away the time watching princes and pages play a game called cırıt. Participants would gallop around on horses hurling javelins at one another and catching those directed at themselves. And in North America people complain that monkey bars are dangerous.

## Haghia Sophia

The least charitable description of the **Haghia Sophia** must belong to Mark Twain: "The rustiest old barn in heathendom." Most people fall over themselves in search of the proper superlative; the Haghia Sophia has, for 1,500 years, been one of the greatest works of architecture on Earth.

The Haghia Sophia, *Tel. 212 522 1750*, dominates the head of the old city peninsula, a looming jumble of domes and buttresses capped by a broad dome. The Haghia Sophia is the centerpiece of Sultanahmet, with the entrance by the park at the bottom of Divan Yolu Caddesi.

## History

The Haghia Sophia (Divine Wisdom) is the third Christian church built on this site. The first two were remarkably short-lived. The first church was built by the son of Contantine the Great just 30 years after the dedication of Constantinople, but was destroyed by rioting just 44 years later in 404 A.D. The second church was dedicated in 415 A.D., but this building was destroyed in the 532 A.D. Nika Revolt that marred the beginning of Emperor Justinian's reign.

Both of the early Haghia Sophias are reported to have been elegant basilicas and centerpieces of the new Roman capital. They were conventional beauties, however, and the young Justinian had more ambitious plans for rebuilding the church. He set the mathematician Anthemius of Tralles on the task, assisted by another mathematician, Isodorus of Miletus, and the two men conceived a structure that took architecture to new figurative and literal heights. We can only assume the ever-industrious emperor was himself surprised when his designers presented plans for the new Haghia Sophia: 182 feet high, more than 24,000 square feet, with a dome more than 100 feet in diameter. The nave, or open area below the dome, extends 262 feet in length, 100 feet across.

A recitation of the statistics hardly does the Haghia Sophia justice; it was a quantum leap in architecture at the time, not rivaled for a thousand years. Even those grand churches that came later – such as St. Peter's in Rome, one of the three edifices with a greater open area than the Haghia Sophia – are felt to lack the Haghia Sophia's soaring aesthetic inspiration.

For five years Isodorus supervised construction of the church – Anthemius died early in the construction. The design was mathematically sound, but in attempting such an unprecedented engineering feat the devil was in the details: hollow bricks had to be created for the towering dome, artisans from throughout the world had to be collected and persuaded to ornament the interior, great quantities of marble had to be quarried.

The Haghia Sophia was dedicated on December 26, 537, only six years after the former church was destroyed. Guests at that dedication, including Justinian, were awed by both the scale and the beauty of the new church. Justinian is quoted as gloating, *"O Solomon, I have outdone you."* The interior was faced with ornate mosaics, glimmering in the light of thousands of candles. No doubt the pious must have felt their belief in God confirmed, and the less-than-pious must have had some misgivings.

The cathedral had a strong hint of magic about it, but this was temporarily dispelled after earthquakes shook down the dome and the semi-dome above the apse less than 20 years later. Justinian lived to see his church repaired by Isidorus, a nephew of the original designer, and reopened on Christmas Eve 563. Justinian died a year later. For the Byzantines the church remained an inspiration, and Christians traveled from around the world to make a pilgrimage here. Even non-Christians admired the building, and it was to the Haghia Sophia that the Ottomans were bound to come.

Constantinople's citizens had retreated here, "an unmeasurable multitude," according to Michael Ducas. "And shutting the gate they stood there fervently hoping for deliverance by the angel. Then – fighting all about, killing, taking prisoners – the Turks came to the church, when the first hour of the day was not yet flown. And when they found the doors shut, they battered them with axes, without compunction." Forcing their way in, the Ottomans subdued the Greeks, then lashed them together and marched them away. The patriarch, according to legend, chose this moment to vanish into the walls of the Haghia Sophia; he will return either on the Day of Judgment or when İstanbul is returned to the Greeks, depending who you ask.

It was later on the day after the city's fall that Sultan Mehmet II entered Constantinople, riding directly to the Haghia Sophia. The conquering sultan wasted no time, issuing immediate orders that the church be converted to a mosque, and in that hour an imam intoned a Muslim prayer in the great hall. Workers set about soaking up the blood and cleansing and fumigating the Christian edifice that it might be rendered a suitable mosque. In later years the mihrab, mimber, and details such as the two Proconnesean marble water urns were introduced.

The Haghia Sophia was held in high esteem, the foremost mosque in the city until Ottoman-built marvels such as the Süleymaniye and the Sultanahmet Mosques drew admirers of their own. One man who clearly spent substantial time studying this building was the master architect **Sinan**, who drew countless lessons from the structure and helped the Ottomans make a quantum leap in design. Sinan was also among those who performed renovations on the old building, correcting earthquake damage and reinforcing weak areas. The Haghia Sophia's minarets were erected piecemeal beginning with the northeast minaret.

The final chapter in the Haghia Sophia's long history began in 1932, when Kemal Atatürk declared that the mosque would be converted to a museum. Art historians descended on the site, searching for figurative mosaics under the plaster, and discovered many in fine condition. Now, 1,450 years after the Haghia Sophia opened, it continues to dazzle a world grown used to skyscrapers and large-scale projects. That this building

## EMPEROR JUSTINIAN

The **Emperor Justinian** must be considered one of history's most ambitious men. His long reign, 527-565, assured that his empire came into conflict with all of its many neighbors, and Justinian's generals were largely successful in pursuing his policy of restoring the former Roman empire. The emperor carefully sought to balance negotiation with the use of military force, now securing peace with the Persians to conquer the Ostrogoths and Vandals in Africa, now pacifying the Africans to deal with the Goth Totila in the west. All the while, however, enemies in the north preyed on the frontiers, taking advantage of weakness when the Byzantine army was engaged far off. The challenge was colossal, and although Justinian doubled the extent of his lands, he is judged to have ultimately weakened the empire.

The **Haghia Sophia**, Justinian's most enduring legacy, can be viewed as a testament to his visionary excesses. When Justinian came to power, the court historian Procopius reports that his predecessor had a vast reserve – 320,000 pounds of gold. Justinian dug into this reserve early and often, funding his wars (and ransoming an expensive peace with Persia), paying for civil projects such as the Haghia Sophia, the Basilica of St. John in Ephesus – even churches in newly conquered lands such as the Church of St. Vitale in Ravenna – and subsidizing fortifications throughout the empire. Ringed by enemies, Justinian had no choice in this final matter, and outposts were erected along the ever expanding frontiers of Africa, Europe, and Asia. The problem with Justinian's ambitious growth was that the gold reserve and the revenue from new territories fell far short of matching his overwhelming expenses. Justinian's recourse was simple and traditional; he burdened Byzantine citizens with heavy taxes that sapped the wealth and strength of the empire. Procopius, in a secret biography of Justinian, saw the damage the emperor's policies were doing and referred to Justinian as "a demon in human shape."

Justinian's reign ended in 565, with the emperor 83 years old. At his death Byzantium was in full flower, having assumed a shape very similar to the Ottoman Empire at its zenith 1,000 years later, but its decline was already assured. The hold on Byzantium's western lands was tenuous, occasionally accomplished through bribe money, which was, ironically, coming at the expense of the poorly paid Byzantine soldiery. The empire was ripe for collapse, and, sure enough, Italy was overrun within four years of Justinian's death and the newly constructed frontier fortresses throughout Europe were soon in enemy hands.

Worse, Justinian's preoccupation with restoring the classic Roman empire in the west had left Persia to grow ever mightier in the east – helped along by an annual tribute from Byzantium. Surging out of the east, one Persian force captured Jerusalem in 614, pushing on into Egypt, while a second marched through the whole of Asia Minor, encamping opposite Constantinople at Scutari. In the chaos, Mohammed, born five years after Justinian's death, galvanized the Arabs with a new religion that would in time be Constantinople's undoing. In the words of one historian, commenting on post-Justinian Byzantium, "There is perhaps no period of history in which society was so universally in a state of demoralization."

should still be standing is miraculous, given its monumental novelty. The building's designers, Anthemius and Isidorus, must be considered two of the most visionary architects in world history.

## Seeing the Haghia Sophia

You enter the grounds of the Haghia Sophia through a gate to the left of the square, paying at the ticket booth and first passing into a small garden. A smattering of columns and stone ornaments from the church are located here, as is the foundation of the former Haghia Sophia.

The first room you enter is the long, slender exonarthex along the northwest side. This opens into the **narthex**, a broader room where the first of the museum's many mosaics are found. The most famous of these mosaics is directly above the Imperial Gate – formerly said to be carved from the wood of the Ark. Christ's right hand is raised in a common sign, thumb to ring finger, identifying him as an Orthodox Christ offering a blessing: upon the book is written *"Peace upon you, for I am the light of the world."* The prostrate figure at Christ's feet is an probably an emperor named Leo VI (886-912), called "the Wise." Leo's wisdom led him to enact volumes and volumes of laws, one of which condemned the evils of third marriages. Leo, his own wives dying with suspicious rapidity, went on to have third, then fourth marriages. In this hypocrisy Leo was opposed by the Patriarch, who Leo promptly let go.

After a brief investigation of the narthex, you enter the nave, or main chamber, through the Imperial Gate. As you pass through the entrance once reserved for the Emperor and his party the Haghia Sophia opens before you, looming higher and higher. The visitor's first reaction is to the sheer scale of the interior. Architects continue to debate the merits of the world's great holy places, but many continue to maintain that the effect of the Haghia Sophia is still unmatched. The great dome's size is a marvel, achieved only with the help of light, hollow bricks and succeeding in giving the impression that it was hung from heaven by a thread.

The interior is especially striking, architects say, by virtue of the two supporting semi-domes. These partial domes open the space lengthwise (from the Imperial Gate to the apse at the front of the church), and reveal the immense dome to the visitor. Unlike later buildings that hold the dome aloft with massive piers, the designers chose to help distribute the weight with two long rows of columns on the bottom floor, and second rows lining the galleries. The towering series of columns on the lower level curtains the side aisles of the basilica.

The exterior of the Haghia Sophia is imposing, but spare. A quick glimpse at the interior reveals that the starkness ends at the door. Intricately executed stonework is on display throughout the space, marble seamlessly joined and precisely cut. The inverted bowl-shaped column capitals are elaborately carved, many of them with a round seal containing stylized insignias attributed to Justinian and the Empress Theodora. Even without the crusting of jewels and gold stripped by the Crusaders in 1204, even without the glittering mosaics that once covered the entire upper section of the basilica, even without thousands of flickering candles, the Haghia Sophia is beautiful in its detail as well as in its soaring structure.

---

### HAGHIA SOPHIA MOSAICS

*When the Haghia Sophia was originally opened in 537, the interior – including the domes, semidomes, narthex, and galleries – was almost entirely clad in mosaic tile, which, illuminated by thousands of candles, created a darkly golden second sky. Today only a few of the mosaics are visible in the old church, many of them having come to intentional harm.*

*Earthquakes aside, the most terrible damage to the mosaics happened at the hands of the Byzantines themselves. Following an edict by Leo III (717-741), icons were banned throughout the empire, and workers undertook to destroy images of people and animals. This was much deeper than a question of aesthetics: blood was spilled over the issue and it helped spark civil war. The work was undone after the Iconoclast period came to an end (843) and new images were created – all of the figurative images in the church were, therefore, executed after 843. The church returned to its former glory, although the decline of the Byzantine Empire resulted in a concomitant decline in the Byzantines' great church.*

*The arrival of the Ottomans in 1453, then, was something of a blessing. The Ottomans were ill at ease with the icons within the Haghia Sophia, but greatly respected the great building. In accordance with the Muslim prohibition against icons the Ottomans covered the offending images, showing remarkable restraint in light of the damage done by the Christian Iconoclasts. At the same time, the vigor of the new empire meant that the church was given much-needed renovation, much of it by Sinan.*

*Following the conversion of the Haghia Sophia from a mosque to a museum by Kemal Atatürk in 1935, restoration efforts – already under way – accelerated. All of the mosaics visible today have been rediscovered and revealed in this century. Other mosaics, many of them simply of geometric shapes and patterns, remain hidden beneath plaster and paint – you will see parts of mosaic through holes cut in the plaster of the south gallery vaults.*

---

The massive wooden **levhas**, six gold-on-black disks bearing calligraphic writing, were not installed until an 1849 renovation. The six levhas depict the names of Allah and Mohammed, as well as the first four caliphs: Abu Bakir, Omar, Othman, and Ali. An attempt was made to remove these disks after the Haghia Sophia was converted to a museum, but workers found themselves unable to squeeze the levhas through the doors. Unwilling to destroy the disks, the supervisors returned them to their places.

On the floor of the mosque are the other major Ottoman-era additions. The small raised kiosk to the left is the **Sultan's Loge**, an area reserved for the prayers of the sultan alone. This was built by Sultan Ahmet III (1703-1730), he of the tulips and turtles bearing candles. The **mihrab**, the small recessed niche facing Mecca, is located in the apse, squared with the rectangular **mahfili** at angle on the main floor of the nave. This kiosk was built for the muezzin singers. The four minarets outside were raised during the reigns of various sultans, the first soon after Sultan Mehmet II's seizure of the city.

One of the most interesting of the Byzantine features is the circle within a square inlaid on the floor of the nave. This is the oddly asymmetric site of coronations and other signal events involving the imperial personage.

Several of the mosaics in the main chamber are now visible. On the vaulted ceiling of the apse, in the front of the church, is a depiction of Mary and Christ. This image was groundbreaking, accompanied by an inscription heralding the reintroduction of mosaics at the Haghia Sophia after the supporters of icons defeated the iconoclasts in a Byzantine civil war. The Archangel Gabriel flutters to one side, also within the apse, while the Archangel Michael, to the left, is in poor condition.

High atop the nave, on two of the four pedentives – the flat-faced seams below the main dome and in the seams between the semi-domes – are mosaics of angels. To the left of the main floor are three sainted Byzantine bishops, from the apse to the back of the church, Ignatius Theophorous, John Chrysostom, and Ignatius the Younger.

Before leaving the nave, stop at the weeping column near the back of the left aisle. The column's lower section is clad in bronze, and someone will probably have a digit stuck in it. The weeping column continues to draw people seeking fertility and simple good luck.

According to one tale, an angel appeared here during a lull in the construction and ordered a boy to run off and return with his father and fellow workers. The boy scurried away to retrieve the workers, but his father cleverly forbade the boy ever to return to the church. The angel waits there still, benevolently haunting the Haghia Sophia forever. The angel, according to the story, blesses anyone who shoves their thumb in the hole in this column. It isn't necessarily enough, however, just to stick your thumb in the hole; these days it's also fashionable to twist your hand around one way, then the other, so that your fingers make a complete circle around the pivoting thumb. There's usually moisture in this hole, and no wonder, with everyone shoving their sweaty thumbs in there.

## Galleries

Leaving the nave through one of the doors near the weeping column, turn right in the narthex and begin ascending the ramp at the narthex's end. This ramp spirals its uneven way upward to the galleries where the basilica's finest mosaics are located. You emerge in the north gallery, which extends along the left wall to the front of the church.

The galleries were the exclusive preserve of women in some periods, in others they were reserved for the imperial family. On one of the great piers in the north gallery is a mosaic of Alexander (912-913), a man content to while away his time accomplishing nothing at all. This suited his almost lifelong role as brother to the emperor (shades of Billy Carter and Roger Clinton), but became a distinct problem when his brother Leo VI (886-912) died. Alexander's listless and truculent rule created problems that would plague the empire for decades – and he managed this in a single year, after which he toppled from a horse and died. At the end of the north gallery, directly beside the apse at the front of the church, is a screen behind which emperors and ladies would sit.

In the central area of the gallery, at the back of the church above the **Imperial Door**, is a distinctive circle of green marble. This was the seat of the empress Theodora, echoing the circle of her emperor husband on the main floor.

Continuing around to the south gallery you arrive at an ornate stone screen. The purpose of this screen is unknown, but it may have been used to bar access to Church synods. Just beyond the screen in an open area to the right is the best preserved mosaic visible to the public. Christ is shown in the company of an aggrieved St. John the Baptist and Mary. This mosaic, known as the **Deisis**, clearly benefits from perspective lacking in so many Byzantine mosaics, dating it to the 13th century or later. Christ is offering an Orthodox blessing with his hand, and his eyes appear somewhat sad and thoughtful.

No wonder, he looks across the hall to the place where the Doge of Venice, **Henricus Dandalo**, was buried. Dandalo, representing Venice in the Fourth Crusade, was the driving force behind the sack and seizure of Constantinople in 1204. He lived only a single year after taking the city, and chose the Haghia Sophia as his resting place. One story holds that his body remained entombed here until the arrival of the Ottomans in 1453, and that it was the Muslims who opened his tomb and scattered his bones to the dogs; if that is the case then the Deisis was executed with the Venetian's body in place. Perhaps a more likely story is that it was the Greeks who, upon regaining their city in 1261, opened the tomb of the man who had sacked their city, enslaved and killed their people, and looted their church, and perhaps it was the Greeks who scattered his bones to the dogs. This also would cast an interesting light on the Deisis, whose Christ might be demonstrating somber approval. The inscribed lid of Dandalo's tomb has been restored to its former place.

Take a moment to note the mosaics peeking from beneath thick plaster in some sections of the gallery vaults; the ceilings here were formerly covered with mosaic patterns, and some remain covered with plaster. Continuing to the very front of the gallery you arrive at the gallery's final mosaics. To the left, closest to the apse, is a depiction of **Constantine IX** (1042-1055) and **Empress Zoe** (1028-1050). There are conflicting stories about Zoe, but it is clear she led a long and eventful life. Zoe was the heir to Constantine VIII (1025-1028), who had no sons. The elderly Constantine gave his 51 year old daughter to her aristocratic suitor **Romanus III Argyrus** (1028-1034). This was commemorated on the wall of the Haghia Sophia. Unfortunately, Romanus the diligent suitor became Romanus the neglectful husband, and, soon afterward, Romanus became dead in his own bathtub.

Now Zoe elevated her juvenile lover Michael (now Michael IV, 1034-1041) to the throne, fixing his face on the body of Romanus in the Haghia Sophia. Michael proved a competent ruler but, once again, an inattentive husband once he had secured the throne. Zoe was watched and kept at arms length, and she was banished entirely when Michael IV died of illness. Upset with her banishment, the Patriarch joined forces with the aristocracy to depose a new emperor and return the throne to the blood princess, the 65 year old Zoe, together with her younger sister Theodora. Once more a marriage was arranged for Zoe, this time with Constantine IX. Now the mosaic of Romanus was given Constantine's head. Zoe died eight years later.

To the right of this mosaic is another of Mary and Christ, flanked by John II Comnenus (1118-1143) and his wife Eirene. The prince, Alexius, is squeezed into a tight space on the right. Alexius died at a young age, but his father was a capable and intelligent ruler.

Now return through the gallery and down the ramp, appreciating the grandeur of this building. When you decide to leave, exit through the door in the narthex opposite the ramp. This exit was the original entrance to the Haghia Sophia. The small chamber separating the narthex from the outside is adorned with a mosaic of two emperors making an offering to Mary and Christ, one, Justinian, offering the Haghia Sophia, the other, Constantine, offering the city itself. This mosaic was probably done during the reign of the great and ruthless Basil II the Bulgar Slayer (926-1025), and is remarkable because Basil II didn't insist on a mosaic of himself.

Exiting the Haghia Sophia, you enter a small **forecourt** filled with smaller buildings. Five sultans are buried here. Mustafa I and Ibrahim, both known as "the mad," warranted respectable burials but not türbes of their own; they were laid to rest in the former Orthodox baptistry building. This is the first building to the left. Selim II (1566-1574), Murat III (1574-1595) and Mehmet IV (1623-1640) are buried in their own türbe in this section.

---

### MELVILLE ON THE HAGHIA SOPHIA

*Herman Melville visited in 1857, and had this to say:*
*"Saw the Mosque of St. Sophia. Went in. Rascally priests demanding "bakshesh." Fleeced me out of one half dollar; following me round, selling the fallen mosaics. Ascended a kind of horse way leading up, round and round. Came out into a gallery fifty feet above the floor. Superb interior. Precious marbles Porphyry and Verd antique. Immense magnitude of the building. Names of the prophets in great letters. Roman Catholic air to the whole."*

---

## Yerebatan Cistern

The cistern is perfect on a summer afternoon, a cool, dark spot in the midst of Sultanahmet's pandemonium. **Yerebatan Cistern** is located just across the street from the Haghia Sophia, in a low building near the ruined outline of the former **Milion**, or first milepost of Byzantium. *The Yerebatan offices can be reached at Tel. 212 522 1259.*

The cistern dates back to Byzantium, but the current, massive incarnation was built during the reign of Justinian (527-565), incorporating pillars and other artifacts from elsewhere in the empire. A total of 336 pillars support the cistern's towering roof, and wide walkways have been installed that permit you to wander through the vast subterranean space.

The cistern fell into disuse during the Ottoman Empire, and was not discovered again until this century. A curious scholar went in search of a great cistern in the region, and discovered it by lowering himself through a hole in the basement of a local residence. The cistern was, predictably, a shambles, but its four meter-thick walls continued to be waterproof. No one knew just how far the subterranean waterways went, and there was a great air of mystery about the structure until its rehabilitation in the 1980s. Herman Melville, visiting in the mid-1800s, noted the eerie, dark interior and commented that it would be a "terrible place to be robbed or murdered in." Finally cleared out and opened, the cistern is an inspiring sight – note that a section of about 50 columns remains walled off. Chamber music is piped in, and there is a small cafe. Keep your eyes peeled for fish in the shallow water.

Midway through the cistern is a weeping column, very much like the weeping column in the Haghia Sophia. As at the Haghia Sophia, you can insert your thumb into the wishing hole on the column and twist your hand around one way, then the other in a complete circle to make a wish. Some people, skeptical of this, just chuck coins in the water nearby. The Medusa heads at the very rear of the cistern are a mystery. They may have come from anywhere – Justinian's engineers were great recyclers, particularly of Chalcedonian material from across the Bosphorous. Why they were used as column bases, one upside down, the other sideways, deep in the recesses of a cistern is anyone's guess. You can still see the snake-hair on one of the Medusa's heads.

Finally, according to rumors, a few people once knew the devious subterranean routes into Topkapi Saray, using the Cistern as their entrance. Among the business conducted were rare, and presumably dangerous, abductions from the Seraglio.

Admission to the cistern costs $1.50. The Yerebatan Cistern is located at the intersection of Yerebatan Caddesi and Divan Yolu, next to the tram line and across the street from the Haghia Sophia. There is another, less frequently visited cistern near the Ibrahim Paşa Palace.

## The Hippodrome

Don't come to İstanbul hoping to see the **Hippodrome**; all that remains is the ground the Hippodrome once stood on. The Hippodrome today is a grassy park immediately in front of the Blue Mosque, but at one time it was a stadium holding almost 100,000 people for large sporting events and celebrations.

The building was erected by the Roman Emperor Septimius Severus (193-211) in the process of rebuilding the city that he had earlier razed to the ground during a military campaign. The most popular past-time here was chariot racing, and the old chariot course is still identifiable by the monuments that stood in its center. The city was desperately fanatical about the teams that raced at the Hippodrome, and over time team allegiance came to have strong political and social overtones.

The most vivid example was the Nika Revolt of 532, when the Greens – named for the livery of their charioteers – rioted against the policies of Emperor Justinian, himself a Blue. The rioters destroyed the Haghia Sophia and forced Justinian to consider fleeing, but in the end he stood firm at the behest of his wife Theodora. Justinian loosed his general Belisarius, who managed to hem the rioters into, appropriately, the Hippodrome. There the Byzantine army massacred as many as 30,000 people, ending the revolt.

All that remains of the grand stadium are the centerpieces. The stadium suffered through repeated fires, earthquakes, and even, it is reported, a hurricane, to which the indignity of the Crusader's looting was added in 1204 – the **Quadriga**, a statue of four horses that stood atop St. Mark's Cathedral in Venice until they were taken down for preservation in 1995, was stolen from here by the Crusaders. Although the Hippodrome survived into the Ottoman period, it had fallen into ruin. The collapsing edifice was finally closed and mined for stone, much of which was used in the construction of the Blue Mosque next door.

As you enter the open Hippodrome area from the direction of the tourism information booth and the Haghia Sophia, you arrive first at the peculiar **Fountain of Kaiser Wilhelm II**. Suffice it to say this wasn't a fixture of ancient Byzantium; it was introduced by the German Kaiser in the late 1800s as part of his campaign to promote German/Turkish unity and, more specifically, a German-built rail line through the Ottoman Empire to the Red Sea. This Hejaz Railway was completed in 1909 and destroyed piecemeal to great effect by the British agent T.E. Lawrence during World War I. Wilhelm was lodged in his two state visits, 1892 and 1901, at an early palace at Yıldız.

The fountain's location corresponds to the former northern end of the Hippodrome, which ran lengthwise around the current grassy arcade. The **Obelisk** is the next monument along this line. The Obelisk is the oldest object in this ancient city, dating to the reign of Thutmose III in the 16th century B.C. The Obelisk remains in good condition, its hieroglyphs remarkably well preserved after 3,500 years of weathering. Thutmose III originally erected this obelisk at the temple of Karnak in present-day Luxor. The hieroglyphic reliefs depict the pharoah making offerings to the god Amon-Ra in thanks for a great victory in Syria and Mesopotamia.

What you see now is only the tip of the original obelisk, one which measured nearly 200 feet high. Even the erection of this modest section, a mere third of the original's size, posed a unique engineering problem almost 2,000 years later when it was shipped down the Nile and across to Constantinople. Finally, under Theodosius the Great (379-395) it was raised and set on the marble blocks you see today. These blocks depict Theodosius accepting tribute from the provinces, enjoying the races, congratulating the victor, and, ahem, helping erect the obelisk. The most interesting reliefs are those lower down, demonstrating how the Byzantines set about raising the great stone. Later obelisk thievery from the Luxor area has contributed to the decoration of Washington, D.C., Paris, and London.

Next along the former racecourse is the **Serpent Column**, a trophy from the great Greek victory at Plataea in 479 B.C. The battle was fought between the united Greeks and the army of Xerxes, whose gigantic army had set out from Persia, crossed bridges at the Dardanelles, and continued by land to Greece in 480 B.C. The vast Persian army – which numbered somewhat less than Herodotus' ridiculous estimate of 5 million – had plowed through Greek resistance to sack and occupy Athens.

Their only setbacks had been at sea, and there was an air of invincibility to their land army until the Greeks met them at Plataea in the second year of the occupation. The battle turned into a rout, and the Persians were forced into a panicked 1,000 mile withdrawal towards friendly territory.

The Greek trophy names the 31 cities that contributed soldiers to the battle, and was crafted from the shields of fallen Persian soldiers. The trophy originally stood at the Oracle of Delphi – which correctly prophesied Greek victory and, Herodotus reports, defended itself from sack by the Persians with lightning bolts and a hail of boulders. Constantine the Great (324-337) ran afoul of none of this, evidently, when he removed the trophy from the Oracle site and transported it to his new capital city. Perhaps some Oracular revenge was visited on the unknown vandal – historians suspect a drunken Polish diplomat – who sawed off the three snake heads in the 1700s, one of which was found a century later and placed in the İstanbul Archaeological Museum.

The final monument is the bedraggled-looking 100-foot **Colossus**. This monument was old and rickety when it was sheathed in bronze by the Byzantine Emperor Constantine VII Porphyrogenitus (913-959), but it seems to lack the pedigree of its fellows. It dates to, at the earliest, Constantine the Great's reign. Nowadays the bronze is gone again, and the Colossus' old bones are looking their age.

## The Turkish and Islamic Arts Museum

Across the Hippodrome from the Blue Mosque is the **Palace of Ibrahim Paşa,** *Meydanı No. 46, Tel. 212 518 1385.* The palace was built for one of Süleyman the Magnificent's Grand Viziers at the height of the Ottoman Empire's power. Ibrahim came to power in 1523, one year before completion of his ambitious residence, and proved an able and intelligent adviser to Süleyman, his most trusted confidante and a brilliant general in the field. The friendship between the two men was deep, and remained so through most of Ibrahim's thirteen year term.

In the end, Süleyman was turned against Ibrahim – as he was later turned against two of his own sons – by intrigue within the palace, particularly from his jealous favorite within the harem, Haseki Hurrem, or Roxelana. After a private dinner Ibrahim was strangled and buried in an unmarked grave, his estates and belongings confiscated by the throne. The palace, considered the grandest private residence in İstanbul, was converted to a Janissary dormitory.

The palace is now converted into the **Turkish and Islamic Arts Museum**, open from 10:00 a.m. to 5 p.m. and, like most places in the area, closed Mondays. The museum has a large collection of religious art, including engravings, tiles, and calligraphy, all of which is introduced by a video that runs through basic Turkish history. The lower floor is recommended for carpet/kilim shoppers; there, in the presence of old looms, you can learn the basics about dyes, fabrics, and styles – a much more relaxed place to learn than in a Sultanahmet carpet shop. The traditional Turkish coffee house on the premises offers caffeinated help if you're unravelling under the strain of jet-lag.

To the north of the museum, three blocks in from Divan Yolu Caddesi on Klodfarer Caddesi, is the **Binbirdirek Cistern**, akin to the Yerebatan Cistern near the Haghia Sophia – ask for directions on your way toward Divan Yolu Caddesi. Binbirdirek ("Thousand and One Columns") is an immense, dry cistern, with a few less columns than advertised.

## The Blue Mosque

The **Blue Mosque**, as **Sultan Ahmet Cami** is known, is probably the most striking monument in İstanbul. Unlike the Haghia Sophia, with its austere and functional exterior, and the city's other mosques, most of which have been enveloped by the city, the Blue Mosque still commands the eye with its beauty and its open location.

The Blue Mosque is best approached from the Hippodrome and entered through the front gate opposite the Turkish and Islamic Arts Museum. This approach allows you to appreciate the heap of smaller domes ascending toward the great dome high above, and will almost yank the camera from around your neck and shoot the pictures for you. You enter through the spacious courtyard, which stands beneath what was once the eastern end of the Hippodrome, and approach the main doors (in the heavy tourist season you may be directed to the left side of the mosque, facing the Haghia Sophia, and enter there).

The Blue Mosque was one of the only true interests of its namesake, Sultan Ahmet I (1603-1617). Ahmet declined to go to war in Asia, sat by while palace intrigue blossomed, and allowed the Ottoman military to decay, but the young lad found plenty of time to lend his frail help at the building site. Beyond his enthusiasm for this beautiful mosque, Ahmet resolutely failed to distinguish himself in any way as a sultan. He died curiously young, at 27.

The Blue Mosque, designed by Davut Aga, was the first in the world outside of Mecca to have six minarets. This design drew condemnation from around the Muslim world until Davut Bey offered to construct a seventh minaret at Mecca. The Blue Mosque, so named for the colors in the interior tiles, not Hippodrome allegiance, stood on par with the Haghia Sophia in Ottoman esteem, and sultans would often bypass the Haghia Sophia to worship at the Sultan Ahmet Cami. It was from here that the dissolution of the Janissary corps was announced in the summer of 1826 by a fatwa, an edict of the caliph.

The interior of the mosque is intricate, light, and pretty. The four massive columns supporting the dome replace the forest of smaller columns in the Haghia Sophia, opening up the interior in the manner popularized by Sinan in the Süleymaniye in İstanbul and the Selimiye in Edirne. The lower sections of the mosque are faced with Iznik tiles from the 16th century, at the peak – and end – of the Iznik workshops' brief heyday. The mimber (the slender, staired pulpit) and mihrab (the niche facing Mecca) are carved from Proconnesean Marble, quarried from an island in the Sea of Marmara.

The stonework is exacting and beautiful, although of a less precise sort than that found in the Haghia Sophia. The interior, too, is lighter, freer and less ... Catholic than the Haghia Sophia. Visitors often prefer the Sultan Ahmet Cami to its moody, ancient cousin, but the Haghia Sophia is a work of greater inspiration and genius. On the other hand, the Blue Mosque is free.

## Mosaic Museum

The Byzantine Royal Palace once stood on the hill now crested by the Blue Mosque, the palace grounds sprawling toward the Haghia Sophia and down toward the sea. Many of the exposed walls and foundations in this vicinity were once part of the palace, but the only significant evidence of the ancient structures are the mosaics in this museum.

Signs direct you to the **Mosaic Museum**, *Tel. 212 518 1205*, downhill of and behind the Blue Mosque on the Haghia Sophia side. You enter through a small court of shops attached to the rear of the Blue Mosque. The museum has become a storehouse for Byzantine oddments that have been unearthed in recent years, but the highlight continues to be the fine mosaic work. The mosaics here are in a remarkable state of preservation, insulated from abuse for centuries by marble flagstones, then by heaps of rubble and new construction. The subjects of the in-situ mosaics are well-executed hunters and their prey, thought to date to the fifth century. The path covered in these mosaics would have led, fittingly, to the Imperial box, or **kathisma**, in the Hippodrome where actual hunters and prey often provided entertainment. Those venturing south toward Olympos and the Chimaera should keep their eyes peeled for a Chimaera mosaic, although we have only managed to locate one of the later adventures of Bellerophon and the flying horse, wherein our hero soars toward Olympos' heights and, like Icarus, pays for his hubris.

The Byzantine Palace on this site was a spacious, gardened pavilion similar to Topkapı Palace. The palace suited Constantinople, for 900 years the world's great city. In 1203 it was described thus: *"All those who had never seen Constantinople before gazed very intently at the city, having never imagined there to be so fine a place in all the world. They noted the high walls and lofty towers encircling it, and its rich palaces and tall churches, of which there were so many that no one would have believed it to be true if he had not seen it with his own eyes,"* wrote Geoffrey Villehardouin, one of the leaders of the Fourth Crusade who was shortly to burn, sack, and loot the city. In the aftermath of the Crusader's victory the palace was badly damaged, and after returning to the city in 1261 its Greek rulers settled in the Palace of Blachernae by the land walls, leaving the Great Palace to decay.

## Near Sultanahmet

The Grand Bazaar is just up Divan Yolu Caddesi (the road with the tramway) from Sultanahmet, then down to the right. Divan Yolu was the main avenue of Constantinople, and some of its former decorations still stand. Conspicuous among them are the **Column of Constantine**, now called Çemberlitaş, or the banded column, because of the iron bands that help hold it erect. The column is near the upper entrances to the bazaar.

The **Beyazid Fire Tower** is another distinctive landmark atop the hill, a tall, thick tower ringed with windows. This is part of the Beyazid II complex, and was just what it claims to be, a fire lookout.

## The Süleymaniye

The **Süleymaniye** is one of the greatest works of artistry and engineering in the Ottoman Empire. You will not see a better mosque anywhere in Turkey except Edirne: you should find the time for a visit.

The Süleymaniye dominates the skyline on the hill above Galata Bridge. You can approach from this side or from the Grand Bazaar. Either way it is a short walk uphill, but a twisting one – you'll probably need to ask directions (*"Süleymaniye Camii nerede?"*).

### Visiting the Süleymaniye

The Süleymaniye is a fitting monument for the man who guided the Ottoman Empire to its greatest conquests and its largest extent. **Süleyman** the Magnificent was loved by his soldiers and his people. "The Magnificent," oddly, is an appelation bestowed on him by the western countries that bore the brunt of his military power. At home he was known as "The Lawgiver," and considered a just and intelligent ruler.

Under Süleyman, the Ottomans cleared the Knights of St. John from Rhodes and cleared the eastern Mediteranean, while on land he led conquests in the east and the west. Süleyman was a contemporary of Charlemagne, but the natural rivalry between the two was never settled in battle; Charlemagne carefully avoided challenging the Ottomans in the field, where no major battle with the west had ever gone against them. The Ottomans were the scourge of the world.

And while Süleyman prosecuted wars abroad and established laws at home, his master architect, Sinan, began a fitting tribute. Sinan, with dozens of mosques already to his credit and a skilled corps of stone carvers, began work on the Süleymaniye atop the Saray Burnu's highest hill, and he was determined that it should be suitable for the ruler of the age.

One famous (possibly anecdotal) story of Sinan's exacting attention is telling: once during construction of the Süleymaniye one of Sultan Süleyman's retainers rushed back to the palace with some disturbing news: the Sultan's master architect was smoking in the partially completed mosque. Süleyman, furious, went to the building site to see for himself. Sure enough, there was the architect Sinan, calmly smoking a water pipe in the very center of the mosque. Süleyman stormed over and demanded an explanation. The old architect pointed to the dome high above, and showed the Sultan how, based on the echo of the water pipe, he was directing workmen to adjust stones in the ceiling. He was making the minute adjustments necessary for perfect acoustics, an effort that, however unorthadox, worked marvelously well. The acoustics in the Süleymaniye remain among the best in the world.

The Süleymaniye is hailed as Sinan's greatest work in İstanbul, second only to the Selimiye in Edirne. The interior is vast and fascinating, more so the closer you look. If you have visited the Haghia Sophia and the Blue Mosque, you have witnessed two very different approaches to holding aloft the great dome. This is a third. The Muslim religious ceremony dictated alterations to a great building from the Christian Haghia Sophia. In place of a long main chamber flanked by aisles, the Süleymaniye has an open central area. To achieve this Sinan rested the dome on great buttresses, then joined these to the exterior walls with galleries. This de-emphasizes the central piers so dominant in the Sultan Ahmet (Blue) Mosque and opens up the side "aisle" areas.

When you tire of admiring the structure, focus on the tiles in the interior. These are Iznik tiles of the best era. If you're interested in how

**HAGHIA SOPHIA**

tiles should look and how they ordinarily do look compare a tile – a trivet, say – from the Grand Bazaar to what you see here. The Iznik blues are deep, the whites have a milky quality, and the reds are sharp and precise. After leaving the interior return to the opposite side, site of the **türbe of Süleyman** and his favorite wife, Haseki Hürrem or Roxelana. Süleyman's love for Roxelana is legend, and she is held responsible for the decline of the empire. Süleyman's eldest son, the promising, intelligent Mehmet, died naturally in 1543, deeply aggrieving Süleyman. Next in the succession was Mustafa, and he, too developed into a strong leader and a favorite among the Janissaries.

Enter Roxelana, who had already convinced Süleyman to kill İbrahim Paşa; now, wanting her own son Selim to assume the throne she slowly preyed on her husband's pride and fear, convincing him that Mustafa was planning his downfall. Süleyman ordered his son killed, clearing the way for Selim to become the next sultan. Selim was a poor sultan, and the father of poorer ones. Selim's reign marks the beginning of the empire's long decline.

If you're interested in a meal, you're in luck. The **Darüzziyafe restaurant**, one of İstanbul's classic dining spots, is part of the mosque complex. From the türbe go back past the visitors entrance to the mosque and out the far gate, crossing a narrow street to the former soup kitchen.

## Along The Theodosian Land Walls
### What Goes Up ...

The original walls of Byzantium have long since disappeared. Any remnants of those walls that were not scattered in the ferocious sack of the city by Septimius Severus in 196 AD were carted off and reused by the selfsame Severus' labor force in the construction of new, greater walls. These walls were dismantled and rebuilt further to the west as part of Constantine the Great's great vision for the city in 325-330. The new walls probably enclosed an area from the Atatürk Bridge, through Fatih, and down to the Marmara, but they didn't last long, either.

In 413, shaken by the news that Rome had fallen to Alaric's Goths (Alaric was, ironically, a former Roman general), Theodosius II's engineers and laborers set about reinforcing the city's land defenses, pushing the cordon of walls out to its current location. This wall was badly damaged in 447 by an earthquake – more than half of the defensive towers fell – but workers immediately set to work rebuilding those walls under Theodosius II, who was still ruling. The rebuilding project took on a decidedly animated aspect as Atilla the Hun approached. Two months after work began, Constantinople was again protected by its 40-foot tall main wall, now surrounded by a second 27 foot wall with 96 towers of its own. Finally, in a burst of Atilla-inspired energy, workers added a deep

## THE CRUSADES

The First Crusade was conceived to wrest back Jerusalem from the Muslims, but from the earliest moments it was a headache for the Byzantines. Most of the Crusaders were crude and vicious even by the low standard of the day, leading undisciplined marches through Byzantine lands. Still, when the main Crusader armies set out in 1097 it offered the Byzantine Empire a great opportunity. The Crusaders swept through Asia Minor, rolling up the Selçuk outposts and ceding them to the Byzantine Empire, continuing on to capture Jerusalem in 1099. On balance the First Crusade helped the Byzantines, leaving them with western Asia Minor. The Second Crusade (1146) was a total failure, highlighted by the Crusader's swath of pillage through Byzantine territories en route to being slaughtered by the Turks on the frontier of the Sultanate of Rum. The Third Crusade (1189) came on the heels of two great Byzantine setbacks, one at the hands of the Selçuks at Myriokephalon (1176), and another in which the invading Normans viciously sacked the Byzantine Empire's "second city," Thessalonika. The Third Crusade itself threatened Constantinople before continuing south, where Richard the Lionhearted failed to retake Jerusalem.

Byzantine blood was in the water. The Fourth Crusade (1203) maintained the pretense of Holy War against the infidel, but from its inception the Venetian leadership viewed it as an opportunity to crush their merchant rival in Byzantium, which after some time they did. Through the darkest of the dark ages, Constantinople had burned brightly as a repository of culture and history. For almost 900 years Constantinople held out against its enemies, enduring more than 20 sieges and serving as the eastern buttress of the Christian faith. Now the city was looted and burned by fellow Christians. "So much booty had never been gained in any city since the creation of the world," boasts Geoffrey de Villehardouin, a chronicler and leader of the Crusade, not realizing how ironically tragic his words would one day sound.

moat outside and below the outer walls, topped by yet another defensive wall. The flurry of activity was a success; Atilla didn't waste his time, taking his rampage elsewhere.

### ... Must Come Down

The walls held for another century, then another, then another. The Persians, Arabs, Saracens, Huns and Avars could seize the Byzantine Empire's land and defeat its armies, but they were always stopped short at the walls of Constantinople itself. Treasure, icons, statues and holy relics accumulated in the Imperial capital during this aberrantly-long period of stability, and by the second millennium Constantinople had the greatest concentration of artifacts in the world.

Finally, however, the walls failed on July 17, 1203, and not to the ravages of pagan hordes or Muslim armies but to the caprice of the fellow Christians of the **Fourth Crusade**. Like all Crusades, it had been headed for the Holy Land, but became distracted by Constantinople's wealth and marched on the city with help from a sizeable Venetian fleet. The first successful siege forced the flight of Emperor Alexius III with part of the imperial treasure and left the city in the hands of a Byzantine puppet government. The people of the city revolted, assassinated the puppet leaders, and again shut the gates of the city against the Crusaders. On April 13, 1204, the Crusaders broke through the walls once again, this time ravaging and looting the city.

The wealth was scattered throughout Europe, with Venice benefiting most conspicuously, and the Latin government installed in Constantinople proceeded to sell off or give away much of the remaining art and treasure.

Constantinople fell back to the Byzantines in 1261, when Alexius Strategopoulus, commander of the revived Byzantine military, happened by and found the walls to the city unmanned and the Venetian fleet off fighting in the Black Sea. Strategopoulus was quite unprepared for this but quickly amassed his forces, wrestled a few guards at the Silivri Gate out of the way, and wandered into the city. This delighted Constantinople's mostly Orthodox residents, who were not fond of the Crusaders' Latin rulers.

The restored Byzantine empire was doomed to undergo repeated sieges, culminating at last in the great siege of 1453. Ottoman Sultan Mehmet II put a stranglehold on the city, cutting it off by sea, then besieged it by land. Massive siege cannons pounded the walls until, on May 29, the defenders were overwhelmed and the city fell for the final time. The Byzantine Empire fell with it, but after the obligatory three days of rampage Sultan Mehmet set his immense energies to revitalizing the city. Constantinople was made the capital of the Ottoman Empire, under whom the walls were rebuilt and the treasury refilled. The city's glory was dramatically renewed as the Ottoman Empire grew to match or exceed the Byzantine Empire at its height.

## Visiting the Walls - From the Marmara

The land walls, originally erected in 413, still stand – they were maintained as part of the city defenses until the late 1800s. Although they are decidedly run down in places, and punctured by railways and highways in others, the five-mile long walls are an impressive reminder of the city's power. You see the section of wall along the **Sea of Marmara** upon arrival. This part of the ancient fortifications, now pierced by John F. Kennedy Caddesi, is where a tour of the walls should begin.

Where the wall once met the sea there are the landlocked remains of a 100 foot-tall tower. Its marble-faced lower walls are hardly characteristic of the sturdy stonework elsewhere, and historians speculate that this may have been part of a small waterfront palace. Today the great tower is surrounded by the miles-long waterfront park built on filled land along the Sea of Marmara, and the tower itself is the backdrop to an apparently bankrupt outdoor theater.

The sea walls that ran in a circuit around the tip of the peninsula are missing from this section, have been destroyed by sea erosion and building material scavengers. The Marble Tower's southern wall is decorated with, of all things, Metallica and Slayer graffiti.

## Yedikule

The six lanes of John F. Kennedy Caddesi have flattened the wall directly beside the marble tower. On the far side of the highway the walls gradually ascend toward **Yedikule** (Seven Towers), a fortress built at this key corner of the city defenses. To reach Yedikule from the sea, pass inside the walls and cross the bridge over the railroad tracks. That road takes you to the Yedikule entrance, where admission is $1. If arriving by train from Sirkeci, follow the signs toward Yedikule, 700 feet beyond the railway station.

The Seven Towers fortress is built around the **Golden Gate**. The Golden Gate is the oldest point in the five mile circuit, a triumphal arch built by Theodosius I to commemorate a victory over the Visigoths who had defeated and slain the previous emperor, Valens. The arch was gilded and decorated with sculpture, and Theodosius II's architects were so fond of it that they chose to incorporate the arch into their defensive wall. It was a Byzantine tradition for victorious armies to return through the Golden Gate, but by the time the Ottomans took the city the gilding had long since vanished, and the arch was bricked up.

Soon after seizing the city, Mehmet the Conqueror ordered that a fortress be built on the spot, the headaches and concerns of a siege still fresh in his mind. A walled garrison within the main city walls – particularly one that could command access to the Sea of Marmara – would pose a problem for invaders even after breaking through the outer defenses. Fatih's industrious foresight was never tested, however. Yedikule housed an Ottoman garrison, but from the moment that Constantinople was taken, the Ottoman Empire's frontiers were hundreds of miles away. Defense of the walls became irrelevant.

In lieu of real martial action, the fortress became a treasury and a prison. The three interior towers – the largest of the seven towers that give Yedikule its name – housed an arsenal, a prison, and a treasury. The wooden innards of these towers are gone, rotted and burned away. All that remains are dark stone staircases that wind their way up to the top of the walls, and thence to the top of the towers themselves. Bring a flashlight, both as a means of finding your way up the dark stairways and of locating prisoners' sad scrawls in the stones of the prison tower.

## CAUTION ALONG THE WALLS

*There are paths or small roads along the entire length of the walls, although İstanbul's expansion has long since spilled outside the walls to the west. The simple, sensible way to hike along the walls is to stick to the outside, where one of İstanbul's main arterial roads skirts the moat and the walls along their entire length. More difficult – and unnerving – are the paths along the inside and top of the walls and between the inner and outer sections. In many places, houses and warehouses abut the land walls, and, indeed, the arched recesses of the land walls are a temporary dwelling for some of İstanbul's poorer inhabitants.*

*The walls are not a tourist attraction, as such, and litter is strewn around their base along infrequently visited sections. Much of the area between the inner and outer walls has been cultivated, and is teeming with begging children and snarling dogs. Finally, climbing atop many of the walls' most inviting sections requires dexterity and a good head for heights. Despite this litany of criticism – and because of it – we find a long walk along the walls an interesting diversion and an excellent way to get acquainted with real life in İstanbul. You can always hop in a dolmuş or cab traveling north (Edirnekapı, Defterdar) or south (Yedikule) if you're tired, or end your trek at Topkapı, midway along, and take the tram directly back to Sultanahmet.*

The **prison tower**, also called the Inscriptions tower, has several stones bearing Greek inscriptions at its base. Rumors tell of a pit in the floor that was open to the sea, into which refuse, and severed human heads, were once dumped. That is the good news: Ottoman executioners here are said to have employed execution by compression of the testicles, as in the case of the deposed Sultan Osman II – although others report he died, mercifully, by common strangulation.

Inside the keep there are the ruins of several old buildings, including the telltale minaret of the former mosque, as well as some of the massive cannonballs used by Fatih Sultan Mehmet II in his assault on the city. The centerpiece of Yedikule is the Golden Gate. Even denuded of the statuary and gilding that once covered it, the Golden Gate is a beautiful triple arcade. The marble-clad pylons to either side of the Golden Gate once had the hurly-burly of torture chambers and execution places, but these are rarely – if ever – on display anymore.

To reach the outer sections of the Golden Gate, follow the road around to the left after exiting Yedikule. After passing through the walls double back toward the sea along the outside. After entering a small portal you find yourself in the forecourt of the Golden Gate, a far more impressive site from the outside than the inside. This secluded, lush spot is excellent for a rest before moving on along the walls.

## From Yedikule

The walls north of the Seven Towers are in good condition for a long stretch. Note the inscriptions atop two of the towers between the Seven Towers and the Belgrade Gate. They denote repairs made in the eighth and fifteenth centuries. The latter repairs were undertaken by John VIII Palaeologus just twenty years before the attack by Mehmet Fatih.

There is little to see at **Belgrade Gate** aside from a cannonball from Fatih's great siege cannon. Beyond the large Belgrade Gate, so named because of the natives of that town forcibly resettled here by Süleyman the Magnificent, the walls continue in good condition as far as the **Silver Gate** (Silivri Kapı). Several towers along this stretch bear inscriptions of the Byzantine Emperors who performed repairs to the land walls. The Latin Crusaders' brief rule of Constantinople ended in the summer of 1261 when the Byzantine commander Alexius Strategopoulos happened by and found the gate undefended and the Latin fleet away. He led a small force through the gate and began a popular uprising that drove the Latins out. Just inside the gate is the **Hadım Ibrahim Paşa Mosque** (1551), one of the prolific Sinan's works. It is named for one of Süleyman the Magnificent's outstanding Grand Viziers.

We strongly recommend taking a side trip one quarter mile outside the double-gated Silivri Kapı to **Our Lady of the Life Giving Spring**. This church dates back only to 1833, the latest in a string of churches that has been located by a small nearby shrine. The church and the shrine are both within a compound surrounded by – and paved with – tombstones. Inhabitants of the city have always buried their dead outside the city walls, and that custom has created a long ribbon of cemeteries from the Golden Horn to the Marmara.

To reach the church, take the left road after exiting the Silivri Kapı gate, then take the right fork (Balıklı Sivrikapı Yolu) up a small rise to the church entrance on the left. (open daily, closed during erratic lunch hours).

The shrine was founded after travelers had a vision of the Virgin Mary at the site in Byzantine times. The church, straight ahead as you enter the outer compound, is frequented by Greek travelers and residents and is lovingly decorated with engravings, woodwork, and dark, moody icons framed in silver. The **spring** (ayazma) is down a short flight of steps to the right of the inner church entrance, behind a sign written in Greek.

The waters of the spring are said to have curative, restorative properties, and even the goldfish that swim in the small, covered pool have been incorporated into the legend of the sacred spring, and are supposed to have supernatural fish powers of their own; they don't seem too extradordinary. Penitents wash themselves carefully in the marble basin, and you're welcome to treat yourself to holy water as well. There are even small containers of water available "to go," for which you can leave a donation.

The next most interesting part of the church is a nondescript square panel high on the wall to your right as you arrive at the bottom of the first flight of stairs leading to the spring/shrine. This hatch, opening into the shrine, is reported to be much more than it appears. During the heyday of the Byzantine Empire there was, some say, a tunnel from Sultanahmet, near the Haghia Sophia, directly to the sacred spring, arriving at this very spot. This astounding tunnel would have been almost five miles from end to end, a secret route used only by the Emperors and other VIPs in times of trouble. It's an absurd theory, and for all we know it might even be true.

Whether you buy into any of the tales surrounding Our Lady of the Life Giving Spring, it makes an excellent goal or rest stop as you walk along the walls. After returning to the walls, we recommend continuing along the outside as far as the huge gate at Topkapı. The most notable feature along the next stretch is the walled up **Third Military Gate**, once ornamented with a statue of the Emperor responsible for the walls, Theodosius II. The statue was spirited away in the years before the Ottoman conquest, probably peddled for cash like so much of Constantinople's artwork in those final, desperate years. The section ends at the **Mevlana Gate**. The current name refers to the founder of the Dervish order, and is so named for a dervish tekke (a monastery or holy place) that was once located in the area. In Byzantine times the gate was known as the Gate of the Reds, taking its name from the Hippodrome faction that supervised work on this section. The gate is heavily inscribed, with great proclamations about the strength of Constantinople.

From Mevlana Kapi continue along the outside of the walls – the inner route drives you away from the walls. Just before reaching the massive reconditioned walls pierced with Millet Caddesi there is a partially buried smaller gate set into the main wall. If you scramble up between the two walls you'll find an inscription on the lintel seeking divine protection from invaders. A small pile of cannon balls just outside the old gate is testimony to the failure of the Greek prayers. If you climb over the lintel you can duck down through a gap in the wall to the left and emerge on the inside of the walls.

## Edirnekapi

Just beyond this is the completely modern gate knocked through the walls for Millet Caddesi, the road down which the city's tram travels. İstanbul has pursued an aggressive beautification program in this region, rebuilding the walls and clearing out parks. A little further along, the wall is pierced at Topkapı Gate by Millet Caddesi. **Topkapı**, or **Cannon Gate**, is named for Sultan Mehmet II's siege cannon Orban, which was place just outside the walls at this point.

When Mehmet the Conqueror's army laid siege to the city in 1453, the sultan encamped near this central gate, joined by his pride and joy Orban the siege cannon. Orban joined the rest of the sultan's unprecedented artillery – Orban's cannon balls weighed 270 pounds apiece – in raining destruction on this section of walls, particularly the section in the valley to the north. To get an idea of just how impressive Orban was, have a look at the specially wrought cannon balls inside the Topkapı Gate. Still, the defenders under cunning Genoese general Giustiniani were able to repeatedly repair the breaches and fight off waves of Ottoman troops.

Continuing north down into the valley you see the disadvantages of this low section of wall, called the **Mesoteichion** (low wall). The last Byzantine Emperor made his final stand in this valley, fighting near the small military gate north of **Vatan Caddesi** (see sidebar below). At Edirnekapı, cut inside the gate and visit the **Mihrimah Camii**, directly within the entrance. This mosque stands at the highest point along the walls, and was designed by Sinan for Mihrimah, a daughter of Süleyman. **Edirnekapı**, the Edirne Gate (see sidebar on the next page, *The Last Emperor*), was long the major entrance to the city, and Mihrimah rises above the walls here like a talisman. This mosque is admired as one of Sinan's masterpieces. The türbe on the mosque grounds, by the way, isn't Mihrimah's; she's buried near her father at the Süleymaniye.

Also in this area is one of the greatest Byzantine historical sites, the **Church of St. Savior at Chora/Kariye Camii**, *Tel. 212 631 9241*. This church is located two blocks within the city walls, and if you wind along the inside of the walls you will either find it or Kariye Camii Sokak, which leads you away from the walls and directly to the church.

## THE LAST EMPEROR

*Edirnekapı was the place the Ottomans finally wrested from the defenders of Constantinople. The way was cleared by a simple mistake – some of the defenders neglected to close a small postern gate to the north (near the end of the main walls). Janissaries poured through, and were soon atop the walls, fighting their way toward Edirnekapı. After seizing the gate and controlling this section of the walls, Sultan Mehmet II and what remained of his 250,000 troops entered the city. The defenders were driven to their ships or killed where they fought.*

*There are as many contradictory stories about the fate of Constantine XI, the last Byzantine Emperor, as there are about Elvis. The standard story is that he fought valiantly even as the walls were overrun, and, realizing that the city had fallen, tore away his insignia and sought his own anonymous death in battle. Afterwards, his body was discovered by those loyal to him and they buried him secretly at one of the nearby churches. Character witnesses seem to accept this account of the brave king. The cynical story is that Constantine XI had unloaded his kingly raiment and was making an anonymous beeline for the boats when he was caught and killed. The most imaginative story, however, is that he disappeared, only to return at the end of time. Like Elvis.*

*Meanwhile, the Sultan handed the city over to his troops for three days of pillage, as was the custom. The ransacking and looting rights did not extend to the buildings, including the Haghia Sophia, which Mehmet II "Fatih" made quite clear were his.*

## Church of St. Savior at Chora
### History

The **Church of St. Savior at Chora** was originally built well outside Constantine's city walls, thus the name "at Chora," meaning "in the country." The Theodosian walls brought the Church within their protective shell in 413.

Although the church remains on the original site, the building was completely overhauled in the 11th century and enjoyed a great revitalization when Byzantium's rulers moved to the Blachernae and Tekfur Palaces, both of which were relatively near.

The restoration work was partly structural, but immense effort was also poured into the Church of Chora's mosaics and frescoes. Because of their late date, the paintings and mosaics at the church were executed with an understanding of perspective and depth lacking in the flat, lifeless Byzantine art of earlier periods. After Constantinople fell, this may well have been the central Greek Orthodox Church, but the period of grace ended under Beyazid II (1481-1512), who ordered the church converted to a mosque. Subsequent to that the plasterers arrived on the scene and covered most of the art, and even so it is apparent that the mosque was not held in particularly high esteem.

Over the years earthquakes and neglect caused marked deterioration to the interior of the building, a process that was finally halted after World War II. The Byzantine Institute of America and California's Dumbarton Oaks Center for Byzantine Studies began carefully restoring the mosaics and frescoes, an extremely successful undertaking.

### Visiting St. Savior at Chora

Today St. Savior at Chora is a museum, closed Tuesdays, and, uniquely, open on Mondays. There is a $3 entrance fee. The art within the pretty church is beautiful, and if ever there was a site where the $3 picture guidebook is worth the money, this is it. There are English language explanations within the building, but they do not elaborate on the particulars of the myriad images within.

You enter the church to the side of the exonarthex. A highlight of the interior includes a depiction of **Theodore Metochites**, the man responsible for rebuilding the church, offering a church to Christ, as Justinian does in the Haghia Sophia. Metochites was eventually forced to live his last years in the monastery on the site, and is among those buried in the south chapel.

Within the inner narthex are two domes decorated with Christ's ancestors: the upper ring of men in the southern dome lists Adam through Jacob, while the upper ring in the northern dome counts down through the kings in the house of David. One might ask questions about how God, Jesus' father, enters into such a genealogy? The most powerful image in the church is surely contained in the funerary area in the **south chapel**; the painting at the front of the chapel shows Christ breaking the gates of hell and forcing the submission of Satan. This is the Anastasis, also known as the Harrowing of Hell, and the souls of kings, saints, and even Eve (who Christ is helping from her tomb) are all being rescued. Elsewhere in this chamber are vivid images of heaven and hell, some quite grim for a funerary chapel.

The Kariye Hotel, next door, has a fine restaurant if all this apocalyptic imagery is making you hungry. If you're a glutton for Byzatine-era imagery, the **Fethiye Camii Müze** is only a ten minute walk back toward the tip of the peninsula on Draman Caddesi, which becomes Fethiye Caddesi. The old church is one block left where the road jogs sharply right. There is a $1 entrance fee to see the mosaics, which include the standard cast of characters.

## Continuing North Along the Walls

Returning to the base of the walls, wind your way along downhill to the **Byzantine Palace**, or Tekfur Saray. The neighborhood is a little dodgy. This old palace is not on many itineraries, and the man in charge keeps some erratic hours, but if he's around or if the palace is open you're might want to look around (it should cost 50¢ or less). "Palace" is hardly a suitable term anymore; this is an empty shell of a palace erected to command the view over the walls and into Thrace. Rather pretty from the outside, Tekfur Saray's interior is a let down. The building was erected by the latter Byzantine Emperors after they seized Constantinople back from the Latin Crusaders. The palace here accompanied the Palace of Blachernae a small distance north, but its most interesting period came after Ottoman conquest when it was first a zoo, then a brothel, a pottery craft center, and finally a poorhouse.

The walls undergo a dramatic transformation just north of Tekfur Saray, where the Byzantine Emperor Manuel Comnenus (1143-1180) built giant new walls down to the Golden Horn. The new walls were erected in response to the weakness of the older stretch, located at an area that many invaders had chosen for their sieges. There are no traces of these sieges today, with the exception of two tombs from the Arab siege of 674 (one of which is the tomb of Eyüp).

The final site of interest along the circuit of the walls is the former **Palace of Blachernae**, a Byzantine-era building that has been reduced to its foundations. If you thought Tekfur Saray was disappointing, we advise skipping this altogether and continuing down to the Golden Horn. The foundations of the palace are located by the Kazasker Ivaz Efendi Cami, inside the city walls and three blocks up the hill from the road along the Golden Horn. There was a palace on this site from the time of Emperor Anastasius I (491-518), but only under the late Byzantine Empire did this palace replace the former Great Palace of Bucoleon on the tip of the peninsula, east of the Blue Mosque.

In the years prior to the Ottoman conquest, the Palace of Blachernae was improved and refitted, becoming the exclusive residence of the Byzantine Emperors of the Paleologue dynasty. Two towers of the palace still stand, as do several vaulted underground chambers.

## Eyüp Mosque

The **Eyüp Mosque** is the most important religious site in the city. Other mosques soar higher, others commemorate great Sultans, but Eyüp was built to honor the resting place of Mohammed's standard bearer and friend, Eyüp. Eyüp fell here during the first Arab siege of Constantinople in 674 and he is held in such esteem today that people from throughout the city make pilgrimages to his mosque and türbe. In the years after the Arabs broke off the siege in 678, the tomb of Eyüp was probably left undisturbed by the Byzantines as a condition of their peace agreement. In time, superstition built up around the site and residents of the city used the tomb as a talisman for summoning rain.

A second, more extravagant story holds that at the time of the Ottoman conquest the tomb had been destroyed. After taking the city Sultan Mehmet II (1451-1481) returned to the area with his greatest imam in tow and began a mystical search, wherein the tomb of Eyüp was revealed in a dream. Mehmet II uncovered the burial site of Eyüp and rebuilt the tomb, later adding an entire mosque complex.

This complex was once the site of the Ottoman coronation – the strapping on of Sultan Osman's sword – but today it is visited by ashen-faced young fellows on their way to a less rarefied coming-of-age ceremony, circumcision. The current version of the mosque and accompanying buildings was completed in 1800.

**Visiting Eyüp**
The Eyüp Mosque is located just outside the city walls on the Golden Horn. Several buses serve the area from Eminönü, departing from the sea-side station, not the main station on the inland side of the seafront road. Walking directly from Eminönü takes about one half hour, but the road is busy. On the way along the Golden Horn between Eminönü and Eyüp keep your eyes peeled for St. Stephan of the Bulgars, a huge, prefabricated cast iron church located on the water's edge. Parts of this church were built in Vienna and shipped here after Bulgaria won its independence from the Ottomans.

Be on your best behavior here; after the great mosques in Mecca, Medina, and Jerusalem, this is the most holy Muslim site in the world. The Eyüp Mosque is like no other site in the city, and there is almost always a large, reverent crowd.

From the parking area, the Eyüp compound is off to the left. Upon entering the courtyard the mosque is to your right, the exit of Eyüp's türbe is directly ahead. To view the türbe, go through the courtyard and turn right into the mosque's sidecourt. You will see people removing their shoes along the magnificently tiled wall and entering Eyüp's chamber. In addition to his dramatically decorated chamber, similar to the shrine of Mevlana at Konya, there is a cast of Mohammed's footprint.

Exiting and reshodding yourself, you can have a look at the mosque, originally built after the Ottoman conquest of Constantinople in 1453. The current structure dates only to the beginning of the 19th century, when it was rebuilt.

After viewing the Eyüp compound, all that's left to do is to climb the cemetery hill to the **Pierre Loti Cafe**. A 15 minute walk up a long, gentle slope, tombstones to every side, brings you to the patio of the Pierre Loti, perpetually busy. Although this cafe has very little to do with the Pierre Loti who wrote so glowingly of life in İstanbul, romanticizing the city for the French, it does have an excellent view down along the Golden Horn and benefits from the fresh air of the parklike cemetery cordon.

Business here suffered during the heyday of slaughterhouses and leather production facilities that created a reek, but these are no longer in operation. Unfortunately, neither are the narghile water pipes that were once a fixture at the cafe.

## İstiklal Caddesi

**İstiklal Caddesi** is a broad pedestrian avenue in the area above Galata Tower. This fashionable district is lined with turn-of-the-century buildings and elaborate facades; all of İstanbul seems to come here on evenings and weekends. İstiklal was the European borough of old İstanbul, where the foreign traders and diplomats lived and worked, and it will feel much more familiar to you than the chaotic warrens of the bazaars.

### Visiting İstiklal Caddesi

İstiklal is an interesting walk from Sultanahmet (see *Getting Around Town, By Foot* above). İstiklal is the main boulevard off of Taksim Square, so you can catch a taxi or bus from virtually anywhere in the city to Taksim and stroll down İstiklal in the opposite direction. The Conference Valley hotels are located less than one mile north of Taksim in Harbiye. This account begins at the top of the tünel line and works north.

İstiklal Caddesi proper begins where the trolley route begins, and you can take a ride along the avenue for the cost of a single 30¢ İETT bus ticket. The lower end of İstiklal is thick with book shops, antique stores and shops with old prints and artwork. The most significant monument is the **Galata Tower**, a short distance downhill. This is an excellent place to stop in for a cup of coffee and one of the city's finest views (see *Where to Eat* above).

Once on İstiklal, you'll find an abundance of shops, theaters and embassies. The city's main **synagogue** is just down the street near Galata tower, and the main Catholic and Protestant churches (**St. Anthony of Padua** and the **Dutch Assembly**) are along the İstiklal to the right. There are many small, good restaurants and cafes along İstiklal and along the back streets behind it. In addition to the places mentioned in *Where to Eat*, consider any of the little cafes in this area for a bite to eat.

One of the only genuine "sights" along İstiklal is the **Galata Mevlevıhanesı**, on the right side as you begin your walk. This was established by a descendant of Celaddin Rumi (Mevlana), the founder of the Dervish order. After Atatürk's proscription against the dervishes, the complex fell into disrepair, but has been recently restored. It now functions as a small **dervish museum**. The appeal of the rest of the route is in the gorgeous, ornate facades and the endless small, interesting shops. The American Consulates is several blocks off of İstiklal – turn left on Asmalı Mescit Sokak and descend down the narrow lane to the entrance on Meşrutiye Cad.

Following Meşrutiet Caddesi uphill, you will pass a modern convention center, then arrive at the British Consulate. This beautiful building dates to 1845 and underscores the weight that the British Empire had with the Ottoman Empire in its later years.

Back on İstiklal, one of the landmarks is the **Çiçek Pasaj**, or "flower passage," a covered arcade with small restaurants and bars. You can get a tasty meal here, but the prices tend to be more than you'd expect, and the low key appeal of Çiçek Pasaj is mostly long gone. Better options await you on the road parallel to İstiklal, behind Çiçek Pasaj, and elsewhere nearby (see *Nightlife & Entertainment*).

As you emerge from İstiklal into the wide expanse of Taksim Square you will see a hulking Orthodox church to your right. This is the **Church of the Holy Trinity**, a 19th century insitution that has predictably suffered since the population exchange of 1924. Other landmarks around the square include the **War of Independence Memorial**, the Marmara Hotel (above the city's best and most risque magazine shops), and the **Atatürk Cultural Center**, home of the İstanbul Opera. Taksim was once the main water distribution center for İstanbul, with pipes fanning out from this hilltop. Today, buses and taxis fan out from here, and so too will the new subway.

## Asker Müze (Military Museum)

Few of İstanbul's visitors make it to the **Military Museum**, but we highly recommend a visit. With rifles and machine guns, battle standards and armor, it's great fun for the males. The museum is located north of Taksim Square in Harbiye, bordering on Nişantaşı. It is closed one hour for lunch.

### Visiting the Military Museum

From Taksim Square, catch a taxi for the short ride to the museum. If you trust your sense of direction, cross the square from İstiklal and continue down the main road on the far side (there's a McDonalds on your right). Continue straight for several long blocks until you see the large police building on your right: the museum is just beyond, also to the right.

The Ottoman military had several distinct characteristics, all of them represented here. The museum's back section features old **Ottoman pavilions** of the type used by Sultans on campaign. The Ottoman sultans continued a legacy that dates back to ancient Persia of traveling with a massive retinue and recreating Imperial splendor in the field. This ostentation contributed to the mystique of the Ottoman military during its rise, and, during the decline, to its shame. No Sultan was on hand at the second siege of Vienna (1683), but in the center of a great crescent of Ottoman tents was the pavilion of Grand Vizier Kara Mustafa and his entourage. When the siege was broken and the Ottomans put to rout by a relief army, the Viennese found in the Grand Vizier's abandoned pavilion a wealth of carpets and furs, caged birds, jeweled weapons, and cases of peculiar black beans, which a clever general hauled into Vienna and used to open the city's first coffee house.

A second signature of the Ottoman military was its **Mehter**, or military band. Unlike the imperial pavilion, military music was uniquely Ottoman in Turkish history. The rhythmic booming of martial songs preceded troops into battle, and the Ottoman's opponents are said to have been dispirited by the mere sound of the army's approach. The military band, marching in uniform as garish as the Janissaries, inspired its own troops and served as a warning in newly occupied territories. Other militaries, and college football teams, learned from the success of the Mehter, and you can still see the original go through its paces – although with artificially enhanced mustaches – at 3 p.m. in front of the museum. The dramatically percussive band is anything but dull.

The museum is divided in two sections. The back section, alongside the courtyard used by the Mehter, houses the aforementioned pavilions, captured battle standards (the Janissaries own were burned after their abolition), uniforms, and a section for Atatürk's several victorious campaigns. The front section houses the chain that was once stretched across the mouth of the Golden Horn, and also features a collection of weapons and armor.

## Bosphorous Cruise

A cruise on the Bosphorous, discussed in *Getting Around Town, By Ferry* above, is highly recommended. The scenery is enchanting, dotted with mosques and fortresses, and the Bosphorous is blessedly cool during İstanbul's long, hot summers. The main sites you will want to visit are described below, starting at the fortress at the top of the Bosphorous at Anadolu Kavağı and working your way back by land from Sariyer to Rumeli Hisar, from which point you can head off to dinner at Körfez or back to your hotel. The alternative to all of this is obvious; enjoy the ferry ride back to Eminönü.

İstanbul's ferries serve the Bosphorous three times daily in the summer, departing from Boğaz Iskele at 10:35 and 12:45 and 14:10. For a $4 round trip price, the ferry chugs up the Bosphorous to Anadolu Kavağı. The trip takes one hour and 35 minutes, stopping at several ports along the way. There are two boats on Sunday (Pazar), at a $2.50 discount rate. Details of the route are included above in *Getting Around Town, By Ferry* .

## Anadolu Kavağı

If you take a public ferry, you will typically have two or three hours in the village of **Anadolu Kavağı**. There are plenty of ice cream and snack food vendors available to ease your appetite, and a number of little waterfront cafes with mildly overpriced coffee and mezes. It's not hard to linger there for your entire stay in the village, but a take the opportunity to ascend to the fortress on the hill above town.

Ferries leave daily from Eminönü's "Boğaz Hatti," one of the main terminals east of the Galata Bridge. You can also pick them up at upstream locations such as Kabataş, Beşiktaş, Ortaköy, and Sariyer.

The fortress is a short taxi ride or a steep hike. To reach the fortress by foot, head to the left after getting off the ferry and follow the cobbled road in front of the Midilli'li Ali Reis Mosque inland and uphill. The road follows the slope of the hill upward, bearing right. You can enter the lower compound by cutting up a path next to the small military compound, or continue to the parking area at the top. There is no fee, and there is a refreshing wind on top, much welcome when you're overheated from the walk.

The fortress, **Yoros Tepesi**, occupies the crest of two hills and commands the Black Sea entrance to the Bosphorous. Like the many other strategic points along the Bosphorous and the Dardanelles, this area has long been occupied by kingdoms vying to exact tribute from passing ships. The hilltop fortress was built to defend a small customs port at Anadolu Kavağı, formerly known as Hieron. The small anchorage was much sought after as traffic through the Bosphorous increased, and it changed hands between Byzantium, Bithnia, Pontus, and Rome. The Romans recaptured the port under Septimius Severus in 196 AD, consolidating Roman control of the entire strait. The fortress reached its zenith in the 1200s, when the walls were extended to their current size, probably under the Byzantines who had been expelled from Constantinople by the Crusaders.

The fortress has been reinforced periodically, notably by the Genoese in the years preceding the Ottoman conquest of Constantinople. Soon thereafter they handed it over to the ascendant Ottomans under Beyazit I, who fumbled it away after getting stomped by Tamurlane. Along came the hyperkinetic Mehmet II, who restored the fortress as a prelude to taking Constantinople. By the time the Ottoman Empire was again threatened from the east, this time by the Russians, warfare had changed and the fortress was decaying.

Today the fortress is a vast picnic ground with an outstanding view of the upper end of the Bosphorous. There are a few nooks and crannies to poke around in, but many of them are filled with litter.

## Sadberk Hanım Museum

A restored Ottoman mansion along the Bosphorous shore road house the educational and interesting **Sadberk Hanim Museum**, *Büyükdere Caddesi 27-29, Sariyer, Tel. 212 242 3813*. The mansion's modern annex is the equivalent of a four-story Cliff Notes book. The bulk of the region's numbingly long history, from the late Neolithic period (5400 B.C.) through the fall of the Byzantine Empire (1453 A.D.), is related in English and Turkish as you ascend from the first floor. Pottery, statuary, cuneiform tablets, and other relics illustrate each period, and the museum is filled with tidbits that not even the best history students remember.

For instance, Assyrian merchants introduced tin to Anatolia, which, mixed with the native copper, yielded bronze, and the Bronze Age; the Cimmerians, vaguely immortalized in Conan comic books and movies, helped found the Lydian empire. The historical section of the museum is an excellent way for newcomers to get their bearings. Compared to the sprawling museums in Sultanahmet, it is very peaceful; on weekdays you're likely to be followed around by a museum employee who turns off lights as you leave each room.

The upper floors of the mansion itself are devoted to art and relics of the last thousand years, and are highlighted by a display of Iznik and Kütahya ceramics. You can see what all the fuss over tile is about firsthand. Nearby is a display of Celadon porcelain from China's Yuan and Ming Dynasties, and while the collection may seem incongruous, it is impressive enough to have merited John Carswell's *Chinese Ceramics in the Sadberk Hanim Museum*, a table top book available at Sotheby's. You didn't come to Turkey to see the Chinese porcelain, but it is quite nice just the same. A final highlight is a section devoted to calligraphy that outdoes the Topkapı Palace.

The rest of this house has its share of oddities, but suffers from poor English documentation: a table with reliefs of Napoleon and his marshalls, displays of Ottoman medals, and even a model of a Ford Probe go unexplained; as for the latter, Sadberk Hanim was the wife of Vehbi Koç, himself a much-loved industrialist and Turkish Horatio Alger character.

## Rumeli Hisar

The "Fortress of Europe," **Rumeli Hisar**, is on the sea road on the European shore, just below the second Bosphorous Bridge. Buses serve Rumeli Hisar along the sea road, and there is parking. There is a $1 admission fee.

If you've taken a Bosphorous Cruise or arrived in İstanbul by bus from the Asian side, you've seen Rumeli Hisar. The fortress is built at the narrowest point along the Bosphorous, and complements the smaller **Anadolu Hisar**, the Fortress of Asia, on the opposite shore. This is the same spot that the Persian King Darius crossed into Asia on a bridge of ships in his campaign against the Scythians (512 B.C.). Herodotus remarks favorably on the Scythians' cunning, and also mentions one of their entertaining habits: they would pack into a warming hut with hot stones in the center and burn hemp, emerging with much whooping and hollering. It seems to have made quite an impression on Herodotus. Darius' campaign eventually failed when the Scythians refused to give battle and made a long, meandering retreat just ahead of Darius' army. An exasperated Darius eventually gave up and marched home.

Control of the strait was always crucial, but this particular point did not play a major historical role until late in the 1300s. At this time Sultan Beyazid I ordered the construction of Anadolu Hisar, on the Asian shore. This was part of his strategy of choking off Constantinople. Beyazid's scheme was foiled by the invasion of Tamurlane in 1402. By 1451, the Ottomans had recovered, and in that year Mehmet II came to power and immediately set about finishing the job his great grandfather had started: he shored up Anadolu Hisar and, with what would become typical industriousness, erected Rumeli Hisar on the European side in the space of four months.

Within Rumeli Hisar's seaside tower he positioned a set of newly forged cannons and 500 men and demanded that any ships passing through the strait submit to boarding and pay a fee. Mehmet II was delighted to hear that the first ship that attempted to run the gauntlet between the two fortresses was immediately holed and sunk. His soldiers merrily fished the survivors out of the sea and impaled them; later sea traffic stopped as ordered.

When Constantinople fell, Rumeli Hisar's purpose was served. It housed an occasional garrison, and was at times used as a prison, but it has had little military importance. Earlier this century the fortress was filled with small wooden houses, but these were cleared out in the 1970s to make way for a park. Today various international musicians perform concerts here in the spring and young couples from Bosphorous University come to neck.

Like so many old fortresses, Rumeli Hisar is a shell, but it is well worth the $1 entrance fee. Be sure to climb to the upper left tower, whose winding stair takes you up through an interior draped in vines, lit eerily from above. The column at the center was used to fix the tower's wooden flooring. Note the care taken to place a recycled Orthodox cross in the floor at the tower's entrance so that the garrison could trample it on every trip in and out of the tower.

## Dolmabahçe Palace

### History
**Dolmabahçe** is just two kilometers north of the Golden Horn's Galata Bridge, directly on the main sea road. The Palace, *Tel. 212 258 5544*, is on the Bosphorous side of the main shore road, and the entrance is marked with an elaborate baroque clock tower. Buses bound from Eminönü for Beşiktaş and points north pass the palace.

Long before the Dolmabahçe was a glimmer in the Ottoman Imperial eye, this was the site that Fatih Sultan Mehmet II sent his ships overland from during his siege of İstanbul. Stymied by the great chain strung across the mouth of the Golden Horn (now in the Military Museum), Mehmet II completely bypassed a siege of Galata Tower and hauled his ships directly into the Golden Horn, advancing a step closer to his ultimate victory. Years later, Sultan Ahmet I, he of the innumerable hobbies, began ordering the deep cove at this site to be filled for the sake of his gardens. Later Sultans continued Ahmet's practice of filling this area, which yielded the name "filled-garden", or Dolma-bahçe.

It was on this auspicious spot that, in 1853, Sultan Abdül Mecit I (1839-1861) completed his new palace. His motivation may have been, in part, to distance himself from the intrigues of Topkapı Palace, but his main influence was a desire to build a palace in the style of the Europeans the sultans had come to admire.

Dolmabahçe is the culmination of the Ottomans' turn to the west. The Empire had been in obvious decline for almost a century, and the only fear the Ottomans now evoked in Europe was that their collapse would be to the advantage of another Western power – especially Russia. In order to shore up the Ottomans, western nations made loans, sent advisors, even threatened its enemies. The Ottoman sultans had grown so comfortable in this role that Abdül Mecit's palace was largely built with loans from Europe.

More vividly, in the same year Dolmabahçe was completed the Crimean War erupted, wherein Turkey's French and English allies fought off the Russians in what had once been the Ottoman's private preserve, the Black Sea. Europe battled the Ottomans' enemies and built its palaces; such a good deal, and such a sad one.

Dolmabahçe underscores the abandonment of tradition: it is a Western palace of the most extravagant kind, with rococo ornamentation and baroque flourishes. There are 285 rooms, 43 halls, and six Turkish baths; it has the world's largest mirror and chandelier, and giant elephant tusks are on hand as was anything else big and resplendent. Designed by the architect Nikoğos Balyan (who was also responsible for the pretty Ortaköy mosque), the Dolmabahçe retains nothing of the Topkapı Palace's simple, functional charm.

Even after the later construction of the Çırağan Palace, Dolmabahçe was the official residence of the sultans until 1922. Afterward, Dolmabahçe was often Atatürk's accommodation while in İstanbul, although he made it plain that İstanbul was not a city he was comfortable in. He stayed here a total of three months between 1927 and 1938, and perhaps his unease was foreboding; he died here at 9:05 a.m. on November 10, 1938. All of the clocks here remain set to that time.

## Visiting Dolmabahçe

Dolmabahçe is on the main shore road along the European side of the Bosphorous, across the Galata Bridge from Saray Burnu (Sultanahmet, Eminönü). You can't miss it, its the ornate palace between Beşiktaş's İnönü Stadium and the Bosphorous. Arrive at 8 a.m. Gates don't open until 9 a.m., but the tour buses begin unloading hundreds of people by 8:30 a.m., even on the cusp of high season. The waiting lines are long and impossibly sluggish, the ticket takers are nasty, and if you arrive later in the day you may have to cool your heels for hours in line, jostling with sweaty people from around the world. It's fun to look at the motionless soldiers on ceremonial guard, but it ain't that fun. If you're on a budget and you've seen Topkapı, spend elsewhere: at $8 for the residence and harem joint tour, Dolmabahçe is not especially great.

Unlike Topkapı, where you can linger over those things you find interesting, you are guided through all of the buildings here. Go to the front hall after entering the grounds and join the cluster around an English speaking guide. You are herded first through the **selamlık** (residence) on a tour, in which you see several of the world's largest chandeliers, masses of crystal, cut stone, elaborate arches, gigantic carpets, and every other gaudy ornament the designers were able to pack inside. After the selamlık you are handed off to a second guide if you have bought the harem tour as well.

The guides do a fine job of explaining the interior, which is highlighted by the **Imperial Ceremonial Hall**. This vast chamber rises almost as high as the Haghia Sophia and covers 6,200 square feet. George Bush,

Helmut Kohl and François Mitterand have dined here, but that was during the summer – the palace is musty and cold in the fall and winter. For a break, the conveniently located cafe by the Selamlık entrance is surprisingly reasonable. You can wander the gardens on your own.

## Miscellaneous Sights of Interest

A catalogue of İstanbul's sites could fill tomes. A few of the more interesting historical sites that you might take the time to visit are listed below.

### Deniz Müzesi (Naval Museum)

The Naval Museum is on the waterfront in Beşiktaş. The displays are less interesting than those in the military museum, but well worth a look if you are at Dolmabahçe or Çırağan Palaces. Highlights of the collection include old naval artillery pieces and photos and paintings of naval battles in both Ottoman and Republican times.

### Kiliç Ali Pasa Camii

This is one of Sinan's final works, built for a successful Ottoman naval officer who died in the company of his harem at age 90.

### Kız Kalesi (Maiden's Castle)

It isn't likely you'll be visiting this monument in the center of the Bosphorous, but you're bound to wonder what it is. This was once a customs point for ships entering the Bosphorous, and has long had a tower or fortification of some kind. It is sometimes referred to as **Leander's Tower**, a reference to the myth of Helle, Leander, and the golden ram related in the Çanakkale section.

### Küçük Aya Sofya (The Church of St. Sergius and Bacchus)

This building was originally commissioned by Justinian, and is much admired by architects for its clever dome. The patron saints of the church were dear to the heart of Roman and early Byzantine soldiery. The church was converted to a mosque after the Ottoman conquest.

### Şehzade Cami (The Prince's Mosque)

Sinan built **Şehzade** early in his long career for Süleyman the Magnificent's favorite son. The son, Mehmet, died of smallpox while still young. This is one of the city's most beautiful mosques.

### Tophane (The Cannon Foundry)

The **Tophane** is a cannon foundry dating back to Fatih Sultan Mehmet II. Under Süleyman the Magnificent, the foundry was rebuilt in its current form and became one of the most world's foremost manufacturing facilities for artillery pieces.

**Aqueduct of Valens**
Constantinople's system of aquaducts was elaborate, extending far outside of the city to the Belgrade Forest. This is the last great evidence of the system still intact within the city, and you're likely to pass beneath its arches as you bus or taxi through the city. Valens was a Byzantine Emperor between 364-378.

**Yer Altı Cami (The Underground Mosque)**
This is an underground chamber where the chain crossing the Golden Horn was once fixed, now converted to a mosque. Two martyrs of the first Arab siege are located here.

**Yıldız Saray (Palace) and Yıldız Park**
In the hills above the Çırağan Palace is İstanbul's largest park, a beautiful strip of mildly cultivated wilderness. If you need a break from urban İstanbul, this is the place. Sultan Abdul Hamid II felt this way and built the last Ottoman Palace in the heights just above, maintaining his own private wilderness here.
The park has several small, pretty kiosks and pools, some of them restored by the Turkish Touring and Automobile Association.

## NIGHTLIFE & ENTERTAINMENT
**Hamams**
There are more than 100 Ottoman-era hamams (Turkish baths) in İstanbul alone. One of the finest examples of a classical bath in the city is the **Haseki Hurrem Hamamı**, designed by Sinan for Süleyman the Magnificent's favorite wife, Roxelana. The structure, between the Haghia Sophia and the Blue Mosque, now houses the Ministry of Culture's kilim and carpet shop, **Döşim** (see section on kilims and carpets for further information). If you're not planning on visiting a bath for bathing purposes, then stop by Döşim and kill two birds with one stone.
Some of the more interesting hamams are:
**CAĞALOĞLU HAMAMI,** *Yerebatan Caddesi in Sultanahmet, near the intersection with Nuruosmaniye Caddesi just uphill of the Basilica Cistern. Hours are 7 a.m to 10 p.m. for men, 8 a.m. to 9 p.m. for women.*
Apparently the proceeds from this bath in Ottoman times were used to maintain Sultan Mahmut I's library in the Haghia Sophia. It is now one of Istanbul's premier tourist hamams, and the prices reflect this. Cost notwithstanding, it is a beautiful place.

**ÇEMBERLITAŞ HAMAMI,** *Vezirhan Caddesi No. 8, off of Divan Yolu. Hours are from 6 a.m. to midnight.*
Built by Nur Banu Valide Sultan in 1580 (wife of Selim II the Sot and mother of Murat III), this hamam is supposedly based on a plan by Sinan. The original womens' section was destroyed in street widening some years ago, but still has sex-segregated quarters, of apparently equal size.
**GALATASARAY HAMAMI,** *Suterazi Sokak 24, off of Istiklal Caddesi in Galata.*
The mens' quarters are lavishly bedecked with marble, the womens' less so. Expect to pay a lot for your luxury.
**PARK HAMAMI,** *Dr. Emin Paşa Sokak No. 10 in Sultanahmet.*
Turn off of Divan Yolu opposite the Hippodrome. The hamam is across from Hotel Petrol and is a simple, small, neighborhood establishment.

### Theater, Opera, & Ballet
**ATATÜRK CULTURAL CENTER** (Atatürk Kultur Merkezi), *Taksim.*
If you're standing in front of the Marmara Hotel facing the Square, AKM is on your right. Built as an opera house, the AKM also houses the State Ballet, the Symphony Orchestra, and the State Theater Company. Friends generally advise against ballet, unless it's a visiting international company, and with theater you'll face the language problem. But the tickets are so inexpensive that it hardly matters.

---

### ISTANBUL INTERNATIONAL FESTIVALS
*Istanbul's international festivals attract some of the world's finest performers, including Turkish ones. You can enjoy theater, film, music & dance, and jazz; tickets are inexpensive to moderate by U.S. standards. You can find out more about the festivals by asking at your hotel or the tourism information offices.*

---

### Art Galleries
Almost all of the major banks sponsor art galleries, and publish books of Turkish artists' works. You can easily find small galleries in **Nişantaşı** and **Teşvikiye,** as well as in the small streets around **İstiklal Caddesi** such as: **Aksanat Cultural Center,** *Istiklal Caddesi 16-18, Tel. 212 252 3500;* and **Yapi Kredi Gallery,** *Istiklal Caddesi 285-287, Tel. 212 252 4700.*

### Movie Houses
Going to the movies is a popular pastime in İstanbul. Many of the theaters along Istiklal have a long history, having been built in the first half of this century.

If you missed the first run of something in the U.S., you may be able to catch it on the big screen after all. All major Hollywood films come to Turkey, not long after release in the U.S. Many other foreign films come through as well, especially during the **İstanbul International Film Festival**. The Istiklal theaters are the main venue for the festival. Matinee prices can be as low as $1.50, but regular rates for new releases are pushing the $5-6 mark. Usually movies are subtitled in Turkish, rather than dubbed. The notable exceptions are childrens' movies, which are always dubbed. There is always an intermission, which disrupts the flow of the film but is convenient for buying snacks, using the restroom, or, of course, smoking a cigarette – which is mercifully not permitted in most theaters. Theaters usually have cafes attached, where you can buy a drink and a snack before or after the film. Some of these theaters should fit your cinematic needs:

**ATLAS**, *Istiklal Caddesi 209, Tel. 212 243 7576* – The main theater has very bad sound, but the smaller one is fine.

**FITAŞ**, *Istikal Caddesi, Fitaş Pasajı 24-26, Tel. 212 249 0166* – five screens.

**BEYOĞLU**, *Istiklal Caddesi, Halep Pasajı 140, Tel. 212 251 3240* – To find the theater, go into the passage and down the stairs ahead of you on the left.

**ALKAZAR CINEMA CENTER**, *Istiklal Caddesi 179, Tel. 212 245 7538* – A restored theater with two screens. Look for sculptures of women on either side of the narrow arched entrance.

**EMEK**, *Istiklal Caddesi, Yeşilçam Sokak 5, Tel. 212 293 8439* – The lobby's not much to look at, but inside is a grand old one-screen movie house.

**FERIYE**, *Çırağan Caddesi, Tel. 212 236 2864* – This theater is along the sea road, next to the Ortaköy municipal bus stop. The modern theater has a lofty ceiling with exposed beams. Have a Bosphorus view with your pre- or post-film coffee at the indoor cafe.

### Nightclubs, Bars, & Other Entertainment

Istanbul's unique summertime nightlife owes much to its peculiar geography. As in other Mediterranean cultures, Turks eat dinner late in the summer, and stay out – on the streets or at cafes and bars – even later. Outdoor restaurants, bars, and discos, especially along the Bosphorus and the Sea of Marmara, figure prominently in İstanbul's summer life. In the wintertime people tend to stay at home more, but there is still a lively indoor nightlife until all hours.

In the following list we recommend some of Istanbul's best nightspots, summer and winter. A couple of alternatives are to spend an evening, and some Lira, at a casino or Turkish floor show. Most major hotels have casinos with live games and slot machines. You'll need your passport, since only foreigners and Turks with special gambling licenses are allowed to participate. This is the case everywhere in the country.

You'll notice we don't recommend bars with Turkish floor shows (usually of the belly dancing variety) aside from the very expensive Galata. Many of the places with floor shows are disreputable and you'll wind up getting gouged. There are plenty of places where you can go that will be just as lively, and, if anything, more "Turkish" because there are Turks enjoying the atmosphere right alongside of you.

Note: Although many of our favorite places are in the Istiklal area, it's probably best to avoid the deserted side streets off of Istiklal at night, especially if you're out alone. Mugging is uncommon, but it does happen. Single men should also be wary of new friends, as explained in the Safety & Avoiding Trouble in Chapter 6, *Basic Information*.

**Q CLUB**, *Çırağan Palace Hotel Kempinski, Beşiktaş, Tel. 212 236 2489.*
Very steep drink prices, but a breathtaking summertime setting on the palace's terrace next to the Bosphorus. In the winter they move into the ground floor of the palace itself. Q Club features Turkish and international jazz musicians, and flaunts a wine and cheese bar.

**HARRY'S JAZZ BAR**, *Hyatt Regency İstanbul, Taksim, Tel. 212 225 7000.*

**EYLÜL**, *Birinci Caddesi 23, Arnavutkoy, Tel. 212/257-1109, 9 p.m.-4 a.m.*
A two floor bar with live jazz, rock, and funk set in an historical Ottoman building. The downstairs is a cozy area, and winding stairs take you to the music club upstairs. The menu includes imported wines. Crowded on the weekends.

**ZIHNI**, *Muallim Nacı Caddesi, Ortaköy, Tel. 212 258 1154.*
Popular among young urban professionals and the cellular telephone set. Expensive drinks, but a commanding view of the Bosphorus in the summertime on their terrace. The Zihni gets crowded after 8 p.m. Takes Amex, Diner's Club, Visa. Just past Ortakoy and the Bosphorus Bridge, on the land side of the sea road. Zihni is closed on Sundays and Mondays.

**PASHA**, *Muallim Naci Caddesi 142, Ortaköy, Tel. 212 259 7061.*
A couple hundred meters more up the Bosphorus and across the sea road from Zihni is Pasha, an outdoor bar and disco open only in the summertime. One of the places to be seen. On weekend nights it can be tough to get in.

**BILSAK**, *Soğancı Sokak No. 7, Taksim, Tel. 212 293 3774.*
To get here, go down Siraselviler from Taksim, pass the German Hospital on your left ("Alman Hastanesi") and turn left at Dilek Market onto Soğancı Sokak. Bilsak (otherwise an arts center) is about 150 meters up on your right. On the first floor is Barbahçe, a bar/restaurant. Or, take

the elevator up to the 5th floor to Beş Inci Kat (Fifth Floor), also a bar/ restaurant, with a great view. Both have dramatic paint jobs, and both are crowded on weekends. For food details, see *Where to Eat* above. Mixed drinks are expensive. Open 6 p.m. to 2 a.m.

**ROXY,** *Arslanyatağı Sokak No. 9, Taksim, Tel. 212 249 4839.*

Go down Siraselviler from Taksim and take a left at the Ismar supermarket, onto Arslanyatağı Sokak. Roxy is on the left. This rock and jazz bar/club is popular with international musicians, who are likely to show up here for jam sessions after their concerts elsewhere. No cover charge on weekdays, but a hefty one on weekends. No credit cards. Open 6 p.m. - 3:30 a.m.

**KEMANCI,** *Siraselviler Cadessi No. 69, Taksim, Tel. 212 245 3048.*

Almost directly opposite the Church of the Holy Trinity on Siraselviler. The arcade entrance says Taksim Sanat Evi – inside you'll see a neon sign for Kemanci. There are three floors for different musical tastes. The floor called Millenium offers some of the city's hottest techno.

**CAFE PIA,** *Bekar Sokak No. 6, Taksim, Tel. 212 252 7100.*

Go down Istiklal Caddesi from Taksim and turn right at the FBI (no relation) clothing store onto Bekar Sokak. Cafe Pia has two cozy floors.

**KAKTÜS,** *Imam Adnan Sokak No. 4, Taksim, Tel. 212 249 5979.*

Kaktüs is another cozy cafe that specializes in light European food. Lots of artists, intellectuals and good cheese cake. Going down Istiklal Caddesi from Taksim, take a right onto Imam Adnan Sokak, opposite the Vakko department store.

**ROCK HOUSE CAFE,** *Princess Hotel Ortakoy, Dereboyu Caddesi, Tel. 212 227 6010.*

When the Hard Rock chain finds out about this place, they'll try to shut it down. The imitation is quite faithful, with guitars on the walls and and nachos and burgers on the menu. Big screen TVs show videos or soccer games. The game room includes video games and pool, popular with kids. Bands perform on weekends.

**FLY INN,** *Nispetiye Caddesi 10, Etiler, Tel. 212 257 8989.*

Another bar popular with İstanbul-style yuppies, just up the road from Akmerkez on the right. The Fly Inn takes its name from the partial airplane suspended in the main room. The Etiler area has its share of lively bars, and the traffic can be bad on weekend nights. Open from 6 p.m.-3 a.m., food served 8-10 p.m.

## SHOPPING

Whether you want the amenities of one of Europe's finest shopping malls (**Akmerkez**), the quirkiness of an arts and crafts market day (Sunday in Ortaköy), or the historic din of the Grand Bazaar, İstanbul has what you're looking for. The weekly neighborhood **pazars** – Thursdays in Etiler/Ulus, for example (in the otherwise empty lot across from Akmerkez – see Akmerkez section below for directions) – offer a 'real-life' shopping scene where you can buy everything from your weekly groceries to fingernail polish and kilims.

As if the madness of Turkey's own cornucopia of goods wasn't enough, a **Russian Market** is held in Beyazid in front of the İstanbul University gate on Sundays; goods from all over the former Soviet Union turn up. If you want to neglect our historical tour itineraries and spend a full week shopping, you'll find there's plenty to keep you occupied.

Remember that the Grand Bazaar and the Egyptian Bazaar are closed on Sundays, as are many shops.

## The Grand Bazaar

*Open 9 AM-7PM, Monday-Saturday, closed Sundays.*

The first shopping destination in İstanbul is usually the **Grand Bazaar**, arguably the mother of all shopping malls. The Grand Bazaar is known to Istanbullus as the **Kapalı Çarşı**, or "Covered Market," for obvious reasons.

To get here, turn right off of Divan Yolu onto Vezirhanı Caddesi. At the Nuruosmaniye Mosque, take a left through the mosque gate. Pass through the courtyard and out the other side. One of the Grand Bazaar's entrances, on Çarşıkapı Sokak (Market Gate Street) will be right in front of you. This doorway brings you onto the Bazaar's main drag, Kalpakçılarbaşı Caddesi. Most of the Bazaar will be off to the right of this street. This may sound like a guidebook cop-out, but rather than sticking to the map, it's really much more enjoyable to let yourself get "lost" in the Grand Bazaar.

### History

The first thing you'll probably notice about the Grand Bazaar is that shops selling similar wares are all clustered together. The roots of this practice are in the guild system, which resulted from the specialization of labor, early economies of scale, and the state's desire to police prices, supplies, and tax revenues. Thus names of the streets in the Grand Bazaar – such as **Jeweler's Street** and **Quilt-Maker's Street** – reflect the guilds that are or were once making and selling their goods there.

Although this may be an urban myth, we've been told that there is still an ethic among merchants whereby a shopkeeper will may refuse a sale if he's already had one that day and knows that his neighbor hasn't. This forces the customer to go next door, which spreads wealth as well as good cheer (except to the confused tourist), and perhaps wards off the evil eye to boot.

The Grand Bazaar got its start as a simple warehouse, or **bedesten**, for Mehmet the Conquerer. The area around this particular bedesten became popular with merchants, who eventually built structures from under which to ply their wares year round. As time went on, **hans** were built around this bazaar; hans were cousins of the larger **kervanserais** on the outskirts of town, places where goods could be stored and locked up. Many of the hans are still functioning in their original capacities, as well as for the manufacture of goods. Feel free to wander into a couple as brief respite from the sensory overload of the Bazaar.

### Playing the Tourist

"A fool and his money are soon parted." P.T. Barnum would have liked it here. Bear that in mind as you ease into this capitalist spectacle, but don't let it paralyze you. If you're in Turkey for a month you can acquire some of the connections to get good stuff a little cheaper; only then do you have the luxury of not being taken for a sucker. Otherwise, you're a stranger in a strange land, baffled by jet lag and exchange rates and the odds are against you getting much of a deal. On the other hand, the Grand Bazaar has a vast amount of stuff that you can't get any cheaper elsewhere. So go ahead, wander the streets asking prices: "*Bu ne kadar?*" (Boo nay ka-dar?) – "How much is this?" – and seeing what's to be had.

You enter the bazaar at a disadvantage: your clothes are sure to brand you as a traveler. In other words, the shopkeepers know about you. They know there's money in your pocket, know you're interested in spending it, and probably know how to string together some fair English sentences. Furthermore, they have your inherent politeness on their side – no matter how cold-blooded you think you are, you will be coerced into one or two booths and set upon with tea and greedy hospitality.

There are the inevitable reports of people being drugged at the Bazaar. It allegedly works like this: you are offered tea, but the tea is spiked to knock you out. After you leave the booth, unscrupulous Bazaar crooks track you like Marlon Perkins tracking a tranquilized Grizzly and roll you in an alley. This is quite a tale, but pretty much unfounded. If you want to have tea in someone's shop, have tea. Shop owners and salesmen in the Bazaar may be irritating at times, but they're not criminals and in a million years they aren't going to destroy their shop's reputation by messing with a foreigner.

Pickpocketing may be a more valid concern. Although this, too, is not common, pickpocketing is on the rise, and by people you wouldn't expect, like groups of older women in headscarves. It works like this: they will feign interest in items that you are also looking at, crowd around you, talk loudly to each other and the shopkeeper, and then move on. If your wallet or another important item was in an exterior pocket, it may not be anymore. So: keep money and other valuables in a neck pouch under your clothing or in a money belt. There are also stories circulating of tourists' bags or backpacks being slashed as they wander around the bazaars.

For all of this, the Grand Bazaar is neither scary nor intimidating. It's just a big, chaotic market. Nothing bad will happen to you so long as you stay frosty. Go, shop, buy. The bazaar is fun.

## The Egyptian or Spice Bazaar
*Open 9 AM-7PM, Monday-Saturday, closed Sundays.*

The **Spice Market**, or **Egyptian Bazaar** (Mısır Çarşısı), is basically a t-shaped structure adjacent to the Yeni Cami in Eminönü, constructed in the 1660s as a part of the mosque complex. It was once known for the folk remedies sold by its merchants. What's left of those remedies today are primarily spices, bins of green henna powder, loofas and sea-sponges, with other items scattered nearby. The tall brass grinders you'll see everywhere are good for either coffee or pepper; a Turkish friend says that one of his fondest childhood memories is of his grandmother roasting some coffee beans in a pan, and allowing him to grind them. The tall grinders work remarkably well, and are more classic and fun than your Braun bean grinder at home. People talk about the pungent aroma of the spices, but it takes a little imagination to make them pungent except when you're up close sniffing.

Tip: Unless you like the convenience of the packaged spices, buy in bulk. The spices will be cheaper and fresher. So, too, with the Turkish Delight and coffee.

The large doors at the foot of the "t" are the Bazaar's main entrance, right on Eminönü Square, across from the Yeni Camii's pigeon-covered steps. Inside to the left is the stairway entrance to the turquoise-tiled **Pandeli Restaurant**. The Pandeli's moderate prices, excellent Turkish dishes, and unusual setting make it one of the best deals in İstanbul. They are open for lunch only (see *Where to Eat* section above).

The real action and pungency is outside the bazaar. In the righthand arm of the "t" (if your back is facing the main entrance), your nose will lead you to Kurukahveci Mehmet Efendi coffee roasters, just beyond the Bazaar's side door. Mehmet Efendi uses Arabica beans, and sells ground coffee in brown paper packets or in sealed tins and plastic bags, whichever you like. Don't forget to ask for the English instruction sheet, because translated directions for cooking Turkish coffee are not on the packaging. Directly across from Mehmet Efendi on Hasırcılar Caddesi are some confectioner's shops, where you can pick and choose fresh

rkish Delight) in various flavors by the kilo. Shopkeepers will
you samples to entice you to buy.

Along the outside of the bazaar that faces the bus station are stalls and stands selling fresh produce, dried fruits, cheeses, meats, olives, and nuts. Indulge in some dried apricots (kayısı), figs (incir), or dates (hurma). Outside on the other side of the "t" opposite the Yeni Camii is a **Sunday bird market** and stalls with gardening supplies. Here you can find tulip bulbs, but look at the label – the bulbs are more likely to be from Holland or Washington State then they are from Turkey, the tulip's original homeland.

Take some time to wander in the narrow streets that lead away from the ferries. In the maze of streets behind the Egyptian Bazaar you'll discover wooden utensils, fake Levis, German department store brand coats, and other everyday items. One steet is filled with woodworkers, another with hardware shops, another with with plastic goods. Many of the things that you find in the shops around Eminönü are also made in workshops here, tucked away in hidden arcades, up stairways, behind walls. These are streets largely inhabited by men, craftsmen, salesmen, shopkeepers and businessmen, suggesting an İstanbul at odds with the cosmopolitan city you see elsewhere.

## Other Shopping Areas
### İstiklal Caddesi

This is the most classically "European" section of İstanbul. This hill opposite the old city has been populated for a long time, but under the Ottomans it became a borough for non-Ottoman traders and, later, diplomats. The major embassies of France, Germany, England, Russia and America are located here, although they have all been demoted to consulate status since the capital shifted to Ankara.

Classic Greek Orthodox and Roman Catholic churches dot the avenue, as do the beautiful old facades and storefronts. This wide pedestrian lane is one of most popular spots for a weekend stroll, to take in a movie, or to do some shopping. Most of the shops offer clothing and household goods that probably aren't what you came to Turkey to find. The lower end of İstiklal has antique and collectibles shops, as described below, and on the Taksim side of İstiklal, just past the bend at Galatasaray, is an market beside the Çiçek Pasaj filled with spices and dried fruits.

If you're strolling along Istiklal near Galatasaray Square and happen to be looking for a good deal on ceramics, you might stop by the **Aznavur Pasaj** just across from the Yapı Kredi Bank building. The kiosks on the ground floor of the pasaj sell ceramics with the same kinds of historical patterns, color schemes, and quality of those in the Grand Bazaar, and come at a lower price because of the lower rents. Open on Sundays.

---

**SHOESHINE BOYS**

*Istanbul's shoeshine boys, particularly in the Taksim area, are bound to get your attention. These tiny young things wander the streets late at night with their banged up shoeshine boxes, while their child colleagues offer candies or packets of tissue. Many of the urchins are persistent to the point of being relentless, especially with tourists. They'll follow you around doggedly, and you can sputter "Git" (go) and "Gerek yok" (not necessary) all day long without it making a bit of difference. The community often keeps an eye on the youngsters, and you'll see shopkeepers and men outside a restaurant offer them some spare change. Sadly, and predictably, many of these kids are addicted to sniffing glue and live together under the "guidance" of shoeshine pimps.*

---

### Nisantası & Teşvikiye

These tony neighborhoods have a concentration of galleries, antique stores, contemporary design stores, and upscale clothing shops. You can easily take a taxi from Taksim to Nişantaşı – ask to be dropped off on Vali Konağı Caddesi at the clothing store called **Yargici** (at the corner of Rumeli Caddesi). Yargici is Turkey's version of a Banana Republic, and the nearby streets have other high profile clothing stores.

Or, if you don't mind a 15-20 minute walk from Taksim, follow Cumhuriyet Caddesi past the Divan Hotel; Cumhuriyet turns left at the Harbiye Military Museum (Askeri Müze) – you want to keep going straight, onto Vali Konağı Caddesi. This puts you in great position to take advantage of Istanbul's prime shopping.

### Ortaköy/Sunday Crafts Market

Sundays in **Ortaköy** are an entertaining confusion of street vendors selling crafts and people stepping out for one of the city's finest views. The baroque mosque, built in the nineteenth century by the creator of the Dolmabahçe, commands the waterfront, with the 1973 Bosphorus Bridge behind. If you didn't bring your camera, this is where you grit your teeth watching the perfect light and the serene Istanbullus soaking up the sun. From about 10 a.m. until well into the evening, the pedestrian zone on Ortaköy's waterfront is filled with tables of inexpensive silver jewelry, handicrafts, and other collectibles. In good weather it's swarmed with young Istanbullus munching on huge baked potatoes and **gözleme**, filo dough cooked with your choice of filling. Have tea or coffee in one of the many indoor or outdoor cafes, stroll among the wares, and people watch.

Ortaköy, literally "middle village," was traditionally a mixed place, with Greeks, Armenians, Turks, and Jews all living together. The Greek

Orthodox church (behind the wall opposite McDonald's) and the synagogue (on the sea road) both still attract small congregations. When the Ortaköy waterfront went through a gentrification/urban renewal phase between 5 and 8 years ago, many bars moved in and there were clashes between alcohol-swilling young people and the elders from each of the three religious establishments. They ultimately came to an agreement, and now none of the cafes near the mosque serve alcohol. Out of sight of the mosque and all along the sea road, however, there are bars and **bakals** (markets) selling booze.

Even if you don't make it to Ortaköy on a Sunday, there are many little shops and restaurants where you can pass the time and spend some money. See *Where to Eat* section for restaurant recommendations in Ortaköy.

### Akmerkez

This two year old shopping mall stole the show from Galeria (see below). For what it's worth, **Akmerkez** has won both the Best European Shopping Mall award for 1995 and the Best Shopping Mall in the World award for 1996. You'll find major upscale Turkish and international brands represented here. Very crowded when the weather is bad. For the Thursday pazar across from Akmerkez, simply ask anyone *"Pazar nerede?"* (pah-zar nair-day?) and they'll point you to it. Akmerkez is open from 10 a.m. to 10 p.m. daily in Etiler.

### Bazaar 54

This is a giant emporium where you can find kilims, carpets, jewelry and anything else you might be looking for. **Bazaar 54** may tempt you by its familiarity – it's much less foreign to people accustomed to department store shopping than may be the Grand Bazaar. They are, however, doing the same thing to smaller Turkish shops they have done in the U.S.: helping to run them out of business. Moreover, Turkish friends recommend against Bazaar 54 and its relations because it's hard to know what you're getting there. If you want to have a look anyway, the address is: *Nuruosmaniye Caddesi No. 54, in Cağaoğlu, Tel. 212 511 2150.*

---

### TO BUY OR NOT TO BUY!

*Everyone has his or her own favorite shop, depending on tastes, dynamics with the shopkeeper, etc. We make only a few recommendations here, based on some personal experience and trusted recommendations. Look around, then buy where you feel comfortable with the shopkeeper, the goods, and the price.*

---

## Kilims & Carpets

If you want a more thorough listing, pick up a copy of *İstanbul: The Halı Rug Guide* published by Halı: the International Magazine of Antique Carpets and Textile Art ($14.50, available at stores with English-language books); it recommends rug dealers by neighborhood.

As background before you leave home, you may also want to find a copy of Henry Glassie's *Turkish Traditional Arts Today*.

**HAZAL KILIM & HALI**, *Mecidiye Köprüsü Sok. No. 27-29, Ortaköy, İstanbul. Tel. 212 261 7233, Fax 212 789 1923.*

An excellent selection of high quality kilims (and a few carpets) just down the street from Ortaköy's lovely baroque mosque. The owners, Engin and Ahmet Demirkol, are knowledgeable and friendly, reasoning, rightly, that the kilims will work their magic without unsolicited sales patter. It's worth going just to see the kilims displayed in the Demirkols' beautifully restored and decorated Ottoman building. Recommended.

**DÖSIM**, *Haseki Hurrem Hamamı, Ayasofya Karşısı, Sultanahmet, İstanbul. Tel. 212 638 0035.*

This shop offers carpets and kilims in a wide a range of prices and quality, but the ministry insists they are all hand made and many of them use natural dyes. Dösim is associated with the Turkish Republic Ministry of Culture and has two goals; to promote the production of traditional Turkish carpets and kilims, and to make a little money while doing so. Prices are set in Turkish Lira and posted; these prices are a good benchmark for bargaining in privately owned shops. One tip: the fixed prices are adjusted for inflation on the first Monday of each month, meaning that in the couple of days prior you're getting the best deal relative to the US dollar. Recommended.

**İPEK YOLU** (Silk Road), *Mevlana Cad., Naci Fikret Sokak No. 1, Konya. Tel. 332 353 2024, Fax 332 352 7658.*

Mehmet Uçar, owner of İpek Yolu, has been spearheading the research into natural dyes. The lost art is now making a recovery, thanks in good measure to his efforts. What this means for you is that his shop, not far from the tourism information office, has a beautiful collection of rugs. Konya has always been a marketplace for good kilim anyway, but with the revival of natural dyes they are irresistible shades of yellow, green and red. Even the least perceptive of us can appreciate these creations. Uçar has a good reputation, and is vastly knowledgeable about the business. Recommended.

**ADNAN & HASSAN**, *Grand Bazaar.*

Adnan and Hassan are perhaps the most well-known rug dealers in İstanbul. In addition to their tourist clients, they sell to locals and expatriates, and their prices are more or less fixed. They don't put undue pressure on you, and they welcome people who would like to stop in just to learn more about kilims and carpets. The majority of their rugs are new.

**SÜMERBANK**, *Istiklal Caddesi, Taksim. Tel. 212 252 0805.*
This state-owned retail chain sells genuine Hereke carpets and other handmade rugs at reasonable, fixed prices.

## Textiles

**VAKKO**, *Istiklal Caddesi 123-125 near Taksim Square (closed Sundays).*
One of Istanbul's first luxury department stores. On the second floor you can find luscious textiles at equally luscious prices. For the determined discount fabric hound, head to **Saraçhane**, on the old city side (behind the aqueduct) near the Atatürk Bridge. There you can find bolt after bolt of export-quality fabric at unbeatable prices.

## Gold

İstanbul is filled with gold shops. See the Gold section in Chapter 9, *Shopping*, for further information.

**TEPOT**, *Nuruosmaniye Cad. No. 86-88, Cağaloğlu, Tel. 212 520 7601.*
This is the jewelry shop where Hillary Rodham Clinton made some purchases on her 1996 spring break trip through the Middle East with Chelsea. The proprietor has a wide selection of traditional and modern pieces and doesn't mind people who browse. Recommended.

## Antiques

There are probably hundreds of antique shops in İstanbul. Some of the best are located in the **Teşvikiye/Nişantaşı** area, while others crowd the backstreets in the **Tünel** area at the south end of Istiklal Caddesi. Remember that it is illegal to sell, buy, or export antiques that might be considered national treasures; you must get a certification from the dealer for customs.

**SELDEN EMRE**, *Teşvikiye Cad. No. 99/1, Teşvikiye.*

**ABDULLAH ÇALABI**, *Mim Kemal Öke Cad. No. 17, Teşvikiye Tel. 212 225 0185.*

**ANTİK KONAK**, *Süleyman Nazıf Sok. No. 14/11, Teşvikiye.*

## Old Books & Maps

If you're interested in finding old books, maps, and collectibles, you're in for a treat. İstanbul has a number of shops, some ratty and run down, others catering to a discriminating clientele. Sahaflar Çarşısı near the Grand Bazaar is an old standby, but the Tünel district near the bottom of Istiklal Caddesi is awash with stores.

**SAHAFLAR ÇARSISI**, *Sahaflar Çarşısı Sok, west of the Covered Bazaar.*
A tiny lane packed with used and old book sellers, also offering

prints, photographs, old Ottoman contracts and official papers. Excellent collectibles. The street is crammed in alongside the Beyazid Mosque, just off of Divan Yolu to the north (uphill) and through a gate on the left.
**ARTRIUM**, *Tünel Pasaj No. 5/7, Beyoğlu, Tel. 212 251 4302.*
**LIBRAIRE DE PERA**, *Galipdede Cad. No. 22, Tünel, Tel. 212 245 4998.*
**OTTOMANIA**, *Istiklal Cad., Sofyalı Sok. No. 30/32, Beyoğlu, Tel. 212 243 2157.*
This short street runs parallel to Istiklal. Recommended.

## Books in English

İstanbul has some excellent English-language book stores that carry everything from contemporary critical theory to beautiful coffee table books on Turkey. Ara Güler's photographic tomes about Turkey are especially striking.
**ROBINSON CRUSOE**, *İstiklal Caddesi 389, Tünel, Beyoğlu, Tel: 212 293 6968.*
Excellent English-language section, with guides, coffee table books and an exhaustive collection of history and classics books. Located at the lower end of Istiklal Caddesi on the east side. Recommended.
**PANDORA**, *Büyük Parmakkapı Sokak 3, Beyoğlu, 212 245 1667.*
A fine selection of philosophy in English, as well as books about İstanbul and Turkey. Coming from Taksim, take a left at the Benetton. Pandora is on the left. Recommended.
**REMZI KITABEVI**, *Akmerkez, Basement Floor No. 121. Tel: 212 234 5475.*
English language books, magazines, and newspapers.

## PRACTICAL INFORMATION

### Consulates

**AMERICAN CONSULATE**, *Meşrutiyet Caddesi No.104-108, Tepebaşı, Tel. 212 251 3602.*
They have a public library here with slightly out of date periodicals.
**CANADIAN CONSULATE**, *Büyükdere Caddesi No.107/3, Gayrettepe, Tel. 212 272 5174.*
**GREAT BRITAIN CONSULATE**, *N. Meşrutiyet Caddesi No. 34, Tepebaşı, Tel. 212 293 7545.*
The British Consulate Library is on İstiklal Caddesi, just uphill of the bend in the middle. Your first visit to the library is no charge.

### Hospitals

İstanbul has several good hospitals and a collection of very able American and European-trained doctors. Ambulance sirens are rarely heard, because response times are too dismal to make ambulances particularly worthwhile. If you need to get to a hospital, get there yourself by taxi. For specialists, consult the U.S. Consulate, which keeps a list of recommended doctors. İstanbul's best hospitals are the: **AMIRAL BRISTOL HASTAHANESI/AMERIKALI HASTAHANESİ** (American Hospital), *Güzelbahçe Sok. No. 20, Nişantaşı, Tel. 212 231 4050.*

The American Hospital is widely regarded as the city's best, with emergency service and some English speaking staff. The hospital is located in Nişantaşı in the hills above Dolmabahçe Palace.

**INTERNATIONAL HOSPITAL,** *İstanbul Cad. No. 82, Yeşilyurt, Tel. 212 663 3000.*

The only other hospital recommended by the American consulate. Several English speaking staff members and doctors.

Many people come down with nose and throat ailments after long flights from North America. If it turns serious, see the U.S. educated Doğan Senocak, *Ear Nose and Throat, Çamlık Sok., Aslan Apt. D. 7, Etiler, İstanbul, Tel. 212 263 1388.*

If you require blood testing or X-rays, you may be referred to a Pakize Tarzı Laboratory. One of the clinics is down the street from the American Hospital and right four blocks *(Valikonağı Caddesi No. 86, Nişantaşı, Tel. 212 241 3895),* and another is in Etiler across the street from Akmerkez shopping center *(Zeytinoğlu Caddesi, Arzu 1, Apt. K, Etiler, 212 287 2560).*

**Places of Worship**

Obviously if you're a practicing Muslim you're in for a treat. Whatever your religion, bear in mind that Mosques are houses of God, and many find them a good place to pray. If you're looking for a little more community, however, try the following places:

**DUTCH CHAPEL,** *Union Church of İstanbul, Postacular Sok. No. 4, İstiklal Caddesi, Hollanda Konsolosluğu, Beyoğlu, Tel. 212 244 5212.*

English language services at 9:30 and 11:00 on Sunday, with tea and coffee after the second ceremony. This is the oldest Protestant church in the city, at the lower end of İstiklal Caddesi two blocks south of the Saint Antoine Church.

**ST. ANTOINE CHURCH,** *İstiklal Caddesi, Beyoğlu, Tel. 212 244 0935.*

This beautiful cathedral, occasionally used for concerts during the early summer İstanbul Festival series, is still used by İstanbul's Catholic community. Mass in Italian nightly at 7:00, with English mass at 10:00 on Sundays. No Latin mass.

**NEVE SHALOM,** *Büyük Hendek Caddesi No. 61, Şişhane, Tel. 212 244 6675.*

İstanbul's synagogue is located between the American Consulate and Galata Tower. Büyük Hendek Caddesi intersects with Galata Tower three blocks downhill.

## Police

The local emergency number is **155**, but there's little chance of reaching an English-speaker on the other end – it is obviously a good idea to have a Turk with an understanding of the problem make the call. Police maintain a fairly high profile, so you'll probably always be fairly near an officer of the law. The bazaars have their own brand of police to settle disputes and maintain order.

## EXCURSIONS & DAY TRIPS

Other area excursions are treated in subsequent chapters because they deserve more than a day or two. In this section, in addition to travel agents, we've listed one main excursion north of Istanbul – **Edirne**.

### Travel Agencies

The Turkish language puts up a fairly impenetrable barrier during a lot of travel planning. A reliable English-speaking travel agent makes your life much easier if you're making travel plans within the country. There are hundreds of travel agencies in İstanbul to choose from, but we reserve our highest recommendation for the infinitely patient staff at Imperial Turizm. The other agencies are helpful within their niches.

**IMPERIAL TURIZM,** *Divan Yolu Caddesi No. 31, Sultanahmet, İstanbul, 212 513 9430, Fax 212 512 3291.*

The staff at Imperial is efficient, helpful, English-language fluent and, above all, honest. They can book planes, buses, and ferries within and without Turkey. Imperial offers a service bus from their office to the bus station. You may have some problems when trying to make arrangements with them from home, however. They give priority to people who are standing in their office.

**TUR-ISTA TURIZM,** *Divan Yolu Cad. No. 16 A, Sultanahmet, 212 527 2531, Fax 212 519 3792.*

Authorized to book train travel throughout Turkey.

**TURKISH MARITIME LINES,** *Rıhtım Cad., Karaköy, 212 245 5366, Fax 212 251 9025.*

They can arrange international ferry travel to Venice and Brindisi, Italy.

**SHE TOURISM,** *Cumhuriet Cad. 309/3, Harbiye, 212 233 3670, Fax 212 233 3673.*

She runs tours around İstanbul of fair quality, but is most useful for organizing things you cannot realistically do on your own, such as private yacht cruises on the Bosphorous and Princes Islands. Schedule well in advance.

**For More Information**
There are **Tourism Information offices** in the railway station at Sirkeci, along Divan Yolu Caddesi in Sultanahmet, and at Atatürk International Airport. Most offices in İstanbul have an English speaking staff member, and they are certain to have free English language maps and scads of photo-packed free literature about whichever regions are of interest. The main office is at the airport, *Tel. 212 663 6363-82.*

---

### ESCAPES FROM ISTANBUL

*If İstanbul threatens to short circuit your brain, try getting away to one of the following spots:*

**Kilios**
*Kilios beach is located on the Black Sea by the mouth of the Bosphorous. This long sand beach is choked with İstanbullus on summer weekends, but is otherwise a good place to escape the city to.*

**Princes Islands**
*Ferries depart from Eminönü (Adalar terminal) and Kabataş for the Princes Islands (See Getting Around). These islands have pretty beaches and a relaxed pace. The islands are very busy on weekends.*

**Yalova (Termal)**
*A springs wells up near Yalova on the Asian shore. The Romans took advantage of it, as did the Byzantines, and even Süleyman the Magnificent and Atatürk lowered themselves into the soothing waters. The healing powers of Yalova/Termal's hot springs are explained thusly in one of the hotel brochures: "with its radioactivity, semi-dead cells are reactivated." If you can bear up to that, Termal is a fairly quick ferry ride from İstanbul, 15 kilometers from the Yalova ferry stop. If you'd like to spend a night here, the Turban Yalova Hotel (Yalova, Tel. 226 675 7400, Fax 226 675 7413. Double: $64) is recommended, an old standby at the area, just uphill from the extensive thermal bath.*

---

# EDIRNE

There is precious little to see in Thrace other than **Edirne**, the former Adrianople. Edirne is a must-see for those interested in Ottoman history and architecture. Interesting for the architecture of its buildings – including Sinan's greatest work – and its Ottoman ruins, Edirne can be seen in a day from İstanbul. The city is not convenient to most travel routes, unless you are continuing into Bulgaria or Greece. This is an excellent place to bone up on mosque architecture.

## ARRIVALS & DEPARTURES

### By Car

Edirne is a 2.5 hour drive up the E-80 freeway from İstanbul. The E-80 is the road that runs across the northern – Black Sea side – Bosphorous bridge, past the Esenler Otogar and continuing north into Thrace and Europe. The route has changed very little since ancient times, when a major Roman road connected Rome, the western capital, with Constantinople, the eastern capital. Keep an eye out for buses, which, as in the city, often run this route at high rates of speed, and are laissez-faire about lane markings.

### By Public Transportation

Several bus companies offer service to Edirne, with buses running hourly. Edirne is a three hour trip from Istanbul's new Otogar at Esenler, unless you happen to be entering the city in the morning or leaving it in the evening.

Cağlar Turism *(Tel. 212 658 0851)* offers nonstop service in big Mercedes buses which can be pleasant. The cost is $2.50.

## HISTORY

Edirne, north of the junction of the Tunja and Meric Rivers, can trace its history back into the distant past. Xenophon's 10,000 probably fought battles near here on behalf of the Thracian king Seuthes, but the city never truly arrived until the much-traveled Roman Emperor **Hadrian** founded Edirne (Hadrianopolis) to command the land approaches to Constantinople.

Through the centuries it indeed proved the key to Constantinople, and thus the key to much of the Mediterranean basin: one of Rome's signal defeats took place here when Emperor Valens and his entire army were massacred by an army of Goths in the fourth century; the Third Crusade wrested the city from Byzantine hands in 1187, paving the way for Istanbul's fall to the Fourth Crusade in 1204; and the Ottomans captured the city in 1360 and made it their capital as a precursor to cutting off and defeating İstanbul in 1453. Thereafter Edirne was a staging ground for Ottoman assaults against Christian Europe.

Fortunately artisans have lavished almost as much attention on the city as generals and pashas, leaving Edirne with a proud legacy of mosques, the ruins of the 14th century Ottoman palace, and even inexpensive baths of Sinan's design. The city retains the aura of an outpost, and the frequency of Cyrillic and Greek alphabet signs attest to the number of Bulgarians and Greeks that cross the nearby border to do business in Edirne's bustling markets. The population is estimated to be more than 130,000.

## WHERE TO STAY

Be under no illusions: Edirne caters to people on their way elsewhere and to hardcore mosque devotees. Neither group demands five star service, and neither group receives it. Hotels in this area have no more than two stars, but those listed below are clean, well-managed, have parking, phones, and at least a little English.

**RUSTEMPAŞA KERVANSARAY OTEL**, *Kapili Han Cad., No. 57, Edirne, Tel. 284 225 6119, Fax 284 212 0462. Rooms: 22 winter, 100 summer. Double: $45 with breakfast. Credit cards. Nightclub, cafe, and billiard room.*

In a town demonstrating the legacy of the architect Sinan, it is fitting to spend the night in a building he designed. The kervansaray, built in 1561, was one of dozens, even hundreds of secure stopover points for caravans making their way to and from İstanbul. The building's contemporary history began with a remodel in the early 1980s. Although gentler than the Russian army's remodel in 1877, when a chapel by a fountain in the courtyard was destroyed, the recent restoration is well done. It's not the restorer's fault the old stone hearth in each room now contains a television that picks up Bulgarian programming.

Despite such indignities to the master architect, the kervansaray has atmosphere in its bones. You'll appreciate the domed ceilings, the old wooden doors, and the broad stone hallways. You may not appreciate the racket from the bar and billiards room downstairs, which can continue until 2 a.m.

**SULTAN HOTEL**, *Talatpasa Asfalti, Edirne, Tel. 284 225 1372, Fax 284 225 5763. Rooms: 90. Double: $38 with breakfast. Restaurant.*

Officials with the tourism bureau are particularly fond of this tidy and nicely run hotel. Manager Mehmet Gokay is friendly and helpful, and the decor is decent. There are 20 rooms with baths in the hotel, the others have showers. Rooms, like all of the rooms in Edirne, are fairly plain. The Sultan may take credit cards in 1997. The restaurant is open May-September.

**OTEL SABAN ACIKGOZ**, *Tahmis Meydanı Cilingirler Cad. No. 9, Edirne, Tel. 284 213 1404, Fax 284 213 4516. Rooms: 34. Double: $41.*

Just four years old, the Acikgoz, just south of the Kervansaray, is one of the nattiest hotels in Edirne, with a spacious, nicely decorated lobby and friendly help. The rooms offer fairly lousy views, but are decent and well cared for. Like all hotels in Edirne, it's centrally located.

## WHERE TO EAT

Chances are your visit to Edirne is a short one, and from a dining standpoint that's just as well. With the exception of Lalezar, restaurants in the city are undistinguished. Hotel restaurants are a good bet – the restaurant at the Park Hotel is deserving of particular praise. Edirne is as good a place as any to try cheap local fare, with several restaurants in the city center serving inexpensive meals that will do nothing to ravish your palate, but can be pretty damn good if you're hungry. **Cati Restaurant** on Talatpasa Caddesi offers good, basic food on this model.

**LALEZAR**, *Karaç Yolu, Edirne, Tel. 284 212 2489. Moderate.*

The Lalezar is a solid exception to an otherwise undistinguished dining landscape. The restaurant is located on the Meric River south of town.

## SEEING THE SIGHTS

Coming from İstanbul you arrive from the southeast on Talatpasa Asfaltı, Edirne's main road. The road bends to the left at the city center heading in the direction of Bulgaria. Most sites of religious and historical interest are only a Koran's throw from here, exceptions being the Kırkpınar wrestling area and the Beyazid II complex, about one kilometer to the north and northwest, respectively. The **tourist information offices** are both on Talatpasa, the first just around the corner from Uç Serefeli *(Hurriet Meydanı No. 17; Tel. 284 225 1518)* and the second, main office is west of downtown *(Talatpasa No. 76A; Tel. 284 225 5260 and 225 1490)*.

Three of Edirne's principal mosques, the Eski Camii, the Uç Serefeli Camii, and the Selimiye Camii, offer a convenient clinic in the evolution of Ottoman architecture. The Ottomans were in all things excellent learners, and as their territory expanded they had an increasingly vast selection of architectural lessons to consider. First there were the designs of the Selçuks, like themselves Turks, which were incorporated in the Ottomans' early mosques and public buildings.

**Eski Cami** (1414), the oldest mosque in Edirne, was built while Edirne was the Ottoman capital and deviates little from Selçuk style. The structural limitations of the old mosque are glaring when compared with the nearby Selimiye, but Eski Camii was a step in the evolution toward such ambitious buildings. In its favor, the pursuit of vast, airy spaces left behind some of the charm of the relatively confining Eski Cami, whose calligraphic inscriptions of Koranic verses are immediate and mesmerizing. Although Eski Cami's architecture has been upstaged by later mosques, it boasts an inch-long sliver of stone from the Kaaba in Mecca, located on the right – southwest – side of the mihrab. The columns on the face of the building were swiped from nearby Roman ruins, accounting for their contrast with the stone and brick used elsewhere.

Two blocks northwest of Eski Cami, **Uç Serefeli Cami** (1447) was built at the behest of Murat II, father of Mehmet the Conqueror. The mosque's name, "three balconies," derives from the balconies high atop the northwest minaret, which was the tallest minaret in the Middle East until the construction of the Selimiye Mosque one century later. In Uç Serefeli the Turks incorporated some of the Seljuk style, but were already making improvements on it to suit their taste and to take advantage of technological advances, as evidenced in the relatively imposing size of the central dome. The forecourt and fountain of the Uç Serefeli were innovations that later became a fixture in Ottoman architecture. Reconstruction work is under way on part of the mosque, but it remains open to the public.

With the capture of İstanbul less than a decade after Uç Serefeli's completion, the Turks had a wealth of Byzantine architecture – including the gargantuan Haghia Sophia – to study and assimilate. It was in this atmosphere that following generations of Turkish architects would fuse the Selçuk and Byzantine traditions and create a distinctly Ottoman style. Sinan, the most renowned of the Ottoman architects, constructed a mosque that is arguably the pinnacle of the alloyed style here to accompany the Eski and Uç Serefeli: the **Selimiye Mosque** (1579), atop a hill in northeast Edirne, dominates the city's landscape – and the Thracian plain below, for that matter.

The mosque was built at the very apex of Ottoman power under the son of Süleyman the Magnificent, who was not particularly magnificent himself. Selim II immersed himself in wine and the harem, engaging in affairs of state only enough to precipitate the fateful battle of Lepanto, which broke the back of Ottoman naval might and signaled the decline of the empire. Selim II eventually slipped in a hamam after drinking a full bottle of wine and cracked his skull. He is probably undeserving of this legacy, the mosque Sinan considered his greatest achievement.

The Selimiye is, however, a fitting testament to one of the world's great architects at the height of his powers (he was 83 upon the mosque's completion) and to the wealth of an empire that commanded the entire eastern Mediterranean, the Middle East, and North Africa. The mosque is a quantum level beyond its predecessors, with a massive open area whose eight mammoth pillars allowed Sinan to incorporate 999 windows, one for every name of God, and achieve marvelous lighting. The symmetry of the windows is beautiful – begging the question where, in this symmetrical building, did Sinan put the odd window? The grand dome – 31.5 meters – makes the Selimiye seem fuller than even the vast Süleymaniye. The Selimiye further benefits from its dominating position atop Edirne's hill, where it is almost completely unobscured, its galleried minarets soaring up out of the earth.

Mosque Design 101 concluded, you may want to have a look around the rest of the city. The **Beyazid II complex**, a kilometer from the city center to the northeast, is definitely worth a visit. The complex, restored in the 1970s, includes a mosque, kitchen, hospital, school, and store rooms. The design of the hospital (Darussifa) in particular was on the architectural cutting edge at the time. The **Archaeology and Ethnography Museum** and **Turkish and Islamic Art Museum**, behind the Selimiye Mosque, are each well worth the 75¢ admission price. The former traces the history of the area from prehistoric times through the Byzantine Empire.

The art museum offers further architectural information about the city's mosques, as well as a selection of glass work, weaponry, and, notably, a pavilion of the type taken on imperial campaigns. Other things to see include the **Muradiye Cami** (1436), a mosque commissioned by Murat II that demonstrates another gradation in the development of Ottoman architecture, between the time of the Eski and Uç Serefeli Mosques – it has a gorgeous prayer niche.

One of the most fascinating events in Turkey is Edirne's annual **Kırkpınar Festival**, held during one week in June or July. Activities surround Kırkpınar, but in the end it is all window dressing for the real event: **Oiled Wrestling**. Thousands of burly men pour into town each year to slather themselves with oil and wrestle in a massive round robin tournament, the winner making off with some cash and livestock, and, most important, the title "Başpehlivan" (Chief wrestler). If your arrival coincides with Kırkpınar, you're unlikely to find room at the inn, but it's worth a struggle to stay awhile and witness this greasy, manly spectacle. The tourist offices will be of great help with tickets, which should be available at the municipality (belediye).

The site of the Kırkpınar wrestling, north of town at a fork in the Tunca rivers, is alongside the ruins of the old **Ottoman Royal Palace**. This was once the equivalent of Istanbul's Topkapı Palace, but it fell into disrepair during the 18th and 19th centuries and was consumed after an Ottoman ammunition depot exploded here during the Russian offensive of 1877. The ruins are decidedly ruined, but the few remaining buildings on the once-vast grounds make for a quiet, interesting walk when the oiled-up madness isn't going on.

If you are visiting from İstanbul, you will definitely want to pay a visit to one of Sinan's baths. The **Tahtakale**, **Mezit Bey**, and **Sokollu** hamams are all of his design, and are all considerably cheaper than baths in İstanbul. The Sokollu Hamam, conveniently next to the Uç Serefeli Cami, is roomy and has separate baths for men and women. The smaller Mezit Bey hamam is to the right of the statue of Sinan as you look at the Selimiye; men and women bathe at different times, but the wooden interior is superior to the Sokollu. Tahtakale, located near the junction of Sarajlar Cad. and Eski İstanbul road south of downtown doesn't get much tourist business, and may be the better for it. Baths in each of these facilities cost about $2, with massages $4.

If it's a beautiful day and you have the time, take a walk or a short drive to the junction of the Meric and Tunca rivers. Between the first and second sections of Sinan's bridges is a pleasant, lightly forested area for a picnic or simple peace and quiet. It is also on the way to Lalezar restaurant, across the second bridge and right.

# 12. SOUTH OF ISTANBUL

On your way to or from İstanbul, try to find a way to shoehorn in some of the interesting sites south of the Sea of Marmara. **Bursa** is the most intriguing city in the area, offering fascinating Ottoman relics, skiing, thermal springs and silk fabric. **Iznik** and **Erdek** are both established on the sites of ancient cities, Nicaea and Cyzicus, respectively, and each is worthy of an afternoon.

## BURSA

**Bursa**, the first Ottoman capital, remains home to some of the most important relics and monuments in Ottoman Empire. Anyone with an interest in the trappings of an ascendant empire will enjoy the tombs and mosques of the empire's first sultans, and the growth of their wealth and artistic assurance. There is little evidence of 2,000 years of habitation that predated the arrival of the Ottomans, but there is more to Bursa than history alone. People flock here for the thermal baths welling up at the foot of **Mt. Uludağ**, the skiing atop the mountain peak, and for markets loaded with silks and other textiles.

"Green Bursa" has also been famed for its beauty, standing atop one of Mt. Uludağ's (an ancient Mt. Olympus) great spurs and looking out over the orchards of the Bithynian plain below. Unfortunately the beauty is slipping away, sacrificed to the industrial activity associated with trade on the Sea of Marmara. Green Bursa is quickly giving way to the reds of tile roofs as far as the eye can see. The city has a population of 1.8 million and is sprawled out over an area 30 miles wide.

Bursa was founded by the Bithynian King **Prusias** in the third century B.C., and through Roman times the city was called Prusa in honor of its builder. The Bithnians were initially thought of as a crude, warlike race, in keeping with their obstinate attacks on Xenophon's 10,000 in 401 B.C. The Bithnians were responsible for shipping in Celts as mercenaries in their ongoing battles, but this proved short-sighted, as the Celts settled near Ankara and became Anatolia's most hated people, forever waging war against their terrified neighbors. The Kingdom of Pergamon eventually put an end to the threat in 230 B.C., and it was soon after that when Prusias established his city.

The city prospered, developing ties with Rome in the west and Pontus in the east. When the two realms came to blows under Mithradites VI Eupator (120-63 B.C.), Bithnia went over to Mithradites, a decision that proved costly. After the Roman General Lucullus' remarkable campaign against a joint Bithnian/Pontic force, the Kingdom of Pontus was forced to recoil to its traditional place on the Black Sea and Bithnia was forced to appease Rome. To this end they accepted their exiled king, Nicomedes IV, who, like Attalus III of Pergamon before him, bequeathed his kingdom to Rome.

The city's command of the fertile Bithnian plain ensured that it remained important under Roman rule, but with the decay of Roman dominion the city was exposed to various invaders, usually en route to Constantinople. The Goths, Arabs, and Byzantines alternately ravaged and rebuilt the city. Bursa fell to the Ottomans in 1326 after a seven year siege, and the Ottoman's first sultan, Osman, entered the city gates only after his death. Sultan Osman's tomb – and the tombs of the next five sultans and many of their kin – can be found here.

Many of Bursa's most famous monuments, such as the Muradiye, the Great Mosque, and the Green Mosque date from the early years of the Ottoman Empire, but even these structures suffered through occasional invasions and natural disasters – notably Tamurlane's occupation in 1402-3 and the quake of 1855, which toppled all but one of the city's minarets. Bursa and its damaged historical sites were rebuilt, usually quite faithfully, allowing us to see the birth of Ottoman architecture with its attendant artwork and craftsmanship.

## ARRIVALS & DEPARTURES

Bursa is located due south of İstanbul, but separated from it by the sea of Izmit; thus land routes are rather serpentine. Sea-land routes are the most popular, with ferries leaving from several sites in İstanbul.

### By Bus

Buses make the trip from Istanbul's otogar (bus station) to Bursa hourly, but take different routes to get there. The best alternative are buses that meet the car ferries at Eskihisar/Darica and shuttle you across the Bay of Izmit to Topçular east of Yalova. From there they continue on to Bursa's central bus station in the north of town. Buses that take the

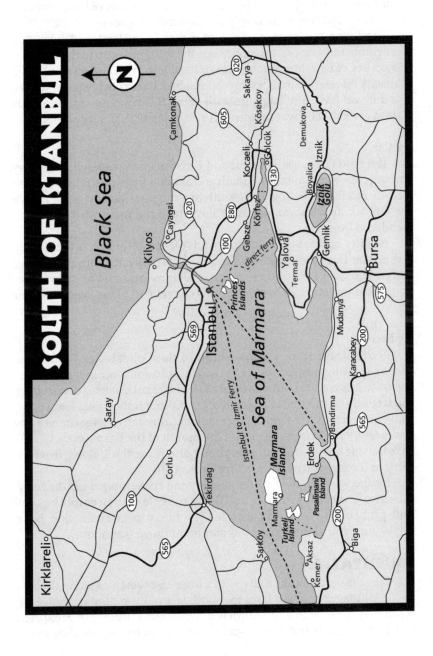

ferry route are marked Feriböt ile and cost slightly more. It is a 4 hour trip. Some buses take the land route, skirting around the Bay of Izmit through Izmit itself, and these are longer and certainly less scenic.

The Bursa bus station is a zoo; if you are patient and relatively unencumbered you can take a city bus the three miles up to the pleasant district of Çekirge (bus number 24), or head into town and transfer at the main city bus station to a Çekirge-bound bus. It is probably wiser to take a taxi if you have any baggage with you – Bursa's buses from the bus station are almost always stuffed. A taxi ride out to Çekirge costs $5.

### By Car

The roads between İstanbul and Bursa are adequate, with freeway driving between İstanbul and Izmit and another freeway stretch between Yalova and Bursa. Follow E-80 south to Izmit, then head west to Yalova via Gölcük and Karamüsel. At Yalova take the main road south via Gemlik to Bursa.

A better option is to follow the signs off of E-80 at Darica to the ferry terminal at Darica and take a Yalova ferry, actually arriving at Topçular just east of Yalova. From there, follow the signs through Yalova to Bursa, about one and one half hours. Bursa is convenient to the İstanbul-Izmir route.

### By Ferry

Ferries leave from Kabataş south of the Dolmabahçe Palace. The seabus, or Denizbus, ferries are two-deck hydrofoil machines that rocket across to Yalova in about one hour ($4). The regular ferries depart from the left side of the Kabataş terminal, and though they take longer and move slower they are a much more enticing alternative on a summer day and pass by the Princes Islands at the mouth of the Bosphorous ($2.50). In Yalova follow just about everybody else filing the 200 feet from the ferry to the big coaches headed for Bursa ($3).

By the way, there is a reason everyone rushes to get off the ferry: buses leave when they're full, and if you straggle onto an empty bus you will probably sit and wait awhile. The bus trip takes another hour, depositing you at the central bus station in Bursa (see above).

## ORIENTATION

Bursa is very simple, a city with a long east-west axis along the base of Mt. Uludağ. Because it hugs the south face of the mountain, however, it can play tricks with you – north is down, south is up. Sights are spread out through town, but the hot springs emerge in the western heights, in a neighborhood called **Çekirge**, and several good hotels make that an excellent base. The main Çekirge road, **Çekirge Caddesi**, runs through the central part of town (changing names to Altıparmak, Atatürk and finally Namazgah Caddesi) and past most of the major sites.

**Tourist information offices** are at the center of town (*Ulu Cami Parkı Orhangazi Altgecidi No. 1, Heykel, Tel. 224 220 1848, Fax 224 220 1848*) and in the lowlands near the bus terminal (*Fevzi Cakmak Caddesi, Fomara Ishanı, 6th floor, Tel. 224 254 2274, Fax 224 253 0411*).

## WHERE TO STAY

The finest hotels are clustered in the **Çekirge heights** of western Bursa, where marble baths are a fixture in even the most spartan accommodations. The top end hotels are staggeringly overpriced and should be negotiated down before arrival. The pensions in town are recommended.

**THE HOTEL KERVANSARAY TERMAL**, *Çekirge Meydanı, Bursa, Tel. 224 233 9300, Fax 224 233 9324. Rooms: 211. Double: $170. Three restaurants, two bars, casino, baths, pool, disco.*

The only one of Bursa's three five-star hotels to really earn its stars, this hotel was built in 1988 to accompany the beautifully domed **Old Springs** (Eski Kaplıca – see Baths under *Sports & Recreation* below). The two are incorporated into a tasteful whole, with halls and open spaces mimicking the domes and arches of the baths. The interiors are light and finished in marble and brass, with greenery cascading down from above. The rooms are done in subtle pinks, with dark wood cabinetry, and have the amenities you would expect. Less tasteful, but quite popular, is the casino downstairs.

A unique attraction of the hotel is its fully equipped physical therapy section, which uses the waters of the Eski Kaplıca to help heal a long list of ailments, including rheumatism, kidney stones, the pain of broken limbs, and gout. Süleyman the Magnificent used waters from a nearby springs for his gout. Use of the Eski Kaplıca is not included in the room rate – neither is use of the springs pool on the first floor or the fitness center – but consultation with a physical therapy professional is free.

**HUZUR TERMAL HOTEL**, *Çekirge 1 Murat Caddesi No. 31, Bursa, Tel. 224 234 5250, Fax 224 234 4576. Rooms: 22. Double: $75. Restaurant, baths.*

This little gem is tucked away in an unassuming corner across from some of the massive four star behemoths. The Huzur opened in 1995, and is refreshingly clean, with unusual attention to detail. The woodwork is splendid, and the decor, from molding to carpet, is very nice, with stained glass in many of the valley-side rooms and natural springwater piped into every room's bathtub through brass spigots. Like all of the

Çekirge hotels it has a bath – unlike the other high end places it has a small mosque upstairs and your room includes prayer beads, a Koran, and various other religious books, including one with the daunting title *"How to Convert an Enemy to Islam."* We adored this place, but be warned: although they are eager for American guests, the staff at Huzur will send you rifling through your Turkish-English dictionary.

**THE ANATOLIA HOTEL**, *Çekirge Meydanı, Bursa, Tel. 224 233 9400, Fax 224 233 9408. Rooms: 93. Double: $170. Restaurant, two bars, baths, pool, disco.*

This eight story hotel has a commanding view of the Bithnian plain, complementing the best standard rooms in Bursa. The Anatolia is pricey considering it does not have the exhaustive list of amenities of Bursa's five star hotels, but it makes up for it with good service under reception manager Güngör Aktepe. Anatolia takes full advantage of Çekirge's waters with gorgeous deep marble baths that can be rented hourly, and the Eski Kaplıca baths are just across the street.

**SAFRAN HOTEL**, *Kale Sokak, Tophane, Bursa, Tel. 224 224 7216. Fax 224 224 7219. Rooms: 10. Double: $65.*

The Safran Hotel is the most attractive and interesting small hotel in Bursa. The Safran's owners have restored a mansion, and take meticulous care of it.

**KONAK PALAS OTEL**, *Çekirge 1 Murat Camii Arkası No. 11, Bursa, Tel. 224 236 5113. Rooms: 26 Double: $15. Bath, no restaurant. No credit cards.*

Do not be put off by the Konak's run-down looks, it is one of the nicest budget accommodations you will find. Scrunched in an alley behind the Murat I Mosque, the Konak is tidy, clean, and managed by a decent gentleman named Mustafa Dörtçelik – you might even say the place is charming. Everything here is bare and simple, with the exception of the fine marble bath in the basement – included at no charge, like the bread and cheese breakfast. Other pensions are scattered nearby.

Otherwise, Bursa's hotels are differentiated only by the number of amenities, not their generally lackluster quality (Çekirge-area marble baths excepted). You will find five star amenities at the redoubtable **HOTEL ÇELIK PALAS**, *Çekirge Caddesi No. 79, Bursa, Tel. 224 233 3800, Fax 224 236 1910. Rooms: 173.*

### In Uludag

**HOTEL KERVANSARAY ULUDAĞ**, *1 Gelişim Bölgesi, Uludağ, Tel. 224 285 2187, Fax 224 285 2193; Rooms: 127. Double: $90 weekdays, $140 weekends.*

The most sophisticated of Uludağ's mountaintop hotels, with immediate access to the lifts. The Kervansaray has a great lobby and amenities, including a pool, but the rooms aren't especially appealing. Half board accommodations available.

**BECEREN OTEL**, *Uludağ, Tel. 224 285 2111, Fax 224 285 2119. Rooms: 80. Double: $80 weekdays, $120 weekends.*

A rickety, atmospheric three star hotel offering full board accommodations, so all you have to think about is skiing.

**GENC YAZICI HOTEL**, *Gelişim Bölgesi, Uludağ, Tel. 224 256 0010, Fax 224 285 2045. Rooms: 47. Double: $75 weedays, $100 weekends.*

Ricketier still, but a fun spot to stay. With the antiquated equipment and decor you'll feel like you're in an early eighties ski movie.

## WHERE TO EAT

Bursa's local specialty is the İskender Kebap, and you should try this if it sounds at all appealing (see Taste of the Town sidebar below); we've had to try it repeatedly as conscientious guidebook writers.

The second dining alternative for anyone in town briefly is to eat on **Arap Şükrü Sokak**, just west of the city center. The cobbled way begins at the fish market on the uphill side of Altıparmak Caddesi, and the lane takes you west past restaurants and cafes. The area pulsates in the summer, with tables out on the street, and it pulsates through the night all year round. The best restaurants are those with the big black seal and stars from the tourism bureau. The name Arap Şükrü seems associated with every one of the restaurants in this strip, and they can be hard to distinguish from one another.

---

### TASTE OF THE TOWN

*Many towns have their culinary specialties, but Bursa's probably tops the list. None of Bursa's top-end restaurants are likely to serve you anything better than the local fare, İskender Kebap. In the İskender, dense pieces of pide bread are covered with slices of doner kebap, which are in turn covered with a tangy tomato sauce and butter. It is served with yogurt. There are lots of small family restaurants that specialize in this dish – do yourself a favor and try one of these away from the main strip. Portions are bigger and quality is better. Iskender places are all over town, but the best ones are the little places in the streets above the Heykel at city center.*

---

**RESTAURANT ARAP ŞÜKRÜ**, *Arap Şükrü Sok., Bursa, Tel. 224 221 9202. Moderate-Expensive.*

Our favorite option in the nest of Arap Şükrü restaurants. Shrimp, appetizers, and a bottle of rakı for two costs $20.

**PICCOLO BAR,** *Arap Şükrü Sok., Bursa, Tel. 224 221 9389. Moderate-Expensive.*
A nice terrace retreat above the bustling market street.
**PIZZA KASRI,** *Çekirge Meydanı, Bursa, Tel. 224 233 9400. Moderate-Expensive. Major credit cards.*
The Italian food turned out at this 150 year-old Ottoman mansion is good and the venue is great, overlooking the domed baths at Eski Kaplıca and the plain below. The ambiance is not the least bit Italian but the pastas are decent and the pizza will hit the spot.

## SEEING THE SIGHTS

Because the rebuilding periods have been far more thorough than the ransacking periods, Bursa is awash with interesting sights and stories. In the likely event you are in Bursa for a short stay, there are a few things it would be a shame not to see.

### The Muradiye Complex

A good place to start a day of sightseeing is at the **Muradiye complex** (from Çekirge follow Çekirge Caddesi towards town, then take a soft right up Murat Caddesi for three blocks ) on the west side of town. The complex was built with a mosque and school (**medresse**), but the cemetery is what truly distinguishes this site. Begin at the **Muradiye Mosque** to the left of the tombs and the school. The building was built on the orders of Murat II, a shrewd ruler who consolidated the empire and built up its resources so that upon his death in 1451 his son, Mehmet Fatih, was able to immediately set about the conquest of Constantinople. In a period of rapid architectural advancement, sure enough, the Muradiye Cami had something new to offer with the "courtyard dome" over the center of the building matched in size and height by the "prayer dome" above the mihrab at the prayer-side of the mosque. The enlarged front area was imitated later, and presaged opening up space in the mosque on a grand scale. The mosque has some beautiful tile work.

There are four major tombs in the garden behind the mosque and the school, with another eight smaller tombs of wives, dignitaries, and even concubines. The garden is well cared-for, with shaped shrubs and winding paths. Clockwise from the tomb of Sehzade (prince) Ahmet, which is the tomb to the left of the path between the medresse and the mosque, you'll find the following tombs:

**Tomb of Sehzade Ahmet:** There is some argument over whose bodies are here, exactly. Ahmet was a son of Beyazid II, but it might also be one of Mehmet's sons, whom Murat II had blinded upon ascending the throne. The latter Ahmet died of the plague together with his brothers.

**Tomb of Murat II**: The largest tomb belongs to the sultan, who asked to be buried in the earth of Bursa, and specified that a "sumptuous mausoleum" not be erected. He got his wish, more or less, with a grave within a simple building, but the artisans could not help sprucing it up a little bit with some grand old columns and later added beautifully carved wooden eaves. Murat II (1421-1451) was the final sultan to be buried in Bursa. The thick-trunked tree across the path from the entrance to the tomb was planted when the tomb was built. Murat II was the father of Mehmet II Fatih, conqueror of İstanbul.

**Tomb of Prince Mustafa**: Mustafa has a sad place in Ottoman history. He was the strongest, boldest, and most just of Süleyman the Magnificent's sons, but palace intrigue turned Süleyman against him. Süleyman ordered his son killed, helping clear the way for the incompetent Selim II to ascend the throne. This is a classic turning point in Ottoman history, for under a worthy successor who knows what heights the empire might have reached? Mustafa's tomb is beautifully appointed with flowered Iznik tiles. Note the differences in craftmanship between the original tiles and their modern replacements – a cluster of three on the left side, another cluster of four on the right.

**Tomb of the sons of Mehmet II Fatih**: Mehmet's first son, Mustafa, died during a campaign in central Anatolia and was buried here. His brothers Cem and Beyazid II were left as rivals for the throne, which Beyazid assumed. Cem tried to establish his own capital in Bursa, but was driven out and forced into exile. He died a political pawn in Italy, and his brother repatriated his remains for burial here. The interior of the tomb is dazzling, with colorful gold-leaf tile, restored painting, and stained glass above a sea of blue and green tiles – a far cry from grandfather Murat II's simple resting place.

The school is used today as a dispensary and a health center. There is some evidence of its old beauty – the tiles and stained glass at the back of the courtyard, for instance – but it is largely run down, and you'll be watched curiously if you have a look at the place.

### Other Sights in Bursa

From the Muradiye, you can follow the signs one half block down the street facing the complex and visit an 18th century Ottoman house. The three story house, its salons and parlors still decorated as they were at the time, suggests the glamour of the Ottoman high classes ($1). Continuing up Kaplica Caddesi from the Muradiye in a winding course, you pass through remnants of the city gates atop the bluff and wind past Şehadet Mosque. Just prior to descending down out of the old fortress, you will see a clock tower to your left, with some structures in the park at its base. These are the **Tombs of Osman and Orhan**, the empire's first two sultans. Their tombs have changed appreciably from their original form, although they remain in the same location. The originals were demolished in the 1855 quake, and were rebuilt by Sultan Abdülaziz in 1863 in the Ottoman baroque style – in other words, the design of these tombs is even younger than the Dolmabahçe Palace in İstanbul.

Descending down out of the **Hisar** (fortress) area puts you on Atatürk Caddesi near the **Ulu Cami**. This mosque, below the intersection of Maksim Caddesi and Atatürk Caddesi, is the center of Bursa's religious life, and it is one of the finest mosques in Anatolia. Like Edirne's Eski Cami, the Ulu Cami was built just as the Ottomans began to find their own sense of style. Consider the evolution in the course of just over a century: in 1388 the empire was ruled by Murat I, a conqueror who gave little thought to art or architecture and was unable to write. By 1515, the Ottomans had become enlightened to the point that when Selim the Grim seized Tabriz and massacred all of his prisoners he spared the artists, shipping them home to help decorate his empire. Ah, the humanizing force of art!

Murat's son, Beyazid I, commissioned Ulu Cami, which was completed in 1399. The construction of the mosque has an interesting story: Beyazid swore he would build 20 mosques in thanks for one of his major victories in Europe, but some of his financial people explained that he couldn't afford 20 mosques. Apparently after some haggling with Allah, Beyazid commissioned the building of a single mosque with 20 domes as a compromise. Allah may have been taking notes, considering Beyazid's grim fate (see below).

The Ulu Cami, six centuries old, is constructed out of massive stones that were cut precisely, then placed flush together without mortar. Although earthquakes have shaken the area, notably the 1855 earthquake that toppled every minaret in Bursa except one of Ulu Cami's own minarets, the mosque has held firm. The same, unfortunately, cannot be said for the 20 domes – most of them were also collapsed in the 1855 quake. Looking at them now, the perceptive person will notice how some of the domes have fine detail work, unlike the replacement domes. The imaginative person, meanwhile, can picture how the interior would have looked with gilding on all of the pillars and 700 small lanterns filling the mosque with light. Much has changed since the mosque was completed – the great entranceway was added after the invader Tamurlane wintered in Bursa, when artists carved the front doors, and one of the minarets had to be rebuilt – but in its structure, its decoration, and its delicately cut walnut mimber, the mosque retains its original spirit.

The covered markets, with a rich selection of silks and other textiles, are below the Ulu Cami in Bursa's urban labyrinth. See the shopping section below.

Getting back on Atatürk Caddesi, continue heading away from Çekirge. As you pass the PTT on the right, the tourist office is just ahead to the left. This is the town square, **Heykel**, and there are a number of good cheap restaurants in the neighborhood. Continuing on Atatürk Caddesi you cross over a small gorge. The second road to your left after the gorge is Yeşil Caddesi, and you will see the dome of the **Yeşil Türbe** ahead of you. Yeşil Türbe (Green Mausoleum) and **Yeşil Cami** (Green Mosque) stand together in this end of town, Bursa's most popular attractions.

The Yeşil Türbe (1421) was built for Mehmet I, and, no, the outside of the Green Mausoleum is not green but a radiant blue. Green, the original color, did honor to Muhammed, but the original exterior tiles were mostly lost and had to be replaced. The restorer inexplicably chose blue. The building's interior imitates the accompanying mosque on a smaller scale, and is adorned with the same fine stone and (original) tile work, and even some brooding stained glass. The same artisans that worked on the mosque turned their attentions to this tomb upon Mehmet I's death. Mehmet I was the son of Beyazid I Yildirim, and had to overcome both Beyazid's crushing defeat and capture by Tamurlane, who ran roughshod over the Ottomans' Asian territories, and his own rival brothers. Mehmet I is characterized as more peaceful in temperament than his father, but he clearly had an iron will to emerge from the bloody interregnum and set the drifting empire in order. He was officially sultan for only eight years, 1413-1421, but the eight years prior were absorbed with seizing control of the empire.

The **Yeşil Cami** (1419) was being built for Mehmet I, but he died just before its completion. Work on the mosque was arrested soon after his death, and among the details left unfinished was the portico before the main door. Otherwise, the mosque is wonderfully complete, lacking Haghia Sophia-inspired volume but making up for it in attention to detail and in the flourishes peculiar to the Ottoman's budding aesthetic. The mosque is decorated with the aforementioned green tiles, as well as tiles of blue that denote the heavens above.

The highlight of the mosque is its **mihrab**. Yeşil Cami's mihrab is a massive work of ceramic that required unparalleled craftsmanship. The mihrab had to be conceived and molded in large pieces, then painted, cut into smaller pieces to fit in kilns, fired, and reassembled. The work was done by craftsmen from Tabriz, Persia. Little wonder, after looking at this cunningly wrought masterpiece that in later campaigns Ottoman sultans, prone to slaying pitilessly, would spare artisans from Tabriz, carting them back to the decorate the empire.

The decoration within the mosque is beautiful, with tile representing alternately flowers of the gardens of heaven, or the heavens themselves with thunderbolts and stars. Opposite the towering mihrab, the sultan's box is visible above the entranceway looking out over the interior of the building. The blues and greens of faience, textured stonework, and stained glass give this room an appropriately regal – and tantalizing – appearance. Unfortunately, visitors cannot ascend to the chambers. The vestibules off of the entranceway (themselves decorated with old Byzantine columns) have a set of stairs that lead to the chambers, but a door within the stairwell is shut and locked.

The **Turkish and Islamic Art Museum** (50¢, closed Mondays) located just down the street has a collection of decorative tile, dervish costumes, and knick-knacks from the Ottoman Empire. There are also some very old hand puppets, for which Bursa has a particular mania. Central to Bursa's puppet lore is Karagöz, a character who has a monument near Çekirge, and his friend Havicat. The characters are based on two men who worked on a mosque in Bursa in the 14th century. The older Karagöz would strike up conversations with Havicat, a Persian, and the two would inevitably fall into misunderstandings that were funny enough to bring work around them to a halt. The sultan at the time, either Orhan or Beyazid, blamed the mosque's slow progress on this mirth, and had Karagöz hanged. Havicat, saddened, left Bursa. Later, feeling sentimental, the sultan had a puppeteer recreate the antics of the two, and the shows became a hit. Television has predictably quashed the puppet shows (Mario is more fun than Karagöz), but the puppets and the name Karagöz still pepper signs around the city.

Isolated in the northeast corner of town is the **Beyazid I Complex**, with its mosque, tombs, and fascinating history. Beyazid was called Yildirim, or lightning, for his rapid marches and the speed of his decisions. He shattered the last of the great crusades in Bulgaria, laid siege to Constantinople, and his martial success further expanded the Ottoman borders in all directions. He appeared set to continue the work of the three sultans that preceded him when Tamurlane appeared in the east.

The ever-victorious Tamurlane would perhaps have been satisfied with leaving the Ottomans in peace, seizing the holy lands to the south, and marching back to pursue his dream of conquering China. However, the hot-blooded Beyazid tempted fate and goaded the eastern armies into battle, where the Ottomans were crushed at the battle of Ankara in 1402.

Beyazid himself, captured atop a heap of Tatar soldiers, was caged and kept for Tamurlane's amusement. He lived one year in captivity while Tamurlane plowed through western Anatolia, stabled his camels in Bursa's mosques, and paralyzed Europe with fear. Tamurlane and his armies disappeared into the east the following year, never to return.

Beyazid's türbe was probably already under way when he was defeated at Ankara – it was customary for sultans to oversee the building of their own burial sites. After Tamurlane's passing, Beyazid's body was recovered and one of his sons took time out from the ferocious civil war to complete the tomb here and inter his father.

Then, in the final chaos of the interregnum, Karaman invaders from Konya, nursing an old grudge, destroyed the tomb and burned and scattered the luckless Beyazid's bones. Sultan Mehmet restored order to the empire and rebuilt his father's tomb, but later sultans refused to visit the site, scorning Yildirim's defeat and capture. The tomb itself is relatively bare, its paint long since disappeared. The mosque, too, has suffered over the years, but the structure is excellent, with marble stalactites and small "lightning" insignias in both tile and marble.

## SPORTS & RECREATION
### The Baths
The baths may hearken back to long before the time of Justinian and the height of the Byzantine empire. Together with the baths at Yalova, Bursa's baths were a retreat for the wealthy, who sought not only relaxation but healing in the piping hot waters. Süleyman the Magnificent was one of the visitors here, and the Yeni Kaplıca bath complex was built for him.

Most hotels in the Çekirge area have their own in-house marble baths, but the best in town are at the **Eski Kaplıca**, *Çekirge's Kervansaray Termal Hotel, Tel. 224 233 9300*, and the **Yeni Kaplıca** lower on the hill.

### Skiing
Skiing is, of course, a fairly modern addition to Bursa/Uludağ's appeal, but the industry received considerable press in 1994-1995 when an American army officer and his son disappeared while skiing at **Uludağ**. Newspapers in North America and Europe speculated wildly about kidnapping and foul play, but the outcome was much less interesting: the two became lost while skiing in the backcountry and had to dig in and wait for a storm to pass. When rescuers located them after a three day search both were fine, a testament to the overreaction of the American press and the father's army training. It was also, alas, a testament to what lengths good skiers will go to find challenges away from Uludağ's lackluster main slopes. The mountain does have some of the best skiing near İstanbul, however, with good, plentiful intermediate slopes.

Transport from Bursa is easy – your hotel will probably help make arrangements for the 45 minute trip by road to Uludağ, or, alternately, you can stay at one of the seasonal hotels atop the mountain (see above, *Where to Stay*).

There is a cable car from Bursa to Uludağ that leaves hourly from the far east side of town ($4 round trip), but you must take a taxi the final few miles to the skiing and hotel area. The mountain's set-up is antiquated, and likely to seem odd if you're accustomed to big-time skiing in Canada and the United States; different companies – hotels, usually – own different lifts. If you are content on one or two runs, buy a day pass for a single lift. Otherwise, think about buying lift tickets for a set number of runs and venturing around the hill.

Note: **Palandöken**, near Erzurum, has Turkey's best skiing. Lodging is available at the Dedeman Palandöken *(Tel. 442 316 2414, Fax 442 316 3607)*, and Turkish Airlines flies to Erzurum several times per week.

## SHOPPING

Bursa was at the western end of the old silk road, and the city has been heavily involved with silk commerce for more than 2,000 years. In the sixth century, agents of Emperor Justinian traveled to China and returned with the secrets – and cocoons – to begin producing silk here as well. Today the bustling Bursa silk market still has local and Chinese silks, and some of them are quite cheap.

One of the reputable local outlets is **Caretta Silk Center**, *Kozahan No. 233, Tel. 224 223 5688*, on the second floor of the silk bazaar below Heykel. Caretta has almost a corner on the market in Turkish patterns – tulips and blossoms that evoke images of Iznik tiles – and helpful staff.

## IZNIK

**Iznik** has a peculiar and wonderful feel to it. This was an important city in ancient times, first the Bithnian capital, then the Roman provincial capital of **Nicaea**. Now, however, many of the landmarks have a Central Asian look, owing to Iznik's early settlement by the Selçuks and Turks.

Iznik was founded by **Antigonus the One-Eyed**. Antigonus was so named because he lost an eye in battle, continuing to fight and allowing no one to pull the dart from his eye until the battle was over. Antigonus was one of Alexander's most brilliant generals, and one of those who made claims to parts of the empire after Alexander's death. He founded Iznik in 316 B.C., and it was seized from him in 301 B.C. by his rival Lysimachos. Under Lysimachos it became capital of Bithnia and remained so even after Lysimachos' own death soon afterward. The name Nicaea derives from the name of Lysimachos' wife.

Nicaea lost its primacy to Nicomedia (Izmit) in the middle of the third century, but it remained an important city. Nicaea passed to Rome peacefully, under whom it was restored to its status as capital of Bithnia. It was under Roman rule that Christianity took hold and Nicaea became an important religious center. The First Council of Nicaea in 325 settled one of the burning, divisive issues of the early Christian Church – whether Jesus was a divine entity or a mortal man possessed with a divine entity. The latter notion, supported by Arian, was solidly defeated and denounced as the Arian Heresy. Jesus' divinity was established beyond a doubt in the **Nicene Creed**, which is a sort of checklist of proper Christian belief.

Nicaea continued to play an important role in resolving theological disputes as late as 787, when the Iconoclastic controversy was finally ironed out here. By this time the Arabs had already flooded the area during their campaigns, and Iznik had held firm, but eventually the constant attacks from the east wore down the Byzantines; Iznik fell to the Selçuks in 1075, an event that badly shook Constantinople. The Byzantine Empire was able to reclaim the city shortly thereafter in the wake of the Crusaders' 1097 campaign.

After the soldiers of the Fourth Crusade took Constantinople, Orthodox royalty retired here and built up the city walls, reviving their moribund empire. The city's importance waned after the Orthodox recapture of Constantinople, and the city soon became a target of the nearby Turkish warlords. The warlord that finally seized the city in 1331 was Orhan, the son of Osman and the second ruler of the budding Ottoman Empire. The city grew in relation to the thriving Ottoman Empire, but it also shared the suffering of the great defeat to Tamurlane in 1403. Iznik was sacked and partially destroyed.

Iznik's remarkable regeneration speaks volumes about the vigor of the Ottoman Empire. After decimation and massacre in 1403, Iznik was rebuilt and rapidly developed one of history's greatest porcelain workshops. The heyday of the Iznik workshops began at the end of the 15th century and lasted for almost 100 years, after which the Ottoman decline drastically reduced the market for faience and Persian artists imported during eastern campaigns were shipped away or slain when the Ottomans went to war with Persia. Iznik's rise was meteoric, and its fall sudden. In less than fifty years it was as if they had forgotten all of what they knew, and the workshops fell into disuse and abandonment.

Iznik has continued to thrive, but its heyday is over. An attempt is underway to revive the ceramic industry, and archaeologists are at work on unearthing the old kilns and excavating the workplaces, but Iznik today is fairly quiet.

## ARRIVALS & DEPARTURES
### By Bus
Iznik is a short trip from Bursa, and not far from İstanbul via the Yalova ferry. Direct İstanbul buses are rare, but dolmuş wait for arriving

ferries and are delighted to shuttle you on to Iznik. Iznik's otogar is inside the city walls, and the tourism office and main sights are several blocks north along the east-west Kiliçaslan Caddesi.

**By Car**
Follow the directions to Bursa, veering off of 575 at Orhangazi and taking the 150 east, skirting Iznik Gölu (Lake).

## ORIENTATION

Iznik's three mile ring of walls attests to its former importance. A walk around the circuit of walls can be enjoyable, but obviously takes a little time. Certainly try to stop in at the main gates in the north (İstanbul Kapı) and east (Lefke Kapı), both of which are in good states of preservation – Lefke has three separate gateways. It's fascinating for most North Americans to watch people going about their lives in a walled city, driving tractors through arched stone gates as if it were the most normal thing in the world.

Iznik's **Tourism Information office** is at *Belediye İşhane No. 130-131, Tel. 224 757 1933.*

## WHERE TO STAY & EAT

People don't often stay in Iznik, but it's a good place to get a bite to eat.

**FRANKFURT PANSİYON**, *Mustafa Kemal Paşa Mah., Sahil Yolu Cad. No. 18, Iznik, Tel. 224 757 3029. Rooms: 6. Double: $12.*

Very cheap and pleasant family operation along the waterfront. Other pensions are located nearby.

**BALIKÇI RESTAURANT**, *Göl Kıyısı, Iznik, Tel. 224 757 1152. Moderate.*

The best of Iznik's waterfront fish restaurants, although they're all pretty good. The price is hardly prohibitive, $2 for trout. The Savorona is also recommended.

## SEEING THE SIGHTS

Historically the main attraction in town was the **Haghia Sophia**, a building that dates from the beginning of Constantine's reign. The cathedral was converted to a mosque under the Ottomans, but the structure collapsed during intense fighting between the Greeks and Turks in the 1922 War of Turkish Independence. Today the ruin, near the center of town, has been partially cleared and restored and you can find mosaics from the original building.

The most interesting site in Iznik today is the **Yeşil Cami**, or Green Mosque, near the Lefke Kapı. This building screams of Central Asia, and that may be because when Tamurlane sacked the town he carted off the artisans already here and put them to work on the Registan in Samarkand and on other great Central Asian monuments. The Green Mosque is now faced partly in replacement tiles from Kütahya, but the pattern is beautiful and surprisingly eastern.

Iznik's **museum**, nearby in the Nilüfer Hatun soup kitchen, is also worth a visit. The carving around the doorway deserves to be stared at from now until the end of time, but you should, instead, enter the museum and have a look at the nice display about the history of tilemaking, old kilns, and artifacts from the city's ancient past. The other reason to visit is to inquire about the **catacomb** outside of town, to which museum personnel can direct you and for which they have keys. The catacomb is Byzantine era and nicely decorated – an intriguing and little-known side trip from Iznik.

The other appeal of Iznik is obviously its beautiful shoreline on **Iznik Lake**. Several restaurants have set up on the lakeside to take advantage of the beautiful view, but you can also opt for a picnic on your own in the area north of Göl (lake) Gate.

# ERDEK

**Erdek** is a rarity on tourism itineraries, but offers several interesting nearby sites and is convenient for its İstanbul ferry service and location on the Bursa-Çanakkale road. There is very little to see in Erdek itself, but the surrounding islands, the ruins of Cyzicus, and Kuş Cenneti National Park are all of interest.

The Erdek **Tourism Information Office** is on *Yalı Mah., 1 Nolu Sok. Şeref Apt. No. 2, Tel. 266 835 1169.*

## ARRIVALS & DEPARTURES

### By Car

Erdek is on Kapidağ Peninsula, just 14 kilometers northwest of Bandırma.

### By Bus & Dolmuş

Buses and dolmuş serve Erdek regularly from Bandırma, and direct buses depart from İstanbul in the summer.

### By Boat

Car ferries link İstanbul and Bandırma, just east of Erdek. Ferries depart İstanbul on Tuesday, Thursday, Friday, and Saturday at 9 a.m., arriving in Bandırma five hours later. The cost is $7 for individuals, $20 for automobiles. People with cars are advised to book ahead. Ferries return from Bandırma on Tuesday, Thursday, Friday and Sunday at 2:30 p.m.

## WHERE TO STAY

The Erdek area has a humble collection of holiday villages and pensions. Foreign travelers are a mild rarity.

**TORONTO HOTEL,** *Çuğra Mevkii, Erdek, Balıkesir, Tel. 266 835 3857, Fax 266 835 2323. Rooms: 124. Double: $85.*

One of the best hotels in the area, offering four star resort hotel service. The Toronto has satellite television, air conditioning, a pool, tennis and its own beach. Not of the same caliber as the Aegean or Mediterranean holiday villages, but this is the best address in Erdek.

Also consider the cheaper **PINAR HOTEL,** *Mangırcı Mevkii, Tel. 266 835 7024,* and, cheaper still, the **ARSEVEN PANSIYON,** *Ocaklar Köyu, Tel. 266 835 1164.*

## SEEING THE SIGHTS

Erdek is a resort area popular among Turks, offering a good collection of quiet beaches scattered around an archipelago in the Sea of Marmara. Ferries from Erdek serve Pasalimanı, Türkeli, and Marmara islands, the latter of which is the former Proconnesus, famous as the site of Proconnesian marble. Both Marmara and Türkeli (Avşa) islands have numerous hotels, and Türkeli has wineries. Inquire at the Erdek Tourism Information office for boat schedules and times.

You are almost guaranteed to have the ruins of ancient **Cyzicus**, six kilometers east of Erdek on the isthmus of the Kapıdağ Peninsula, to yourself. The city was founded by colonists from Miletus in 756 B.C. and grew rapidly, becoming so prosperous that, according to the local folklore, the city erected a large bridge between the island and the mainland. Jason and the Argonauts paid a tragic visit during their voyage, accidentally slaying their friend, the Cyzicene king, and, later, King Mithradites's dreams of conquest were foiled here at the hands of the Cyzicene's Roman allies. The city grew to be one of the most glorious in Asia Minor, but has faded dramatically into obscurity.

Time has wrought great changes on this once-powerful city. The island is an isthmus now, and the city is a peaceful wreck. One of Turkey's two genuine **amphitheaters** can be found here (theatres are semicircular, ampitheatres circular), as can sections of an aquaduct, the old city walls, and the site of the acropolis. You won't run into tour groups here, and there's no one to take an admission fee. It's a wonderful

## MITHRADITES' DEFEAT

In the Third Mithraditic War (69-66 B.C.), the Roman general **Lucullus** confronted the marauding armies of **Mithradites VI Eupator at Cyzicus**. Mithradites' Pontic army was far larger than the Roman force, and it was already besieging the important Roman city of Cyzicus when Lucullus arrived in the winter of 67 B.C. Lucullus was unwilling to engage the Pontic army, and chose instead to harry its supply lines. While his small force busied itself with isolating the Pontic Army, Lucullus encamped on a hill within sight of Cyzicus. According to Plutarch's account, the inhabitants of the city believed the force to be their enemies' reinforcements, Mithradites' Armenian allies, and the Cyzicenes were thrown into despair. Some advised surrender to Mithradites. By lucky chance, a boy managed to steal his way through the cordon from outside and make his way into Cyzicus. The despondent citizens asked him if there was any word of their Roman allies. At this the youth "laughed at them, supposing them to be jesting," Plutarch writes. "But when he saw they were in earnest, he pointed out the Roman camp to them and their courage was revived."

At this point, Lucullus' strategy was already taking a toll. Mithradites army was on severe rations, and that strain was compounded by an unseasonable storm that blew in and wrecked many of the Pontic siege engines. Mithradites, realizing his plight, was forced to try to retire. While Lucullus was away with the bulk of his troops raiding a Pontic supply caravan Mithradites sent his cavalry, injured soldiers, and horses away toward Bithnia. Lucullus began a pursuit through the snow, overtaking the Pontic force at the river Rhyndacus (Kocasu Çayı) and massacring them, capturing 6,000 horses and 15,000 men. These they marched back the way they had come past Mithradites' siege army, now itself under siege. The Pontic army lost heart, and was routed in a long, harried retreat to the east that culminated in the sacking of the Pontic capital on the Black Sea.

place for a short visit or a long, determined hunt, but the ruins are overgrown and difficult to explore.

### Kuş Cenneti National Park

You cannot fight the militant fanaticism of birders, but you can satiate it for a while. **Kuş Cenneti National Park** on Küş Gölü (Bird Heaven Park on Bird Lake) will soothe anyone so afflicted, with more than 220 different species numbering in the millions. It is Turkey's undisputed birding capital, smack dab in the middle of the migratory routes north and south. The high season occurs between March and June, when birds arrive and nest in vast numbers. By May many of the young have hatched and fill the air with a mad peeping, and by August most of the birds have flown away.

If the birds lure you to this place you know to bring your bird guide, binoculars, and a camera, although the visitors center addresses some of those needs. The national park is equipped with blinds for peering out at the birds. Even if you don't fancy birds, the park is a sun dappled idyll in the spring and summer and an excellent place to break up a Bursa-to-Çanakkale drive.

You will want a car to explore the reserve, which is located just off of the E-90 Bursa-Çanakkale highway. Eight miles east of Bandırma, turn south off of E-90 on the Aksakal road, then turn right at the signs two miles later. The entrance is just over a mile from there.

# 13. ANKARA & CENTRAL ANATOLIA

The Anatolian plain is Turkey's breadbasket, as it was the Ottoman's and the Byzantine's before them. The plateau often looks desolate, particularly in the heat of summer or during the long, bitter winters, but control of the area and its web of trade routes has been crucial since long before recorded history began in 2000 B.C. So much has changed, and so little; Turkey's capital, **Ankara**, is not far from the Hatti's pre-2000 B.C. capital city and the city that the Hittites adopted afterward, **Hattuşas**. Another capital, **Gordion**, is just to the west of Ankara.

Ankara, Turkey's capital, carries on regardless of the weather, but some of the nearby travel destinations can be rendered inhospitable. Hattuşas, Gordion, and nearby **Cappadoccia** are best avoided in the winter, although Cappadoccia's hotels can take care of you despite the cold – and that region's Bizarro world landscape will still dazzle with a dusting of snow.

## ANKARA

For thousands of years, **Ankara** has been a crossroads and administrative center, and in a land of constant change that, at least, remains the same. If you are in Ankara, you're probably passing through, picking up a visa at one of the local embassies, or here on business. And you are in luck, because while Ankara may not get marquee billing on a trip itinerary, it has more than its share of charm. With embassies from around the world and two fine universities (Bilkent and Middle East Technical), the city has international flavor to go with its Anatolian hospitality.

Ankara is best as a staging area for trips west to Gordion, east to Hattuşas, south to Cappadoccia, and north to Amasya and the Black Sea beyond. One night in Ankara is usually plenty for tourism purposes, but there's plenty to see if you remain longer. Ankara's tourism highlights include the **Anatolian Civilizations Museum**, concentrating on pre-Hellenistic history (Hittite, Assyrian, and Urartian), scattered ruins from Roman **Angora**, and **Atatürk's grand mausoleum**.

The pace here is different, and this is even reflected in holiday habits; Ankara has a July and August lull (think discount reservations) while vacationers head to the coast. Even in the dog days, though, Ankara is a pleasant place to visit.

## History

Ankara is an ancient settlement, and was already old when the **Hittites** occupied it in the second millenium B.C. The easily defensible fortress here was occupied later by the Lydians and Persians, and it was still officially under Persian dominion when **Alexander** arrived in 333 B.C. After cutting the knot at Gordion, Alexander made for Ankara (then Ancyra, later Angora). The people of Ankara, however, thought better of challenging the young king and surrendered, diverting him from what would have, at best, been a damaging march through their countryside. Alexander accepted the submission of Ankara and headed south toward Cappadoccia.

Ankara passed on to Seleucus after Alexander's death, but the city was seized by the Gauls who came to Anatolia as Bithnian mercenaries in 279 B.C. The Gauls dominated the local area, terrorizing their less aggressive neighbors until their great defeat at the hands of Eumenes of Pergamon in 230 B.C. Soon afterward the city was occupied by Pergamon, and was thereafter inherited by Rome after the death of Attalus III. The city's Gallic identity remained in the name of the Roman province, Galatia. Ankara was the capital of that province, and it was here that St. Paul addressed the Galatians.

Ankara's long period of peace ended with the Persian invasion of the seventh century, and after several damaging battles the Arabian Caliph Mutasim captured and decimated the town in 838 A.D. The Byzantines recovered quickly, but their hold remained weak. The city fell and was recaptured several more times, finally slipping away to the Selçuks, then the Ottomans. The Ottoman occupation dramatically interrupted when Tamurlane and Beyazid I fought the Battle of Ankara in 1402.

The confrontation pitted two relentlessly successful generals against one another, young Beyazid Yildirim (Lightning) against the old, shrewd Tatar emperor. Beyazid squandered the advantage of the high ground and water at Ankara by marching out against Tamurlane who, after some shrewd maneuvering, encamped alongside Ankara himself. The ensuing battle, west of Ankara, was long and ultimately decisive, ending with the Ottoman army shattered and Beyazid captured. Ankara, like most Ottoman cities in Asia, was sacked and partially destroyed by the Tatars.

The city was recovered by the Ottomans under Mehmet I in 1414. Almost 500 years later this dark period in Ottoman history was followed by a glorious moment in Turkish history.

## The Founding of the Turkish Republic

Ankara was established as the Turkish seat of power in the uncertain period between the end of World War I and the Turkish War of Independence. It was chosen partly because it reflected Turkey's return to the values of the Anatolian heartland, partly because Atatürk mistrusted İstanbul, and partly because both peacemakers and rival armies were on the verge of seizing İstanbul, Turkey's last and grandest European possession.

In the years following the Central Powers' loss to the Allies in World War I, Ankara was a hive of activity. The postwar peace had carved up the nation; Russia had a chunk of the northeast, Armenia everything east of Giresun, England everything south of Lake Van, France a block of territory extending east of the Mersin-Tokat line, Italy the rest of the Mediterranean coast as deep as Afyon. İstanbul and the rest of the northwest not ceded to the Greeks was placed in a jointly administered occupied territory. The Turks, despondent after a series of painful defeats in the Arabian theater and the subsequent collapse of the Ottoman Empire, were relegated to a chunk of the Anatolian heartland centered on Ankara. Worse, the Turks seemed resigned to defeat and partition, ready to let their homeland of 600 years slip away.

But in their darkest hour, they were saved by, of all things, the Greeks. Antagonism between the Greeks and Turks had festered since the mutual atrocities of the Greek's own War of Independence in the 19th century, and, some might say, since the Greeks ransacked Troy in 1250 B.C. The post-WW I peace treaty called for the Greeks to occupy Smyrna (Izmir), and, after the judicious reluctance of the Greek King Constantine, prime minister Eleutherios Venizelos jumped at the opportunity. Greek forces landed at Izmir on May 15 , 1919, and began penetrating into the Turkish hinterland.

The Turks, written off as beaten and exhausted, were awakened by the invasion of their longtime subjects. Four days after the landing at Smyrna, the newly resolute Turks began piecing together resistance. One year later the nationalist Turks, whipped along by Mustafa Kemal (later known as Atatürk), had taken refuge at Ankara and formed an army. When the Greeks and Turks finally met, the new nationalist army was ready, stealing the initiative from the Greeks in the first battle of İnönü (January 10, 1921) and driving them back in the second (March 31, 1921). Atatürk was responsible for the military victories, as well as for fielding an army in the first place.

What began as a surge against the Greeks became, in Atatürk's skillful hands, a surge for a strong Turkish nation. The allies, having in some ways prodded the Greeks into aggression, stood by while the Turkish nationalists surged out of their Treaty territory. The allies, licking their wounds from the nightmare of WW I, had no stomach for further warfare. Even when the Turks drove the Greek army back to Izmir and out into the sea, neither the British, French, or Italians showed any signs of resistance. The Russians, mired in their own civil war and its horrible aftermath, were otherwise occupied. The **Treaty of Lausanne** confirmed the Turkish victory, restoring their borders to the current size.

Having successfully defended Ankara, the Turkish nationalists now began to appreciate its spartan virtues. Atatürk was in favor of permanently shifting the Turkish capital from İstanbul to Ankara, and, as ever, he won the day. Ankara became the centerpiece of the new Turkish nation, and remains a sophisticated and appealing town.

## ARRIVALS & DEPARTURES

### By Air

Both internal and international flights serve Ankara's **Esenboğa Havalimanı**, including one non-stop flight per day from New York on Turkish Airlines. Ankara's airport has direct service to several points in Turkey, but most flights are funneled through İstanbul's Atatürk Airport.

The airport is 32 kilometers outside of town. The easiest access to and from the airport is using Havaş buses, which run from the bus and train stations every half hour from 6 a.m. to 11 p.m., or Turkish Airlines' own shuttle bus to their office in Kavaklıdere/Gaziosmanpaşa. The new subway is not expected to serve the airport.

### By Bus

Ankara's otogar, **Yeni Terminal** (New Terminal), is worth a visit all by itself. The facility opened in 1995 and is shockingly slick and organized. Buses whisk in and out with crisp precision, ticket offices are organized numerically along one long concourse, and giant information boards tell you when each company's bus is leaving, and where it is headed. If you're going somewhere slightly peculiar, you'll find that the best method to get where you're going is still to ask a tout which buses serve that region. Ulusoy and Varan have separate terminals near the otogar on Eskişehir highway, but they also have ticket offices at far western end of the main otogar.

Getting to and from the Yeni Terminal is also easy. Many bus companies offer ongoing service to Ankara's major neighborhoods – but you have to ask. The new subway system begins here, serving Kızılay in the center and other neighborhoods east and west. Failing that, municipal buses arrive on the bottom level bound for Ulus and Kızılay, and, if that doesn't suit your purposes, taxis hover in the otogar using the same cheap city rates as İstanbul. Finally, Havaş buses leave half-hourly for the airport from 7 a.m. to 11 p.m. from the lower level, alongside the municipal buses ($2.50).

Varan, one of the leading bus companies, has the following rates to destinations from Ankara: Izmir $18; Antalya $19; Alanya $21; Didim $20; Kuşadası $20; Bodrum $23; İstanbul $22.

### By Car

All roads lead to Ankara, and most of them are in excellent shape. Konya is 255 kilometers south, Nevşehir 297 kilometers southeast, Boğazköy 200 kilometers east, Gordion 76 kilometers west, and İstanbul 385 kilometers northwest. The slick new six lane version of the highway between Ankara and İstanbul should (should) be complete in 1997.

## ORIENTATION

Ankara is a comfortable, coherent city, with lawns, broad streets, and several large parks. Diplomats from around the world mix with students from some of Turkey's top universities, creating a cosmopolitan feel and a good night life. Note that tourism sites shut down on Monday.

The main **Tourism Information** office, *Ismet Inönü Sok. No. 5/7, Bahçelievler, Tel. 312 212 8300, Fax 312 213 6887*, is mildly inconvenient, but staffed by a knowledgeable group.

## WHERE TO STAY

For all its international character, Ankara is lacking in small, appealing hotels. The best bets are at the top end and the budget travel end, with precious few quality hotels in the mid- and upper ranges.

**SHERATON ANKARA HOTEL & TOWERS,** *Noktalı Sk. Kavaklıdere, Ankara, Tel. 312 468 5454, Fax Tel. 312 467 1136. Rooms: 311. Double: $240.*

**ANKARA HILTON HOTEL,** *Tahran Cad. No. 12, Kavaklıdere, Ankara, Tel. 312 468 2888, Fax Tel. 312 468 0909. Rooms: 324. Double: $235.*

The two hotels are differentiated mostly by shape. The Sheraton is tall and cylindrical and easy to spot. The Hilton is more boxlike. The Hilton's traditional shape is complemented by a slightly more old world feel than the Sheraton, and the latter's lobby teems with the young and hip. Otherwise both boast first class services, outstanding amenities, and solid, polished, comfortable rooms; these are far and away the best hotels in the Ankara area. Each hotel has a casino, a pool, a fitness center, and a business office. As usual, these hotels are not designed for actual people to pay the room charges and extras; they are intended as line items in your expense account. Still, if you can afford it, you can book directly to cut 15-30 percent off the price (See Chapter 11, İstanbul, Where to Stay).

**HOTEL METROPOL**, Olgunlar Sk. No. 5, Bakanlıklar, Ankara, Tel. 312 417 3060, Fax Tel. 312 417 6990. Rooms: 32. Double: $75.

The Metropol is an excellent small hotel in the city's bustling Kızılay area. This is one of Turkey's several hotels that rates only three stars because it lacks a casino and other large scale amenities, instead squandering its attention on tidy, attractive rooms, good service, and an excellent lobby. This gem far surpasses the rest in its class, and its city-center location is convenient. Fax ahead and mention this Open Road guidebook for a discount of 30 percent. The Metropol has satellite television and a restaurant.

**TURIST HOTEL**, Çankırı Cad. No. 37, Ulus, Ankara, Tel. 312 310 3980, Fax Tel. 312 311 8345. Rooms: 148. Double: $38.

As the name indicates, this hotel was built to accommodate tourists in 1978. Its preeminence in the field is now something of the distant past, but the hotel still serves nicely as a midrange accommodation. Everything is a little ragged at the edges, but clean, and the hamam and sauna downstairs are most welcome during the long Ankara winter. The Turist overlooks the extensive ruins of the old Roman baths, and is located in the old heart of the city.

**HİTİT HOTEL**, Hisar Park Cad., Firuzağa Sk. No. 12, Ulus, Ankara, Tel. 312 310 8617, Fax Tel. 312 311 4102. Rooms: 44. Double: $30.

The Hitit has an elaborate, interesting lobby and a wonderful location at the base of the fortress hill. The rooms have baths and small desks. Like other hotels in the area the Hitit is a little ragged, but the lobby is nice and well-suited to a brief stay.

**HİSAR OTEL**, Hisar Park Cad. No. 6, Ulus, Ankara. Tel. 312 311 9889. Rooms: 24. Double: $9 (plus $7 for two baths).

The Hisar makes a virtue of its shortcomings. The modest little budget hotel doesn't claim to have 24 hour hot water, it has none at all. Instead, it is attached to a hamam where, for an additional fee, you can treat yourself to the baths. The hotel is clean and, come nightfall, quiet. Several rooms have good views. The Hisar is centrally located.

**LALE PALAS**, Hükümet Meydanı Telegraf Sk. No. 5, Ulus, Ankara, Tel. 312 Tel. 312 5220. Rooms: 45. Double: $15.

A tidy, exacting little Turkish hotel with genuine charm. Located near the Column of Julian in the center of the old town.

## WHERE TO EAT

The Byzantine-era fortress atop Ankara's main hill has several of the city's best restaurants. Many of the restaurants are located in houses dating to the dawn of the nationalist era. They offer excellent views of the city. Prix-fixe menus are common, with prices ranging between $12 and $25 per person. American fast food restaurants are also beginning to appear on prime corner real estate.

**KALE WASHINGTON RESTAURANT**, *Ankara Kalesi, Doyuran Sk. No. 5-7, Kaleiçi, Ankara, Tel. 312 311 4344, Fax Tel. 312 324 5959. Expensive-Very Expensive.*

An exacting Turkish acquaintance of ours maintains this is the only authentic Turkish food outside of İstanbul and private kitchens. The Washington is an Ankara institution since 1955, the work of a family which has, to answer the obvious question, ties to Washington, D.C. In 1994 the family moved the restaurant to its new location atop the fortress hill, a marvelous location in a sprawling old house that offers a patio view of the city below.

Slightly more expensive than its rivals, the Washington is worth it. Mezes, dinner and spirits shouldn't exceed $30. The restaurant excels at making the standard dishes properly; su boreği (pastry), eggplant salad, and grills, for instance. The most dubious item on the menu is the "munched fish," but the kazandibi, milk pudding with chicken, is surprisingly good. Stay on your toes; there are serenading musicians.

**AGORA ET VE BALIK EVI**, *Ankara Kalesi, Kale Kapisi Sok. No. 14, Ankara, Tel. 312 310 7675, Fax Tel. 312 310 1555. Moderate-Expensive.*

Another of the fine restaurants within the old Ankara hilltop fortress. For $15 the Agora serves up bread, butter, salad, several hot and cold mezes, a Turkish entree such as lamb kebap, a half bottle of wine, and belly dancing. The idea is, of course that you'll fill up on drinks while watching bellies undulate. The Agora is located in an 80 year old stone house on one of the narrow lanes in the old city, grape vines climbing through its wooden rails. Very nice.

**CHINA RESTAURANT** (Çin Lokanta), *Irfan Baştug Caddesi, Altınpark, Ankara, Tel. 312 318 1207, Fax Tel. 312 318 1407. Moderate.*

Beijing and Ankara are sister cities, and these are the fruits of that relationship. The Chinese government subsidizes the prices at this restaurant as a gesture of goodwill, and apparently the Embassy personnel police the quality of the food. The setting is unbeatable, on a hill overlooking a sprawling expanse of lawn and an artificial lake at the city's Altınpark. The restaurant itself is beautiful, with wood and sliding panels in a traditional Chinese building.

Finally, best of all, the food is marvelous. A big dinner, with drinks, tea and water, won't cost more than $15. If you've been losing patience with aggressive Turkish food touts, this restaurant is a haven of serenity. The cooks, staff, and management are Chinese. Get bus 612 from Kızılay, or ask a taxi for Altınpark.

**CHEZ LES BELGES**, *Sahil Cad. No. 24, Gölbaşı, Tel. 312 484 1478. Expensive.*

A half hour drive south of Ankara on the Konya Highway (Konya Devlet Yolu), this small French restaurant has a pretty setting on Lake Gölbaşı. The food is excellent, the prices French ($40 per person).

**SANTINI**, *Sheraton Ankara, Noktalı Sok. Kavaklıdere, Ankara, Tel. 312 468 5454. Very Expensive.*

Northern Italian cuisine. The prawns are worth squandering your expense account on, every single day.

**TIME CAFE**, *Attar Sok. No. 6, Kavaklıdere, Tel. 312 468 3393. Moderate.*

Popular among the diplomatic types. Good food and an outstanding bar. Chatty foreign service flavor until the wee hours.

**PAUL**, *Arjantin Cad. No. 18, Gaziosmanpaşa, Ankara, Tel. 312 427 1246. Moderate.*

A French bakery and coffee shop with two locations, the second in Bahçelievler. The croissant, by the way, is allegedly Ottoman, not French, to begin with, a puffy, flaky "crescent."

**HACİ ARIFBEY KEBAPÇİSİ**, *Güniz Sk. No. 48, Kavaklıdere, Ankara, Tel. 312 467 6730. Moderate.*

A nice alternative if you're in the Kavaklıdere area; it's just downhill of the Hilton. Good food and moderate prices; popular among locals.

**KÖŞK**, *İnkilap Sokak No. 2, Kızılay, Ankara, Tel. 312 432 1300. Inexpensive.*

In the heart of the Kızılay district, Köşk has a chokehold on the local kebap business with excellent, cheap kebaps and lahmacun.

**MEŞUR 49 PIDE AND KEBAP SALON**, *Işiklar Caddesi, No. 9/A, Ulus, Ankara, Tel. 312 311 7260. Inexpensive.*

A good, honest hole in the wall restaurant serving food cooked by men, for men. Tavuk şiş (chicken shish) is $2, iskender kebap is $1.50, and lahmacun is 50¢. A short walk downhill from the Ancient Civilizations Museum.

## SEEING THE SIGHTS

With the notable exception of Anıtkabir, most of Ankara's historic sights are clustered on and below the city's hilltop fortress, **Hisar**, above downtown. The fortress itself is ornamental, its southern end occupied by restaurants and the rest by an old neighborhood. There are some inscriptions built into the fortress walls, but there is no access to the towers.

Ankara's principal site, the **Anatolian Civilizations Museum**, is located down the street from the citadel's western gate. The museum has the world's preeminent collection of Hittite and Urartian art and sculpture. If Hattuşas, Gordion, or eastern Turkey are in your plans, this

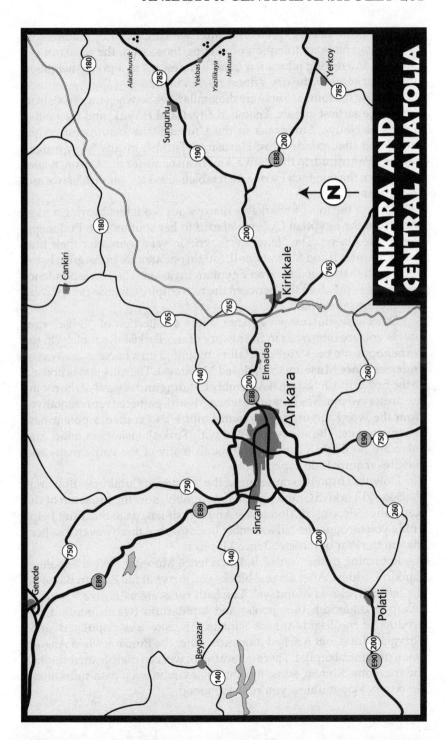

museum is a must-see (preferably after viewing the sites themselves). Even if you have no intention of visiting those sites, the museum is a painless, interesting education (and, besides, it's in a pretty neighborhood near some of the city's finest restaurants).

Among the things to note are the similarities between the reconstruction of the earliest known Anatolian city, Çatal Hüyük, and the pueblo homes of Native Americans in the United States' southwest. While pondering that, ponder this; Havasu in Turkish means "sky/water," similar, we are told, to the Native American name for the Arizonan lake. Note, also, the one inch by one inch tablets used to "publish" laws and track finances.

Among the most remarkable discoveries is a tablet bearing a message from the Egyptian Queen Nefertiti to her counterpart, Pudahepa, the Hittite Queen. The "letter" was written very soon after their husbands, Ramses II and Muwatallis II, fought one another in the great battle at Qadesh that turned back an Egyptian invasion. The correspondence underscores the close ties between the two empires, whose nobles were often of the same blood.

Otherwise, downtown Ankara offers a collection of "B-list" sites unless you are interested in the history of the Turkish Republic. On the corner opposite the statue of Atatürk mounted on a horse is the **War of Independence Museum** (50¢, closed Mondays). The museum is housed in the first Turkish National Assembly building and several of the rooms are preserved much as they were when Atatürk gathered representatives from the wreckage of the Ottoman Empire and crafted a potent new renegade state. The site is designed with Turkish visitors in mind, and there are no English captions, although many of the battle maps and pictures require little explanation.

Downhill from this museum on the left side of Cumhuriet Bulvari is the Second Turkish Grand National Assembly, now the **Museum of the Republic** (50¢, closed Mondays). An English-language brochure helps guide you through the old assembly building, but there's even less here than in the War of Independence Museum.

Returning to the War of Independence Museum, take a left along Cankiri Caddesi. After several blocks you arrive at the **Roman Baths** on the left (50¢, closed Mondays). The bath ruins are extensive – with an enlarged calderium (hot pools) and tepidarium (warm pool), a byproduct of the frigid Ankara winters. The site was populated since Phrygian times, but reached its zenith under the Romans when Angora was a provincial capital. There is a scatter of worked marble surrounding the site, some Roman, some Byzantine. If you've seen bath ruins along the coasts, skip it unless you're in the mood.

Cutting uphill and right, in the direction of the hilltop, you pass the **Column of Julian**. The column is tall and rifled, erected in honor of the Roman Emperor Julian (361-363). A statue of the young emperor once adorned the column, but the statue toppled hundreds of years ago. The column is now crowned with a massive bird nest, and is perhaps much improved.

Continuing uphill, you arrive at the **Hacibayram Mosque**, across the street from the big new market of the same name. The mosque is side by side with the **Temple of Augustus**. The temple is on the site of an earlier shrine of Cybele, the Anatolian fertility goddess. The Cybele shrine was converted to a temple by the Kingdom of Pergamon around 200 B.C., and when Rome appropriated Pergamon's lands it encouraged worship at the site, creating a Diana/Artemis/Cybele connection as at Ephesus. As religious sensibilities changed, so did the religious habits at the temple. Perhaps seeking to curry favor with the emperor, Angora's city fathers dedicated the temple to Augustus. After his death the history of his reign was inscribed on the outer face of the building and worship here continued, perhaps including Cybele. The final phase here, as at so many temple sites, was its conversion to a church. Note the small opening directly beneath the main altar. This area was once the holy precinct of Cybele, although its use afterwards is uncertain.

The local boys who happily show you around the site claim that a tunnel once connected this chamber to the Kale on the hill above. Given the vast tunnels at various ancient sites, it's hard to dismiss the idea out of hand; still, the claim is totally unfounded. If you take a particular interest in Latin and Greek inscriptions, the outer face of the temple will be a pleasure. As mentioned, the well-preserved inscriptions document Augustus' life, his will, and later, general history and even the expenses of the empire, like a giant stone scribble pad. Scaffolding was erected recently as part of the restoration work at the site, allowing better access to the inscriptions.

The Hacibayram Mosque takes its name from the founder of one of the dervish orders. The mosque was originally built by the Selçuks in 1290, and is a classic Selçuk design with a large wooden ceiling. It is the oldest and most important mosque in the city, although the voluminous new Kocatepe Mosque southeast of Kızılay has stolen much of the limelight. The Hacibayram Mosque is surrounded by several additions on two separate floors, with the old main building directly alongside the Temple of Augustus.

If you have a particular interest in railways, you may be interested in visiting the **Railway Museum**, very near Anıtkabir. A lot of what you need to know about Turkey's checkered railway history is detailed in T.E. Lawrence's classic *Seven Pillars of Wisdom*.

## NIGHTLIFE & ENTERTAINMENT

**Bilkent University** has concerts on Wednesday and Friday nights during the fall, winter, and spring. Contact the ticket office, *Tel. 312 266 4382.*

## SHOPPING

If ever you are going to buy an Angora sweater, Ankara, ancient Angora, is the place. The people in the Tourism Information office have up-to-date advice on where to shop. The city's premier shopping area is **Karum Shopping Center**, located in the long, vaulted building beneath the Sheraton. The **Kızılay** area, on the north side of the first pedestrian bridge, has Ankara's English language bookshops and a collection of other stores.

**Kavaklıdere winery**, based out of Kavaklıdere in Ankara, releases its own Premier Beaujoulais on the third Thursday in November. For information about wine tours and wine tasting, contact the winery (or Tourism Information), **Kavaklıdere Şarapları**, *Akyurt, Ankara, Tel. 312 847 5773 (847 5075), Fax 312 847 5077.*

## PRACTICAL INFORMATION

### Church Services

The **Vatican Embassy Chapel**, *2 Sok. No. 55, Çukurca Mahalle, Çankaya, Tel. 312 439 0041*, has an English Mass at 10 a.m. Sunday, and Masses on holy days are at 7 p.m. The **Ankara Baptist Church International**, *Atatürk Bulvarı No. 195, Kavaklıdere, Tel. 312 440 6127*, has services at 10 a.m. on Sundays. The **synagogue**, *Birlik Sok. No. 8, Samanpazarı, Tel. 312 311 6200*, is open only on the Jewish Sabbath (Friday sunset to Saturday sunset).

## EXCURSIONS & DAY TRIPS

### Gordion

**Gordion** is located about two hours west of Ankara on the E-90 to Polatlı and Sivrihisar. There are two routes, one north at Polatlı, then, 14 kilometers along, left to the site, five kilometers. The dependable route is to turn right 17 kilometers past Polatlı, following the course of the Sakarya River 12 kilometers to Gordion and the modern town of Yassıhüyük.

Public transportation is possible from the Polatlı otogar, but there's no telling when minibuses will make the trip. Guided tours are arranged in Ankara; contact the Tourism Information office for information about their own tours.

Gordion has little left to show for its legacy of **Midas and the Golden Touch** and **Alexander and the Gordion Knot**. Like Troy, the evidence of a settlement here is widely scattered and difficult to make sense of, but archaeologists from the University of Pennsylvania have been busy doing just that. The **Phrygians**, a dimly understood people who reigned after the Hittites and were defeated by Persia, reigned from this city. The ruins and hillocks are difficult to appreciate, but a **museum** of recent finds has rendered a visit worthwhile. The museum contains some of the artifacts from an undisturbed royal tomb.

## Anıtkabir

**Atatürk's burial site** is treated with something akin to religious reverence by the secularists who come here. It is a vast, impressive edifice to celebrate one of the most influential men of the 20th century.

Anıtkabir's main entrance is on Anıt Caddesi in Ankara, just off of Gazi Mustafa Kemal Caddesi, which runs from the city center at Kızılay. By public transport (transfer at Kızılay) look for buses going to Tandoğan, and ask for Anıtkabir. The entrance is just two blocks away from the intersection.

If you are bothered by the hasty construction technique evident throughout the country, bricks and concrete prone to immediate decrepitude, Anıtkabir will help restore your faith. Atatürk's (1881-1938) mausoleum is as visionary as the man himself. Atatürk, for all his appreciation of western dress and military discipline and alphabet, was deeply respectful of the people of his country and the Anatolian heart he believed beat in the chest of the Turkish nation.

His tomb draws on that heritage. The flourishes and baroque flair of the final sultans, as typified in Çirağan and Dolmabahçe Palaces, are discarded. In its place are Hittite and Urartian themes, and a spare, immense space approaching the tomb. Even the location is significant, atop a hill that was an ancient necropolis. Two Turkish architects, Orhan Arda and Emin Onat, captured the character of Atatürk perhaps better than they might have believed: consider that no Ottoman Sultan, possessor of Mohammed's Holy Mantle and a claim to the defender of Islam on Earth, had ever been buried in such glory. Perhaps Lenin provided a contemporary precedent; otherwise Anıtkabir hearkened back thousands of years to the Pyramids, the Mausoleum, and Nemrut Dağı. Atatürk's resting place is an ironic throwback to a time when rulers were on an equal footing with God, and this for a man who worked passionately to drive home secular lessons in his young state.

The strangest part is that Atatürk deserved it. Rarely in human history have a people owed so much to a single man. Atatürk exercised his immense will to build a nation out of broken pieces, then steered that nation, often against immense resistance, toward western thought, western dress, a western secular government, and even western alphabet and surnames. Even those who did not like the west grew to appreciate the advantages the new ideas gave Turkey over its fellow Islamic states.

In a single generation the Turks regained military status absent since the heyday of the Ottoman Empire. Atatürk secured trade relations with countries throughout the Middle East and Europe, but was careful to avoid entangling alliances that might drag Turkey into a new world war. His former second-in-command and successor, Ismet Inönü, faithful to this philosophy after Atatürk's death in 1938, kept Turkey out of WW II as part of this policy.

Anıtkabir stands atop a low hill west of town. The main entrance is at the end of a long, gently rising road. By this main entrance you walk along a long arcade lined by Hittite sphinxes, arriving at a great square below the mausoleum. This square is enclosed with museum buildings containing Atatürk's possessions and other heirlooms (note the photographs of clouds in the shape of Atatürk, one of the oddest curiosities in the exhibit.)

The towering flagpole in the courtyard was donated by Nazmi Cemal, a Turkish-American. Finally, ascending the stair past motionless soldiers (someone make a note to add "Motionless Soldier" to the worst jobs list), you enter the mausoleum. Anıtkabir is visited on state holidays by the president and prime minister, and there is a light and sound show on summer evenings.

## HATTUSAS

The great forests of Anatolia were home to one of the world's first great Empires, the **Hittites**. The empire and the forests are long gone now but the capital city remains, and it comes as a shock to most people. **Hattuşas** is not the small, crude ruin that you might expect from a 4,000 year old kingdom; Hattuşas is a vast, complex city, surprisingly intact despite the 3,200 years that have elapsed since its final sack.

Tucked away amid dry rolling hills, Hattuşas, near modern **Boğazköy**, is a worthy destination, deserving of a day and benefiting from a night's stay in the area.

### History

The ruins of Hattuşas represent its last, greatest incarnation under the Hittite Empire. The city – principally the section atop **Büyükkale** – had earlier been settled by the Hatti, and upon arrival the Hittites sacked it and cursed the site. Later, seeing the advantages of the easily defensible acropolis at Büyükkale, the availability of water and the excellence of nearby arable land, the Hittites disregarded their own curse and moved in. The king at the time went so far as to give himself the name Hattusili (1650-1620). The 17th and early 16th centuries marked a period of great expansion, followed by incursions into Hittite territory that culminated in the destruction of Hattuşas at the hands of the Kaşka (about 1500 B.C.), who apparently emerged out of the northeast.

The Hittites overcame the loss of their capital and launched a second campaign of expansion, and it was in this period that modern scholars deem the Kingdom ended and the Empire began. **Suppiluliuma I** (1380-1340 B.C.) is usually acknowledged as the first Hittite emperor, although the classification is almost purely academic, and the Hittite leaders are usually referred to as kings anyway. The Hittite kings occasionally moved their capital when Hattuşas was threatened, as Muwatalli II (1306-1282 B.C.) himself did around the time of an Egyptian invasion. Under Muwatalli II (1306-1282 B.C.) the Hittites took the field against an Egyptian invasion under Ramses II, the irrepressibly successful pharoah immortalized in Percy Byshe Shelley's *Ozymandias*. Ramses II was defeated, beaten at the battle of Qadesh (1286 B.C.) and forced to withdraw through Palestine. Upon his arrival home, the pharoah put a positive "spin" on the battle of Qadesh, and hieroglyphs at Karnak speak only of a great victory. Through it all, the wives of the King and the Pharoah continued trading letters and gifts, one of which, the great green stone sent by Neferteri, remains at Hattuşas today.

After the death of Muwatalli II, the Hittite Empire was shifted back to Hattuşas, but the empire was soon thrown into disarray by civil war. The timing for such chaos was bad: the Babylonians, or Persians, were threatening the southeast, the barbarous Kaşka were harassing borders in the northeast, and Greek and Mycenaean colonists and traders had at last appeared to the west and along the coasts. The Trojan War ended in the middle of the 13th century B.C., and in the aftermath the Greek "Sea Peoples," a confusing agglomeration of colonizing Greeks and the coastal natives displaced by their arrival, began scattering the native populations inland. This only increased the pressure on Hattuşas. Within a century of its victory at the battle of Qadesh, the Hittite Empire had collapsed. Hattuşas was sacked and burned to end the 13th century B.C.

Hattuşas was only identified in the late 19th century A.D. Curiously, the burial places of the Hittite kings have proven less interesting than those of the pharoahs. Skill at war is not an indication of artistry or wealth, but considering Muwatalli II's victory over Ramses II, and the latter's elaborate, treasure-filled burial complex, it seems reasonable to assume that Muwatalli would have been buried in glorious style. This still may have been the case, but the tombs discovered near Hattuşas have never revealed anything on the scale of the Egyptian tombs.

## THE HITTITES

*Beginning around 2000 B.C., Assyrian traders from the south imported tin to Anatolia, which, combined with local stores of copper (probably secured through trading elsewhere) allowed local kingdoms to pursue large-scale production of bronze. The production of bronze weapons and art allowed the Anatolian kingdoms to thrive, and that's one story. More important, perhaps, is that the traders, being good businessmen, kept records on small tiles of clay in cuneiform script. This was a watershed; the beginning of written history (although there is some inevitable disagreement about which people intrdouced writing). Whereas earlier kingdoms – the Sumerians, for instance – left a large, shadowy footprint, the Hittites' laws, wars, and finances were immortalized.*

*The Hittites, like so many cultures to appear later, entered Anatolia from the east and soon were masters of the native Anatolian population. The new arrivals, however, were no cultural imperialists; they adopted the religion and much of the language of the indigenous people, largely Hurrians. In the 20th Century B.C. this alloyed race built its first major city, Kanesh (near Kültepe), from which it began to dominate the rest of central Anatolia. In the 18th Century B.C. the capital was shifted to Hattusas (Boğazkale), and soon the Hittite Empire was in full flower, encompassing Babylon in the east, all of Anatolia, the Mediterranean east of Antalya and, many believe, sections of the Aegean coast near Izmir.*

*The Hittite culture was not so different from the more famous culture in Egypt at the time. While it endured, so powerful was the Hittite Kingdom that in the 14th Century B.C. the widow of King Tutankhaman sought a Hittite prince to be her new husband. Her hopes were not realized; the son of the Hittite King Suppiluliuma I was killed on the journey to Egypt.*

*The Hittite's final legacy was one of a surprisingly restrained and fascinating set of laws. Murder and assault were punished by fines, and only rape, treason, and bestiality were punishable by death (the latter because the Hittites were wary of breeding monsters).*

## ARRIVALS & DEPARTURES

### By Bus & Dolmuş

The only public transportation to Boğazköy departs from Sungurlu in the north and Yozgat in the south. Sungurlu, along the main Ankara-Samsun highway, is the most convenient. From Sungurlu, municipal buses depart for Boğazköy at 7:30 a.m. and at irregular intervals thereafter, passing in front of the Hittite Motel before veering south to Boğazköy.

The Ankara Tourist office arranges tours direct from Ankara in the high season. Dolmuş make trips back and forth as well, more frequently in high season. From Ankara consider joining a trip through the Tourism Information office, which offers a cheap, direct way of seeing the site with a guide.

**By Car**

Boğazköy is 23 kilometers off the main Ankara-Samsun road and 31 kilometers from Sungurlu. You can visit Boğazköy from Ankara on a long day trip. Seeing Hattuşas by car should take less than two hours, but adding the time spent at nearby Yazılıkaya and the museum and returning to Sungurlu, plan on making a day of it. If possible, try walking the long, steep loop road and exploring the minor stone buttresses.

## ORIENTATION

Hattuşas was the Hittite capital at the height of Hittite power, and the six kilometer circuit of the city walls is mute testimony to this dead empire. There is no tourism information office, but the museum in Boğazköy has information about the site and sells Kurt Bittel's excellent *Guide to Boğazköy*.

## GETTING AROUND TOWN

Getting around Hattuşas requires lots of hiking or letting a cab drive you around. Reaching Yazılıkaya also requires a lift unless you are staying in Boğazköy and have time to walk two kilometers uphill. Seeing both sights in one day on foot under the blazing sun is probably possible, and so is heat exhaustion.

Alacahüyük, a third Hittite settlement in the area, is located 30 kilometers from Boğazköy, 14 kilometers back toward Sungurlu, then right at Salmanköy for 11 kilometers, and left to Hüyük.

## WHERE TO STAY & EAT

Boğazköy's hotels are cheap and serviceable. Consider staying at Sungurlu, on the main Ankara-Samsun road, one of whose better establishments is reviewed below.

**HATTUSAS MOTEL/PANSIYON**, *Boğazköy, Çorum, Tel. 364 452 2013. Rooms: 18. Double: $15.*

The most popular place in town among those who choose to stay, mostly backpackers. The Hattusas is on the main square, opposite the dolmuş stop and just up the street from the museum. Owner Mustafa Baykal is conscientious and helpful, and the hotel even serves meals.

**BAŞKENT MOTEL,** *Yazılıkaya Yolu Üzeri, Boğazköy, Tel. 364 452 2037, Fax Tel. 364 452 2567. Rooms: 6. Double: $17.*
Another option in the immediate vicinity of Boğazköy, run by the cheerful and knowledgeable Osman Bey.

**In Sungurlu**
**THE HITTIT MOTEL,** *Ankara-Samsun Karayolu, Güzergahı, Sungurlu, Tel. 364 311 8409, Fax Tel. 364 311 3873. Rooms: 25. Double: $37.*
The Hittit Motel is an unassuming place off the side of the road to the left as you approach Sungurlu from the Samsun direction. The Hittit has decent, clean rooms and a garden and pool in the back. An otherwise adequate hotel gets an exotic cachet from Charles, the Prince of Wales, who stayed here several years ago. The prince stayed in room 40. Alone, we are told. The pool was probably full for him, but it probably won't be when you get there. The garden is a good place to return to after a day scorching at Hattuşas. The Hittit is joined with a restaurant serving good, basic fare.

## SEEING THE SIGHTS

As you ascend past the entrance gate above Boğazköy, the great bastion of stone to your left was once covered with buildings and may have bridged the river. During most of the year you will probably be approached by one of the men who work with archaeologists in the digging season and asked if you would like a guide. Ideally you would have a chance to see the site and accumulate questions on one day, and take the guide along on the second. Consider seeing Hattuşas without a guide and taking one along for Yazılıkaya afterward (see below).

The huge foundation just uphill to your right is the **Great Temple of the Storm God.** This vast structure was dedicated to both a Storm God and a Sun Goddess, and built in the 13th century B.C. Little is known of either of these deities, although they appear to have been worshipped by the Hatti peoples well before their domination by the Hittites. As you follow the road around to the entrance, you find a large stone basin broken into different parts and decorated with the head and shoulders of lions. This was probably used as part of a ritual. A fellow nearby whittles away small lions out of green stone, or anyway, he appears to; he usually pretends to carve and buys in bulk.

Entering the precincts of the temple from this side there are several anterooms that were once guarded. The entryway opens into a hall, and another right takes you in the direction of the lower road and one of the temple chambers. The chamber is entered through three small chambers, and the chambers appear to have had deep pools of water, making access to the temple chambers difficult until someone on the interior slid a bridge across. There are small alcoves to the sides of these small rooms where guards were once posted. Statues of the two gods, each in their own temple chamber with their back to the entrance road, were the main adornment. The building would have been roofed with wood. As you exit back through the main entrance, look off to your right for a distinctive green stone. This was originally a sharp cube but it has been smoothed by weathering. This was a sacrificial stone, probably a gift to the Hittites from Queen Neferteri of Egypt.

Two of the most interesting sites at Hattuşas are rarely visited, the **stone buttresses** just up the road from the Great Temple and off to the right. These are pocked with evidence of old structures, with channels and dowels cut into leveled areas of stone. The first buttress is divided by a cleft in the rock which may have been used as a gate or, instead, had some ritual significance. There is evidence of caves cut into the bases of these outcrops. The view over the Great Temple is excellent. Just below the fork in the road is another mysterious stone outcrop. This one, called the **Kızlar Kaya**, or maiden's rock, may have had a role in blood sacrifice of the aforementioned maidens, but the deliberate shapes and channels cut in the stone are only dimly understood.

At the fork in the road continue straight (right), ascending in a loop around the interior of the former northwestern walls (now disappeared). At the top you will see signs for the **Lion Gate**, one of the three great gates still in place at Hattuşas. On the many occasions when there is no one visiting, this is one of the most silent places in Turkey, with the wide eyes of the lions staring out to the west. The lions adorn the outer gateway, giving way to a small entrance chamber that was, in turn, gated on the interior side. The sign suggests looking for an inscription here at high noon, and we can attest that it is invisible otherwise. Archaeologists are puzzled by the floor just inside of the gate, where the doors have a horizontal groove. This may have been the footing for an interior barricade.

Hattuşas' marquee site is ahead, but take some time to wander back down to the rocky outcrops in the center, most of which were carved and fashioned into small buildings and fortresses. Back on the main road, you ascend to the **Yer Kapı**, or the **Earth Gate**, so named because it dives down out of the city through a tunnel. This fascinating gate is located at the highest point in the city, and was built through a vast artificial hill that runs along the upper section of town, itself walled and punctuated with towers. The tunnel, more than 180 feet long, cuts through the center of this long, slender hill, and has puzzled archaeologists.

Another gate, the **Sphinx Gate**, is located directly above the tunnel, and appears to have been the main entrance and exit. Guesses about the purpose of the tunnel have run to the idiotic, such as speculation that

Hittite soldiers may have used this route to mount sneak attacks on the enemy army, but the tunnel may well have served a ceremonial purpose for Hittite armies marching away to war. The overall appearance of this smooth stone hill – it may, too have been clad in marble – beneath a high wall and a series of towers would have been impressive, but the rising terrain outside of the wall means it was not easy to spot from afar. Tunnels also appear to have also been used at some of the lower gates.

The third upper gate, the **King's Gate**, is so called because of a carved figure here thought to be a king. The figure has been carted off to Ankara, and was not, anyway, a king; it was probably a god, perhaps the storm god himself. A copy has been installed in its former place. This entrance was more complex than the others, with a road leading past the high southern walls and through a series of towers and compounds culminating in the gate itself. This was probably a major entry point into the city.

Around the interior are a collection of temple sites, all fenced off. The stone outcrops ranged along the upper half of the interior are all accessible, but require hiking over stony ground. Among these are some outstanding examples of early architecture, with massive stone blocks combining with natural rock formations to create smooth walls and terraced surfaces for houses and temples. **Yenicekale** is the chief example of this, near the center of the interior field, and the precipitous **Sarıkale** is another example. The latter, a short distance downhill of the King's Gate and off to the left, probably had a set of upscale residences.

Just to the interior of the road is yet another outcrop, **Nişantaşı**, this one with a long inscription in Hittite hieroglyphs. The inscriptions date from the years just prior to the fall of the empire. A ramp or stair once climbed this rock just to the left of the inscription. Across the road recent excavation has yielded small chambers and what may have once been a reservoir. This area is sometimes referred to as the southern citadel.

The road continues now to **Büyükkale**, with a draw (a small valley) descending down toward the gorge below – this, too, may have been the site of a bridge across the river. Büyükkale is the location of the palace and citadel, and also the site of original settlements here. The outline of the palace is distinct, but the great collection of rooms and roads is bewildering even to those who study the site. Suffice it to say, the imperial chambers were probably located atop the buttress, looking out over the gorge.

### Yazılıkaya

If you have time, consider visiting **Yazılıkaya**, where an outdoor shrine has some of the most impressive Hittite carvings in existence. A sacred road once linked Hattuşas with Yazılıkaya, probably crossing the bridge at the gorge to the south side of Büyükkale. Yazılıkaya was centered around two chambers, natural clefts in the stone, and was ornamented with various buildings as its importance grew. The last of the inscriptions here date from the final years of the empire.

The storm god, Teshup, figures prominently here as at Hattuşas, and the quality of the various reliefs are outstanding considering their age. Teshup is just one of the hundreds of dieties worshipped by the Hittites, and their rank can usually be determined by the number of horns on their hatwear. It is difficult to make sense of the great variety of reliefs, and a guide is of particular use here.

Yazılıkaya is two kilometers northeast of Boğazköy, with a road heading off toward the site from near the Hattuşas entrance gate.

# 14. CAPPADOCCIA

Cappadoccia is a former Roman province, a former Hittite province, a timeless plain of softly curved stone located in the heart of the Anatolian plateau. The eerie landscape is a natural wonder: the terrain is carved into soft, rounded shapes by thousands of years of erosion, and boulders perch impossibly atop slender steeples of rock.

Cappadoccia would have been a marvelous tourism destination had development never happened; but fortunately development did happen, first by the settlers worn down by the bitter winters and the injustices of passing armies, then by Christian refugees. Both dug rooms out of the soft rock, then more rooms, continuing deeper and deeper with amazing artistry and cunning. Cappadoccia today is pocked with small holes, some giving way to a shallow room, others to painted churches, still others unfolding into staggeringly complicated labyrinths connected to one another by miles of subterranean passageways.

The region has several sights that are almost always busy, but the troglodytic inhabitants burrowed throughout the valley. For every one of Cappadoccia's marquee sites on the standard tour – **Göreme**, **Zelve**, and **Derinkuyu** – there are a handful of other interesting places tucked away, and still more waiting to be discovered.

**History**

Cappadoccia was just another Anatolian farming community, evidently distinguished by horses (Cappadoccia is, literally, land of the beautiful horses) and by its peculiar terrain of soft stone. More important to the area's development, Cappadoccia was a crossroads. The earliest trade routes wound through the area, passing under the shadow of **Mt. Argeus** in their 2,000 mile circuit from Susa in Babylon to Sardis near the Mediterranean. Other routes came from north and south, connecting the communities on the Black Sea, formerly the Euxine Pontus, with the eastern tip of the Mediterranean, and forming the overland route from Syria to the Dardanelles and the Bosphorous.

No one knows when people began burrowing into the earth for shelter, but the only requirements were tools and a moment of inspiration during the bitter winter months. Xenophon reported stumbling across a village with underground chambers during his 400 B.C. winter retreat in modern Armenia, but people had been tunneling in stone since long before Hittite times and it seems likely that the people of the area have had humble underground shelters for thousands of years. These shelters were more than refuges from the harsh winter; armies march the same roads as traders, and the Cappadoccians surely found it convenient to round up their food and cattle and retire out of sight underground.

The agrarian region underwent its own small Renaissance during the early days of the Christian religion. The area was a substantial Roman province, governed out of **Caesarea** (Kayseri), and was itself occupied as evidenced by Roman graves atop Uçhisar and other areas, but the Romans were reluctant to police the endlessly winding valleys of Cappadoccia. **Antioch** (now Hatay) and Caesarea were centers for the budding faith, and Cappadoccia became a refuge and a spiritual haven for the embattled religion. While the Romans busied themselves torturing and murdering Christians elsewhere in the empire, the Christians who survived the early purges consolidated their views and their canon here, helping form a religion that has, in turn, shaped the world.

As early as the second century, anchorites (religious hermits) and solitary mystic Christians were settling here; by the fourth century Cappadoccia was home to a large population of Christian ascetics. Monks carved out small rooms in the valley walls and perched there. The Christians' habit of forgoing worldly pleasures spoke powerfully to Rome's poor, held at arms length from the largely hedonistic pagan religions. The message that there was a better life after this one resonated with those whose lives were miserable; that the holiest of the Christians suffered in small holes or, like St. Simon Stylites in Antioch, perched atop pedestals for their entire lives trusting to a good afterlife, was a credit to the Christian faith. It is tempting to dismiss them as nuts, but Christianity owed much of its potency among the masses to the actions of these ascetics.

In time the isolated monks formed communities, working together to carve small churches. As Christianity prospered, the monks began establishing rituals and habits that were reinforced when, in the seventh and eighth centuries Arab armies came coursing through the region. The most sophisticated monastic communities, those at **Göreme** and **Zelve**, were established in the ninth century. The summers were spent tending to fields and livestock, and cultivating wine, while the winters were given over to cutting away at the rock. While the monks busied themselves with churches and dormitories, Christian villagers were also eager to escape the ravages of invading Arabs, tunneling ever deeper into the soft, easily carved stone of the plains. The results, **Derinkuyu**, **Özkonak**, and **Kaymaklı**, to name but a few, were much more than store houses, granaries, and simple shelters; each was a defensible underground city descending hundreds of feet and many levels into the earth. And though there is no record of it, there may have been underground fortifications far earlier; fanciful modern drawings of Roman soldiers attempting to storm the Cappadoccians' subterranean hive may have a kernel of truth to them.

With the arrival of the Turks, things changed. The Turks did not sweep through, but stayed. The monks could not hide out forever, and the Christians nearby never intended to live their lives underground, just to hide there. By the 13th century, most of the Christians had left, and most of the cities were abandoned. Some people remained, keeping track of the almost forgotten cities, and some people live in underground dwellings still.

Cappadoccia provokes intense curiosity. The best information available is in Spiro Kostof's *Caves of Gods*, Oxford Press; *The Dictionary of Christian Lore and Legend*, Thames & Hudson Publishing; and Guillaume de Jerphanion's *Une Nouvelle Province de l'Art Byzantin*.

## CAPPADOCCIA'S NATURAL HISTORY

*Everyone who visits Cappadocia wonders how it happened. According to geologists, volcanic activity buried the area long ago, and the lava and ash from the earth's interior cooled and settled into a plain of soft stone. Most of the deposits eroded quite rapidly, creating a network of ravines and channels. At the same time, occasional deposits of harder stone hardly eroded at all, forming what today are spires, hills, and, in the extreme, the massive earth towers of **Uçhisar** and **Ortahisar**, rising far above the plain and offering a commanding view that armies and traders would later appreciate. The same phenomenon explains the "**fairy chimney**," stones perched atop slender shafts of stone: hard material did not weather as quickly as the surrounding terrain, and the softer stone directly beneath was protected from erosion by the harder block of stone above. The soft stone, **tufa**, is not unique to the region, but the vast quantity of soft rock in the area made it the favored building material.*

*There are parallels here with Petra in Jordan and the mesa cliff dwellings in the southwest United States, but the sheer scale of the human-carved caves and warrens and underground cities here is entirely unique, and a function of the particularly malleable stone. (It seems a disservice to continually emphasize the "soft" in "soft stone." Have a feel for yourself when you visit: tunneling into this rock took a lot of work.)*

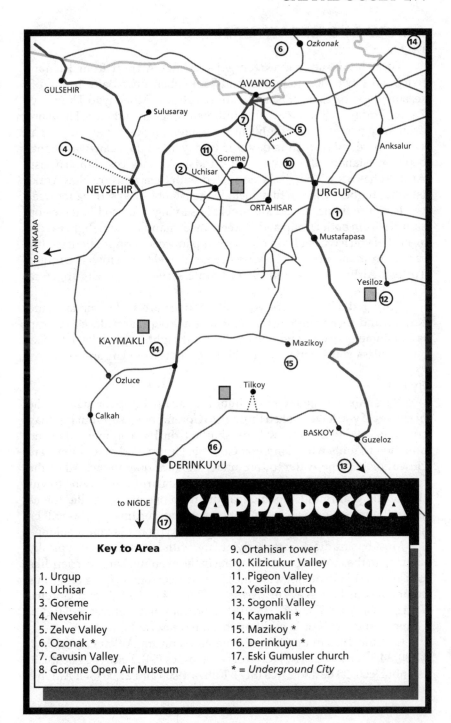

**CAPPADOCCIA**

## Key to Area

1. Urgup
2. Uchisar
3. Goreme
4. Nevsehir
5. Zelve Valley
6. Ozonak *
7. Cavusin Valley
8. Goreme Open Air Museum

9. Ortahisar tower
10. Kilzicukur Valley
11. Pigeon Valley
12. Yesiloz church
13. Sogonli Valley
14. Kaymakli *
15. Mazikoy *
16. Derinkuyu *
17. Eski Gumusler church
* = *Underground City*

## ARRIVALS & DEPARTURES

**By Air**

Turkish Airlines serves Kayseri's **Erkilet Airport** from İstanbul twice daily between June and mid-September, once daily in the off season; departures from İstanbul are at 9:20 a.m. Monday to Thursday, 7 p.m. Friday to Sunday, with additional times in summer. There are ordinarily two weekend flights in the winter. Flights depart Kayseri at 11:45 a.m. Monday to Thursday, 9:15 Friday to Sunday. One-way flights between İstanbul and Kayseri on Turkish Airlines cost $73. Turkish Airlines has occasional deals associated with their nonstop New York-İstanbul flights, wherein they include the İstanbul-Kayseri leg for free.

If you're flying in you are probably staying at a good hotel; co-op shuttles from both Ürgüp and Göreme meet many Kayseri flights at the airport. If you have booked a night in Cappadoccia, enquire about shuttle service from the airport. Likewise Argeus Travel (see below) is Ürgüp's Turkish Airlines office and offers shuttle service; $5 to Ürgüp, $6 to Göreme.

During daylight hours your alternatives are to bus or taxi into Kayseri and get an ongoing bus, or to take a taxi to Cappadoccia (Ürgüp is 85 kilometers away and will cost $45). At night you will have to take a taxi unless you are met by the shuttle or a car from Ürgüp.

**By Bus**

**Nevşehir** is the main transit hub, and the final stop for many of the big buses. If you have booked through to Göreme or Ürgüp your bus may continue, otherwise you will be shuttled on by a minibus. Pay no attention to touts who claim that Göreme, Ürgüp, and other towns are closed, or have no water, or are under medical quarantine. All of the towns in the region, Göreme and Ürgüp particularly, are thriving towns that bustle year round. Upon departure from one of the smaller towns you will, on rare occasions, be met by your bus; ordinarily you will be shuttled to Nevşehir from the town in which you made your booking.

Most bus traffic departs early or late, with İstanbul buses typically arriving in the morning and departing in the evening. Large carriers like Ulusoy and Varan do not serve the Cappadoccia region. Long range bus companies include NevTur *(Nevşehir, Tel. 384 213 1171)* and Göreme Turizm *(Nevşehir Tel. 384 213 0191)*, and they have offices in Ürgüp, Göreme ,and Uçhisar, in addition to main offices at Nevşehir.

Göreme Turizm departures from Nevşehir for Ankara are at 9:00, 11:30, 14:30 and 17:30 ($8); Kayseri seven times ($4); Fethiye 21:00 ($20); İstanbul 9:00, 20:00 and 21:00 ($17); Konya 19:00 and 21:00 ($7); Antalya 19:30, 21:30 and 22:00 ($15).

Note: If you don't want to shell out the $18 for a bus, there is a free bus from the Backpackers' Underground Cafe in Sultanahmet, İstanbul, on Mondays and Thursdays at 8 a.m. from June until October.

**By Car**

The roads to Cappadoccia from all points west are heavily traveled and in good condition. The journey from İstanbul takes 10 hours, passing through Ankara. The favored route from Ankara to Nevşehir is along the E-90, turning east at Aksaray. From the south the E-90 is also the best route, heading inland from the Mediterranean just west of Adana. From Antalya and the Lycian Coast the quickest route is via Konya.

## ORIENTATION

We have divided sprawling Cappadoccia up differently than other regions of Turkey. First we discuss where to stay and eat in various towns, then we recommend several trips that combine underground cities, churches, and Cappadoccia's daunting beauty. We highly recommend spending at least one day hiking, biking or horseriding through the various valleys (see *How to See Cappadoccia*, below). Wherever you rent a mountain bike, you should be offered a map and directions to the nearest convenient valley.

Nevşehir is convenient to the roads west, and is close to Cappadoccia's largest, most amenity-packed hotels. At the far end of the spectrum, **Göreme** has a slew of cheap pensions and a predictably boisterous nightlife down in the valley. Falling somewhere in between are the towns of **Ürgüp** and **Uçhisar**. Both have small pensions and some impersonal hotels, but both are also graced with some of the finest accommodations in the country.

## URGUP

Morning in **Ürgüp**: the air is clean with a trace of wood smoke, the sky a vast chalky blue, and swifts whirl madly clockwise, around and around. The mesas on the near horizon are undercut by entrances and windows in the stone, and off in the east snowcapped **Argeus** rises out of the mist.

Ürgüp is a clean, pretty town at the heart of Cappadoccia. It is convenient to rarely visited monastic valleys and the popular sites of Göreme and Uçhisar alike. We think of Ürgüp as the perfect place to wake up after a long flight in from North America, an excellent place to shake off jet lag and undergo a pleasant stupor of sensory overload.

The **tourism information** office is on *Kayseri Caddesi, Tel. 384 341 4059, Fax 384 341 4059.*

## ARRIVALS & DEPARTURES

Ürgüp is 20 kilometers east of Nevşehir, and half-hourly dolmuş serve the town center. Dolmuş also serve towns further afield such as Avanos. As mentioned, dolmuş do not serve Göreme, although perhaps by the time of your arrival this moronic turf war will be over. Meanwhile you must go all the way to Uçhisar and await a bus bound for Göreme from Nevşehir, hoping it is not full. Make it clear to the dolmuş driver from Ürgüp that you are going to Göreme and he will drop you off where you need to be. The otogar at the center of town has bus ticket offices.

## WHERE TO STAY

**ESBELLI EVI,** *Turban Girişi, Çeşme Karşısı, PK 2, Ürgüp, Tel. 384 341 3395, Fax 384 341 8848. Rooms: 7. Double: $64.*

In Cappadocia's Zelve valley, monks spent 800 years poring over the Bible, living simply, and slowly chipping away at the soft tuff to create churches, living areas, and bedrooms. Being monks, they were busy, but rarely rushed. They could take their time deciding where to carve a window out of a cliff face, where to connect two spaces with a tunnel, where to build a shelf.

Travelers today come from thousands of miles to wind through the labyrinthine corridors, entering unlikely looking holes at ground level and emerging hundreds of feet above. But lost in 700 years of abandonment and erosion is the careful attention to detail of monks with a lifetime to contemplate the stone and the greenery of the valley below.

The Esbelli Ev in Ürgüp probably comes close to capturing the sense of precision and detail that would have once been found here. The Esbelli is not the product of many lifetimes; in fact in some ways it has been put up in a terrible hurry. After purchasing property in the hills above Ürgüp village in 1979, Esbelli Ev owner and host Süha Ersöz mulled over the site and set to work in 1987. He cleaned and recarved three rooms from the living rock, rehabilitating the stone houses above. Four years later he began inviting guests. In the following years he purchased some adjoining land and completed a few more rooms. "Seven rooms in seven years is not the way most people do business," says Süha Bey.

And seven rooms is all the Esbelli will ever be. Seven sets of guests are probably too many, the owner laments. He enjoys best of all getting to know the people who pass through his hotel, cultivates an almost familial relationship with them. Repeat guests arrive with gifts of CDs and photographs, and send photographs and postcards throughout the year.

The only affront that seems to register with Süha Bey is when guests rush off in the morning and stagger in at night. Ersöz is not in the business of processing customers, he wants people to visit and enjoy his hotel. In 1995 he was forced to scuttle an arrangement with a tour company; the guests were up at 8 a.m. and limping in ten hours later. He'd much rather you lingered over your excellent breakfast on the patio, then read a paper for a little while until it is seemly to mix yourself a gin and tonic (in the refrigerator with all the other beverages, no charge). Ersöz has created a halfway house in the old style, a place to relax and catch your breath. Monks spent lifetimes here just sitting and looking, and they weren't as crazy as they sound. If you're going to see where they lived, you might as well see why they lived here.

Selected as one of our best places to stay – see Chapter 10.

**OTEL SURBAN**, *Yunak Mahallesi, PK 55, Ürgüp, Tel. 384 341 4761, Fax 384 341 2025. Rooms: 64. Double: $32.*

This ten year old hotel is aging nicely. At $32 for a double it is an outstanding bargain with simple, solid stone and wood interiors. The hotel is built above a basement that dates back much further than the rest of the hotel. The Surban is a favorite for tour groups, and has half board buffet dining. The roof terrace is beautiful. Half board accommodations are available.

**ALFINA HOTEL**, *Istiklal Cad., Ürgüp Girişi No. 25, Ürgüp, Tel. 384 341 4822, Fax 384 341 2424. Rooms: 32. Double: $55.*

The Alfina offers several underground rooms and hallways, and gives you the enjoyable experience of spending the night in a cave, but the decor is not on par with the area's finest hotels. The restaurant bar and restaurant are enjoyable, but feel unnervingly like they are designed to imitate the interior of a large modern hotel. A restoration effort begun late in 1996 could dramatically improve this hotel.

**HITTIT OTEL**, *Istiklal Cad. No. 46, Ürgüp, Tel. 384 341 4481. Rooms: 16. Double: $40, breakfast.*

If you want to stay in something less like a cave and more like a real building, stay in this restored stone house. The management is thoughtful and friendly and the quality is outstanding. The hotel has secret perks in the form of tunnels and rooms carved in stone on the interior.

**PANSIYON SUN**, *Hamam Sok. No. 6, Ürgüp, Tel. 384 341 4493. Rooms: 8. Double: $10.*

Just off of the main square, the Sun is a reliable family pension.

## WHERE TO EAT

**ŞOMINE**, *Cumhuriet Meydanı, Ürgüp, Tel. 384 341 8443. Moderate.*

With the Sofa and the Hanedan both probably out of the picture, the Somine becomes the town's best. A very nicely arranged restaurant with a view from its outdoor terrace. Prices are fairly reasonable, with grilled chicken and rice $3.50, spicy Adana kepap $2.50.

**HANEDAN RESTAURANT**, *Yunak Mah, Ürgup, Tel. 384 341 4266. Moderate-Expensive.*
Probably Ürgüp's fanciest restaurant, just next to the Surban Hotel. Meals are a bit more expensive than elsewhere, but the food is well-made and the interior is hospitably Turkish. The restaurant is moving to Avanos in late 1996, and may close its Ürgüp location.
**SOFA LOKANTA**, *Yunak Mah., Ürgup, Tel. 384 341 4006. Moderate.*
Just down the street from the former Hanedan, there are rumors the Sofa may not reopen after the winter break. Hopefully it will; its prices are good and its location in a large courtyard is very nice. Grills and güveç stews are very good.
**ARMAĞAN DISCO**, *Fabrika Cad. No. 19, Ürgüp, Tel. 384 341 4060, Fax 384 341 4061. Expensive.*
A favorite of tour groups, the Armağan is a cavernous underground establishment with food and belly dancing late into the night. Can be great, loud fun.
**OCAKBAŞI**, *Terminal Üstu, Ürgüp, Tel. 384 341 3277. Moderate.*
Ürgüp's premier kebap house, widely acclaimed by the locals. Traditional setting and friendly service.
**KARDEŞLER PIZZA RESTAURANT**, *Suat Hayri-Dumlupınar Cad., Ürgüp, Tel. 384 341 4357. Inexpensive.*
Kardeşlar Pizza Lokanta has good, cheap food in the very center of town. Located on the main square in Ürgüp, the big, friendly proprietor, Mehmet Sofularlı, offers excellent borek and the local specialty, guveç, in a clay pot sealed shut by baking bread. He saws through the bread "lid" at your table, revealing the eggplant, tomato, onion, garlic and (optional) meat still boiling. Neat trick, and good food.
**BARIUM BAR**, *Karahandere Mah. No. 14, Ürgüp, Tel. 384 341 4198. Moderate.*
Ürgüp's best standard bar, with live music in an underground atmosphere.

## SEEING THE SIGHTS
### Wine Tours
Göreme has its own wine festival in June, but the true center of wine production is in Ürgüp. Your hotel or the tourism information office can help pinpoint the various nearby wineries, most of which welcome visitors and offer wine tasting. The best of the lot, with good whites and reds, is **Turasan**, near the Turban Hotel and Esbelli Ev.

### Devrent Valley
Just west of town on the Nevşehir road is a classic set of "**fairy chimneys**," tall steepled stones topped by a massive boulder, like a bean

on the head of a pin. There is a parking area off the side of the road for those who want to see the sun rise or set from here. Another place of interest is the **Pancırlık Valley**, a good hike winding seven kilometers up toward Ortahisar.

# UÇHISAR

On the rim of the valley, above both Göreme and Ürgüp, **Uçhisar** lies in the shadow of a giant buttress of natural stone that has been used as a fortress since Roman times. This is a peaceful town, with fine views down into the Göreme Valley below and an excellent selection of hotels.

## ARRIVALS & DEPARTURES

Uçhisar is on the main Nevşehir-Ürgüp road. Dolmuş speed back and forth through here all day, and those coming from the west also dive down into the valley below to serve Göreme.

## WHERE TO STAY

**LES MAISONS DE CAPPADOCE**, *Semiramis A.Ş., Belediye Meydanı No. 24, BP 28, Uçhisar, Tel. 384 219 2813, Fax 384 219 2782. Houses: 7. House for 6: $1,300 per week. Studio for 2: $400 per week.*

French architect Jacques Avizou came to Cappadoccia as a tourist in 1987, returning home with some photographs, tourist chotchkes, and some inspiration. Since then he has returned annually, often flying back to Orly Airport with more substantial souvenirs, such as title deeds. Through his Turkish company, Semiramis, Avizou has renovated a clutch of houses and studios in Uçhisar, doting over them and mending them in exacting fashion. There are five houses and two studios currently available, with a further seven houses probably available in 1997.

Each is faithful to the peculiar architectural legacy of the area, with arches, stairs, and rooms carved out of the valley wall, finished with blocks of stone. Each house and suite is equipped with a kitchen, and you should solicit advice on some Turkish recipes while here. Patios command Pigeon Valley below and you are free to use the pool at the nearby Kaya Hotel. Unfortunately you may never make it that far from the house, let alone all the way to Göreme and Zelve.

Houses and studios, accommodations for anywhere from two to six people, are available for weekly rental. Contact Semiramis for information about shorter stays. Open April through October.

Selected as one of our best places to stay – see Chapter 10.

**KAYA OTEL**, *Uçhisar, Nevşehir, Tel. 384 219 2007, Fax 384 219 2363 (in İstanbul Fax 212 233 8517). Rooms: 60. Double: $64.*

The Kaya is the Club Med offering in Cappadoccia, and is highly thought of. The building is decorous and attractive, with stone block rooms looking out over the valley. The pool and grounds is a welcome bit of cool greenery during Cappadoccia's hot summers. The restaurant, too, is the best in Uçhisar. The Kaya is not the friendliest hotel in the area, but it is clean, enjoyable and efficient. French spoken. Open April through October.

**PANSİYON MEDITERANEE,** *Üçhisar, Tel. 384 219 2210. Rooms: 24. Double: $22.*

The Mediteranee costs more and offers more than standard budget accommodations. The Mediteranee is often full, and you'll have a chance to bone up on your French. There is an excellent view over Pigeon Valley.

## WHERE TO EAT

Uçhisar's affordable restaurants are hidden far from the Kale. The area caters mostly to tourists.

**KAYA OTEL,** *Ürgüp Caddesi, Uçhisar, Nevşehir, Tel. 384 219 2007, Fax 384 219 2363.*

The Kaya's restaurant serves up excellent buffet meals, suitable for one of the area's elite hotels. The restaurant serves a well-conceived combination of traditional Turkish fare and food from around the world.

**BINDALLI RESTAURANT,** *Ürgüp Caddesi, Uçhisar, Tel. 384 219 2690.*

Bındallı is built back into the hillside and offers delicious Turkish cuisine in a traditional setting. Open only for lunch.

**HISAR RESTAURANT,** *Uçhisar, Tel. 384 219 2764.*

If you're looking for a good, inexpensive meal in Uçhisar, this is your best bet.

## SEEING THE SIGHTS

The **Uçhisar fortress**, which dominates the skyline in all directions, is well worth a visit. This natural shaft of rock was tunneled and fortified by the Romans, and probably before. From the top of the fortress you have a commanding view of the plain below, as well as of other natural fortresses in this circuit, such as those at Ortahisar and Ürgüp. There is evidence of Roman burial sites atop the fortress, which – like so many things in Cappadoccia – is as interesting as you are daring, with tunnels and shafts shooting every which way.

## GOREME

Just one kilometer from the Göreme Open Air Museum and deep amid the Cappadoccian valleys, **Göreme** has become the center of budget travel in the area. The town has a raucous feel to it, unlike the somewhat quieter towns nearby.

The tourism information cooperative has a new location next to Gulliver's Travels, but has no phone.

## ARRIVALS & DEPARTURES

Dolmuş leave for Göreme from Nevşehir and Avanos hourly throughout the day, passing Uçhisar on the way. There is no dolmuş service between Göreme and Ürgüp, but there are hourly dolmuş to Avanos. The dolmuş stop is at the otogar in the middle of town.

## WHERE TO STAY

A cooperative enforces standardized pricing among Göreme's many budget hotels, and its restaurants as well. The restaurants seem to adhere to pricing based on some arbitrary set of borders, with ground zero at the city-center square. The farther away from the center you go, the cheaper the prices.

**ATAMAN HOTEL**, *Göreme, Nevşehir, Tel. 384 271 2310, Fax 384 271 2313. Rooms: 33 (43). Double: $120, half board.*

Another of Cappadoccia's beautiful rock-hewn hotels. The Ataman is located on the edge of Göreme village, at the opening of a long, winding valley. Orchards packed with apricot and nut trees range in front of the Ataman terrace, and a stream winds past shaded by aspens. The cozy facade of the Ataman conceals a massive cavern-hall and a network of rooms and hallways carved into the tufa, although most rooms on the front side are more Cappadoccia-conventional, built with stone blocks. The Ataman is lovingly decorated and even has an excellent small library collected by the owner, an archaeologist and guide.

The restaurant on the premises is outstanding (see below), and the owners Şermin and Abbas Ataman are thoughtful and conscientious. The Ataman's greatest drawback is its cost, which is on par with the large Nevşehir hotels but dramatically undercut by the remarkably affordable good accommodations in the area. Like most hotels, the Ataman will happily come off of its high season individual room price if you inquire by fax or phone. The Ataman remains open in the winter.

**THE OTTOMAN HOUSE**, *Orta Mahallesi No. 36, Göreme, Tel. 384 271 2616, Fax 384 271 2351. Rooms: 35. Double: $24. Restaurant.*

A well-run, smallish hotel on the road leading up the canal from Göreme's otogar. The Ottoman House is constructed from stone blocks and operated by a friendly Australian/Turkish couple. A cheap, reliable choice in Göreme. Be advised that this cheap, appealing hotel is subsidized by its in-house carpet shop, and that you are likely to strike up an acquaintance with someone who stands to make a commission. There's nothing wrong with the practice, so long as you're aware of it. Breakfast costs $5 for an open buffet, and a set menu dinner is $8.

Budget accommodations: The best cheap hotels in a city filled with them are the **PARADISE PENSION**, *Tel. 384 271 2248*, in the direction of the open air museum, and the **UFUK PANSIYON**, *Tel. 384 271 2157*, at the corner between downtown and the open air museum.

## WHERE TO EAT

**ATAMAN HOTEL**, *Göreme, Nevşehir, Tel. 384 271 2310, Fax 384 271 2313*.

Abbas Ataman opened his restaurant in 1986, and it became popular enough that he opened a hotel to go with it in 1993. The cuisine at the Ataman is overwhelmingly rich, baked shrimp, quail, sauteed artichokes and chicken, followed by heavy, decadent desserts. One of the most vulgarly satisfying restaurants in all of Turkey, and relatively inexpensive at $20 for a prix fixe meal.

**ORIENT RESTAURANT**, *Göreme, Tel. 384 271 2346*.

Located on the main Nevşehir road just before leaving town, the Orient is the area's most honest and reliable inexpensive restaurant, serving good food at reasonable prices. The restaurants along Göreme's main strip prey on disoriented foreigners, but the Orient is a relaxed respite from that. Plus, bless its soul, it offers pancakes in the morning.

**FRED FLINTSTONE'S CAVE BAR**, *below Paradise Pansiyon on the way toward the museum. No phone.*

Everyone seems to stop in here, and everyone loves it. Probably the most fun dive bar in Göreme, with an eccentric cast of beer swilling foreigners. Good place to dig for information, as someone here will have been where you're going.

## NEVSEHIR

Cappadoccia's regional center is at **Nevşehir**, but that does not mean you want to stay here. Aside from the **Selçuk fort** on the crest of the hill above town and the relaxed byways of **Nar** (old Nevşehir) across the gorge, there's very little to see here. You are sure to pass back and forth through town, but you won't feel inclined to stay.

The **tourism information** office, *Atatürk Bulvarı, Tel. 384 213 3659*, has good information but is disinclined to actually give you any.

## ARRIVALS & DEPATURES

Nevşehir is a transit hub on the western end of the Cappadoccian plain, with roads fanning out toward Mersin, Konya, and Ankara. If you arrive in the area by bus, you will probably be dropped off at Nevşehir's main bus station, out of town to the north.

Dolmuş pass every 15 minutes or half hour en route to the center of town. At the center of town, on Atatürk Bulvarı near the tourism information office, is Nevşehir's major dolmuş stop. Dolmuş bound every direction stop here, and if you are using public transportation you'll become familiar with this place. Not only do dolmuş from here serve the underground cities of Derinkuyu and Kaymaklı and sites farther afield, such as Niğde, but at the moment you may have to pass through Nevşehir on your way between Ürgüp and Göreme, owing to some municipal bickering.

## WHERE TO STAY

HOTEL KAPADOKYA DEDEMAN, *Ürgüp Yolu, Nevşehir, Tel. 384 213 9900-9915, Fax 384 213 2158. Rooms: 349. Double: $120.*

This is Cappadoccia's lone five star hotel, with satellite television, pools, basketball, and a casino. The Dedeman chain is very well run, and this hotel is no exception. If you need convenience and the standard amenities of a major hotel, this is the place.

## TOURING CAPPADOCCIA

There are countless things to see in Cappadoccia, and no matter how much time you have you will have to skip things of interest. We have broken the sights down into areas, with some out of the way spots thrown in for good measure. There are, as mentioned, more than 30 underground cities and hundreds of churches; the only way to see Cappadoccia thoroughly is to buy a house and live here.

Don't kill yourself trying to see everything; Cappadoccia is a good place to simply relax. You can see all of the major sites by public transportation and judicious taxi rides – some places, like Göreme, Derinkuyu, and Kaymaklı are easy to see by dolmuş. Many smaller sites require a rented scooter, motorcycle or car. Bring a flashlight, a light jacket for the dark interiors, and (who knows) a long piece of string or breadcrumbs. Most of the valleys and underground cities in the area have an admission fee of between $1 and $2.

## HOW TO SEE CAPPADOCCIA

Taxis charge roughly $45 for eight hours of shuttling around three or four people – although prices fluctuate according to the season and your bargaining ability. Rental cars are ideal, and both scooters ($25 per day), motorcycles ($30 per day) and bikes ($8 per day) provide other options.

Unless you have such transportation and a doctorate in Byzantine art, a guided trip can be useful. Cappadoccia is a relentless oddity, with new peculiarities down every hole and around each corner. A good guide, with years of experience in the area, can explain what you're looking at and even give you tips on how to spend your unguided time. Moreover, if you have less than four days in the area, your only hope of hitting all the high points is to sign on with a guided tour company.

Bear in mind, however, there are distinct problems with guided tours that are often compounded in Cappadoccia. Although the guided tours visit many of the area's most interesting sites, they don't give you the time to get off the well-worn paths and poke around in out of the way areas, or climb through a warren of caves to the top of a cliff and rest. You are on someone's clock, which isn't always enjoyable on your own vacation.

Second, guides take you on a circuit that can get congested, and most guides are inclined only to show you what they want to show you. You may stand in line while 200 feet away a collection of churches sits empty. Third, the amount of time spent visiting the ruins can be equivalent to, or even less than, the amount of time at carpet, pottery, and rug-weaving shops, and these establishments are no great bargain. The prices aren't especially good, even before the shopowner tacks on the commission he is turning over to your tour company. Perhaps you don't mind, but if you do mind, if your time in the area is limited and you want to see what you came to see, then the detours and delays of a guided tour can be frustrating. Finally, there are some downright disreputable tour companies in the area.

One of the local companies, Ürgüp's **Argeus Travel Agency**, *Istiklal Cad. No. 13, Ürgüp, Tel. 384 341 4688, Fax 384 341 4888; E-mail: argeus@ada.net.tr*, is free from most of these vices. Argeus has higher rates (roughly $15 per day more) than its competitiors, but it deals honestly with its clients, skips the side trips to pottery factories, feeds you at top notch restaurants, and has a brace of knowledgeable guides. Argeus arranges bicycling tours and even skiing packages in the winter. The company occasionally works with American outfitter REI, and is Ürgüp's licensed agent for Turkish Airlines offering shuttle service to Kayseri (70 kilometers).

Among the ferociously competitive second tier of companies, we recommend **Alan Turizm**, *Yunak Mah. PK 55, Ürgüp, Tel. 384 341 4667, Fax 384 341 2025*, and advisedly recommend **Red Valley Tourism and Travel Agency**, *Cumhuriet Meydanı No. 4, Ürgüp, Tel. 384 341 5061, Fax 384 341 2551*. Your tour price is partially subsidized by miniature tours of local ceramic outlets, but both are conscientiously managed.

## CAPPADOCCIA ALTERNATIVES

*Consider seeing Cappadoccia the way very few people do, on an extended trip by bicycle or horse.*

*Caroline Williams, an Englishwoman, organizes and guides bicycling tours throughout Turkey, but lives in Ürgüp and focuses primarily on the Cappadoccia area. Single or multi-day trips can be arranged around Cappadoccia, getting you into the fascinating nooks and crannies that few people are able to see. Contact Caroline Williams directly (PK 36, Ürgüp, Nevşehir, Tel/Fax 384 341 3328, E-mail: carolinw@doruk.com.tr), or contact Argeus Tourism, with whom she often works (see above). Argeus is one of the several agencies that rents mountain bikes daily (nine hours, $9).*

*As an alternative you can take a two to nine day horseriding trek with Beyaz Yele (white mane) out of Ürgüp. Beyaz Yele takes advantage of Cappadoccia's ancient association with beautiful horses to organize multiday guided tours through the area between April and October. The company offers horses for a range of skill levels, from beginners to advanced, and its excursions can cover 40 kilometers a day. Accommodation is provided in private houses or camps. For more information, contact Beyaz Yele at Karandere, Sucuoğlu Sok. No. 12, Ürgüp, Tel. 384 341 5175, Fax 384 341 8089, or, again, Argeus.*

*Several local tour companies also offer multi-day hiking expeditions into Cappadoccia's backcountry. Check with Argeus and Alan tour companies. Another entertaining way to see the area is on a balloon trip over Cappadoccia. These trips typically last between one and two hours and include a bite to eat, which isn't too much to ask considering the individual selling price is a (negotiable) $250 per person. Contact Cloud Nine, Nevşehir, Tel. 384 213 9945, Fax 384 213 5092.*

# NORTHERN CAPPADOCCIA

## Zelve

**Zelve** is a peculiar spot, long inhabited by monks who carved great arcades and living spaces out of the tufa. Zelve is particularly beautiful first thing in the morning, when tour groups have not yet arrived and the site is achingly quiet. Evidently it was rarely this quiet historically. Christians settled here very early on, perhaps as early as the first century, and they began work on cooperative monastic living quarters in the fourth and fifth centuries.

At its height, 5,000 people may have populated this area, but by the 12th century the arrival of the Turks had driven most of the Christian communities away. Reportedly, one of the ways to tell who built caves is to note their height. If they wind in and up, or the only opening is on the rock face, they were constructed by Christians concerned about defending themselves from Persians, Arabs, and, later, Turks. Caves at ground level were created by Turks less worried about their security.

Unusually heavy rains in 1950 were responsible for the collapse of the great chamber in the right valley, and the government relocated residents from here in 1952. The Ministry of Tourism began restoring the area in 1960.

Of particular interest here is the great hall on the right wall of the rightmost valley, whose facade has collapsed. You can still ascend to the upper sections. The highlight of the area is the warren of tunnels and rooms linking the right valley to the middle valley.

## Özkonak

Less refined than Derinkuyu and Kaymaklı, this underground city is in some ways far more fascinating. Özkonak may have once been as large as Derinkuyu and Kaymaklı, but large sections have not yet been explored. Features of those cities such as the great rolling defensive stones are present here, too.

One distinctive aspect of Özkonak is the drainage system, not present in other underground complexes. The city appears to have been designed by people who had the advantage of critiquing other underground complexes. The oft-quoted population figure for this city is inexplicably 60,000 people (40,000 more than the figures given for Derinkuyu), which seems completely preposterous. Less than 5,000 live in Özkonak today.

To reach the underground city (once again, "Yeraltı Şehir") pass through Avanos and follow the "Özkonak/Göynük" road north. The road is signed for the Özkonak underground city 11 kilometers past Avanos. The Kayseri road is slightly more roundabout, but also posted. Dolmuş depart Avanos for Özkonak about once every two hours from in front of the PTT, and are especially frequent on market days in Avanos (Friday) and the weekend.

## Çavuşin

Çavuşin is located on the road between Göreme and Avanos. This area has at least two churches of interest. The first, **St. John's Church**, is the oldest surface church still standing, dating to the 6th or 7th century. The second is another underground church, the **Bishop's Church**, for which a fee is charged. The interior has some interesting mosaics depicting the life of Christ, and a powerful image of a late Byzantine emperor, Nicephorus II. Several churches are located up the Kızılçukur from

## CAPPADOCCIAN SYMBOLS

*Cappadoccian churches and monasteries are carefully decorated with innumerable inscriptions and other forms of art. When the iconoclasts banned figurative art, monks began forming rebuses to depict important stories.*

*Here's what the symbols represent:*

**The Cross** – *Christianity.*

**The Fish** – *Both Jesus Christ and Christians were symbolized by the fish. The Greek letters in "fish" were also strung out to form a holy acronym meaning Jesus, son of God, saviour, while Christians considered themselves fish caught in his holy net.*

**The Peacock** – *The adoption of Christianity.*

**The Deer** – *Resurrection.*

**The Lion** – *Victory.*

**Grapes** – *Baptism.*

**The Chicken** – *The annunciation.*

**The Triangle** - *Someone espousing the Holy Trinity, an evangelist.*

Çavuşin, including the stunning White Church (Beyaz Kilise), making this a good place to head out on hikes.

## Göreme Open Air Museum

This is the most beautifully decorated site in Cappadoccia, at the heart of Turkey's Göreme National Park. Monks living here carved out a collection of churches above a small, fertile valley, decorating their holy places with painting and frescoes. Many of the frescoes remain in good shape, although most are marred in some way, usually with their eyes gouged. Again and again while in Cappadoccia you will see frescoes and paintings defaced in this way. This practice was supposed to "kill" the images, according to iconoclastic Muslims. In addition to the damage done on religious grounds, standard vandalism has taken a toll. Ironically, many frescoes were damaged when Greek Orthodox residents chipped bits of the art away to use in healing balms.

**Tokalı Church** is one of the crowning glories of Cappadoccia, a beautiful cave church ornamented with remarkably well-preserved frescoes. The church is located outside of the Göreme Open Air Museum's main gate, down the road toward the car park. With the beautiful detailing of the columns and arches within Tokalı you can almost forget you are in a cave. The foyer was initially the entire church, when local Christians began hollowing out places of worship in the second century. Over time the larger interior space was opened up, and with the victory over Iconoclasts in 843 B.C., the monks were free to decorate the interiors with representations of Christ and other figurative images. Note the difference in the artwork; the outer section is painted directly on stone, while the interior chamber is covered with frescoes. The life of Christ is represented on one section of the arched ceiling in six long rows, separated in the center by depictions of the apostles. The lower level was a crypt. UNESCO restored parts of this church after a collapse in the sixties.

Within the park all of the churches are signed, each given a name that has something to do with the art within. The **Elmalı Kilise**, or Apple Church, for instance, is so named because Christ is depicted holding what was thought to be an apple. The new theory, that it is a globe, is fairly absurd considering the general conception of geography in the middle ages. The frescoes probably date to the 11th century.

One of the sights that never fails to disappoint is the **Yılanli Kilise** (Snake Church), which has a painting of an old bearded man, St. Onophrius, who is in fact an old bearded woman. It seems that as a young girl Onophrius sought God's help to steer her away from the temptations of being a beautiful young woman, and God granted her wish by transforming her into an old man. Onophrius' breasts are visible, but her genitals are delicately obscured.

The **Karanlık Kilise**, or Dark Church, was reopened in late 1996 after a long restoration project. The artwork inside was once exposed only to the light of a single window, but the interior was exposed after a section of the facade broke off and collapsed. The restoration has sought to ensure that the paintings remain vivid. The chief subjects of art within this church are the beautifully decorated last supper and Judas' betrayal. A surcharge at the church should be dispensed with after 1997.

Elsewhere at Göreme, **Kızlar Kilise** was not a church at all, but probably the home of several hundred nuns. Another church is down the road toward Göreme and off to the left.

## Ortahisar

An entire village bustles at the foot of Ortahisar's towering **fortress** of living stone. The fortress is laced with tunnels and rooms, more so, even, than the Uçhisar fortress. Ortahisar means, literally, middle fortress, and was part of a security circuit from Göreme to Uçhisar. It's a wonder the peak still stands at all with the honeycomb of caves through its foundations.

Some impressive painted churches are located up Balkandere valley from Ortahisar, and it is a good point from which to set out on a four kilometer hike to İbrahimpaşa, two kilometers off of the main Ürgüp-Nevşehir road. Ortahisar is three kilometers off the road.

## Kızılçukur (The Red Valley)

This valley, so named because of the red-hued stone, is an excellent place to spend several hours exploring. The valley is located on the Nevşehir-Ürgüp road four kilometers west of Ürgüp. From the road you descend to the north, where an old path twists among steepled stone, passing small tunnels and chambers. People frequently watch the sun set from atop the valley, but the valley is worth visiting for much more than its passive scenery. Tucked away in the valley are remarkably preserved churches carved out of the cliff face. The valley empties out at Çavuşin on the Göreme-Avanos road.

## Pigeon Valley

Pigeon Valley extends from Uçhisar down to Göreme, offering an excellent hike in both directions. The trail along the valley floor offers a hushed, pretty walk past several tombs and caves.

## SOUTHEASTERN CAPPADOCCIA

### Yeşilöz

You'll find Yeşilöz well off the beaten track southeast of Ürgüp. The mystery of this site is still intact, and you're likely to be the only ones here; it is not worth the trouble unless you have several days in Cappadoccia. Signs direct you to the Theodora Kilisesi Church, an isolated and well-preserved chamber with inscriptions. Dolmuş go to Yeşilöz, but you'll spend an entire day getting back and forth without your own transportation.

### Soğanlı Valley

Until recently this area was spared heavy bus traffic, but the word is out and trips to Soğanlı are becoming more common. Soğanlı is located a little more than 50 kilometers south of Ürgüp, and is just seven kilometers west of Yeşilhisar (near Yeşilöz). Public transportation is so difficult as to not be an option, and even most locals hitch back and forth. A map at the entrance (near where they take your $2) shows you the various churches scattered through the dry valley, although many of them are easy enough to find, telltale windows and passages in the face of a stone spire giving them away on the right side of the valley.

Several of the monasteries and churches at Soğanlı are fascinating, notably Kubbeli Kilise for its incredible multi-storied chambers and Yılanı Kilise with its depiction of St. George in battle with a dragon (misidentified in Turkish as yılan, or snake).

# SOUTHWESTERN CAPPADOCCIA

## Kaymaklı

Contrary to popular belief, "Kaymaklı" is not Turkish for bad posture. This cramped underground city is south of Nevşehir on the way to Derinkuyü. This complex has fewer floors than its neighbor Derinkuyu, but snakes into the earth in a tighter, more disconcerting way.

Kaymaklı is, if anything, more complex than the open sections of Derinkuyu. It is interesting to see the differences in tunneling and internal design; note, for instance, the holes for passing along messages from floor to floor. Kaymaklı, like Derinkuyu, had access to water from an underground river. Also, like Derinkuyu, when the population re-tired underground it was in the habit of dumping its waste into the section of river furthest downstream; unfortunately Kaymaklı's down-stream was Derinkuyu's upstream, which, nevertheless, does not seem to have fouled relations since they seem to have cooperated in building a tunnel connecting their cities. As at Derinkuyu, there is an arrow system to help you determine whether you are ascending or descending.

## Mazıköy

Located 30 kilometers south of Ürgüp and 10 kilometers east of Kaymaklı, **Mazı Yeralı Şehir** is one of Cappadoccia's secrets. Unlike the other cities, Mazıköy is built back into a mountain. This fairly remote, rarely visited area is ideal for getting away from the lines and crowds during the summer. The underground city is usually open but poorly lit; new lighting may be installed by the summer of 1997.

## Derinkuyu

Along with Kaymaklı, this is the most visited underground city in Cappadoccia. The underground city is identifiable mostly because of the tour buses that congregate in southeastern Derinkuyu-town. The open-ing is a humble staircase opening into a large chamber, which is in turn attached to further chambers descending eight floors and 180 feet deep. Upon entering, the bulk of the city is around to your right, while livestock areas, the school, and the winery are off to your left. Try to avoid Derinkuyu between 10 a.m. and 3 p.m. during high season, when you have to squeeze in between huffing, sweating busloads of people.

According to one account this city was besieged three separate times by the Arabs, to no avail. The Arabs could not dislodge the Christians, who were supplied with food and water, and they could not seal them in since the natives could burrow out at will. It now appears that a long suspected tunnel leading from Derinkuyu to Kaymaklı – almost six miles – really existed, and that the people of Derinkuyu could carry in provisions along a six foot wide avenue. The tunnel has not been fully excavated, nor has the rest of Derinkuyu itself. The section tourists see today is probably 15 percent of the entire city, with the remainder now walled off. Try to make your way to the very bottom, down a last passage from the church. Here you arrive at the lowest accessible section of the vertical shaft and can look up at the pinpoint of natural light far above.

## Eski Gümüşler

The rock cut church of **Eski Gümüşler** is 85 kilometers south of Nevşehir in the foothills of the Taurus Mountains. The site is five kilometers north of Niğde, off the road four kilometers to the left. Eski Gümüşler is worth the long trip out of the way. This former monastery is in excellent condition, and its well-defended entrance suggests that it was built at a time of great threat.

Eski Gümüşler is most impressive for its interesting design, but its frescoes are appealing as well. Adding to the aura of mystery about the cunningly designed chambers is the suspicion that they connect with an underground complex like those in Nevşehir and Kaymaklı.

## IHLARA VALLEY

In a region full of wonderful oddities, this is frequently the favorite. **Ihlara** can be seen on a day with other sites in the southwest region, but it is worth a day all by itself. Bring a small pack full of food, clothes you can get grubby, a good book and some hiking boots (sneakers are fine, too).

The Ihlara Valley rises up in sheer cliffs to either side of the **Melendiz River**, and the river valley is a thick ribbon of green, sharply contrasting the sere grasses of the plain above. What makes Ihlara peculiar instead of merely dramatic is the collection of painted churches, dormitories, and individual dwellings that litter the walls. The monks lived austere lives, but they were no fools; this gorge is a beautiful, peaceful, thriving place filled with whirling birds and wide-eyed frogs. There are trails along the entire river edge, although they are difficult to negotiate when the river level is up in the spring. Churches and monastic dwellings are located on either side of the Melendiz River, which is easy to cross in the summer and is spanned by several bridges.

## ARRIVALS & DEPARTURES
### By Bus

The Ihlara canyon is not served by public transportation from the Nevşehir area; Aksaray is the regional hub. Municipal buses serve Ihlara and Selimiye from Aksaray, and there is occasional transportation to

Belisırma. Municipal buses depart Aksaray, 47 kilometers west of Ihlara, three times daily, beginning at 11 a.m.

You can try to inquire about Belisırma buses while in Aksaray (Do you go to Belisırma? *"Belisırma'ya gitiyor musunuz?"*), as one dolmuş or bus daily should serve the town – although it's often probably the Ihlara bus. If you are comfortable hitching, have the Ihlara bus drop you off at the Belisırma intersection and await one of the many empty tour buses headed down to the valley floor; otherwise, taxi from Ihlara.

**By Car**

Ihlara is the least convenient of the sites in the greater Cappadoccia area. With a car, Ihlara takes time to reach, but is not a particular problem. Signs direct you west from Derinkuyu, making that a possible morning stop before continuing on to Ihlara. The quickest way from Nevşehir to Ihlara is to follow the highway from Nevşehir toward Aksaray. This road takes you past the impressive Ağzıkarahan caravansaray on the left hand side of the road, worth having a look at.

After turning south onto the Ihlara/Selimiye road continue until the main rim entrance for day trips, just before Ihlara town. A stair descends to the floor of the gorge, and a $2 admission fee is charged. If you hike along the gorge to its end at Selime, you can find a taxi to shuttle you back to the entrance.

## WHERE TO STAY & EAT

Instead of rushing out to Ihlara and away you may want to stay here. Consider staying at Belisırma, midway along the valley, where humble hotels and guest pensions are only beginning to appear. This small, friendly town is beautifully situated near the middle of the gorge, and is accustomed to people emerging from the upstream (Ihlara) trail, getting a bite at the **AŞLAN RESTAURANT**, and getting on the bus to head back to Nevşehir. There are monk dwellings and churches on both sides of the gorge, both upstream and downstream of the town.

This is one of the last truly central and truly undiscovered places in Turkey – backpackers tend to crowd into Ihlara town or come on day trips from Cappadoccia proper. Of the limited accommodations available in Belisırma, **AŞLAN CAMPING VE PANSIYON** is the most reliable. There are several accommodations in Ihlara town as well, with the noisy but efficient **RIVER VIEW HOTEL** topping the list. The most popular accommodation in the area is probably the **ANATOLIA PENSION**, *Tel/Fax 382 453 7439*.

## SEEING THE SIGHTS

There are innumerable holes in the cliff walls, many of them with interior passages that ascend or descend, occasionally giving way to new rooms and new views. There were more than 90 churches along this 6 mile stretch of the Melendiz River, and many are still intact. The churches at the upstream end of the valley show more eastern influence in their frescoes, while those downstream are more Byzantine, perhaps suggesting later occupation. As at Göreme and Zelve, Muslims damaged many of the frescoes around the eyes in order to "kill" the spirit within the painting.

One of the favorite churches is **Yılanlı Kilise**, on the east bank of the river near a bridge upstream of Belısirma. This church is well decorated, although the frescoes and paintings are difficult to make out without your own light. The "yılanlar," or snakes, in question are sometimes ferocious lizard creatures, but all manner of reptilian creatures are devouring and nibbling at evildoers in hell. Another Gothic image is that of the forty *Christian Martyrs of Sebaste* forced into freezing water and forbidden to leave until they renounce their religion. This 39 of the men refuse to do, but one man leaves the pool and, as depicted, is replaced by a Roman guard who strips off his own clothes and enters the pool. An exasperated devil looks on, grimacing.

One of the secrets of the valley is the stretch below Belisırma, descending toward Selime. This section is lightly traveled and small paths wind up to churches and chambers in the valley wall.

298

# 15. THE BLACK SEA COAST

The **Black Sea coast**, from Akçakoca to Trabzon, is Turkey's most peaceful frontier. The ancient allure of Troy and Ephesus, the mystique of İstanbul and the temptation of the Mediterranean beaches attract most of Turkey's visitors. This is understandable, but at least consider a spin out along the Black Sea. Languishing, or thriving, along this moody sea are sites that are older, more significant, and less understood than their counterparts in well-traveled Turkey. Even the climate seems to conspire to keep tourism interest low; the rain arrives in late August and continues at a tropical rhythm until October, when the temperatures begin to drop. May and June are warm again but wet, leaving July and the bulk of August as the ideal time unless you can deal with afternoon rains.

The moist climate has also encouraged dense greenery, which has in turn done its level best to hide or obscure the ruins scattered across the landscape. Still, for a few months of the year, this is one of the most rewarding places to travel in Turkey today. You don't need to forgo beaches nestled beneath Hellenistic city walls; they're here, too. You don't need to hole up in fleabag pensions; we've found plenty of good hotels, and some that are wonderful. You don't need a car; bus transport along the Black Sea coast is easy and cheap, on good, well-maintained roads. You don't even need to be wary and weathered; Turkish honesty and decency is at an extreme in these little traveled areas. Every time we think we're ripped off on the Black Sea, we're adding incorrectly.

What you do need along the Black Sea route is a willingness to climb and hike and, at the end of the day, not quite understand what you've seen. Somewhere beneath the vegetation and thousands of years of history are traces of the Amazons, Jason and the Argonauts, the Kingdoms of Pontus and Phyrgia and Rome, the Armenians, Hittites, and Urartians, the monasteries of Sümela and Georgia, the outposts of the Trapezuntine Empire, and, finally, the Ottomans. Archaeologists have

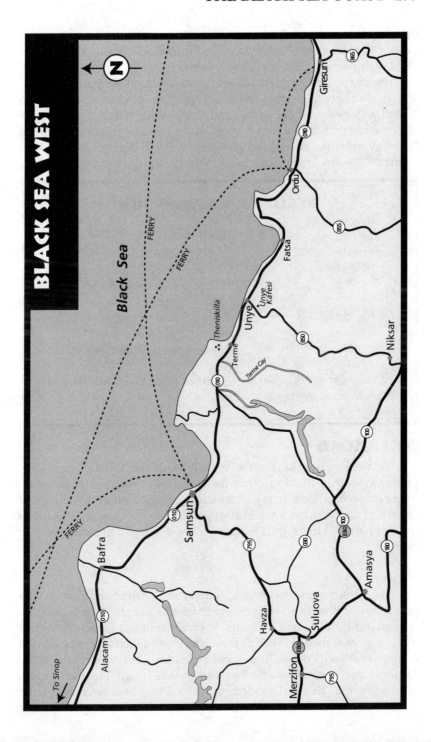

been hard at work along this coast for a century, but it's slow going; the known sites are a tangle of mystery and rumor, and no one knows what else lay unknown in the thick undergrowth.

The first stretch, from **Akçakoca** to **Amasra**, is off the main highways and particularly peaceful. The coast between **Amasra** and **Sinop** is dotted with perfect little beaches and quiet fishing villages, but lodging is rare – often in the form of a guest room. Just east of Sinop the main highway emerges at **Samsun** and carries most İstanbul and Ankara traffic on toward **Trabzon**, then on to the Georgian Republic.

---

## BLACK SEA SEASONAL FISH

| Season | Fish |
|---|---|
| Dec./Jan. | Hamsi |
| Feb./Mar. | Istavrit, Hamsi, Kalkan (small) |
| April/May | Barbuniye, Mezgit, Kalkan (small) |
| June/July | Midye (mussels), Kefal, Mezgit, Istavrit, Iskarpit, Barbuniye |
| Aug./Sept. | Zargan, Palamut, Lufer, Istavrit, Hamsi, Iskarpit, Barbuniye, Mezgit |
| Oct./Nov. | Palamut, Lufer, Hamsi, Mezgit |

Note: Shrimp (karides) are not native to the Black Sea. **Alabalik**, freshwater trout, is always available.

---

# AKÇAKOCA

On weekends, **Akçakoca** is usually fairly busy with Istanbullus getting away from the city, otherwise it is subdued even in high summer. There are several hotels here and the city is going through a development spurt that may turn the town a little ugly. There is not much of historical interest here, but there are a few diversions when you tire of the nearby beaches.

### History

Akçakoca has always played a minor role in Black Sea affairs. As the port town for Prusias ad Hypium, 15 miles inland at modern **Konuralp**, it often did bustling trade, and its rich plantations of hazelnuts were a major source of income, then as now. The town, called Diapolis, carried on under Bithnia, Pontus, Rome, and Byzantium, but its only remaining fortification is a small Genoese keep to the west of town. This fortification was built in the 1200s and handed over to the Ottomans one century later.

Two of Sultan Orhan's generals, Akçakoca and Konuralp, seized this territory around 1355, leaving their names to the conquered towns. They are celebrated in a statue at the town center, by the new mosque (although Orhan is mislabeled Osman).

Akçakoca continues churning out hazelnuts, and there is a festival to celebrate the pending harvest on the third weekend in July.

## ARRIVALS & DEPARTURES

### By Bus
Several bus companies offer service to Akçakoca, leaving you at the intersection west of town. From there it is a simple matter (during daylight hours) to get a dolmuş into town. The route into town passes the Hotel Akçakoca and follows close to the beach, leaving you in the city center. The tourist information office is one block away on Cumhuriet Meydanı. You can continue on to the Diapolis by foot, or take another bus on the Kale route that passes Tezel Kamping, the city's best pension/campground.

Ulusoy has daily service to the area from Ankara and İstanbul, but Üstün Erçelik offers the most frequent buses.

### By Car
From the south and west the quickest way to Akçakoca is following the main E-80 highway to Düzçe, then following the 655 through Konuralp to the coast and following the signs left into Akçakoca. A brand new highway along the Black Sea coast from Karasu in the west was still under construction at the end of 1996. To the east, the highway hugs the coast as far as Ereğli, then ascends into the mountains, emerging just west of Zonguldak.

## ORIENTATION
Akçakoca is only a pilgrimage for Nutella lovers. This quiet town has had only glancing attention from the tourist masses making a beeline to the southern beaches, and is the better for it. The beaches in the area are excellent – along a 20 mile stretch, half of the coastline is beach, most of it deserted. To the west the coastline is both prettier and less accessible, and there is an excellent sand beach about five kilometers west of town.

The **tourism information** office is near the dolmuş stop at the center of town, on *Cumhuriet Meydanı, Tel. 374 611 4554, Fax 374 611 4448.*

## WHERE TO STAY & EAT
As at most mid-sized towns on the Black Sea, the Tourism Information office is a clearing house for people willing to rent out their homes

or rooms in their homes. Akçakoca's old houses, on the hill above town, are much prettier than the new hotels.

**HOTEL AKÇAKOCA**, *Ereğli Cad. No. 23, Akçakoca, Bolu, Tel. 374 611 4525, Fax 374 611 4440. Rooms: 76. Double: $55.*

The first four star facility on the Black Sea coast, the Akçakoca opened in 1990. A nice, unpretentious holiday spot on a long expanse of gritty sand beach. Tennis court, pool, cafes, a restaurant, and several bars. Closed in winter.

**DİAPOLİS HOTEL**, *ınönü Cad., Akçakoca, Bolu, Tel. 374 611 Tel. 3741, Fax 374 611 3790. Rooms: 120. Double: $55.*

An unusually attractive holiday hotel overlooking Akçakoca's small port. An excellent place to watch the sun set while boats chug home after a day fishing. All of the standard amenities, including three bars and a pool.

**MESEN HOTEL**, *Edilli Köyü, Çanak Çanak Mevkii, Akçakoca, Tel. 374 611 4436, Fax 374 611 2574. Rooms: 20. Double: $42.*

Isolated outside of Akçakoca, this small hotel is away from whatever hustle and bustle Akçakoca has, ideally located for relaxation. The hotel has a small pool, sauna and in-house restaurant. To truly get away, try one of the bungalows.

**TEZEL CAMPING**, *Hürriyettepe Mevkii, Akçakoca, Bolu, Tel. 374 611 4115, Fax 374 611 4115. Rooms: 12. Double: $7.*

Charming little campground/pension on terraces above a cliff, with a stairway leading down to the surf. The rooms are no-frills, but the staff is friendly and there is, lest we forget, a perfectly situated clifftop bar. On the western side of town.

**AK-BEY BALIK LOKANTASI**, *Atatürk Caddesi, Akçakoca, Tel. 374 611 3233. Moderate.*

There's little to distinguish one of the waterfront restaurants from the others, but this little spot is a good, reliable option. The fresh palamut is excellent in season; mezes are a little more than $1, and beer is $1.

In addition, Akçakoca has a collection of fine standard seafood restaurants. The Diapolis and Akçakoca Hotels have their own restaurants. Don't forget to try a handful of fresh hazelnuts in the late summer.

## SEEING THE SIGHTS

The fortress to the west of Akçakoca is badly ruined, hardly even yielding good photographs. Ruins enthusiasts will be likewise disappointed by the ruins of Prusias ad Herculeum at Ereğli, which were picked over for building material by Sultan Mehmet II's work crews while Rumeli Hisar was under construction. The area's finest ruins are at **Prusias ad Hypium** in Konuralp, 20 miles inland from Akçakoca. A small museum at the site has sarcophagi and other things of interest. Prusias ad Hypium was one of three cities founded by Prusias, the King of Bithnia. The other cities were Prusias ad Heculeum (now Ereğli) and Prusias ad Olympium (now Bursa).

Cave enthusiasts will be pleased with the meandering **Caverns at Fakıllı**, just 8 miles from Akçakoca (follow the signs from the bridge intersection on the east side of town near the Hotel Akçakoca. Continue following signs, finally taking a left at the Fakıllı mosque. Park in front of the Kayalar Aile Çay Bahçesi). Bring a light and some grubby clothes; the caves wind through some tight, muddy spots. Local boys will be happy to guide you – there's even a small underground lake if you descend far enough. This is, experts say, not the cave the ancients called The Cave of Hades, the route by which Hercules entered and escaped the underworld. That cave is in Ereğli, not far to the east.

The Fakıllı cave is, nonetheless, a remarkable spot, with a little of its own history. Turks are supposed to have holed up within the cave when the region was Greek-occupied after WW I. It is a one and one-half hour walk from the entrance of the cave to its (blocked) end, with many more hours required to explore its nooks and crannies. Electric lights are strung deep into the interior, but a flashlight is necessary insurance. If no one is around to show you, the electricity box is just inside the entrance.

The next stop on the Great Caves of the Western Black Sea excursion are the aforementioned **Caves of Hades** (Cehennum Mağarası), one half hour east by dolmuş or car. The caves are located in the northwest of Ereğli, about 400 feet inland of the Black Sea on the ancient river Acheron – the river of the dead. The river of the dead is more realistically suspect today, its waters carrying effluent from the industrial plants lining the river out to the sea. The ruins of **Herecleias ad Pontus** are scattered around the northeast section of Ereğli. The ancient town was at one time quite extensive, but in its current condition it doesn't merit a visit. Fatih Sultan Mehmet II, the conqueror of Constantinople, raided the site for material while building Rumeli Hisar on the Bosphorous. Ereğli is renowned for iron production, a smoke-spewing industrial town not well suited to most conceptions of a beach holiday. Iron lovers will want to stop by the Erdemir factory.

### Waterfall Hikes

Back in the Akçakoca area, consider a hike to one of the two waterfalls just inland, **Aktaş Selalesi** and **Sariyayla Selalesi**. If you lack your own transport, contact the Tourism Information office in the center of town. They arrange occasional tours, and the tourism information director is exceptionally helpful.

# AMASRA

**Amasra** is one of the highlights of the Black Sea. You arrive after winding through lush hills, finally descending to a long spit of land – really a tiny archipelago linked to the mainland by a narrow isthmus and a small bridge. Amasra's natural advantages have made it an important trading center for thousands of years, and although its primacy has been brought to an end by the more easily accessible ports at Zonguldak, Ereğli, and elsewhere, Amasra still supports a thriving fishery.

Amasra's industrial loss is the traveler's gain. Amasra today is an infrequently-visited combination of historic ruins, natural beauty, a sand beach, a small, interesting museum and vigorously healthy, friendly people. Even the bread is wonderful.

## History

The early history of the area is unknown, but the city was settled by Greek colonists, calling it Sesamos, which in time became Amastris and, eventually, Amasra. Homer refers to Sesamos, but the best thing he can think to say about it is that it is where "wild mules are engendered." The leader of the Paphlagonians is described as "the equal of Ares," but, three lines later, is stabbed through the chest and killed by Menelaus. Amastris supplanted Sesamos in the fourth century B.C. and soon fell under the sway of the Kingdom of Pontus, based in Amasya and Sinop. Amastris paid for its allegiance when the Roman General Lucullus, pursuing the routed Pontic King Mithradites VI, stopped here and sacked the town.

Amastris recovered, but its later history was undistinguished. The city was always a haven for ships and a commercial center, and the Romans held it in a little esteem. Rivals for the throne of the Byzantine Empire struggled over the town, but its strategic location atop an isthmus, with a secondary position higher up on Boztepe, made it difficult to take by force. Sultan Mehmet II had a remarkably indirect strategy. As a prelude to taking Amasra he secured the Bosphorous, the Dardanelles, besieged and took Constantinople, seized the towns near Amasra, and seized Trabzon. Only at this point, with a reported 50 healthy soldiers defending the city walls and a ragtag collection of pirates at sea, did the sultan sail and march his army to Amasra (1461). After a long bleak look at the alternatives, Amasra opened its gates without a fight.

# ARRIVALS & DEPARTURES

## By Bus

Most people come to Amasra via Bartin (dolmuş between Amasra and Bartin are half-hourly and hourly, 50¢). The roads are good and frequently traveled, with several bus companies serving Bartin from İstanbul, Ankara, and other major towns. The alternative route to Amasra is from the east, via the remote and dramatically undulating road from Cide. Getting to Cide is itself a chore, but from there dolmuş frequently come and go to Bartin via Amasra.

Özemniyet bus line serves Amasra direct from İstanbul, a six hour trip. İstanbul departures are at 9:00, 12:00, 15:00, 19:00, 21:00, and 23:30.

## ORIENTATION

Amasra is ideal for relaxed exploration. Even on August weekends the town is relatively uncrowded.

The **tourism information**, open long hours, is located near the end of the isthmus beneath Amasra's old walls. It's easy to find, but since road names aren't posted you'll have to ask: *"Turism danişma şube nerede?"* The tourims office in nearby Bartin can be reached at *Tel. 378 317 6116.*

## WHERE TO STAY

Amasra's hotel selection is cheap and generally uninspired. Space is sold by the bed, so if you'd like solitude make this clear *("Bir oda istiyorum.")* You'll pay for all of the beds in the room. Expect some bugs and squat toilets, and pick up a mosquito coil or device.

The helpful folks at the tourism information office *("Turism Danişma Şubesi")* are located near the end of the neck of the isthmus, just south of the mosque. The office is on the corner. They can direct you to these hotels and other family-run establishments.

**BÜLBÜL PANSIYON**, *Boztepe Mah., Uçpalamar Sk. No. 38, 74300 Amasra, Bartin. Tel. 378 315 1288. Rooms: 3. Double: $10.*

The Bülbül family lives at the end of Uçpalamar Sokak and runs the pension next door as an extension of their house. You're treated like an extension of their family. Charming and quiet, with views of the western bay, a kitchen, and the family's own boat. Follow Küçük Liman Caddesi through the isthmus around to the left, passing through a gate, cross the old stone bridge to Boztepe, enter another gate, and turn left on Uçpalamar Sokak.

**OTEL BELVÜ PALAS**, *Küçük Liman Cad. No. 20, Amasra, Bartin, Tel. 378 315 1237. Rooms: 11. Double: $12.*

Spacious budget accommodation for almost 30 years. Excellent terrace and balconies overlooking Amasra's western (quiet) bay.

**AMASRA OTELI**, *Büyük Liman ıskele Cad. No. 59, Amasra, Bartin, Tel. 378 315 1722, Fax 378 315 3025. Rooms: 8. Double: $14.*

One of the best in the area, convenient, clean and appealing views in two of the eight rooms. The rooftop bar next door troubles some, however. The hotel is located by the base of the walls at the eastern end of the isthmus.

**SÜR PANSIYON**, *Kale, Amasra, Bartin, Tel. 378 315 1251. Rooms: 4. Double: $12.*

Located atop the isthmus hill, overlooking the long pier. Pleasant garden and family atmosphere.

**OTEL TIMUR**, Kum Mahallesi, Gen. Mithat Ceylan Cad. No. 57, Amasra, Bartin, *Tel.* 378 315 2589, Fax 378 315 3290. Rooms: 18. Double: $16.

A decent standard hotel with phones and baths. Unremarkable views. Open year round.

**MUKADDER CEBECIOĞLU** (owner, not hotel name), *Tel.* 378 315 3244. Rooms: 7. Double: $12.

Small, spartan apartments overlooking the eastern beach, atop the walls of the citadel. A small stove and kitchen area, but otherwise no frills whatsoever. A great place to hole up for a while and sit out on the balcony. Bring mosquito coils. Open year round.

## WHERE TO EAT

Amasra has many good, small restaurants, and it is hard to find seafood cheaper in any town you'd enjoy being in. Don't miss the greasy, ketchupy fried mussel (**midye**) sandwiches sold out of carts in the summer.

**CANLİBALIK RESTAURANT**, *Kücük Liman Cad. No. 8, Amasra, Bartin, Tel. 378 315 2606. Moderate.*

An Amasra institution since 1945. One of the town's two status restaurants, but it still offers good, cheap food. Mezes are $1.30, fish range from $1 for barbuniye to $6 for istavrit. Beer is 70¢, rakı 80¢.

**LIMAN LOKANTASI**, *Büyük Liman Cad., Amasra, Bartin, Tel. 378 315 2148. Moderate-Expensive.*

The Liman may be a bit less charming than the Canlı Balık, but no one can argue with the freshness of its fish. The purse seiners pull up right in front of the restaurant and the Liman is among the first to see what they've brought back. The Liman is at the end of Büyük Liman Caddesi beneath the city walls. Prices are akin to CanlıBalık.

## SEEING THE SIGHTS

At the lower, southwestern end of the island (the left, as you look away from the mainland) an ancient road winds through several gates from the isthmus toward the island of Boztepe. As you look below you'll notice the peculiar Byzantine tower jutting into the sea. This tower, called **Direkli**, is thought to be an old watch tower or lighthouse. On the same spur of land is the foundation of a much older Hellenistic building, perhaps a temple to Poseidon, the sea god popular among the Amastrians.

The island attached to the northwestern shore of Kaleiçi is called **Boztepe**. It is reached via a small bridge. The small strait below the bridge was cleared in 1995, recreating the natural moat that existed in Hellenistic times. The double-gated archway is just about large enough to squeeze a car through, and the local residents do (as evidenced by the gouges scraped through the stone). Once through the gate, follow the small roads up the right side of the island, ascending sharply along the old walls until they terminate at the point of redundancy – the cliffs below served well enough.

From there, cut left and across the island, taking in ruined walls. Tucked away on the southern face of Boztepe, just above the present town, are large square cuts in the stone, rooms dating to at least Hellenistic times. Local boys will show you some graves and bones they shouldn't. The view from the top is predictably brilliant. At the far western point you can shinny down the long, flat sloping rock to the seaside like the local kids do, and trace the course of the fallen walls.

The main citadel is on the main hill at the end of the isthmus, now the center of Amasra town. The old Genoese-era walls and gates are still in place, and the gates remain in use. There is a Byzantine church within the compound, now unroofed and in ruins.

When you tire of the beaches and wandering the Amasra's winding streets, Amasra's **museum** is pleasantly small and concise ($1). There's nothing here worth traveling from Ottawa or Los Angeles for, but it's well worth a short walk down Amasra's cobbled lanes. The museum has a fine collection of Hellenistic and Roman statues and inscriptions gathered at Amasra, and the workmanship on the statuary is very good. Take a moment to look at the snake carved from a single block of stone, which you'll appreciate even if you don't appreciate snakes. There are also some Byzantine and Ottoman items here to round out the collection, and an interesting set of inscriptions in the garden surrounding the museum.

## TEA GARDENS & BACKGAMMON

*On your way back from Amasra's museum, stop in at one of Amasra's many relaxed, friendly beachfront **tea gardens** (çay bahçesi). You can retire in the trees for a cheap beer or a sandwich and a game of **tavak** (backgammon). This is an obsolete phenomenon in most parts of Turkey – real estate this outstanding is usually trampled with pricey waterfront disco spots. Enjoy it while you can.*

## SPORTS & RECREATION

### Beaches

Most people, reasonably, make a beeline for the long sand beach on the **eastern side** of the isthmus and stake out a space. It's busy on summer weekends, but nothing like the lines of roasting people in Marmaris or Kemer. The east side of the isthmus may be the conventional place to swim, but anywhere around the islands is good. On the western side of the isthmus, in the **Küçük Liman**, kids play like otters beneath the Direkli tower, for instance, and on the eastern side of Boztepe.

### Boating

Renting a boat is inexpensive and easy. A small fleet of rowboats ($1.50 per hour) and motorboats ($5 per hour) awaits on the north (fortress) side of the main beach. A guide will be happy to escort you around and deliver pleasant patter, but a better idea is to bring some food and paddle out around the sea wall – weather permitting – and back to the outer side of town, perhaps stopping off for a look at the monastery ruins on uninhabited **Tavşan Island**. A motorboat can get you to the beach at **Çakroz**, in the east, in 45 minutes.

### Caving

The **Gürcuoluk Mağarası**, near Çakroz town, is fairly deep and worth visiting. Check with the Tourism Information people about getting to and from this labyrinth.

## ALONG THE COAST FROM AMASRA TO SINOP

Most people opt to skip the coastal route between Amasra and Sinop, instead taking the relatively quick inland route to Sinop or Samsun via Kastamonu.

If you choose to hug the coast you'll be rewarded with fine views along a winding road that serves village after tiny village. Some of the towns have small hotels, some have little beaches. The next significant town is **Cide**, followed by **Inebolu**, but most people find even these provincial centers too, ah, provincial. The smaller towns, too, while pretty, are not necessarily places you will, or should, feel comfortable spending the day on the beach. Your best bets, if spartan accommodation and isolation from other travelers is what you want, include:

**Tekkeönü**: A ruined isthmus fortress is off to the west of Tekkeönü's town center.

**Gideros Koyu**: This pretty natural harbor 12 kilometers west of Cide offers some accommodation.

**Cide**: at the eastern end of a long stretch of sand and gravel beach. This, with Inebolu, is a transportation hub, more or less, and you can get minibuses several times daily to the east, west, and south (Kastamonu). The **Cafe Yalı Restaurant and Pansiyon**, east of the town dock and near the beach, is the destination of choice (or very little choice) for the occasional visitors.

**Denizkonak**: 27 kilometers east of Cide, has a camping site upstream of a pretty beach.

**Akbayir**: 42 kilometers east of Cide, has some small pensions and the standard access to a small cove.

**Inebolu**: There was once a great Hellenistic city on this site, but the city (probably the former Ionopolis) has only the barest trace of its antiquity. Mostly, the old fortifications have become retaining walls for a pretty assortment of Ottoman houses on the city's main hill. The houses have not been converted into pensions, the ruins are disappointing, and the waterfront is gravelly and, to the east, industrial. If you choose to stay, the bread is marvelous and there are some cheap pensions. The best in town is the **HOTEL DENIZ**, *Zafer Yolu Cad. No. 18, Inebolu, Tel. 366 811 3448, Fax 366 811 3449*, on the east side of town across the road from the sea. Across the street from the beach on the west side of town, the **SAHIL PENSION** is recommended over the generally poor hotels in town.

The favored dining spot is the obvious choice, the **CANLİBALIK LOKANTA** at the city center by the PTT. Prices are reasonable ($1 beer). For excellent, even cheaper food, try the Palmiye, just inland on Cumhuriet Caddesi. Many dolmuş and minibuses will drop you in Inebolu on the sea road at the center of town, but the genuine otogar is four blocks inland on the east bank of the Inebolu River. If you've made it all the way to Inebolu treat yourself to the local **köfte**, which some Turks consider the country's finest. The regional bread is also heavy and excellent. A road crawls steeply inland to Kastamonu from here.

# SINOP

The history of **Sinop** is longer and more glorious than any other city on the Black Sea, but has little left to show for its rich heritage. Today the town is a fairly busy port city located off the beaten track, but is less pretty than Amasra or Amasya. There are good beaches nearby, and some beautiful natural scenery.

### History

There have been settlements at Sinop since well before the Bronze Age (3,000 B.C.), but details are difficult to find. Visitors to this region were clearly impressed by the great natural harbor at Sinop. Like those who came after, the first settlers probably established themselves on the isthmus south of Sinop Burnu. Herodotus reports that the Cimmerians founded a city here in roughly 700 B.C., fleeing persecution by the Scythians along the northern Black Sea. The Cimmerians themselves were ferocious by the standard of Asia Minor and went on to sack and destroy towns thoughout the area.

At roughly the same time the Cimmerians arrived, perhaps slightly before, settlers from Miletus on the Aegean are also thought to have built a town here. Whether the settlements were simultaneous is not known, but the Milesian legacy was lasting, and this colony, in turn, established other towns to the east including Cerasus (Giresun) and Trapezus (Trabzon).

The name **Sinope** was an invention of these settlers. The name supposedly derives from Sinope, the beautiful Amazon daughter of a minor god. Sinope caught the eye of Zeus, who desperately sought to consummate his godly love with her. Sinope, with Amazon resoluteness, refused his advances, prompting Zeus to offer her any wish if she would change her mind. Sinope agreed, wishing that she be allowed eternal virginity. Zeus, outwitted, took this well and allowed Sinope to live out her life here.

The next great character in Sinop's history was its wry son, the philosopher **Diogenes**. Diogenes (the Cynic) was well known for his disdain for common beliefs; he lived outside in a tub and exercised his bodily functions in full view, obeying his own appetites for sleep, food, and sunlight in the way he chose. No wonder he was sent packing by the people of Sinop, but while in Corinth he was well enough respected that Alexander sought him out. Finding the old philosopher sunning himself, Alexander asked if there was anything he could do for him. Diogenes replied that, yes, there was: Alexander should stand back out of his light. This startled Alexander and delighted his friends. Later, while his entourage was joyously recalling the story, Alexander said *"Nevertheless, if I were not Alexander I would be Diogenes."* On another occasion, when someone was comparing Diogenes' life unfavorably with that of Aristotle, Alexander's tutor in the court of Philip, Diogenes said simply *"Aristotle dines when Philip chooses, Diogenes when Diogenes chooses."*

Sinop was conquered by Pharnaces I (185-169 B.C.), King of Pontus. His successor Mithradites III consolidated the young kingdom and shifted the capital here from Amasya. Sinop remained the capital of Pontus for a full century, and was decorated as befitted one of the most powerful cities in the world at the time. The Pontic kings were careful to stay on good terms with the Roman Empire, which was emerging on the Mediterranean, and Pontus contributed to the force that subdued Rome's hated enemy, Carthage.

With Carthage out of the way, however, Rome became increasingly belligerent. Pontic resentment came to a head under Mithradites VI Eupator (the Great), who lived from 120-63 B.C. A series of Mithraditic Wars ensued, in which the Romans were forced to directly intervene against the Pontic King, who styled himself as a liberator of the heavily taxed Roman subjects in Asia Minor.

Mithradites' kingdom proved no match for the Roman Empire, however, and his armies no match for the Romans, either. Between 90 and 69 B.C. some of Rome's finest generals first stalemated and finally defeated the Pontic armies, seizing Mithradites' homeland and driving the King across Anatolia into Armenia. General Pompey's pursuit continued even there, and with the Roman victory over Armenia at Tigranocerta Mithradites ended his own life.

---

### MITHRADITES, HE DIED OLD

*Mithradites' name lives on. The long lived scholar-king is reported to have mastered 22 languages, and secured his long reign by building up his immunity to various poisons by sampling them little bits at a time. Prisoners and criminals paid dearly for Mithradites' curiosity, and were often forced to test his various antidotes and exotic concoctions. The King's methods certainly saved him from various intrigues, but in the end he was ironically stymied in an attempt to end his own life with poison after the Romans had pursued him to his last refuge in Armenia. In desperation to avoid falling into Roman hands, Mithradites had one of his servants run him through with a sword.*

---

Sinop was destroyed following an earlier defeat by Lucullus, and slowly built its way back up. Both the Romans and the Byzantines made great use of this port city, far and away the best natural harbor on the southern Black Sea coast.

Russian ships shelled Sinop in 1853, an attack that decimated the Turkish fleet and killed more than 2,000 Turks. The "Massacre of Sinop" stirred up anti-Russian sentiment in both France and England and helped precipitate the Crimean War. The most recent footnote is the relatively recent passing of a U.S. Air Force facility atop the Sinop peninsula. With the end of the Cold War this facility was closed; many residents of Sinop worked there and seem to have fond memories of the facility. English is predictably common.

## ARRIVALS & DEPARTURES

### By Bus

Sinop is not directly on the main bus route, which emerges from the interior at Samsun and heads east, but there are hourly buses from Samsun. Dolmuş serve Sinop from both Boyabat and Cide in the west. The otogar is located alongside the outer city walls. Dolmuş serve the center of town, continuing on to isolated Karakum beach. They also head in the other direction, toward Kumsal beach.

### By Car

From the west, either follow the coast road from Cide – slow going – or do what most people do and cut north just before Boyabat. The road descends through the misty, green highlands and emerges on the coast road just east of Sinop.

### By Ferry

The Black Sea ferry arrives from İstanbul on Tuesdays at 10 a.m., departing for points east at 2:30 p.m. The ferry returns on Thursdays, departing at 5 p.m.

## GETTING AROUND THE AREA

### By Tour

For tours around the area, the best choice is **Sinop Tours**, *Kıbrıs Caddesi No. 7, Sinop, Tel. 368 261 7900, Fax 368 261 0810*, run by the Mephistophelian Adem Tahtacı. Sinop Tours does an excellent job organizing boat tours, cruises, cave trips, and guided day trips that take in the area's natural beauty – an American working in the area described the tip of Ince Burnu northwest of Sinop as looking like Tierra del Fuego. Most tours cost between $15 and $20.

## WHERE TO STAY

Sinop's accommodations are scattered along the east side of the isthmus, with the concentration of cheaper spots just below the main city walls, another half kilometer into town from the outer walls by the otogar.

**OTEL MELIA KASIM,** *Gazi Caddesi No. 49, Sinop, Tel. 368 261 4210, Fax Tel. 368 261 1625. Rooms: 57. Double: $32.*

Not necessarily attractive to look at, but Sinop's status address. Central location and made of brick, like the smart pig's house. The hotel is located on the eastern bay, just beyond the old city walls, and has a good restaurant and helpful service. The hotel boasts in-room television, complete with the movie channel Cine5, full baths and other amenities. A solid, serviceable choice.

**OTEL 57**, *M. Kapı Mah., Kurtuluş Cad. No. 29, Sinop, Tel. 368 261 5462. Rooms: 20. Double: $24.*

Probably the nicest spot in town. An odd location on the top of the isthmus, but that just means you're a four minute walk from the waterfront. Clean and interesting, with a pleasant second floor lobby and, of course, breakfast.

**BELEDIYE YUVAM TESISLERI**, *Kumsal, Sinop, Tel. 368 261 2532. Rooms: 24. Double: $32.*

A basic municipal hotel on a good stretch of beach.

Other options include the **KARAKUM TATIL KÖYÜ**, *Tel. 368 261 2694.* For pensions, try the **KARAKUM PANSIYON**, in a quiet location beyond town on the peninsula, or the **IKIZLER PANSIYON** overlooking the harbor.

## WHERE TO EAT

Diyojen and Melia Kasım hotels have decent restaurants. Other options include:

**SAHIL RESTAURANT**, *Iskele Caddesi, Tel. 368 261 1729.*

The best of the many small restaurants on the eastern waterfront in the center of town.

**EVIM CAFE & BAR**, *Kıbrıs Caddesi, Sinop, Tel. 368 261 7900.*

A pleasant, exactingly built spot just up the hill from the waterfront. Good bar food, $1 beer, and a comfortable feel.

## SEEING THE SIGHTS

The **fortress** that straddles the isthmus was the last in a long line of fortifications on the site, the handiwork of the Selçuks. Today the outer walls bisect the isthmus at the otogar, to your left on entering town. Just inside the outer fortifications on the southern (right) side is a large keep, a 19th century addition to the fortifications. You'll notice it appears to be in good condition; it should be, as it is the regional prison. The main road follows the crest of the isthmus. The inner walls of the town, farthest from the mainland, divide the city. Two large gates are still in use, and atop the walls is the **Burç Çay Bahçesi**, with cheap tea and excellent views.

The beaches on the southern side of the isthmus are the most immediately tempting, and that's good. The undercurrent on the north side – and out along the northern side of the Ince Burnu peninsula – are notorious, and should be avoided unless you spot bright, reliable people (read: not teenage boys) swimming there. The beaches along the developed southern and western shore have safe swimming, such as **Kumsal** and **Karakum**. **Sarıkum** (Yellow sand) beach 20 kilometers west is also supposed to be safe.

The **Sinop Museum** in the center of town has an average collection, unless you are a particular fan of Byzantine art. There are several Byzantine paintings recovered from a Byzantine palace at the site, as well as an assortment of ornaments, vases, and a few gruesome weapons. The Sinop area is of keen interest to anthropologists and archaeologists. An interdisciplinary team that includes students at the University of Chicago has been pursuing research in the area, interested in the tiny settlements that sprang up in many of the small, isolated coves around the region. The museum is set on a plot of land that has the foundations of the former Temple of Serapis, an Egyptian god you might not expect to find way up here; according to Tacitus, Hellenistic worship of Serapis may have even begun here.

For an out of the way jaunt, try a drive around the **Erfelek** area, just south of the inland westbound road. The area offers atmospheric old houses in the heavily wooded mountains. If it's a Friday, you're in particular luck; it's slaughtering day, and the kebaps here are reputed to be the best in Turkey.

While wandering around Sinop, keep your eye peeled for Tarzan Kemal, a 50 or so year old guy who walks around town in a loin cloth. You'll know him if you see him.

## AMASYA

The eastern end of the Black Sea is covered in forests and topped with alpine meadows. The Ankara-Trabzon route passes near Amasya en route to Georgia and the former Soviet Republics. You want to make Amasya your first stop, and perhaps your last as well.

**Amasya** is a small, fascinating town on the road from Ankara to the Black Sea. Amasya is near the route most people take to the Black Sea, and a far more interesting destination than Samsun on the seaside. The town sits in a narrow river valley, its old houses hanging over the edge of the usually placid Yeşilirmak River. A great fortress looms directly above town, originally of Pontic design and later restored and improved by the Byzantines and Ottomans. This city, once the capital of the Kingdom of Pontus, is further decorated with the tombs of its former kings and an interesting collection of Ottoman buildings. The days of glory seem to be in the past now, but Amasya maintains a tidy, bustling spirit and makes an interesting diversion for one or two nights.

### History

As is the case in so many places where nature offered an ideal site for fortification, Amasya's citadel area was probably settled quite early, but no traces have been discovered under the fortifications built and rebuilt in the thousands of years since. Amasya began to emerge from obscurity at the time of Alexander's campaign. Alexander's conquests only grazed this area, but the turmoil of the young king's victories and the chaos that followed allowed a dynasty started in 337 B.C. to grow near the shores of the Black Sea. The borders of the Pontus were initially modest, well within the area delineated by the modern cities of Sinop, Samsun, and Amasya.

The Pontic kings took advantage of the 301 B.C. defeat and death of one of the most initially successul Diadochi, Antigonus the One Eyed, and established Amasya as their capital in 300 B.C. under **Mithradites I**. The Pontic kings clung to the Persian system of rule while the Persian Empire itself was crushed under Alexander's heel. The budding kingdom played a cautious diplomatic game with the rivals for Alexander's empire, alternately forging alliances and fighting against the Seleucids, and went on to foster a similar relationship with the Romans. Mithradites V went so far as to contribute men and arms to the final Roman campaign against Carthage (147-146 B.C.), at the same time pushing the borders of his own kingdom south into Cappadoccia and the heart of Anatolia and west until it came into conflict with the Kingdom of Bithnia based at Nicaea, modern Iznik.

Amasya lost some of its importance after Pharnaces I established a new Pontic capital at Sinop. The Roman General Pompey underscored Amasya's continued importance, however, by razing it to the ground during the final stages of Mithradites VI's (120-63) failed anti-Roman wars. Near the end of Mithradites' reign, the writer **Strabo** was born in Amasya. Strabo would later travel much of the world and amass more than 17 volumes of historical and geographical facts, only a few of which survive today.

Amasya was chosen as a Roman provincial capital, then faded into obscurity during the Byzantine years. The area was overrun by Arabs, retaken by the Byzantines, and passed back and forth between various local lords before falling to the Ottoman Sultan Beyazid I in 1392. According to one account, Amasya's citadel was one of the few places in Asia Minor to remain in Ottoman hands during Tamurlane's rampage of 1402-1403, and it was from here that Beyazid I's son Mehmet I embarked on the campaign that won for him his father's empire.

Amasya maintained an important role under the Ottomans thereafter as a frequent staging area for campaigns into the east and as a proving ground for Ottoman princes. The most momentous events in Amasya's later Ottoman history were the earthquakes that often rocked the city, including three times in the past three centuries. Finally, Atatürk came here via Samsun in 1919, ostensibly as a British agent seeking to pacify the Turks. His intention was far from what the British thought, however;

Atatürk's first order of business was to meet with several Turkish separatist leaders and begin organizing the nationalist movement that, four years later, ended with the restoration of Turkey.

Atatürk's arrival at Amasya is commemorated on its anniversary, 12 June, with a week long festival.

## ARRIVALS & DEPARTURES

**By Bus**

Amasya is not directly on the highway between Samsun and Ankara, but many buses swing through town anyway. The otogar is about two kilometers northwest of town, and it is frequently served by dolmuş as well as taxis. A rail line passes through Amasya en route to Samsun from Sivas, but buses are preferable.

Buses serve many cities on the Marmaris and Aegean directly; some nearby destinations and distances to note: Ankara (Sungurlu/Hattuşas) buses depart several times an hour, five hour trip, $12 ($6); Samsun buses depart once an hour, two hour trip, $7; Kayseri buses depart in the morning and evening, eight hour trip, $13.

**By Car**

Amasya is 130 kilometers south of Samsun on the Black Sea, 261 kilometers north of Nevşehir, and 528 kilometers northeast of Ankara. The distance from Hattuşas is 157 kilometers. Roads to the north, west, and east are in good shape.

## ORIENTATION

Apart from the train and bus stations, Amasya is fairly compact and easy to see on foot. The citadel is the most daunting walk, a half hour hike up a steep incline, but is well worth the effort.

The **Tourism Information** office is at *Mehmet Paşa Mah., Mustafa Kemal Paşa Cad. No. 27, Tel. 358 218 5002, Fax 358 218 3385.*

## WHERE TO STAY

**ILK HOUSE**, *Gümüşlü Mah., Hittit Sok. No. 1, Amasya, Tel. 358 218 1689, Fax Tel. 358 218 6277. Rooms: 6. Double: $32.*

Guests roundly enjoy both the architecture of the Ilk House and the architect responsible for it, Kamil Yalçin. Yalçin has been working incessantly around Amasya since renting and restoring the Ilk Pansiyon in the late 1980s, and among his current projects are a boardwalk on the river and restoration of some riverfront houses. These good intentions, combined with painstaking detail and tempting prices have made the Ilk

Pansiyon a standard first stop on the Black Sea circuit. Breakfast is $3, dinner is $8. Open year round.

**YUVAM PANSIYON,** *Atatürk Cad. 24, Amasya, Tel. 358 218 1342, Fax Tel. 358 218 3409. Rooms: 20. Double: $20.*

Another of the restored Ottoman mansions that has been converted into a hotel. The decor is rural Ottoman, with appealing wooden furniture and kilims. The courtyard serves as a dining area in the summer, and a wooden house in the garden is used for additional accommodation in the summer. Another of the Amasya's genuinely friendly places to spend the night. Open year round.

**MELIŞ PANSIYON,** *Yeniyol Cad. Torumtay Sok. No. 135, Amasya, Tel. 358 212 3650, Fax Tel. 358 218 2082. Rooms: 12. Double: $37.*

One of Turkey's "special class" hotels, with television and lots of pleasant features, including television. Decor is busy Ottoman. Open year round.

## WHERE TO EAT

Hotels have their own restaurants with good set price meals, but if you want to venture out for dinner try the **SEHIR KULUBU,** *Tel. 358 218 1016,* on the north shore of the river beneath the fortress. This club opens its doors to visiting foreigners.

Among the cheap, filling restaurants, **ELMAS KEBAP SALONU,** *Tel. 358 218 1606,* is highly esteemed among kebapçis in the area; it's a good, cheap place to grab a bite.

## SEEING THE SIGHTS

Amasya's **fortress** dominates the heights above a bend in the Yeşilirmak River, as it has for at least 2,200 years. The summit of the hill was once crowned with the Pontic acropolis, which had a temple to the Persian god Ahura, akin to Zeus. Today the fortress is a shell, but the views are tremendous and there are stone cut chambers and even long, descending tunnels on the grounds.

These tunnels, occasionally found on hilltop fortresses in the Black Sea region, were probably used to guarantee the citadel's water supply, but may have had a religious role, probably associated with Mithra or Ahura. The towers date from the Pontic Kingdom but the walls have been extended over time by various rulers; note their former course down to the river, where they encircled the northern town.

The **rock tombs** lining the cliff below the citadel are also interesting. This somewhat perilous collection of tombs was for the burial of royalty, but there is little evidence for which tomb belonged to which king. Mithradites is always a good bet, since, over the course of 260 years, there were six kings named Mithradites plus an earlier Mithradites who was an ancestor to them all. Still, the one identified tomb is that of Pharnaces I, (185-169 B.C.), and it appears unfinished. Pharnaces helped expand Pontic control over the Black Sea, paving the way for the capital to shift under his successor, Mithradites IV (169-150 B.C.).

One of the nearby tomb entrances connects to a tunnel leading down from the acropolis, but, deeper down, the tunnels are choked with the debris of several thousand years. A group spearheaded by the local governor and assisted by Kamil Yalçin of the Ilk Pansiyon has discussed an effort to clear the tunnels. The **Pontic Royal Palace** (called Kızlar Saray, or Maiden's Palace) was located on the terrace just below the tombs.

Most of the sights within town are from the last 800 years. Particularly interesting is the **Bimarhane Medresse**, an insane asylum completed in 1308 under the Mongols, who occupied the area until the arrival of the Ottomans. This interesting old building, long since roofless, has an ornate facade, and is not far inland from the tourism information office. The insane asylum was, some might say appropriately, dedicated by a Mongol lord to his wife. The museum, located in an old house, has both archaeological and ethnographic areas, the former with a mishmash of items found in the region, some pieces dating back to Hittite times.

# ÜNYE

Ünye rarely makes it onto itineraries for the simple reason that no one knows about it. The city is itself boilerplate, offering the barest glimpse of its former Hellenistic glory. Ünye, however, is located just to the east of long stretch of sand beaches that are well-served by pensions and hotels. Inland, the lush green interior hides some truly fascinating sites, sites that, at the least, you'll want to stop by on your way through the area.

### History

Precious little is known about Ünye's history, but it seems clear that if there is any truth to the stories of **Amazons**, they once lived in this area. The legendary range of the Amazons is bounded by Thermodon (modern Terme) on the west and Giresun on the east. No hard evidence of their existence has ever been discovered, but even the most ancient writers, skeptical of many things, had no doubts that Amazons existed.

**Ünye Kalesi** was pre-Byzantine, and probably pre-Roman. Tunnels at the site like those at Amasya, together with a rock tomb at the entrance, suggest that the fortress was erected by the Kingdom of Pontus, but even this might have been built on an earlier foundation. The settlement on the coast was known as Oiniaon in ancient times, eventually yielding the modern name, Ünye. Pompey either sacked or accepted the surrender of the fortress from Pontus during his campaign, and the city was subject to Roman control after 63 B.C. Ünye's fortress maintained a garrison, but it largely faded from view for several centuries. There are mentions of the popularity of Ünye wine, although wine is no longer made in the area.

Several Turkic tribes seized and held the city after the Empire of Trabzon began deteriorating. The Ottomans took the town as a prelude to the capture of Trabzon in 1459.

## ARRIVALS & DEPARTURES

### By Bus

If you are arriving from the west, keep your eyes peeled several miles before Ünye, where the beach and hotels are located. The main otogar is located three blocks inland of the PTT; this is where dolmuş depart for Ünye Kalesi. Another bus and dolmuş station is located just to the northwest of this intersection on the sea road; dolmuş headed west and east are green and white, while those heading inland are red and white. Dolmuş serve Kumsal beach (the good hotel strip) half-hourly.

Ulusoy is the best bus company running the Ankara-Trabzon route, with Metro another good option.

### By Car

The main coast highway passes right through Ünye. The strip of good hotels is to the west of town on the main highway.

## ORIENTATION

Ünye has beaches to all sides, including Çamlık, Gölevi, and Uzunkum, although you're likely to be satisfied with the beach directly below wherever you're staying. Ünye retains fragments of its old walls, but the compelling things are outside of town. Check in at the tourism information office for more nearby sights, including the tombs at Delikkaya and other fortresses.

Ünye's **tourism information** office, *Tel. 452 323 4952, Fax 452 323 4952*, is usually staffed by some very helpful and English-savvy people.

## WHERE TO STAY

In Ünye proper there are a few desultory options, but there are several nice pensions, hotels, and campgrounds at Kumsal Beach to the west of town.

**PINAR PANSIYON**, *Gölevi Devrent Mevkii, Ünye, Tel. 452 323 3496. Rooms: 7. Double: $17.*

The Pınar is simply one of the nicest pensions in Turkey. It comes as a surprise here along the Black Sea coast, a carefully maintained large house with old wardrobes and other nice furniture in spacious, tidy rooms. Guests have access to the kitchen, as well as the patio outside amid the lush, colorful garden. Ünye beach is just across the road. The owner, Münir Altınay, is a kind, helpful man who built the house and maintains it as a hobby. The hotel is on the inland side of the highway.

**OTEL KUMSAL**, *Ataturk Mah., PK 9 Kumsal, Ünye, Tel. 452 323 4490, Fax 452 323 4490. Rooms: 32. Double: $45.*

A longtime favorite in the area. The Kumsal (just across the road and west from the Pınar Pansiyon) has the relaxed, lazy atmosphere you'd hope to find, with a sauna and television in the room (and VCRs and videotapes floating around). The in-house restaurant serves good Turkish food.

**OTEL TALIP**, *Atatürk Mah., Devlet Sahil Yolu, Ünye, Tel. 452 323 2738, Fax 452 323 7032. Rooms: 15. Double: $45.*

An attractive hotel that opened in 1996. The Talip is directly on the seaside, with plain, serviceable rooms. The owner, however, has moments of imperiousness that can make guests a bit uncomfortable.

**IPEK YOLU PANSIYON**, *Atatürk Mah., Ünye, Tel. 452 323 2643. Rooms: 12. Double: $11.*

A clean, friendly spot also to the west of Ünye, but closer to town. Cheap and simple lodging.

## WHERE TO EAT

Most hotels have their own restaurants, and pensions let you cook for yourself. Dining in Ünye is a matter of selecting good, hearty fare that any one of a number of restaurants can offer.

**KÜÇÜK EV**, *Atatürk Mah., Ünye, Tel. 452 323 4447.*

A small hotel and campground near the recommended hotels with, Ünye's locals say, the best köfte in town.

**KALEDIBI LOKANTA**, *Ünye Kalesi Altı, Ünye, Tel. 452 323 4978.*

A small, excellent trout restaurant just a short distance below the path to Ünye Kalesi. Two trout, bread and a salad cost about $4.

## SEEING THE SIGHTS

### Ünye Kalesi

**Ünye Kalesi** is located just five kilometers inland of the main highway just off of the Akkuş road. Check with the Tourism Information office for an area map if you're heading up on your own.. The fortress appears ahead and left as you ascend into the valley on Akkuş road, and you take the road that dips to the left as you approach, which then ascends to the trailhead about 700 feet past Kaledibi Lokanta (it is a leisurely 25 minute walk to the top).

The fortress is very much in the tradition of Black Sea citadels; it crowns a sheer crag, offers several defensive rings, has steps and buildings carved in the living stone, and is, today, overgrown and open free to the public. Upon arrival, you enter between two great pylons just below an old rock cut tomb. One of the pylons is fixed to the crag at the left, the second stands free on the right. These walls are probably Hellenistic, thus Pontic. The most adventurous, and those with no concern for tearing holes in their clothes, can take the difficult, steeper path to the left and scramble along old staircases, through thick bushes, and past old walls to the lower cave. Otherwise, wind around to the right and approach the cave from below. The lower tunnel is an impressive piece of work, 15 feet wide and eight feet high, a perfectly arched and sealed staircase descending at a ridiculous 35 degree angle – an impossible descent now that the stairs have worn and weathered. The peculiarity of this tunnel is leavened by its abrupt end less than 50 yards deep, the result of either collapse or intentional filling.

On the same terrace, before ascending, you can examine some old walls and cuttings in the stone, as well as an overgrown upper gate. Be careful of uncovered cisterns. The ascent to the next level squeezes between two great stones, emerging in a flat, open area looking out in the direction of the sea. On the northern rim, facing the sea, is a broken sarcophagus. Stairs have been carved into the final great stone outcrop at the center, but before ascending the solid – if rickety looking – wooden ladder, round the corner to the left.

Here you find the entrance to the upper tunnel. Like the lower tunnel, it is cut steeply and neatly into the stone, descending rapidly in the direction of the sea, five kilometers away. Unlike the lower tunnel, this tunnel has no apparent end. Toss a smooth stone or marble into the tunnel and listen. And listen. This is an eerie place, and rumors swirl in town; some say it is an old well, others an ancient shrine, others an escape tunnel. Tearing yourself away from here, ascend the ladder to the acropolis, where more steps and foundations are carved in stone, and from where you have an excellent view in all directions.

## Toskoparan Cave

Perhaps the most truly weird site in Turkey is four kilometers to the east of Ünye. **Toskoparan Mağarası**, or the Toskoparan cave, is less than two kilometers off the main coast road. To get there, stay to the left at the first main intersection by the cement plant and look for the battered sign on the right. Follow the path just to the right of the landowners' stairs through a thick hazelnut grove. As you ascend you'll see the rock cut tomb carved into the surface. The tomb is not unusual, and reports of art in the interior are greatly exaggerated. The tomb is only vaguely interesting if you've been through the Lycian coast or Cappadoccia, where they'd carve something like this before breakfast.

Returning to the path, continue following the trail around the stone buttress. Arriving at the uphill face, look carefully at the regular courses of one and one-half foot wide layers of stone, and the seams in the rock, and the sealant that is corroding in those seams. Toskoparan Mağarası, on close examination, appears at least partly manmade, like a low, squat pyramid. A winding path leads to the top of the hill, which offers traces of old cut stone. Continuing around the buttress you arrive at a great trench along the face of the rock; when we visited in 1996 a work crew was digging out this trench under the watchful eye of some armed soldiers.

During the 1922 exchange of populations, we were told, a Greek took with him a map indicating that five meters directly beneath a sign carved into the stone there were gates to this hollow formation, and a treasure of gold. Having bought rights to the map, a small team of investors secured digging rights from the Turkish authorities and spent four days digging for treasure at the proper spot. Our initial impression of strangeness was vouchsafed by the diggers; this was once a site of worship, may well be hollow, and some speculation about its origin involves, yes, space aliens. No treasure was recovered, but the trench remains and curiosity mounts.

## Ancient Home of the Amazons?

Farther afield is a battered, ancient fortress commanding the heights above Terme, ancient Thermodon, the former home of the Amazons. **Karpu Kale** requires a substantial drive out of the way, and is only accessible by car. Turn inland of the main coast highway at Terme, 26 kilometers west of Ünye. From here to **Salıpazar** is 20 kilometers – there are some signs, but ask for the correct road to Salıpazar (*"Salıpazar'a gitiyorum. Salıpazar nere'de?"*). The turn-off is just before Salıpazar. If you miss it, from Salıpazar follow signs toward Yenidoğan, and once out of Salıpazar keep your eye peeled for battered signs. While on the mountain road, stay to the left at each turn (most of which are signed), continuing for 10.5 kilometers from the town center. The roads in the mountains above are rough and winding, but in pretty good condition.

Upon emerging in full view of the mountaintop fortress, pull up by the Suluca Koyu sign and hike 25 minutes from there. The upper sections, within the old mountaintop compound, are steep and usually wet – be extremely careful. Some may want to content themselves with the lower sections. The site has not been adequately explored, and most of what is believed is speculation. This was clearly an ancient site, perhaps

Paphlagonian, or, based on sheer speculation, Amazonian. The hilltop is crowned with a ring of walls, where walls are necessary, and at the summit are cisterns and stone-cut rooms, long since collapsed. The view down over the Thermodon valley is glorious.

## GIRESUN

Like Terme, **Giresun** has a direct tie to tales of the Amazons. The small island just offshore of Giresun to the east, now known as **Giresun Adası**, was probably the one mentioned in the tale of Jason and the Argonauts. The city has only a few things to see, and unless you want to spend time nosing around the island of the Amazons, you'll probably want to use it as a break on the way to Trabzon or, nearer, Tirebolu.

### History

Giresun may have been an Amazon stronghold, as evidenced by their association with little Giresun Adası just offshore. The island was thought to have been an **Amazon shrine**, but by the year 400 B.C. there was no trace of the fierce women warriors. At that time Xenophon's 10,000 stopped here on their long march home, finding a normal Greek settlement, one of the colonies of Sinop.

Their stay was uneventful, although they were much intrigued by the native Mossynoici people they found just to the west. *"When they were in a crowd they acted as men act would act when in private, and when they were by themselves, they used to behave as they might do if they were in company; they used to talk to themselves, and laugh to themselves, and stop and dance wherever they happened to be,"* reported Xenophon. Most startling were the wealthy boys fed on boiled chestnuts until *"they were practically as broad as they were tall,"* and decorated head to toe in flower tattoos.

Pharnaces I, King of Pontus, seized the city in the second century B.C., after which it was known as Pharnacos until the Romans destroyed the kingdom. Giresun was one of the many Pontic strongholds quashed by the Roman General Lucullus, who not only sacked the city but, adding insult to injury, took its cherries. Cherries grew naturally in this area, and Lucullus, fond of the fruit, shipped some seeds home to Rome where they became justly popular. Lucullus is sometimes credited with changing the name of the city from Pharnacus to Cerasus, Latin for cherry, but he was only restoring the city's former name.

The Kingdom of Pontus, however, was not dead yet. Pharnaces II (63-47 B.C.) used Giresun as a base to begin cautiously restoring the broken kingdom after the death of his father, Mithradites VI, the Great. Pharnaces II worked doggedly at rebuilding key fortresses and piecing together an army, and was rewarded by a victory over Rome that opened the way to Cappadoccia and Bithnia. From the ruin of his father's last days, Pharnaces seemed on the verge of restoring the Kingdom of Pontus, when he ran headlong into Julius Caesar at the battle of Zela in central Anatolia. In just four hours, Caesar routed Pharnaces' army and destroyed Pontus forever, and it was in recalling this brilliant, rapid battle he said laconically, *"Veni, Vidi, Vici."*

Giresun's fortress was restored and used into Byzantine times, then taken over by the Trapezuntine Empire in its desperate rearguard action against the Ottomans. The Ottomans took the city in 1461. Giresun marked the eastern border of Turkey in the post-WW I partition.

---

### THE AMAZONS

*According to the legends, the ancient land of the Amazons was bound by Themistikos (near Terme) on the west and an island – probably Giresun Adası – on the east. Themistikos was the capital city. The Amazons allowed no man to live among them, and to sustain the tribe they mated anonymously with men of the inland tribes in the middle of the night. Boy children they returned to the inland tribes, girls they kept and raised as Amazons. One custom was to sear the right chest to stop the right breast from growing and interfering with spear casting. Their only known shrine, on their Black Sea island, was devoted to a war god.*

*When Homer chronicled the Iliad in the eighth century B.C., there were no Amazons left. He refers to them as Bronze Age contemporaries of Troy in the centuries before the Trojan War. If this is the case they were contemporaries, too, of the Hittites, perhaps bounded by the Kaşka on the east and the Trojans far to the west.*

*The problem is that evidence is all apocryphal – Hercules fighting for the girdle of the Amazon queen, King Priam of Troy and Theseus battling invasions of the women warriors, Bellerophon sent against them on an impossible mission. The stories are legion, but the hard evidence is slim. Some have suggested that Amazons were simply matriarchal tribes living along the Black Sea before the arrival of the Greeks, but most of us can't help believing that there is an element of truth to the tales. As Arrian, Alexander's biographer, wrote in the second century A.D., "I cannot bring myself to believe that this race of women, whose praises have been sung so often by the most reputable writers, never existed at all."*

---

## ARRIVALS & DEPARTURES
### By Bus

Giresun has constant bus service to both the east and west, with Ulusoy and Metro bus companies offering the best service.

**By Ferry**
Westbound ferries arrive at 1 a.m. Thursday, eastbound ferries at 5 a.m. Wednesday.

## WHERE TO STAY & EAT

The eastern Black Sea coast is notorious for its "Natashas," prostitutes who often hail from the former Soviet Union. Many cheaper hotels cater to the trade, and often it is obvious. Occasionally it's not. A good idea is to stick to hotels with the word "Aile" (family) in them. Strongly consider staying on Girsesun Island if at all possible, or in Tirebolu further east.

**GIRESUN ADASI**, *Giresun Island, Tel. 454 216 4707. Camping.*

If you have a tent along, the best place to stay, bar none, is the former temple island of the Amazons. The caretaker is resupplied with necessities every three days, but you'll want your own stove and food along. There is no charge, great swimming, and perfect little campsites. This is the best kept secret on the Black Sea coast. See the site description below for information on getting to the island.

**KIT-TUR OTEL**, *Arifbey Cad. No. 2, Giresun, Tel. 454 212 0245, Fax 454 212 3034. Rooms: 50. Double: $55.*

Giresun's status address, with a nice lobby and helpful staff, but the rooms are disappointing at the price.

**BULUT OTEL**, *Fatih Cad. No. 10, Giresun, Tel. 454 216 4115. Rooms: 14. Double: $10.*

A budget option in a town filled with Natasha hotels and their expensive alternatives. Located away from most of the other budget hotels, west and behind the tourism information office on the far side of the park.

**DENIZ LOKANTA**, *Alparslan Cad., Giresun, Tel. 454 216 1158. Moderate-Expensive.*

The "sea restaurant," has, predictably, an excellent selection of fish. Somewhat expensive by the local standard, a full meal will cost about $11.

**KERASUS RETAURANT**, *Ayvasıl Cad., Giresun, Tel. 454 314 4236. Moderate.*

Traditional Turkish fare.

### In Tirebolu

**EREN PANSIYON BOARDING HOUSE**, *Plaj Mevkii, Tirebolu, Tel. 454 411 4600. Rooms: 12. Double: $12.*

Giresun's budget hotels are generally sleazy and urban, while the Eren Pansiyon, one half hour east, is starkly clean and comfortable, and across the highway from a perfect sand beach. Each floor has its own kitchen and the town's nicest restaurant is a stone's throw away. Tirebolu boasts an old Ottoman castle and dolmuş depart Giresun hourly.

**TRIPOLIS PLAJ-RESTAURANT**, *Plaj Mevkii, Tirebolu, Tel. 454 411 4339. Moderate.*

Tucked away between a stand of trees and a hill at the base of Tirebolu town, this is the obvious (and right) choice if you're staying at the Eren Pansiyon.

## SEEING THE SIGHTS

Giresun has two interesting places to visit. The first is the citadel looming above the city. On your way uphill toward the hilltop fortress, take a moment to appreciate the valor of a distinguished Ottoman soldier. While storming the fortifications, one of Sultan Mehmet II's lieutenant's had his head lopped off by one of the Trapezuntine defenders; no matter, Seyit Vakkas fought on valiantly, leading the attackers up the hill. His comrades, much impressed, erected a türbe that still stands next to the road up to the fortress.

Even with your head still on, it is a steep walk up to the **citadel**, which now encloses a city park and fills with children and picnickers on weekends. The walls make a long circuit, and the entrance is at the site of the original main gate. The walls and buildings within are badly damaged, and the addition of layers of soft earth have made the layout of the old structure difficult to understand. Even so, the large compound with its commanding view is compelling. What remains of the walls is mostly Selçuk and Trapezuntine, but the raw steps and footings carved in the rocks at the summit date back to an earlier time, perhaps Pontus, perhaps before.

On the western side of the hill, within the citadel compound, is a series of large **caves**. Rumors swirl about another northern cave, since collapsed. Locals say it led to a labyrinth beneath the citadel. Another entrance was supposed to have been to the left of the main gates, now hidden behind houses. Yet another tunnel wound down to the area near the **museum** on the east. Some even say a tunnel extended to the Giresun Adası offshore, a distinct impossibility.

If you have the time, the island of **Giresun Adası** is the other thing you should try to see. Since the tunnel option doesn't work, you need a boat. There is no ferry service, but one of the fishermen along the shore will agree to shuttle you out and back for $10 or less. The Çerkez Lokanta east of town usually has a few men with boats available, as does the Uç Kaya harbor nearer town. You can also contact (or have the information office contact) the island's Turkish-speaking Grizzly Adams-looking caretaker, Yusuf Dinç, *Tel. 454 216 4707.* He occasionally has time to shuttle people across, for a fee.

Giresun Adası is thought to be the Amazon's sacred island, Aretias. This was the site of their altar to the war god, the place where Jason and the Argonauts landed and were attacked by birds dropping darts.

The Amazons worshipped a black stone on their island, according to the second century B.C. account, and that stone remains on the island today. The "mystic power source" remains an object of veneration; once a year, during the **Aksu Festival** in the third week of May, people of the area gather at the mouth of the Aksu Çayı, on the mainland, and boat out to the island to visit the stone. Circling the stone three times – once for every point of the rock touching the earth, the mystic number three – is supposed to bring good luck and fertility, but the rock juts out into the sea and is virtually impossible to negotiate without getting wet. Other parts of the ritual include jumping into and out of a metal pot hanger and tossing pebbles, representing troubles, over your back and into the Aksu.

Whether this is residue of the Amazons is anyone's guess. The walls that once surrounded the island are mostly fallen, although a fairly intact large tower still stands on the west side, looking out toward Giresun.

The most substantial ruins are those of a Byzantine monastery in the middle of the island. Large amphorae once filled with wine are now inhabited by croaking frogs. The island has several campsites, with beautiful, peaceful views to all sides, but few people are aware of them and the campsites are rarely used.

## TRABZON

**Trabzon's** days of charm and glory are mostly behind it. The town is a hub of the bustling suitcase trade over the border with Georgia and it is an important port, but it is a gritty, industrial town in the throes of tremendous growth even by Turkish standards. The population has doubled to almost one million in just seven years. There are several interesting things to see in Trabzon, but the best sights are in the interior or along the coast in either direction.

Many people check into Trabzon in order to see the Sümela Monastery, but that's not necessary. If you'd just as soon avoid Trabzon's bustling urban scene you can; on the other hand, Trabzon is a vital, interesting city whose past is not yet completely buried and whose present can be intriguing.

Our favorite observation is that the burgundy and blue Trabzonspor soccer club banners waving throughout the city mimic the colors in Trabzon's glorious sunsets.

## History

Trabzon's history is long and impressive. **Xenophon** is among the first to mention the city, which was well-established when his fugitive army descended out of the mountains in 400 B.C. The city was located on a small plateau above the Tabakhane Dere, a site so advantageous that the relatively unprotected harbor barely dented the city's growth. Trapezus, as it was first known, was settled by people from Sinop. These colonists originally came from Miletus soon after the Trojan War broke the stranglehold on Hellenistic commerce.

Trabzon's high water mark was in the 12th and 13th centuries. With the Latin capture of Constantinople, the rulers of the Byzantine Empire scattered into Anatolia. The Comnenis took advantage of their family ties and settled in Trabzon, founding a Greek Orthodox splinter empire out of the broken bits of Byzantium. The new empire of Trebizond proved a short lived success. The rulers of this peculiar little empire were adept at playing their predatory neighbors off against one another and securing their alliances with one currency they are said to have had in abundance – beautiful princesses. Even after the Byzantine empire was reestablished at Constantinople the Comnenis were content with their corner of the Black Sea, nestled among the Orthodox monasteries and good trade routes.

The pressure mounting on the Trebizond Empire, however, was immense. Even with fortresses at the mountain passes and lining the sea approaches, the empire was prey to ceaseless incursions from the east and harassment along its southern border. The empire's troubles were compounded with the conquests of Tamurlane, who rode roughshod over the whole of Anatolia in 1401. When, in 1402, Tamurlane vanished into the east, Trebizond struggled to right itself, but its brief golden age had passed.

In 1453, the Trapezuntine Empire, shot through with fabled decadence and vice, stood by as the Ottomans seized Constantinople. In the aftermath, **Sultan Mehmet II** demanded and received substantial tribute from Trabzon. So might affairs have continued, had not the cautious Emperor John IV died and been replaced by his hot-headed brother David. Emperor David secured an alliance with the ever-more fragile Venetians and Genoese, and arranged a further alliance with Uzun Hassan, a Turkish prince who held sway in the east. Having made these arrangements, the Emperor David demanded a reduction in tribute. The Sultan's response was a sudden attack by land and sea, rolling up the enemy outposts on the Black Sea by siege and negotiation.

The Emperor David's erstwhile allies proved useless, with even the formidable Uzun Hassan's armies melting away at the Sultan's approach.

When the Ottoman armies arrived at Trebizond, completing the encirclement begun by the navy, Emperor David met the Ottoman's rapid march with an equally rapid capitulation. The terms of the peace were akin to total surrender: the population was enslaved and deported, the palace stripped of valuables, and Emperor David became a pet on a short leash. The Emperor, and the other males of Comneni blood, were executed at Yedikule in İstanbul in 1564.

The execution of the Comneni males was to end, once and for all, the hereditary claims to the throne of Constantinople, but Sultan Mehmet II's efforts were partially undermined by the irrepressibly beautiful princesses of Trebizond. Sultan Beyazid II fathered Selim I (The Grim) by one of the captured princesses, thus ensuring Comneni blood in the veins of the sultans themselves.

## ARRIVALS & DEPARTURES

### By Air
Trabzon's airport is just to the east of town. Turkish Airlines has two flights daily (except Thursdays) to İstanbul during the low season; departures are at 6:10 a.m. and 4 p.m., departures from İstanbul are at 8:25 a.m. and 8:15 p.m. The cost is $70 one way. Turkish Airlines operates a shuttle bus between the airport and their office at Kemerkaya Mah. on Meydanı Park (*Kemerkaya Mah. Meydan, Parkı Karşısı, Tel. 462 326 6433*).

### By Bus
Trabzon is Turkey's northeastern hub, and buses from all over the country go directly there. Among the destinations and rates: Ankara, 11 hours, $30; İstanbul, 20 hours, $35; Kars, 12 hours, $20. Ulusoy is the premier carrier along this route, with Metro and As Turizm also offering buses with good ventilation. The bus station is two kilometers east of the city center, between the town center to the west and the airport to the east.

### By Car
The Black Sea highway from Samsun is in good condition, but it is extremely busy with truck and bus traffic. Many bus and truck drivers make the İstanbul-Trabzon stretch in a single shot, and they get a shade ragged as they barrel along this highway. Drive by day.

### By Ferry
If you're fortunate enough to have the time, spend two days taking a mini-cruise between Trabzon and İstanbul. Ferry service operates between late May and September, leaving İstanbul at 2 p.m. Monday, arriving at Trabzon about 9:30 a.m. Wednesday. The ferry continues on to Rize, then returns to İstanbul, departing Trabzon at 7:30 p.m. Wednes-

day. Arrival in İstanbul is at 3 p.m. Friday. There is a bewildering array of classes, with prices running between $30 for a seat and $80 for a first class cabin.

İstanbul Maritime Lines charges $55 for car transport between İstanbul and Trabzon. Bring food along, as the food on board is relatively expensive and of uncertain deliciousness ($10 for fixed menu dinner, $3 for breakfast). For a reservation from within Turkey contact the **İstanbul Turkish Maritime Lines** offices at İstanbul, *Tel. 212 249 9222, Fax 212 251 9025.* English speakers are usually available.

In Trabzon, your best bet is to contact the tourism information office and ask them to make a reservation for you – they are accustomed to this. From abroad consider making arrangements through the Turkish Maritime Lines sales office in England: **London Sunquest Holiday Ltd.**, *23 Princes St., WIR 7RG, London, Tel. (44) 171 499 9992, Fax (44) 171 499 9995.*

## ORIENTATION

Before racing off to see Sümela, take the opportunity to have a look around Trabzon. Tucked away throughout the city are sights from the city's Byzantine heyday, some of them well-preserved. The Haghia Sophia is more than two kilometers west of the city center.

The **tourism information** office is in the city center park, *Meydanı Park, Tel. 462 321 4659.*

## GETTING AROUND TOWN

Within town, Trabzon has a good public transportation system. City buses converge at the "Park" in the center of town by the tourism information bureau. Helpful bus routes departing regularly from the Park include the "Ayasofya" (Haghia Sophia), "Garajlar" or "TIP" (bus station), and "Havaalanı" (airport).

The most common mode of transportation is the peculiar, and excellent, dolmuş car arrangement. Compact station wagons are operated like dolmuş, traveling along set routes through town. Tell the driver your destination and he'll let you know whether you should get in. Fare is roughly the same as the bus (30¢).

## WHERE TO STAY

Trabzon's hotels are uninspired, but there is some decent lodging in the lot. One of the problems is that the constant influx of people from the former Soviet Union, traders who are lousy pension neighbors. The easterners have yet to get the hang of many traveling niceties, and the number of busy "Natashas," as prostitutes from across the border have come to be known, renders budget accommodations a shaky prospect.

**OTEL ANIL**, *Güzel Hisar Cad. No. 10 Trabzon. Tel. 462 321 9566, Fax 462 322 2617. Rooms: 45. Double: $35.*
Here, as at other hotels near the city center, the tourism information office can secure a better rate than you are liable to get on your own. The Anıl is one of the newest hotels in the area, pleasantly appointed and offering decent rooms that stop short of being garish. The hotel is conveniently near the information office, tour offices, and non-stop hustle of commerce-sodden Trabzon.

**HISARSARAY PANSIYON**, *Ortahisar Mah., Zağanos Cad. No. 22, Trabzon, Tel. 462 326 3162, Fax 462 326 2669. Rooms: 9. Double: $28.*
The Hisarsaray is dramatic exception to Trabzon's poor range of accommodations. The sprawling house is perched atop a foundation of stone that was once the western wall of Trebizond, and the west-facing rooms look out past the stream below in the direction of the Haghia Sophia. The house was originally built in 1920, and its classic, clean lines were restored in 1992. Today the pension is meticulously cared for, with simple, tasteful interiors, hard wood floors and large sitting rooms. The suite room, $50, is spacious and offers a fine balcony. Guests are free to use the kitchen. The pension is located away from the hive of tourist hotels, across from the Ortahisar (or Fatih Büyük) Cami in the Kale. Reservations necessary.

**COŞANDERE PANSIYON**, *Maçka, Sümela Manastırı Yolu Üzeri 5 km. Trabzon, Tel. 462 531 1190. Rooms: 14. Double: $14. Turkish spoken.*
The Coşandere solves the Trabzon accommodation problem by getting you out of Trabzon. An industrious family on the Sümela Road, 40 kilometers inland, opened a restaurant ten years ago, and in 1995 added a small guest house. The guest house is set above the same stream that spills past the Sümela Monastery, high on a slope in a grove of hazelnut trees.

The ten room farmhouse-inn is at the top of a steep gravel path, with small spare rooms built of wood and stone. The restaurant offers the only food for miles, but it is cheap and excellent. For breakfast (and lunch and dinner) treat yourself to an omelet and trout, breaded with corn meal and pan fried.

To get here follow the directions toward Sümela by car; the Coşandere is just across a small bridge five kilometers past Maçka. Getting there without your own car is a slight bother, but quite easy: stop by the tourism information office in Trabzon and ask one of the helpful staffers to call ahead. Take a Maçka minibus from the station east of the tourism information office at the bottom of the hill, and get out at the end of the line, by Maçka's town square. From here, phone the Coşandere (*"Bu akşam pension'da kalacağız. Şimdi Maçka'da bekliyoruz. Geliyor musunuz?"* This is a halting and gramatically poor way to say "Tonight we're staying at your pension. Now we're waiting in Maçka. Can you come?"). Some-one will be along shortly to give you a ride – if your party's greater than two, someone may make the trip in the bed of the family's pickup.

You can also stay in bungalows at Sümela if your timing is right (see Sümela section).

**CHURCH OF SANTA MARIA,** *Istiklal Mah., Sümer Sok. No. 26, Trabzon, Tel. 462 321 2192. Rooms: 10. Double: Donation.*

Only 500 meters downhill from the tourist information office in the center of town is an intriguing accommodation option, a boarding house in a Catholic Church. In a city with the rampant vice of Trabzon it's a wonder the priests and nuns have time to keep the modest rooms tidy, but as you would expect, they do. If you phone from the otogar you can even get a lift to the pension. You pay what you feel is right, which can get downright expensive for good, conscience-ridden Catholics. Little English, mostly Italian, French, and Turkish.

Failing these, the **UZUNKUM HOTEL,** *Tel. 462 223 4041, Fax 462 223 4042,* at the western entrance to town, costs $40, and the **YILMAZLAR OTELCILIK,** *Tel. 462 325 7967, Fax 462 325 8053,* on the sea road east of downtown, runs $20. Both are reasonable value. Trabzon is a good place to check with the tourism information office; the staff there can help locate decent accommodations and secure a room.

### In Rize

**DEDEMAN RIZE HOTEL,** *Ali Paşa Köyü, Rize, Tel. 464 223 5344, Fax 464 223 5348. Rooms: 82. Double: $75.*

The sole four star hotel on the Black Sea coast. The Dedeman meets the high standard of the chain despite its unusual location far off the tourist track. Very popular among people doing business across the Turkish-Georgian border. A beach is being constructed, and is due to be ready in 1997. Satellite television, sauna, pool, restaurant and attentive service. The Dedeman is located to the west of Rize, but dolmuş pass back and forth regularly. One hour from Trabzon.

## WHERE TO EAT

Trabzon has been welcomed into McDonald's' wide embrace (on the main square). You didn't come to Trabzon to playfully entice your palate, and that's a good thing. Trabzon's restaurants tend to offer substantial, traditional food. Any of the places around the city-center square are good and reliable; check with the tourism office for the latest update.

**KIBRIS RESTAURANT,** *Trabzon, Tel. 462 321 7679. Moderate.*

A good, filling meal of mezes and köfte izgara washed down with a couple of glasses of beer won't run any higher than $9. Traditional Turkish fare.

**KAVAKLIK RESTAURANT**, *Trabzon, Tel. 462 321 7646. Moderate.*
Another reliable restaurant serving traditional Turkish cuisine.
**TAD PIZZA AND BURGER**, *Belediye Karşısı 11, Trabzon, Tel. 462 321 1237. Moderate.*
If you feel yourself weakening for McDonalds, rush yourself to Tad Pizza and Burger, where you can get yourself an actual western-style pizza as well as spaghetti and grilled chicken. It's still much more Turkish than a box of McNuggets.

**In Akçaabat**
**KÖSK RESTAURANT**, *Inönü Cad., Akçaabat, Tel. 462 228 3223. Moderate-Expensive.*
Acclaimed for a hundred kilometers in both directions, the Kösk is worth the trip from Trabzon. The restaurant is across the street from the Hotel Sümela. Try the seasonal (mevşim) fish, which will be cheaper and almost certainly delicious. Lufer and palamut are always good choices.

## SEEING THE SIGHTS

One of Trabzon's great sites, the **Haghia Sophia**, is more than two kilometers west of the city center, requiring either a dolmuş-car or an "Ayasofya"-bound bus, both of which depart from the lower end of the main city square. The Haghia Sophia has been marvelously restored, largely through the efforts of a team from the University of Edinburgh, Scotland. Restoration work began in the 1950s, ending centuries of neglect by the Ottomans, who covered over the frescoes and used the Haghia Sophia as a mosque. Today the Haghia Sophia is a museum, closed Mondays, and there is a $2 entrance fee.

The Haghia Sophia (Divine Wisdom, the same name as İstanbul's great cathedral) was erected by Emperor Manuel I in the 13th century on the site of an older, smaller church. The structure is on a much more modest scale than the vast İstanbul cathedral of the same name, but Trabzon's Haghia Sophia benefits from the immense talents of Selçuk stone workers who pitched in during construction. The truly distinguishing characteristic of the church, however, is the quality of its frescoes. The paintings are titled with English plaques, although you need to know that the pendentives are the joints between the top of two arches and the dome on top, and north is toward the sea.

Some of the most striking of the many vivid frescoes within are in the narthex, where Christ's miraculous acts are depicted. The vibrant paintings are a quantum leap from the flat Byzantine artwork of earlier centuries, and this has been traced to a late 11th century journey by monks from Europe. These monks brought with them a book whose vivid illustrations used tricks of depth and scale, forever altering the art of the places they visited. The clock tower alongside the church was here before the Comnenis began construction of the Haghia Sophia.

Just off the main road through the citadel, Uzun Yol, is the **Ortahisar Cami**, also called **Fatih Büyük Cami**, formerly an Orthodox church. The basic structure of the Panaghia Chrisokephalos, as it was once called, dates to the 10th century, with extensive remodeling in the 13th century heyday of the Trebizond Empire. During the reign of the Comnenis, this church was the site of their coronation ceremonies, and was appropriately resplendent with a golden dome. Comneni family members were buried on the church grounds.

Like most churches of the period, the Panaghia Chrisokephalos was decorated with frescoes that are now either plastered over or fallen. The church is a fine engineering exercise, with ascending vaults and arches that create a dramatic effect. The building has changed very little in the past thousand years, although a stairway had to be removed to fit a wooden mihrab, and the stone floor, like the frescoes, is covered over.

Due south of Ortahisar Cami, the road climbs to the centerpiece of old Trebizond, the hilltop **Golden Palace of the Comneni**. Be warned, the palace is neither golden nor even palatial. Follow one of the likely looking paths through backyard gardens to the ruins. Children are very likely to come along and offer to show you around (disputes develop: what the boys call "dungeons" the girls call "kitchens"). The highest tower is topped by a flag and visible from a distance.

While the Trebizond Empire controlled affairs in its corner of the world, this palace was its glorious centerpiece. The author Rose Macaulay in *The Towers of Trebizond* has helped fix the beauty of this labyrinthine palace in our minds, but it can be difficult to square that image with the tumbling and overgrown ruin found today. Vines, grasses, and trees have sprung up amid the palace walls, taking advantage of Trabzon's fecund climate. Once the home of royalty, of galleries, wind towers and great audience halls, the eastern palace is now a warren of small residences and garden plots. After winding your way to the outer ramparts, you can scale to the top and look out over the western city. This was once just a remote corner of a palace that straddled the hill from east to west. The western battlements rise directly out of the shallow valley on the west side of the hill, and that, at least, remains quite dramatic. Most of the interior sections have collapsed or burned, but you can still get a sense of the palace's size. This was part of the upper keep, one of three terraced levels that descended toward the sea.

**Gülbaharhatun Cami**, located across the bridge to the west of the citadel and one long block south, bears the name given to the beautiful and generous Comneni princess, Maria. Gülbaharhatun, or "spring rose" was among the spoils of Fatih Sultan Mehmet's conquest of Trebizond, and she was introduced into the harem of his son Beyazid II. She was a great favorite of Beyazid II, and bore him the son that became the next sultan, Selim I.

The apple, it seems, fell far from the tree. No spring rose, Selim was called Yavuz, or "the Grim. He was a great conqueror with little regard for human life, slaying his grand viziers and attendants with the same alacrity his armies showed in massacring Shi'ite armies and doubling the size of the empire. Historians say nothing about the relationship between young Selim and his mother, but it can be said that the mother won a measure of vengeance for the Ottoman massacre of her male relations, the destruction of Trebizond, and her own "imprisonment" within Beyazid II's harem: Selim forced his father Beyazid II from the throne in 1512 and probably poisoned him.

For his mother, the lad showed much more respect. In the same year, 1512, Selim began construction of a mosque in his mother's ancestral home. Gülbaharhatun is interred in a türbe alongside the mosque.

## NIGHTLIFE & ENTERTAINMENT

### Hamams

Both the Sekiz Direkli Hamam and Fatih Hamam are interesting, attractive Turkish baths. The **Sekiz Direkli**, *Moloz Mevkii, Tel. 462 322 1012*, or Eight Column bath is open to women on Thursdays from 8 a.m. to 5 p.m. The **Fatih Hamam** is open to women on Wednesdays at the same hours. A bath and full scrub costs $6.

## SUMELA MONASTERY

**Sümela Monastery** is one of Turkey's great sights, however construction work is expected to continue until 2000. With much of the structure teetering there was no choice but to begin restoration in 1990. As often happens, however, the restoration is robbing the site of some of its mystery. The process is necessary, but somewhat regrettable and inconvenient.

### History

It all began when St. Luke painted a black figure of Mary on a piece of the True Cross. Two Athenian monks set out along the Black Sea in the fourth century, at the time of Theodosius the Great, bearing with them the holy icon. Led by dreams and visions, they came upon a cave high above a remote area and established a small church and monastery there, with the icon as its centerpiece. In ensuing years the monastery grew into both an Orthodox religious center and a Byzantine outpost guarding one of the most important passes into Trabzon. Justinian and his general Belisarius are said to have visited and caused a series of lookouts to be built as an early warning system for the city below.

The Persians and Arabs who besieged Byzantium in the seventh century thus had good cause to sack the monastery, and did, although monks were able to spirit away most of the valuables and religious icons and reestablish the monastery when the threat ebbed. Trabzon helped secure funds for the rebuilding project. The monastery continued in its role as a guardian of the critical Zigana Pass down to the Black Sea, and was occasionally attacked by bandits, which led the monks to begin constructing the high walls now in place.

Under the Trapezuntine Empire, Sümela rose greatly in esteem, and **Emperor Alexius Comneni III** (1349-1390) chose the monastery for his coronation and helped fund construction and decoration of the site. The Trapezuntine Empire was, however, nearing its end. When Fatih Sultan Mehmet II seized Trabzon in 1461, he showed characteristic – but remarkable – indulgence of his Christian subjects and left the monastery in peace and the monks with most of their lands intact. While Sultan Mehmet II's grandson **Selim I** (1512-1520) was governor of Trabzon he once fell ill on a campaign and was restored to health at the monastery. In thanks for the monks' help, Selim – a frequent visitor during his eastern campaigns – bestowed lavish gifts on the monastery, including five ornate oil lamps.

The monastery continued to thrive for centuries, and at one point the Ottomans made it a virtual dumping ground for troublesome priests. The population declined from an estimated 1,000 monks and nuns to just 100 by the end of the 19th century, but contributions and alms continued to pour in. Armenians retreated to the monastery during the purges prior to WW I. During the severe economic crisis and warfare of the time the monks were forced to abandon the monastery.

Following the war, the Treaty of Sevres partitioned Turkey, and Sümela was now located outside of Turkey in a Russian/Armenian administered zone, under the oversight of a French governor. The French governor helped restore the monastery, but the partition was never really enforced before Kemal Atatürk's nationalists routed the Greek occupation army in the west and Turkey reclaimed its current lands. The monastery's long life came to an abrupt end in the summer of 1923, when the monks were deported to Greece in the exchange of populations.

## ARRIVALS & DEPARTURES
### By Bus Tour from Trabzon
Several companies run tours from Trabzon to Sümela, and the tours are both cheap and fairly informative. The best of the tours is offered by

**Afacan Tour**, *Iskele Cad. No. 40C, Trabzon, Tel. 462 321 5804, Fax 462 3217001*, with buses departing at 10 a.m. from in front of their offices, just east of the tourism information office. The cost is $6 per person. Ulusoy also offers a tour one half hour later, departing from the tourism office. It is slightly more expensive.

### By Car

The main southern E-97 highway out of Trabzon, serving Maçka, Bayburt, and Erzurum, also takes you in the direction of Sümela. At Maçka follow the signs to the left marked Sümela and Maryemana, which ascends the left side of a steep gorge, crossing back and forth as you ascend. The ticket booth is 17 kilometers along, and there is a restaurant and gift shop at the trailhead.

## WHERE TO STAY

The Çosandere Pansiyon, mentioned in Trabzon's *Where to Stay* section, is located halfway up the Maçka-Sümela road. There are also eight bungalows available at the Sümela trailhead, open year round. Reservations at the bungalows are necessary, however; have the tourism information office call ahead, *Tel. 462 331 1061*.

## SEEING THE SIGHTS

In addition to a charge at the entrance to the park, there is another fee at the top of the trail. The **monastery** is built into a great natural cave high above the valley floor. The ascent from the parking lot is steep and the trail is usually a little muddy. After a determined 15 minute climb you begin catching glimpses of the monastery's dramatic face, eventually and you ascend a long staircase beneath the old aqueduct and enter the compound from above.

Sümela's facade is one of the best-preserved parts of the monastery, so don't be surprised to descend into what is mostly a set of ruins. If it appears a bomb must have gone off, one did. In the aftermath of the monk's abandonment, an explosion destroyed part of the interior; the Greeks accuse the Turks, the Turks accuse the Greeks. Adding to the damage, the venerable collection of wooden houses burned in the 1930s.

The current restoration work may undermine the mystery of the site, but it has certain clear advantages; you now begin to understand the layout of the interior. The highlights are the chapel and the holy spring. A spring on the underside of the cave's roof drops a trickle of water down through open space into the "fountain," and this water was considered to have healing and purifying properties. The same fountain was also used as a cistern, and connected to the aqueduct.

The chapel, like most of the buildings and frescoes hugging the back wall of the cave, is fairly well preserved. Vandals have gone to great pains to chip away at and scar the many images here, but a beautiful collection of art remains. In many cases the frescoes are at least two layers thick, done and redone over a period of centuries. Despite the damage, the Greek writing and artwork is still largely intact, and you can make out several Biblical tales in the succession of panels by the main church, including the Creation. In the interior of the church – the first thing constructed – are Jesus and Mary paintings that shimmer on the rare occasions when sunshine breaks through the clouds.

During the exchange of populations, the monks were wary of bringing the monastery's great collection of valuables and icons along and secreted them in a hole near the smaller church outside the compound, along the upper path. Later, in secret, they recovered their treasures. There is an alternate path down to the restaurant and parking lot from here.

# 16. THE EAST

Artvin is the gateway to the east, a dramatic change from the lush landscapes and the easy life on the Black Sea. The northeast interior of Turkey was once the territory of the **Bagratids**, Christians with a great love of churches and monasteries; many of these monasteries remain today, and are the goal of travelers who head inland. However the landscape and the stark culture alone should lure you through the passes and into the interior.

Hikes in the **Kaçkars** are popular, rafting on the **Çoruh River** can be arranged, and for those of you who want to see what the State Department insists you shouldn't, we give you details for a trip through the east. Note that a car is excellent in the northeast corner of Turkey for getting to and away from the monasteries, and that viewing the **Georgian churches** is extremely slow, difficult, and tedious by bus and dolmuş. Conversely, you should stick to major forms of public transportation for any travel southeast of Erzurum, where you are safer from (extremely rare) terrorism than you would be in a car.

## ARTVIN

Artvin is historic, but has little historic to see. The fortress guarding the mountain pass below is on the grounds of a military installation, thus off-limits. Otherwise Artvin is a simple, quietly bustling town with staggering views and quick access to some of the Georgian monasteries. You get the sense that something has changed with your arrival here; the heat lightning, the watchful people, and the steep, barren, silent landscape can be unsettling. You are in the east.

### History

The creases in this mountainside have always been used as trade routes, and Artvin sits atop one of the most important routes, following the Çoruh River down to the Black Sea. The distant history of the area is lost, although it was certainly occupied under the Arabs in the seventh

---

### CATCHING A BUZZ IN ARTVIN

*The honey in the mountains west of Artvin is infamous. Twice, once during Xenophon's passage in 400 B.C. and again during the Roman General Pompey's campaign against Mithradites in 65 B.C., armies were ravaged by the hallucinogenic effects of the local honey. Pompey's army suffered the most: during their journey through the area the natives left great quantities of honey out for the soldiers to eat, waiting for the men to descend into delirium and illness before attacking and butchering hundreds of helpless soldiers.*

---

century. The Georgians of the **Bagratid Kingdom** established themselves in this mountainous region in the early ninth century, and their rule lasted until the 13th century.

Most of the monasteries and churches date from the 9th and 10th centuries. The Bagratids control of the mountain passes made its neighbors wary of invasion, and the Bagratids proved very able at repelling invaders; only the Selçuks broke through and successfully seized the Bagratid cities (in 1071), and they were forced out just 30 years later. With the Bagratid collapse, the Ottomans seized these lands under Selim I, and they remained crucial to the Ottomans' eastern defenses until the Russians forced the passes during the Russian war of 1886-87.

At that time the Russians seized Kars, Erzurum, and Ardahan, penetrating as far as Artvin. The lands were restored in the Treaty of Lausanne in 1922.

## ARRIVALS & DEPARTURES

### By Bus

If you have arrived by public transportation, you should probably keep going to Yusufeli. The monasteries near Artvin almost all require a car, although taxis will gladly help guide you around the area. Artvin's otogar is located at the riverside, but Artvin itself clings to the mountain slope high above, even above the fortress. From the otogar to the city center you can walk (three hours straight uphill) or catch the minibus at the otogar for 30¢, a ten minute ride.

Public transportation can be excruciatingly slow if you are on a schedule. Buses from Artvin serve Ardahan, Kars (once per day), Yusufeli, Erzurum and other northeast towns, as well as Trabzon, and there is one bus daily continuing all the way to İstanbul.

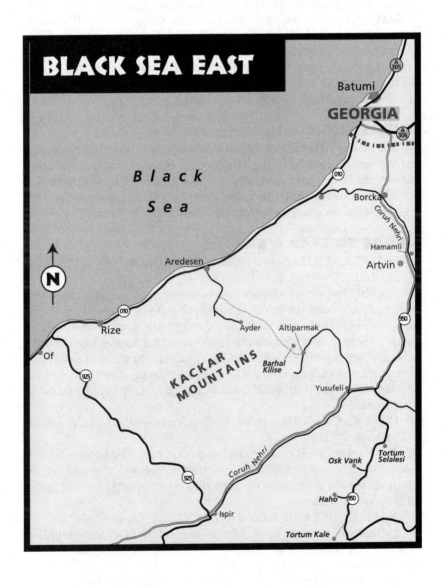

## By Car

Getting here is half the fun. From the direction of the Black Sea you wind your way up the Çoruh River through great gaps in the local mountain range. On the journey, along a surprisingly good road, you're treated to glimpses of old fortifications, many of them tumbled, but some of them, like the old Ottoman post at Borçka, in good condition. From Erzurum in the opposite direction you descend through similarly stark terrain. Upon arrival at the Artvin's otogar, you see a slender tower high above on the far side of the river, a defensive position dating to Selim I's eastern campaigns.

## ORIENTATION

The road to Artvin climbs up more than a dozen switchbacks, finally turning onto a relatively flat road called **Inönü Caddesi**. The city's restaurants, hotels, and government buildings are all located here. The city's former lament that it had nowhere flat enough for a soccer field has been solved with a large concrete platform across from the PTT.

## WHERE TO STAY & EAT

**HOTEL KARAHAN,** *Inönü Cad. No. 16, Artvin, Tel. 466 212 1800, Fax 466 212 2420. Rooms: 48. Double: $35.*

The Karahan's rooms have a Frankensteinian aspect, as if made with odds and ends from the building supply, but this is the old standby for lodging in Turkey's northeast. The owners are helpful and well-acquainted with guests who are interested in seeing the Georgian monasteries, so they can offer advice and background. The hotel's front rooms have gorgeous, endless views. The restaurant serves good, hearty food. One of the Karahan brothers also has a pension in Altıparmak that can be a useful base.

**OTEL KAÇKAR,** *Hamam Sok. No. 5 (below Inönü), Artvin, Tel. 466 212 3397. Rooms: 24. Double: $14.*

The Kaçkar offers clean rooms and a kitchen. The hotel is located below Artvin's centerpiece Valiliğli building just off the main street. Ahmet-Bey runs a remarkably tight ship when you take a look at his budget competitors.

**KAFKASÖR TATIL KÖYÜ DAĞ EVLERI,** *Tel. 466 212 5013.*

In the style of the Yaylas that Turks adore in the Black Sea's highland meadows. A collection of bungalows 20 minutes from Artvin's city center. Phone ahead and enquire.

**EFKAR LOKANTA,** *Inönü Cad., Artvin, Tel. 466 212 2963.*

At the bend in the road as you begin your descent out of Artvin, Efkar has cheap food, beer, and an almost perilous view, perched at the edge of a sheer drop-off.

## SEEING THE SIGHTS

**Visiting the Churches & Fortresses Near Artvin**

You won't be able to miss the fortress perched above the Coruh River as you enter town. This is reportedly a fascinating spot, but you'll be unable to visit until the Turkish Army moves to a new location. The picturesque ruins date from the campaigns of Selim I, the Grim. It was Selim who plowed through the enemies that had plagued the Ottomans' eastern borders, wiping out several Persian armies and sacking cities well into modern Iraq. At the end of his campaign he fortified the passes in eastern Anatolia, of which this was one.

The reason for visiting Artvin is to visit the Georgian monasteries nearby. The bulk of these are on the highway linking Artvin to Şavşat, an area sometimes compared to Greece's Mt. Athos. Nearest Artvin is the **Hamamlı Church**, south on the main 950 highway and left at the intersection for Şavşat. Nine kilometers from the intersection a road turns off abruptly for Hamamlı, a harrowing five kilometer drive. The village has a 10th century church with several large paintings. Descending back to the road at the bottom of the gorge, several battered old yellow signs lead you to monasteries above the gorge. Some of the churches and monasteries require a hike, such as that at **Pırnallı**. Following the gorge you emerge at a formidable Bagratid fortress just west of Şavşat. Six kilometers northeast of Şavşat is another church in modern Cevizli, this one offering reliefs of Georgian luminaries.

Returning back toward Artvin, the Ardanuç road cuts off across a bridge to the left and passes south through the spectacular **Cehennum Deresi Kanyonu**, or Hell's Creek Canyon. Unfortunately the Ardanuç road doesn't get you anywhere but Ardanuç, but there you are rewarded by beautiful views and a ruined Bagratid fortress. **Ardanuç** was the Bagratid capital from the 9th century onward, and the clifftop citadel is a 12th century Bagratid structure. In the interior of the battered old fortress is an old Georgian church.

On the road between Artvin and Erzurum, beyond Yusufeli, are several more excellent monasteries and churches, highlighted by the church at **Ösk Vank** and, further south, **Haho** (Bağbaşı).

## TREKKING IN THE KAÇKARS

There are innumerable trekking options in the region. Below we detail one such trek. Good maps are difficult to locate; Turkey does not have the love of highly detailed contour maps so popular in the west.

This route takes you directly through the mountains from south to north, and assumes you won't want to return for a car. From Trabzon, get a bus into Yusufeli, 75 kilometers south of Artvin. The town has an old west mining town flavor to it, although the image is skewed by people putting in at the class 4 and 5 Çoruh River and itinerant trekkers (for information on rafting, contact **Alternatif Turizm**, İstanbul, Tel. 216 345 6650). Zeytinlik, downstream, has a hot springs.

From Yusufeli get one of the several dolmuş to Barhal/Altıparmak that leave each day, climbing up and out of barren Yusufeli to the moist greenery of the mountains. There are several small family pensions at Barhal, and someone will almost surely meet you as you emerge from the dolmuş if you need to spend a night before getting underway. The **Barhal Kilise**, a 10th century Georgian church, is in good condition and merits a visit. Guides are always willing to lead you across the range (not, officially, the Kaçkars, although this **Altıparmak** – Six Fingers – range is every bit as beautiful) if you are unable to locate a map.

If you have failed to bring a map along, you can usually get a map from backpackers emerging from the opposite direction or convince someone to draw something up. If this seems chancy, it is and it isn't; trails are in good shape and receive steady use, but there are a lot of them. If you take a wrong turn, someone will be able to set you right soon enough. If you follow the valley to the Altıparmak massif there's no getting lost, you follow the valley. The Turkish Tourism Ministry publishes a mountaineering guide with a vague map of the **Altıparmak-Ayder route**.

A five day trek through the Altıparmak range deposits you at Ayder, one of the upland meadows on the Black Sea side of the mountain. A map is a very good idea given the various side trails. There are hotels (and hot springş) at Ayder, and dolmuş to Pazar on the Black Sea coast.

## THE EASTERN CIRCUIT

This book does not cover eastern Turkey owing to the continuing unrest, and we advise against travel here on that basis. However, you may not be able to resist the temptation. What follows is the traveling circuit that has developed in the past few years, and on which you can be fairly confident of safety. Cars would offer wonderful freedom, but are not a good idea. Stick to major public transportation between cities, and try to travel by day.

Here we offer only the bare necessities; you will want to grill others during your travels and make a beeline for the Tourism Information offices in each city, where they may have some helpful warnings or suggestions.

## ARRIVALS & DEPARTURES

You can, believe it or not, get a bus from İstanbul to **Kars**, though it makes a lot more sense to come via Trabzon or Erzurum or, most directly, by air via Turkish Airlines' daily flight from İstanbul at 6:30 a.m., via Ankara at 8:15 a.m. There is also a mind-bendingly cheap train between Kars and İstanbul, a 44 hour trip costing less than $10.

"Kars?" say a few Canadian readers. Yes, Kars. This Kars has a sister city of the same name near Ottawa, after the Canadians renamed East Wellington during the Crimean War. The Canadians were impressed by the city's conduct in fighting off the Russians.

## VISITING THE EAST

In Kars your first stop is the **tourism information** office. Here the friendly and somewhat bored staffer will check your passport and issue a permit for visiting **Ani** (which is in a restricted zone along the Armenian border). Sometime before departing for Ani you must stop off at the **Kars Museum** to pick up your ticket for the ruins, and you should consider a quick run around the museum while there. The city's fanciest hotel is **ANIHAN MOTEL**, *Tel. 474 223 7404*, followed by the **HOTEL KARABAĞ**, *Faikbey Cad. No. 84, Kars, Tel. 474 212 3480, Fax 474 223 3089*, each costing about $30.

The following day you can drive the 43 kilometers to Ani, or get a taxi. Hitchhiking is an obvious option, with Westerners making the trip back and forth during high season, but the return leg can be monstrously difficult once evening comes. Complicating things, there are mean dogs on the road. A taxi will usually be there when your willpower gives out. $30 should get you to Anı and back to Kars, with a couple of hours for visiting.

Visitors agree that Ani is worth the trouble. This city was one of the grandest in the world, the centerpiece of Armenia at the height of its power at the end of the first millenium. Many of the beautifully crafted churches are still recognizable, particularly **St. Gregory**. The stonework here provided inspiration for the Selçuks who, under Alp Arslan, seized the city in 1063. The city's decline was dramatic, as successive conquerors from the east, first the Turks, then the Mongols, then the Tatars, damaged and ultimately destroyed the city.

From Kars, head south to **Doğubeyazit**. Buses make the two-leg trip via Iğdir several times daily. The city has a interesting circuit of walls, but is not especially appealing. It is, however, in the foothills of **Mt. Ararat** of Noah's Ark fame. Ararat treks are increasingly difficult to arrange, with occasional PKK (Kurdish rebel) incursions in the area, but you can enquire with a local travel agency. There is a large population of Kurds here, accompanied by a large population of soldiers.

The sight you must see is five kilometers from the city center, **Ishak Paşa Palace**. The palace is four kilometers uphill. Dolmuş make the trip infrequently, and taxis are glad to offer a ride for about $10 both ways. The Palace was built for the local governor, an almost completely autonomous lord of this far-flung Ottoman province. The grandeur of the palace, completed in 1801, reflects the paşa's ability to keep a little something from the tax money generated in his realm. The Silk Route wound past, and one important provincial business was tolling passing caravans. The palace is decorated with beautiful stonework, and almost half of the interior space was dedicated to the paşa's harem. As incredible as the palace is, it was more ornate still before the Russians took advantage of their brief possession of this land to cart off many of the most beautiful relics to the Hermitage Museum in St. Petersburg.

Accommodations in Doğubeyazit include the top end **OTEL ISFAHAN**, *Tel. 472 215 2048*, and the **ISHAKPAŞA HOTEL**, *Tel. 472 215 5243*. Both are near the center of town and cost about $30 for a double. Or you can try **ORTADOĞU OTEL**, at $26 for a double with cramped little rooms.

From Doğubeyazit, take one of the frequent buses to **Van**. This stretch of road skirts the Iranian border before veering off toward **Lake Van**. The otogar is outside of town, but shuttle buses ordinarily meet arriving buses. Van is the ancient capital of **Urartu**; the Urartians were industrious, talented fortress-builders who emerged from the wreck of the Hittite Empire. They figure prominently in the bible; Ararat, for instance, is written consonant for consonant identically in the vowel-less characters of the time. **Van Kalesi**, the Rock of Van, was their original citadel, reinforced and rebuilt through the years, with the final improvements by the Byzantines and Ottomans.

Most of the basic defense works, such as the long trenches, were built by the Urartians. This citadel still commands the surrounding area from its bluff between the town and the lake.

The lake is vast and well over 1,000 feet deep. The **museum** in town has a striking collection of near Eastern pieces. **Çavuştepe**, 20 kilometers south of Van, was the Urartian royal citadel, and on the same road, 59 kilometers from Van, is **Hosap Kalesi**, a Kurdish fortress dominating another sheer peak. This mazelike castle, located near Güzelsu, was built by Kurdish separatists in the 17th century; that much, at least, has not changed.

While in Van, consider staying at the **OTEL VAN**, the backpackers' popular choice (there will be someone from the hotel looking for business at the bus station). The **AKDAMAR HOTEL**, *Kazi Karabekir Cad. No. 56,*

*Tel. 432 216 8100, Fax 432 212 0868*, and the **BÜYÜK URARTU HOTEL,** *Hastane Sok. No. 60, Tel. 432 212 0660, Fax 432 212 1610*, are both three star options.

You can try to catch the ferry across Lake Van to Tatvan and bus from there, but the ferry keeps irregular hours and is typically commandeered on the whim of the army. It is usually disciplined enough to meet arriving trains (Vangölu Ekspresi, arriving Van 8:30 p.m. Friday (or so), departing 7:20 a.m. Saturday). Outside of Fridays and Saturdays it is often better to bus directly on to Malatya from Van. There are also Turkish Airlines flights and a rail service that passes through Malatya, Sivas, Kayseri, and Ankara on the way to İstanbul.

**Malatya** is the first or final stop in the circuit. Malatya has a few interesting sights, but is most useful for its convenience to **Nemrut Dağı.** Kahta in the southwest is closer to the peak and well accustomed to booking trips to Nemrut Dağı, but is itself a difficult place to reach. In Malatya, stop in at the tourism information office, where the staff arranges good tours to the mountain. Minibuses typically depart in the early afternoon, arriving at the top four hours later for sunset.

After getting this initial view, often with some helpful information about the surprisingly unspectacular Antiochus I for whom this was built, you descend to a small hotel. After dinner and some cards you sleep, with a second trip to the summit at sunrise. This, plus the ride back to Malatya and a cheap breakfast, costs $25. There are more thorough ways of seeing Nemrut Dağı, but this is a remarkably good option, and less expensive by hundreds of dollars than the deals arranged by most of the people you see at the mountaintop.

If you arrive late and are spending a night in Malatya, try the **MALATYA BÜYÜK OTEL,** *Yeni Cami Karşil, Zafer Işhanı No. 1, Malatya, Tel. 422 321 1400, Fax 422 321 5367.* Likewise, if you want to stay very near Nemrut Dağı, try the **ZEUS MOTEL,** *Nemrut Dağı Karadut Köyü, Tel. 416 715 2428,* near the summit.

From Malatya there are daily Turkish Airlines flights to Ankara at 5:30 p.m. with ongoing service to İstanbul and Ankara, trains to Kayseri, and buses to all of the above, plus Adana and Mersin on the eastern Mediterranean coast.

348

# 17. THE MEDITERRANEAN COAST

Turkey's most captivating collection of ruins and beaches are toward the western end of the Mediterranean shore, but some beautiful places dot the shore between Mersin and Antalya. If you have the inclination, you should take a trip along the eastern shore, but its sights are scattered more widely and traveling along the mountainous coast is slow.

We've intentionally focused this book on the outstanding sights in the west, but you can find critical information on the Eastern Mediterranean in Chapter 22, *Other Points of Interest*. The best route for those making the trip between Cappadoccia and the Antalya area is inland via Konya.

## ANTALYA

As a base from which to see many of the most interesting ruins from the ancient world, **Antalya** is ideal. Among the nearby sites are **Termessos**, easily defensible within its canyon walls; **Perge** sprawling between two mesas; **Aspendos**, whose ancient theater is the best on earth; **Sillion**, perched atop a barely accessible bluff; and **Selge**, high in the interior at the end of a deep, beautiful gorge.

Antalya has a few ruins of its own, but its greatest assets are a central location and an excellent collection of old houses that have been converted to hotels and pensions in the city's old quarter. There are several good beaches less than one-half hour away, but if you want a beach outside your back door continue on to the west.

### History

One version of Antalya's founding has it that **King Attalus II** of Pergamon (160-139 B.C.) sent forth his minions to find the perfect site for a beautiful new city, and those minions picked this spot. Beautiful though the site certainly was, perched in the greenery on the cliffs above

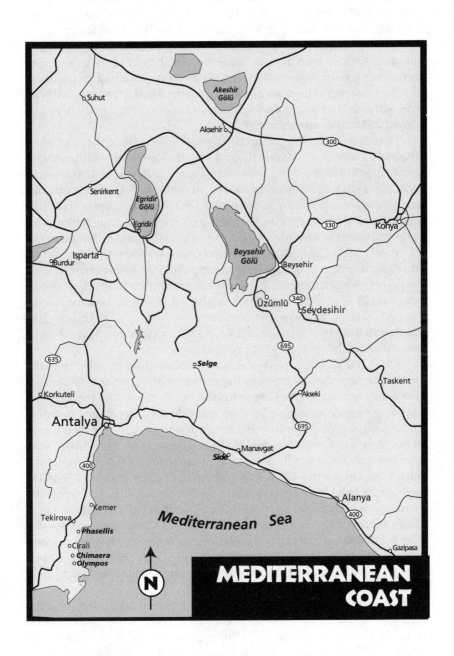

**MEDITERRANEAN COAST**

the Mediterranean, a more realistic reason for Antalya's founding was its strategic position commanding the wide **Bay of Antalya**, the first major anchorage west of the Lycian Mountains. Attalus II's search for a port city coincided with the high water mark of ancient civilization in the region; Side and Aspendos to the east were near the height of their power, as were other coastal cities to the west. Rome was extending its influence into the eastern Mediterranean, and had completed a trading deal with Side. **Attalus II**, needing a secure port of his own, built a city here and named it Attaleia, after himself.

The Kingdom of Pergamon hardly had time to build the city before Attalus II's successor, Attalus III, broke up the kingdom, willing most of it to Rome. Antalya did not pass immediately to Rome, and pirates and other ne'er do wells moved in, taking advantage of Antalya's fine bay (the world's navies still anchor there). The **Roman Empire** had little tolerance for interference in its trade and waged several brutal campaigns to clear the area of piracy, the most notable under Pompey in 66 B.C. Afterwards, the region was cleared of pirates and port cities such as Antalya came directly under Roman control. Rome, unfortunately, used the eastern Mediterranean as a dumping ground for its shadiest noblemen, and local governors systematically looted and abused the coastal towns. Unlike Perge and Aspendos, however, Antalya's brief history had left it with little to steal or desecrate, and the city grew apace while its venerable neighbors were stripped and brought low.

Antalya's fortunes never seriously declined, although for many years it remained a footnote to the activities at Perge and Aspendos. Eventually the inland cities began to fade, but Antalya, with the last good anchorage easily accessible by road from the east, continued to thrive under fairly steady Byzantine rule. Crusaders used the city in their forays to the Holy Land, but they fumbled the city away to the Selçuks, who adorned it with some of its landmark monuments. The Ottomans finally seized the city in the expansion campaigns of Beyazid I (1389-1403), capturing it from their Turkish rivals, the Karamanlıs. The city remained an important commercial center throughout the Imperial period, eventually assuming the dominant role along the Mediterranean. Following WW I, Antalya was partitioned to the Italians in the Treaty of Sevres, and was occupied by the Italians between 1918 and 1921, when Kemal Atatürk seized back the Turkish heartland and all of the allies abandoned their claims.

Today Antalya is one of Turkey's main industrial centers, and the hub for tourism along the southern coast. The World Bank-funded tourism zone near Kemer is fed through Antalya's airport, and even without this help the city is a natural destination for connoisseurs of ruins and fine accommodations.

## IT'S A PIRATE'S DEATH FOR ME!

*A pirate tale you don't usually hear: While still a young Roman officer, young **Gaius Julius Caesar** was seized by pirates on his way to Rhodes and held for ransom. The charming young Roman developed a friendship with the pirates in the weeks he awaited payment of the ransom, playfully telling them that someday he would crucify them all for his current indignity. One account even says that he was insulted when the pirates failed to ask a high enough ransom, and voluntarily increased it fivefold. When payment arrived from Caesar's friends in Miletus the parting was tinged by sadness. Several years later, Caesar was helping the powerful Pompey in his effort to clear the eastern Mediterranean of pirates, and it so happened that Caesar's past captors fell into his hands. According to the policy of the times, and his own past assurances, Caesar was compelled to crucify the pirates – but out of sentiment for their past acquaintance he had their throats cut first.*

## ARRIVALS & DEPARTURES

### By Air

Antalya's economy hinges on processing sesame, cotton, and tourists. The latter industry has been carefully masterminded to funnel through Antalya's airport and disperse in the huge resort hotels between here and Tekirova in the west. Flights can be booked directly to Antalya via İstanbul, or booked from İstanbul for roughly $85 per person on Turkish Airlines or $60 on İstanbul Airlines. Flights to other points in Turkey cost about the same, using either İstanbul or Ankara as a hub.

Turkish Air has contracts with American and United, and a round trip from New York with a stay of less than one month costs $740 in the high season, $690 in the low. West Coast departures cost an extra $400.

Buses and dolmuş run regularly between the airport and the main bus station (otogar), costing 40¢. Ask for the airport bus *("Hava'alani otobus nerede?")*. Taxis to Kaleiçi cost roughly $10, although the better hotels will of course arrange transport. Turkish Airlines runs a shuttle service between its office on Cumhuriet Cad. near the tourism information office and the airport. For more information, contact **Turkish Airlines**, *Cumhuriet Cd. Özel Idare ışhanı Altı, Tel. 242 243 4383.*

### By Boat

A ferry leaves Antalya's main Konyaaltı harbor bound for Venice on Wednesdays at noon. Book well ahead; see Chapter 6, *Planning Your Trip*, Getting Around Turkey section.

## By Bus

Antalya's main otogar is now several kilometers distant from the Kaleiçi district on Kazim Özalp Caddesi. The major companies (Kamil Koç, Ulusoy, and Varan) are represented, as are a handful of smaller competitors. There is service to almost every major city in Turkey. Kamil Koç serves the Lycian coast to the west. Varan, one of Turkey's premier lines, offers non-smoking buses to and from İstanbul for $20, Ankara for $15, and Izmir for $15. Taxis into Kaleici should cost less than $8, and there is dolmuş service.

Many dolmuş pass through the otogar, but the official dolmuş station is to the east of Kaleiçi. From Kaleiçi follow Cumhuriyet/Atatürk Caddesi east to the Doğu Garaj parking lot, on your right. Some dolmuş (Serik, for instance) must be met even further down Atatürk Caddesi at the Mevlana Caddesi intersection.

## By Car

Antalya is easy to reach, since most highways terminate here.

## ORIENTATION

The city is laid out along the clifftop, sprawling east to west. To reach Kaleiçi (the old city) follow signs directing you toward Kaleiçi or "Liman."

Antalya is a base from which to see nearby ruins, but its own are not particularly compelling. They are worth appreciating on your inevitable way past. The major ruins of Selge, Aspendos, Sillion, Aspendos and Termessos are listed below in *Seeing the Sights*.

The **tourism information** office is on the main waterfront road, three blocks west of Kaleiçi, *Cumhuriyet Caddesi, Tel. 242 247 0541*.

## WHERE TO STAY

Antalya's hotel selection is wonderful. The following pensions and hotels are within the maze of Antalya's old city, **Kaleiçi**. The Historic Preservation Society and the Turkish Touring and Automobile Association have conspired to bar development of new buildings in the area, so the thicket of charming 100 and 200 year old patios and compounds is safe, although the infusion of tourist dollars into this fascinating neighborhood has ensured that most of the houses are being converted into pensions, restaurants, and hotels.

Rates given are for the high season and are typically one-third lower in the fall and spring, and can drop dramatically in the winter. Rates and seasons are typically set by the municipality, so haggling is not technically necessary – but it always helps. Breakfast is usually included.

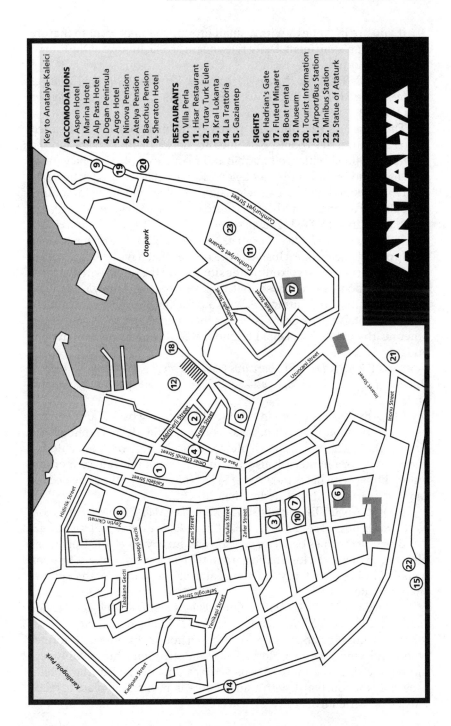

# ANTALYA

**Key to Antalya-Kaleici**

**ACCOMODATIONS**
1. Aspen Hotel
2. Marina Hotel
3. Alp Pasa Hotel
4. Dogan Peninsula
5. Argos Hotel
6. Ninova Pension
7. Atelya Pension
8. Bacchus Pension
9. Sheraton Hotel

**RESTAURANTS**
10. Villa Perla
11. Hisar Restaurant
12. Tutav Turk Eulen
13. Kral Lokanta
14. La Trattoria
15. Gaziantep

**SIGHTS**
16. Hadrian's Gate
17. Fluted Minaret
18. Boat rental
19. Museum
20. Tourist Information
21. Airport/Bus Station
22. Minibus Station
23. Statue of Ataturk

If you are in Antalya with a small group, you may want to inquire into renting an apartment. Daily rates begin at $35. Inquire at the tourist information office.

**1. ASPEN HOTEL**, *Kaleiçi Mermerli Sok. Turizm Müdürlüğü Yani 16-18, Kaleiçi, Antalya, Tel. 242 247 0590, Fax 242 241 3364. Rooms: 40. Double: $105.*

The Aspen is exceptionally pretty, with marvelously landscaped patios and attractive rooms. Balconies are decked with flowers and the gardens are filled with aged marble and manicured plants. The view is excellent, and includes the bay below. Rooms 106-110 are particularly pretty. All rooms have satellite television, minibar, and air conditioning.

Selected as one of our best places to stay – see Chapter 10.

**2. MARINA HOTEL**, *Mermerli Sok. No. 15, Kaleiçi, Antalya, Tel. 242 247 5490, Fax 242 241 1765. Rooms: 42. Double: $125-$80. Restaurant.*

Probably the most exclusive of the houses that have been converted to hotels. Prices vary according to the situation of the room, with the most expensive rooms being those that look out on the Antalya Bay. The Marina's courtyard is attractive, with a pool and the mother of all date palms in Antalya. The decor is busier than the Aspen and some of the other nearby hotels. The Dom Perignon, at $290, may put a dent in your budget.

**3. ALP PAŞA HOTEL**, *Barbaros Mah., Hesapçi Sok. No. 30-32, Kaleiçi, Antalya, Tel. 242 247 5676, Fax 242 248 5074. $50, $68, $80 double. Restaurant.*

The Alp Paşa is housed in two buildings dating back 200 years, but its transformation into a hotel was completed in 1995. The hotel has simple, classy charm, attractive tilework, nicely crafted wooden floors, and the A list of amenities. It also has a boutique pool and an oxymoronic buffet dinner with black tie service ($11). Note: keep your eye peeled for "surprise service," duly listed in their brochure.

**4. DOĞAN OTEL & PANSION**, *Kılıçaslan Mah. Mermerli Banyo Sok. No. 5., Kaleiçi, Tel. 242 241 8842, Fax 242 247 4006. Rooms: 30. Double: $42.*

Blurring the lines between pension and luxury hotel, the Doğan has pleasant rooms and a lush patio garden with cascading water. The pool, installed in 1996, is a fairly functional alternative to most of the kidney-shapes in the area.

**5. ARGOS HOTEL**, *Atatürk Orta Okulu Karşısı, Kaleiçi, Tel. 242 247 2012, Fax 242 241 7557. Rooms: 15. Double: $125-$80. Restaurant.*

The Argos is an appealing old Ottoman house, restored to its former wood and white painted glory. The standard rooms are notably less impressive than the more expensive ones, but the rest of the hotel – especially the courtyard, with a small pool – is an excellent place to relax. Particularly friendly service.

**6. NINOVA PENSION**, *Barbaros Mah. Hamit Efendi Sok. No. 9, Kaleiçi, Tel. 242 248 6114, Fax (İstanbul) 216 352 0479. Rooms: $19. Double: $35.*

This spacious old house has high ceilings, wood floors, and a large, peaceful garden. A wonderful place to return to after a day searing on the beach or at the ruins.

**7. ATELYA PANSIYON**, *Barbaros Mah. Civelek Sok. No. 21, Kaleiçi, Tel. 242 241 6416, Fax 242 241 2848. Rooms: 16. Double: $30.*

The Atelya has high ceilings, wood floors, shower in every room, and a large patio garden; it's just another of Kaleiçi's perfect, clean little pensions.

**8. BACCHUS PENSION**, *Kılıçaslan Mah. Zeytin Çikmazı Sok. No. 6, Kaleiçi, Tel. 242 243 5092, Fax 242 241 6941. Rooms: 14. Double: $17.*

The Bacchus Pension is Antalya's best budget alternative. The rooms are clean and appealing, the sitting areas are pleasant, and there is even a good terrace on the roof. The owner, Celil, speaks good English. And yes, fittingly, the Bacchus has wine.

**9. SHERATON VOYAGER ANTALYA**, *100 Yıl Bulvarı, Antalya, Tel. 242 243 2432, Fax 242 243 2462. Rooms: 400. Double: $195-$170. Restaurants.*

Many giant hotels deteriorate rapidly and pitifully. A select few escape that fate. The Sheraton, an Antalya institution, is taking the latter course. The grounds are a bucolic pleasure, the rooms are done to a tee, service is engaging, and you'll often find a rose or some Turkish Delight in your room at the end of the day. Five star "full service" hotels are springing up in bunches, but few are done with the precision and evident care taken with the Sheraton.

If it seems we are biased against large hotels, we are. Typically guests at such hotels discover a raft of silly indignities that include indifferent service and extra charges for the health club, hamam, or fresh squeezed orange juice. The Sheraton carefully avoids the appearance of parsimony, although you'll still pay a fee for the squash or tennis courts, and outside phone calls are, as usual, staggeringly expensive. Note that room prices are always negotiable by fax beforehand, and published rates drop to $155-$130 in the off season.

The hotel is located atop Antalya's waterfront cliffs, with dedicated park and convention center land to one side and Antalya's outdoor sports facilities behind it. The acclaimed Antalya Archaeological Museum is just a short walk away. The location leaves plenty of room to run or stroll and watch the sun set. The Sheraton even has a story; it was the brainchild of Del Monte tycoon Asıl Nadir. While the hotel was being built, fortune turned on Nadir and his empire collapsed. He left England just prior to being nabbed by British police for shady financial undertakings and returned to his native Northern Cyprus. Since Cyprus does not have relations with Britain, he cannot be extradited so long as he remains in Cyprus – meaning that the man who built the hotel is prevented from viewing it – let alone staying here.

## In Belek
**IBEROTEL BELPARK PALACE**, *PK 37 Belek-Serik, Antalya, Tel. 242 715 1300, Fax 242 715 1317. Rooms: 160. Double: $140.*

A full service hotel on the beach at Belek, east of Antalya. Iberotels are good, reliable holiday alternatives, with satellite television inside and lots of athletic pursuits outside. Half board arrangements are standard.

## WHERE TO EAT

Predictably, the critical mass of foreigners in the Kaleiçi area has led to the development of good restaurants. Many of Kaleiçi's hotels have restaurants, and though we only mention Villa Perla below, we have found most to be very good. In addition to the high quality restaurants there are many places serving cheap, fresh squeezed orange juice and small stores selling a delicious array of fruit preserves.

**10. VILLA PERLA**, *Barbaros Mah., Hesapci Sok. No. 26, Kaleiçi, Antalya, Tel. 242 248 9793, Fax 242 241 2917.*

The Villa Perla was opened by the matron in 1990 based on her experience during years of guiding Italian tourists. Bad experiences with local eateries led her to establish her own restaurant featuring traditional Turkish cuisine, and the painstakingly prepared dishes include mezes (appetizers), grills, and kebaps done up with the attention to detail of a Turkish mother with Italian culinary skills riding herd on an excellent chef. About 90 percent of the dishes here are vegetarian. The restaurant (and a pleasant 11-room hotel) happens to be in the former Italian embassy. The Italians picked this out of all the houses in Kaleiçi, and they knew Antalya well – it was their provincial seat during Italy's brief reign in the region following the partition of WW I.

**11. HİSAR RESTAURANT**, *Cumhuriet Alanı, Kaleiçi, Antalya, Tel. 242 241 5281. Moderate.*

The Hisar has one of the most remarkable settings in Antalya, near the Atatürk Statue. The Hisar is alongside the Tophane tea gardens and has a commanding view of the harbor. The food is a very good collection of seafood and Turkish staples.

**12. TUTAV TÜRK EVI**, *Mermerli Sok. No. 2, Kaleiçi, Antalya, Tel. 242 248 6591. Expensive.*

Alongside the Tutav Türk Evi Hotel are its Pink House and Green House restaurants and the Kale Bar. All of these are slightly full of themselves, but the location atop the Kaleiçi battlements shouldn't be missed. The restaurants have a beautiful view out over the harbor and are very popular on summer evengings. Meals and drinks are not as expensive as you might expect, with entrees costing about $8 and a beer $2.

**13. KRAL SOFRASI**, *Kaleiçi, Antalya, Tel. 242 241 2198. Moderate-Expensive.*

Kral has long been a reliable dining option, depending as much on delicious food as its harbor-view balcony. The service, food, and setting are excellent.

**14. LA TRATTORIA**, *Fevzi Çakmak Caddesi No. 3C, Antalya, Tel. 242 243 3931. Moderate-Expensive.*

A pretty restaurant, but it is the fine Italian food that makes this restaurant tick. Some excellent seafood pasta dishes.

**15. GAZIANTEP**, *Balbey Mah. 410 Sok. No. 4, Bazaar, Antalya, Tel. 242 241 7121. Moderate.*

Akin to Haji Abdullah's in İstanbul, Gaziantep offers excellent Turkish cuisine in a family atmosphere.

## SEEING THE SIGHTS

The maze of Antalya's **Kaleiçi** district is enjoyable to wander in, and since you'll lose your hotel a few times you *will* wander here. The yacht marina is pretty, as are the parks that line almost the entire length of Antalya's clifftop waterfront.

At the northeast boundary of Kaleiçi is **Hadrian's Gate**. Most cities in Asia Minor commemorated the visit of Roman Emperor Hadrian (130 A.D.), and Antalya was no different. The gate is one of the only residual elements from the ancient city. The triple arcade marble gate has been restored and is in good condition. Another old structure is the **Hıdırlık Kulesi**, a cylindrical tower on the clifftop overlooking the bay just south of Kaleiçi in the Karaalioğlu municipal park. The building dates to the second century A.D., but its use is unknown; it was probably a watch tower or a tomb. The park is a good place to wander on warm evenings.

Other historic elements of the town are more recent. Antalya's signature **Fluted Minaret** (Yıvlı Minare) dates to the Selçuk occupation, and was erected in 1230. This minaret is located on the northwestern outskirts of the Kaleiçi district, and is visible from afar. The minaret was originally attached to a converted Byzantine church, but it is all that remains of the original structure.

Near the fluted minaret in the park above the yacht harbor is the **Atatürk Statue**, in which Atatürk is depicted on a wildly rearing horse amid a crowd of youths.

The most impressive historical sights in Antalya are housed in the **Antalya Museum** (closed Mondays, $3.50), which has a beautifully organized and presented collection from throughout the region. We highly recommend setting aside half of a day for a visit here. You will appreciate the information in the exhibits here during excursions to nearby ruins, and the education goes down easily with the pleasure of seeing a marvelous collection of sculpture. Highlights include a room with statues of Greek and Egyptian gods, from Athena to Zeus; a register explains their roles and powers. An inscribed chunk of Saint Nicholas' skull is also on hand.

A relatively new addition is a stern rebuke to the Museum of Fine Arts in Boston in the front court. There, the bottom half of a statue is displayed, together with a photograph of the perfectly matching upper half now on display at the American museum. Turkey continues to be burned by thievery of antiquities, and is understandably outraged when a respectable foreign museum benefits from the practice. The museum is a long walk or a short cab ride from the Kaleiçi along the waterfront road, Cumhuriet Cadessi.

## SPORTS & RECREATION
### Beaches
The long band of **Konyaaltı Beach** joins Antalya to the resort areas in the west, and the better **Lara Beach** is located to the east. Dolmuş and buses travel to both.

### Boating
A boat tour out of Antalya is enjoyable – although perhaps redundant if you've already had the good fortune to have a gulet cruise. Particular companies are as evanescent as their reputation, so the best policy is to get a personal recommendation: Regatta and Dragon are recommended *against*. The Kaleiçi harbor is filled with tour boats and their touts.

Itineraries vary little: a five hour tour will usually include a short sail out to **Rat Island**, where pirates once holed up. Your day is divided between swimming and some mild sightseeing at the island. Lunch is served. The cost is about $14 per person, but you can do better. Another destination is the **Lower Duden waterfalls**, a shorter trip.

### Golf
The **National Golf Club**, *Tel. 242 725 4620, Fax 242 725 4624*, is located in Belek, one half hour east of Antalya. The course has an 18 hole championship course and a nine hole par 3 course, as well as a driving range.

**Rafting/Canyoning**

Several companies lead guided rafting tours down the lower Köprüçay (Eurymedon) River, and **Get Wet** *(in Side, Tel. 242 753 4071, Fax 242 753 4073)* is a local favorite. The same company offers "canyoning" day trips through a steep, beautiful gorge east of Side, allowing you to swim, jump, and clamber your way down. Highly recommended. You can take a 50 minute bus ride to Side to join the tour before its 9 a.m. departure or, better, drive to the staging area by 11 a.m. Make reservations at least one day ahead, or make arrangements through National, Tantur, or Robinson Club tours.

**Medraft Tours**, *Konyaaltı Cad. Derya Apt. No. 68-16, Antalya, Tel. 242 248 0083, Fax 242 Tel. 242 7118*, runs the best trip of the lot, a half day visit to the distant ruins of Selge combined with a half day descent down the Köprüçay River by raft. Medraft. Medraft Tours and **Parkur Turizm**, *Kemer, Antalya, Tel. 242 814 4823, Fax 242 814 4824*, run excellent adventure tours around Antalya, the former with Side as its main base, the latter based in Kemer.

## SHOPPING

Antalya's **Bazaar** is just outside the Kaleiçi area in the direction of the otogar. Antalya has a slew of international retailers, including Benetton and Ralph Lauren in addition to the regular assortment of shops selling leather, carpets, and other Turkish goods.

## EXCURSIONS & DAY TRIPS

Using Antalya as a base you can see three of the following ruins in a day – Aspendos, Sillion, and Perge. Selge and Termessos pose the biggest problems, accounting for almost a day each.

### Perge

**Perge** sprawls through a plain between two high hills. One of the hills once held the former acropolis; that is gone, but most of the city's public buildings remain. Perge is the closest and most convenient ruin to Antalya.

Perge is the easiest of the ruins in the Antalya area to see. If you're driving, follow the main coast road (E400) east out of Antalya to Aksu, 13 kilometers on. Just after entering Aksu from Antalya look for a sign directing you left to Perge, one mile off the main road.

Dolmuş and normal buses serve Aksu en route to cities further east. Aksu buses depart from the main otogar, and are the best option; dolmuş do a broad circuit around the center of town, meaning a long walk east on Cumhuriet Caddesi to Doğu Garaj or the Mevlana Caddesi intersection.

## History

Until the upstart Antalya came along in the second century, Perge was the first major city east of the **Lycian Mountains**. Owing to its (former) coastal location and its position near the Cestrus River (Aksu Çay), trade funneled through the area and it was already established at the time of the **Trojan War**. Hittite records mention a city called Parha on the Kashtraha River, which seems a match for Perge on the Cestrus. Then as now, Antalya probably produced an abundance of crops, including citrus.

Perge did not enjoy the defensive advantages of its truculent neighbors Termessus and Sillion, nor did it share Aspendos' bad judgment; when **Alexander** arrived in 333 B.C., Perge welcomed him, appointing guides and whatever assistance he asked. Alexander moved on quickly, ensuring his flank was secure before continuing north and east to confront the retreating Persians, but in the aftermath Perge's position among the Pamphlian cities was elevated. Following Alexander's death, Perge passed back and forth between all of the principal rivals for Alexander's Empire, but after Pergamon and Rome united to defeat the Seleucids in 188 B.C., the kingdom spawned by Lysimachos, Pergamon, won control of the city.

Even at this time, the port at Side was considered much superior to Perge's shallow bay. King Attalus II of Pergamon, clearly dissatisfied with Perge's diminishing value as a port, sought to establish his own port city, Attaleia, modern Antalya, in 160 B.C. This nearby city would eventually supplant Perge, but not for centuries. The Roman period burdened the town with some inept and corrupt governors, but was generally a time of prosperity. In the first century Perge reached its greatest extent, a population of 100,000.

Among Perge's advantages over the upstart Antalya was a renowned **Temple of Artemis**. This temple, mentioned in Strabo's *Geography* and on inscriptions still at the site (search through the tumbled inscriptions inside the pylons of the Hellenistic gates), has not been located. It may have been dismantled and scattered by especially thorough Christians.

Two large basilicas at Perge establish that the city was still powerful into the fifth century B.C., but the one-two punch of siltation and a new rival with a superior bay eventually sent Perge into decline. The city's great arcades and lanes have become the province of goatherds.

## Visiting the Ruins of Perge

As with so many cities that once were built on the ancient shore, Perge can be hard to envision. Upon arrival clamber up the **theater** (if restoration work is complete). When it was built, the theater would have looked directly out over the sea, which continued on around the acropolis hill to the left, on the far side of the ruins. The course of walls remains in good shape, excluding the theater and stadium just below, but including everything north of the parking lot, including the acropolis hill.

The ticket booth is by the parking lot beyond the theater. Admission costs $3. The necropolis is outside of the city proper east of the parking lot. Just before entering the city, the tomb of **Plancia Magna** is to the right. Plancia Magna was a wealthy priestess of Artemis who contributed generously to buildings and statues in Perge – you will find inscriptions of her name here and at the Antalya Museum. Continuing now through the outer gate you enter a great paved area with a variety of levels; this was the site of the **baths**, which began at the frigidarium, progressed to the tepidarium, and ended in the hot water of the caldarium. The scale of these baths is impressive.

Two great rounded pylons constitute the inner, older gate. This **Hellenistic Gate** was rendered into a pretty municipal centerpiece by the aforementioned Plancia Magna after the outer gates were erected. The semicircular court with its twelve niches and two smaller niches honored many of the city's great men, including some members of Plancia Magna's own family (M. Plancius Varus and C. Plancius Varus) and the irrepressible **Mopsus and Calchas**, who were a sort of Homeric Rosencrantz and Guildenstern, members of the Greek army that besieged Troy. Following the war they sailed south, and many of the Mediterranean cities seized upon them to create a Homeric pedigree, when in fact Perge was already well established when the Trojan War ended. Some of the inscriptions have been replaced in their niches, with others scattered around the floor of the court.

The main marketplace is just inside the Hellenistic Gates, and a wide paved lane continues directly to the acropolis. This lane was once covered, and runs on either side of an open-air **water channel**. The details of ancient city planning are often impressive, and this is such a feature; given the area's warm summer temperatures, a colonnade with water flowing past would have been greatly appreciated by the citizens of the town. If you continue to the base of the hill, you find the water issuing from an elaborate fountain. **Cestrus**, god of the local river, probably reclined atop the fountain.

If you wish to continue to the acropolis, continue up the dirt paths behind the fountain. The acropolis' ruins are unimpressive, and defensive walls skirting the hill are not visible. Bear in mind that there are reports of snakes in the area, but they are not especially venomous. Reassuring, huh? An alternative is to wander left, west, toward another set of baths. These baths are directly at the end of one aquaduct course, and require some bushwhacking to reach.

## Aspendos

Aspendos is home to one of the world's great ancient theatres, with other ruins on the hill just above.

The route is well signed if you're driving, three miles north off the main road east of Antalya between Serik and Side. Aspendos can also be reached easily by public transport. Take a bus or dolmuş to the Serik otogar and transfer to an hourly Aspendos-bound dolmuş. Fare to Serik from Antalya or Side is $1, and the Aspendos leg is 40¢. There is also a coven of taxis waiting at the Aspendos turn-off on the main road, their meters ratcheted up full blast – no need to have them wait at the site, there are always other taxis (and the hourly Serik dolmuş) to bring you back.

You can also visit by tour. Every Antalya and Side tour company includes Aspendos in a one day trip that also includes Manavgat Falls and Perge, with average rates of about $22 and a trip to a carpet shop or jewelry store cutting deeply into your time.

### History

Aspendos is an Anatolian name, so there was probably a settlement here before the arrival of colonizing outsiders. According to an apocryphal but accepted theory, the colonizers in question were Trojans fleeing the ruin of their empire in the 13th century B.C. This theory was popular in the ancient world, where cities around the Mediterranean basin, Rome included, sought to cultivate a worthy, if revisionist, heritage by establishing roots among the Trojan heroes. If in fact the Greeks did colonize the area, it was probably already settled by Asian natives of some stripe, perhaps Hittites.

The citizens of Aspendos were not particularly good at warfare, and it's no wonder their trade routes were preyed on by the Pisidians at Termessos and Selge, but their spotty martial record is at least entertaining. The city followed the normal course in the region, falling under Lydian, then Persian, control. While still a Persian possession, Aspendos was the site of a critical battle between the Greeks and Persians. Persian King Xerxes, desperately trying to recover from the failure of his Greek invasion, gathered the remnants of his army and navy near Aspendos in 467 B.C. The Athenian navy, having won over the Lycian cities to the west, advanced eastward and descended on the Persian encampment. The naval battle went quickly and predictably to the Greek admiral Cimon, who followed up his success the same evening by outfitting his army with captured ships and uniforms and crushing the confused and demoralized Persian and Aspendian soldiers at the mouth of the river Eurymedon.

Having been thus fooled, in 333 B.C. the citizens of Aspendos sought to use some guile of their own. They made a great declaration of peace with **Alexander the Great** on his approach. Alexander accepted the terms and busied himself with the siege of Sillion to the west. Aspendos' citizenry then used the breathing space to begin fortifying and arming their city against Alexander's army. Messengers informed Alexander of the treachery, and the young general, already exasperated by the time-consuming siege of towering Sillion, marched his army back to Aspendos. The illicit building effort was unfinished, and the conqueror's unexpected arrival caused much consternation. The town fathers cowered, paid double the initial tribute, handed over hostages, and accepted a garrison.

The heavy payment aside, Aspendos' fortunes rose following Alexander's arrival in 333 B.C. Piracy blossomed along the coast, but Aspendos probably had a tidy stake in the pirating business. In fact, the Roman onslaught that finally broke local piracy (70 B.C.) had a deleterious effect on local affairs; Rome saddled Aspendos with a series of avaricious governors who famously stripped the city of its sculpture and artwork.

Aspendos remained a viable city throughout the first millenium A.D. – the theater was built in the second century A.D. – but its fortunes waned. The Byzantines had a respectable city at the site, and the ruins of a grand basilica are atop the hill behind the theater. Arab depredations finally drove the Byzantines away, and the Selçuks occupied the deteriorating city from the time of **Alaeddin Keykobad I** (1219-1236 A.D.). Under the Selçuks the long-empty theater came to life again; its stage building became headquarters for the local Selçuk governor.

### Visiting the Ruins of Aspendos

The parking lot is located directly beneath the grand Aspendos **theater**, which is the finest Roman-era theater in the world today. Unless you are in town for the June **Balat Arts Festival** (contact the Antalya Ministry of Culture for schedules, *Tel. 242 243 3810*) the sublime acoustics are squandered on foreigners hooting experimentally. The theater is like the many others in Turkey, only more complete. The statues that once lined the top of the theater are missing, as is most of the detail from the stage, but the theater is fundamentally the same as it was when it was built in the late second century A.D. during the reign of Marcus Aurelius (161-180). According to one theory, the massive theater was built to compensate for Aspendos' decline into relative unimportance.

Perhaps the most wonderful thing about Aspendos' theater is that it attracts tour groups to the exclusion of all else. The only entrance fee at Aspendos is for the theater ($4), and the rest of the site costs nothing to visit. The theater is not particularly more interesting than those at Perge, Ephesus, or elsewhere unless you have a background in Roman architecture. The gentle hill above the theater has the balance of the city's ruins. The trail begins to the right of the theater. The right fork takes you out past a sprawling temple building and continues out past several smaller structures to the old city walls, pierced in a draw by the old Northern Gate.

As at Sillion, there are several **deep cisterns** scattered around the site; be careful. To the west of the gate is the **aquaduct**, an astounding piece of engineering. The aquaduct carried water to Aspendos from the foothills to the north, delivering it in under enough pressure to supply the entire town through a long tube hollowed from pieces of stone and erected 40 feet high. The entire aquaduct structure is twice that height, even with the top of Aspendos' hill. The aquaduct's course within the city is impossible to determine.

The stadium and necropolis at the eastern foot of the hill are in bad shape, overgrown and broken.

As mentioned, the stripping of Aspendos began in 60 B.C. and has been carried on today by the world's museums. The town center offers several large, nondescript structures and the foundations of others, but the statues and ornamentation that accented Aspendos are long gone. One of the last remaining pieces of interest is a white column bearing Greek inscriptions.

## Sillion

There are three yellow signs along the main D400 road indicating Sillion. The westernmost sign takes you through Abdullah Rahman, where another sign directs you to the right toward the Sillion mesa. If you keep your eye on the imposing Sillion mesa, however, any of the occasionally confusing roads will bring you to the gravel parking area at the southern side of Sillion and the small store. If you feel lost, say *"Sillion istiyorum. Sillion nair-duh?"* (I want Sillion. Where is it?) and at least get a general point in the direction of the ruins. The roads are perfectly manageable.

Leave your car at the small refreshment stand on the southwest (Antalya, sea side) and have a look at the battered metal historical marker sign, as it is the only tourism-friendly object at the site.

No dolmuş serve this remote site, but it is less than 10 kilometers from the main road. On a Serik or Side-bound bus from Antalya ask to be dropped off at the Belek turn-off, where taxis can take you directly inland to the site. This is most sensible in small groups, since transport and a few hours at the sight will cost about $20 or $25.

## History

Sillion challenged **Alexander the Great** in 333 B.C., and Alexander besieged the city. The siege of towering Sillion rapidly promised to become time consuming, however, and Alexander wanted to move along. Alexander, gritting his teeth at the citizens hurling boulders down on his troops and dancing mockingly atop the outcrop, eventually withdrew to Aspendos. As a result, it is one of the few places to have successfully held its own against the conqueror.

Sillion emerged from obscurity during Alexander's campaign only to lapse back into obscurity once again. How earlier and later conquerors dealt with the city is unknown – probably in much the same way Alexander did, cutting it off and letting it fall in good time of its own accord. It was always associated with Perge, even claiming the same legendary and fabricated founder, Mopsus. Both the Byzantines and the Selçuks maintained garrisons here, and some of the ruins are of their creation.

## Visiting the Ruins of Sillion

Reaching the top of Sillion requires a 30 minute climb from the valley floor to the top, plus exploration time. Allow yourself three hours at the site. To reach the top either rent a lad to show you the way or follow the path that meanders gradually upwards to the right of the mesa, cutting back up past a spring. You can reach the top by a fairly direct route up this south side, or follow the old road as it climbs the west (left) side of the mesa and doubles back. As at most sites, try to be here before the heat of the day. You are likely to have Sillion virtually to yourself.

Sillion's ruins are curious. After passing the outer ramparts and checkpoints and scrambling to the top, you'll find yourself in heavy undergrowth with walls and buildings poking out. It's a disorienting place, so get your bearings to assure a swift and hassle-free descent.

The first reward for the sweaty hike up the ridge into Sillion is appreciation for Alexander's frustration. The city was perfectly defensible with strong walls augmenting the sheer rock faces. The remaining rewards are for determined bushwhackers, because the upper area of Sillion is thick with underbrush. First, work your way into the middle of the city, behind the great Hellenistic walls, and poke around for a stone doorway. Here, on the inside of a door jamb, is the longest example of the undeciphered Pamphlian writing. It has been partially destroyed by a deep rectangular hole cut into the jamb, and was apparently recycled as a door jamb after a more dignified role elsewhere.

Continue past the old Hellenistic walls to the southern edge of the mesa. Be careful: Sillion's upper level is pocked with **deep cisterns**, and their flared openings are convenient for falling through and inconvenient for escape. To the southwest is Sillion's **theater**. The theater was built into the top of the hill, but its lower sections have toppled away, crashing to the earth hundreds of feet below. Only the upper rows of the theater remain, and all the world is its stage.

Beyond this, further along the southern edge, are several small buildings and a number of deep fissures. The most intriguing of these fissures is located just in front of a temple structure, separating the temple from the main body of Sillion. There is a small Hellenistic bridge spanning the narrow chasm. The fissure itself may have once had a sheer, **secret path** winding down to the valley floor. This is partially supported by a tunnel sunk into the earth below the city in the neighborhood of the fissure's opening. The path, if it was indeed a path, is no longer suited for any traffic whatsoever; a treacherous jumble of fallen stone that appears blocked near the bottom. The temple itself is constructed of both blocks of stone and living rock, but there is no indication of its denomination. At the far eastern edge of Sillion is a tower with a predictably magnificent view of the Pamphlian plain below.

The aforementioned tunnel requires effort and determination to reach. After descending from the top, circle back around to the left by whatever paths you can find. The explorer George Bean describes the tunnel, which he speculated to be a water channel, as two feet wide and 75 feet long, with several rooms at the end. Bean visited the site about 30 years ago, and we have yet to locate it ourselves, but we wish anyone intrepid enough the best of luck.

## Selge

This remote city is difficult to reach, but rewarding for those who persevere. The site is high in the mountains above the **Köprüçay River**, surrounded by cedar forests and stone that bears a resemblance to the bizarre landscape of the Cappadoccian interior. The ruins are at an elevation of 3,000 feet, and get only determined visitors; their inaccessibility has helped preserve them from museum-funded depredation. Plan on spending more than three hours at the site; take a lunch along, a sweater for the altitude, and, as always, lots of fluid.

If you're driving, turn off the main E400 road five kilometers east of the Aspendos turn off, passing through Taşağıl to Beşkonak, 37 kilometers inland. Ignore the first set of Selge signs, continuing to Beşkonak and then a further 18 kilometers to Selge, following the signs to Altınkaya/Zerk. Six kilometers beyond Beşkonak turn left at the Altinkaya sign, cross the bridge, and follow the road right and up the final gravelled 11 kilometers.

Dolmuş serve Beşkonak, but from that remote town you must cross the Köprüçay River and ascend another 18 kilometers. There are a few taxis in Beşkonak willing to shuttle you to the site for a flat fee, but it begins making more sense to arrange a full day ruins excursion unless you really want to see the ruins on your own. Anyway, you begin to understand why invaders like Pergamon's Attalus II usually gave up.

## History

Oddly, the residents of Selge had a running feud with their equally inaccessible and recalcitrant western neighbors, the residents of **Termessos**. Why the two fairly distant cities came into conflict is un- known – perhaps over control of the mountainous interior in between – but their antipathy was evident whenever a third party invader would march on either one of the cities. When Alexander besieged Termessos the people of Selge dropped what they were doing and raced to his assistance. After Alexander abandoned the siege, the people of Selge were only too happy to lead him against another of their Pisidian allies, Sagalassus. The Termessans, for their part, were happy to return the favor when Selge provoked Attalus II to attempt an invasion.

Both cities succeeded in resisting these and countless other sieges, and Selge was ordinarily left alone in its lofty perch. During the prosper- ous early Roman years, an estimated 20,000 people lived in this town, a seemingly remarkable number for so inhospitable a site, but the citizens traded heavily in wine, olives, livestock, and a local perfume made with the resin of the styrax bush. The trade augmented the toll business, but in time the trade routes shifted (and perfume tastes changed) and Selge's importance waned. Selge, initially ranked behind only Side in the esteem of the Byzantine Empire's Mediterranean bishoprics, dropped quickly out of sight in the 400s.

## Visiting the Ruins of Selge

Selge is notable for the beauty of its situation, as you begin to understand on the long, winding ascent to the old city. The deep gorges and peculiarly weathered stone are blanketed with coastal cedars in the lower climes, then heartier pines – and light-hued styrax bushes – at the higher elevations. The old Roman bridge that you cross on your ascent has given its name to the former Eurymedon River; Köprüçay, or "Bridge River."

Selge is built in the heights above Zerk, where the road terminates. The theater, facing you, initially dominates the ruins. This theater has a predictably excellent view, and may have been large enough to hold half of Selge's Roman-era population, 10,000. At the foot of the theatre is the large market square, or **agora**, while to the south – the right as you look out from the theater – a long **stadium** runs in the direction of the slope and the city walls. The ancient town occupies the high ground south of Zerk, and is ringed by a wall.

The walls, mostly broken or borrowed on the Zerk side, are in good condition on the far side of the slope, on the southern face of the hill. A necropolis is located in the section of town just above the theater, with another necropolis on the eastern spur. Some of the stones bear inscriptions in Pisidian. The city's truly dominant feature is the **Temple of Zeus** standing on a spur above the rest of the town, in what amounts to Selge's acropolis.

## Termessos

Termessos is not an easy ruin, requiring a hike and patient investigation through thick undergrowth, but it is extremely rewarding.

By car, follow the main highway north (650) from Antalya toward Isparta, turning right at the Korkuteli turnoff (E87). Some 25 kilometers along you will see the entrance to **Güllükdağı Milli Parkı**, at which you pay an entrance fee (at a place corresponding closely to the former Termessan toll site), and continue nine kilometers to Termessos. If you've arrived with a car, it's worth the trouble to drop in at the **Karain Caves**, the spot with the oldest evidence of human civilization in Turkey. Material found in the caves dates to the Paleolithic Age, before 10,000 B.C., and it may have also been the site of religious ceremonies in Hellenistic times. The caves are seven kilometers off of the Korkuteli road (E87) opposite and just east of the Güllükdağı/Termessos turnoff.

By public transportion, it's more tricky. Take a Korkuteli dolmuş and ask to be dropped off at the Termessos intersection, at the entrance to Güllükdağı Milli Parkı. In summer you should find taxis waiting to shuttle you the nine kilometers to Termessos for $5. In the off-season be content with collecting enough people for a taxi from Antalya to the site – $50 total, or stick with the guided tours. You can hazard the dolmuş to the gate, still, but you may have to hitch to the site.

### History

The **Solymi**, as the people of Termessos called themselves, had a unique reputation for skill at warfare from an early date. They crept into Homer's tale of Bellerophon as the indomitable warriors against whom the young hero is sent to battle (Bellerophon, of course, gets the better of them by hurling rocks down from soaring Pegasus). Homer's tale dates to the eighth century B.C., but the martial skill he immortalized was still in evidence many centuries later, as when, in 333 B.C., Alexander uncharacteristically called off a siege here.

Termessos was one of two cities in Turkey to repel **Alexander the Great**, and, unlike his abortive siege of Sillion, Alexander had time to make a game attempt. Alexander even had the eager assistance from the people of distant Selge, who saw his arrival as an excellent opportunity to settle an old score with Termessos, their fellow Pisidians. Arrian, chronicling the campaign of Alexander, mentions a skirmish at the site, Alexander's encampment outside the walls, and the arrival of fresh troops from Selge anxious to besiege the city; then, after all of this, Arrian breezily says that Alexander marched on to Sagalassus.

Termessos eventually came around on its own, cooperating with the world Alexander had recast. Soon after Alexander's death, **Alcetas**, one of Alexander's infantry generals, withdrew here after suffering a shattering defeat at the hands of Antigonus. Alcetas, one of the many men who made a bid for parts of Alexander's empire, was welcomed here, and the city endured a siege by Antigonus. With the siege stalled, Antigonus coerced a group of older Termessans to assassinate Alcetas, which they did while the younger Termessans who supported the general were fighting outside the city walls. In the aftermath the younger Termessans began to destroy their own city, later relenting and giving Alcetas a suitable burial in an elaborate tomb. Some suspect that his tomb is the one located on the western wall of the valley above the colonnaded street.

The Termessans continued to rely on their ability to withdraw behind their natural defenses. They were at war with the entire Lycian League at the end of the third century B.C., a war that the Lycians never chose to prosecute to the extent of a siege. Termessos was often at odds with its neighbors, and even in times of relative peace the ongoing feud with the people of Selge was simmering. Roman administrators seem to have sized up the situation quickly, leaving the city an unusual degree of autonomy and partial exemption from taxes.

Termessos is clearly defensible, but the visitor must wonder how the natives supported themselves. The answer appears to be through **tolls** levied on the Korkuteli road, which was heavily trafficked owing to the difficulties of the Lycian coast. The city faded in the third century A.D., never to regain its former power.

### Visiting the Ruins of Termessos

Termessos is a beautiful ruin, thickly overgrown with shrubs and trees. Its distance from the sea probably spared it much of the archaeological depredation that has stripped other sites in Turkey.

The parking lot is located one half mile below the town. The **Propylon of Hadrian**, a grand entrance gate to a temple, is dedicated to the

Emperor Hadrian, whose second century B.C. whirlwind tour of his empire is commemorated in many ancient cities. You can enter Termessos the same way people entered – or tried to enter – the city for millenia, following the King's Road through the cleft between two high hills. This approach gives you some appreciation of the site's defensive advantages.

As you approach the site you see the former guard tower designed to alert the Termessans of approaching danger. At the entrance to the outer fortification wall, inscribed on the inside of the gateway is a **dice oracle**. No hurly burly of secret ceremonies and rites here; roll the dice and read the corresponding fortune (whose translations are suspiciously like those of Sidney Omarr or Jeanne Dixon). After climbing the path, the valley opens onto Termessos itself, a dense, picturesque ruin that was a suitable home to a fiercely independent people.

The town is littered with interesting sites, most of which are well-signed. The **theater**, with its stunning view of **Güllük Dağı** (Mt. Solymos) above, remains in fine shape. The stage area was the site of some late remodeling so that wild animals could be released and slaughtered without danger of the animals dragging audience members from their seats. This theater, with a capacity of no more than 5,000, was a relatively minor venue for the brutal entertainment of the time.

## SOUTH FROM EPHESUS

*"Bestiarii, the professional slaughterers, fought lions and tigers, bears and bulls, but these as often fought each other, or alligators, or hippopotami (imagine the time that it takes for a great defenceless hippo to die, for no big cat could throttle it or break its neck, and only shock and exsanguination would bring it mercy as small parcels of flesh were torn from it under the leather hide), or slew a host of such defenceless creatures as deer, giraffes and ostriches. Suetonius noted with seeming pleasure the death of 5,000 animals in one day at the inauguration of the Roman Colosseum, and Trajan saw 3,000 slaughtered in two days; even if these great numbers died only on Imperial occasions, and the ordinary venatio accounted for comparatively few, those smaller figures must be multiplied by the number of theatres spread across the Empire, and the frequency of the occasions; scale too must have had its effect, for there would be little point in filling the great circus of El Djem in Tunisia for the death of a single ostrich, though it might have made a flurry in Termessos. Five centuries of slaughter wiped out the Caspian tiger, the Assyrian lion, and the Numidian forest elephant – the tough pygmy that carried Hannibal over the Alps."*

*—Brian Sewell,* South from Ephesus; Travels in Aegean Turkey, *1988, Arrow Books Limited.*

The tomb of Alcetas is located at the top of an overgrown trail on the northwest wall of the valley. The trail veers off from near the Agora, or marketplace, winding up the side of the valley. Alcetas' cave tomb remains in good shape, and you can see the details; shelves, for instance, to take along knick knacks into the afterlife. The fading depiction of a soldier on horseback at the entrance is inconsistent with Alcetas' career as an infantry general, but the tomb is probably his, anyway.

More tombs, lids askew and stone surfaces rent and cracked, are located in the upper necropolis at the top of the path that climbs past the theater. This upper area has a fine view over the foothills below, with a Biblically melodramatic foreground of broken sarcophagi.

## KONYA

The southern interior rises steeply away from the sea, giving way to a section of Anatolia that has evidence of the earliest moments in human civilization.

Konya is an oasis breaking the monotony of the Anatolian plateau. The city has prospered since ancient times, and was called **Iconium** under the Romans. The vestiges of Hellenistic and Roman times are gone now, replaced by a serene Central Asian character that stems from when the Selçuks made the city their capital. The cool blue and green tiles of the holy places, the precise stonework of old facades, and the strong religious belief of Konya's people contribute to a feeling that is unique in western Turkey.

### History

Konya was inhabited before 3000 B.C. by people living on Alaeddin Tepesi, the site of today's Alaeddin Camii and the former palace of the Sultanate of Rum. Konya's early history is fragmentary, but the town changed hands repeatedly, falling under Hittite dominion, then passing to the Phrygians, who were defeated by the Lydians, who were themselves defeated by the Persians in 546 B.C. The subsequent centuries were full of such monotonous activity; even Alexander thought the story was tired in 333 B.C., skipping past the city and leaving it unmolested. Rome brought respite from the repeated invasions, but the peace was similarly dull; whatever empire controlled Konya, the city's lot was the same, a trading post on the road to somewhere better.

Konya's long slumber ended with the appearance of the Turks, when the Selçuks established their capital here after defeating the Byzantines at the **Battle of Manzikert** in 1071. The Selçuks held the city in great esteem, founding here the Sultanate of Rum, as the Selçuk kingdom was known. The kingdom suffered growing pains as the Byzantines and the Crusaders, not to mention rival Muslim forces, sought to bring it down. Still, the Selçuks put their stamp on the region, and the city itself, with mosques and public buildings of intricate beauty.

The high water mark of the Sultanate was under **Sultan Alaeddin Keykobad** (1219-1237), who ringed the city with new defensive walls and buildings. During this period it could fairly be said that the Sultanate of Rum, with its great respect for learning and science, was one of the few bright spots in a world gone dark. It was not to last. In the years before Alaeddin's death, the Selçuks, once invaders themselves, faced the first motley bands of Mongols out of the east, like the first drops of rain.

The Selçuks began bracing for the storm that was certain to come; in 1243 the Sultanate and Byzantium entered into a truce, hoping to unite in the face of the Mongol threat. Byzantine assistance did the Selçuks precious little good. Later in the same year the Mongols plowed through the Selçuks and their allies at Köse Dağı, dividing up the lands in eastern Anatolia. The loss did not cost the Sultanate of Rum its capital city, which remained under Selçuk control, but the Selçuks were forced to seek an expensive peace.

The Sultanate remained on the brink of collapse for long years afterward, eventually losing the capital, then gaining it back in 1276. The last Selçuk Sultan was killed by the Mongols in 1307. The Mongols were run off by the Karamans several years later.

Meantime, the Ottomans were blossoming while the Sultanate of Rum faded away. The Ottomans were initially established in northeastern Anatolia by the Selçuks, where Ertuğrul, father of the Ottoman dynasty, was a march lord for Alaeddin. The decay and collapse of the Selçuk Empire in the south and the rickety Byzantine Empire in the north proved the perfect climate for a young empire, and the Ottomans seized the mantle of Turkish leadership. Sultan Beyazid I brought the process full circle by taking Konya after defeating the Ottoman's great Turkish rival, the Karamans, at the **Battle of Ak Tchai** in 1393. The classic storyline was ruined, however, after Tamurlane crushed Beyazid at the Battle of Ankara.

Konya was lost, and in the chaotic aftermath the Karamans revenged themselves on Beyazid by seizing Bursa and scattering his bones to the dogs. The Ottomans did not retake Konya until 1466, 13 years after the fall of Constantinople.

## ARRIVALS & DEPARTURES

### By Bus

Most major bus companies have offices in Konya. Some rates and departure times include Izmir, 0:30, 7:30, 10 a.m., 2:30, 6:30, 11 p.m.; $11.

Ankara, hourly; $6. Antalya, 6:30, 9, 11 a.m., 12:30 p.m., midnight; $8. İstanbul, 7, 8:30, 10 a.m., 10:30, 11 p.m.; $14.

The Konya otogar is adjacent to a dolmuş stop and just a block from Konya's rail line, in the middle of the major street you arrived on. Both options cost 30¢. A taxi to the main hotel area on the far side of downtown costs $7.

**By Car**

Most travelers pass through Konya because it is on the way from Cappadoccia and Ankara to Antalya, and we're guessing you are, too. The roads are generally fine, with some rough spots on the direct Ankara-Konya route.

## ORIENTATION

The town radiates out from **Alaeddin Tepesi**, a park topped with the Alaeddin Mosque and a favorite gathering place on weekends and evenings. The rail system terminates here, and dolmuş depart from the eastern side.

## WHERE TO STAY & EAT

**HOTEL BALIKÇILAR**, *Mevlana Karsısı No. 1, Konya, Tel. 332 350 3920, Fax 332 351 3259. Rooms: 48. Double: $70.*

The hotel spends heavily on lobby and public spaces, leaving rooms a shade uninspired. Clean and well managed, with a perfect location if you don't mind Turkey's finest muezzins in the Mevlana Museum across the street. A bar? *Var* (Turkish for "yes, we have."). The terrace is directly across from the Selimiye Mosque.

**OTEL DUNDAR**, *Feritpaşa Mah. Kerkük Cad. No. 34 Konya, Tel. 332 236 1052, Fax 332 235 9130. Rooms: 106. Double: $100.*

The city's lone four star hotel, the Dundar is ambitious and hums with tour bus traffic. Everyone in town agrees its the best place, what with bidets and CNN and all, but it will age quickly.

**OTEL YENI KÖŞK**, *Yeni Aziziye Cad. Kadınlar Sok. No. 28, Tel. 332 352 0671. Rooms: 18. Double: $18.*

A relief after hunting through Konya's backstreets for a decent, cheap place to stay. The nearby Bey Otel is also a good option.

**PANSION MUSTAFA**, *Mevlana Caddesi, Bostan Çelebi Sokak No. 14, Konya, Phone/Fax 332 350 7504. Rooms: 4. Double: $10.*

Just around the corner from the information office and the Mevlana, this is a simple alternative to the uninspiring hotel selection. The pension is named after its charming proprietor, a helpful young man born in 1972 who is wed to a Scottish woman. You have free run of the kitchen, he has excellent English.

**KÖŞK LOKANTA**, *Akçesme Mahallesi, Topraklık Cad. No. 66, Konya, Tel. 332 352 8547. Inexpensive-Moderate.*

An old local home converted into Konya's most charming eatery. You enter a small garden and pass through the immaculate outer kitchen. The price has a lot to do with the charm – $5 will feed you very well – as do the wonderful borek pastries, soups, and grilled meat. No alcohol.

**OPERA RESTAURANT & BAR**, *Meram Bağları, Konya, Tel. 332 325 0009.Moderate-Expensive.*

A somewhat surprising French/Turkish restaurant in the country-side near Konya. The Opera is run out of a tall Ottoman-style house, offering good food and drinks – this is where, in a fairly dry town, you'll find oversize mai-tais and Kamikazes. The Steak Süleyman Paşa, a pepper steak, is good and inexpensive. Open year round.

## SEEING THE SIGHTS

The first time you pass Alaeddin Tepesi, if you're coming from Cappadoccia, you pass a great open dome structure. This covers part of the defensive walls of the old Selçuk palace.

Above and behind the old palace walls are a collection of çay bahçesilar, or **tea gardens**, ascending toward a structure atop the hill. This building is the **Alaeddin Mosque**, which houses a complex of tombs and former meeting areas and libraries. The interior is decorated in blue and white tile, and recent renovations have mixed new wooden roof panelling with a collection of Iconium's old Hellenistic and Roman columns.

Most of the building's redecoration has the feel of a YMCA, but there's no disguising the beautiful bones of this structure. The Selçuk's contribution included the gloriously precise **mimber**, or slender prayer platform. The tombs of the earliest sultans are in the courtyard and at the bottom of a stair; scattered around the courtyard are Meşud I, Kılıçarslan, Rukneddin Süleyman II, Giyaseddin Keyhusrev I and Alaeddin Keykobad I, Keyhusrev II, Izzeddin, Kılıçarslan IV and Keyhusrev III, the sixth to sixteenth rulers of the Sultanate of Rum (1116-1283).

On the west side of the hill, across the street, is one of the many gorgeously crafted buildings in the area, the **Ince Minare and Medresse** (Thin Minaret and School). The tall minaret is beautifully faced in yellows and blues, and the entrance to the medresse may be the best of the many exquisite portals in the city. The interior houses a collection of Selçuk carving and art. Continuing around the hill to the north you'll come to **Karatay Çini Eserler Müzesi** (Karatay Tile Museum), in which many of the best tiles are the originals still covering the walls. This is a surprisingly impressive exhibit, with hundreds of oddly shaped tiles and Escher-like patterns.

Proceeding now to the east side of the hill, head away from the hill on the main road, Alaeddin Caddesi. Many of the cities best shops and restaurants are located along this road. The eeriest place in town is hidden away a block off Alaeddin Caddesi to the left, or north. The **Türbe of Kara Aslan** crouches in the space between buildings near the Serefettin Camii. Kara Aslan, or Black Lion, was a ferocious Karaman warrior during the period that the Karamans broke the Mongol stranglehold on the area. His türbe is clearly neglected, and even used for dumping rubbish, but if you peer through the broken door you can just make out a sarcophagus decorated with stunning blue faience and, in the shadows, a dark set of antlers.

The **Selimiye Mosque** is further along, where the road curves off. The tourism information office is just to the left. The Selimiye is one of several mosques in Turkey celebrating Sultan Selim II, who was a governor here before ascending the throne. The mosque was not completed until 1587, a 29 year project from beginning to end. The mosque is imposing and pretty within, suiting this religious city, but suffers a little in comparison to Selim II's other mosque, Edirne's Selimiye. The latter building is usually cited as the greatest Ottoman architectural achievement and Sinan's piece de resistance. Selim II was an uninspired sultan, but inherited an empire at the height of its wealth and glory from his father, Süleyman the Magnificent. Mosques were built for him because there was money for such projects, not because he was particularly deserving.

Konya's great site is the **Mevlana Museum**. The museum's pacific green-blue tower is visible from a distance, directly above the tomb of one of Islam's great religious philosophers and mystics, **Celaleddin Rumi**, later known as Mevlana. Mevlana's works fill 22 volumes of poetry, and his lectures and letters form a daunting collection.

Tourists pay $1 on entering the mosque complex; Turks pay 25¢, in a clear violation of Mevlana's ecumenical teachings. You leave your shoes outside of the interior building. The tombs are located in a cluster below the ornate interior of the tiled tower. Mevlana is buried here, together with his father, wife, children, and some family friends. The interior of the museum is filled with cunningly wrought Korans, rugs, wood stools and Koran stands, and musical instruments. Some of the latter are **neys**, the reedy flutes whose whine is so appropriate and haunting within the complex or during a dervish ceremony. There is usually ney music in the background during your visit. Away from the confines of the Mevlana Museum you're unlikely to seek out ney music; it seems to be an acquired taste.

## THE FATHER OF THE DERVISHES

*Celaleddin Rumi was born on September 30th, 1207, the son of a renowned religious philosopher. The family migrated west from Afghanistan in the face of Mongol expansion, settling in Konya at the behest of Alaeddin II in 1228. Upon his father's death, Rumi assumed the role of religious teacher (Mevlana), and was soon held in the same esteem enjoyed by his father. He lived to the age of 66, his teaching corresponding to some of the most trying times in the Sultanate's short reign; the Sultanate's armies were beaten by the Mongols in 1243, the city occupied several years later.*

*Mevlana's Sufi message of dedication to Islam was tempered with a powerful message of toleration and loving one another. His teachings combined bits and pieces of familiar philosophy, but had one manifestation that was dramatically new: to this day Mevlana's most famous teaching is that an epiphany of love is possible by whirling, the left hand face down, the right hand face up. The position of the hands indicates the receiving of blessings from Heaven and the passing of those blessings along to mankind. Other teachings were more strictly ascetic, befitting a Sufi, such as 40 day periods of bread and water. In general, however, Mevlana's teaching was neither stark nor unyielding:*

*Come, come again, whoever, whatever you may be, come*
*Heathen, fire worshiper, sinner in idolatry, come*
*Come, even if you have broken penitence 100 times,*
*Ours is not the portal of despair and misery, come.*

**Dervishes** still whirl at tourist dinner places throughout the country, but they truly whirl in December in Konya. During the week leading up to the anniversary of Mevlana's December 17th death, dervishes whirl for real at a gymnasium in Konya; the former grounds are no longer large enough to accommodate their many visitors. The dance is riveting, with dervishes whirling in their snow white dresses, while a dervish master walks among them, ensuring that they are performing properly.

Before the dance, the dervishes drop their black coverings and emerge in white to whirl their way closer to God, symbolizing the abandonment of their earthly cares. Mevlana's teaching inspires deep curiosity among most people unfamiliar with it, but the good-hearted kernel of his philosophy is probably there in front of us the entire time, in the giddy whirling of the dervishes.

Konya's **Archaeological Museum** is deserving of a visit. Empires and kingdoms have littered this region with artifacts and statues for thousands of years, and Konya enjoys the spoils. The finest pieces in this interesting museum are the sarcophagi, one of which depicts Hercules performing his 12 tasks. The artistry and complexity of the sculpted exteriors is difficult to believe. In most cases, the nobles buried in this grand fashion are unknown. The museum is south of the Alaeddin hill.

## SHOPPING

Among those harmed by Konya's relegation to "lunch break" status on the standard trip itinerary are the local **kilim shops**. Shed no tears for them, they still sell plenty of kilims, but trade is down. This is good news for kilim buyers, as Konya has rich a kilim-making tradition.

We are wary of recommending carpet dealers, but if you are in the market for high quality pieces, consider trying **Ipek Yolu**, *Silk Road, Mevlana Caddesi, Bostan Sok. No. 14A, Tel. 332 352 7658*. The owner, Mehmet Uçar, exports to the United States and has a solid reputation in the business. He is among the first to return to traditional natural dyes, which yield vivid, beautiful colors. We're probably the only people who say we aren't getting a commission who really aren't.

## EXCURSIONS & DAY TRIPS

**Çatal Hüyük**, which most archaeologists take to be the oldest civilized human settlement yet discovered, is located about 55 kilometers from Konya, via Çumra in the south. The site is more significant than it is immediately gripping, but it's worth a visit.

**Gökyurt** is a rarely-visited, little known counterpart to Cappadoccia, with several elaborate churches carved from the stone. Gökyurt is near Alahan in the mountains beyond Karaman on the Silifke road.

# 18. THE LYCIAN COAST

The **Lycian Coast** extends roughly between **Phaselis** in the east and **Dalyan** in the west, encompassing some of the most remote and picturesque terrain in Turkey. Mountains rise from the sea like blades, and the rugged terrain was the last section of the Mediterranean to be pacified by the Romans. The cities in the region formed the **Lycian League**, a body led by six cities – Xanthus, Patara, Pinara, Tlos, Myra and Olympos – that now constitute the core of Turkey's most fascinating and beautiful set of ruins.

Waves of development have hit the eastern edge of the Lycian Coast, knocking the charm out of the cities near Kemer for the sake of beachfront holiday playgrounds. The World Bank has helped Turkey finance the slew of resort hotel operations here, envisioning the Turkish Riviera as a highly profitable tourism destination. The region has all of the requisite characteristics: mountains tumble directly into the sea, pine forests and fragrant flowering plants give way to long sand and pebble beaches, and of course there are ruins.

The only problem, ironically, is the intense development. The streets of Kemer resemble nothing so much as a sunny Atlantic City boardwalk. Large hotels squat behind columns and columns of beach umbrellas, and with the influx of tourists has come the inevitable wave of carpet, ceramic, and knick-knack hustlers.

There are some nice hotels in the lot, but in high season they range upwards of $100 per night. If that's a concern we recommend skipping past the hotel zone to **Çirali/Olympos**, a plummeting 6 kilometers below the main coast road. The ruins and the wraith-fire of the Chimera merit a visit to this stubbornly undeveloped oceanside village. Continuing east, the **Kaş/Kalkan** area is marvelous, offering antiquated fishing-village charm, quality lodging, and convenience to many days worth of ruins and beaches. **Patara**, too, wins a recommendation for its sleepy

atmosphere, convenience to ruins, and its boggling 16 kilometer fine sand beach. Finally, anchoring the western end of the region, **Dalyan** boasts a rich, interesting collection of ruins, baths, and beaches.

Getting around the Lycian Coast is remarkably easier than it once was, when pirates prowled the coastline and a particularly ferocious strain of Lycians, the Termessans, extorted money at the mountain passes. A winding, scenic, and well-maintained road serves the length of the coast, although it is occasionally forced miles inland by the vagaries of the local terrain. The Antalya and Dalaman airports bookend the region, through which Kamil Koç and Pamukkale buses pass several times daily.

A number of the sites in this chapter are ruins only, with very little in the way of accommodations. You can pick any number of towns for your base, with Antalya or The Olympos area your leading choices for Eastern Lycia (there's a greater range of places to stay in Western Lycia).

## EASTERN LYCIA

This region is one of Turkey's garden spots, the very place that Alexander the Great chose to settle in for the winter. Some of its character has been buried beneath walls of hotels, but some of the new hotels are all they're cracked up to be. If you want to live cheaply, keep heading west to Olympos or beyond.

## ARRIVALS & DEPARTURES

### By Bus

Buses travel between Antalya and the resort towns regularly; Kemer, for instance, is hourly in the summer. In addition, many hotels in the area offer transfers from Antalya – contact your hotel before arrival to enquire. If you are taking a bus, they depart from Antalya's otogar just north of Kaleiçi. It is a good idea to get buses directly to Kemer and Tekirova, since both are a kilometer or two off the main highway.

## WHERE TO STAY

There's little point in staying in this area unless you're going to stay at a **holiday village**. If that's your intention, you have a lot of top quality hotels to choose from. Outside of August, most of these hotels are willing and able to bargain; in the bad times four and five star hotels sell off packages of rooms for as low as $20 per, not that you will approach this figure bargaining alone. Winter rates are less than half of the high season.

Caveat Emptor: If you envision peaceful mornings with bougainvillea twined through the rails of a whitewashed hotel, the strip west of Antalya may disappoint. In place of traditional Turkish hospitality there are signs warning you against bringing food or beverages to your room. Half- and full-board accommodations are common, and the hotel will always have pet rental car and daily tour companies for getting away to the ruins (and they will be charging captive audience rates).

If you aspire to lie in the sun, swim, eat, and play – and who, really, can argue against that – then we have striven to pick out the best of the bunch.

### In Beldebi

**ANTALYA RENAISSANCE HOTEL**, *PK 654, Beldebi, Antalya, Tel. 242 824 8431, Fax 242 824 8430, North American Reservations: 1 800 HOT ELS1. Rooms: 335. Double: $170.*

A full service, five star luxury hotel offering a more refined experience than most of its jet ski-mad neighbors. The huge hotel complex is set back from the beach in a forest of pines, offering a glorious view of Mt. Olympos above and the beautiful blue-greens of the Mediterranean below. Satellite television, tennis courts, pools, excellent half-board buffet meals and a friendly staff are all included.

Be aware that in the battle against unrefined behavior there are some innocent victims: the Renaissance has an evening dress code that insists on "full length trousers and closed footwear." The garden rooms are preferable to the normal rooms. Note that the rack rate between November and March is only $70.

### In Kemer

**MAGIC LIFE DER CLUB KEMER**, *PK 170, Göynük, Kemer, Tel. 242 815 1511, Fax 242 815 1510. Rooms: 240. Double: $145.*

Like the name suggests, der club offers a methodically thorough agenda of sun, fun, and fitness. The room rate is all inclusive, meaning the Magic Life is like a large cruise ship run aground. The bungalows are preferable to the main hotel rooms.

**MAGIC LIFE DER CLUB WORLD**, *Kiriş, Kemer, Tel. 242 824 6950, Fax 242 824 6970. Rooms: 746. Double: $150.*

The Club World virtually squeezes the fun out of you, every last pitiful drop. You will run, dance, sing, eat schnitzel and visit the beer garden, then hit the wave pool, play some tennis, and jump in the ocean. Everything, but everything, is included in the room price. Zeus would have abandoned Mt. Olympos, high above, for this. Popular among Germans on weekly vacations.

**In Tekirova**

**TEKIROVA CORINTHIA**, *Tekirova, Antalya, Tel. 242 821 4750, Fax 242 821 4653. Rooms: 402. Double: $120.*

A nice beach, secluded and thus not staked end to end with umbrellas. Helpful staff and the gamut of activities from tennis to diving and catamaran rental. Half-board accommodations are the typical arrangement, and make sense since the Corinthia is a short hike from town. The architect was a cubist.

**PHASELİS ROSE**, Tekirova Köyü, Kemer, Tel. 242 821 4780, Tel. 242 821 4792. Rooms: 300. Double: $85.

A collection of bungalows leading down to a section of private beach. Half-board accommodations are standard. The Phaselis' amenities are less comprehensive than many of the other hotels in the area, but the important things – lodging, half-board dinner and beach – are all very good.

# PHASELIS

This beautiful little ruin has three beaches beneath a cover of pine trees. The air is good and you can go for a swim in the southern bay, where Alexander the Great himself once bathed.

**History**

Phaselis' origin is similar to Manhattan's in New York City. Colonists from Rhodes arrived in the area and rightly judged this site to be the perfect piece of land. They found a shepherd nearby and arranged to purchase the property from him – never mind that he probably didn't "own" it anyway – for a supply of dried fish. The shepherd accepted the offer and the Rhodians settled in to make a perfect little fortress town. The story may even be true, but there was probably some sort of port at the site during the Phoenicians' explorations in the second millenium B.C.

Phaselis' three harbors, one on the southwest, two on the northeast, were ideal for warfare as well as trade, and in the latter pursuit Phaselis proved very successful, trading timber from the interior. Their first historic battle went less well. Phaselis sided with the Persians against the Athenian Cimon in 467 B.C. Cimon, in hot pursuit of Persian King Xerxes' fleet following the Greek victories at Salamis and Plataea, wanted to roll up the Persian defenses along the entire coast before squaring off against the main body of Persians.

He settled in for a siege of Phaselis that led to a Phaselitan capitulation, after which he settled for money and the assistance of the Phaselitan navy against Xerxes. Cimon went on to crush the Persians at the Eurymedon River, near Aspendos.

## THE SISOE

*With tombs to discover and great mysteries to solve, some historians still find the time to speculate about the Phaselitans' hair. The citizens of Phaselis wore a sisoe, a hairstyle that is forbidden in the Book of Leviticus in the Bible (King James, somewhat at a loss, translates this as "thou shalt not round the corners of thine head."). What, exactly, a sisoe was is unknown, although it may have been a shaved head with a long topknot, as popularized by Baal worshipers and Yul Brynner as a Native American in Western movies.*

Phaselis' peculiar situation between the territories of Lycia to the west, Pisidia to the north, and Pamphlia to the east helped give it an independent character in choosing policy. When the Persian satrap **Mausolus** (377-353) of Helicarnassus sought to reestablish Persian rule in Lycia, the Lycian League (of which Phaselis was a sometimes member) waged a long, successful war for its independence, while Phaselis chose to come to terms with the Persians.

The Phaselitans' ongoing allegiance to the Persians didn't cloud their good sense. When **Alexander the Great** began marching through Lycia to the west, accepting the peace offers of Xanthos, Pinara, and Patara, Phaselitan envoys approached him with a golden crown, vowing allegiance. With the summer campaign season drawing to a close, Alexander chose to winter in Phaselis (334-333), reportedly helping dislodge a small Pisidian fortress just inland as a favor to his hosts. Phaselis shared the Lycian's fate after this, eventually being given back to their colonizing forebears, the Rhodians, as part of a Roman peace agreement.

When the pirate **Zenicetes** built a small piracy empire out of Olympos, he seized Phaselis as well. With the two best ports on the long, sheer coastline west of Antalya, Zenicetes had excellent bases from which to control local shipping. In 67 B.C. Pompey judged the pirate's continued depredation of Imperial Roman shipping to be an official burr in his saddle and launched the campaign that bloodily cleared the area, shifting the two towns to the Roman province of Cilicia.

Phaselis flourished through Roman times, eventually succumbing to the persistent invasions of the Arabs and finally disappearing in the medieval period as Antalya's naval supremacy was firmly established.

## ARRIVALS & DEPARTURES

Phaselis is two kilometers off the road between Kemer and Tekirova. If you arrive by public transportation expect to walk the two miles – taxis rarely wait at the main road. The road is gently sloping, with a ticket gate just before entering the ruins. Dolmuş from Tekirova go directly to the Phaselis gate, if there is enough interest.

## SEEING THE SIGHTS

Phaselis' location alone is worth the $2 price of admission. Pine trees pad the earth with needles, and sand dunes have engulfed parts of the old town. There are many well-shaded areas and you can swim in the southern bay. The large north harbor, to your left upon arriving at Phaselis' parking lot, is below the necropolis. This harbor was inferior to the other two and little used. Parts of the wharf of the smaller, central harbor are visible. This harbor, protected to the north, or Antalya, side by a long breakwater was topped with a tower. This harbor could be closed with a chain. The third harbor, on the opposite side of the isthmus, was Phaselis' main moorage.

The **acropolis** was probably the site of the **Temple of Athena**, in which Achilles' spear was housed. How the Phaselitan's came by this item is unknown, but it might have made a great impression on Alexander, who, in his stop at Troy, had danced naked around Achilles' tumulus. The exact site of the temple is unknown, and Phaselis has not yet been worked over by archaeologists (although, local guides say, the holes in the floor of the theater are the work of some amateur archaeologists-cum-treasure hunters). The acropolis is relatively barren.

The final significant structure at the site is the marble **gateway** at the south end of the main avenue by the south harbor. This gateway was dedicated to the Roman Emperor Hadrian (117-138 A.D.), and ceremonial gates seem to have been the potato salad of Hadrian's traveling potluck – "you're making him a gate? But *we're* making him a gate!"

## OLYMPOS/THE CHIMAERA

**Olympos** is, in a nutshell, why you have come to Turkey. The ruins of the ancient city rise above a pretty estuary that empties into the Mediterranean alongside a perfect strip of sandy beach. The ruins here are scattered and rough, half buried in thick vegetation. A short distance north along the beach is the **Chimaera**, a patch of living fire that has burned for thousands of years and been central to ancient religious ritual.

Accommodation is mostly cheap and simple, although a couple of nicer hotels have been established in nearby Çıralı – nothing on the scale of Kemer. The area is frequented by the backpacker and yachting sets, with little in between.

### History

Olympos sounds quite important, but, actually, it wasn't. It was a decent sized town, but never became famously embroiled in warfare or politics (which, many would say, speaks well of the local inhabitants). The city held enough sway that it had maximum votes among cities of the Lycian League, but it seems to have been a fair-weather member, and was usually overlooked when a new conqueror sought to bring the League to heel. Olympos drew its name from **Mt. Olympos**, towering directly above. This was one of a handful of Mt. Olymposes scattered around Turkey.

Olympos' history, if not dramatic, was interesting. Owing to the proximity of the blazing **Chimaera** – whose flames have for thousands of years burned so brightly that they serve as a beacon to passing ships – Olympos became a sort of pilgrimage. Olympos was linked to the flames of the Chimera by a paved road, and the residents of the city worshipped **Hephaestus** (the Roman Vulcan), the god of fire and metal smithing. Curiouser still, the area became central to worship of the god **Mithra**, a warrior religion that grew to be hugely popular among the Roman soldiery and competed with Christianity into the fourth century. Mithra worship involved secret ceremonies and initiations that now appear destined to remain secret. Locally, the ceremonies took place with the Chimaera as a backdrop.

Mithra worship was imported by a pirate named **Zenicetes**, who seized the city and made it his home at the beginning of the first century B.C. Zenicetes' piracy was so successful, and so irritating, that the Roman general Pompey sailed to the region with a huge Roman force. Pompey completed a determined and bloody purge of the area's pirates in 67 B.C., and Olympos was incorporated into the Roman empire soon thereafter.

Olympos eventually became an honest Roman town, but by the third century A.D. pirates had returned to the winding Lycian Coast and resumed preying on local shipping. Olympos continued to make do, however, and under the Byzantines a church was established atop the old pagan worshipping sites near the Chimera and a fortress was built on a hill above the beach. In the 12th century, the Genoese expanded the Byzantine structure, establishing a fortified trading post at Olympos. This venture was a ringing success for almost 200 years, but the rapid expansion of the Ottoman Empire on land and at sea forced the Genoese out, out, out. The old city has been its serene, dilapidated self ever since.

Olympos' great structures have collapsed or been shipped off to the world's museums, so the ruins are less a tourist attraction than the backdrop of a tourist attraction. The determined ruins enthusiast can nonetheless pick over these ruins for hours with gratification, finding arches bursting up out of thick vegetation and ancient walls above the meandering river.

## THE CHIMAERA

*The Chimaera was one of the most formidable beasts of mythology, the monstrous spawn of* **Typhon**, *himself the son of Gaia. Typhon was powerful enough that a concerned Zeus connived against him, succeeding in shackling the giant god in the bowels of the earth, eternally consumed in flames. Typhon's offspring was a gargantuan thing, with a snake's long, reptilian tail, the belly of a goat, the chest and forelegs of a lion, and a firebreathing goat head. There are some variations on this theme, but it is in any event a terrible and fearsome combination. This mishapen creature was given to terrorize the people of ancient Lycia, descending on them unawares and burning their cities.*

*Against this terrible monster the Lycians had no recourse. Their savior arrived in the unlikely form of a young man named* **Bellerophon**, *who arrived in Lycia bearing coded instructions for his own assassination. He had run afoul of his previous host, who mistakenly believed the lad to have had an affair with his own wife. The Lycian King at the time, Iobates, obligingly sent Bellerophon off on the impossible task of battling the Chimaera. The resourceful young man, however, was a favorite of Athena. Visiting his plight, she lent him the bridle with which to tame and mount Pegasus, formerly Perseus' winged horse (by the way Perseus was claimed as an ancestor by, you guessed it, the Persians). Astride Pegasus, Bellerophon set off to battle the Chimaera.*

*For this purpose he had fashioned a great spear of lead, which he hurled into the creature's furnace mouth from high above. As Bellerophon hoped, the spear melted as it fell, raining into the monster's innards and killing it. The Chimaera's resting place is still marked by guttering flame. Bellerophon, for his part, returned to Iobates unexpectedly triumphant, and eventually unseated the wily old King and assumed the throne himself. Glaucus, one of the famous Lycians who fought alongside the Trojans in The Iliad, claimed to be his grandson.*

## ARRIVALS & DEPARTURES

### By Bus

Public transportation to Çıralı is tricky, but it is possible. There is allegedly direct dolmuş service to Çirali from Antalya's main otogar once daily, Monday through Saturday, except in winter or when the whim of the driver says otherwise. Dolmuş leave from Antalya in the afternoon (stopping at some towns on the highway along the way), returning to Antalya in the morning.

What most regular people do is get one of the frequent buses to Kaş or Demre/Kale and get out at the "Çıralı 7" sign. Dolmuş wander up and down the hill a few times a day, and taxis will always be on hand unless it starts pouring down rain and you really want one. There are also daily dolmuş to and from Kumluca in the west.

## By Car

After a long ascent from the east you arrive at a sign telling you quite clearly "Çıralı 7, Yanartaş, Chimaera." This is the best of three alternatives, and if you're coming from the west we suggest this route as well, unless you're just dropping by Olympos for a day trip (or going to Kadir's; see below). In that case take the turnoff by the blue Ulupinar restaurant farther west. The first route takes you to the lazy seaside town of Çıralı, an intermediate point between the Chimaera and Olympos, and yields the greatest number of pensions and small hotels.

## ORIENTATION

From Çıralı, simply follow the beach south (right) down the beach to the ruins of Olympos. By car from the main road the Çıralı route is also good, although you can get closer by following the signs to the main coast road to Olympos. Both routes may be blocked by swollen streams in the winter, but the distance to the ruins from the flooded road is short. There is a $1 entrance fee when the guard is on duty.

Arriving at the city along the beach, the acropolis rises atop a peak above the sea, falling steeply toward the stream to the south. The city is divided by the slough, itself interrupted by the pier of a broken, ancient bridge.

## WHERE TO STAY & EAT

There is a collection of quaint hotels and pensions in the area, typified by Kadir's at the low end and the Olympos Lodge at the high end. Hotels typically offer their own dining, and there are lots of small open air **kebapcis** open in season.

The best meal in town is, predictably, at the Olympos Lodge, but you'll find most dining is perfectly good. The kitchen at the Canan's is recommended. In the off season the trees are filled with oranges and lemons, which you can have mashed into juice. Çıralı is largely spared mosquito problems by its location on the beach, but they can be a problem at Kadir's.

**OLYMPOS LODGE MOTEL**, *P.O. Box 38, Kemer/Çıralı. Tel. Tel. 242 825 7171, Fax 242 825 7173. Rooms: 8. Double: $100.*

The Olympos Lodge is one of the most beautiful little hotels in the whole of Turkey, admirably blending into the landscape behind a screen of orange trees and a large landscaped garden. Where most of Çıralı's hotels are rough around the edges (and wonderful in their own right), the Olympos is done to a tee. A handful of cabins are scattered along the course of a stream, beyond which the beach trails off toward the Olympos ruins. The shaded lawn is ideal for retreating in the heat of the day and having a drink. Management has endeavored to keep the Olympos Lodge understated, and has largely succeeded.

The hotel remains the only refined lodging in Çıralı, and it does an excellent job of maintaining the bucolic charm of Çıralı without sacrificing craftsmanship or the details of good hotels. The manager was reticent about being written up, which is one of the sure signs that his hotel deserves to be.

**CANAN HOLIDAY HOUSES,** *Çıralı. Tel. 242 825 7251. Rooms: 8. Double: $25.*

The Canan Pansiyon is one of the first accommodations you find on entering Çıralı from the main road. The owner, Cavit, has built a beautiful, simple set of two-story cottages along the stream running through town. All of the buildings are faced in river rock and offer baths, screens on the windows, tasteful, spartan furnishings, and patios. The centerpiece is a restaurant-lodge with a big stone fireplace, where guests can sample excellent kebap, fresh trout, or delicious cabbage dolmas.

**AZUR HOTEL,** *Çıralı. Tel. 242 825 7072, Fax 242 825 7076. Rooms: 8. Double: $40.*

The Azur is open year round, and is one of Çirali's nicest hotels with a fireplace, orange trees in the yard, and 24 hour hot water.

**KARAKUŞ PANSIYON,** *Çıralı. Tel. 242 825 7062, Fax 242 825 7061. Beds: 26. Double: $18.*

A set of small bungalows with friendly, helpful management. The **Çıralı Pansiyon** and the **Orange Pansiyon** on the right of the road bearing toward the Chimaera from the Çıralı Market are also good options.

**KADİR'S YÖRÜK TREE HOUSE,** *Olympos. Tel. 242 892 1250. Beds: 150. Double: $12.*

Kadir's is on the Olympos side of the beach, and has been a good home to thousands in the past several years. Kadir's resembles a MASH unit in a deep valley one mile inland of Olympos, and there is a constant hum of cards, chess, drinking and Jurassic Park on the VCR. Seasoned, cynical backpackers are happily processed here, churned through Kadir's $6-per-night-all-you-can-eat-breakfast-and-dinner-included wonderland.

Locals aren't too impressed with Kadir's scruples, but his guests are delighted. Getting here is the only trick, and it isn't too hard. While on the main coast road, disembark the dolmuş at the turnoff with the baby blue Ulupinar restaurant. From there, wait for a ride going down or drop in and call Kadir's – management doesn't mind because Kadir is his son. The setting is beautiful, but mildly distant from the ruins and the beach. Mosquitoes can be a problem in the high season.

## SEEING THE SIGHTS

Olympos is divided by the slough; on the near side the **acropolis** is a steep scramble, but rewarding for its complex network of walls and broken towers and, of course, its excellent view. In the thick vegetation below, accessed from the river by a well-worn path, is a colossal gateway, ornately decorated and surrounded by fallen blocks and pillars.

This presumed to have been a **temple**, its back to the reedy area north of the ruins, but the divinity in question is unknown. It is a true prize to stumble upon in the tangle of undergrowth. Not far along are Roman era baths complete with the Romans' beloved mosaics.

Continuing upriver you come to the ticket booth and a small set of backpacker hotels and restaurants just beyond. Across the ancient bridge – or, for our purposes, the sand choked mouth of the stream – you find more remnants of the ancient city, including industrial waterfront structures from the time when the river opened into a serviceable lake. Immediately across the bridge is a Byzantine church surrounded by Greek and Roman structures. The highlights of this bank are the wreckage of the theater a little inland and above the stream, and, above that, Olympos' **necropolis**. The necropolis has a smattering of tombs – not, oddly, Lycian in style despite Olympos' important place in the Lycian defensive alliance.

Inscriptions abound – again, not Lycian script – including one 24 line inscription that is a letter oracle of the kind found at Termessos. The messages were presumably thought to offer advice from beyond the grave. The Genoese fortress sprawls deceptively on the steep hillside south of the beach. Most of the fortress walls are fallen, but individual buildings, towers, and chapels still stand. A great stone pier, mostly hauled or washed away, pokes out into the sea.

---

### OLYMPOS: THE MOVIE

*In late 1996, a film crew arrived in Çıralı with secret big name stars and massive sets. Locals were hired by the hundreds as extras, and carpenters built palaces on the shore. Rumors swirl as this book goes to print, but the movie is apparently "The Odyssey," also filmed in Malta. Reports on who star in it range from Marlon Brando to Anthony Hopkins.*

*The locals, for their part, gave big time Hollywood's month-long stay mixed reviews: the money wasn't bad, but stage crews erected giant fans to blow mist over the sets, and everyone came down with head colds.*

The **Chimaera** (Yanartaş) is best visited from Çıralı, a sometimes steep hike into the mountains above town (it is a 45 minute walk from Çıralı to the trailhead plus another 25 minutes up to the lower Chimaera). The parking lot is about three kilometers north of Çıralı (follow the signs), and the flames of the Chimera itself are a further two kilometers along a winding trail. You have arrived when you see the ruins of a great temple to the right of the path, and, above it, a large church still decorated with frescoes. Above the church the flames spout at various openings in a large stony area, burning on water and stone.

Amateur scientists and frustrated vandals quench the flame with dirt, but they burn on beneath the earth and re-erupt later. The flames are most arresting beneath the canopy of stars late at night, but you'll definitely need a flashlight for the hike. If you're adventurous, seek out the second Chimaera fires another twenty minute hike above the lower flames – the trail is badly marked.

## WESTERN LYCIA

This is the Lycian Coast that daunted sailors and soldier alike. The once indomitable landscape is now opened up by a highway in fair condition, and a new highway is under construction along the western end of the route.

## FINIKE

**Finike** is a sleepy little town that hasn't been overwhelmed by the influx of tourists because there hasn't been much of one. Finike is not ugly, it's just plain. There is a new moorage here, and the town is en route to the ruins at **Arycanda** and **Limyra** (see *Excursions & Day Trips* below) Finike is not derived from the home of the Phoenicians, as you might expect; the Phoenicians emerged out of the Red Sea area and established themselves on the eastern coast in present day Syria.

Curiously, though, Phoenicia is thought to have used Phaselis as a base, and may have had dealings with this section of coast before going on to settle sections of Spain.

### ARRIVALS & DEPARTURES

You are here with the intention of seeing Limyra and Arycanda, and those ruins are both located up the excellent Elmalı road, which turns off from the main coast road in the Finike city center on the west bank of the Yaşgöz Çayı, formerly the Arycandus. The Finike otogar is several hundred feet up this road, and minibuses for the interior depart from the otogar hourly. Elmalı dolmuş can drop you at the Arycanda turn-off (Arıf village) 41 kilometers inland, from which the ruins are a one kilometer hike.

Catch a return dolmuş and, if you have the desire, backtrack to the Limyra/Turoncova intersection where you can hike three kilometers in to Limyra. Dolmuş run between 7 a.m. and 6 p.m., later in the summer.

## WHERE TO STAY & EAT

Accommodation here is cheap and not especially marvelous, but Finike is a good base for excursions inland.

ŞENDIL PANSIYON, Finike, Tel. 242 855 1660. Rooms: 22. Double: $10.

Alaadin Şendil has been running a hotel here for years. Rooms are tidy and simple, hot water is guaranteed, and the establishment is open year round. The terrace bar has wonderfully cheap beer.

BİLAL HOTEL, Kumluca Cad. 29, Finike, Tel. 242 855 2199, Fax 242 855 2199. Rooms: 30. Double: $15.

The Bilal is a more standard offering than the Şendil, and a good family spot.

PETEK RESTAURANT, Liman Girişi, Finike, Tel. 242 855 1782.

When yachtsmen stop in, this is where they often go.

## SEEING THE SIGHTS

Other than the fortress and the waterfront fish restaurants, Finike's best feature may be a new Turkish bath by the otogar. Women's days are Saturday and Sunday.

Finike's finest beach is five kilometers west, Gökliman Plaj. The new coast road passes long stretches of beach to the east of town, but these are unpopular. There are some tiny beaches along the winding section of road to the east and west, but parking can be difficult.

## EXCURSIONS & DAY TRIPS

### Arycanda

As Turkish archaeologists continue their archaeological dig at Arycanda, ruins aficionados are becoming a little breathless in their praise of the site. His work has elevated Arycanda from a minor backwater ruin (of the kind scattered liberally throughout the region) to a major find, and his efforts continue. The ruins are not only substantial but gorgeous, with thick stone-walled buildings climbing toward the Temple of Helios above.

## History

Arycanda's position atop an eagle's nest controlling the main Elmalı-Finike pass through the Toros Mountains suggests a role similar to the one enjoyed by Termessos, charging for access to a toll road through their land. The city predates Greek settlement, as evidenced by its patently un-Greek name. Little is known about the people of the town beyond Plutarch's denunciation of the Arycandans as a lazy bunch of spendthrifts.

## Visiting the Ruins of Arycanda

Like other inland cities, Arycanda was spared the ravages of nineteenth century archaeologists/treasure hunters. The ruins are in a remarkable state of preservation, descending **Mt. Akdağ** in a series of tiers. The upper terrace is the site of a Hellenistic stadium, which was built coeval with the nearlyperfect theater below. During the Roman period reconstruction was undertaken on the theater. The lower terrace is the site of an almost intact Roman bath, missing only its roof. More mosaics can be found here, and note that fresh water sometimes still flows through the town, carried in by an old water system. The necropolis is perched just above the baths in a series of buildings.

One of the most arresting structures in the city is the odeon on the middle terrace; it opens on to the grand marketplace, itself suspended above a backdrop of mountains. Similarly, the Temple of Helios, off to the left of the stadium as you approach from below, is stunning, green and silent..

## Limyra

**Limyra**, a less impressive ruin than Arycanda, has a far better history. If you have to choose between them, choose Arycanda.

## History

Unlike Arycanda, Limyra appeared late, perhaps in the fifth century B.C. Limyra was for a time the capital of the Lycian League, led by the Limyran Pericles (393-370 B.C.) who refused to submit to the Persian satrap Mausolus. His leadership galvanized the Lycians and kept the coast independent, setting a precedent for the Lycians' bullheaded dealings with outsiders.

Limyra's period of leadership ended after Pericles' death, but it remained a member of the Lycian League and eventually an autonomous territory of Rome. It was under this arrangement that the heir-apparent to Caesar Augustus, Gaius Caesar, died at Limyra in 4 A.D. Caesar died of natural causes while traveling through the area, and the Limyrans did their utmost to dignify his death, and were evidently not held to blame. This unfortunate turn of events left the Roman succession in disorder, with the mantle passing to Tiberius in 14 A.D., a role played so memorably by Peter O'Toole in *Caligula*.

Limyra's tale descends thereafter into the standard banalities; bad quake damage in 141 A.D. followed by some reconstruction, a conversion to Christianity and the appointment of a bishop, slow strangulation by Arab raids and shifting trade routes.

### Visiting the Ruins of Limyra

The **sarcophagus**, or cenotaph, of Gaius Caesar was the greatest structure at Limyra, but today it is badly weathered and difficult to reach until late summer – it is in the middle of a sunken bog at the foot of **Mt. Tocat**. The citizens of Limyra, knowing the beauty of the heroon (a small temple or sarcophagus for someone of semi-divine status), are said to have used the monument as a tool when negotiating with Rome, and it was formerly decorated with depictions of the 20 year old Caesar's many exploits, or how, at least, his exploits would have been.

The sarcophagus is located in the western of two walled sections, with the eastern section housing the later Byzantine Church. The necropolis is on the slope above the theater. The most important native Limyran tomb is probably that of **Pericles**, atop the acropolis. The Heroon of Pericles has been stripped and removed to the Antalya Museum, but the steep forty minute climb is enjoyable. The tomb is on the small terrace to the right as you look down off the acropolis, but for all of its pretty relief work archaeologists are still uncertain who was inside, finally judging it to be Pericles because, after all, who else could it have been? If you don't mind climbing all the way up there only to find a cut up tomb, take the steep, winding trail that begins at the back of Turunçova. The acropolis itself has little left to see, but it offers a stunning view

Like Sura, Limyra had a fish oracle, but the site of the oracle is unknown. The entire bog surrounding the cenotaph of Gaius Caesar could be home to oracular fish.

## DEMRE (KALE)

**Demre** is roughly on the site of the former Lycian city of **Myra**. The ruins of that city, and the legacy of its most famous citizen, St. Nicholas, are the highlights of a visit here. Accommodation is available. Note that the official name of the city is Kale, but the locals continue to call it by its traditional name, Demre. This all becomes especially confusing if you are going to Kale, or "Kaleköy," otherwise known as Simena, in nearby in Kekova Bay.

## History

**Myra** was another of the Lycian League's chief cities, commanding the large plain that is today choked with tomato greenhouses. The city like Priene, was once astride a navigable bay, but the silting of the river narrowed the watercourse until it narrowed all the way out to the sea near the Andriake garrison. The contemporary names of the ruins at the site, the sea necropolis and the river necropolis, hearken back to a time when the sea was much nearer, and the river's course much wider and closer.

Myra appears little in the historical record, typically lumped together with its fellow intractable Lycian cities chafing under outside rule or raiding sites elsewhere in the Mediteranean. The city and its two garrison towns (the aforementioned Andriake and Sura) carried on independently, pirates to the east and uncertain Roman rule to the west. In 42 B.C., the Romans were forced to assault the city to bring it under their control (although the Myrans proved more flexible than their allies at Xanthus, submitting after the Roman navy broke through the defenses at Andriake). St. Paul put in here briefly during his travels, but his visit is overshadowed by a later Christian, St. Nicholas.

Perhaps owing to the fame of St. Nicholas, Myra became the provincial capital of Lycia in the fifth century, although this success evaporated as the Byzantine Empire was beset by waves of Persians and Arabs in the 600s. The river's continued silting and intermittent invasions from the east finally undid the city, which faded into agrarian obscurity.

## ARRIVALS & DEPARTURES

### By Bus

Dolmuş leave Demre for Kaş and Fethiye frequently between 7:45 am and 11 p.m., and they depart for Antalya until 8:45 p.m. The daily bus to Üçağız passes through town around 5 p.m. Demre's otogar is on the main road, one quarter mile shy of the city center, inland. The Church of Saint Nicholas (Noel Baba) is signed to the left at the city center intersection, and Myra is also signed, straight through town to the foothills behind.

Andriake in Demre/Kale is remote from transport and hotels, but much closer and cheaper to visit (from-$6) than Kaş.

### By Car

Demre is at the western end of a large alluvial plain, and the road westward toward Kaş is forced up the mountain behind Myra. The main road takes a circuitous route through town, but it is well signed in both directions and toward Myra. To reach the docks at Andriake, follow the Müze Caddesi road past the Church of St. Nicholas due west.

## ORIENTATION

Follow the signs from the main coast highway to the city center (merkez), which is posted with yellow signs for Myra and Noel Baba Kilesi (The Basilica of St. Nicholas). Myra is built up against the foot of the mountain inland of town.

The tourism information office for Demre is in **Kaş**, *Tel. 242 836 1238, Fax 242 836 1238.*

## WHERE TO STAY & EAT

Although somewhat distant, we recommend staying at one of the towns to the west; either sleepy Kale or Üçağız in the Kekova region, or the seaside towns of Kaş or Kalkan. The following hotels and pensions in Demre are serviceable, but uninspired.

Regarding restuarants in town, Demre's a reasonable place to stick to the bus stop beans and rice lokanta.

**KENT PANSIYON**, *Alakent Mah., Alakent Cad., Demre, Tel. 242 871 2042. Rooms: 11. Double: $9.*

Directly on the road to Myra, a ten minute walk from city center and fifteen minutes from the bus station, the main section of this pension is a nice old house, with decent, well-maintained rooms. Service is a little shaky, and try to avoid the Alec Guiness-in-Bridge Over the River Kwai hotbox huts in the front garden.

**NOEL PANSIYON**, *Gökyazı Mah., Demre, Tel. 242 871 2267. Rooms: 12. Double: $13.*

Ali, the proprietor, is friendly and helpful despite the language barrier. Decent, cheap lodging.

**ŞAHIN OTEL**, *Gökyazı Mah., Müze Cad. No. 2, Tel. 242 871 5686.*

Worn but reliable.

**Grand Hotel**, *Göyazı Mah. Ortaokul Cad. No. 37, Tel. 242 871 3462, Fax 242 871 5366.*

The town's biggest hotel, but also a bit worn.

**GÜNEYHAN RESTAURANT**, *Gökyazı Mah., Müze Cad. No. 24, Demre, Tel. 242 871 5019.*

Assuming you're here for lunch, this spot adjacent to the Church of St. Nicholas is fine. There is a patio garden and tour bus ambiance, with average food at average prices.

**HOTEL ANDRIAKE**, *Finike Caddesi PK 62, Demre. Tel. 242 871 2249, Fax 242 871 5440. Rooms: 52. Double: $70.*

Demre's status address, with a ribbon-cutting ceremony at the end of 1996 attended by former Prime Minister Tansu Çiller herself. The location is odd, marooned inland of the beaches along the main road, but this three star hotel has free shuttles to the two nearby beaches and all of the comforts like satellite television, air conditioning, a big pool, and a nice terrace. The hotel is convenient to Myra and the St. Nicholas church, and even a good base for day trips inland of Finike or by boat to Kekova.

## SEEING THE SIGHTS

The **Basilica of St. Nicholas** (Noel Baba Kilesi) dates to the eighth century, and is obviously built on a far more grand scale than the chapel used by St. Nicholas himself. There is a $3 entry fee, a small price to pay if you are a sailor, virgin, pawnbroker, or Russian seeking spiritual guidance. The church is interesting but not especially exceptional. The current incarnation of the basilica was pieced together by a Russian prince in 1862, and makes use of recycled stones bearing old pagan inscriptions to Artemis and her ilk. The conspicuous broken tomb within the church's southern aisle may be that of St. Nicholas, but that is as dubious as the claim by the Antalya Museum that they are displaying the skull and jaw of the old saint. Note the small looped passage behind the apse, identical to the passage in the chapel on the lowest level at Derinkuyu in Cappadoccia.

On Dec. 6 every year, the Greek Orthodox Church still observes the feast of St. Nicholas at the site, a tradition that blossomed in England during medieval times.

### The Story of Father Christmas

Who really knows how legends grow and perpetuate themselves, but the kernel of truth left in St. Nick's tale is no deeper than the name, St. Nick. Before settling in for a long winter's nap, the rosy-cheeked children may be surprised by some of the differences between the traditional and actual accounts of the saint's life.

St. Nicholas grew up in Patara, west of Demre, in the third century. The details of his upbringing are vague, but he appears to have been elected bishop in Demre during the reign of Diocletian (285-305 A.D.). His good deeds won him fame throughout the Mediterranean, but what deeds, and how good, is impossible to tell. One story foreshadows a modern Christmas tradition: told of a poor man unable to provide his three marriageable daughters with a dowry, St. Nicholas stole up to the house one night and dropped three small bags of gold down the chimney – or, more likely through a window opening. These anonymous gifts were credited with saving the young women from lives of prostitution. Other tales are less familiar: St. Nick refusing to suckle at his mother's breast on the sabbath, or St. Nick resurrecting three dismembered lads (an act that would have put Christ's resurrection of Lazarus to shame).

The truth of St. Nicholas' life is difficult to separate from the folklore; for instance, a reasonable-sounding account of St. Nicholas slapping the renegade Bishop Arius at the 325 A.D. Council of Nicaea suffers from the unfortunate arithmetic: St. Nick was imprisoned and tortured under the wave of persecution sponsored by Diocletian in the final years of his rule. It is unlikely that he was ever released, instead becoming a martyr to the Christian cause.

Whatever his fate, St. Nicholas' fame and reputation appeared to blossom in the centuries after his death. In the seventh century a church was erected in his name at Constantinople, and he was adopted by pawnbrokers, children, the Russian nation, and even the conflicting pairing of sailors and virgins as a patron saint. A Byzantine named Simon Metaphrastes wrote a preposterous account of the saint's life in the early 900s, perpetuating all of the rumors that had circulated during the past 500 years. This account helped make St. Nicholas more popular than ever, and surely contributed to the next grim chapter: in 1087, a motley bunch of merchants from Bari sailed to Myra. There, ignoring the animated resistance of some clerics, the merchants disinterred the myrrh-covered bones of St. Nicholas and hauled them back to Italy. These bones fetched a fine price among those under St. Nicholas' protection, and were popular both as talismans and medicinals.

For those who complain that Christmas has become too commercial, it's also interesting to note that prior to the theft of the bones, the Greek Orthodox clergy at Myra's Church of St. Nicholas turned a nice profit selling myrrh they claimed came from a bottomless supply in St. Nicholas' tomb.

## Ruins of Myra

The **ruins** of Myra are inland of the Church of St. Nicholas on Yeni Cami/Alakent Caddesi, west of the church. The Myra ruins are a fine bit of tourism sleight of hand. The ticket booth is located at the westernmost part of the site, and allows entrance to the Myra theater and the "sea" necropolis. After running a gauntlet of mystifying curio sellers (porcelain rabbits and ducks, Santa Claus statuettes) you arrive at the base of the hill. A few tombs are down at ground level, but the majority are on the steep ridge and cliff face above. Signs discourage climbing, but curious folk will be sorely tempted. The collection of largely inaccessible tombs is pretty, but most visitors find little else beyond, sigh, another theater and a $1 entrance fee (7:30 a.m.-7 p.m. summer, 8 a.m.-5:30 p.m. in winter).

For the intrepid, Myra offers much more of interest. Instead of turning left at the yellow "Myra 200 meters" sign, continue on the same road (Guvercinlik Cad.) for another 1,500 feet, rounding the southeastern spur of the mountain, and turn left at light pole #34. Continue to another road just after light pole #20 and take another left by the concrete cistern.

The road heads directly into the draw past more tombs and climbs the ridge to a big new industrial building halfway up the slope. If you climb to the top of the mountain, you find the battered ruins of the old **acropolis** and a Selçuk **fortress**.

If you want a jumble of ruins to yourself, the ascent virtually guarantees it. The large exterior walls are a Byzantine construction, while the inner, more finely hewn walls are Lycian, dating to the fifth century B.C. The hilltop also has the remains of a watch tower and a Roman-era temple.

The most interesting ruins in the area are in the **river necropolis**, to the left of the aforementioned acropolis road just before it begins climbing out of the valley. You can approach the base of the hill from the popular sea necropolis by winding your way right through greenhouses or by following the directions toward the acropolis. The ruins of the river necropolis are fun to look through, but only if you have a good head for heights; many of them require heavily exposed scrambling. You will see the tombs as you approach, carved into the rocky mountainside, and there is an ancient network of steps and paths cut into the stone to help ascend to them. Many of the paths have fallen into an understandable state of disrepair.

The tombs in the area are often adorned with lengthy Lycian inscriptions and even artwork. The two most interesting tombs – some of the best in the whole of Lycia – are also three of the most obvious, on the eastern flank of the mountain between the acropolis road and the sea necropolis. The two tombs are on the left side. The first, more easily accessible tomb is decorated with reliefs of the deceased's family, four to one side of the opening, four to the other. The interior columns of the tomb itself are topped by the heads of lions in a curiously Hittite style. They were once decorated with paint, but the paint has worn even less well than the stone itself.

The second tomb is accessible after a long ascent topped with a mildly nasty carved stair. This tomb, the finest of a good lot, has a square opening divided with living stone into four panes, the bottom frame broken. A group of people, presumably the family, is carved in relief to either side of the tomb. To the right is a peculiarly Egyptian-looking relief of a woman offering a small box to the deceased (myrrh, for all we know, which some have suggested was the root of the name Myra). These tombs were almost certainly carved after the 5th century B.C., but the Hittite and Egyptian imagery could hearken back to the Lycians', sometimes referred to as the Lukka or Lukki, persistent raids and warfare against both great empires.

## EXCURSIONS & DAY TRIPS
### Andriake

**Andriake** (Çayağzı) is three kilometers from Demre. Follow the road in front of the Church of St. Nicholas (Müze Cad.) away from the city center; signs guide you, but it's basically a beeline. Scheduled boats depart Andriake for Kale/Kekova at 10 a.m., but there are always captains on the docks willing to shuttle you there or take you fishing for a little extra money. Fishing will cost at least $20 for 5 hours, and a special charter to Kale is typically $25 for the boat. The trip from Andriake to Kekova is shorter than the trip from Kaş to Kekova, but the scheduled departures are less regular.

Little is known about Andriake. The town was founded as a garrison port for the metropolis of Myra up the Androkos River. Today Andriake is overgrown and partially buried in fine white sand, which is a shame for archaeologists, but marvelous for beach-lovers. Andriake's long, pretty beach is hardly a secret – weekends find it busy with local residents – but it is almost always bypassed by tourists on their way to Kale/Kekova by boat. A new port here has renewed Andriake's historic role as a seafaring terminus – boats frequently ply the old routes back and forth between the dead cities to the west and the dead city here.

The new road winds along the Androkos River in what was once one of the coast's finest bays. The **ruins** of the former town are distributed to either side of the old bay, with the majority of ruins inland of the new road and another collection of walled ruins on the opposite shore in the area behind the restaurant. A pedestrian bridge allows access to the far (northern) bank. The buildings on the road shore were dedicated to commerce from Myra and include a great granary built during Hadrian's reign (117-138 A.D.). On the far shore there were also commercial buildings, although to a lesser extent. The necropolis is further inland on the northern bank, outside the ring of walls.

### Sura

Several kilometers inland of Andriake is another of Myra's outposts, **Sura**. This city stood on the western road, then as now. The scattered ruins are located in the vicinity of the second turn as you ascend from the plain (begin counting after the large, square Roman-era temple by the intersection). The perfectly rectangular walled city guarded the upper entrance to Myra's plain, and may have been immediately above a navigable section of river or sea, today a soupy marsh.

Sura's only distinction from the garrison towns that pepper the Lycian Coast is that it was host to a **"fish oracle."** Priests of the oracle would feed fish chunks of meat and make their determinations on the basis of what food the fish ate. This sounds ridiculous until you visit another of history's great budget oracles at Termessos and Olympos.

Andriake's Temple of the Fish Oracle was associated with **Apollo**, who was also the patron of the great oracle at Patara. The Doric Apollo temple is located below the main town, and a spring still trickles past. There are no fish here anymore to offer prophesy, nor have there been since oracles were given the kibosh by Theodosius the Great (378-395 A.D.).

## KEKOVA BAY

If you want sheer escape, **Kekova** is your place. Two small seafront towns are located at the site, **Kale** and **Üçağız**, and both of these fishing and farming villages remain what all of the developed towns along the Mediterranean claim to have once been: pretty and unassuming spots with thick cascades of bougainvillea, whitewashed buildings, and lush greenery. Here, too, there is an overwhelming collection of Lycian ruins – it is here we saw a weary old spaniel bitch eating from her bowl while lying prone in her stylish doghouse, a Lycian tomb with a hole punched in the front. The **Teimussa ruins** in Üçağız are related to the ruins just outside the mouth of the bay at Kale, ancient Simena. Capping this, sunken ruins sprawl into the bay, and **Kekova Island** is just offshore.

Visitors stay here for weeks and months at a time, taking advantage of the town's several pensions and private guest houses. Writers, burn-out victims, and backpackers take up residence and are lulled by the peace of the little town. The only "disturbance" is the activity on the waterfront, where several daily tours from both Kaş and Andriake/Demre visit the town and anchor offshore, and that remains a fairly benign sort of irritant, although it has served to nudge food and accommodation prices upwards. You can't rent a place in Üçağız for pennies, but it won't cost you much more than $10 for a double in winter, $20 in summer. Everything's negotiable, of course, and if you want to stay for a while your bargaining power rises accordingly.

Also, between the good paved road connecting Üçağız and the main Antalya-Fethiye highway and the frequent yacht and tour boat visits, Üçağız manages to be a lot closer to civilization than it might appear – if you must have your *Herald Tribune* or *Turkish Daily News*, you can have it shipped in with a little something for the trouble.

## ARRIVALS & DEPARTURES
**By Bus or Boat**

Yes indeed, there is a dolmuş to Üçağız. During the summer dolmuş leave Üçağız for Antalya at about 8 a.m., at the discretion of the driver.

After arriving at Antalya they will wait around, usually between noon and 3 p.m., then head back down to Üçağız. The dolmuş passes through Demre on its way to Üçağız – on those days it is running – sometime after 5 p.m. There are reports of a dolmuş from Kaş to Üçağız, but no one has actually seen one.

If all of this seems a little vague to you, the best alternative is to get a ride aboard a boat from Andriake or Kaş (Kaş is the more convenient choice wherever you are coming from – Andriake is remote from transport and hotels), get a taxi, or to hitch from the main road the way the locals do.

## By Car

The turnoff for Üçağız is posted just three miles east of the Kaş/Antalya/Elmali intersection, taking you 16 well-paved miles down through the mountains. En route you pass through Kılıçlı, a fairly lifeless valley town that is the unlikely site of the ruins of Appolonia. The Appolonia ruins are atop a hill just south of town; nothing is known of the town. Üçağız has a main parking lot by the waterfront, from which you can get your bearings.

Kale (Simina) is just outside the mouth of the bay, around to the left as you look out at the sea from Üçağız, and is perhaps an even better retreat. Kale's sole contact with the outside world is by boat – no one has yet managed to punch a road through to the inaccessible village. If you have a rental car you'll want to stay in Üçağız or arrange to leave your car there while you stay around the corner in Kale. From Üçağız a small launch takes 15 minutes to reach Kale and costs, oh, $2. Simina has its own collection of small guest houses and pensions, and the same casual litter of Lycian ruins, including a Byzantine fort atop the hill behind the village. It is a pretty 45 minute walk from Üçağız to Kale.

## ORIENTATION

The idea for many of those who go to the trouble of getting here is to do nothing at all. Read, go on boat rides, draw, wander through the ruins and up to the Byzantine castle, and swim at the beach on Kekova Island or at the cove across the bay near the old stone house. If you want to head into Kaş or Demre, it is fairly easy to do by boat, although it can involve some expense unless you make arrangements beforehand.

When you bestir yourself to investigate the region, you are in for a pleasant surprise; Kekova is more than beautiful, it's also strange and interesting. **Kekova Island** protects a small bay, deep and navigable in some places, shallow and peculiar in others. The peculiarity arises from the staircases carved out of living rock that descend into the depths and from a sprawling collection of submerged buildings and tombs. **Kekova** is touted as a sunken city, when in fact it is a set of partially sunken cities (or, according to especially dramatic locals, the massive lost city of Atlantis).

## WHERE TO STAY & EAT

Pensions and small fish restaurants are divided between Üçağız and Kale/Simena. You'll be able to size up the restaurants yourself soon after arriving and asking at your hotel, but obviously any of the restaurants catering to the tour boats are serviceable. Water is a problem – all of the water is shipped in and can run low on occasion. Your host will love for you to bathe in the sea.

Some of the most impressive accommodations in Kale are rented only by **Savile Row Tours and Travel,** and you should at least have a copy of their annual booklet to inspire you: *39 Savile Row, London, W1X 1AG, UK, Tel. (0171) 287 3001.* Savile is in the business of arranging full transportation to and from your accommodation, offering exclusive service and prices.

**LEYLA PANSIYON,** *Üçağız, Kekova. Tel. 242 874 2038, Fax 242 874 2039. Double: $20.*

Ms. Aliçavuşoğlu rents out six rooms in her house, just two blocks up the street from the waterfront. The pretty garden has a fine Lycian tomb as its centerpiece, and is an excellent place to while away the time. Water can be a problem. Upon arrival, follow the road that runs parallel to the waterfront, past the Fisherman's Inn, and another 100 feet to the Kekova Market. Inquire at the market with Ahmet Aliçavuşoğlu.

**ONUR PANSIYON,** *Üçağız, Kekova. Tel. 242 874 2071.*

This pension directly on the water is unprepossessing, but the sort of place that people are satisfied with for months at a time. Open year-round.

**FISHERMAN'S INN,** *Üçağız, Kekova, Antalya. Tel. 242 874 2024.*

A fine, dark, wood-trimmed hideout reminiscent of San Felipe's Barefoot Bar, with one dollar beers. The relaxed little spot is convenient to the waterfront, run by Uğur Yilmaz.

The **BABA VELI PENSION**, also in Üçağız, should be ready to open in 1997.

### In Kaleköy

**MEHTAP PANSIYON,** *Kale. Tel. 242 874 2146. Rooms: 10. Double: $20.*

The Mehtap's great feature is a stunning, simple wooden porch wrapped around several rooms and a restaurant. The Mehtap, uphill of the dock and slightly left, commands a view of Kale and the archipelago. Irfan Tezcan, the relaxed, friendly proprietor has been in business since 1982 and has got it right. There is a small lending library, excellent food (like Irfan-Bey's kalamar), and pleasant, clean rooms.

**KALE PANSIYON,** *Kale Iskele. Tel. 242 874 2111.*

Perched just above the water to the right of town, this little pension has been in business for years. The scenic little spot offers fine views over the bay and is run by Salih Bey, a helpful man who can help direct you around the area and make arrangements. This pension is included on one company's exclusive tour itinerary and said to epitomize relaxed living.

**MURAT PANSIYON** and **SALIH PANSIYON** are also good choices, both within minutes of the boat landing.

**CAFE ANKH,** *Kale. Tel. 242 874 2171.*

Ahmet and Hasan Takır have built their tasteful little empire on a foundation of ice cream. Ice cream's not all they offer, but it's what smart gület captains bring their guests miles for.

## SEEING THE SIGHTS

**Aperlae,** to the west of Kekova Bay and at the head of a long, narrow bay, is the westernmost of the ancient sites. The most substantial ruins at Aperlae are the old stone jetties, which now stand submerged, and the walls of the former town. The Aperlae walls remain in good condition, although one of their gates has settled into the sea. The main gate is on the southern wall, and if you choose to adventure through the undergrowth you will find sarcophagi and a walled acropolis.

**Üçagız,** ancient Teimussa, is almost entirely in the form of a spawling **necropolis** – and it's easy to wonder whether the unwalled area wasn't simply the necropolis for nearby Simine. Teimiussa is a city without history, known only from a few inscriptions. If it was more than a necropolis for Simina, it may have been a small associated fishing village – there are sunken piers just offshore. The name Üçağız derives from "three mouths," identical to the Greek "Tristomo," which refers to the mouth of the small Üçağız bay and the two narrow mouths of the Kekova Bay to either side of Kekova Island.

While looking through Üçağız's great collection of tombs, fashioned with such care and artistry, you cannot help but be impressed with the efforts of living for the dead, since the tombs here were not made for great Lycian rulers, only for citizens of this parochial town. Sarcophagi lay scattered throughout the little town, but the main section of the ancient town is supposed to have been located to the east, behind the Koçlar Turizm pension. An especially picturesque tomb is located here, perched atop a stone with a natural cleft.

If you've arrived by boat you've already begun seeing ruins in the shallows beneath the sea, and the greatest concentration of these curiosities is on Kekova Island. The Üçağız side of the island is liberally sprinkled with structures just beneath the surface; mostly small chambers and stairways, with more sarcophagi. This section of Kekova, called **Tershane** (or boatworks), is supposed to have been the main necropolis for Simina, in modern Kale. The structure that gives the area its name is a long stone building near a sand beach on the northwest side of the island. The locals suppose it to have been a boatworks, although it also suggests a small church. Unfortunately, the bulk of the remaining walls collapsed in 1996. More ruins are located in the thickly overgrown interior. Good boots and heavy pants are handy for a real investigation. Tiny islands jut from the sea throughout the bay, many of them cut and quarried for building material

Continuing now along the leeward side of the island and crossing to the mainland we arrive at the final town in this idyllic archipelago, **Simina** (Kale, or Kaleköy). Simina is located at the eastern entrance to Kekova Bay. Such a fine, well-protected bay needed some protecting of its own, to which end the pretty **Crusader Fort** was built atop Simina's steep hill. The present form of the fortress derives from the Knights of St. John, although there was doubtless a fortification prior to the 13th century. Based on the likely occupation of pirates and Crusaders, it seems this perfect little bay was seized for its remote character, its excellent harbor, and its ability to control shipping lanes. Merchants must have made a wide detour around this spot.

The path to the castle is direct, and the view from the ramparts is excellent. While atop the fortress you can take in the entirety of Kekova Bay, as well as the steeply descending town below. The town's present scattering of houses probably varies little from its Hellenistic forebear, indeed the modern houses incorporate the same stone quarried by the residents of Simina. A cute seven row theater set just inside the castle looks out over the turquoise sea, the ruins of a small bath lay near the pier, and a necropolis descends in the direction of Üçağız.

You can rent rowboats in Üçağız and, obviously, Kale, where they constitute the main mode of transportation.

## SPORTS & RECREATION

The Kekova Island area may have been designed with sea kayaks in mind, and we are fortunate that one company rents them: **Bougainvillea Travel**, based in Kaş (*Çukurbağlı Cad. No. 10, Kaş, Tel. 242 836 3142, Fax 242 836 1605*), offers day long kayaking tours (putting in at Üçağız, transportation from Kaş included, $40) and kayak rentals to experienced boaters

($75 for three days). Paddles, skirt, flotation device and a map of the suitable campgrounds on and near Kekova Island are all included. Bougainvillea also has sleeping bags and tents if you haven't come prepared for outdoor adventure.

---

### ATLANTIS?

*Probably not, but Kekova poses some tricky questions. Why, when so many ancient cities in Asia Minor were left high and dry by siltation, quakes, and possible drops in the elevation of the sea, did this anomalous city drop into the sea? One theory is that the ruins haven't sunk at all, but that there was a local tradition of hewing sarcophagi and small buildings out of stone already in the water. In other words the ruins may have come pre-sunk. Any examination of the ruins suggests that this may be part of the explanation, but it doesn't account for everything, such as the sunken gates at Aperlae.*

*Other explanations are that plate shifting dropped the entire shelf into the sea and that massive siltation has more than compensated for this in nearby cities such as Meis, now high and dry. This would help explain other flooded ruins near Fethiye, Letoon, and elsewhere. Also possible is that there was a regional seismic event that coincidentally dropped the Kekova area into the sea. Finally, ancient conspiracy theorists can amuse themselves with the notion that the Knights of St. John, related to those shadowy Knights Templar, had something to do with it; after all, they built and resided at the castle above Kale.*

---

## KAŞ

Kaş has long been a pit stop on the great backpacking road, past Kuşadası, on the way to Kathmandu. When the new coast road was punched through in 1980 Kaş seemed a natural pit stop, with a smattering of ruins and beaches. What began with the completion of the coast road continues gaining momentum today, but Kaş remains a good destination.

Kalkan has better accommodations if you're on a $40 or over budget, but Kaş has ruins of its own and its own boat tours to Kekova/Üçağız/Kale. Plus, Kaş has a much more developed shopping scene (Benneton again), rounding out the arts, crafts, and kilim merchants that thrive in both towns.

### History

Before it was Kaş it was **Antiphellos**, the port city to inland Phellos in the mountains above. This arrangement, started in the fifth century

B.C., was shortlived, as Phellos fell on hard times before the first century B.C., and Antiphellos became the more important of the two Phelloses.

Antiphellos did well for itself into Roman times, but, like the other cities in this inhospitable stretch of Lycia, was not significant enough to make invading armies detour across the barrier of mountains at its back. Pliny the Younger, the Cliff Clavin of antiquity, notes that Antiphellos produced excellent sponges.

## ARRIVALS & DEPARTURES

Kaş is on the main coast road, easily accessible by car or bus. Buses depart regularly for Bodrum (six hours, $15) and Fethiye (two hours, $4) to the west, and Antalya (four hours, $8) in the east. At least one İstanbul-bound bus is available per bus company, per day (15 hours, $25).

## ORIENTATION

The Kaş **tourism information** office is just inland of the harbor on *Cumhuriet Meydanı No. 5, Tel. 242 836 1238, Fax 242 836 1238.*

## WHERE TO STAY

The hotels in Kaş are good by most standards, but they're not as appealing as their neighbors to the west in Kalkan (see next destination below).

**OTEL MEDUSA**, *Küçükçakı Mevkii No. 61, Kaş, Tel. 242 836 1440, Fax 242 836 1441. Rooms: 40. Double: $45.*

The Medusa is a tall, modern hotel with a small pool and attentive service. The sea view rooms have an excellent view of the Mediterranean.

**OTEL SARDUNYA**, *Hastane Cad., Kaş, Tel. 242 836 3080, Fax 242 836 3082. Double: $29.*

A pleasant, family run hotel. Request rooms 207 or 208.

**MELISA PANSIYON**, *Recep Bilgen Cad. Tel. 242 836 1162. Rooms: 22. Double: $15.*

Another pretty pension covered in climbing vines and flowers. Excellent view from the terrace.

**AY PANSIYON**, *Yeni Cami Mah., Tel. 242 836 1562. Rooms: 12. Double: $10.*

A simple, pretty pension a few blocks away from the sea. Rooms are clean and bare, with a toilet and shower.

## WHERE TO EAT

**SMILEY'S**, *Uzun Çarşı, Ara Sok. No. 22, Kaş, Tel. 242 836 2812. Moderate-Expensive.*

You'll find Smiley's packed, and there are two good reasons for it.

Smiley has an informal deal with budget travelers; eat here and you can stay free in a large public room upstairs. That's reason one: backpackers are obliged to eat here, reassuring people who hold to the belief that a packed house means good food. Reason two is that, in this case, it is good food, and reasonably priced. Oh, and there's a third reason: the wily Smiley guarantees that if you flash our recommendation you can have a ten percent discount.

**ERIŞ RESTAURANT**, *Gülsoy Sok. Orta Sok. No. 13, Kaş, Tel. 242 836 2134. Moderate-Expensive.*

Formerly housed in part of a church, this restaurant has become an institution in Kaş. The restaurant serves the best food in Kaş, now operating out of an old Ottoman house behind the tourism information office, near Smiley's.

**BAHÇE LOKANTA**, *Anıt Mezar Karşısı No. 31, Kaş, Tel. 242 836 2370. Moderate-Expensive.*

A lovely garden restaurant just uphill of a conspicuous city center rock tomb. Excellent mezes and a wide selection of vegetarian dishes.

**MERCAN LOKANTA**, *Çarsı İçi, Liman Başı, Kaş, Tel. 242 836 1629. Moderate.*

Just up the street from the tourism information center, serving good Turkish food.

## SEEING THE SIGHTS

Some Lycian sarcophagi are scattered around town, and the **Antiphellos theater** is located slightly west of town just inland of the waterfront road. This 26-row theater often remains humming into the wee hours, as rogue campers and the guests at nearby Kaş Camping strum their guitars and commune with the Antiphellians. If you stay in town you can also visit the base of the hill behind town, where rock-carved tombs are located.

The sea in the immediate vicinity of Kaş isn't too clean, as you're likely to notice. Two beaches, **Küçük Çakil** and **Büyük Çakil**, offer good swimming not far away. Otherwise, get a dolmuş to **Kaputaş Beach** in the west. Another alternative is to go on one of the several boat tours out of Kaş (see below).

## SPORTS & RECREATION

**Boat Tours**

The daily Kekova boat tours depart at 10 a.m. from the town's main harbor, located between the tourist information office and the central mosque, visiting the sunken city, the island, the town of Simena/Kale, and pulling in at Uçağız for a bite. The cost is between $10 and $15 per person, and should include lunch and a stop for swimming. Another tour chugs off in the opposite, western direction, visiting some of the impressive sea caves along the coast, passing through the Kalkan Bay and calling at some of the small islands. Kahramanlar has been around for years and tends to have straightforward touts and standard prices.

Another sailing possibility is the boat trip to **Meis**, a Greek island just offshore. This is one of the busiest small ferry routes in the country, kept bustling by foreigners leaving Turkey for an afternoon to get their travel visas renewed as well as standard tourists. The Greek community of Meis and the Turkish community in Kaş have been conspiring to give Turkish/Greek relations a good name, cooperating between themselves and doing their best to tone down the ongoing disputes between their respective nations. During the 1996 Kardak Rocks crisis, a band of inflammatory Turkish journalists traveled to Kaş, intending to stir up patriotic trouble by planting a Turkish flag on a tiny Greek island near Meis. The residents of Kaş firmly and sensibly refused to rent the journalists a boat for the purpose, and the members of the media slunk off dejected.

For an afternoon on this charming island, turn your passport in to Rekor Turizm the day before traveling. That office will run your passport through the port authority so that you can sail the following day. Travel time is just over one half hour. Spending an afternoon in Meis does not require a special visa, but if you intend to stay longer than a single afternoon you'll be asked to fill out a form. Cost of a single day excursion is $22, plus $20 if you need to renew your Turkish visa. Note that this is subject to change in the same way that relations between Turkey and Greece are subject to change.

### Diving, Walking, & Sea Kayaking Tours

**Scuba diving** lessons are an interesting local possibility, with 6 day P.A.D.I. deep water certification courses costing $350, including equipment. Bougainvillea Travel is a reliable company, handling diving lessons in addition to walking tours and sea kayak rentals out of Kekova Bay. Contact **Bougainvillea Travel**, *Çukurbağlı Cad. No. 10, Kaş, Tel. 242 836 3142, Fax 242 836 1605*.

## SHOPPING

Like Kalkan, Kaş has a lot of shops with art and crafts. In addition to the requisite leathers and carpets you'll find some interesting silver work. One good, honest silver shop is **Mencilis Art**, *Uzunçarşı No. 17, Kaş, Tel. 242 836 2897*.

# KALKAN

**Kalkan** is spared the fate of its neighbors in the Kemer area by its geography. The town clings to a mountainside and can sprawl very little. A quite sensible government edict against development in Kalkan has further forced developers to refine the small houses already in place. There are a few jarring notes, such as the colorful Pirate's Club hotel in the west of town, but Kalkan strikes a good balance between resort area and quaint Turkish coastal town.

## ARRIVALS & DEPARTURES

The coast road runs directly through town if you're driving. Kamil Koç offers dolmuş and regular bus service in the area, serving Kaş hourly, Antalya and Fethiye seven times daily, with İstanbul departures at 7 p.m., Ankara at 4:30 p.m., and Marmaris at 8:30 a.m. Pamukkale's buses maintain a similar schedule, with an additional Izmir route at 10 a.m. and 10 p.m. Additional service is added in the high season.

There are dolmuş to Patara beach several times daily in summer, and regular service to Kaş via Kaputaş Beach.

## ORIENTATION

Kalkan is a simple fishing village; no ruins, no mythology (and as such no *Seeing the Sights* section; we go straight to *Sports & Recreation*). The town is remarkably picturesque, dropping steeply into the sea from the mountains at its back. It was founded a mere 150 years ago by settlers from Meis, and it had a large Greek population until the exchange of Turkish and Greek populations in 1923.

Kalkan's enlightened community leaders have legislated against the construction of large hotels (the Pirat Hotel notwithstanding), ensuring that Kalkan remains as classic and appealing as it is today. Kalkan has a collection of great hotels, restaurants, and bars, as well as high quality arts and craft sellers.

## WHERE TO STAY

It's difficult to go wrong with accommodation in Kalkan. The following are just our favorites out of a much larger pool of good hotels:

**KALKAN HAN**, *Kalkan, Tel. 242 844 3151, Fax 242 844 2048. Rooms: 16. Double: $65.*

The Kalkan Han embodies Kalkan's ideal: simple and elegant. The hotel was designed by Haydar Karabey, who helped the municipal government establish its far-sighted zoning standards and locked Kalkan into its charming shape before giant hotels could move in and sweep away what makes Kalkan so appealing. The design mirrors the Greek/ Turkish architecture native to the area, but there's really nothing tricky about it; wood and stone construction on clean, simple lines. Rooms are good-sized and spartan, with ceiling fans, well-appointed bathrooms, and balconies along the upper floor. Amid all of this simplicity, however, the Kalkan Han has a remarkable way with the complex, whether serving the finest dinners in the area or helping you make arrangements.

The Kalkan Han is smartly managed, with a courteous and likeable staff. The Han is located at the upper end of town just uphill from Kalkan's single entry road.

**TÜRK EV PANSIYON**, *Kalkan, Tel. 242 844 3129. Rooms: 9. Double: $30-$45.*

All the way at the top of the town, the former Eski Evı is a small, creatively bustling place. The food is delicious, the ambiance wonderful, and the owners, Önder and Selma Elitez, are relaxed and kind. The Türk Ev is open in winter, but is an excellent refuge year round. Ideal for single women.

**PATARA PANSIYON**, *Kalkan, Tel. 242 844 3076, Fax 242 844 3753. Rooms: 9. Double: $28.*

The Patara Pansiyon is a resounding success, offering a collection of tasteful rooms with fans and showers in a wonderful restored house. Bougainvillea climb the walls, the terrace looks out over the bay, and the staff, led by owners Claire and Uluç, are very friendly.

Even cheaper is the **Deren Motel**, *Tel. 242 844 3256*, away from the center of town.

**PATARA PRINCE HOTEL**, *PK 10, Kalkan, Tel. 242 844 3920, Fax 242 844 3930. Rooms: 120. Double: $140.*

The Patara Prince is substantially different than the other hotels we recommend in Kalkan, because it is a hotel. Part of Kalkan's charm is its excellent collection of restored houses and winding streets, and the Patara Prince Hotel is not only not a restored house, it is not even on Kalkan's winding streets. The Patara Prince Hotel is located just across the bay from Kalkan, set amid the villas of Club Patara, a retreat for Turkey's wealthy and famous. The hotel is built to the exacting Club Patara standard and offers the whole slew of amenities, from satellite television to a casino. If this is you, check in.

## WHERE TO EAT

Our restaurant picks mimic our where to stay suggestions, with the Kalkan Han and the Patara Prince Hotel topping the list. Kalkan is home to innumerable seafood restaurants, and all of those along the waterfront are at least decent.

**KALKAN HAN**, *Kalkan, Tel. 242 844 3151, Fax 242 844 2048. Moderate-Expensive.*

The Kalkan Han offers a fixed menu each night at a reasonable price. Check the board in the downstairs lobby as a formality, but be assured that whatever is prepared will be to your liking. Dinner is served on the terrace.

**BELGIN'S KITCHEN**, *Yalıbolu Mah. No. 1, Kalkan, Tel. 242 844 3614. $10. Moderate.*

A staple of repeat visitor's diets, Belgin's stakes its claim to old fashioned Turkish food. The restaurant often has live music and is occasionally marauded by musicians with violins.

**YAKAMOZ**, *Yalıboyu Mah., Kalkan, Tel. 242 844 2070. $10. Moderate-Expensive.*

One of the fun, noisy waterfront places, the owner recently took a new tack and is offering Italian dishes on the sea food strip. He's doing a good job, and makes a peculiar but excellent pizza.

At the far end of the row, another restaurateur has taken the same tack with a different cuisine and opened **SHANG HAI RESTAURANT** for Chinese food. Reports are that the food at Shang Hai is surprisingly good.

## SPORTS & RECREATION

Kalkan does not have a proper beach, but there are concrete landings on the west side of the bay accessible by ferry. These landings have entire hotels attached with restaurants and other services. Kalkan does have fairly convenient access to one of Turkey's prettiest beaches, **Kaputaş** five kilometers east, and to the longest, cleanest beach in Turkey, the 16 kilometer beach at **Patara**, 15 kilometers west of town.

Boat tours leave out of Kalkan for the nearby sea caves and small islands that dot the bay, and you can make arrangements for a Kekova Boat Tour, shuttle to Kaş included, for $22. **Adda Tours**, *Yalıboyu Mah., Tel. 242 844 3610, Fax 242 844 3501,* does boat trips, trips into the interior, and a canoeing trip from Xanthos down the Esen Çayı 17 kilometers to Patara Beach.

If you are interested in seeing what local guide companies have to offer, drop by Armes Travel, *Yalıboyu Mah., Yat Limanı, Kalkan, Tel. 242 844 3169, Fax 242 844 3468.* Adda Tours is also recommended (see above).

Finally, there is a reason Kalkan is so silent and peaceful in the morning; everyone has been out all night at the local bars and dance places, which are kept muffled after midnight, and often surge right through Kalkan's periodic power outages on the strength of their generators.

# PATARA

**Patara (Gelemiş town)** has Turkey's finest beach, 16 long kilometers of clean, peaceful, white sand. Development is prohibited and access is difficult, meaning you are virtually guaranteed a patch of beach to yourself, and you can certainly find the company of others at the two entry points. There hasn't always been a beach here; it was once a lovely little bay dominated by the Lycian city of Patara, but the bay is gone and, gradually, the city is disappearing beneath sand dunes.

The small town has a relaxed charm and is served by a few nice small hotels. Take real shoes with you if you go walking in the sand. There is a lot of it, and it burns.

**History**

Patara's history is peculiar among the four major Lycian cities located in the Esen Çayı Valley, owing first to its ancient roots and second to its role as a transportation hub. Patara stems from Pttara, a word in the ancient Lycian dialect, predating the arrival of the Greeks. How much evidence of the town's advanced years is still located at Patara no one knows, since much of the site has been lost beneath advancing sand dunes.

One of the greatest mysteries is the whereabouts of the **Temple of Apollo**, a famous oracular shrine based in Patara. Apollo retired to Patara during the winters, during which time the oracle began issuing its predictions. The temple was built on a grand scale, but no evidence of it has been found.

Patara finally appears in the historical record in an inscription at Xanthos in 400 B.C., and the two cities were always closely linked by trade and proximity (Xanthos is only 12 kilometers inland), with Xanthos making great use of the harbor at Patara. The inscription postdates the first recorded cataclysm to befall the region, when the Persian Harpagus led his armies into the valley seeking to subjugate Lycia and was forced to witness the self-immolation and battlefield suicide of Xanthos' entire population. The catastrophe at Xanthos would surely have sent shock waves through its neighbor Patara, whose citizens apparently capitulated following the destruction of Xanthos.

The bond between the citizens of Xanthos and Patara was evidently a little elastic – on at least one occasion they went to war – but they were generally tight friends. Patara irked Xanthos because of its cosmopolitan aspect as the host most of the eastern Mediterranean's traffic, while the Xanthians were much more set in their ways, a charge for which there is ample evidence; the Patarans would never have destroyed their own population.

This alliance formed a kernel of the **Lycian League**, which was assembled under Pericles in the early fourth century B.C. to maintain independence from the Persian Satrap Mausolus, and after conflict that probably included naval action the Lycian League won. The cities of the league were more amenable to the passage of Alexander, who was ushered through without incident.

**Mithradites VI**, King of Pontus, brought his long campaign against Rome to the walls of Patara in 88 B.C., allegedly hacking up sacred trees at Letoon to make siege engines. His siege engines failed, his campaigns failed, and 19 years after felling the holy trees Mithradites VI had lost his kingdom and ended his own life.

Just 46 years after Mithradites VI, Julius Caesar's assassins **Cassius and Brutus** assaulted Lycia during a Roman civil war, and once again Patara watched the citizens of Xanthos massacre themselves, shook their heads wearily and surrendered.

St. Paul passed through briefly, not even stopping long enough to give a speech. Another famous Christian, Nicholas, spent his childhood in Patara before joining the clergy and moving to Myra, where he was eventually sainted as St. Nicholas. The rise of Christianity eventually spelled doom for one of Patara's greatest attractions, the oracular Temple of Apollo, and the evils of pagan oracles was codified by Theodosius I, The Great. Patara's fortunes faded even further when siltation finally closed the harbor, and the city began its long, slow submersion beneath the sand.

A final event with bearing on the ancient history of the site occurred in 1842, when the battleship *HMS Beacon* anchored offshore for six months and waited while a huge team of British sailors cut apart the ruins of Xanthos and packed them into 78 huge crates. These they loaded aboard the Beacon and sailed back to London, where they are on display at the British Museum.

## ARRIVALS & DEPARTURES

### By Bus

Dolmuş serve Kalkan and Kinik/Fethiye ten times daily in the high season, but service is much less frequent in the off season. Inquire for specific times, and try to purchase a return ticket early at one of the dolmuş stands in town. The math is fairly clear; ten dolmuş plus sixteen kilometers of perfect white sand plus 85 degrees equals bad news trying to get home.

### By Car

Patara is just three kilometers off the main coast road, 15 kilometers from Kalkan in the east and 12 from Kinik in the west. If the ruins are your goal, drive straight through town and pay at the entrance gate. If the beach is all you're after, turn right in the center of town and follow the signs toward the Beyhan Hotel, continuing to the end of the road and descending to the beach.

## WHERE TO STAY & EAT

**MERHABA HOTEL,** *P.O. Box 223, Patara, Tel. 242 843 5199, Fax 242 843 5133. Rooms: 14. Double: $30.*

The Merhaba is run by Mithat Ünnu, a doctor who was forced out of İstanbul following the revolt in 1980. He has made the most of his exile, performing some medicine when he has an opportunity and opening this hotel in 1989. The hotel blends into the hills above town, just to the north of the beach. It is run with the ruthless efficiency of a doctor; mosquito netting, an elaborate water filtration system, and exacting Turkish decor. Rooms have balconies and desks, but you'll want to spend your time at the small lobby bar or down the road at the beach.

**XANTHUS HOTEL,** *Patara, Tel. 242 843 5015, Fax 242 843 5069. Rooms: 16. Double: $27.*

A small, sprawling hotel on a hill just above town. The Xanthos Hotel has a pool, half board, and a tennis court that isn't quite fully operational. The hotel has a nice setting that has been allowed to go a little to seed in an inexplicably British way.

**HOTEL SISYPHOS,** *PK 57, Patara, Tel. 242 843 5043. Rooms: 16. Double: $27.*

Just to the left as you enter the main part of Patara, the Sisyphos has a small pool and a pretty vine-covered terrace. Thre's a relaxed atmosphere here. The restaurant may be the best in town, offering chicken curry, crepes, even banana splits.

**HOTEL BEYHAN PATARA,** *Patara, Tel. 242 843 5098, Fax 242 843 5097. Rooms: 128. Double: $75.*

Patara's only large scale hotel, the Beyhan has a commanding view of the Patara beach from atop a hill in the west of town. Rooms are functional and air conditioned, but without much style. The music continues well into the night, but the hotel is large enough that you may not notice. Convenient to the best beach access. You will see this hotel upon entering town, perched above town to the right.

**MEDUSA BAR,** *Patara, Tel. 242 843 5193.*

An excellent, unexpected place to get a beer and a big sandwich or to kill time into the wee hours. The Medusa attracts a strange set of expats and young collegiate types, and conversations that begin normal are likely to veer strange. The owner, Pamir Yilmaz, is a fount of knowledge about the ruins and is willing to explain what he knows. The Medusa is near the center of town just off of the main road out to the ruins.

## SEEING THE SIGHTS

The first indication of the former city is in evidence at **Kısık Boğazı**, the cleft in the high rock walls as you enter Patara. This was once walled and fortified, giving way to a small valley. In Patara's heyday the bay reached up deep into the valley, probably as far as the city center where the road to the western beach turns off. The majority of the Patara ruins skirted the eastern side of the bay, generally along the course of the main Patara road. The road was widened in 1995, at which time several **underground chambers** were discovered, which still lay open in the cutting at the side of the road. There is discussion of displaying the artifacts found within at a museum.

The first significant ruin is, appropriately, the **ceremonial gateway** just beyond the ticket booth. Close inspection is not possible, as the gateway is fenced off, but there are inscriptions concerning Mettius Modestus and identifying statues of his family that are no longer there. It wasn't this particular Modestus that gave us the term modest, apparently. Immediately beyond the arch is a hill of special interest to archaeologists, where new discoveries have led some to hope the Temple of Apollo may be located. The hill stands just above the former bay, whose opposite shore corresponded to the long low granary building to the west. The granary is the counterpart to the granary at Andriake, built during Hadrian's reign (117-138 A.D.).

Fields cover much of the terrain between here and the other acropolis hill at the beachside, but a collection of tombs and walls winds to the highlight of the ruins, the half-sunk Patara **theater**. Above the theater is the most likely true **acropolis**, topped by the foundation of a smallish temple of Athena. There is also a deep cylindrical hole, possibly a cistern, that has puzzled archaelogists. Scan the hills above you to the east; an old Byzantine **fortress** is secreted up there, one of several curious things found on the hill. The Patara aqueduct also winds through the hills, an engineering feat of unusual cunning.

If the aqueducts are of particular interest, turn off the main coast road east of Patara at the Yeşilköy sign, where a three kilometer drive brings you to the upper end of the waterway. There a massive and precisely constructed channel harnessed the pressure of dropping water to eliminate the need for a raised aquaduct. The view is outstanding as well.

## SPORTS & RECREATION

If it's the **beach** alone you're after, the best access is from the west side of town. Take the right turn at the town's main intersection, following the signs toward the Hotel Beyhan Patara.

# XANTHOS

**Xanthos** was the dominant city throughout most of the Lycian League's history, a powerful inland city populated by strong-willed, determined people. Today the city's sprawling ruin is in the heights above the modern town of Kınık, on a steep bluff above a bend in the River Xanthus (**Esen Çayı** in Turkish).

### History

Xanthos' history is epic. Sarpedon, one of the heroes of the Trojan War, was a King of Lycia from Xanthos; he was the grandson of Bellerophon, slayer of the Chimaera, and the son of Zeus besides, according to Homer. "Godlike Sarpedon" was a good warrior and the leader of the Lycians who fought with Troy, eventually falling to Patroklos. The reality of this man and this war is probably less important than the great reputation of Lycia synonymous with Xanthos, so often referred to as the "rich country of Lycia" and "bountiful Lycia."

It was perhaps with this legendary wealth in mind that the Persian General Harpagus was dispatched to subdue Lycia in 545 B.C., seeking to complete Persian domination of Asia Minor. Harpagus arrived with a great Persian army after clearing the western coast of opposition.

What happened then, according to Herodotus' *History* (The University of Chicago Press, 1987) was this: *The Lycians, when Harpagus drove his army into the plain of Xanthus, came out against him and fought; they were few against many, but they performed great deeds of bravery. Still, they were defeated, and, being driven into the city, they gathered their wives, children, property and servants into the citadel and then set fire to the entire citadel, to burn it all. Having done so, and sworn mighty oaths to one another, they issued forth and died in battle, all the men of Xanthus.*

The city rose from the ashes relatively quickly, when the few families that had been outside the walls at the time of the siege returned and the Persians settled others here as well. It is surprising to note that just 60 years later the Lycians marched and sailed against Greece with the Persian King Xerxes, wearing, Herodotus notes a little jarringly, "feathered caps on their heads." Alexander the Great was greeted warmly, freeing the Lycians from the constant threat of Persian domination, and Xanthos (callled Arna in the Lycians' own tongue) regained its former importance, earning the maximum number of votes in the Lycian League.

But the shadow of the ancient massacre was long. In 42 B.C. two of Julius Caesar's assassins, **Crassus and Brutus**, descended on Lycia, seeking to finance their civil war against Marc Antony. Once again the Xanthians were outnumbered and overwhelmed, and once again, rather than surrender to the invader they rounded up their citizens and massacred the entire population.

Xanthos recovered yet again, but the city's strength was largely spent. Roman rule proved to have its advantages, and this section of Lycia was at peace for centuries. Xanthus was later the site of a Byzantine cathedral.

## ARRIVALS & DEPARTURES

Xanthos is easily accessible, just off the coast road in Kınık. Dolmuş and buses from Fethiye in the west and Kalkan in the west serve the site.

## SEEING THE SIGHTS

Xanthos is bisected by a modern road curving between the theater and the ruins of the main city in the heights above. The ruin lacks the dynamic nature of the cities high in the mountains, such as Tlos, but its convenience and importance makes it a staple on most tours. Xanthos also has two classic pillar tombs, a sizeable necropolis, and one stunning spot on the hill behind the theater.

Upon entering the site you pass the site of the Nereid Monument, which once stood here and does no longer, having been crated up and shipped to London 150 years ago. The **Nereid Monument** is one of English antiquity thief Charles Fellows' great prizes, now reassembled in the British Museum in London. The monument was cast down when Fellows arrived, and its reconstruction was a puzzle for over a century. The museum believes it has finally got it right, but that does the visitor to Xanthos a fat lot of good. The Nereids for whom the monument was named were twelve water nymphs, but they've since been identified as Aurae, wind nymphs. All of which is academic, since only the platform at the base remains. The monument may have been a memorial to the tragic defeat to Harpagus, a small temple, or an elaborate tomb.

The Nereid Monument was just within the ring of walls erected in the third century, walls that extended around the tops of both hills and off a considerable distance to the east. The city was refortified by the Romans and Byzantines and intermittently sacked, which resulted in much destruction and recycling of buildings; it is therefore much less comprehensible than cities that fell into disuse earlier.

Ascending the hill to the right, you arrive at the site of a great Byzantine church whose mosaic floors have recently been uncovered. Continuing around the base of the hill you pass some deep tomb openings and arrive at the picturesque **necropolis**, the site of several square cut rock tombs and a soaring pillar tomb of a kind particular to Lycia; this sight is a fixture of local hotel brochures and personal slideshows. The tombs here are some of the only structures in this section of Xanthos that pre-date the Roman period, hailing from the fourth century. The hilltop above the necropolis is the site of the acropolis in the Roman era, a much more sprawling version of the city that in earlier times had been centered on the hill above the theater. The chief feature of the hilltop today is a Byzantine basilica and the Roman walls, which continue until they are redundant in the heights above the modern road.

Descending now to the road you come to the area of Lycian Xanthus. Notable here is the **Xanthos Obelisk**, whose long inscription tells of a great Xanthian leader from the end of the fifth century. This man, the son of Harpagus, but not the aforementioned Harpagus, is credited with slaying seven men in a day and other great feats of virility and derring-do. His various exploits were commemorated in reliefs now found in the İstanbul Archaeological Museum, and included leading the Xanthians against the Athenians in one of the battles that helped Sparta to victory in the Peloponnesian War.

The **Harpy Tomb** is also here in the vicinity of the theater, opposite the open space that formed Xanthos' marketplace. The reliefs atop this tomb have been copied and returned to Xanthus (the originals are in London), and depict small flying bird women. As with the Nereid Monument, the Harpy Tomb now seems hastily named; the Harpies may in fact be Sirens hauling spirits of the dead to Hades, one of their various duties. The tomb was built for an unknown man in the third century B.C., and was the combined work of Lycian and Greek artists.

Ascending above the theater you find a great hodgepodge of buildings from various eras. Structures dating to ancient and Hellenistic Lycia are no longer recognizable. Complete your tour at the tip of land jutting out above the river, the likely site of a former temple or defensive tower. While here consider that the account of the siege under Brutus mentions Roman soldiers trying to break through the Xanthos defenses by swimming, a method that would seem to leave them at the base of this sheer acropolis hill, stones raining down on their dripping wet heads. Anyway, the swimmers were foiled and entangled by nets dropped in the river, and the city was eventually taken by a standard storming of the walls. The remaining citizens, having retreated to this high point, engulfed their acropolis and themselves in flames, and acrid black smoke rose over the valley for the second time.

# LETOON

**Letoon** bookends the huge beach of Patara, with the Patara ruins at the eastern end. Lycia had a great collection of oracular shrines and temples, but Letoon was the spiritual center. It is a relatively minor ruin.

**History**

Letoon's history begins with a legend. **Leto** was special among Zeus' many conquests in that the King of the Gods evidently felt real affection for her, which was a threat to Hera. Hera banished the pregnant Leto, who gave birth to both Apollo and Artemis on the Greek island of Delos, then made her way to Lycia in order to wash the children in the waters of the Xanthos River. As the story goes, Leto was turned away from the river by shepherds, perhaps fearing the wrath of Hera. With the assistance of a wolf pack she made her way to the river, drinking from it and bathing her children in its good water. Not content to let the shepherds get away with their lack of chivalry, she returned, godlings tucked under one arm, and turned the foolish men into frogs.

Leto's spirit continued to inhabit the place, and frogs still do too. It was Leto who changed the Lycian's name from the Termilae, out of respect for the wolves (lycos), and, more subtly, perhaps lent the Lycians their name for woman, lada (and English speakers ours – lady?). Herodotus, it should be noted, has an altogether different conception of the origin of "Lycian," claiming it comes from a certain Lycus, a son of Pandion and a citizen of Athens. Letoon has a great sanctuary to Leto, as well as somewhat lesser sanctuaries to Apollo and Artemis. The layout of the city, one temple immediately beside the other, underscores its religious focus. The Lycian League held its gatherings here, and Letoon's high priest was considered the high priest of all Lycia.

Letoon was a holy place, not a military fortification, and it was seemingly left in relative peace by invaders. One account of Mithradites VI's siege of Patara notes that the king destroyed not Letoon's buildings, but its trees in the manufacture of siege engines. Even in this he was discouraged by a dream, and abruptly stopped; the damage may have been done, as Mithradites' warfare against Rome came to naught, and he lost his home, his empire, and, in 69 B.C., his life. Roman rule was beneficial throughout Lycia, but Letoon ceased to thrive after Theodosius I's edict against pagan worship. The city was finally destroyed in the seventh century during Arab incursions.

## ARRIVALS & DEPARTURES

Just two kilometers west of Kınık signs point to Letoon, four kilometers south of the main road. Without a car you can hike the flat road or hope for a dolmuş, which leave intermittently from Kınık, although a better policy is to enquire about departures for Letoon at the Kınık otogar or get a taxi. With so many easily accessible ruins nearby, we don't recommend visiting Letoon without a car.

## SEEING THE SIGHTS

The **three temples** were the centerpiece then, and are now. The foundations of the three lay side by side, with Leto's temple the largest building on the west and the temple of Artemis and Apollo on the east. The middle temple may be the oldest, but the identity of its spiritual occupant is unknown, and various permutations have been suggested for the three central gods and the three temples. The western temple was built above a holy spring, and the presumed Temple of Artemis and Apollo is so named for its mosaic of a bow and quiver, surely less Leto's province than her warlike offspring.

The elaborate semicircular building just south of the temples is often partially flooded, suggesting that this region underwent the same seismic activity that apparently dumped the ruins near Kekova into the sea. This was the **nymphaeum**, an ornamental fountain found in many towns, but rarely on this grand scale. The distinctive ruins of a Byzantine church are located on the higher ground.

Finally, Letoon's **theater** was grand for a city of Letoon's small size, but this owed to the pan-Lycian meetings held here. There are several small reliefs just outside the northeast passage, on the far side of the theater from the ruins, and a small cafe is open here during high season.

# PINARA

**Pınara** is shocking and gratifying beyond most of Turkey's inaccessible ancient sites. As you approach, high cliff walls honeycombed with tombs rise before you. Other cities' necropoles, even Myra's, pale. Pınara has the sheer, mysterious power of Petra and Cappadoccia.

### History

Pınara was probably a settlement of **Xanthos**, and grew to be of such importance that, like Xanthos and the greatest of the cities in the Lycian League it had the maximum votes in League affairs. Pınara shared the fate of its fellows in the League, falling to Harpagus, surrendering peacefully to Alexander and enjoying a period of prosperity under Roman rule. The original city was located atop the acropolis, eventually dropping down to the more accessible level that most of the ruins are on today. Earthquakes badly damaged the city in the second and third centuries, but remained important into the middle ages, as evidenced by the ruins of a medieval fortress atop the acropolis.

## ARRIVALS & DEPARTURES

### By Bus

Tours travel to the site, and dolmuş serve Minareköy from Esen, but service is rare and unpredictable. Taxi drivers will be loathe to bump their way up the long, steep hill, but, as always, have a price. The hike from Minareköy is not a good idea in the heat of the day. Some would say it's never a good idea.

**By Car**
Four kilometers north of Esen take the Pınara/Minareköy exit. Minareköy is four kilometers along, from which there is a steep three kilometer road to the site.

## SEEING THE SIGHTS

Pınara is rarely busy, and the local caretaker enjoys showing you around for a small fee. Given the thickly overgrown nature of the site, he is a good buy.

Pınara spills over the sides of a small valley high in the mountains above the Xanthian plain. The walls surrounding the city soar more than 1,000 feet to the acropolis, decorated throughout with rock-cut tombs. The tombs were carved out by workers lowered from above; at least that's what people speculate. It's the only conceivable way of performing work so difficult on a sheer wall. It doesn't appear that anyone has catalogued the tombs, although it seems that the facade is no more than it seems, with simple square cut burial chambers. The walls would offer some wonderful challenges for historically-minded rock climbers.

On the floor of the small valley are the ruins of the Roman-era city with several interesting buildings socked in amid thick underbrush. The **Royal Tomb** is located at the southern end of town, near the origin of a small stream, and it remains decorated with a fine set of reliefs. British archaeologist Charles Fellows, recognizing the difficulty of transporting the actual reliefs away, made plaster casts. The reliefs have deteriorated badly in the brief period since Fellows made them in 1839, but they depict a set of people that may be the deceased's family, together with city that is not Tlos. Your guess is as good as anyone else's. The identity of the tomb's occupant is unknown, but his importance can be surmised by the scale of the tomb.

The **theater**, facing the wall of tombs, is cleared and a good place to rest, as is the creek that winds through the site beneath a set of weathered oaks. The **acropolis** is accessible, barely. If you want to climb to the acropolis wind your way up toward the top from near the Royal Tomb.

## TLOS

**Tlos** is credited with having the most commanding view of any Lycian city, a great boast and a probably a fair one. A visit here should be combined with a visit to the gorge at **Saklikent**, less than six kilometers away.

**History**

Tlos' history has spanned more than 3,000 years, from Hittite times to an 18th century feudal baron who resided at the site. Discoveries at Tlos date occupation here to the Hittite era, which corresponds to mentions of a Dalawa in 13th century Hittite texts (akin to the Lycian name for Tlos, Tlawa). The inhabitants of this towering city probably enjoyed great success in the toll trade, owing to their proximity to the routes into and out of the Xanthos plain.

Tlos and Pınara were sister cities, sharing the mountainous high ground. Both rose and fell with the Lycian League, bearing the brunt of land invasions that entered Lycia from the northwest. Tlos' own history mirrored that of its fellows, and it was one of the Lycian League's leading members, but there seems to be no records of the battles that surely occurred here. The one anomaly on Tlos' record is its relatively recent use by a brigand during the late Ottoman Empire. Kanlı ("Bloody") Ali Ağa retired to this castle after a brush with Ottoman law, allegedly after killing a man. Rehabilitating the castle, Kanlı Ali Ağa went on to set up a remote feudal system amid the debris of a badly overextended Ottoman Empire.

## ARRIVALS & DEPARTURES
**By Bus**

A daily dolmuş departs Fethiye in the afternoon, and if there is enough demand a dolmuş driver may weaken and shuttle you up to the ruins. It's nice if a dolmuş is returning in time for you to make it back down to Fethiye (*"Dolmuş dönecak ne zaman?"* When will the dolmuş return?) without the long five kilometer walk to the highway.

**By Car**

Tlos is easy to spot, but can be infernally difficult to reach. Tlos is located alongside the village of Yaka, four kilometers south of Guneşli village. The easiest way to Guneşli is via the Fethiye-Korkuteli road, eight kilometers north. Turn off of the Fethiye-Korkuteli (350) road at the Tlos sign just one kilometer east of the intersection of the coast and interior roads to Antalya.

There is another route to Guneşli from the coast road, involving a serpentine passage through Çamurköy, but the route from the north is easier to follow and more heavily traveled.

## SEEING THE SIGHTS

Tlos is built around a stony outcrop, which is now topped by the ruin of the remarkably recent **fortress** of Kanlı Ali Ağa. Arriving at the village of **Yaka**, you are near the center of the smallish city, the theater off to your left, the fortress above a tangle of old walls and buildings to your right. The fortress is built on the obvious site of the former acropolis, which has a spectacular view of the valley below, reminiscent of Karpu Kale on the Black Sea. Yaka is alongside a long set of ruined foundations, probably of Tlos' marketplace. A church was built on the site, this just past the curve in the road bearing off toward the theater. The **theater** has several friezes, but is thickly overgrown and far less gratifying than the **acropolis** area with its tombs and fortress.

You've already glimpsed the best of Tlos' tombs on your way up to Yaka, and these are reached via several paths, according to your agility. The easiest approach is from below, following the stream, dry in the high season, and climbing up to have a look around. The most remarkable tomb in Tlos is far and away the **tomb of Bellerophon**, so called not because Bellerophon was interred here but, like Alexander's sarcophagus in İstanbul, the named individual is depicted on the tomb. In this case Bellerophon is in midflight, about to choke the Chimera with his leaden spear. This is to the left, but other decorative carvings are also found in the large open area at the mouth of the rooms. There are tombs to the left and right, with resting places for the deceased.

One of the reasons this site was chosen for a citadel is the abundance of fresh water, filtering down from the Akdağ Mountains and welling up here. **Yaka Park**, near Tlos, is thick with springs and even some pools. They are what the English might call "bracing." The **castle** atop the acropolis is badly beaten up considering its recent use, but it's still a fine destination. This was the site of the ancient settlement, later used for the citadel of Hellenistic Tlos. For a quick education in wall construction, have a look at the walls along the east side of the acropolis, facing the town. These have been built and rebuilt over the course of more than 2,000 years. If you're in a hurry, accept the nearly certain offer of a local kid; he'll be able to whisk you through the most interesting of the area's sights.

### Saklikent

You turned off the road leading to Saklikent on the way to Tlos. Consider retracing your steps and continuing on to this beautiful gorge. In addition to the now plentiful signs there is a thick trail of köfte and gözleme restaurants along the correct route. Dolmuş serve Saklikent directly from Fethiye, better than we can say for Tlos.

If the roadside restaurants don't stir your fancy, the **MOUNTAIN LODGE**, *Tel. 252 638 2515*, which you pass on your way to Tlos from the highway, might; it offers a surprising range of well-prepared food, from Chinese stir fry to Indian curried meals. The Mountain Lodge also offers accommodation.

# FETHIYE

The **Fethiye** area is a hub for visiting the ruins and beaches in the vicinity, but it lacks the appeal of Dalyan to the west and Patara, Kalkan, and Kaş to the east. The city has some ruins of ancient Telmessus, and is ironically improved by the booming growth in Ölüdeniz, which has left Fethiye a little quieter and more relaxing. The once-great attraction of **Ölüdeniz Beach** is a thickly overdeveloped mess, and Ölüdeniz town squats beside it growing exponentially.

### History

There has been a settlement on this excellent harbor since at least 1500 B.C. The ruins undergirding Fethiye are of **Telmessus**, the Lycian League's westernmost outpost. The city's name echoes the name of the original Lycian name for Lycia, Termilae, which is odd considering that Telmessus was not considered part of Lycia proper until Pericles welcomed the city to his new Lycian League in the campaign against the Persian satrapy at Helicarnas/Bodrum. Telmessus' bay was known as the Bay of Glaukos after one of the Lycian heroes of the Trojan War.

The city shared the fate of its neighbors in Lycia, opening its gates to Alexander, chafing under Rhodian rule in the second century B.C., and suffering badly under Arab attacks in the seventh century. The Crusaders probably left a garrison at the hilltop fortress here in the 15th century, and the Crusaders certainly staked a claim to the islands dotting the Fethiye Bay, where they have left evidence of their occupation.

Fethiye's modern name derives from **Fethi Bey**, a Turkish military pilot who crashed and died here in 1913. The former name of the city was Makri.

# ARRIVALS & DEPARTURES

### By Bus

The otogar is inconveniently distant from the town center, about two kilometers. Dolmuş run into town from the road you enter town on, Ataturk Caddesi, and major bus lines should offer service buses to new arrivals. Driving times from **Dalaman Airport** (see Dalyan, Chapter 19) will be cut dramatically by a new highway being punched through the mountains.

Note: the curious broad stripes cut into the bare hillsides approaching Fethiye are firebreaks.

**By Car**

Fethiye is one of Turkey's largest cities on the southwest coast and is laid out along a long central road running directly through town that proceeds to bend around the bay.

## ORIENTATION

Between the town's new name and devastating earthquakes, Fethiye has few traces of its former self. The sole remnants of ancient Telmessus are at the theater, near the tourism information center at the town center, and in the scattering of tombs at the base of the steep hill directly above town. A Crusader-era castle stands on the acropolis, surely fashioned from – and covering over – ruins of Telmessus' temples or fortifications.

Fethiye's **tourism information** office is just inland of the marina on İskele Karşısı, *Tel. 252 614 1527, Fax 252 614 1527.*

## WHERE TO STAY

You must choose whether to stay in the relatively quiet hotels of Fethiye as a base to see ruins outside of town, or nearer Ölüdeniz Beach in Ölüdeniz. Fethiye is the better option if you're on a budget or passing through; Fethiye has quicker transport, better hotels, and, if you want to go to Ölüdeniz, dolmuş make the trip constantly.

**VILLA DAFFODIL**, *Il. Karagözler Fevzi Çakmak Cad. No. 115, Fethiye, Tel. 252 614 9595, Fax 252 612 2223. Rooms: 15. Double: $56.*

A well-run small hotel just across the shore road from the Fethiye Bay, one kilometer from the harbor. The Villa Daffodil, opened in 1995, has air conditioning, satellite television and a pool. The suite room, 301, is truly special in its interesting attic space. The hotel restaurant offers a top-notch fixed menu dinner.

**YACHT MOTEL**, *Il. Karagözler Cad.,Fethiye, Tel. 252 614 1530. Rooms: 33. Double: $20.*

Open six months a year, the Yacht is simple and cheap, offering convenience to the city center and a beautiful location. The front room in the main building has an outstanding view of the harbor, and the annex building and pool are also well-situated.

**MER PANSIYON**, *Dolgu Sahası Sahil Yolu No. 1, Fethiye, Tel. 252 614 1177. Rooms: 20. Double: $19.*

An excellent, clean, inexpensive pension.

**GÖREME PANSIYON**, *Dolgu Sahası, Stadum Yanı No. 25, Fethiye, Tel. 252 614 6944, Fax 252 614 6944. Rooms: 14. Double: $20.*
Like the Mer, a solid budget choice.

### Near Ölüdeniz

**MONTANA PINE HOTEL**, *Ovacık Köyü, Fethiye, Tel. 252 616 6252, Fax 252 616 6451. Rooms: 154. Double: $95.*

Set in the pine trees 1,200 feet above Ölüdeniz beach, the Montana Pine Hotel is built in the image of a mountain village. The rooms are scattered among various cottage buildings, each building done in wood as designed by an 85 year old architect whose traditional construction has been awarded by the Ağa Khan. The Montana Pine is in neither Fethiye nor Ölüdeniz, although it is closer to the latter. Its mildly remote location makes it necessary to have a car.

The hotel has an unusual and wonderfully conceived set of public areas, long patios and arched interior spaces with traditionally decorated couches and tables, ideal for unwinding after a long day. The rooms are simple and complete. The hotel is perched above forest, through which you can just glimpse the sea. Half-board accommodations are recommended here; dolmuş travel back and forth on the road one kilometer below the hotel.

**ROBINSON CLUB LYKIA WORLD**, *Kıdırak Mah, Fethiye, Tel. 252 616 6410, Fax 252 616 6410. Rooms: 163. Double: $135.*

One of the Mediterranean's hotels for gluttons: food, fun, and recreation, 24 hours a day. There is an all-inclusive arrangement that covers drinks and meals as well.

**OTEL MERI**, *Ölüdeniz, Fethiye, Tel. 252 616 6060, Fax 252 616 6456. Rooms: 83. Double: $115, Half board,*

An old standby on the inner bay at Ölüdeniz. The dramatic growth of the area has now engulfed the hotel, but it remains protected by the mountains behind and the end of the beach beyond. New units are being developed – complete with a small escalator car – in the heights above the main hotel.

**OSMAN'S PLACE**, *Ölüdeniz, Fethiye, Tel. 252 616 6002. Bungalows: 14. Bungalow: $8.*

Directly next to the Otel Meri, Osman's Place has a set of simple bungalows (read: clapboard shacks) and a strip of beach alongside its affluent neighbor. The most savvy among the backpackers pick this spot despite the long walk. Dilapidated, cheap, and always interesting.

## WHERE TO EAT

There are dozens of fish restaurants in the area. Quality varies a little, atmosphere a lot.

MEĞRİ RESTAURANT, Çarsı Cad. No. 13-17, Fethiye, Tel. 252 610 4046. *Moderate; second location – Eski Cami Geçedi Likya Sok. No. 8-9, Fethiye, Tel. 252 614 4047, Fax 252 612 0446.*
A local favorite, serving nicely prepared Turkish dishes and fish. An excellent and reasonable place to try the in-season seafood specialties. A second Meğri is now open and seems to be upholding the same good quality. Rafet Restaurant is also a good choice in Fethiye proper.
PEKING CHINA RESTAURANT, *Dispanser Sok. No. 60, Fethiye, Tel. 252 614 0706. Moderate.*
Some of the dishes may not quite be what you expect, sweet and sour things, for instance, but the food is good.

**In Ovacık**
ŞADİRVAN, *Ovacık, Fethiye, Tel. 252 616 6140. Moderate-Expensive.*
The Şadirvan is in Ovacık, atop the hill between Fethiye and Ölüdeniz. Good food and a very personable staff.
BEYAZ YUNUS, *Ölüdeniz, Tel. 252 616 6799. Moderate-Expensive.*
The best choice in Ölüdeniz; note that the "white dolphin" in the restaurant's name is not reflected on the menu. Particularly overpriced seafood, but the other dishes are fairly reasonable by Ölüdeniz standards.

## SEEING THE SIGHTS

The castle and acropolis is reached after a hike up the road behind the theater or up Kale Cad. from the east, and is signed in both directions. The **Knights of St. John** probably built the fortress in the 15th century, fortifying the mainland ports opposite Rhodes as protection against attack from Asia Minor and to better command shipping. The castle is bare, but it is worth a visit simply for the view.

The **rock tombs** at Fethiye constitute the city's most interesting ruins. The cluster of tombs in the eastern part of the city, above the dolmuş station in the direction of the city center, has Telmessus' finest remaining relic, the **Tomb of Amyntas**. The tomb has been dated to the middle of the fifth century, but about Amyntas not much is known. The necropolis is meager compared with areas such as Pınara, but the set of tombs here is lovely at sundown.

The **museum** has one very important piece, the **Letoon Trilingual** that helped scholars untangle the Lycian language, but the museum is not particularly instructive.

## SPORTS & RECREATION

**Beaches**

**Ölüdeniz beach** is one of the most beautiful and overcrowded stretches of sand in the world. Dolmuş travel back and forth between Fethiye and Ölüdeniz half-hourly in the summer. The beach is served by a great variety of restaurants and cafes, and shops selling everything from sunglasses and Ölüdeniz T-shirts to paragliding from Babadağ mountain high above. There's a $1 entry fee.

There are cruises to **Haghia Nikola Island**, a small, pretty spot with Byzantine ruins and a good beach. From Fethiye you can visit **Çaliş Beach**, on weekdays less crowded (but less pretty) than Ölüdeniz beach.

**Boating**

Day cruises out of Fethiye are excellent, sailing around the many islands poking up out of Fethiye Bay. Prices vary with the season and the number of people along for the trip – the cost rises if you insist on a semi-private cruise.

Cruises depart from the Fethiye Harbor every morning, spending the day visiting various islands and selling you drinks. Lunch is included, as are opportunities to swim from the boat or, if it is the will of the boat, from beaches on various islands. Your hotel can set you up with a specific company, which is ordinarily easier than hunting down a boat on your own.

**Rafting/Canyoning**

Several companies arrange trips on the **Dalaman River** west of Fethiye, and canyoning trips are also available into **Saklikent**. Never been canyoning? Hell, no one else has either. **Alternatif Turizm**, based in Marmaris but with a base camp on the Dalaman River, is recommended. Contact them at: *Şirinyer Mah. Çamlık Sok. No. 10, Marmaris, Tel. 252 413 5994, Fax 252 413 3208*. Their Ölüdeniz agent is **Aventura Turizm**, *Belcekiz Tatil Köyü, Ölüdeniz, Tel. 252 616 6427*.

## SHOPPING

Tuesday is Fethiye's **market day**, an excellent opportunity to browse, watch people, and perhaps even pick up some irresistible vegetables or souvenir.

## EXCURSIONS & DAY TRIPS

### Kayaköy

This once-bustling town in the mountains above Fethiye was emptied in the trade of Greek and Turkish populations in 1923. The Turks relegated to this area proved unwilling and unable to assume the role of their Greek predecessors, and the city was eventually abandoned. The ghost town is animated by a few inhabitants, but the overall effect is a powerfully sad testament to a powerfully sad event. The recent interest has led to the establishment of a hotel to put you up, but we can't vouch for it.

The ghost town is reached via Fethiye's Kaya Cad., following the signs. Tours visit the town as well, but guides have little to say that the town doesn't say itself.

## Cadyanda

This ancient ruin is located in a thick pine forest in the hills above Fethiye to the northeast. Signs direct you from the main Muğla/Marmaris road, and **Cadyanda** is near Üzümlu, a total of thirty kilometers from Fethiye. Archaeologists from the Fethiye Museum are at work here, giving some order to what has always been a confusing muddle of old stone foundations. The highlights of a visit to Cadyanda, aside from the view, are the sarcophagi cut from within boulders.

# 19. THE CARIAN COAST

This section of coast, once home to the cities of **Caria**, is far more heavily developed than the Lycian Coast to the east, but there are still plenty of secluded spots, fine hotels, and impressive ruins. **Marmaris** and **Bodrum**, two of Turkey's largest marinas, are located in this stretch, and filled throughout summer with yachts and Turkey's traditional two masted wooden gulets. **Caunos** and **Cnidos** are two of the best preserved and interesting ancient cities in Turkey, and there are dozens of other, less impressive ruins along the lush coast.

Dalaman Airport serves the region on the east and the new Bodrum Airport at Güllük is scheduled to open in 1997.

## DALYAN (CAUNOS)

**Dalyan** has a charm all its own. The small town hugs the eastern side of the **Koyçeğiz delta**, a pleasant and abundantly fertile place that pulses with birds, turtles, and fish, with the bray of frogs and, unfortunately, the whine of mosquitoes. Shallow draught boats ply the channels back and forth between the four mile long sand beach and the town three miles inland, passing the outstanding ruins of Caunos on the way. The boats continue puttering upstream to mud baths, sulphur springs, and, finally, **Koyçeğiz Lake**. The entire course of the river is unbridged, choking off development of the western shore and ensuring that boat travel remains the main means of transportation.

Dalyan boasts one of the most remarkable ancient cities in the Mediterranean in **Caunos**, a short distance downstream. The endless city walls enclose two spurs of a mountain and a towering crag that rises out of the river and commands the entrance to the delta. This sheer spire was once topped by Caunus' acropolis, but today offers only the remains of some Hellenistic and Byzantine fortifications. Upriver of the acropolis are 4th century B.C. rock cut tombs overlooking the town.

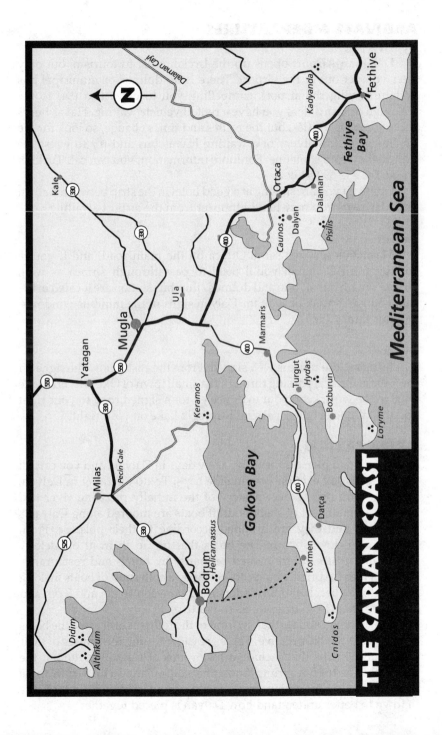

THE CARIAN COAST

## ARRIVALS & DEPARTURES

### By Air

**Dalaman Airport** opens up the Lycian coast to tourism, but only after you get out of the airport. There is no dolmuş or municipal bus system serving the airport, compelling you to get a taxi ($4) to the Dalaman otogar unless you have a rented vehicle waiting. Havaş buses serve some local cities, but the routes and times change, so look for the green and yellow livery of a waiting Havaş bus and try to wrest the destination from someone. For more information, you can call **Turkish Air** at *Tel. 252 692 5499.*

Finally, if you are staying at a good hotel in the strip between Kalkan and Marmaris you may have a transfer from the airport awaiting.

### By Bus

Major bus services serve Ortaca on the main road, and if you're coming from Dalaman you'll need to pass through Ortaca as well. Ortaca's main bus station and dolmuş/minibus station are located in the same otogar, so ask or look for Dalyan signs in the minibus windows. Dolmuş fare is 75¢.

### By Car

As usual, the route is well signed. From the east follow the signs off the E400 at Ortaca, passing through the small town of Okcular. From the E400 in the west, keep your eyes peeled for a signed road to your right about 4 kilometers after passing Koyçeğiz Lake on your right.

## ORIENTATION

It's good to plan on spending a few days in Dalyan, and you can fill a week with day excursions and side trips. To do anything in Dalyan, however, you need some mastery of the initially puzzling **river taxi** system. A small fleet of shallow draft boats are moored along Dalyan's waterfront, and they are grouped according to their purpose. From upstream to downstream: The boats that tie up in front of Melody Restaurant upstream are owned primarily by hotels and restaurants. Next is a pier for private boats, followed by a collection of boats making the trip to the beach and back (departing between 10 am and 3 pm and returning from 1 pm to 7 pm; $3 round trip).

Downstream still further, in front of the tourism office, are the boats belonging to the cooperative. Touts are eager to sing the praises of their five hour, $6 trips that include a token look at Caunos, a stop at the mudbaths and the hot springs, and a final stop at the beach. In truth, these trips are a good time and we recommend joining in on your first full day in town to better understand how Dalyan is pieced together.

River taxis, freelance boats willing to take you anywhere along the river, are parked a little further downstream (If you pay more than $2 per person for a trip to Caunos and back you're not haggling very well). At the bottom of the boating food chain are the rowboats, located furthest downstream at the end of a gravel path. These small boats leave from behind the health clinic and Caria Hotel, crossing to the small town of Çandir on the opposite shore. Once across you can find your own way to the tombs, upstream, or the ruins, downstream. You can rent rowboats for less than $15 per day, finding your own little pool amid the reeds and swimming, or exploring the coastline.

That clear, Dalyan's local attractions are plentiful, although it is a two hour drive to ruins farther afield such as Tlos in the east. Dalyan is an excellent place to relax and fall off the ruin-a-day pace, exploring a town with ruins and rock cut tombs of its own, plus lots of interesting cafes, shops, and a great beach to relax on.

## WHERE TO STAY

Dalyan's popularity has grown through the years, but the terrain – and some careful restrictions on development – has dictated that growth be limited. At a distance of three miles from the beach, Dalyan is prohibitively far for genuine "beach resort" status. That is the town's saving grace, since it is otherwise an idyllic vacation spot (mosquitoes notwithstanding). Speaking of mosquitoes, all of the hotels listed offer fans or electric devices to keep mosquitoes at bay. Most hotels in the area are closed during winter.

Because the town is built up against the Dalyan River it is easy to figure out – unfortunately this has made the municipality slow to post street signs. Koyçeğiz, on the main coast road at the head of the Koyçeğiz Lake, has accommodations which blur the line between restful and dull.

**SULTAN PALAS HOTEL**, *Dalyan, 48840, Mugla, Tel. 252 284 2103, Fax 252 284 2106. Rooms: 26. Double: $550 per week, high season;$450 per week, mid season. Half board. Closed October 30 to April 1.*

The Sultan Palas is a charming retreat tucked away on the "other side" of the Dalyan River, alone in a small valley at the base of the sprawling Caunos ruins. The hotel's centerpiece is the stone tower that serves as a late evening bar, although some might claim that the generously sized pool is the crucial bit. Rooms are practical and have their own balconies, but the real fun is in lounging at the poolside or joining in on one of the many day trips. The Sultan Palas caters to vacationers who are in the area for several days or a week – and hosts Taifun and his English wife Linda excel at keeping you as busy as you care to be. The hotel has its own boat service between the hotel dock and town. The hotel offers cheap, interesting day excursions around the Dalyan area.

**HAPPY CARRETTA**, *Dalyan, 48840, Mugla, Tel. 252 284 2109, Fax 252 284 3295. Rooms: 18. Double: $30. Breakfast. Open all year.*

Clean and simple, this hotel has a pretty waterfront location made all the better by a painstakingly tended lawn and garden. Like most of the hotels in the south end of Dalyan, the Happy Carretta has a grill in the back on the river, where you're welcome to sip drinks amid the roses and bougainvillea and watch the boats putter past.

**DERVIŞ HAN**, *Gulpınar Cad., Dalyan, 48840, Mugla, Tel. 252 284 2479, Fax 252 284 3539. Rooms: 9. Double: $35. Breakfast. Closed November-March.*

The Derviş has managed to remain a secret, despite opening in 1990. It's off the beaten track on the north end of town in the neighborhood of the Denizatı, the Sultan Palas, and Dalyan's new soccer field. If you take the trouble to find it and sort out language difficulties with owner Hüseyin Kural (Turkish and German) you'll find a stunning garden looking up at the sheer slopes beneath Caunos. Rooms are tidy and practical, but the garden is one of the reasons to visit Dalyan.

**ASUR HOTEL**, *Dalyan, 48840, Mugla, Tel. 252 284 3232, Fax 252 284 3244. Rooms: 34. Double: $90. Half board.*

Dalyan's status address is a comfortable, slightly cookie-cutter set of cottages designed by Nail Çakirhan – the Ağa Khan Architectural award winner who also designed the Montana Pine Resort. The hotel just misses being charming – despite the clutter of "traditional Turkish" knick-knacks in each room. It mortgages charm for an A-list of amenities, such as satellite TV and air-conditioning, and a slightly jaded staff. The hotel is at the southern end of Dalyan, nearest the sea, and has its own dock.

Good budget pensions costing less than $15 for a double are the **LIKYA PENSION**, *Tel. 252 284 2233*, and the **SAHIL PENSION**, *Tel. 252 284 2187.*

### In Sarigerme

**IBEROTEL SARIGERME PARK**, *Ortaca Postanesi PK 1, Ortaca, Tel. 252 286 8031, Fax 252 286 8043. Rooms: 372. Double: $160, Half board.*

A short drive – or a one hour pair of dolmuş – east of Dalyan is one of Turkey's finest holiday villages.

In a land filled with hotels that are less than the sum of their parts, the Sarigerme Park is a bewitching exception. The Sarigerme Park is precisely what most of the large beachfront hotels intend to be, a full-service retreat with archery, soccer, horse riding, volleyball, and a whole range of beachside diversions. Nighttime even brings the noisy "animations," Turkey's ubiquitous and typically unsuccessful humor and dance numbers, and here they work. Here everything works.

The Iberotel benefits from its great size – it is more than 140,000 square meters – and from the happy coincidence that the property is on the grounds of **ancient Pisilus**. The bulk of the ruins are off the path to the beach to the right. Here you can clamber up a hill and poke around the acropolis, trampling through the thick undergrowth to investigate tumbled Roman structures and the large ring of 6 foot wide city walls. The necropolis is built on the buttress just above the beach, with other ruins scattered around the hotel grounds. Amateur archaeologist Heinz-Otto Lamprecht has identified many of the Pisilus ruins, and the hotel staff leads occasional tours of what amounts to its own ruins.

Just as the hotel takes care of the big things, it is mindful of the small things as well. You get a pot of coffee in the morning, not a tiny cup; you get good potatoes and eggs if the standard bread, jam, cheese and tomato diet is wearing thin. Getting a dolmuş to the local transit hub of Ortaca is easy since the route is partially funded by the hotel. Most rooms have a balcony bedecked with flowers, and air-conditioning and CNN/NBC is standard. The beauty salon even offers a six-day regimen of massage and every other form of relaxation and beautification.

The grounds are nicely tended, with paths down to a long sand beach that offers beach lounging furniture and umbrellas. Europeans love these things. The hotel buildings are low and unassuming, and many rooms are located in smaller two story bungalows. The hotel's largest building is set back into a hillside hardly visible from the beach, with flowers tumbling from the balconies. As you would expect from such a well-run hotel, the staff is helpful and professional.

Note: the Pisilus ruins are open to the public, and the Sarigerme beach is also public, accessed from the main road to the west.

## WHERE TO EAT

Dalyan, predictably, is stuffed with fish restaurants. Heads up, though – a Chinese food restaurant is expected to open in 1997. As is normal along the Mediterranean, your hotel is likely to have a tempting meal plan.

**DENIZATI**, *Dalyan, Muğla, Tel. 252 284 2129, Fax 252 284 2635. Moderate-Expensive.*

A Dalyan institution, the Denizatı has a full assortment of fresh seafood. The restaurant is a mile north of Dalyan on the east bank of the Dalyan River, across from the Sultan Palas dock – a $4 cab fare or, better still, a similarly priced boat ride. The slight inconvenience of getting here from Dalyan is worthwhile; the mezes (appetizers), in particular, are expertly prepared. Prices are comparable to those in town (meze are $1.30, beer $1.00, entrees $4-8). The **Deniz Yıldızı** in town is a recent spinoff of the Denizatı

**BEYAZ GÜL**, *Dalyan, Muğla, Tel. 252 284 2304. Moderate.*
As close as Turkey comes to a riverside barbeque. The Beyaz Gül is an excellent, reasonable option in a neighborhood that is going upmarket.
**THE PINK BAR**, *Dalyan, Muğla. Moderate.*
Never mind the name, the Pink Bar serves good meals. This restaurant/bar is located not far inland from the tourism information booth.
**THE MEDITERANEAN FRUIT BAR**, *Dalyan, Muğla. Inexpensive.*
Near the center of town, the employees here squeeze a wondrous assortment of fruit into icy cold shakes and smoothies. Just the thing after, well, anything at all.

## SEEING THE SIGHTS

The ruins of **Caunos**, just across the river from Dalyan, are sprawling and, like the greater Dalyan area, can be explored for days.

You get to Caunos via Dalyan, unless you arrive from the sea. Tours to Caunos put in at the harbor on the seaside, two kilometers downstream of Dalyan. If you catch a boat to Caunos independently you will be dropped off at the end of a long dirt track at the base of the Acropolis hill. Forge your way inland along the road and around the peak and after ten minutes you arrive at one of the ticket booths. The main entrance to Caunos is at the end of a long boardwalk downstream of the acropolis.

### History

It is unclear who initially settled the site of Caunos, and historians agree it was probably not the Greeks. It may have been a native settlement or a colony of Rhodes, but whoever settled the area left it with odd customs and language. The early tongue of Caunos, like Carian, remains uncracked by scholars. Herodotus commented on the oddity of the Caunians: *"In their customs they are different from the Carians, and, indeed, from the rest of mankind. The finest thing for them is to keep company together, men, women, and children, in groups according to age and friendship – for drinking."* Evidently they were like the British.

As often happens in history, the first news about Caunos is bad. Like the Lycian cities to the east it resisted the Persian general Harpagus and was badly defeated, although apparently not with the drama of Xanthos' self-immolation. Harpagus was seeking to tame the whole of Asia Minor, and probably valued the harbor at Caunos. The harbor, which extended to the foot of the city, has long since silted up, but was the key to the city's prosperity for almost 1,000 years.

The advantages of the well-protected and easily defensible harbor were somewhat offset by the problems of living on the delta. Mosquitoes in the area were probably malarial in ancient times, and anopheles took its toll on the local inhabitants. Neighboring cities enjoyed making jokes at the expense of the Caunians: One unkind wit said that the greenish pallor of the Caunians gave meaning to Homer's phrase "the generations of men are like the leaves of trees." At the time the blame for the citizens' ill health fell on fruit.

Given the popular opinion of the city, no one was especially interested in moving here. The Persian satrap Mausolus (377-353 BC) had his own ideas, however, and extended and reinforced the city walls until they formed an immense ring around the city. This work went on during his campaign against Lycia, when Caunos was very near the front lines.

Despite Mausolus' optimistic building program, Caunos' appeal does not appear to have grown much, and it certainly never occupied the grand space within its walls. The cycle of deterioration was relentless: the Dalyan River silted up the harbor and the rest of the delta, mosquitoes increased, trade fell off, and, in time, the city died behind its magnificent walls.

## Visiting Caunos

Admission to the site is $1.50. Most of the space within Caunos' impressive circuit of walls is empty, but the area at the inland foot of the **acropolis**, near the theater, has a dense set of ruins. The summit of the acropolis itself is mostly bare, excepting a few defensive walls, but its dominant position above the **Dalyan River** makes it an enjoyable twenty minute climb. To reach the acropolis follow the paths from behind the theater. The theater is substantial, looking out in the direction of **Sülüklü Lake**, the site of the former harbor.

Inland of the theater are market areas and a small church. Slightly downhill are several inscribed stones and the foundations of a temple to an unknown deity. A collection of buildings descends toward Sülüklü Lake, where old harbor buildings border the water. The lake's unappealing name, literally "Leech Lake," surely refers to the leeches famous in this area; English traders once imported medicinal leeches from east of this area. Don't let the name put you off swimming in the waters around Dalyan – leeches like stagnant water best. By the same token, it may be prudent to avoid swimming in this particular body of water.

Caunos' **baths**, auxiliary to those at Sultaniye on Koyçeğiz Lake, were built in the higher ground above the church and behind the ticket booth. Another temple is located above the baths complex.

By the downstream boardwalk entrance there is a small restaurant and some tombs on the southern hill.

The lower end of the city's great ring of walls begins on the ridge to the west – seaside – of the city, on the opposite side of the lake from the theater. The walls continue in a great circuit along the steep ridge high above town and end at the top of a cliff above a bend in the river near the mud baths. The ashlar walls were an awesome engineering project using an immense wealth of great stone blocks, but the millenia of disuse have carpeted them with pine needles and soil. (Ashlar walls are walls built with precisely cut rectangular blocks of stone, unlike the cobbled together Roman walls that followed them or the giant oddly shaped Cyclopean walls that predated them.)

If you spend a long morning ascending along uncertain trails to the top of the walls, you may want to return to town via the dirt road on the far side of the ridge, which terminates at the Dalyan River at a small dock just across from the Denizati Restaurant, two hundred feet upstream of the mud baths.

Dalyan's most distinctive features are the Caunian **rock-cut tombs** carved out of the cliffs on the western bank of the river. These tombs date from Mausolus' time, the mid-fourth century B.C. A few tombs hug the bottom of the cliff, and you can spend an intrepid few hours nosing around them, but the reward is inevitably your own sense of adventure; the interior of the tombs are uniformly square and uniformly bare, except for goats or garbage. Somehow the most interesting of the tombs to marvel at is the unfinished tomb, which is easy to spot amid a cluster somewhat downstream. The tomb began in an ambitious fashion, but work was inexplicably cut short after workers had completed the upper half of the tomb. The 2,300 year-old work-in-progress offers a glimpse of how these tombs were created.

## SPORTS & RECREATION
### Mud Baths
Dalyan's mud baths are less than one kilometer upstream on the far bank of the river. The best mud is toward the back of the mud hole, and you should dig deep for the freshest and healthiest mud. So we are told. For the full beauty and health benefits, cover yourself well, with particular care for areas troubled by mosquito bites, and wait in the sun for the mud to dry before washing yourself off in the river. Keep your eye peeled for the large Nile turtles who bask in the sun just downstream of the mud baths.

### Hot Springs
**Sultaniye** has best sulfur springs, but plan on a dip and an extended mud bath afterward. The sulfur at these springs is potent stuff, liable to cling to you for an evening. The springs are located on Koyçeğiz **Lake** to the west of the entrance to Dalyan River. The springs were developed in

ancient times by the citizens of Caunos, and the Byzantines established their own hot springs here. The ruins of the old bath buildings have been partially swamped by a water table that has risen as the delta silted up. You can conceivably spend your day shuttling back and forth between the mud hole and the sulfur springs, with dips in the river in between.

## Beaches

Dalyan's **Iztuzu Beach** is more than four kilometers long, a clean, sandy spit of beach extending almost across the mouth of the delta. The northern tip of beach has small refreshment stands, but the beach is otherwise bare, and the central reaches are usually empty. Most people wind through the reeds to this beach on boats from Dalyan, which shuttle back and forth between 10 a.m. and 3 p.m., every half hour, returning between 1 p.m. and 7 p.m. for $2.50. You can also reach the beach by road, heading for Gökbel at the southern edge. Dolmuş serve Gökbel periodically throughout the day, departing from Dalyan's otogar, but the river ferries are far the better option.

The beach is best in the morning. Afternoons are windy and crowded. With the exception of a stand of trees at the tip of the peninsula, there is no cover, and beach umbrellas are strongly discouraged owing to the turtle eggs beneath the sand. The eggs belong to Caretta Caretta, an increasingly rare turtle native to this long spit of beach. The turtles bury their eggs by night and the eggs incubate beneath the sand, which remains at a cozy temperature, neither too hot nor too cold. In September the young turtles hatch and scurry for the sea, a race against birds and other predatory wildlife that is wise to the rhythms of turtle hatching. The beach is closed at night to protect the turtles and allow them to breed unimpeded.

If you should inexplicably find yourself dissatisfied with Iztuzu Beach, consider **Ekincik beach** to the west. The beach is accessible by road, but only after circumnavigating Koyçeğiz Lake and following the signs to Hamitköy, then a winding 14 kilometer road to Ekincik. Most people arrive here by boat, which is much easier.

## Birding

Dalyan's delta is a musical stew of peeping and chirping during the spring and fall. Birders should contact Linda at the Sultan Palas Hotel for further information about the bird watching season.

# GOKOVA/AKYAKA

**Akyaka** is a relaxed town at the head of **Gökova Korfezi**. The town has pine trees and beaches off to the northwest and a large delta, officially a wildlife sanctuary, to the south. Akyaka is just north of the Marmaris intersection on the Fethiye-Muğla road, at the bottom of a steep hill. The town has an excellent campground just past the northern town border and some pleasant hotels. Few foreigners come here, despite its convenience to the main north-south road.

## ARRIVALS & DEPARTURES

### By Bus

Dolmuş travel between Akyaka and Muğla in the interior on the half hour, departing from Akyaka's park, near the Belediye (municipality building). Getting to Marmaris or anywhere else can be more tricky, as dolmuş directly from Akyaka are infrequent, and you'll probably have to walk or hitch the long distance from the intersection.

### By Car

You probably don't want to stay in Akyaka without a car. The town is two kilometers north of the Marmaris turn off, up the steep grade toward Muğla, then down a road to the west.

## WHERE TO STAY

Akyaka has several good hotels, as well as some smaller pensions. Few foreigners visit.

**HOTEL DEDEĞIL**, *Akyaka, Gökova, Tel. 252 243 5054, Fax 252 243 5301. Rooms: 48. Double: $75.*

Akyaka's nicest accommodation, designed in accordance with local regulations that insist new buildings be constructed of pine. The Dedegil has the same pine construction as the Montana Pine Hotel above Ölüdeniz, with nicely designed public spaces and a pretty patio dining area and pool. The Dedeğil also offers service to the beach during high season, and is closed during winter. Rates change dramatically during the Dedeğil's seven months of operation owing to high highs and low lows.

**YÜCELEN HOTEL**, *Akyaka, Gökova, Tel. 252 243 5108, Fax 252 243 5435. Rooms: 75. Double: $70.*

Akin to the Dedeğil in design, but less well conceived.

## WHERE TO EAT

The **VILLA CARRETA** in town and the **OZMAK RESTAURANT** on the lower road between Akyaka and Gökova are recommended.

## SEEING THE SIGHTS

Hugging the lower road to the south you pass some rock-cut **tombs**, turning into a steep-walled valley. This was the site of ancient **Idyma**, but it has been largely buried beneath rockslides from the northern canyon wall. Tombs are still visible high on the canyon walls. The ruins of an unidentified medieval **castle** can be seen on a steep hill to the south and above Akyaka. These may be visited by various paths from the base of the hill. Continuing forty rough kilometers past Çinar beach (see below) brings you to the ruins of ancient **Ceramos**.

## SPORTS & RECREATION

There is a **beach** at the base of town, with the southern half free, the northern half beneath the campground charging one dollar. **Çinar beach**, to the northwest of town, offers good swimming on a gravel beach. Boats departing from Cleopatra Island make Çinar a destination, but it is relatively quiet on weekdays.

# MARMARIS

**Marmaris** is a popular yacht harbor and package vacation spot, with large hotels and large foreigners making neat rows along the thin strip of sand north of the harbor. Marmaris' waterfront is lively from dawn 'til dawn, but the go-go pace is suited to some. Bodrum provides the same things Marmaris does with an equivalent marina, better ambiance, a far superior fortress, and better hotels.

Marmaris offers boat service to its several seafront ruins, but the town itself is less appealing than some of the smaller towns surrounding it. The peninsula's most interesting ruin, **Cnidos**, is best seen by boat from Datça.

### History

Marmaris is the site of ancient **Physcos**, a surprisingly small town given the impressive nature of the Marmaris bay. The fortress above the harbor probably stands atop some older ruins, but the Physcos ruins are located in the mountains at the northern end of town.

The modern fortress is the work of the Ottomans, built one year in advance of their use of this bay for the invasion of Rhodes in 1522. After a failed attack under Sultan Mehmet II, conqueror of Constantinople, Süleyman the Magnificent amassed a huge force of ships here to ferry an army of 100,000 men across to Rhodes, where less than 3,000 Knights of St. John fought for eight months before accepting terms and abandoning their fortress. The small Marmaris fortress could easily have been built on the foundations of a structure once used by the knights themselves, for whom the extremely convenient Marmaris bay would have been important.

## ARRIVALS & DEPARTURES

**By Bus**

Because of its distance from the main sea road, Marmaris can require patience if you do not have a car. Most dolmuş and buses pass the turnoff by, leaving you at a small service station across the road from the turnoff. In this event cross the road and wait for a dolmuş to make the turn toward Marmaris, although they often seem to come tightly packed. The bus station is in the flats behind the Netsel Marina at the east end of town. The dolmuş station is inland of the Atatürk statue on the main road out of town, Ulusal Egemenlik Bulvari.

Kamil Koç bus schedules: Izmir, hourly, 5 a.m. to 2 a.m. $8; İstanbul, five times, 8:30 a.m. to 9 p.m., 9 p.m. non smoking. $20; Ankara, three times; 9:30 a.m. to 10 p.m., $16; Antalya, four times; 1 a.m., 9:30 a.m., 3:30 p.m., 8:00 p.m. $15

**By Car**

Marmaris is 30 kilometers south, less than 100 kilometers west of the airport at Dalaman.

## ORIENTATION

Marmaris is a wonderland of leather, carpets, gold, yacht cruises and discotheques. Marmaris has a long strip of sand beach, backed by Marmaris' sea road, itself beneath a long row of cookie-cutter hotels. The beach can be fun, but there's no elbow room, and the smell of slowly cooking human flesh wafts inland from the beach.

## WHERE TO STAY

The hotel selection around Marmaris is dispiriting. A collection of hotels so vast should have more distinguished alternatives. Some of the towns skirting Marmaris are being assimilated by the giant white boxes. If you must stay in the area, we recommend visiting one of the smaller towns and settling in there. Bear in mind that most of Marmaris closes down in the off season.

**HOTEL BEGONYA**, *Kısayalı Hacı Mustafa Sok. No. 101, Tel. 252 412 4095, Fax 252 412 1518. Rooms: 24. Double: $44.*

This hotel is a tiny oasis of taste, but it still suffers indignities from Marmaris' noisy bar street. This renovated old house seems to have been beamed in from Antalya's Kaleiçi area, complete with a lush patio garden. Reservations are necessary. Closed in winter.

**ÇUBUK HOTEL**, *Atatürk Cad. Konti Sok. No. 1, Marmaris, Tel. 252 412 6774. Rooms: 27. Double: $35.*

A fairly standard hotel with an unusually good standard of hospitality and service. Rooms are spic and span.

**INTERYOUTH HOSTEL**, *Tepe Mah., 42 Sok. No. 45, Marmaris, Tel. 252 412 Tel. 3787, Fax 252 412 7823. Rooms: 125. Double: $17.*
An accredited youth hostel in the best tradition, clean, simple, and honest. The hostel has common kitchens, a terrace bar, and boasts of no mosquitoes. It's a hostel, so you can't hear a pin drop, but everyone here has some advice, and it's usually good. Take the hostel up on its offer of a transfer from the bus station or port, which are highly recommended given the hostel's location within the bazaar labyrinth. This hostel has a competitor that's also good; it's alright to be led astray.

**Outside of Marmaris**
**ROBINSON SELECT CLUB MARIS**, *Hisaronu Mevkii, Datça Yolu, Marmaris, Tel. 252 436 9200-9210, Fax 252 436 9228. Rooms: 293. Double: $160, half board. Reservations 212 288 6310, Fax 212 288 9304.*
If you want to stay at a luxury resort near Marmaris, you should stay at the place that the others are trying to imitate. The Robinson is perched atop a hill with a sea view to both sides, and offers an exhaustive list of amenities that includes every athletic pursuit under the sun (40 surfboards, 11 catamarans, basketball, volleyball, diving equipment). The Robinson earns its five stars, and is fairly convenient to Datça. Besides, it is near the historical point where the citizens of Cnidos once tried to cut their city off from the mainland.
**IBEROTEL MARMARIS PARK**, *Pamucak Mevkii, Içmeler, Marmaris, Tel. 252 455 2121, Fax 252 455 2146. Rooms: 200. Double: $150.*
This is another of the exceptional hotels operated by Iberotel, with a full range of services and amenities and a private beach. Closed in winter.
**SABRINA'S HAUS HOTEL**, *Bozburun, Tel. 252 456 2045, Fax 252 456 2470. Rooms: 18. Double: $40.*
An excellent little retreat not far from Bozburun, but seemingly all to itself. Sabrina's is right on the water, with a ragtag collection of boats, a verdant garden, and a pier. Sabrina's has a restaurant and, as you might have guessed, some German influence in its management.
**OLIMPOS HOTEL**, *Koru Mevkii, Datça, Tel. 252 712 2001, Fax 252 712 2653. Rooms: 30. Double: $65.*
The only one of Turkey's special class hotels in the region, in a building that is a cross between Ottoman and English colonial.

**Area Hotels Offering Peace & Quiet**
If you want a small, peaceful hotel you must go considerably out of your way, but these fit the bill.
The town of **Orhaniye**, in the hills above the Hisarönü Körfezi, has the fine little **CEREN** and **PALMIYE** pensions. There is good swimming in this bay, and a sand beach is reported. To reach Orhaniye go to the

roundabout at the entry to town, where, with your back to town, the minibus station is to the right. Buses serve a whole set of towns, often en route to Selimiye or Bozburun.

Be aware that the routes to Datça and Bozburun are different, and be sure to confirm your destination before hopping aboard a dolmuş in Marmaris. The roads are in fairly good shape as far as both Datça and Bozburun.

## WHERE TO EAT

The city's best cuisine is in the neighborhood of the Netsel Marina, including Pineapple, La Campana, and Fellini Restaurant. It's difficult to keep up with the ever-shifting restaurants along the waterfront, but here are some to look for. The smaller towns all have at least a couple of restaurants; ask which one is enjoying primacy.

**TÜRKAY RESTAURANT**, *Mustafa Sok. No. 107, Marmaris, Tel. 252 412 0741. Expensive.*

International fare.

**BAMBOO RESTAURANT**, *Atatürk Cad. No. 9/10, Marmaris, Tel. 252 455 3954. Moderate.*

A long-time favorite among Marmaris' regulars.

**HALIL IBRAHIM SOFRASI**, *PTT Çıkmazı No. 31, Cem Oteli Alti, Marmaris, Tel. 252 413 1445. Inexpensive.*

Seek this place out in the center of the bazaar, around the corner from the youth hostel, for good Turkish food.

## SEEING THE SIGHTS

The city's lone classic feature, the small hilltop **fortress**, is somewhat obscured by development nearby. It is not a particularly impressive fortress, and no less discerning a connoisseur of fortresses than the man who commissioned it says so. Süleyman the Magnificent, in his displeasure at the small, badly designed fortress is reported as saying "*Mimarı as,*" "Hang the architect." Some say that Marmaris' name derives from this very term. Today the fortress houses a pretty but uninspired **museum**.

The peninsulas west of Marmaris are filled with ruins, most of them along the seaside. Boat trips are available past the ruins from Bozburun, Datça, Selimiye, and Marmaris proper. These often remote ruins give gulet cruises through the area much of their charm, but the most significant of the ancient foundations, other than Cnidos and Cedrae, mentioned below, is at **Loryma**, accessible from Bozburun. The ruins remain in forbidding shape above tiny Bozukkale.

## SPORTS & RECREATION

### Boat Cruises

Marmaris is a base for gulet cruises, and also offers a few day trips. Be wary of "boat trips" that actually involve a long bus shuttle, such as that to Dalyan and Iztuzu beach: if you want a day-long boat trip the bus component may be unwelcome. One enjoyable trip goes to **Cleopatra Island** (Sedir Adası), located on the northern side of the peninsula, costing about $14. This requires a short bus ride across the peninsula, with a boat to the island.

An entertaining bit of folklore suggests that the white sand along Cleopatra Island was shipped in specially from Egypt prior to the famous queen's stop here on her romantic voyage with Marc Antony. Geologists can disabuse you of this notion. The ruins of **Cedrea** are located on the east side of the island. This city's one brush with history was grim; as punishment for its opposition, the Spartans sold the inhabitants as slaves in 450 B.C.

Other trips take in **Paradise Island** at the opening of the bay; **Ciftlik Beach**, a phosphorous cave; and other islands just outside of Marmaris Bay, although most of these merely offer a pretext to lounge around on the boat and swim every time the boat drops anchor.

Dolmuş boats depart from near the Atatürk Statue, serving small towns along the coast. We recommend the hourly boat to **Turunc**, a good destination for a day trip. Turunc is hardly unspoiled, but it offers more room than Marmaris and the boat trip helps you get your bearings. Turunc has a collection of hotels and small pensions.

### Ferries

Flying dolphin hydrofoil ferries to Rhodes depart daily at 9 a.m., leaving Rhodes at 4:30 p.m. The cost is $40 for a single day round trip, with the price rising in accordance with visa fees if you choose to stay in Rhodes. The Interyouth Hostel occasionally has even cheaper tickets. Always check visa information with the tourism information bureau, as arrangements change in accordance with Turkish/Greek diplomacy. Ferries depart from the far eastern side of town, beyond Netsel Marina on the way toward Günlucek National Park.

Ferries depart from Körmen, opposite Datça, for Bodrum daily at 9 a.m. and 5 p.m. in the summer, at a cost of $7 one way, $18 for a car and driver. Automobile reservations are important; contact the **Bodrum marina**, *Tel. 252 316 0882*, where an English-language speaker is usually available.

Ferries depart Marmaris for Venice at noon on Wednesdays, arriving on Tuesday at 2 p.m.

### Gulet Cruises

There are many companies selling gulet cruises out of Marmaris. See the Bodrum section later in this chapter for details. **Bozburun**, south of Marmaris, is one of the centers for construction of gulets.

## SHOPPING

Marmaris' **bazaar**, inland of the Atatürk statue and winding in the direction of the hilltop fortress, offers leathers, kilim (including wool rugs from nearby Milas), jewelry, and endless souvenirs, including the popular local honies. For specialized shopping, say the accessories for fashionable yachting, try the Polo, Vakko, and Beymen outlets in the Netsel marina.

If you are in need of detailed charts or other nautical supplies, check in at **Taka Bookstore**, *33 Sok. No. 20/4, Tel.* 252 412 2242, just across the waterway from the bus terminal, inland of the yacht harbor.

## PRACTICAL INFORMATION

### Laundromats

There are always laundromats in the vicinity of a marina. Check at the Netsel marina.

## CNIDOS

**Cnidos** has a truly romantic setting, surrounded by the waters of the Mediterranean. Contributing to Cnidos' romance was the presence of the greatest shrine to Aphrodite, Goddess of Love, on the southern Turkish coast. History says that ships anchored here to wait out the meltem, the north wind, but it would be a wonder if sailors weren't also encouraged to stay by a city that worshipped the Goddess of Love.

### History

Cnidos' history began at modern **Datça**, 30 kilometers east. On that location Cnidos was an extremely successful Greek colony, master of the local seas as well as an active settler of far off lands, including Sicily. Trade and good fortune helped Cnidos grow in wealth and power, all of which seemed liable to come crashing to an end in 540 B.C., in a tale related by Herodotus. The Persian Harpagus, charged with subduing the entire coast of Asia Minor for his King, Cyrus, was crushing all resistance and appeared certain to march on wealthy Cnidos.

Trusting to their proven naval skills, the citizens of Cnidos set to work at the narrowest point of the peninsula inland of their city and began digging away at the land in the hopes of isolating the peninsula from the rest of Asia Minor.

In the midst of this frenzied activity a suspiciously large number of workers were injured by bits of stone in their eyes and the Cnidans, nonplused, sought advice from the Oracle at Delphi. The Oracle returned a blunt answer: if Zeus had wanted the peninsula to be an island, he would have made it an island. The Cnidans are reported to have quit their work and returned home, surrendering to Harpagus on his arrival.

In the middle of the fourth century Cnidos, now under the control of the Persian satrapy in Helicarnas/Bodrum, moved. This traumatic undertaking – the new site had very little fresh water and vegetation – seems to have been brought on by financial concerns. In its new position at the head of the peninsula, Cnidos could offer a safe harbor to ships unable to round the tricky cape during bad weather. The large southern harbor is still discernible, having been built to shelter northbound ships during the cape's strong, steady northerlies. As if difficult weather and the illicit charms of the new port city weren't enough (see sidebar), Cnidos also had a reputation for producing good wines.

With all of this inspiration, several luminous figures hailed from Cnidos, most notably **Sostratus**, the designer of the Pharos Lighthouse in the third century, one of the Seven Wonders of the World. The sculptor Praxiteles was not from Cnidos, but from Athens.

Alas, Cnidos' glory ebbed under the Romans, perhaps in direct proportion to Christian assaults on the rampant vice of **Aphrodite's Temple**. As its sea power faded, its position at the tip of the peninsula turned from a strength to a weakness, and Cnidos was probably preyed on by successive waves of invaders.

---

### NOT JUST ANY PORT IN A STORM

*Cnidos had more than shelter for a weary sailor. In what may have been an early example of clever marketing, the new city of Cnidos was built around a Temple of Aphrodite of Fair Voyages. Here sailors could view the legendary statue of Aphrodite by Praxiteles, a scandalous work of art, but one that four centuries later Pliny the Younger considered the finest statue in the world. Sailors, always eager to learn more about fine art, were enthusiastic to stop at Cnidos. View the statue and visit the Aphrodite 'priestesses.' Cnidos was not only a necessary anchorage, but a much anticipated one.*

---

Evidence of Aphrodite Temples are rare, and no evidence of them remains on Turkey's southern coast. There may have been no way to identify the Temple of Aphrodite at Cnidos if it hadn't been so famous that archaeologists were searching specifically for it. An American archaeologist, improbably named Iris Love, located pieces of what appears to be the statue's pedestal amid a collection of broken stone. Temples of Aphrodite were probably stamped out with especial enthusiasm when Christianity supplanted the traditional forms of worship, and the Cnidos' Temple of Aphrodite was clearly broken up almost stone by stone. The statue's fate is unknown, but the Metropolitan Museum in New York has a possible replica, as does, ironically, the Vatican Museum.

## ARRIVALS & DEPARTURES

The best way to see Cnidos is on a cruise from Datça, departing daily in the high season at 9 a.m. Remember that Cnidos' entire wealth was based on tricky weather at this furiously boiling point, forcing ships to seek harbor here and await more favorable conditions. You may get a little of this yourself in the interest of historical flavor.

Public transport does not serve the remote ruin, but with a car you can reach Cnidos by ignoring the Datça turn and continuing straight along what becomes a dirt road, staying to the left at unsigned intersections. There are cafes at the site, but no accommodation.

## SEEING THE SIGHTS

The **Cnidos ruin** tumbles along for about two kilometers at the end of the peninsula. Few ruins give a sense of what their inhabitants must have been like so well as Cnidos, whose distance from the mainland on this long, sparsely vegetated spit of land has an isolated, desolate feel. The location is unique in the style of mountaintop cities that controlled trade routes, but without the reassurance of much water or arable land.

The central feature of the city is the **isthmus**, formerly a bridge. This connected the two sections of Cnidos and divided its two harbors into the commercial harbor on the south (left as you look out from the mainland), and the military harbor to the north. Sunken sections of the breakwaters and wharves are visible beneath the sea. The northern harbor has the smaller mouth, which is fortified with a tower.

The **acropolis** is on the mainland, as are most of the temples and other public buildings. Climb the steep hill behind the north harbor to reach the site of the former Temple of Aphrodite. This was built on a circular foundation, surrounded by columns and centered on the Praxiteles statue. Another temple, that of Demeter and Kore, is located nearby, and was itself involved some risque traditions (see Priene). Demeter's statue was located here and transported to the British Museum. The city walls are another staggering example of laborious ashlar construction, a circuit of great cut blocks running along the spine of the peninsula. The city's deliberate foundation allowed the use of central planning, so streets are designed on a grid system akin to that at Priene.

If you arrive by sea you will have a chance to see the ruined **Lion Monument**, a trophy of an Athenian victory over Sparta here in the years before the new Cnidos was built. The lion from which the monument draws its name is also in the British Museum. The monument is located at a section of shoreline inaccessible by land. The necropolis is at the inland end of Cnidos by the road, scattered along a hill.

# BODRUM

Like Marmaris, **Bodrum** has been discovered and developed mostly in the course of one decade. Unlike Marmaris, Bodrum has retained its charm, owing, perhaps, to the lack of beaches immediately along the waterfront. There is a selection of excellent accommodations in and around the Bodrum peninsula and a great variety of ways to entertain yourself while here, although the number of legitimate historic sights falls off dramatically after the attractions in Bodrum itself.

## History

The fine, defensible anchorage at **Helicarnassus** made this site one of the first settled by the waves of Greek colonists, perhaps as early as 1200 B.C. There were probably people here earlier than that, but the evidence is buried beneath the daunting Castle of St. Peter on the isthmus.

Helicarnassus was a member of the **Dorian Hexapolis**, a union of six cities with ties to the Peloponnese that also included Cnidos and four cities in modern Greece. These ties were broken after Cyrus' Persian Army swept Asia Minor, seizing Helicarnassus; thereafter the city, together with Milas inland, was often the seat of Persian power in the region. **Artemesia I**, Helicarnassus' ruler, sailed for Greece with Xerxes' invasion force in 480 B.C. During the battle of Salamis, with Xerxes watching from his throne on shore, she distinguished herself on a day when the Persian navy suffered a grave defeat; **Xerxes** commented sourly that his men were fighting like women, his women like men.

In addition to cementing Xerxes' lousy reputation in modern eyes (he also whipped and shackled the Hellespont, earning the ire of environment lovers), this account is of particular interest because it was written by Herodotus, a citizen of Helicarnassus only slightly younger than Artemesia I. His account of the period from 560 B.C. to Xerxes' failed invasion less than a century later offers entertaining insight into the peoples and conditions of the time, and earned Herodotus the title "father of history."

Shortly after Xerxes' defeat, Helicarnassus slipped away from Persian control, but it was returned to the Persian fold early in the fourth century. The Persian satrap Mausolus (377-353) made Helicarnassus the provincial capital, undertaking an ambitious building program. The city was completed during Mausolus' rule and adorned with Mausolus' own massive funerary monument, later considered one of the Seven Wonders of the World.

During this time, two major cities under Mausolus' command, Caunus and Cnidos, were rebuilt on a massive scale – Cnidos was moved to an entirely new location – while Mausolus prosecuted a war against the Lycians to the southeast.

Thus it was with the city in a state of prosperity, secure behind high new walls, that Alexander the Great arrived just twenty years after Mausolus' death. Alexander met heavy resistance here, as a large Persian garrison had been left to challenge him, commanded by Memnon of Rhodes. A prolonged siege finally succeeded in breaching the walls, but once within the city Alexander was met with the prospect of another long siege against the inner citadel – on the site of the Castle of St. Peter. For this he had no time, and Arrian reports that he "razed the town to the ground;" but with the mausoleum still standing Helicarnassus could hardly be considered "razed." Leaving the Persians within the small harbor citadel, Alexander passed control of Caria to Ada, Mausolus' sister, and continued south.

Helicarnassus was put in order during the busy, confusing period following Alexander's death. The rivals for Alexander's empire refortified the town in order to defend themselves from one another, and when it passed to Rome in the second century B.C. it was in good condition.

The city declined under the Byzantines, who were unable to protect their provinces from the ravages of Arab and other corsairs and invaders. The Knights of St. John seized the city in the chaos following Tamurlane's invasion in 1402 – the burgeoning Ottoman empire was smashed and the Knights' own fortress at Izmir was destroyed. After establishing themselves here, the Knights remained secure until the great Crusader fortress at Rhodes capitulated to Süleyman the Magnificent (1520-1566), at which point they sailed away. The Ottomans occupied the fortress, but with the eastern Mediterranean secure and the interior under control, the fortress was irrelevant to the empire's defense.

## ARRIVALS & DEPARTURES
### By Air
A new airport at nearby **Güllük** is scheduled to begin service in 1997. The **Bodrum-Milas Airport** will be the largest in the Aegean, able to serve 4 million passengers annually. The **Turkish Airlines** office is at *Neyzen Tevfik Cad., No. 208, Tel. 252 313 3172.*

**By Bus**

Buses between Bodrum and most sites in western Turkey are available. Buses depart for Milas and Selçuk (passing Didyma, Miletus and Soke) on the half hour, with service. Bodrum's otogar is several blocks inland of the city center. Follow Cevat Sakir Sokak slightly downhill and you arrive at the tourism information office on the isthmus below the Castle of St. Peter. Dolmuş are centered at the same place, serving the surrounding towns on the half hour, including Bitez, Yalıkavak, Turgutreis, and Türkbükü.

**By Car**

Bodrum is just over an hour's drive from Milas on the main 330-525 coast road.

## ORIENTATION

Bodrum has two significant historical sites, the **Castle of St. Peter** and the **Mausoleum at Helicarnassus**, and we highly recommend both despite the latter's sad decline. Most of the city's significant ruins, including the once mighty Temple of Mars erected under the Romans, have disappeared. The 10,000 seat theater was the site of gladitorial contests and combat against wild animals, although the lower seats no longer seem quite insulated from the floor of the theater.

Other seaside historical sites in the region include **Myndos** on the far western side of the peninsula near Gümüşlük and **Karyanda** near Türkbükü. The ruins of **Pedasa** are located at the inland city of Gökçeler, north of Bodrum. These ruins are well-worn, as Pedasa's heyday passed before Mausolus' reign, but they have not been confused by much rebuilding on the site.

## WHERE TO STAY

Bodrum has excellent accommodations, as do other cities on the peninsula. Prices are halved in the off season, a time when merchants also lower prices, and many hotels close their doors in winter.

**ANTIK THEATRE HOTEL**, *Kıbrıs Sehitleri Caddesi, 243, Bodrum 48400. Tel. 252 316 6053, Fax 252 316 0825. Rooms: 20. Double: $110, Half board $148.*

Once a hotel is given the smart title "best small hotel in Turkey" by *The New York Times*, it can't really be considered a secret anymore. Despite the enthusiastic recommendation, the Antik Theatre Hotel remains a quiet, comfortable place, and doesn't feel like its been the least bit spoiled.

The hotel's architect, Cengiz Bektaş, built the terraced hotel into the side of the hill just below the ancient Helicarnas theater, with every room looking out on the picturesque Castle of St. Peter through its shuttered door and windows. Every level has its own small patio with a deliberate jumble of gravel and stepping stones and greenery sprouting by the rail, with bougainvillea crawling up wooden frames and old terracotta pots tucked in corners. On the bottom tier is a deep swimming pool. Guests gather here on summer nights, toasting the magnificent castle and bay below.

The decoration is simple whites and marble, with spare wood furnishings. You'll find a candle and an old framed nautical chart or boat diagram for decoration. The suite room, with its long couches, private terrace, fireplace and steepled skylight, is simply one of the finest rooms available in the country. The aesthetics are helped along generously by a good staff that, far from aloof, is engaging and friendly; in this the tone is set by the manager, Altan Karabelen.

The hotel is directly across Kıbrıs Sehitleri Caddesi from the Bodrum theater. The patios are ideal for late evening dining, the castle illuminated and the harbor alive with lights. The hotel has an excellent chef, and at $38 extra half board accommodations should be considered. At least spend an evening at the Sunset Bar.

Selected as one of our best places to stay – see Chapter 10.

**BAÇ PENSION**, *Cumhuriet Caddesi No. 18, Bodrum. Tel. 252 316 1602, Fax 252 316 7917. Rooms: 18. Double: $55.*

The Baç is an extremely comfortable small hotel located along the seaside in Bodrum's city center. The hotel is a bewildering bargain, with carefully detailed interiors, pretty balconies, and quality wood furniture. The rooms have air conditioning and, on the seaside, small balconies. The terrace has a cool interior bar and a nice patio for keeping an eye on the bustle of boats in the harbor. Open all year.

**MANASTIR HOTEL**, *Barış Sitesi, Bodrum. Tel. 252 316 2854, Fax 252 316 2772. Rooms: 59. Double: 118, Half board.*

The Manastir is one of a handful of hotels in Turkey that warrants three, not five, stars simply because it lacks perks such as a casino and archery. What it lacks in elaborate amenities it makes up for in appeal: the Manastir is an attractive, peaceful hotel, offering good rooms and all the amenities you really want: television, air conditioning, and a swimming pool. Some room decor shades to pink pastels, surely one of the things that the monks who once lived on this very site would be not at all pleased with.

**MARINA VISTA HOTEL**, *Neyzen Tefvik Cad. No. 226, Bodrum. Tel. 252 316 2269, Fax 252 316 2347. Rooms: 87. Double: $125.*

Just across a small bay from the Castle of St. Peter, the front door of this hotel opens onto the waterfront.

**Around Bodrum**
**BITEZ TURIZM**, *Neyzen Tevfik Caddesi 142, 48400 Bodrum, Tel. 252 316 2454, Fax 252 316 3101.*
If you plan an extended stay on the Bodrum peninsula, consider letting a house or villa from Bitez. The company has quaint studios and houses scattered throughout Bodrum and out in the peninsula. Within Bodrum are four small houses and a studio with prices ranging from $140 per week to $1,200 per week. Bitez offers many accommodations outside of Bodrum, including a flower-decked Greek house on the beach at Gümüşlük near the Mindos ruins for $500 per week, a large villa at Turgutreis for $3,000 per week, and restored stone houses at Karakaya on the hill above Mindos for $600 per week.
The accommodations are maintained in excellent condition and often decorated with paintings, old furniture, and ceramics. Contact Bitez for further information.
**BAHÇELI AĞAR PANSIYON**, *Yat Limanı Sok. No. 4, Tel. 252 316 1648. Rooms: 14. Double: $17.*
A nice budget accommodation: clean, pretty, and central.
**SERHAN OTEL**, *Gümbet, Tel. 252 316 5315. Rooms: 29. Double: $35.*
A pleasant old standby, rough around the edges but pretty. Suffers a little from encroachment of large hotels at Gümbet.

## WHERE TO EAT

Bodrum has excellent dining, some of the best in the country. Restaurants, unfortunately, move around.
**ANTIK THEATRE HOTEL**, *Kıbrıs Sehitleri Caddesi No. 243, Bodrum, Tel. 252 316 6053, Fax 252 316 0825. Expensive-Very Expensive.*
Highly acclaimed food, and for good reason. A new chef in 1996 has proven as capable as his predecessor.
**SUNNY'S RESTAURANT**, *Rasathane Sok., Bodrum, Tel. 252 316 5286. Moderate-Expensive.*
Sunny's is the local favorite, with a varied menu that includes Indian and Chinese dishes.
**MAUSOLUS RESTAURANT**, *Neyzen Tevfik Cad., Bodrum, Tel. 252 316 4176. Moderate-Expensive.*
For a good, reliable dinner at no great price, try the Mausolus.
**AMPHORA RESTAURANT**, *Neyzen Tevfik Cad. No. 164, Bodrum, Tel. 252 316 2Tel. 378. Moderate-Expensive.*
The ideal place in the heart of Bodrum's waterfront to eat excellent mezes and drink rakı and dither over whether to have an entree. Fish entrees are the specialty.

**BUĞDAY VEGETARIAN RESTAURANT**, *Türkkuyusu Cad. No. 72, Bodrum, Tel. 252 316 2969, Fax 252 346 6995. Inexpensive-Moderate.*

Some people disembark from a Blue Voyage craving meat; others have had enough. The Buğday opened in the hopes the latter spirit would eventually win the day, a tough prospect in a meat-loving country. Victor Ananias has openeed a vegan restaurant offering delicious food in a classic setting. Some dishes have a very Mediterranean twist, for instance olive and hummus sandwiches and tofu mezes; others, like muesli and carrot cake, are more standard. You will want to try the fruit juices.

**SAPA RESTAURANT**, *Türkkuyusu Sok., Bodrum, Tel. 252 316 2553. Moderate-Expensive.*

A converted old residence, with dining in the garden.

**PİCANTE**, *Türkkuyusu Sok., Bodrum, Tel. 252 316 0270. Moderate-Expensive.*

Remarkably good Mexican food next to Sapa.

**LADDA'S THAI RESTAURANT**, *Cızdaroğlu Sok. No. 10, Bodrum, Tel. 252 313 1504.*

In the mood for good Thai cuisine? Ladda's, opposite the marina, has fine food, but isn't the least bit cozy.

Note: If you get out to Bitez, try the new BarbeQ restaurant.

## SEEING THE SIGHTS
### The Castle of St. Peter

The city's centerpiece is the castle separating Bodrum's harbors. This remarkable fortress was constructed atop the site of the archaic acropolis, which was itself replaced with Mausolus' fortified palace. The archaic acropolis was on an island once known as Zephyrion, now the isthmus of the **Castle of St. Peter**. The Knights of St. John set to work on the castle in 1402, taking advantage of Tamurlane's crushing defeat of the Sultan Beyazid I at the Battle of Ankara and the near collapse of the young Ottoman Empire. The new castle was intended to extend the Rhodes-based Knights' naval power, and by the time the Ottoman Empire had recovered its strength the Castle was complete and the Knights were harassing Moslem shipping.

The castle was a thorn in the Ottomans' side, but it did not prove an insuperable obstacle to Ottoman armies and navies, who avoided the area as they swarmed on to Egypt and the Holy Land and extended their power. Still, the consistent shipping losses to the Knights demanded action. When the Ottomans finally sought to dislodge the Knights they headed directly for Rhodes via a safe harbor in Marmaris, again bypassing Bodrum. Sultan Mehmet II Fatih encountered a rare setback at Rhodes, failing to take the city in 1479. Forty-three years later Süleyman the Magnificent, too, thought better of besieging the Castle of St. Peter as a preamble to an attack on Rhodes, his ultimate goal. He attacked Rhodes directly, and after a six month siege forced the Knights of St. John to surrender on Christmas Day, 1522. The Knights at the Castle of St. Peter surrendered only after the installation of the high gigawatt speakers at the Helicarnas Disco across the water, although history would have us believe that the Knights at the Castle of St. Peter sailed away without a fight in January 1523 as a condition of the peace at Rhodes.

The castle was alternately a fortress and a prison, and is today one of the most imaginative and informative museums in Turkey. The **Museum of Underwater Archaeology** is among the attractions here. One building houses a complete recreation of an 11th century shipwreck, as discovered and moved by Texas A&M. The contents of the wreck are also on display, as is the cargo from fourth and seventh century wrecks.

The **Carian Princess Hall** exhibits the contents of a burial chamber found in 1989. The tomb chamber of a Carian princess – probably Queen Ada, Alexander the Great's ally – was intact, and forensic scientists have used the bones to recreate the features of its occupant. This is the woman who Plutarch reports would send Alexander "dainty dishes and sweetmeats and at last presented him with pastry cooks and bakers who were considered to be very expert." The young conqueror, who felt much fondness for Ada, would nevertheless reject her entreaties; his strict tutor Leonidas had taught him to prefer "for breakfast a night's march, and for dinner a scanty breakfast."

The **English Tower**, the dominant fortification at the back corner of the fortress, is filled with battle standards and wooden tables that look out on the Aegean; wine is served by men and women in page costumes and knight grafitti is etched into the walls. The exterior's west wall has an archaic lion relief, evidence of past occupation of the site and the source of the name **Lion Tower**. In the castle's front court there is even a **Medieval Grocery**, offering an odd selection of herbs and peculiar medicinals. The sole discordant note is at the **German Tower** on the inland wall, where the **Torture Chamber** is witlessly animated by flashing lights and a Halloween tape. The bits of reality, including the inscription above the entry – *"Inde Deus Abest,"* "the place without God" – are all that's necessary here. Most of the exhibits in the museum are open from 8 a.m. to noon, and from 1:30 p.m. to 5:30 p.m., closed Mondays.

## The Mausoleum of Helicarnassus

In the center of town, on Turgut Reis Caddesi directly between the theater and the Castle of St. Peter, is the site of the **Mausoleum at Helicarnassus**. The greatest highlight in the city is gone now, tumbled in an earthquake and picked apart by Crusaders preparing for a battle that never took place. The Mausoleum at Helicarnassus was one of the Seven Wonders of the World, and like the Temple of Artemis at Ephesus and six of the seven wonders, it is gone now.

Like the Cheops Pyramid – the only Wonder still standing – this structure was built to honor a dead ruler. The ruler in this case was **Mausolus**, not even a king but a particularly powerful and autonomous satrap of the Persian Empire. Mausolus' rule was distinguished by several military campaigns and the establishment of the regional capital in Bodrum; his solid but unspectacular rule may not merit such a monument, but the playwright Diogenes has the satrap explain why he merits such a great funerary monument thus: "I am handsome and tall and mighty in war." Professor Kristian Jeppeson, the Danish archaeologist who has driven the research at the site since 1966, offers a different explanation: "Archaeology has always been a symbol of power," he says. "Any potentate who wants to be remembered by posterity will make efforts to leave some outstanding monumental building."

This Mausolus certainly did. A 300 yard by 100 yard area was set aside as grounds for Mausolus' tomb complex, and work on the monument within this complex was started during Mausolus' reign. The mausoleum itself measured 130 feet square at the base, rising to a height of 150 feet. With the exception of the small burial chamber under an arched space in the foundations, the monument was constructed entirely of dressed stone, fitted one to another with metal pins. To this solid, sheer stone mountain were added beautiful works of artistry. The four greatest sculptors of the day were brought in and set to work at the site, each responsible for the work on one side of the monument. The competing artists sheathed the mausoleum in marble, then added row after row of statues and columns. Reliefs and sculpture of Mausolus' exploits ringed the building at several levels.

Alas, Mausolus died too soon, and his resting place was incomplete, but Mausolus' devoted wife and sister Artemesia II proved a devoted widow as well. (The practice of sibling marriages was commonplace among the Hecatomnid royals, and, sure enough, the quality of the gene pool seems to have withered rapidly.) She pressed forward with the construction, aided by the desire of the four principal artists – Scopas, Bryaxis, Timotheus, and Leochares – to leave the temple as their legacy.

During Artemesia's brief reign, the Mausoleum was completed, and Mausoleus' remains secured in the tomb. The satrap was burned on a pyre, and his bones were bathed in wine and collected in an ornate gold sarcophagus. After interring a farmload of slaughtered animals to feed the dead ruler in the netherworld, workers slid a massive stone "plug" into the entrance, and it was fixed in position by a set of cylindrical dowels that clicked into place. The grand mausoleum was basically intact as late as the 1100s, according to accounts.

When the Knights of St. John arrived they found the monument ruined, probably toppled by a great quake in 1304. The Knights began work on the Castle of St. Peter in 1402, and they are likely to have made a habit of using cut stone from the mausoleum's huge pile just across the harbor; they were definitely using cut stone from the Mausoleum during the refortification of the castle in 1494.

A Crusader named Claude Guichard describes his colleagues' appreciation of the ruins: *"Having at first admired these works and entertained their fancy with the singularity of the sculptures, they pulled it to pieces and broke up the whole of it."* Guichard has long been thought to have told the next chapter in the tale, telling a picturesque story of Crusaders discovering a tomb beneath the mountain of stone, but having time only for a cursory look before being recalled to the castle for the night. In the morning, he writes, thieves had broken into the tomb, removed the lid from the sarcophagus, and run off with the treasure.

The Danish archaeological expedition has found evidence that the Crusader-era thieves came far too late. Stymied by the plug stone – which remains scarred by efforts to dislodge it – and stopped cold by the thick courses of lava stone on all sides, earlier thieves apparently burrowed through the softer tufa rock beneath the mausoleum and thus entered the tomb chamber. A few small gold buttons and pins were found in the tunnel outside of the chamber, indicating their success. None of the other, more magnificent valuables from Mausolus tomb have ever come to light.

A small **museum** within the Mausoleum compound explains the archaeology at the sight and offers several possible recreations of the original building. The grounds themselves are unimpressive unless you take the time to look them over carefully. A large indentation indicates where the tomb was located, with its original access opposite the museum. The greenish plug stone is still in its place, too heavy and unwieldly for use in the Castle of St. Peter.

A series of irrigation channels radiate from the lowered tomb area, and there are two other interesting features in the stone beneath the mausoleum. The first is the stairway and set of chambers skirting the southern end of the mausoleum site, opposite the museum entrance; this tomb predated the Mausoleum, and its complexity leads some to wonder whether it was the tomb of Artemesia I. The second thing to notice is the shallow indentation along the southern side of the Mausoleum's burial chamber; this is thought to be evidence of the tomb-robbers tunneling, first overshooting the mark, then returning and knocking loose a block of stone to gain entry. Finally, many of the column drums scattered around the site are engraved with a three-legged **triskele**, whose purpose not even the chief archaeologist can quite explain. The triskele is an inverted V with an additional line going straight up and down.

## Touring By Ferry

A cheap, enjoyable way to leave Bodrum for the south is to take the *M/F Fahri Kaptan 2* ferry across the Gökova Körfezi to Körmen on the Cnidos peninsula, from which point dolmuş and taxi depart for both Datça, just across the peninsula, and for Marmaris on the mainland. This is a car ferry, and an excellent way to continue a journey south, but you will need to make reservations and arrive early. Another car ferry departs Bodrum for the Greek island of Coş.

Both ferries launch from the marina jutting out from the Castle of St. Peter, departing at 9 a.m., returning at 5 p.m. Contact the main office of the **Bodrum Ferryboat Guild**, *Neyzen Tevfik Cad. No. 180, Tel. 252 316 0882, Fax 252 313 0205*, located near the marina on the waterfront road.

Also consider using Bodrum's ferries for seeing some of the Aegean's most important ruins. The Bodrum-Körmen/Datça ferry is excellent for continuing on to **Cnidos**, with departures at 9 a.m. and 5 p.m. in both directions. The two hour trip (round trip, one day) costs $9 per person, $28 with a car and driver. Automobile reservations are necessary. Dolmuş are occasionally on hand to shuttle people the 40 kilometers to the Cnidos ruin, but ordinarily visitors will have to share a taxi. The May-November ferry from Torba, a short dolmuş ride north of Bodrum, to Altınkum is ideal for seeing **Didyma** (it is locally called the Didim ferry) and, once there, continuing on to **Miletus** or **Priene**. This ferry departs both ways at 9 a.m. and 5 p.m. on Mondays, Wednesdays, and Saturdays, with a same day round trip for $13 and a one way trip for $8. Cars can travel on this ferry, but automobile reservations are a good idea.

Information about both ferries is available from Bodrum's **ferry information** office, *Tel. 252 316 0882*, where an English speaker is usually available.

## NIGHTLIFE & ENTERTAINMNET

**HELIKARNAS DISCO**, *Cumhüriet Cad. No. 128, Bodrum, Tel. 252 316 8000, Fax 252 316 1237. Expensive.*

There is dining here, but dining isn't why you come. Helikarnas booms into the early morning throughout the summer, with DJs from London, whirring laser lights, hordes of people and a $10 cover. Don't worry, uncool people are filtered out. Just so you know, Sundays are Ladies Night, Mondays are half-price, and Tuesdays offer free beer. A boat for Helikarnas departs from the center of the west dock.

## SPORTS & RECREATION

### Beaches

Bodrum's own waterfront is neither sandy nor clean, so plan on swimming elsewhere. Beginning in mid-May, regular boats begin shuttling visitors to the best beach sites in the area, including **Bitez**, **Bağla**, and sand beaches at **Ortakent Yalısı** and **Akyarlar**. Dolmuş also serve **Karaincir** and **Akyarlar**, as well as places farther afield such as **Turgutreis**.

### Boat Trips

In addition to the boats between Bodrum and the nearby beaches, there are day trips to **Kara Ada**, Black Island, beneath which is a cave with orange mud that is said to beautify the skin. A hot springs also issues from the cave into the sea. This is one of several stops on a day tour, the others varying according to the boat company.

**Türkbükü** is as close as Bodrum's peninsula comes to a charming hideaway. Türkbükü does not have its own beach, but offers small family pensions and has regular minibuses to the beach at Turgutreis and elsewhere. The ruins of Karyanda are nearby.

We also recommend **Gümüşlük**, where you'll find the site of **Myndos** and a small decent beach. Like Türkbükü, Gümüşlük has many small pensions. Other important peninsula towns include **Turgutreis**, with the peninsula's best beach, stuffed with tourists in the high season. Directly across the peninsula from Bodrum, the active sea port of **Torba** serves local islands and even the ruins of **Didyma** far across Güllük Bay.

## PRACTICAL INFORMATION

### Laundry

There are several laundromats near the marina.

# 20. THE IONIAN COAST

Owing to the **Ephesus** ruins, this is probably the most popular section of the Turkish coast. Ruins buffs gawk at Ephesus. The sprawling beauty of this ancient city earns its place on any but the most cramped itinerary, despite thick summer crowds. Ephesus is the best recognized, but the ancient cities of **Priene**, **Miletus**, **Didyma**, and **Heracleia** hug the coast as well, while three of the greatest ruins in the interior – **Sardis**, **Artemesia**, and **Pamukkale** – are just to the east. Between visits to ruins you can while away your time at excellent beaches.

In addition, there are dozens of virtually unvisited sites barely even mentioned on maps. This region has excellent public transportation and getting around is generally easy. The metropolis and air hub of İzmir is in the north, and Bodrum's new Güllük Airport will provide quicker access to the south.

Beginning in Bodrum, the three principal sites south of Ephesus can be visited in a day, ending at Kuşadası or Selçuk. Didyma offers a slightly eerie glimpse into the maw of an oracle, Miletus is a landlocked wreck of stone, and Priene is a towering, column-strewn beauty. From Bodrum you can begin by taking the seasonal ferry to Altınkum and working your way north from Didyma. By this route you can even go to Didyma in the evening and check in at one of the pensions by the oracle, continuing on to Miletus and Priene the next day.

From the north consider the reverse: see Priene and Miletus, then make it to Didyma where you can sleep in the shadow of the oracle and visit in the morning. If you take the road from Bodrum north, consider stopping in at the wildly overgrown ruin of Heracleia.

## HERACLEIA UNDER LATMUS

This city is one of the most potent examples of siltation in Asia Minor; **Heracleia ad (under) Latmus** was located on a great bay that extended past Miletus. Now the bay is an inland lake, and the former city is scattered along the shore and onto the mountain above. An excellent ruin

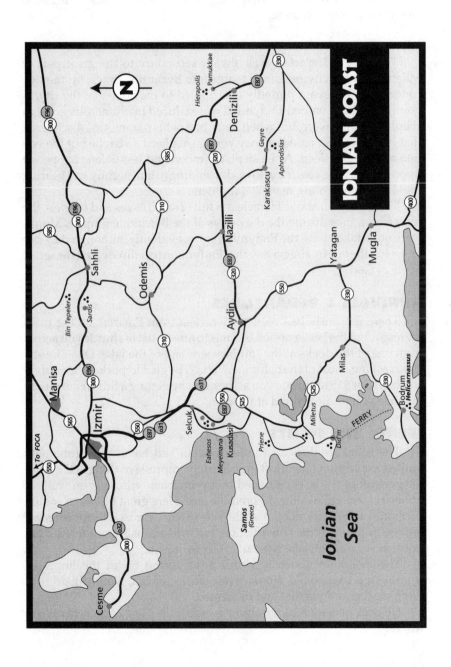

for the intrepid wishing to find things off the beaten track. Bring food along, as the site is remote.

## History

The port at Heracleia was always secondary to the great port of Miletus, but the city remained viable into Byzantine times. Mythology concerning the area reportedly contributed to the appeal of the city. A young shepherd named Endymion was seduced by numerous gods, as shepherds often were, but when Zeus, one of his paramours, discovered that Hera had also paid the busy young shepherd a visit he put the boy into a perpetual sleep. As he slept, the moon goddess Selene happened upon him and she, too, fell in love, descending to him nightly and bearing the slumbering young man 50 daughters.

The mountain above Heracleia is full of small caves and chapels, the refuge of monks during the dark days of the Byzantine Empire. Monks were quite taken with the Endymion story, evidently, although they put a gloss on the tale by suggesting that Endymion had discovered the secret name of God.

## ARRIVALS & DEPARTURES

There is a fairly bad road to Heracleia from Pınarcık on the main highway, but the better option by far is to hire a boat to shuttle you across from one of the docks at the southeastern end of the lake. Don't be shy about asking, most of the fishermen would be glad to pocket the equivalent or $10 or $15 to shuttle you across, maybe getting a little fishing time in while you fiddle around at the ruin.

## SEEING THE SIGHTS

The ruins are difficult to see in detail and have undergone only limited excavation. The most immediately impressive thing is the stunning circuit of walls, constructed by Lysimachos, whose great walls at Ephesus were alike in their incredible size. Here great blocks of square cut stone run in a circuit high up the side of Mt. Latmus. The more recent fortress is a Byzantine construction, but was probably rendered irrelevant as soon as the lake was cut off from the sea.

The mountain above is worth adventuring on in the hopes of stumbling across an old monk cave, some of which, like their peers at Cappadoccia, are painted and decorated.

Helpful phrase: *"Kilise mağaralar nerede?"* – The church caves are where?

# DIDYMA

Herodotus lists eight sacred oracles in the ancient world, and **Didyma**, or Branchidae, was one of the greatest of these. In Hellenistic times it was housed in one of the world's largest buildings. There is no mention of how the oracles were selected, but at Didyma we know that the small spring and grove of olive trees were venerated even before the arrival of the Greeks. There's really not much to see at Didyma, just a single, fascinating building.

## History

This was a mystical place before the arrival of the Greeks, and some say it has remained mystical long after. The source of the mysticism is a fissure in the earth, at which priests labored, undertaking to glimpse the future. There is debate about whether oracles were originally Anatolian or Greek, but this one, at least, appears to have predated the Greeks. This is especially odd given that the Oracle at Delphi was already in use, and underscores the peculiarity of such a belief crossing cultural lines; we are told the Greeks and the Anatolian natives both revered oracles, as did the Anatolian-based Lydians. Only the Persians were skeptical, and Herodotus reports that they got theirs when the Oracle of Apollo at Delphi mowed down part of Xerxes' army with lightning and stones.

Didyma was a temple, not a town. Its inhabitants were the temple priests, whom Herodotus refers to as **Branchidae**. The name was a reference to their descent from Branchus, an oracular priest from Delphi who in his younger years was one of the many wandering shepherds seduced by a god, in his case Apollo. It was Branchus who founded the Temple of Apollo in the tenth century B.C., soon after Herodotus reports Athenian settlers to have seized Miletus and put the entire male population to the sword. Apollo, by the way, had led the settlers to Miletus in the form of a dolphin, and the Delphinium sanctuary at Miletus commemorates that (Delphi being the root of "dolphin," and the Delphi Oracle thus, too, related to the dolphin.)

The Oracular Temple at Didyma was not a city in its own right, but the property of **Miletus**, to which it was connected by a 20 kilometer road called the **Sacred Way** (basically the same as today's Highway 09-55). The oracle attracted pilgrims from throughout Asia Minor intent on glimpsing the future, each bringing a suitable gift. The Lydian King **Croesus** was a particularly generous donor. Despite favoring the Oracle of Apollo at Delphi (see Oracle sidebar), Herodotus reports that the king made sacrifices "equal in weight and alike to those at Delphi" at Didyma, on one occasion alone burning sacrifices, offering 117 gold bricks, each two feet long, one foot wide and four inches high – in all more than 250 talents-weight – and donating a lion made of refined gold.

This wealth was tempting to the Milesians when they rose up against Persia in 499 B.C., but they refused to use the treasure at the Oracle to fund their war. Unfortunately, four years later King Darius destroyed Miletus, then looted and burned the oracle and its sacred grove. The great wealth was used to send a massive fleet against Athens, but this effort failed at the Battle of Marathon in 490.

The Oracle lapsed into disuse, but, according to one of his chroniclers, with the appearance of Alexander the Great the Oracle's fortunes were restored. The water of the sacred spring suddenly flowed anew at his approach, and the Oracle anticipated that Alexander would be victorious in an upcoming battle. Alexander was duly impressed by this and helped fund the reconstruction of the temple. The temple's association with Miletus continued, and under the Roman Emperor **Trajan** (98-117) the sacred way between the city and the oracle was paved with stone. There were repeated upgrades to the structure, but it is largely the one designed soon after Alexander's time.

The Persians, Celts (285 B.C.), and Goths (237 A.D.) all managed to severely damage the temple, but it took the Christians to wreck it for good. Under the staunchly Christian Theodosius I the Great (378-395) the temple had to be abandoned. The rise of Christianity, combined with the steep decline of Miletus, resulted in the abandonment and neglect of Didyma.

---

### THE ORACLE

*That the oracles delivered judgments and forecasts of the future we know, but did it work? The Lydian King Croesus wondered the same thing in 555 B.C. and set about finding out. The King needed the best possible mystic intelligence before mounting a campaign against the Persians in the east, and he tested the oracles to find which was most accurate. He arranged for messengers to seek the answer to a single question from each of the world's oracles at the same time on the same day. On that day he secreted himself in the kitchen and set about an unguessable task, boiling diced tortoise and lamb in a bronze cauldron.*

*As the weeks passed his messengers returned with various answers that disappointed the king. Finally, the messenger returned from Delphi with the answer "A smell steals over my senses, the smell of a hard-shelled tortoise, seethed in bronze with the meat of lambs, mingled together." Croesus, impressed, did business almost exclusively with the Delphic oracle thereafter, flooding Delphi with golden gifts and pestering the oracle with repeated questions about the campaign he was considering. As related in the story of the campaign on Sardis, Croesus fatally misinterpreted the oracle's answers and was crushed by the Persians.*

## ARRIVALS & DEPARTURES

**By Bus**

Dolmuş from Milas and Söke go to Didyma (Didim), continuing on to the beach at Altinkum. Dolmuş between Akköy and Didyma are frequent, but reaching Akköy from Miletus on public transportation takes time. A good time to spring for a cab. See the Miletus section for further information.

In the summer season a ferryboat plies back and forth between Altinkum and Torba on the Bodrum peninsula, departing Altinkum in the morning and returning in the evening. The cost is $5 per person. Service is canceled in the stormy and tourist-less winter months.

Packaged, unguided dolmuş trips to Didyma, Miletus, and Priene typically cost about $16 per person for one or two hours at each site. It isn't a bad option, but it dramatically restricts your ability to see the ruins, particularly at Priene and Miletus. These tours can be arranged through your hotel or the local dolmuş station in Selçuk, Kuşadası, Didim, Söke, or even at Didyma. Larger groups can bargain the price down.

**By Car**

The direct route to Didyma is from the main coast road, 525, via Akköy. A smaller road runs parallel to 525, connecting Didyma (Didim/Yenihısar) with Miletus and Priene. See information about the car ferry below.

**By Ferry**

A ferry serves Altinkum from Torba, just a few kilometers from Bodrum on the Bodrum peninsula. Service is limited to Monday, Wednesday and Saturday between May and November. Ferries depart in both directions at 9 a.m. and 5 p.m., and the one way, one person cost is $8. It is a car ferry, but car reservations should be booked with the Bodrum office, *Tel. 252 316 0882.*

## WHERE TO STAY & EAT

Didim, near the temple site, has limited accommodations. Altinkum, on the coast four kilometers south, has a few fairly pleasant small pensions as well as a strip of larger hotels.

**ORACLE PANSIYON**, *Didim, Tel. 256 813 1585 or 256 813 5503. Rooms: 18. Double: $22.*

A simple, cheap place to bed down for the night, in keeping with the legacy of the Oracle's lodging its supplicants. Excellent location by the temple. Dine at nearby **Kamaçi Restaurant**, also by the temple. Closes in mid-winter.

**TEMPLE HOTEL**, *Adnan Menderes Bulv. P.K. 5, Altınkum Girişi, Didim, Tel. 256 813 5971, Fax 256 813 4670. Rooms: 66. Double: $60*

A normal three star hotel, a few kilometers from the temple and a good hub. Satellite television and other amenities.

**CLUB PATIO LIGAMAR**, *Çamburun Mevkii, Akbuk, Didim, Tel. 256 856 4273, Fax 256 856 4281. Rooms:134. Double: $70.*

If the ruins have worn you out this may be a good destination – mini golf, a private beach, everything but a television in your room. It's the best of an uncertain lot, and offers a minibus from Altınkum/Didim.

**APOLLO PANSIYON**, *Çiçek Sok. No. 8, Altınkum, Tel. 256 813 1055. Rooms: 7. Double: $13.*

The Apollos is a good quality small pension not far from the beach. The Çamlık Pansiyon, nearby on Çiçek Sokak, is recommended by the tourism ministry.

## SEEING THE SIGHTS

The **temple**, which may have never been completed, was conceived to be as grand as the Temple of Artemis at Ephesus, and is far more intact than that vanished structure. The Oracle's massive temple had 122 columns, a forest of stone. Today the forest is felled, the columns broken. A colonnade two columns deep surrounds the central area, and the entrance is five columns deep. Climbing the stair and entering into the interior you wind toward the small antechamber, where two standing columns give way to a door; this was the spot where visitors would ask the oracle their questions. A staircase leads down to the open central area, the site of the sacred spring and an olive tree, or possibly an interior grove. A statue of Apollo was housed here. Adjacent to the entrance small staircases once led down to the fissure beneath the temple.

The structure at Didyma now is basically the same one begun soon after Alexander's arrival, and on which work was done for centuries. The temple is Ionic, quite traditional and quite Greek, and it relied on the great height of its columns, rather than its location, to impress the visitor. The exterior had a band of friezes above the columns, one of which, the Medusa head, is near the entrance. For the proper perspective, duck down and look up at the face the way it was designed to be seen, from below. The relief is much improved. The marble work throughout is of high quality, much of it coincident with the most skilled work at Aphrodisias and possibly supplied by that inland city.

Two roads of note began here. The first, lined with statues, descended to the sea. The statues were stolen in the name of British archaeology in the early 19th century. The second, the paved **Sacred Way** leading to Miletus, is being excavated alongside the temple.

# MILETUS

Miletus, the most powerful of the three cities, is today the least impressive. If you are at Priene, with the intention of visiting Didyma (or vice versa), then by all means visit. Like so many ruins, Miletus benefits from time spent wandering around.

## History

Miletus' former situation was ideal for a settlement, a long isthmus into one of the Aegean's finest bays topped by a hill. It requires a Cray II supercomputer mind to recreate today, but Miletus was both beautiful and prosperous.

Homer mentions a Carian contingent among the Trojan allies, referring to Miletus in the same breath, but this suffers from Homer's having written his centuries-old account at least 400 years after the fact. In any event, Homer was not impressed with the leader of the Carians, a man named Nastes who "came like a girl to the fighting, in golden raiment." Nastes was duly slain by Achilles, who paraded around with his foppish armor.

Despite fighting on the side of the Trojans, Miletus made some of the most concrete gains as a result of Troy's defeat. With Troy out of the way, the furiously colonizing Milesians were able to establish towns at Cyzicus on the Sea of Marmara and at Sinop on the Black Sea; but then these Milesians were probably Greeks, and no longer Carians at all. Miletus' fortunes improved, not those of its Carian population. This is dramatically supported by Herodotus, who says that the Greeks massacred every male in the city and took the women as their wives; and that, as a result, the women of Miletus would neither eat nor sit with their own husbands.

Miletus was the principal maritime city along the Aegean coast when the Persian King Cyrus wrested control of the area from Lydian King Croesus, and it was always a source of unrest. The Milesians, almost always in close contact with the cities of Greece, eventually stoked the Ionian revolt against Darius. One of the key moments in the ill-fated uprising concerned Miletus' relationship with its Oracle at Didyma.

Great wealth was stored at Didyma, including Croesus' spectacular gifts and other prizes from as far away as Egypt. In 499 B.C., the Milesians were sorely tempted to seize the treasure and build a great navy. With such a navy, some argued, the coastal cities considering revolt against Persian rule could establish mastery of the sea. The people of Miletus, however, feared the wrath of the Oracle more than the possibility of defeat. Within five years the revolt had ended in disaster, with King Darius himself on hand for the naval defeat of Miletus and the comprehensive annihilation of the city. The population was massacred and enslaved, and for good measure Darius looted and destroyed the Oracle at Didyma. The priests of the temple willingly handed over their treasures, and were thus branded traitors and forced to flee into Persia in later years.

Miletus was rebuilt and repopulated, and it slipped Persian control after Darius' army was beaten at Marathon. For a full century Miletus struggled to regain its former status, and had made great strides when the King's Peace of 387 B.C. returned the city to Persian control. Perhaps Miletus had reformed its rebellious ways, or perhaps a large Persian garrison left no option, but during Alexander the Great's campaign 54 years later Miletus chose to contest his passage in concert with a powerful naval force. With Alexander encamped by the city the Milesians wavered, offering Miletus as a neutral port, but that wasn't good enough; the next morning Alexander's armies stormed the walls and took the city. For once the population of men was not systematically massacred.

Alexander continued quickly south, while Miletus set once more to putting itself in order. After the dissolution of the Kingdom of Pergamon, Miletus passed under Roman control in 133 B.C. Shortly afterwards, Miletus finally picked a winner, backing Rome against Mithradites VI in the Pontic Wars while neighbors like Ephesus backed Pontus. Rome was grateful for the support, and Roman rule was good to Miletus. It was during the Roman period that most of the current structures were built. It was also at this time that St. Paul passed through Miletus and spoke to the Ephesians.

Miletus' final undoing was much less cruel than those at the hands of Darius and the Greeks before him, it was simply siltation. The only thing that isn't difficult to conceive of about Miletus is its harbor's relentless recession to the west.

Following the loss of Miletus' harbor it faded from historical view. George Ostrogorsky's definitive Byzantine history mentions the city only once, and then indirectly, as a site near a minor Byzantine principality following the fall of Constantinople in 1204. That Miletus remained mildly important is certain; there is a Byzantine fortress atop the acropolis as evidence, and the fortress, Kastrion, was apparently occupied into the 13th century, but it may have been vacated before the Turks occupied the region.

## ARRIVALS & DEPARTURES
**By Bus**

Miletus is the weak link for cheap transportation. Dolmuş serve Miletus from Söke and from Priene/Güllübahçe in the north, hanging a

Balat or Milet sign in their window. Once in Miletus, however, continuing southward to Didyma is tricky since you must wait to get to Balat a few kilometers south, then wait again for the next dolmuş to Akköy, then wait yet again for a dolmuş to Didyma, whether Didim- or Altınkum-bound.

One solution is to spring for a taxi from Miletus to Akköy, about 10 kilometers south. Akköy has relatively frequent service to Didyma, or to Söke if you've had it and you want to go home.

### By Car
From Priene, continue toward the sea, away from Güllübahçe. A few minutes after passing Atburgazı a road signed "Milet" and "Balat" forks off to the left, across the plains. About 15 kilometers along another signed road directs you the remaining few kilometers to Miletus.

## SEEING THE SIGHTS
On your way to Miletus from Priene you pass the island of Lade, the site of two historical naval battles. The "island," however, is now a nondescript knoll, helping set the tone for Miletus. Miletus was not only left high and dry, but, like so many coastal ruins, picked over by early archaeologists on behalf of their native countries.

Near the car park get your bearings by the map and the great open face of the theater. The **theater** is immediately compelling, but with its sea view stolen it's slightly forlorn. Begin by ascending the theater to the fortress, after which you have a long, clockwise descent. The theater had a capacity as great as the theater at Ephesus and was clad entirely in marble. It was successively rebuilt and improved over the course of 600 years, with the final changes in the fourth century A.D.

The **fortress** is just a shell, offering a good opportunity to understand Miletus' layout. The military harbor was located opposite the theater, with two great lion statues at each side of the harbor mouth. A raised road now cuts across the mouth of the harbor. Beyond the harbor the ground rises, but the sea once encircled this, too. The neck of the isthmus was located to the south, in the direction of Balat and Didyma. Walls encircled the entire isthmus, and they are still in evidence along most of their course. The main section of the city lay in the low area at the head of the former military harbor, continuing around toward the car park.

From the fortress, head down the slope opposite the theater to the raised road crossing the mouth of the harbor. Just after you begin crossing the road look to your right for the top of one of the two lion statues, both of which have started dramatically settling. The second is almost covered in mud, the top of its head poking out just after leaving the road and turning right. If you have plenty of time you can double back from the statue and follow the peninsula around the long way, returning on the opposite side. Otherwise skirt the edge of the former bay past a Byzantine church toward the mass of ruins at the center of the former town. Here, during most of the year you will find the former marketplace flooded, the ironic twist for a city left stranded by siltation: the water is land, the land, water.

The **gymnasium** is the first well-preserved building you come to, followed by the **nymphaeum**, or fountain. Signs give some hints about your whereabouts. The area is difficult to navigate but its tumbled ruins are appealing. The finest monument in the city, the market gate, once stood to the southeast of these buildings, facing the open area from the side and marking the beginning of the processional to Didyma. Picking your way back to dry land, the **baths of Faustina** are a particular highlight of Miletus, a remarkably large baths complex built on behalf of the wife of Marcus Aurelius. Within the bath is a statue of a lion and of the local river god, Meander; given the city's sorry state, the river god was not appeased. The **Delphinium** is alongside the bath, a sanctuary for Apollo who, in the form of a dolphin, led the colonists here.

Other highlights include the nearby **Ilyas Bey Mosque**, at the end of a winding path from the baths, away from the theater. This abandoned building has some excellent stonework and is cool in the summer heat. Also worth finding is the **Temple of Athena**, across the road on the far side of the museum. This is on the site of the original Mycenean settlement. If you continue to the walls, or get out as you drive by them in the direction of Balat, you will be rewarded with a view of foundations of the six foot thick walls that Alexander stormed during his siege.

## PRIENE

**Priene** is well worth the trip out of your way. This Hellenistic fortress city is a picturesque gem, perched on a steep bluff beneath a towering 1,217 foot crag.

### History

The city clearly owed its existence to maritime trade, having little room to spare for agriculture in the immediate vicinity. The bay that it once served, however, was well and truly silted up by the time Strabo happened by at the end of the first century B.C. Though the silting destroyed the town's fortunes, it saved the Hellenistic ruins for posterity; neither the Romans nor anyone else took much interest in building atop the original ruins once Priene's usefulness as a port ended.

Priene's still-evident beauty was attended by its citizens' reputation for intelligence. Foremost among them was Bias, one of the Seven Sages (see The Shrewd Bias sidebar). Priene was responsible for administering the **Panionium**, a congress of coastal Greek cities that gathered on the opposite side of Mt. Mycale. On a clear day one of the other principal members of the Panionium, Miletus, is visible across the valley floor. Priene and Miletus had an often adversarial relationship as they battled for commerce. Miletus was a huge, economically dominant city, however, and when Priene wasn't directly under Miletus' thumb Priene still usually had the worst of it. Priene's military history is punctuated by its affable surrender to Alexander the Great, who graciously supplied enough funds to Priene's new Temple of Athena that the structure was dedicated to him. After his welcome in the city in 334 B.C., having secured his flank, Alexander marched around the bay and, to the delight of the citizens of Priene, besieged the stubbornly pro-Persian Miletus. The distant land-sea battle must have been a fine spectacle from atop Priene's acropolis. Alexander, incidentally, won.

When Alexander arrived, Priene was in the act of building the city at its current site. The original site is probably buried in the alluvial plain below and farther inland, and the new city was probably, like Ephesus to the north, chasing after a receding sea. The rebuilding occurred at roughly the same time of rebuilding at Cnidos and Helicarnassus in the south, and, like Cnidos, was done on a grid pattern. Although silting eventually left even the new city commercially and strategically bankrupt, it left its charm intact. Priene is thick with crafted marble and stone, including a playground of column drums by the Temple of Athena. The adventurous can spend hours wandering around the forested upper slopes of the bluff, and even take a winding stair up the right side of the crag to the dizzying acropolis.

## ARRIVALS & DEPARTURES

### By Bus

Dolmuş run regularly from the well-signed dolmuş stop in nearby Söke, and Söke can be reached from anywhere in the region. Don't mistake one of the small dolmuş stops for the main transit hub, a large municipal parking lot with dolmuş arranged by destination.

### By Car

From the north, take the main (525) road south from Söke toward Savulca/Bodrum. Three miles after passing through tiny Savulca, take a right turn on the Güllübahçe road and drive ten kilometers to the other side of Güllübahçe, where the familiar yellow signs direct you up the hill to Priene. If you are quite adventurous, you can try the mountain road from Güzelçamlı on the other side of the mountain range at the entrance to the Dilek Yarımadası Milli Parki. According to maps, it passes the ruins of the Panionium on the north slope and descends to Atburgazı, where it meets the Priene road three kilometers west of Priene.

## WHERE TO STAY & EAT

The most inviting spot for a bite to eat is ŞELALE RESTAURANT at the base of the hill. In the dog days you may be unable to resist the cascade of water and greenery and the shaded patio here. The Şelale has good food, but it isn't a bad idea to visit one of the small local shops for some bread, fruit, and a bottle of Villa Doluca and pack it along with you to the lightly forested upper slopes of the ruin.

There are some small hotels at the base of Priene's hill, but they're tiny local places, good only in a pinch.

## SEEING THE SIGHTS

After entering Priene through a gap in the battered old walls near the East Gate, the main path takes you to a signed intersection. Turn left and descend one block to the **bouleterion**, a small theater, on your right. This building was the meeting place of the city council, erected around 170 B.C. and holding about 500 people. The intimate space opening out on the valley and sea below is typical of the aesthetically pleasing structures in the city. The small theater structure was covered with a wooden roof, which would have been an unfortunate addition on clear days when the view of the cliff face above is as appealing as the land and seascape below.

As you may have gathered on the walk in, the city is laid out on a perfect grid pattern despite the difficulties of the sloped site. Hippodamus of Miletus is responsible for this contribution to civic planning. The small ruins to the left of the bouleuterion, the way you entered, is the **prytaneion**, or city administrative office. The city's sacred flame was located here, and members of the city council would dine by its light. Directly in front of the bouleuterion and across the street is the **Temple of Zeus**, an Ionic temple (tall, slender columns) that was partially demolished when a small Byzantine fort was erected that overlapped its east side, and was more recently emptied by German archaeologists who were bravely seeking to out-plunder the British in their bizarre antiquity race. The altar remains.

Ahead and out of sight against the lower city walls are the **gymnasium** and the **stadium**. If you aren't on a tight schedule the steep walk down to these buildings is worthwhile, though less so than the hike to the summit. The two old structures formed the academic and athletic heart of the city. The gymnasium was both an athletic training facility and an institution of higher learning. While in this building, note various inscriptions etched into the interior walls of the gymnasium – they are roughly equivalent to "Phileas Son of Pausanius was here." The 600 foot long stadium was the site of all sorts of athletic contests, ranging from boxing and javelin hurling to running and the pancration – a no holds barred wrestling/kickboxing match.

About 750 feet west (seaward) along the road in front of the bouleuterion is the **House of Alexander**. This building was clearly venerated, but there is argument as to whether it was out of respect for Alexander's brief stay here or because this was a shrine to gods of the underworld. The underworld adherents use the small fissure in the floor of the building as exhibit A of their Chthonic argument – supporters of the thesis that this house was associated with some form of underworld worship cite the small fissure in the floor as evidence.

A hundred feet uphill of this on a flat open space northwest of the Bouleuterion is the **Temple of Athena**, a good place to sit on a fallen column drum and rest. The Temple of Athena is the city's centerpiece, a large complex with a splendid view. A handful of the tumbled column drums have been collected and set up to reproduce five columns, but the original temple boasted 61 more, in six rows of eleven. The 120 foot long temple was designed by Pytheos, and Priene's city fathers were probably impressed that he had one face of the Mausoleum at Helicarnassus – one of the Seven Wonders of the World – on his resume. Unlike the mausoleum, this was a classic Ionic temple. City fathers dedicated the temple in Alexander's name, thankful for his financial assistance in its construction, but the inscription is now in the British Museum in London. Just below the temple is the footprint of a thinner, longer Doric colonnade whose thick column drums are mixed in with the Ionic pieces.

If you head through the scrub and pine trees directly uphill from the Temple of Athena you will arrive at the **temple of Demeter and Kore**. The two goddesses were linked with the prosperity of crops, and the sanctuary here has a pretty situation but is otherwise enigmatic. Herodotus singles out the rites of Demeter as particularly secret, and the Egyptians called the acts of Demeter – or Isis – worship of the "Mysteries." A contemporary historian, W. Berkert, reports that the sea god Poseidon assumed the form of a horse and mated with Demeter, and rituals may have celebrated this unlikely union. All the uncharacteristically tight-lipped Herodotus will say is that the ritual was "an exhibition of the Gods' sufferings."

Rounding the hill and ascending to the east you arrive at the area where the eastern defensive walls meet the cliff face. There is a defensive tower here alongside settling basins that purified water entering the city by aquaduct. A path follows a mildly harrowing route to the small acropolis, which is also walled.

Looking up at the crag from below, note the squared section slightly recessed into the natural rock; this was probably the site of a statue or monument, the ancient equivalent of a big letter "P" in the local high school's colors.

After descending, Priene's main theater is slightly lower than the temple of Demeter and Kore, around the ridge toward the entrance. This fine old building is surrounded by small trees and is a good place for a final rest before heading out. Five chairs are still arranged around the floor of the building for VIPs, a status symbol as well as a dubious perk – no napping during drawn-out speeches – and they seem to establish beyond a doubt that the Romans' violent forms of circus entertainment were not on display here. Behind the stage is another Byzantine addition to the city, a small church that constituted the local Bishopric.

---

### THE SHREWD BIAS

*Priene's most famous son was* **Bias**, *considered one of the wisest men of ancient times. Herodotus passes along accounts of his wisdom in* **The History**, *including this exchange with the powerful Lydian King, Croesus:*
*"After defeating the cities along the Aegean coast, the Lydian King Croesus returned to the inland capital of Sardis and began contemplating a campaign against the island kingdoms of Greece. Upon hearing that Croesus was preparing to create a navy, Bias approached him and said "Sir, the islanders are buying up ten thousand horses, as they have in mind to make a campaign on Sardis and yourself." Croesus imagined he spoke seriously and said "Would that the gods would put this idea into their heads; that islanders should come against the sons of the Lydians with horses." Bias answered "Sir, you seem to me to pray very earnestly that you might catch the islanders riding horses on the mainland, and your hope in this is very reasonable. But do you believe that the islanders have any other matter for prayer than that they will catch the Lydians at sea and so take vengeance on yourself?" Croesus was extraordinarily pleased with this answer and gave up his shipbuilding."*

---

## KUŞADASI

"Make your spending a memorable experience," chirps the **Kuşadası** tourist bureau's brochure, which is your first clue to the nature of this bustling port. We recommend you don't make your spending a memorable experience here, as the prices are at least as inflated as those in İstanbul. If you aren't foolish enough to pay $75 for a standard ceramic plate, someone from one of the luxury cruise liners is and – poof! – there goes the shopowners' incentive to haggle.

For all of its congestion, Kuşadası is convenient and fun, and has the region's best hotel.

## History

Kuşadası's history is relatively short, having been ushered in by the siltation at Ephesus. Upon conceding the uselessness of Ephesus' receding port the Byzantines began settling here, referring to the city as Scala Nova, or New Ephesus. The fortress was probably constructed by the Byzantines, but it was modified and improved by the Venetians and, later, the Ottomans.

In recent history, Kuşadası was a pit stop on the great hippie trail of Western backpackers.

## ARRIVALS & DEPARTURES

Kuşadası is less convenient than Selçuk, and arriving from the north or east you will pass through Selçuk on your way here. The strip of hotels along the coast between Selçuk and Kuşadası offers holiday and tour group accommodation, and if you plan to stay put awhile they can be a good option; otherwise, don't pay for amenities you won't use.

## WHERE TO STAY

Kuşadası has long since surrendered its former "sedate" status for "rambunctious." If you don't mind the change, stay here. The anachronistically peaceful Kismet, one of our favorite hotels, is an eddy of calm.

**KISMET HOTEL**, *Akyar Mevkii, Kuşadası, Tel. 256 614 2005, Fax 256 614 4914. Rooms: 102. Double: $110. Half board available. Restaurant.*

One of the country's best hotels. The 31 year-old Kismet is the grand old institution of Kuşadası, a sparkling relic of old world calm and decorum that has seen guests such as Jimmy Carter and Queen Elizabeth II (separately). In a region where three-year-old hotels appear tattered, the Kismet is natty, with marvelously manicured grounds and a charm like San Simeon. The rooms are attractive and peaceful, with shutters that open and allow the sea breezes to blow through. It is the ideal English colonial location for an afternoon gin and tonic under the trees, despite its construction by descendants of the last Ottoman Sultan. The tennis court is one of the most beautiful anywhere, but a mis-hit backhand will float to Egypt. Open April-October.

Selected as one of our best places to stay – see Chapter 10.

**CLUB CARAVANSERAIL**, *Atatürk Bulvarı No.2 09400, Kuşadası, Tel. 256 614 4115, Fax 256 614 2423. Rooms: 40. Double: $85. Restaurant.*

Built during the heyday of the Ottoman Empire, the building is a sturdy old fixture on the Kuşadası waterfront. The wagonloads of traders have given way to busloads of tourists, but if you're so inclined, this is the place to indulge in a late night belly-dancing experience, which is part of the extra $30 price for an open buffet in the courtyard garden. They will cram fun down your throat here until late, and your nicely furnished room will shudder and throb until midnight. Best not to be in it.

**DERİCİ HOTEL**, *Türkmen Mah. Atatürk Bulv. No. 40, Kuşadası, Tel. 256 614 8222, Fax 256 614 8226. Rooms: 90. Double: $50. Restaurant.*

The Derici is the best of the standard hotels in Kuşadası, with clean, pleasant rooms and a view out over Kuşadası's waterfront.

**ADAKULE HOTEL**, *Bayraklidede Mevkii, Kuşadası, Tel. 256 614 9270, Fax 256 614 5085. Rooms: 330. Double: $135. Restaurant.*

The heavyweight champion, a sprawling luxury seaside hotel with all of the things you would expect (air conditioning, sailboard rental, satellite television, private beach) plus a few you might not, such as a big fancy restaurant tower and in-room Atari. If the staid, refined world of the Kismet is not to your liking try the Adakule – this place is over the top.

**HOTEL ROSE**, *Aslanlar Cad., Aydınlık Sok. No. 7, Tel. 256 614 1111. Double: $12.*

Given Kuşadası's backpacking legacy you'd expect more budget hotels to have figured out how to do it right; unfortunately this is one of the few. It has the slew of comforts that you just don't find in expensive places; laundry, English movies on the VCR, discounts on long distance bus trips, and cooking by the proprietor's mom. The Rose is just up the hill behind the tourism information office.

Slightly more expensive, with an excellent view, is the **HAZGÜL PANSIYON**, *Tel. 256 614 3641*, up the hill to the south. Hazgül is closed in the off season.

## WHERE TO EAT

Most hotels offer dinner as part of a half-board price, and many of the buffet extravaganzas are excellent (the Kismet distinguishes itself). The reasons to eat out are to dine at one of the fish restaurants, enjoy some entertainment like that at the Caravanserail, or to get something cheap. You'll find many of the latter in Kuşadası's inland streets.

**KAZIM USTA**, *Liman Cad., Kuşadası, Tel. 256 614 1725. Moderate-Expensive.*

Asked where the best restaurant is, most locals will reverentially point toward one of the restaurants on the waterfront by the harbor master's office. This is one of these, and a veteran of the fish restaurant trade. You should find the food delicious and the service very good. Agree on what you're paying up front, although the Kazım Usta usually makes prices fairly clear. To find out what's in season ask *"Mevsimlık ne var?"* **ALI BABA**, nearby, also has a good reputation.

**ADA RESTAURANT**, *Güvercin Island, Kuşadası, Tel. 256 614 1725. Moderate.*

You'll want to walk out to the island anyway, so you might as well take the opportunity to eat here. The island has had a thorough going over by the municipality with paths and tea gardens, but it remains a pretty spot, benefitting from the charm of the old harbor fortress. The food is at least as good as the food in town, and no more expensive. There are several good, cheap restaurants tucked in elsewhere on the small island.

## SEEING THE SIGHTS/EXCURSIONS

The three cities of Priene, Miletus and Didyma constitute a full day trip from Kuşadası. The thin layer of ruins at Panionia is dicussed below, as is the source of Kuşadası's rise to prominence, Ephesus.

**Pigeon Fortress**, the small castle at the southern end of Kuşadası's harbor, is a Byzantine fortification, now given over to a collection of small çay bahçesi (tea gardens) and restaurants. The main keep is kept locked tight, but the fortress remains relatively intact, including, even, the pigeons.

In the summer, ferries depart to **Samos Island** in Greece at 8:30 a.m. and 5 p.m., with a two hour travel time. Departures from Samos are on the same schedule. Ferries may not depart between 1 November and 31 March due to weather or lack of bookings, but there tends to be one ferry daily.

Contact one of the travel agencies to find out if a departure is planned. One way trips cost $30, with $35 for same day returns and $50 for open ended returns. A visa is required. Contact any of the following: **Azim Travel**, *Liman Cad. Yayla Pasaj, Tel. 256 614 1553*; **Diana Travel**, *Kıbrıs Cad. No. 4, Tel. 256 614 1399*; or **Scalanova Travel**, *Yalı Cad. No. 17, Tel. 256 614 3268.*

## NIGHTLIFE & ENTERTAINMENT

If you are staying in Kuşadası you should take advantage of the bar scene. Even the fairy tale fortress just offshore on tiny **Pigeon Island** throbs with dance music late at night.

One convenient pub crawl opportunity is on **Eski Pazar Cad.**, inexplicably a shamrock-spangled Irish wonderland. The gauntlet of bars includes Molly Malone's, The Green House, Shamrock Steak House, The Irish Watering Hole, Murphy's, The Asgard Irish Pub, and the Log Cabin Irish Bar. You walk in one way and lurch out the other.

## SPORTS & RECREATION

**Kustur Plaj** to the north of town is a popular beach, as is the slightly better beach to the south, **Kadınlar Plaj**. Both are below a row of hotels. The best beaches are at the national park (see below). Dolmuş serve both beaches, with trips to Kadınlar every half hour in the summer.

You can combine a day at a relatively isolated swimming area on the coast with a visit to an obscure ruin. The national park at **Dilek Yarımdası Milli Parki** is 26 kilometers south of Kuşadası and accessible by dolmuş. The town of **Güzelcamlı**, located just outside the park, is on the slope below the ruins of **Panionia**. Panionia was the meeting place of the **Ionian League**, and, like Letoon in Lycia, the spiritual capital. The area is dense with foliage, and has not been picked over by archaeologists. There was temple to Poseidon, he of the seas and the earthshaking, at the city. The north slope of the 4,000 foot Samsun Dağı also has the remnants of fortifications that once stood watch over the straits of Samos.

If you have a rented vehicle, you can hazard the route that is supposed to exist past Panionia, over the hill and down to Priene on the far side. The park, with its numerous coves and small beaches, shares Panionia's lush plant life. The sand beaches further along are, predictably, more secluded, but the whole lot is a step up from the strips of sand beneath the new hotels.

On weekends the national park is packed. If you are with a group of four, consider shelling out $40 for a full-day taxi to the park. Dolmuş usually serve Güzelcamlı and turn back, except in the high season. Some dolmuş will post "Güzelcamlı/Milli Park" signs, indicating they shuttle you directly to the beach.

## SHOPPING

As noted, the literature advises us to make our spending a memorable experience, so let's start there. Kuşadası is thick with bars, nightclubs, and shops. Cruise ships and bus tours dump people here just long enough to pick up food, meerschaum pipes, leather goods and Turkish rugs. It is, for many who arrive by cruise ship, the only exposure to Turkey's goods and price structure, and the shopowners have discovered that they can charge a lot. "You will enjoy the fun of bargaining with smiling salesmen," wheedles the Kuşadası tourism bureau, but they're smiling a little too broadly. Unless you're in Turkey for a day and that day is spent in Kuşadası, consider waiting to make that big purchase.

The **Doluca Şarap Fabrikası** (wine plant) is located just outside of town to the south. If you stop in during business hours and boldly ask around, they'll happily let you taste some of the local stuff.

# SELÇUK & THE EPHESUS RUINS

Selçuk *is* Ephesus, located at the site of the original Ephesus settlement. Ephesus is now located little more than two kilometers away, as emperors kept scooting it in the direction of the receding harbor. They didn't scoot it fast enough, unfortunately, and the city died. In addition to the Ephesus ruins just down the road there are several wonderful things to see within Selçuk itself.

Today, the Byzantine Ayasoluk Castle commands the crest of the main hill, not far above the nicely restored ruins of the Basilica of St. John, which is itself just above the İsa Bey Mosque. Together with the town's outstanding Ephesus Museum, you might enjoy Selçuk as much as the famous Ephesus.

The mass of historical sites has generated a powerful tourist gravity, drawing hundreds of thousands of people annually. As a result, Selçuk has its share of aggressive lads selling carpets, hotel rooms, meals, and guided tours to vacationing Westerners. They are a persistent nuisance in town, but it's pretty peaceful outside of the town center.

## ARRIVALS & DEPARTURES

### By Bus

The main bus station in Selçuk doubles as the dolmuş/minibus stop for most routes (Şirince is an exception, with dolmuş leaving from the railway station). The bus station is at the northeast corner of the town's main intersection; here in the city that had so much to do with civilization's birth, the intersection is decorated with a dynamically inappropriate monument to Fulda tires.

Selçuk is a good place to catch buses in every direction, since it is at the junction of the main highway and the southbound coastal roads. Fares (negotiable with larger groups): Bodrum: $6.50, Marmaris $8, Fethiye $8.50, Antalya $10, Cappadoccia $17, İstanbul $15. Crazy Michael at Hakiki Koç is probably the most helpful and honest of the bunch.

### By Car

Selçuk is on the main İzmir-Aydın road, just 50 miles south of İzmir and 55 miles west of Aydın. Selçuk is essentially the end of the line on this main road; hereafter it dives inland to Denizli, then cuts through the interior to Antalya.

The quality of roads along the coast to the south falls off slightly, but is not bad; Kuşadası is 21 kilometers, Bodrum 163 kilometers, and Marmaris 230 kilometers.

## ORIENTATION

Selçuk's sites are mostly clustered around the hill in the center of town. The **tourist office** is across the main road from the bus station in the direction of "Efes/Artemesion," *Tel. 232 892 6945.*

## WHERE TO STAY

Tourists flock to this area, and the coast from Selçuk to the far side of Kuşadası is littered with big luxury hotels. There are plenty of expensive, uninspired places in the mix, but also some excellent options.

**HOTEL KALEHAN,** *Atatürk Cad. No. 49, Selçuk, Tel. 232 892 6154, Fax 232 892 2169. Rooms: 54. Double: $55. Restaurant.*

The Kalehan is a charming inn on the outskirts of Selçuk. Once the centerpiece of a large cotton and fig plantation, the inn has been one of Selçuk's best kept secrets since 1981. The hotel also offers two newer buildings in a compound behind the main house, as well as a small Ottoman-style guest house and a swimming pool. In the evening, guests gather around the hearth in the main hall. The help is carefully attentive, and the rooms simple and pleasant. The atmosphere, while nice, is a bit staid, with shut doors at 11 p.m. The owner, Erol Ergir, grew up here after his family was transferred from Crete in 1920. Credit cards are accepted only in theory; the machine doesn't appear to function. This, by the way, is where George B. Quatman of the George B. Quatman Foundation of Lima, Ohio used to stay (see Basilica of St. John the Apostle under *Seeing the Sights,* below).

**AUSTRALIAN NEW ZEALAND PENSION,** *Prof. Miltner Sokak #7, Selçuk, Tel. 232 892 6050. Rooms: 24. Double: $10.*

This is how pensions should be. Family run since 1986, the Australian New Zealand Pension quite remarkably refuses to maraud people at the bus station, thriving on word of mouth. Vines cascade down into the court of the three-story building, which has a carpet-bedecked rooftop lounge with an appropriately nomadic air. An excellent place to swap travel-gossip, watch English-language videos, get a good, cheap meal, and puzzle over a staggering array of in-house bar tricks. There's even a zero pressure carpet shop downstairs and the pension organizes four day trips into the mountains at Karakaya. Yanks and Canadians welcome, despite the name.

**EPHESUS RICHMOND HOTEL,** *Pamucak, Selçuk, Tel. 232 892 7077, Fax 232 892 6731. Rooms: 196. Double: $130. Restaurant.*

On the coast several kilometers south of Ephesus, the Ephesus Richmond is a convenient seaside behemoth in the luxury hotel mode. A well-managed chain of hotels, but slightly ragged around the edges and appealing only in the high season when you can take advantage of the many things to do at the beach. The "apart rooms," or rooms with kitchen services located in small buildings outside of the main hotel building, are remarkably better than those in the main hotel.

**In Sirince**
ŞIRINCE EVLERI PANSIYON, *Şirince, Tel. 232 898 3099 (In İstanbul: 0 532 223 2907). Rooms: 5. Double: $45.*
Quiet and peaceful, located in a town perched far above Selçuk. This old Greek village becomes wonderfully peaceful at night after the day's crowds leave, and you can empty a few bottles of the local $1-2 wine and gaze off into the valley toward Selçuk. There is regular, cheap dolmuş service to Selçuk. If the Şirince Evlerı Pansiyon is full, try the more humble pensions nearby.

## WHERE TO EAT
Selçuk's dining has been fairly summed up as "average food at average prices." That may be charitable, since the prices on the heavily touristed main roads are pretty exorbitant by Turkish standards. It's remarkable, however, how much more affordable food is just off the main street.
HOTEL KALEHAN, *Atatürk Cad. No. 49, Selçuk, Tel. 232 892 6154, Fax 232 892 2169. Moderate-Expensive.*
Fine dining on the days that the owner is in town, although the standard seems to slip when he isn't around. A fixed menu, varying each night.
ÖZDAMAR RESTAURANT, *Atatürk Mah. Cengiz Topel Cad. No. 65, Tel. 232 891 4097. Moderate.*
It doesn't take a genius to locate this place, a block up from the Artemis statue by the fountain. Mustafa Özdamar, the manager, runs a fairly slick operation that can't help but succeed in this city, at this location. Very reliable and convenient.
YENİ HİTTİT RESTAURANT, *Atatürk Mah., 1070 Sok. No. 2, Tel. 232 892 6920. Moderate.*
Yeni Hittit is a good, reliable option in Selçuk at the same prices as most of the other restaurants in town. Give the çop şiş a try, or anything else from the grill. The Yeni Hittit is open all year, but it closes up early in winter.
OKUMUŞAR PİDE SALONU, *Eftal Doğru Pasaj No. 12, Selçuk, Tel. 232 892 2987. Inexpensive.*
Okumuşlar is just down the street from the Artemis statue. This is a good place to stop in for pide and other cheap, filling fare.

## SEEING THE SIGHTS

The **Basilica of St. John the Apostle** is well worth a look, a pleasantly situated ruin that has seen some faithful restoration by, of all things, the George B. Quatman Foundation of Lima, Ohio. The basilica was erected in the 6th century directly above the tomb of St. John. Owing to the standard confusion that swaddles the apostles, St. John either died a natural death, was boiled in oil, or disappeared and will appear in Ephesus on Judgment Day. Adherents of the first story built a small church at the site of his supposed tomb. The Byzantine Emperor Justinian chose to massively renovate the church, sparing the taxpayers no expense and creating a cathedral that was one of the largest in the world at the time (even today it would have been the seventh largest).

The grand cathedral proved, in the words of Procopius, to be one of Justinian's many "crazy building schemes." Ephesus' problems with the silting bay were already serious, and this was compounded by the deteriorating fortunes of the Byzantine Empire. Ephesus was in foreign hands within 150 years, together with its stunning cathedral, and was thereafter an afterthought in a chaotic theater of war. The ill-fated structure was pressed into service as a mosque and a bazaar and damaged by earthquakes, yet it continued to command enough respect that in the 14th century Selçuk architects erected the minaret of the İsa Bey Mosque on a line with the Basilica entrance, like a punctuation mark at the base of a crucifix. Check out the beautiful inscriptions on many of the pillars, and the crude but effective relief maps of the area just inside of the southern entrance.

On the hill above the cathedral is the citadel of the **Ayasoluk fortress**, rebuilt, like the basilica, during Justinian's reign as part of a massive overhaul of the Byzantine Empire's defenses. The citadel was at the northern end of the original fortress, an immense walled city that enclosed the Basilica. Today only a suggestion of the original walls remains. Impressive as the fortress was, it did not help the Byzantines stop repeated invasions of the area by Persians, Arabs, Crusaders, Selçuks and, finally, Ottomans. The citadel's last serious occupation was by Selçuks, and it has been partially restored in recent years. Today the citadel is a nice backdrop to the town, but relatively dull inside – there is a converted chapel, a mosque, broken ground where storehouses and cisterns have caved in, and crumbling ramparts. The name Ayasoluk derives from the Greek name for the Church of St. John. The fortress is almost always closed, but it is almost always easy to climb into, as the locals often do. You aren't supposed to, technically.

The **İsa Bey Mosque** is directly to the west of and below the basilica. It was built in the 14th century by one of the Turkish tribes who scattered throughout Anatolia in the wake of the Mongol invasions. Like the basilica, the mosque took advantage of the dressed marble scattered on the grounds of the temple of Artemis (perhaps also the city walls and basilica). The long building has a beautiful western entrance, clean lines, and an attractive forecourt on the northern side. Just above this, between the mosque and the Basilica of St. John, is a large sloping pasture littered with marble. Take a break here and have a look out over the area's sites.

The aqueduct running through the center of Selçuk was one of three major lines that supplied Ephesus at its zenith. Water was rerouted from 10, 12, and 25 miles away to supply Ephesus with 1,600 gallons of water per minute. The aqueduct in Selçuk carried water from a valley below nearby Şirince.

Before venturing to Ephesus, stop in at the **Ephesus Archaeology Museum**, *Kuşadası Caddesi, behind the tourism information office, Tel. 232 892 6010; open 9 a.m. to 5 p.m. daily*, where your $2 and one hour is well spent. The Ephesus museum is just to the northwest of the town's main intersection, and its collection breathes life into Ephesus, which has been picked over for many of its best pieces. Our favorite item is the massive marble slab with 63 paragraphs of Roman customs laws for Asia; and you can't miss the gargantuan statue of Emperor Domitian – if St. John the Apostle was boiled in oil, Domitian is the one who boiled him. Try to miss the adjoining museum of modern art, with pieces for sale that are likely to double or triple in value in the next 3,000 years.

There was some confusion as to the whereabouts of the Virgin Mary's resting place, but the Holy See put an end to that in 1950. Based partly on the vision of Katharina Emmerich (1774-1824), a Bavarian nun, the Catholic Church ruled that Mary's resting place was on a small hill near Ephesus. After her son Jesus entrusted her to the care of St. John, she followed John here and lived out her final days. The current chapel, the **House of the Virgin Mary**, is located on the site of a small Byzantine church, and the church appears to have been associated with a monastery. Catholics often make a pilgrimage to the site, and typically give the restorative water from the fountains here a try. Pope John Paul II visited here in 1979 so if you're Catholic you have to go; otherwise drop by if you have a car and some extra time. Some visitors claim to have been relieved of maladies. To get there follow the road from the upper Ephesus gate. Taxis from the Selçuk otogar will shuttle you back and forth with one half hour to see the site for $10.

The town of **Sirince** is high in the mountains above Selçuk, an old Greek village that was emptied in the population exchange. Two Greek Orthodox churches are located here, one of them in mid-remodel thanks to the ever-busy George B. Quatman Foundation of Lima, Ohio. The villagers sell lace, cheap red and apple wine and even olive oil. This is a beautiful side trip, costing only 50¢ by dolmuş, which depart throughout the day from near the railway station. There are several pensions in Sirince, providing a relentlessly peaceful option to life in Selçuk after the day trippers depart at 4 p.m. Tuesday is market day, although most days are market day in the tourist season.

## NIGHTLIFE & ENTERTAINMENT

Selçuk hosts two dramatically different festivals. In the third week of January camel wrestling fans congregate here for, yes, Selçuk's acclaimed **Camel Wrestling Festival**. In May, the **International Music and Folk Dancing** festival arrives, and the Great Theatre at Ephesus has been used for performances.

The crowds for the two festivals are alike only in that they make lodging difficult. Information is available at the tourism information office, *Tel. 232 892 6550*.

## EXCURSIONS & DAY TRIPS

### Nearby Ruins

On your way to or from Selçuk, consider stopping at **Belevi Mausoleum** (signed, 12 kilometers northeast of Ephesus, on the road to İzmir), near where the road branches to Tire. Near the village is a burial mound and the remains of a huge structure that may have been akin to Mausolus' tomb at Helicarnassus. This great block of stone was clad in courses of ashlar . A passageway 65 feet long led to the center, where the sarcophagus was located. The tunnel, unfortunately, is now obstructed by the spoil of persistent treasure hunters. The sarcophagus is on display at the Ephesus Museum in Selçuk. The **Goat Fort** (Keçi Kalesi) is located on a bluff to the west.

The three ruins of Priene, Miletus, and Didyma are a good day trip from Selçuk, and you can make it to Aphrodisias or Pamukkale in the interior and back in one long day. Trips depart almost daily in the high season from the otogar.

### The Temple of Artemis

The most significant ruin at Selçuk is the **Temple of Artemis**, which we recommend stopping by en route to Ephesus, on foot. If you like your history straight, the Temple of Artemis is the place for you; a big muddy field, a column, and fascinating history. This was one of the Seven Ancient Wonders of the World, ranked by one Spartan as the best of the lot. Unfortunately, in the words of an Australian friend, today "Ya look and ya wondah."

Leaving Selçuk for Ephesus, you pass the Temple of Artemis at Ephesus on your right. The site is just adjacent to Selçuk to the west, a short walk from the otogar. The road from Kuşadası in the south cuts across the mountains and arrives from the west.

In its heyday, the temple was three times larger than the Parthenon in Athens, and, if long dead observers are to be believed, far more ornate and glorious. Doric temples, like the Parthenon and the Temple of Athena at Assos, were relatively squat structures that crowned hills. Ionic temples were built with tall, slender columns, and the Temple of Artemis was the most massive of the world's Ionic temples, with 127 columns 60 feet tall covering the area of a football field.

Artemis-worship was not restricted to Ephesus, but it flourished here like nowhere else. Upon arrival in 1000 B.C. the seafaring Greeks grafted their goddess of chastity, Artemis, with the native Anatolian fertility goddess Cybele. The result was the many-breasted deity that adorns postcards and statues throughout Selçuk. The priests and followers of Artemis had a set of rituals as elaborate as their temple, mostly revolving around agriculture and procreation. If you want a root cause for confusion about sexuality, look no further: ceremonies at the fertility/chastity temple included orgies and great spectacles of self-abuse that evidently included self-castration. Eunuchs were responsible for affairs at the temple, and perhaps castration was the hazing ritual for the administrative good life.

There were several versions of the temple, which was old when Herodotus wrote about it. In 560 B.C., the Ephesians attempted to save their city from King Croesus of Lydia by stringing a cord between the temple and the city wall, thus currying Artemis' favor. Herodotus does not tell us how Croesus overcame this obstacle; presumably he sent a Lydian soldier shinnying up a column with a pair of scissors. At any rate the Ephesians' ploy failed, and Croesus' army sacked the city. Croesus, a great believer in the mystical, helped fund restoration of the temple, helpfully contributing several golden cows.

The temple again came to harm in 356, when an arsonist allegedly burned it down. Legends recount that on the day of the fire the goddess Artemis had left the temple to be on hand at the birth of Alexander in Macedon. When the precocious 22 year old arrived in 334 B.C. he was evidently apologetic, allowing the Ephesians to devote their tax money to renovating the structure. The ensuing temple, even more incredible than earlier versions, was the structure deemed one of the Seven Wonders of the World. Worship at the temple continued under the Romans, who knew Artemis by the name of her Roman equivalent, Diana.

Christianity began to erode Artemis-worship. St. John may have settled here in the company of his adoptive mother, Mary, the mother of Christ, and organized the spread of Christianity from this Roman capital of Asia. By the time his colleague St. Paul arrived, the local silver smiths at Ephesus were becoming concerned about Christianity's affect on their trade in Artemis/Diana figurines. St. Paul's evangelizing about the evils of their icons was the last straw, and they rioted, storming around and declaring "Great is Diana of Ephesus." St. Paul, sensing that Christ was not fully in their hearts, did verily split. Eventually, however, the ingenious city fathers (see *Economics of Religion* sidebar below) built a thriving tourism industry around Christian pilgrimage to the site of the Virgin Mary's death, and the silversmiths beat their Diana figurines into crucifixes.

The combined forces of Christianity, a receding sea, and a good, sound sacking by Goths in 237 A.D. finally put an end to worship at the temple. Thereafter the temple site was plundered for its vast wealth of dressed stone and picked over for its best statues and artifacts. Principally, Justinian looted the ruins during the construction of the Basilica of St. John – although the temple columns do not appear to have been shuttled to İstanbul to construct the Haghia Sophia, as is often claimed. What remained was buried by the silting of the Cayster River until it was unearthed and hauled off in the 19th century. Many of the best artifacts from the temple now reside in the British Museum in London and the Kunsthistorische Museum in Vienna.

There is little left to see at the temple. A token column has been assembled from spare drums, but the foundation is gone and what hasn't been carted off has been buried. The only thing of note is on the side of the temple distant from Selçuk, where the remains of the temple altar have been found. This was, like most major temples, by the side of a spring or fissure, although no trace remains. What was sacrificed at the altar is not known.

---

### DID THEY HAVE A SANTA BUNNY?

*Worshippers of the fertility goddess Cybele had an oddly familiar celebration each spring to mark the beginning of the growing season and to bring themselves luck. A pine tree was decorated with a garland of flowers and became the focus of a three day period of mourning for Cybele's lover Attis, the god of flora. After three days the mourning would end with a festival to celebrate Attis having arisen from the dead, and the coming of spring.*

---

## Ephesus

Ephesus is the most marvelous Hellenistic ruin in the Aegean, and, some say, the world.

Once upon a time, everything about Ephesus was impressive. This was the capital of Asia and the most bustling metropolis in the world, with a population of 250,000 at a time when 20,000 was impressive. Ephesus had streetlights and running water, a grand stadium, a theater, avenues paved with marble, and one of the wonders of the world just cubits away at the Temple of Artemis. It was a nerve center for the world's commerce, joining the western end of the Royal Road to Babylon with Mediterranean sea trade.

Even a plague of 19th century archaeologist/looters have not managed to destroy Ephesus' charm. Sites from Assos to Xanthus have been emptied by the battleship load, but museums have not floated the fleet that could strip Ephesus bare. True, some of the ancient city's masterpieces have been hauled off to Europe, but long dead builders and artists seem to have stocked Ephesus well against just such a possibility. There remains a remarkable sprawl of engraved marble and cunningly wrought sculpture, great columns and capitals, mosaics and theaters and wide streets.

Ephesus' great fault is that it numbs you, a drudgery of ornate marble. Advice: Ignore guided tours to the site and see it on your own, lingering over what you enjoy. There is always a covey of guides waiting to help, for a small fee, at both gates.

### Getting to Ephesus

Many Selçuk hotels will provide transportation to Ephesus. The two kilometer distance from Selçuk to Ephesus begins along a wide tree-lined pedestrian path alongside the five kilometer Selçuk coast road. At the sign you bear left and follow the road to the site. The road is well-signed. A slightly longer route takes you to the Magnesia Gate at the upper end of the city, but that route is less pleasant by virtue of the highway's short shoulder. The main parking lot is at the bottom gate, where knick-knacks and snack food are on sale.

Taxis between Ephesus and Selçuk cost $3, and there's no need to let the taxi wait for your return since there are ordinarily plenty here anyway. From Kuşadası a round trip with three hours at the site is $30.

### History

The ruins of Ephesus are from one distinct phase in the wandering city's past. Alexander seized early Ephesus without a fight in 334 B.C., but after his death 11 years later possession of the city was hotly disputed among his squabbling generals. Around 300 B.C. one of the Diadochi (squabbling generals), Lysimachos, took control of the city. He brought a fresh perspective to the problem of Ephesus' increasing distance from the sea, abruptly ordering everyone to build an entirely new city at the present site. The Greeks were the founders of democracy, but not these particular Greeks, and everyone reluctantly did as they were told.

The move put the new harbor flush with the sea and fixed Ephesus' place in maritime commerce for the next thousand years. The city was massive, with walls completely encircling **Mt. Pion** (the hill behind the theater) and marching along the ridge far above the slope houses. Within 500 years continued deposits of silt had forced Roman emperors to order massive dredging operations, none of which delayed the inevitable. The sea receded, and is no longer even visible from the city. Ephesus, too, lapsed into obscurity, hardly meriting footnotes in later Byzantine history.

---

### REPLY HAZY, ASK AGAIN LATER

*According to a myth shrouded in legend, the Greeks who settled here first consulted the Oracle at Delphi. The oracular insight was that a fish and a boar would reveal the site of their new home. Sure enough, the settlers found a few fish and wild boar near Ephesus – as they would have at any site within 2,000 miles. A low point for the Oracle.*

---

**Visiting Ephesus**

If you genuinely enjoy wandering in ruins, you can plan to spend an entire day here – or years. Several hours is enough for most people, especially in the summer. A guide at the site will cost about $13 for a small group, much lower in the off season. Bring along water, sunscreen, and a bite to eat, as you may want to spend a while here and refreshments are isolated in a corner by the entrance. The sun cooks these ruins and visitors fresh from the pasty north. We divide Ephesus' ruins into three sections: the north area by the theater, the center of town, and the upper town to the east. From the lower gate, begin by making your way to the theater. Be sure to visit the Ephesus Museum in Selçuk – better before than after visiting the ruins.

Despairing of the florid prose that has tried to animate the **Great Theatre**, Mark Twain wrote: "One may read the Scriptures and believe, but he cannot go and stand yonder in the ruined theater and in imagination people it again with the vanished multitudes." He's right, but the theater is one of the most accessible parts of the city. Any sports or concert enthusiast has heard the roar that once filled this place during plays, concerts, and, in the end, gladiatorial combat. There's less need to use your imagination in the month of May, when the **Ephesus Festival of Culture and Art** uses this venue for concerts and performances *(information about performances is available at Tel. 232 892 6550)*. The main stage is three stories high, and the 25,000, 100 foot high theater obviously drew performers from around the world. Taking a seat high in the theater gives

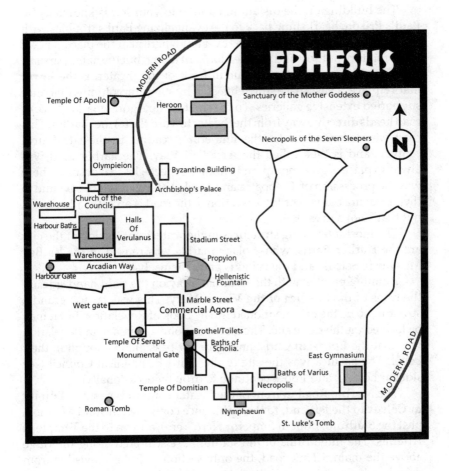

EPHESUS

Temple Of Apollo

MODERN ROAD

Heroon

Sanctuary of the Mother Goddesss

Necropolis of the Seven Sleepers

N

Olympieion

Byzantine Building

Archbishop's Palace

Church of the Councils

Warehouse

Harbour Baths

Halls Of Verulanus

Stadium Street

Warehouse

Propyion

Arcadian Way

Harbour Gate

Hellenistic Fountain

West gate

Marble Street

Commercial Agora

Temple Of Serapis

Brothel/Toilets

Baths of Scholia.

Monumental Gate

East Gymnasium

Baths of Varius

Temple Of Domitian

Necropolis

MODERN ROAD

Roman Tomb

Nymphaeum

St. Luke's Tomb

you an excellent perspective on the ancient city. When work began on the theater under Emperor Claudius around 50 A.D., it had the great Ephesian bay as a backdrop. Today the sea is gone, having receded behind the spur of Mt. Koressos on the left, and the great colonnaded road that once served the shipyards ends abruptly near the great heap of the harbor gates.

The building on the distant hill a little to your left is known as **St. Paul's Prison**, hearkening back to the evangelizing Paul's troubles with the Ephesians. It's unlikely he was ever anywhere near the place, since it was a military outpost and fortified lookout tower, but the name persists.

To the left, across the avenue in front of the theater, is the **lower marketplace**, a vast space still delineated by standing columns that once supported extensive galleries. To the right of the Agora (marketplace) a road heads directly away from the theater toward the former harbor. This road was extended under the Emperor Arcadius in the late fourth century, and is thus called the **Arcadian Way**. The harbor road was always a place of great pomp, and one of the spectacles that occurred here was the procession of Cleopatra and Mark Antony down the avenue to their pleasure barge. The lower section of the road is occasionally closed, but that's not a great loss.

The most interesting structures in the waterfront section of the city are the **Harbor Baths**, whose black marble was reused in the İsa Bey Mosque in Selçuk, and the ruinous gates themselves.

Running parallel with the Arcadian Way on the right hand side are the ruins of the **Basilica of the Virgin Mary**. This was far too grand a structure to be the one mentioned in The Book of Revelation, but it may be located on the same site. The gist of St. John's message in Revelation was that the Ephesian Christians were not passionate enough in their belief. The basilica was the site of the Third Ecumenical Council (see sidebar below), and Popes continue to drop by occasionally.

The **Marble Road** in front of the theater continues past the **Library of Celsus** to the left and, to the right, once continued around Mt. Pion, past the **Stadium** (built in Emperor Nero's era), and on to the Temple of Artemis. The huge ruins of the stadium are scattered along the ridge above the main Selçuk road, the only section of Ephesus visible from Selçuk today. Contests, gladiatorial combat, and races too unruly for the Great Theatre were held here. From the theater, continue up the Marble Way toward the city center to the left.

## THE ECONOMICS OF RELIGION

*In 428, Nestorius of Antioch became the patriarch of Constantinople, bringing with him the belief that Jesus Christ was a mortal man forced to come to terms with his divinity. Other religious thinkers maintained that Christ had a wholly united divine spirit, a single perfect God and Man. This fairly obscure theological debate became the pretext for persecution and unrest throughout the empire. Finally, in 431, Emperor Theodosius II summoned members of the clergy to Ephesus to settle the matter, convening the Third Ecumenical Council.*

*It was a fortunate choice for the city fathers of Ephesus, who had a vested interest in the outcome. They reviled Nestorius' rationalist idea that Christ had the spirit of a mortal man, since that meant, too, that Mary was simply Mother of Christ and no longer Mother of God. In short, the patriarch Nestorius' theology threatened to kill Ephesus' revenues as the site of Mary's tomb and a place of holy veneration and pilgrimage.*

*During the council, Nestorius was outmaneuvered by the Alexandrian patriarch Cyril, who, playing before the sympathetic Ephesian crowd, managed to not only have Nestorius' theology denounced, but get Nestorius condemned as a heretic and exiled to Egypt. The Ephesian city fathers were surely much relieved. Lest you think this all an unlikely subject for such great debate, the 1987 film The Last Temptation of Christ stirred up the same passions by portraying Jesus as a troubled man, and provoked demonstrations and widespread opposition among the religious establishment.*

**From the Theatre**

The centerpiece of Ephesus is the **Library of Celsus**, the grand structure at the juncture of Curettes Street and the Marble Way. The reconstruction is the work of a team of Viennese archaeologists, and if the library didn't quite look like this in antiquity, well, it should have. The building dates back to 117 A.D., when the governor at the time built it for a hero of the Empire, his father Gaius Julius Celsus Polemaeanus. The academics and wise men of the age would collect here to pore over a great collection of papyrus scrolls, or, alternately, duck through a secret tunnel that led to the brothel across the street. The library was one of the world's great repositories of writing, with all of the scrolls administered by an early librarian. The Library and its works suffered badly during the sack of the Goths, no great lovers of books.

To the left as you near the end of the Marble Road are the **Baths of Scholastica**, once a vast three story spa complex of swimming pools, baths, libraries, and private rooms. Some suspect it was associated with a **brothel** here at the city's main intersection, but this may just as well be the prurient fantasizing of archaeologists digging in the sun too long and is based largely on the discovery of the small but distinctive Priapus statue (now in the Selçuk museum). An inscription of a woman, a heart, and a foot on the main street is said to suggest that if a man's foot is not of that size he isn't old enough to be welcome.

In any event, the sprawling baths complex, accessed from higher on Curettes Street, underwent its last great renovation in the fourth century under its namesake, and offers an interesting warren of rooms, heating tunnels, and statuary (some pilfered from the Temple of Hestia Boulea). One of the great matter-of-fact places of antiquity is located in the collection of buildings just beyond the baths. A long L-shaped marble bench with forty-six holes cut in the seats once served as a restroom, and waste was carried away by running water in the pit below. This elegant system surrounded a large, columned pool.

The facilities were apparently reserved for the upper classes and rumor has it that during winter wealthy cityfolk would send their slaves ahead of them to warm a seat. No word on where, or if, the poor were able to go to the bathroom. This section of buildings has several interesting mosaics that are worth hunting for, and the multi-layered flooring is ideal for kids to clamber through.

The **Temple of Hadrian** is to the left of Curettes Street, its back to the Baths of Scholastica. This is one of the city's great sites, part of the great wave of construction that swept every site in Asia Minor, even Petra in Jordan, when Hadrian (118-138) went on his grand tour of the provinces. The ornate building has a detailed frieze that relates the legend of the city's founding. The front arch has the face of Tyche, the Goddess of Fortune, and the interior arch has Medusa, whose role was to protect the temple by turning vandals and miscreants to stone.

To the right as you ascend are some fine mosaics, more of which are contained in the modern buildings on the slope above the library. These buildings contain the **Slope Houses**. For centuries this section of town was Ephesus' toniest neighborhood, and archaeologists continue to unearth a wealth of artifacts and architectural curiosities. The mosaics, frescoes, statues, and central heating system inside will help dispel any lingering 20th century arrogance – the residents of Ephesus were sophisticated. The Slope Houses are a powerful part of the city's story, and worth the $1 surcharge when the area is open.

After viewing the temple, slope houses, brothel, and the Baths of Scholastica take a left up the sloping road just above the baths. Ascending this road gives you a good overview of this part of the city and, hopefully, gets you away from the crowds. This road ran to the top of **Panayir Dağı** (Mt. Pion), meeting the top of the great theater.

Continuing on up the Street of Curettes you pass some remarkable reliefs, including the winged goddess Nike (whose cult has been revived in Beaverton, Oregon) propped up by the side of the road near the **Monument of Memnius**. Memnius was a local hero, and the grandson of Sulla, emperor during much of Julius Caesar's rise to power. Further down the road you pass through the columns of the **Hercules Gate**, built relatively late in the city's history with statues and reliefs recycled from elsewhere in the city. The **Fountain of Trajan** celebrates the emperor (98-117) who replaced the out-of-control Domitian. You have to piece together the emperor's appearance based on a hunk of his chest and his two feet.

Continue directly up Curettes Street to the small theater on your right, the Odeon.

### At the Odeon

First of all, understand that the entire hill at your back was once populated and surrounded by a defensive wall, and the wall ran up the slope ahead of you and along the top toward the distant hill to your right.

This theater was Ephesus' junior version of the main theater in the city below. It was built in the 2nd century B.C. by the local philanthropist Vedius and seated about 1,500 people. The **Odeon** was covered, and was used for slightly more bourgeois purposes than the main theater; city council meetings, conferences, and sophisticated drama. When work began at the site this building had almost disappeared into the hillside, but it has been excavated and repaired.

The building to the left of the Odeon is the **Basilica of Augustus**, which served as a sort of early stock exchange and financial institution. The capitals atop this ancient stock exchange's columns were adorned with, optimistically, bull's heads. Beyond the Basilica is a substantial structure built into the hillside, which at one time served as the public baths. These **Varius Baths** were, like most things in this neighborhood, Roman era.

The colonnaded **Curettes Street** that you have ascended was one of Ephesus' three main roads. It extends from the Magnesia Gate to your left into central Ephesus. The road's name derives from the city fathers' Council of Curettes, not to the coincidental discoveries pointing to Ephesus' early importance in surgery and medicine – the curette of Diokles, the earliest device found to remove arrowheads, was located here. Like the other major streets in Ephesus, the road ran atop a water and sewage system. Beyond the road is the wreck of the **Upper Agora**, strewn with marble. Agoras were market areas, sometimes used for political and religious meetings. The foundation of the **Temple of Isis** is sunk in the earth ahead and to the right. The temple was sacked in the third century, like the Temple of Artemis.

If you look beyond the temple you see a series of arches built into the hillside; this was once the **Temple of Domitian**. Domitian (81-96) was a steadfast opponent of Christianity and a champion of anti-Christian persecution, and no wonder; he was in direct competition. His immense likeness, bulbous forehead and all, once adorned the temple, but is now kept in the Ephesus Museum in Selçuk. The remaining interior precincts of Domitian's massive temple are in use today at the **Museum of Inscriptions**. Definitely stop in here and have a look at the tablets and miscellaneous pieces of inscribed marble and their accompanying translations from the Greek and Latin. The inscriptions may be a shade disillusioning if you are caught up in the mystery of ancient tongues, since most of the translations are downright lawyerly: "four heads of cattle and a fourth share of the ... " Still, it's a captivating exercise, and you can pick out names and places with a handy Greek alphabet guide. Best of all, it's in the shade.

Directly to your right are two structures, the **Council Palace** (Prutaneion) and, beyond it, the **Sanctuary of Hestia Bouleia**. The Council Palace is your standard wreck, dating back to the city's initial construction in 300 B.C. by Lysimachos. The Sanctuary was built at the same time, and was the site of the city's eternal flame, long since snuffed out. The Sanctuary was the town's heart and soul for hundreds of years, but after the comprehensive ravages of the Goths in 263 A.D. it became a source of building material.

As you leave the Odeon and pass the great blocks of stone in the direction of the Museum of Inscriptions, you will notice a tall, slender arch. This is a heavily refinished recreation of the Pollio Fountain's main arch, whose cast of fourth century characters from *The Odyssey* now resides in the Selçuk museum.

Exiting the Magnesian Gate you can usually find a taxi ($9 for one half hour) to shuttle you the three kilometers to the **House of Mary**, or you can descend to the main parking lot, having one more lingering look at the city. The **Cave of the Seven Sleepers**, located on the opposite slope of Mt. Pion, has nothing much to see and a lame story about seven boys who fall asleep and wake up hundreds of years later, like Rumplestiltskin but more tiresome.

If you want to get the most for your admission fee, strap on a day pack and haul some water along with you along the two hills flanking Ephesus. The hill behind the theater has a scattering of ruins, and the course of the Lysimachos-era walls are intact along the great ridge to the south that heads out toward the former sea. Most of Ephesus' best pieces have been removed to the local museums, but there are still buildings – and excellent views – atop Mt. Pion and Mt. Panayir.

# APHRODISIAS

The inland trade routes from Ephesus have been important for many thousands of years, and vital, thriving cities have emerged at the inland passes and mountaintops. One of the cities enjoys fame for its white mineral pools, Pamukkale, while the other, **Aphrodisias**, would find itself on the cover of Archaeology Magazine's "Hot" issue. If they had such a thing. Which they don't.

There were always hints that Aphrodisias might be an important ruin, and recent excavations have borne that out in dramatic fashion. Aphrodisias was not as large as Ephesus, but it was an important religious site with a population of skilled craftsmen and artists. Aphrodisias is worth taking the trouble to visit, and can be given as much time as Ephesus. Many people make it an adjunct to a visit at Pamukkale, which makes good sense. If you're traveling with a sketch pad, this is a place you must visit.

### History

Aphrodisias' history dates back to the distant past, when there was a Bronze age trading center on the site, but the first evidence of its mystical importance appears in its name during the middle of the second millenium B.C., Ninoe, from Nin, an Anatolian goddess of love and war. Nin was probably a precursor to Ishtar, who was later adapted into Aphrodite.

But Aphrodite was a goddess of love without war. In *The Iliad* she appears on the battlefield to retrieve a stricken Aeneas, but in the midst of her rescue the Greek warrior Diomedes recognizes her as "a god without warcraft" and takes the opportunity to strike her with his bronze sword. Athena would surely have wiped up the battlefield with him then and there, but Aphrodite tumbles to the ground wounded and drops Aeneas, who is spirited away by Apollo. Aeneas, according to the legend, went on to found Rome. It is fitting that the city of the goddess of love was unwalled in Roman times, trusting to its status as a shrine of art and peace.

A temple to Aphrodite was built in or before the third century B.C., but before the city passed into Roman hands in the second century B.C. it was rarely mentioned in historical records (then as Megalopolis and Plarasa). The citizens of Aphrodisias (as the city gradually came to be known) found security under Roman rule, and during the Pontic Wars of Mithradites VI (120-63) against Rome, while Mithradites was ranging from his base on the Black Sea as far south as Lycia, Aphrodisias remained loyal to the empire. Rome was grateful for the contribution of fighting men and support, and this gratitude was to prove extremely valuable to the city.

It was under Rome that the city blossomed. Not only did the shrine of Aphrodite, with its celebration of loves both sacred and profitably profane, attract visitors and wealth, but the great success of the Roman Empire provided a ready market for the city's great export, **marble**. With the quarrying of marble came an expertise in working the stone, and one of the world's foremost schools of sculpture developed here. The works of Aphrodisian sculptors are scattered throughout the Mediterranean basin, many in Rome itself. Roman Emperors, not forgetting the city's service during the Pontic Wars, extended special allowances and privileges to Aphrodisias. These began under Julius Caesar and continued for well over a century. Trajan (98-117 A.D.) pronounced that Aphrodisias' ambassadors would have places of honor in Rome.

The city's prosperity continued until Christianity began asserting its hold. Since the Bronze Age a kernel of love goddess-worship had survived all the changes at Aphrodisias, but Christianity brought the practice to an end; Christians occupied the temple and converted it to a basilica. As at Cnidos, Aphrodite seems to have posed a particular threat to the more puritanical Christians, and, as at Cnidos, the church endeavored to supplant her.

The city of Aphrodisias, so ornate and beautiful, began a long decline. Some of the damage was self-mutilation caused by the construction of city walls. Perhaps the city was under pressure to get the walls up quickly; in any case workers dismantled nearby buildings to provide stone. Under the Byzantine Empire Aphrodisias became **Stavropolis**, the City of the Cross. The traffic of Aphrodite's pilgrims died, and without a vigorous empire to serve, the market for marble, let alone sculpture, died with it.

The city's economy a shambles, the new walls were no help. Invaders from the east repeatedly ravaged the city, and soon after the coming of the Selçuks Stavropolis was abandoned. The city of **Geyre**, now beside the ruin, was located directly atop the city when archaeologists began work.

## ARRIVALS & DEPARTURES
### By Bus
Nazilli is the public transportation hub for Geyre town and Aphrodisias. Trains and buses serve Nazilli, and Nazilli has several minibuses daily to Geyre. In the slower season they depart only on the

morning and evening. You can also get a dolmuş as far as Karacasu, 10 kilometers shy of Aphrodisias, every half hour or so. From Karacasu you should be able to catch a dolmuş once an hour, bound for Aphrodisias/ Geyre and beyond. This is the weak link, and you may have a wait.

As an alternative, Kamil Koç offers morning minibuses from Pamukkale in the high season, charging $12 and staying three hours at the ruins. This offers the appealing option of arriving at Pamukkale in the morning and spending the day there, booking a trip to Aphrodisias for the next morning and your ongoing journey the next evening. You can also get to Aphrodisias on a package tour from Selçuk, which makes things simpler but, like the Pamukkale trip, may rush you through the site. Aphrodisias is an excellent place to have time.

### By Car

Aphrodisias was never convenient, and is not now; traveling to the site and back from the Aegean coast near Selçuk requires a full day and an early start by car. Better to plan on a night here or at Pamukkale afterwards. Aphrodisias is by the town of Geyre, 35 kilometers south of the main Aydın-Antalya road by Kuyucak and 50 kilometers west of the same E 87 road at Kazıkbeli. This secondary 585 road that serves the site is in decent condition.

## ORIENTATION

The walled city of Aphrodisias is about 1.5 kilometers in diameter. The parking lot is located alongside a breach in the east wall by a necropolis. A man at the ticket booth at the site will charge $3, open 8 a.m. to 5:30 p.m. There is an outstanding museum here.

## WHERE TO STAY & EAT

If, as mentioned above, you will not be staying in Pamukkale, there is limited lodging at Karacasu and Nazilli, as well as the following options near Aphrodisias. There are several trout (alabalık) restaurants along the roadside nearby.

**CHEZ MESTAN**, *Afrodisias, Karacasu, Aydın, Tel. 256 448 8046, Fax 256 448 8132. Rooms: 28. Double: $15.*

This appealing hotel is just shy of the ruins on the Karacasu road. The Mestan is a large house converted into a country hotel, offering nice rooms and a large deck. If there is no room here they will send you down the road to their other hotel, the Aphrodisias Hotel. The Mestan serves breakfast and dinner. There are also several tour bus restaurants with perfectly decent food on the road near Aphrodisias. This is one of our favorite spots; you feel more interesting by simply spending a night. Like the ruins, it may be problematic to reach by public transportation.

**In Aydın**

**TURTAY HOTEL**, *Aydın, Muğla Karayolu, Tel. 256 213 3003, Fax 256 213 0351. Rooms: 72. Double: $57.*

If being near the waterfront is not a particular imperative for you, consider this hotel in Aydın, ancient Tralles, with its convenience to Pamukkale and Aphrodisias to the east, Ephesus, Priene, and Didyma to the west, and the ruins of Nysa, Alinda, and many other cities nearby. The hotel is very well run, with four stars from the tourism bureau, a pool, satellite television, and air conditioning.

## SEEING THE SIGHTS

The **museum**, just inside the wall, is mostly a collection of statuary (probably the elite 20 percent of the vast discoveries here). It's both educational and impressive, and can be visited for $2.

The centerpiece of the city was the **Sebasteion**, down the street from the museum. This colonnaded way celebrated Roman Emperors and gods together, and may never have seen completion. The lower level of this three story structure was decorated with Doric columns, topped by Ionic columns, while the upper course had Corinthian columns. Statues and reliefs celebrated the successes of the gods and the emperors, and provided some of the lucrative flattery that helped Aphrodisias thrive. Many of the statues from this building were destroyed by Christian zealots, but some have survived and are on display at the museum. The Sebasteion opened onto a temple to the east, on the side where the walls are located. Part of this temple may have found its way into the walls.

The Sebasteion's entrance is on the city's central marketplace, to the south of the acropolis. The **acropolis**, the site of the early city and the final refuge of the dying city, has an excellent theater opening onto an extensive bath. The theater was restored under Marcus Aurelius at the same time work was underway at Aspendus. Another bath is located to the north, this bath at least as extensive and dedicated to the emperor Hadrian. These baths were built at the time of Hadrian's tour of the provinces, and were surely a welcome relief from the arches he was honored with almost everywhere else he went.

The **Odeon**, buried at the time work at the site began, has been cleared of soil. This pristine little meeting area was used by the city's leaders. The Odeon backs up to a small area that is believed to have been the city's sculpting workshop. In the same area is a building whimsically referred to as the **Bishop's Palace** due to the number of Christian artifacts found here.

The Bishop's Palace is, suitably, beside the city's great basilica. The layout of this building, with an apse and two side aisles, is conspicuously Christian, but it was built on the foundation of the **Temple of Aphrodite** in the fifth century. Aphrodite's temple was on the site of an earlier shrine to Ishtar, but that shift was probably less traumatic than the move to Christianity. In addition to dramatically altering the building's structure to suit their needs, Christian reformers were required to change the nature of the worship; Aphrodite's priestesses prostituted themselves, as did the temple slaves. Romans offered marvelous treasures to the temple, seeking surcease from amatory woes or in thanks to the city.

The world's best preserved Roman **stadium** is north of the temple. The stadium, initially used for races and similar athletic events, seems to have been bisected with a wall in the seventh century to provide the city, now firmly Christian, with a better venue for gladiator games.

The **propylon**, the ceremonial entrance to the Temple of Aphrodite, seems to have stood at the crossroads of a road running south past the entrance to the Sebasteion. This building has been completely reconstructed. The man responsible for the research and reconstruction at Aphrodisias between 1961 and 1990, Kenan Erim, is buried nearby.

# PAMUKKALE

**Pamukkale**, in Turkish "Cotton Castle," is a staple on tourism brochure photos, a set of snow white mineral pools descending in picturesque terraces from the tumbled ruins of **Hieropolis**. Pamukkale is a fairly long trip from Ephesus/Selçuk, but quite convenient to those traveling the inland route from Ephesus to Antalya. It can be either an excellent half-day stop or an overnight.

Pamukkale is also a good place from which to see Aphrodisias by public transportation (see above).

### History

The phenomenon is a result of a chemical reaction. As water emerges from underground (at Mt. Cokelez), it is rich with calcium bicarbonate. Reacting with oxygen, this breaks down to carbon dioxide, calcium carbonate, and water. The calcium carbonate has collected over time, slowly forming hard surfaces that rise higher and higher, in turn forcing the water to fan out, seeking a new course. The result of thousands of years of this is the white confection you see spread through more than one and one half miles of pools.

In a less scientific age the explanation was simpler. The moon goddess Selene descended to earth by night to seduce the handsome shepherd Endymion. Endymion, much distracted, neglected his flocks, whose milk spilled out in a torrent down the side of the hill.

The waters of Pamukkale are thought to be good for rheumatism, high blood pressure, heart trouble, nervous disorders, urinary problems, and even ugliness (see sidebar below under *Seeing the Sights*). Today we know that the waters have iron, magnesium, and sodium chloride, perhaps accounting for some beneficial effects. Residents of the area have long made use of these waters, both for their curative and beautifying properties and more practical things; according to Vitruvius, area farmers would make an annual harvest of the newly formed limestone, stripping it from the walls of their irrigation channels. This limestone they would use as field markers.

The city of **Hieropolis** was founded here not because of the water's marvelous properties, but because of the area's strategic importance. At the beginning of the second century B.C. Eumenes II of Pergamon founded Hieropolis, probably naming it after Hiera, the wife of the dynasty's founder. The city's purpose is clear from a map – it straddles trade routes in four directions – but the area was also a center of mining and wool production. One story has it that the travertines are huge sheafs of wool left to dry by giants.

Little is known of Hieropolis' history, although it was clearly prone to earthquakes, and had a major quake earlier this century. Quakes plagued the area, despite supplication to Poseidon the Earth Shaker, but the town repeatedly recovered. Several Roman Emperors, attracted by word of the medicinal waters, even made the long trek to the city. The city made a transition to Christianity, but finally faded under the failing Byzantine Empire.

## ARRIVALS & DEPARTURES
### By Bus & Train
In the high season direct buses serve İstanbul, Ankara, Antalya, Fethiye, Bodrum, Marmaris and Selçuk, but these are much less frequent than buses passing back and forth through Denizli, 18 kilometers away. Dolmuş from Denizli to Pamukkale leave throughout the day from right in front of the bus station, and people can help direct you since they already know where you're going. In Pamukkale buses and dolmuş drop you in the center of town below the cliffs. To reach the baths and ruins head directly up.

Note: if you make an ongoing reservation, bus companies will hold your luggage while you head off to see Pamukkale, but out of high season dolmuş make only a few runs. If you intend to do this, avoid Pamukkale bus company in Denizli, which is not to be trusted. Trains also call at Denizli on their way back and forth from İzmir, and a sleeper train travels back and forth between İstanbul and Denizli. It is more expensive than the bus and, likewise, much more interesting.

**By Car**

Pamukkale is 18 kilometers from Denizli, 14 kilometers from the 320 highway connecting with Dinar and Ankara. The road is in good shape.

## ORIENTATION

An excellent **tourism information** office is located in Denizli, *Atatürk Cad. Ufuk Apt. No. 8, Tel. 258 264 3971*, staffed by very helpful and knowledgeable people. A second office is in Pamukkale proper, near the bus station, *Tel. 258 272 2077*.

## WHERE TO STAY & EAT

Accommodations are stratified between backpacker pensions and big hotels. The pensions tend to have nicer service. Most hotels offer meals, and you're not missing anything by staying in to eat.

**ÖZEL IDARE PAMUKKALE MOTEL,** *Pamukkale, Tel. 258 272 2024, Fax 258 272 2026. Rooms: 55. Double: $70.*

The Pamukkale Hotel is built alongside Hieropolis' sacred pool, with columns and bits of ancient stone beneath the clear water. You've seen it in photographs. There has been talk of destroying this hotel, and those immediately around it, for the sake of the springs, but nothing has been done, and nothing continues to be done at breakneck speed. While the Pamukkale Hotel waits for the ax to fall, its owners are predictably reticent about dropping lots of money on upkeep, maintenance, or performance reviews, so that the hotel may collapse all by itself fairly soon. Until it does, it's a peculiarly wonderful place to stay, with its very own somewhat ratty charm.

**TUSAN HOTEL,** *Pamukkale, Tel. 258 272 2010, Fax 258 272 2059. Rooms: 47. Rooms: $75.*

A more modern hotel offering a springs-fed pool.

**ERGÜR,** *Karahayit Köyü, Tel. 258 271 4170, Fax 258 271 4146. Rooms: 214. Double: $65.*

The Ergür is clean and well-managed, although clearly accustomed to large tour groups. Besides, it has a faux-Chinese restaurant. Three kilometers away from Hieropolis.

**MOTEL KORU,** *Pamukkale, Tel. 258 272 2430, Fax 258 272 2023. Rooms: 132. Double: $62.*

Probably the best value for money among good hotels in Pamukkale.

Among the pensions at the base of the hill try the **HALLEY PENSION,** *Tel. 258 272 2372,* and the consistent **HOTEL TÜRKÜ,** *Tel. 258 272 2181,* which boasts a small pool. Both cost roughly $20 for a double.

## SEEING THE SIGHTS

There are precisely two things to do in Pamukkale, visit the ruins of Hieropolis and take a dip in the springs, and we recommend doing them in that order. Upon arrival you pay a $2.50 entrance fee and ascend into the dry and dusty city.

### The Ruins of Hieropolis

**Hieropolis** catches many visitors off guard; they come for the bright white travertines and discover an impressive ruined city. The ruins back up to the edge of the cotton cliffs, sprawling outside their walls to all sides.

In a city filled with interesting sites, the most interesting feature is surely the **Temple of Apollo**. To get there walk directly in from the terraces, passing the Pamukkale Motel on your right, then the former city fountain before arriving at the Temple of Apollo, which is posted with a sign. This was the central deity of Hieropolis, having supplanted Cybele, but one intriguing aspect of worship remained unchanged; priests of Cybele and Apollo were both guardians of the **Plutonium**, a cave to the south of the temple, on the far side of the current road, wherein noxious gases accumulated, lethal to whatever entered.

The priests were immune, whether by height or the ability to hold their breath, but the gas proved deadly to the unwitting sacrificial birds and livestock they ushered in. The deadly gas was associated with Hades, both venerated and feared. Gases still escape from the collapsed cave, which has led to the opening being closed off from those more curious than sensible. The **theater**, near the temple, is in remarkably good shape, with a partially intact stage building and a collection of reliefs and columns.

Now that you are in the right spirit, the **northern necropolis** is deserving of a visit. One of several necropoles outside the city walls, the northern section has the most impressive set of tombs. From the Plutonium, return to the main avenue and take a right, following the path north (parallel to the travertine slope, Pamukkale town on your left). This takes you in the direction of the Colonnade of Domitian (81-96 A.D.), where you pass a former basilica on your right just before exiting the walls. The main route takes you past the **Arch of Domitian** into the necropolis, and was once the road to Ephesus.

Hieropolis proved a crossroads even in death, as the citizens of the city chose to be buried in various ways according to different traditions. Perhaps the most outstanding tombs are the **circular tombs**, some of which remain roofed. The tomb of the Apostle Phillip, by the way, is located just outside the city walls to the east, right of the old Hellenistic theater. It is a square building with several chambers, and was akin to a Christian temple.

### Baths & Hot Springs

After taking in more of the ruins, head back toward the baths. You're welcome to settle where you like, but to enjoy the baths to their fullest stop in at the **Pamukkale Motel**, whose pool is at the back of the springs. Here, for an hourly admission fee ($2 per hour), you can steep in the fresh water as it rises from beneath the earth. You may also find yourself your own pool on the terraces below and let the water trickle past. The **Pamukkale Museum** is next to the motel and the exhibits are captioned in English. Museum entry is included with the admission fee.

If you can't get enough of healing waters, the region has other marvelous baths, with deposits and curative effects of various kinds. The **Karahayıt** and **Kıllegen baths** cascade down in pools similar to those at Pamukkale, only vibrantly colored like something from Willy Wonka. These baths are five kilometers north of Pamukkale, and are supposed to help those with arthritis, rheumatism, high blood pressure, obesity, diabetes, gout, and digestive disorders.

---

**FORGET EVIAN**

*Once upon a time, a young woman of marrying age grew despondent as years passed and no suitors came forth to ask for her hand in marriage. Finally, poor and homely, she gave up hope and pitched herself off of a cliff at Pamukkale, only to land in a large pool. A young lord came upon the girl, unconscious and injured by the fall, and tended to her. Upon her recovery, the young woman, transformed suddenly into an ethereal beauty by her immersion in the water, was asked to marry by the lord.*

---

# IZMIR

The main road north from Selçuk is a major highway, whipping you through the flats toward İzmir. All of this territory was part of the Ionian League. Most ruins are tucked away off the beaten track, but some, like the Belevi tomb (see Selçuk) are accessible.

İzmir is the major city on Turkey's Aegean coast, having taken up the mantle Ephesus dropped so long ago. This is a bustling sea port and a city of three million people, almost entirely rebuilt since the ravages of the Turkish War of Independence, when it burned to the ground. For all its 3,000 years of history, İzmir has very few historical sites to show. Today İzmir is a pretty and cosmopolitan spot (NATO has a headquarters here), and some view it the way Americans view the San Francisco Bay Area.

İzmir is worth considering as a base for visiting **Sardis**, directly inland, but it is not especially convenient to other ruins or beaches. Other options are to stay in Foça to the north, Selçuk in the south, or to the west on the Çeşme peninsula.

## History

There were native Anatolian settlements at İzmir (ancient **Smyrna**) throughout the second millenia B.C., possibly including the Hittites. This has never been established as a certainty, and would shed an interesting light on the Hittite's dealings with Troy. Some legends suggest that the area was an early Amazonian settlement, unlikely because of the distance from the Amazon's native Black Sea region. The area may have simply been ruled by a matriarchy.

Greek settlers made a habit of mistreating local populations, and Herodotus reports they were true to form here. Ninth century B.C. Greek settlers arrived and were welcomed by natives of mixed Greek blood from an 11th century wave of settlement; while the hosts held a festival outside the city walls, the Greek newcomers seized the empty city.

Smyrna is honored as the birthplace of Homer, though there is really very little to indicate the claim is true. Homer is probably from somewhere in Asia Minor, but nowhere in *The Iliad's* innumerable references does he mention the Smyrnaeans or make other allusion to the region. It seems likely that the great poet would have made mention of the natives of his own city, and this he probably did, but Smyrna was not that city.

Smyrna dropped out of sight for hundreds of years after the Lydian King Alyattes decimated it in the early sixth century B.C. The great bay was still served by a minor town when Alexander the Great arrived in 334 B.C., and he spurred his generals to found a new city on the site. Ever obedient, they built a formidable trading center. Smyrna emerged from the post-Alexander wars intact, shifting peacefully to the Kingdom of Pergamon, then Rome. The Roman peace was relatively uneventful, punctuated by the contributions of Marcus Aurelius to the city after a severe earthquake.

Smyrna was the site of one of the seven churches of Revelation. In Revelation 2:9-11, St. John reassured Smyrna's congregation that the persecution it was enduring would be rewarded: "Only be faithful until death and I will give you the crown of life. He who is victorious cannot be harmed by the second death." The site of the church may have been at Tepekule, inland of Turgut Özal Parkı in the northeast of town, but this early settlement had been largely abandoned after the foundation of a new town by Mt. Pagus.

The Byzantine peace did not last as long. The city fell to the Arabs in 672, and the Muslim hold on the city proved fairly tight. In 1090. the Emir

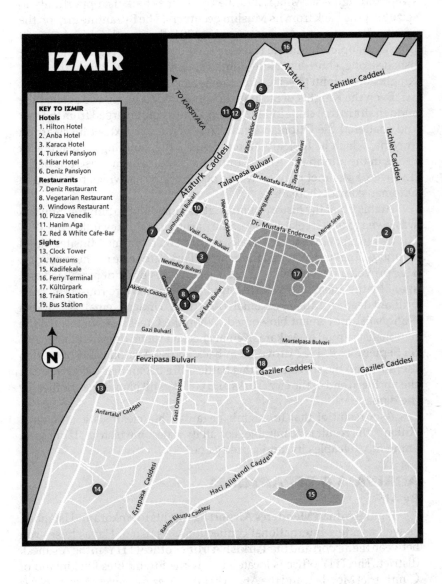

# IZMIR

**KEY TO IZMIR**
**Hotels**
1. Hilton Hotel
2. Anba Hotel
3. Karaca Hotel
4. Turkevi Pansiyon
5. Hisar Hotel
6. Deniz Pansiyon
**Restaurants**
7. Deniz Restaurant
8. Vegetarian Restaurant
9. Windows Restaurant
10. Pizza Venedik
11. Hanim Aga
12. Red & White Cafe-Bar
**Sights**
13. Clock Tower
14. Museums
15. Kadifekale
16. Ferry Terminal
17. Kültürpark
18. Train Station
19. Bus Station

TO KARSIYAKA

Ataturk

Sehitler Caddesi

Ataturk Caddesi

Kıbrıs Sehitler Caddesi

Talatpasa Bulvari

Dr.Mustafa Endercad

Ziya Gokalp Bulvari

Suleat Bulvari

Ischler Caddesi

Dr. Mustafa Endercad

Mimar Sinai

Cumhuriyet Bulvari

Vasif Cinar Bulvari

Piliksame Caddesi

Nevresbey Bulvari

Gazi Osmanpasa Bulvari

Akdeniz Caddesi

Sair Esref Bulvari

Gazi Bulvari

Murselpasa Bulvari

Fevzipasa Bulvari

Gaziler Caddesi

Gaziler Caddesi

Gazi Osmanpasa

Anfartalar Caddesi

Esrepasa Caddesi

Haci Aliefendi Caddesi

Rahim Elkutlu Caddesi

N

of Smyrna contributed to a siege of Constantinople that seemed likely to breach the walls, but was eventually stopped by the diplomatic maneuvering of the Byzantines. A mere seven years later the First Crusade swept through Asia Minor, and the Byzantines took the opportunity to seize Smyrna back from its Muslim occupiers. The Byzantine grip on the area became even more sure when, in 1204, the Fourth Crusade seized Constantinople; Byzantine rulers fanned out into the region and established strong, short-lived kingdoms, though Izmir was left for the Latin Knights of St. John to seize after the Byzantines retook Constantinople.

Even the Knights of St. John, however, stood no chance against the sudden storm that came in 1402, when **Tamurlane** emerged from the east and shattered the Ottoman army. The conqueror next set his heart on Smyrna, which he took after a ferocious battle, building a great pile of heads in the aftermath. After Tamurlane's return to the east, one of the first acts of Mehmet I's reign was to occupy Smyrna, which remained in Ottoman control thereafter.

At this point the history of most cities fades. Not so Smyrna. Smyrna was given to the Greeks as part of the partition of Turkey following WW I. It was from here that the Greeks, spurred on by Prime Minsiter Lloyd George of England, invaded the heart of Turkey to seize further territory. This proved a fatal mistake, as the Turks, to this point demoralized and spent by the anemia of the late Ottoman Empire, were roused by their brilliant leader, Mustafa Kemal (Atatürk). Under Kemal, a Turkish Nationalist movement blossomed. When the Greeks drove toward the nationalist capital at Ankara, Kemal checked them, defeated them, and on September 9, 1922 drove them back across Anatolia and out, often literally, into the sea. During this battle a fire began that raged through the northern end of the city; Turks and Greeks still blame one another for the damage.

As a result of that fire, Izmir began with a clean slate, and, as at Ankara, the result is admirable. For all its gruesome history, İzmir is an eminently liveable city, and a pretty one.

## ARRIVALS & DEPARTURES
### By Air

İzmir's **Adnan Menderes Airport** has flights to Ankara and İstanbul, as well as a few international connections. As usual, Havaş buses run between the airport and the **Turkish Airlines** office (**THY**) in the Alsancak district. The THY office is located below the Büyük Efes Otel inland of Cumhuriet Meydanı and the Atatürk statue (*Gaziosmanpasa Bulvarı No: 1/ F, Büyük Efes Oteli Altı, Tel. 232 425 8280*).

## By Bus

Buses serve İzmir from throughout the country. If you are a glutton for punishment you can make the end-to-end run to Trabzon, if you so choose. The otogar is always busy, and always confusing, without signs or directions. Fortunately, taxis are always on hand (insist they take you where you want to go, not a hotel of their choosing), and someone is always willing to point out the appropriate buses for Alsancak, if you're going there, or for Basmane, centered on the Basmane station and 9 Eylül Meydanı. Do yourself a favor and drop by the Belediye office at the otogar for a big city map.

## By Car

İzmir is the hub for traffic along the coast north and south, and also for traffic to Çeşme and İstanbul via Manısa.

## By Ferry & Private Boat

Turkish Maritime Lines cruises depart from İzmir for Venice, Brindisi and Ancona, Italy (see Chapter 6, *Planning Your Trip*). The **Turkish Maritime Lines** İzmir office is located on the waterfront at *Deniz Yolları Acen., Yeni Liman, Tel. 232 421 1484, Fax 232 421 1484.*

Direct ferries to İstanbul depart on Sunday mornings, although this schedule was probably being revised as we went to press. For information, contact the **Alsancak Liman**, *Tel. 232 421 0094.*

If you're traveling by private boat, İzmir's main marina is located far on the south of town at *Levent Marina, Tel. 232 277 1111, Fax 232 259 9049.*

## By Train

Train travel is not viable between most Turkish cities, but you may want to consider taking a train to or from İzmir. The İzmir-Ankara sleeper route and the İzmir-İstanbul Marmara Expresı, a combination train/ferry route, are two good options.

Both trains depart from the Basmane train station, due south of İzmir's Kültürpark (İzmir is listed as "Basmane" on schedules). The İzmir-Ankara sleeper train, **Ankara Mavı Tren**, departs at 8:30 p.m., double sleeping compartments $60, dinner $10. The Mavı Tren arrives at Ankara at 10:30 a.m. The **Marmara Expresı** train departs at 8 a.m.; you transfer to a ferry at Bandırma and cruise into İstanbul around 7 p.m. This journey is a beautiful alternative to the highway route, and comparable to the bus. No service on Fridays.

Also of interest if you want to visit Selçuk/Ephesus, Nazıllı/Aphrodisias, or Denizli/Pamukkale from İzmir are the thrice-daily Denizli trains, which makes the entire run in five hours. Mark Twain took the train to Selçuk, and the price is probably the same, less than $3 for the entire journey. Some Ankara-bound trains also stop in Sart, near the Sardis ruins.

Information is available at the **Turkish Railways** office in the Basmane station, *Tel. 232 484 8638.*

## ORIENTATION

The former settlement of İzmir was located between the acropolis and the waterfront directly west, by the clock tower in the Konak district. This is, conveniently, the center of the city today, and a good place to begin a walk through town. **Konak Iskelesi** is directly beside the clock tower, and this is where ferries ply the way back and forth to **Karşıyaka** (which, sensibly, means opposite shore). Several good restaurants are located at Karşıyaka.

The interior of the city has broad, logical streets, nothing like the maze of İstanbul. One of the most blatant peculiarities is the completely digitized street-numbering system, but that spares you the problems that go along with unfashionable or forgotten historical figures having their streets renamed. Major streets have real names.

### Tourism Offices
• *Adnan Menderes International Airport, Tel. 232 251 5480, Fax 232 251 1950.*
• *No. 1D, Büyük Efes Oteli Altı, Tel. 232 489 9278, Fax 232 489 9278.* Located inland from the waterfront Atatürk statue and Gaziosmanpaşa Bulvarı.

## WHERE TO STAY

İzmir has excellent luxury hotels and pensions, but does not have a good selection of tourist accommodations in the middle range.

**İZMIR HILTON**, *Gaziosmanpaşa Bul. No. 7, İzmir, Tel. 232 441 6060, Fax 232 441 2277. Rooms: 381. Double: $130.*

If you have a terrible sense of direction, this hotel is for you. The İzmir Hilton towers above the city, visible from miles – let alone blocks – away. The hotel has all of the comforts you would expect of a Hilton, including satellite television, swimming pool, a squash court, a no-smoking floor, and a heliport. If you need any of these things, or if you just want the best service and rooms among İzmir's big hotels, then this is the place.

**ANBA HOTEL**, *Cumhuriet Bulvarı No. 124, Alsancak, İzmir, Tel. 232 484 4380, Fax 232 484 4383. Rooms: 53. Double: $60.*

**KARACA OTEL**, *1379 Sok. No. 55, Alsancak, İzmir, Tel. 232 489 1940, Fax 232 483 1498. Rooms: 69. Double: $70.*

The Anba and the Karaca are reliable hotels in the Alsancak area used to catering to foreigners. Both offer good rooms and locations.

**TÜRKEVİ PANSIYON**, *1480 Sok. No. 9, Alsancak, İzmir, Tel. 232 463 4826, Fax 232 463 9739. Rooms: 8. Double: $25.*

The Türkevi is in a restored house – the only such accommodation in İzmir – but would never be mistaken for a boutique hotel. An interesting local choice not far from the city pier.

**HİSAR HOTEL**, *1378 Sok. No. 2, Fevzipaşa Bul. No. 153, Basmane, İzmir, Tel. 232 484 5400, Fax 232 425 8830. Rooms: 63. Double: $45.*

A decent choice in the hotel district near the Basmane train station. The Hisar has standard three-star amenities, phones, non-satellite television and mini-bars in the rooms. The staff, unfortunately, is harried and impatient. For something cheaper, shop around among the hotels just up the street on 1378 Sokak. Basmane is the budget hotel neighborhood.

**DENİZ PANSIYON**, *Kıbrıs Şehitler Cad., 1478 Sok. No. 1, Alsancak, Tel. 232 421 0187. Rooms: varies. Double: $20.*

The Deniz Pansiyon is actually a set of student dormitories rented out in the summer months. Clean, plain, and fairly quiet compared to the noise and chaos of Basmane. A very good option in a nice part of town.

In Çeşme

**ÇEŞME KERVANSARAY OTEL**, *Çeşme Kalesi yanı, Çeşme, İzmir, Tel. 232 712 7177, Fax 232 712 6491. Rooms: 44. Double: $70.*

A charming old restored kervansaray, formerly a halfway house for traders and military people traveling along the coast. The trip to Çeşme is worth it for the sake of Çeşme's fortress and restaurants alone, but the Kervansaray offers another reason to take a spin out to the end of the peninsula.

The Kervansaray is relatively expensive and can be noisy, but these venerable old buildings are always an interesting experience. The plumbing in the building has come a long way in the past five centuries, by the way: the hotel has in-room showers. The Kervansaray is closed in winter.

## WHERE TO EAT

İzmir has some of the country's best dining, so take advantage of it while in town. Pizza Hut and McDonalds are adding their inimitable style to the mix in Alsancak.

**DENİZ RESTAURANT**, *Atatürk Cad. No. 188, Kordon, Tel. 232 422 0601. Expensive.*

Reputedly the best fish restaurant in the region. Judge for yourself. The Deniz is just one block north of Cumhuriet Meydanı (the place with the statue), and is best visited in the summer and in good weather to take advantage of its outside dining and pretty view.

**VEGETARIAN RESTAURANT**, *1375 Sok. No. 11, İzmir, Tel. 232 421 7558. Moderate.*
The Vegetarian seems to be holding its own in a world of meat eaters and NATO warriors. A good selection of dishes that includes some delicious mezes.
**WINDOWS ON THE BAY**, *31st floor, Hilton Hotel, Gaziosmanpaşa Bul. No. 7, İzmir, Tel. 232 441 6060. Expensive.*
Windows is a bar with a predictably incredible view of the bay and the city. A good place to stop in for a drink and a snack on a hot afternoon or on any evening at all.
**PIZZA VENEDIK**, *1382 Sok. No. 10B, İzmir, Tel. 232 422 2735. Moderate-Expensive.*
With direct ferry service to Italy, you should expect no less. Pizza Venedik is located just inland of the NATO headquarters and serves great, reasonably priced Italian dishes to a crowd of colonels from around the world. Ah, the 20th century; the Italians shelled İzmir in 1912, and now they make stuffed shells here.

**In Karşıyaka**
**HANIM AĞA**, *Yalı Caddesi No. 424, Ağa, Karşıyaka, İzmir, Tel. 232 323 5395.*
This restaurant does marvelous things with some of the staples of Turkish cuisine such as mantı and gözleme. Incidentally, one of their specialties is Gözleme mantı, definitely worth a try. To get to Karşıyaka take a regular ferry from Alsancak Iskele or Konak Iskele.
**RED & WHITE CAFE-BAR**, *Karşıyaka, İzmir, Tel. 232 362 6060.*
A popular night spot with reasonable prices in Karşıyaka's cosmopolitan seafront atmosphere.
**1841 KONAK**, *1688 Sok. No. 3. Karşıyaka, İzmir.*
Another nice place.

## SEEING THE SIGHTS
The clock tower in the center of town beside Konak Square, was a gift from Abdül Hamid in 1901, and it displays the same elaborate flair as other late Byzantine structures. Just south of the clock tower is a cluster of public buildings, including the Fine Arts Museum and the Atatürk Cultural Center.
Inland and uphill of these, behind Turgutreis Parkı, is İzmir's **Archaeological Museum** (8:30 a.m. to 5:30 p.m., closed Mondays, $1.50). The museum has a solid collection of pieces from the ruins in the area, as well as some fine statuary from Smyrna itself. The **Ethnographic Museum** next door has a collection of furniture, textiles, and crafts that is not especially compelling.

Returning to the clock tower you can dive into the city's bazaar inland and north. The **bazaar** is closed on Sundays, otherwise it is as chaotic and interesting as that in İstanbul. We strongly recommend against a visit to the agora; an agora (marketplace square) is by nature flat and dull, and should never be a sight unto itself. There is an altar of Zeus in Smyrna's agora, which does little to invigorate the site.

The **Kadifekale**, atop Mt. Pagus, is much more interesting, and accessible by dolmuş from back at the Konak Square. This is the latest iteration of the fortresses that were built and rebuilt here. It is difficult to determine which of the many armies that occupied Smyrna were responsible for which sections of the fortress.

Today the fortress is filled with residences and birahanes (beer houses). There is no charge to enter the fortress. Note that this is one of the few sites on which the theater, once below the fortress and facing the harbor, is gone, erased by time and stone bandits. From atop Kadifekale you have an excellent overview of the city and out into the Bay of İzmir. While atop Mt. Pagus make a mental note of the green Kültürpark just beyond the Basmane railway station, particularly if you have children along; there is an amusement park there.

The peninsula is dotted with historical sites, enough to keep the intrepid ruin seeker very busy for days on end. None of the ruins are especially spectacular, but there are several worth a visit, including Teos, Colophon, and Çeşme.

## NIGHTLIFE & ENTERTAINMENT

İzmir's **International Festival**, an annual June/July event, is the opportunity to see concerts at ancient theaters in the vicinity, including rare performances at tthe Great Theatre at Ephesus.

## PRACTICAL INFORMATION

The **United States Consular Agent** can be found at the *Amerikan Kültür Derneği, on Sehit Nevres Bulvari No. 23, Alsancak, Tel. 232 421 3643.*

## EXCURSIONS & DAY TRIPS
### Sardis

The ancient Royal Road that connected the Mediterranean with Susa in Persia officially began in **Sardis**, three days march from İzmir. Today, fortunately, it's a two hour trip, one well worth taking. Continuing along the ancient road past Sardis in the direction of Afyon gets you wholly off the beaten track. There are dozens of ruins and hilltop fortresses, once way points along the storied trade route.

Sardis is slightly isolated from the great ruins of the coast, and doesn't see too many visitors. So much the better, since the remains of the **Temple of Artemis** and an impressively restored set of Roman ruins are easily worth a 90 kilometer side trip from İzmir. The setting is strange and beautiful, with peaked stone hills like those in Cappadoccia.

## History

Homer counts the **Maeonians**, the original name of people from Sardis, among those who fought with Troy, but Sardis enters history much more substantially in Herodotus' *History*.

The Lydian Empire reached its zenith under King Croesus (560-546 B.C.). Herodotus concerns himself at length with Croesus, and it is possible that some of Herodotus' information came from Aesop, a teller of fables who lived in the area at the time. Sardis was the official beginning of the **Royal Road** to Babylon and Susa, a 14,000 furlong (2,000 mile) course that wound past forts, inns, and border crossings. The road continued to Ephesus, but glorious Sardis was the true destination for those arriving from the east. The city's wealth and power had been waxing for a century when Croesus came to power, aided by gold deposits in the Paktolos River, and Sardis had developed the world's first system of coinage.

Croesus' reign was punctuated by a further succession of victories that allowed the Lydians to secure domination over the cities of the Aegean. Croesus, prospering in his great city, his armies riding roughshod, wealth pouring into the state coffers, once asked one of the Seven Sages who was the world's most fortunate man. The answer, to Croesus' surprise, was not himself but a man long dead, and the sage explained that Croesus' life, perfect in every regard, was not yet over.

The wisdom of this was soon evident. Croesus began to concern himself with the Persians, whose campaigns had pressed ever further west along the Royal Road until they now were at the Lydian frontier. Croesus' preoccupation with oracles (see Didyma) compelled him to seek advice on whether he should go to war with the Persians. The oracle answered famously that if he went to war with the Persians he would destroy a great empire. Croesus, unfamiliar with the inscrutable ways of the oracle, assumed that the oracle was talking about the Persian Empire and unleashed a massive army, which was summarily beaten in central Anatolia.

In the battle the Persian King, Cyrus, used the horse's distaste for camels to his advantage, mounting his soldiers on camels and routing the powerful Lydian cavalry. The Persians pursued Croesus' army back to Sardis, where they invested his city and took it after several Persian soldiers scaled the steep southern wall of the fortress.

Sardis fared well under the Persians, basically continuing its dominance over Asia Minor as a Persian satrapy rather than a Lydian capital. During the 499 B.C. revolt of the Greek coastal cities Sardis was sacked, an act which roused the Persians and ended with the leading city of the revolt, Miletus, destroyed, and its population enslaved. There was still a Persian garrison here when Alexander arrived, but they chose the better part of valor and opened the city gates. Alexander found a good deal of treasure here with which to pay his troops and fund the next steps in his campaign. Nor did he forget the local population, commissioning a great Temple of Zeus. While considering where to locate the temple, Arrian reports, an isolated electrical storm occurred at one of the proposed sites, and Alexander located the temple accordingly.

Alexander's conquest went smoothly, but the consistency of the Persian peace was sorely missed during the relentless campaigns of Alexander's generals after his death. Sardis eventually fell to the Kingdom of Pergamon, and Attalus III bequeathed it to the Romans in 133 B.C.

Roman rule meant a long spell of peace here as elsewhere, although Mithradites VI's campaigns caused a bloody interruption at beginning of the first century B.C. Christianity found a receptive audience at an early date, and one of the Seven Churches of Revelation was located here. John's mention of the Sardis congregation is fairly critical. He scolded Sardis' Christians for an appearance of piety not borne out in their acts: "I have not found any work of yours completed in the eyes of God," he explained.

The city fell to the Arabs, but was back in Byzantine control in 743, when it was the site of a major battle between rival Byzantine Emperors. The iconoclast Constantine V defeated an icon defender named Artabastus here, clearing the way for a march on Constantinople and an important victory for those opposed to icons and portraits. Turkish tribes failed to seize the city until the 14th century, and then their occupation was cut short by Tamurlane in 1402. Typically, his visit was unpleasant, with much looting and hewing of human heads. Following Tamurlane's sack, Turks returned to the site, but the fortress here was not restored.

**Getting to Sardis**

Buses and minibuses serve **Sart** from İzmir throughout the day, and the ruins are just east and south of town. İzmir-Ankara trains also stop at Sart. Reaching Bin Tepe to the north should require a taxi, although you can try to get a northbound dolmuş from Salihli to drop you at the Bin Tepe turnoff and continue to the necropolis on foot. You may also inquire at Sart's dolmuş station.

By car, Sardis is just off of the main E 96 east-west highway, 93 kilometers east of İzmir. The most accessible ruins are next to the modern town of Sart, with the Temple of Artemis one kilometer south and the necropolis at Bin Tepe ten kilometers north.

## Seeing the Ruins

Sardis has various clusters of ruins. Straddling the highway are considerable Roman ruins, with a second century synagogue and gymnasium along a marble road. This area has been painstakingly restored by a team of American archaeologists from Harvard University. Several mosaics are now on display here. Researchers have also investigated a set of Lydian ruins on the southern side of the hill. Sardis' badly damaged theater is on the same southern slope further to the east.

The highlights of the Sardis ruins are along the Paktolos south of Sart. First, on the east bank, there are several buildings that archaeologists have determined were for heating and separating gold.

The **Temple of Artemis** is located further south. The Temple of Artemis was not as ambitious as the Artemis temple at Ephesus, but it was certainly an impressive work. The footprint of the structure is obvious, starkly beautiful with its thick, broken columns against a scorched, mountainous backdrop. This temple was originally built under King Croesus, but it was probably converted or used for another purpose during the Persian occupation.

Alexander may have funded reconstruction – perhaps this was the temple he built, not a Temple of Zeus as Arrian reported – but the restoration could also have begun under a later ruler. In any case, the temple was built in fits and starts, not wholly completed even in the fourth century A.D., when it was probably abandoned with the enforcement of Christianity. The temple altar, possibly predating the temple itself, is located at the west end of the temple closest to the river. A Byzantine church is located to the south, a standard attempt to confront the pagan religion.

The **acropolis**, the site of the Lydian citadel, is difficult to reach but has a few curious tunnels and some remaining walls from the last fortress.

Sardis' **necropoles** are scattered along the river valley, some on the east and some on the west bank. The great necropolis is at **Bin Tepe** (1000 Hills), visible from the gymnasium on the far side of the highway. If you have a car and you've already come this far, we highly recommend continuing to Bin Tepe. The clearest way to Bin Tepe is to simply return across and follow the posted signs north of Salihli. If the signs are down, ask. The watchman or ticket-taker at Sardis can be of help.

The **Royal Necropolis of Sardis** included the massive tumulus of Alyattes and other kings who preceded Croesus. Alyattes' grave site is the most incredible of these, a gigantic circular monument mentioned by

Herodotus. This tumulus, which contains the father of Croesus and thus the last man to die ruler of Lydia, is more than 300 yards in diameter – three football fields – and ascends to a height of more than 160 feet.

The tumulus was penetrated by a trench long ago, and Alyattes has long since surrendered his grave goods. This tumulus is akin to the Phrygian tumuli at Gordion.

# 21. THE NORTHERN AEGEAN

Jason and the Argonauts and Odysseus once sailed in these waters, where the swirl of legend, myth, and fact is more intense than anywhere in the world. This forgiving landscape of cyprus, olive groves and cultivated land has been the site of epic battles recorded first at **Troy** and last at **Gallipoli**.

In the south are the beautiful ruins of **Assos** and the great city of **Pergamum**, capital city of the Kingdom of Pergamon. Just offshore is the peaceful island of **Bozcaada**, the town in the shadow of a massive Genoese fortress. The region's most enchanting accommodations are at the beautiful stone hotels on the waterfront at **Assos/Behramkale**, **Foça**, and the simple lodgings on Bozcaada island.

## FOÇA

**Foça**, a short distance from the Izmir-Çanakkale (E 87) highway, is one of the most beautific little towns along this stretch of Aegean coast. A subtle change begins coming over the landscape as you continue north; the soil becomes redder, the olive trees thicker.

Foça is suitable for a stop in lieu of Izmir, but getting to Pergamon and back may take some time without a car. Foça is a cozy alternative to Izmir, where you have to get to the otogar then into town. Foça is 65 kilometers north of Izmir, and hugs the sea as it did in its day as Phocaea when its seafaring citizens settled Marseilles in the 8th century B.C. As mentioned, Foça is a good base before or after a visit to Pergamon, and a good place to unwind.

### History

The **Phocaeans**, Greek settlers themselves, never seemed to get the wanderlust out of their blood. Greeks settled the area in the ninth century

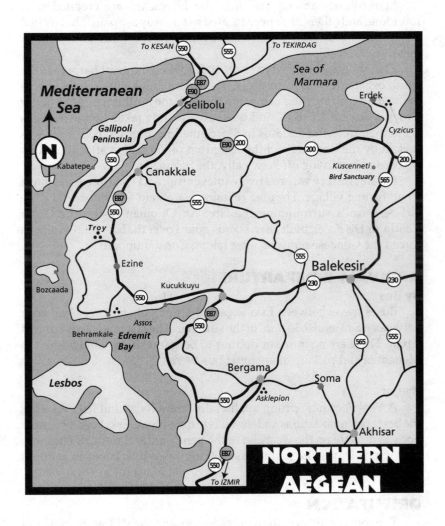

B.C., although they may have replaced or mixed with an existing population. The excellent, protected harbor served the Phocaeans well, and they carried on heavy sea trade and made great voyages through the Mediterranean and the Black Sea.

Marseilles is among the cities the Phocaeans are credited with founding, and others have been located as far away as Spain. The city had an advantage in such long haul voyages, in the form of unusually massive oared ships.

The city was relegated to lesser status when the great harbors to the south began exerting themselves. The autonomous city probably fell to the Lydians during their campaign through the northern Aegean under Croesus around 555 B.C., and was subsequently taken by the Persians upon their defeat of Croesus in 546. Sometime after 190 B.C., Foça was sacked by the Romans and the Kingdom of Pergamon after those two succeeded in driving off Foça's ally, the Seleucids.

Its later history was relatively uneventful, and Foça devolved into a small fishing village. The area remained strategic, as evidenced by the Genoese walls surrounding the city. An Ottoman castle (the **Outer Castle**, or Diş Kale), built later, stands guard over the bay. The Ottomans forced the Genoese out soon after taking Constantinople.

## ARRIVALS & DEPARTURES
### By Bus
Buses travel between Eski Foça and Izmir's otogar every half hour between 6 a.m. and 9:30 p.m. in the summer. The last bus leaves Izmir at 9 p.m. There are no buses or dolmuş to Bergama or Ayvalık; bus out to Menemen and pick up an ongoing bus there.

### By Car
A Yeni Foça has sprung up, literally "new Foça," but Eski Foça has the best accommodations and the nicest atmosphere. Eski Foça, or simply Foça, is directly on the west end of the peninsula at the end of Highway 250, which leaves the main coast 550 highway 10 kilometers north of Menemen.

## ORIENTATION
The **tourism information** office is opposite the PTT at the center of town, *Atatürk Bulvari No. 1, Tel/Fax 232 812 1222*.

## WHERE TO STAY & EAT
The hotels in Foça are generally clean, simple, and pleasant, fitting this seaside town.

**AMPHORA HOTEL,** *Ismetpaşa Mah. 208 Sok. No. 7, Foça, Tel. 232 812 2806, Fax 232 812 2483. Rooms: 18. Double: $42.*

The Amphora is located in an old structure, but it's an old, boxy structure. Nevertheless, it is one of Turkey's special class hotels, and the rooms and service are both good.

**VILLA DEDEM,** *Sahil Cad. No. 66, Foça, Tel. 232 812 1215, Fax 232 812 2838. Rooms: 18. Double: $40.*

The Dedem is another friendly spot on the waterfront. Unlike the Amphora and Karaçam, it isn't a special class hotel, but it is just as charming.

**KARAÇAM OTEL,** *Sahil Cad. No. 70, Foça, Tel. 232 812 1416, Fax 232 812 2042. Rooms: 24. Double: $44.*

Nearby, also on the waterfront, the Karaçam is a classic whitewashed stone building looking out over the bay. Rooms are stark but pleasing. The only jarring aesthetic note is the terrace roof, and you'll appreciate that if you stay here. The Karaçam even offers satellite television in the lobby.

**ALI BABA RESTAURANT,** *Büyükdeniz Sahil Cad., Foça, Tel. 232 812 1173.*

One of Foça's deservedly popular restaurants. Like all of the restaurants in town it has a good selection of fish, but more alternatives than many of the others.

**CELEP RESTAURANT,** *Küçükdeniz Sahil Cad., Foça, Tel. 232 812 1495.*

The Celep's waterfront location makes it a beautiful place to relax in the early evening and watch the sun set. The restaurant offers fish dishes and grills.

**In Yeni Foça**

**CLUB MEDITERANEE FOÇA HOLIDAY VILLAGE,** *Yeni Foça, Tel. 232 812 3691, Fax 232 812 2175. Rooms: 350. Double: $90.*

A nice, standard holiday village, with food and lots of toys. The French management seems to have trained some of the staff to be rude, but its fun anyway. A wide range of rooms and half board/full board arrangements are possible.

## SEEING THE SIGHTS

There are several pretty beaches near Foça, including some at the rocks offshore. These are known as the **Siren Rocks**, and like the Sirens in *The Odyssey* they sing when the wind whips through them. Locals will tell you these are the genuine Sirens. There are a smattering of ruins around town, including some restored city walls and mosaics – check in at the tourism information office for more information. The **Outer Castle** (Diş Kale) can be visited by boat.

One of the most interesting things at Foça is the **Taş Evi**, or stone house, seven kilometers east of Foça on the main road. This 8th century B.C. stone cut tomb dates almost to the arrival of colonists here and has a melange of ornamental styles reflecting native influence, such as a typically Persian stepped base. The tomb is unique, although its various elements can be found at other sites. There is no evidence of who was interred here.

# PERGAMON

**Pergamon** is one of the greatest sites in Turkey, and, like Ephesus, belongs on a touring itinerary. Pergamon, a site that can keep you busy for days, is usually lodged between a departure from Izmir or Selçuk and an arrival elsewhere. Budget at least five hours to see the major sites by car, a full day without. The ruins are located near the modern town of **Bergama**.

## History

Pergamon emerged from obscurity when one of the Diadochi, the old general **Lysimachos**, stashed his hoard here during a campaign. He entrusted his vast treasure to his lieutenant, **Philetarus**, then marched out against the Seleucids, where he was defeated and killed in 281 B.C. Philetarus, much aggrieved, solaced himself by going on a great shopping spree for new city monuments and setting himself up as king in Lysimachos' stead. Philetarus (281-263) proved a competent leader, and left the kingdom to his nephew, Eumenes. Eumenes I (263-241) was tested almost immediately, forced to take the field against the old king Antiochus I. Eumenes won the day at the Battle of Sardis, holding off the Anatolian threat, and won the budding kingdom breathing space.

Pergamon had a wealth of arable land, and the town excelled at cultivating valuable crops and promoting trade. Both Eumenes and his successor, Attalus I, fended off a new threat from a settlement of Gauls along their eastern border. These Gauls had been shipped in by the Kingdom of Bithnia to serve as mercenaries, but they proved terrible neighbors to the Bithnians and the rest of Asia Minor, and Attalus I determined to put an end to their truculent, ceaseless warfare. Contriving to imprint a message saying "Victory for the King" on the innards of a sacrificial animal, Attalus inspired his army to believe that Zeus had made his judgment, and, awash with confidence, the Pergamene soldiers defeated the Gauls. Subsequent rulers began cultivating a relationship with Rome that paid off handsomely when, under Eumenes II (197-160), the Kingdom of Pergamum and Rome combined to defeat the troublesome Seleucids, again, at the Battle of Magnesia. Pergamum reached its zenith in the years that followed, extending its reach into the interior and establishing Attaleia (modern Antalya) on the southern coast. It was under Eumenes II that the library was built and the **Asklepion** achieved fame as a place of medicine.

Pergamon's fall from greatness was extremely unusual. Attalus III (138-133) was an oddball, busying himself with designing and testing poisons on prisoners and trifling with sculpture. None of his hobbies seem to have endeared him to his subjects, and upon his death Attalus III, with no heir, left his kingdom to Pergamon's former ally, Rome. Many smelled a rat, and there was serious opposition to Roman occupation, which the Romans dealt with in their typically forthright fashion, posting a garrison and executing the opposition. The shift to Roman rule was unusual, but relatively smooth, and the city became a favorite of the Empire. Pergamon became the administrative capital under the Romans.

Pergamon is the site of one of the Seven Churches of Revelation, and John the Apostle was later honored by the dedication of the **Red Basilica**. The end of Roman rule and the deterioration of the Byzantines left Pergamon to be ravaged throughout the middle ages by the Arabs, the Crusaders, and a host of others as well. The city fell to the Ottomans in 1336, and they regained their grip on the city following Tamurlane's 1402-1403 invasion of the area.

## ARRIVALS & DEPARTURES

### By Bus

Bergama is located east of the main highway, and many buses passing this way unload Bergama-bound passengers at the junction. This is not ordinarily a problem, since dolmuş await by day and taxis by night, but occasionally people find themselves alone at the junction like something out of a Beckett play, and may want to try hitching the five kilometers to town. A taxi will come, eventually. Within town there is no public transportation to the acropolis, making the taxi drivers happy and $5.50 wealthier with your fare.

Just as getting to town can be difficult, leaving is likewise made tricky by the fact that long distance buses fly past on the main highway. The smartest thing to do, unless a bus happens to be going your way, is get the next hourly bus to Izmir ($2.50) and transfer from there.

### By Car

Pergamon is located at Bergama, 93 kilometers north of Izmir and five kilometers off of the coast road. Pergamon is an especially fine place to bring a car, as the distances within the ruin are so unwieldy otherwise.

## ORIENTATION

Modern Bergama is superimposed atop sections of the former city, but the greatest ruins stand revealed (albeit some in Berlin). Pergamon's acropolis (to the left upon entering town) and the Asklepion on the plain just east of town are the major sights, although the looming Red Basilica shouldn't be missed. The archaeological museum is good for statues in the shade, but is not one of Turkey's best.

The **tourism information** office, *Tel. 232 632 3988*, is located at the southern end of town, where you enter, at the intersection with the road to the Asklepion.

## WHERE TO STAY & EAT

If you decline to stay along the coast, you'll find a serviceable range of accommodations in Bergama and a good collection of cheap restaurants.

**BERKSOY HOTEL, Izmir** *Yolu, PK 19, Bergama, Tel. 232 633 5345, Fax 232 633 5346. Rooms: 57. Double: $70, half board. Restaurant.*

An old standard in the country, one mile out of Bergama in the direction of Izmir. The Berksoy is a nice little spot of green if you arrive in the area in late summer when the grasses are drying up. The hotel has a large pool, satellite television, and friendly staff, although the tendency is toward German speaking, not English.

**BERGAMA İSKENDER OTEL**, *Izmir Cad. Ilıca Önü, Bergama, Tel. 232 633 2123. Rooms: 60. Double: $60.*

The İskender is a decent hotel, popular with group tours. It has air conditioning to keep you cool in the dog days.

**TUSAN BERGAMA MOTELİ**, *Bergama-Izmir Yolu, Çatı Mev., Tel. 232 633 1173.*

Not particularly distinguished, but a clean, tidy place to lay your head for the night.

**PERGAMON PENSION**, *Bankalar Caddesi No. 3, Bergama, Tel. 232 633 2395. Rooms: 4. Double: $10.*

Housed in a 150 year old mansion, this pension offers good, spartan accommodations. The Pergamon has a central location just down the street from the tourism information office. Closed from November to April.

**MEYDAN RESTAURANT**, *Bankalar Caddesi No. 18, Bergama, Tel. 232 633 2318.*

The Meydan overlooks the Red Basilica, just down the main street from the mosque. The Meydan has good food in a pretty, shaded setting, ideal after hours of watching army exercises at the Asklepion and hiking around the acropolis. The food here is exactly what you've come to expect: şiş, rice, soups, and lots of bread, of course, and it's well prepared.

The cheaper restaurants are up the street near the Pergamon Pansiyon and the police station.

## SEEING THE SIGHTS

### The Acropolis

The **Acropolis**, above town to the north, has the main concentration of Pergamene ruins. We advise beginning at the parking lot atop the Acropolis and working your way down. The German archaeology team responsible for excavating and studying here have done a good job of posting the identity of various ruins. The **Altar of Zeus**, above the agora, was built to commemorate the Pergamene victory over the Gauls under Eumenes II. The altar was decorated with statues and a frieze of giants doing battle with the gods and was perhaps the most stunning monument in the city; it is now located in Berlin's Pergamon Museum. This altar may have been what John the Apostle referred to as "the Throne of Satan" in the Book of Revelations – although John may have been referring to Pergamon's role as Roman provincial capital.

The terraced palaces along the rim of the Acropolis were occupied by various kings of Pergamon, including Eumenes II, nearest the parking lot. Heading toward the summit, you arrive at the **Library** once adjacent to the **Temple of Athena**. At the top of the hill are a set of buildings for storing food and arms against the possibility of a siege.

Backtracking to the lower levels on the theater side, the emerging form of the **Temple of Trajan** is of particular interest. Archaeologists have been piecing together bits of rubble, now strewn across the ground at the temple, trying to recreate the building. If they have continued success, this may become another Turkish photographic cliche, like the Library of Celsus at Ephesus. Even in its badly damaged state it shines like a beacon across the valley floor. The building originally had 54 columns and was dedicated to both the Emperor Trajan (98-117) and his heir, Hadrian (117-138).

Descending steeply below the acropolis is the **theater**, a peculiarly high and narrow structure owing to the cramped space. There is a stair from the Temple of Athena to the theater, which has 80 rows. Around to the side of the theater is the lower section of the city, including the **Temple of Demeter**, goddess of the harvest, and gymnasium and bath buildings. If you continue to the foot of the acropolis you arrive at the **Acropolis Gate**, a partially intact Hellenistic fortification.

### The Asklepion

The **Asklepion**, on the valley floor across the river, is partially in a military zone and thus you have to be careful what you do with your camera. This was a medical center, one of the leading medical institutions of the Roman age. The Asklepion functioned like a spa, with springs, water therapy, and dream analysis. Emperor Caracalla was among the patients, and the presence of a library and theater on the site suggests that convalescence was fairly luxurious.

A colonnaded **Sacred Way** connected the Asklepion with the main city. In the Asklepion's forecourt you'll see the first of many snakes in relief; snakes were, then as now, a symbol of the medical profession. The significance of snakes as icons is allegedly that snakes could regenerate, but it seems likely that the early doctors would have known better. Here, as on the Acropolis, there was a library. Archaeologists are uncertain about an underground passage from the main court to a round chamber just off the premises; it may be a temple of Telesphorus, a god of healing, but it was probably related to a course of medicine. One entertaining theory is that patients were told to walk through the tunnel while doctors dropped snakes through the gaps in the ceiling as shock therapy.

## THE LIBRARY OF PERGAMON

*Under Eumenes II (197-160 B.C.) the **Library at Pergamon** had 200,000 books and scrolls, and the extent of the institution was considered a direct challenge to the status of Alexandria's famous library. Accordingly, the Egyptians refused to sell papyrus to their rivals, thinking that would bring to a halt the expanding collection at Pergamon. In response Pergamon created its own alternative, thin sheets of specially treated goat hide that came to be known as Pergamon-paper, and emerged in modern English as **parchment**. The shift away from papyrus, in turn, forced the Pergamenes to shift from scrolls to pages, the first step in the evolution of books as we now know them.*

*The great collection continued to grow even after Pergamon came under Roman control, attracting scholars from around the world. In the end the destruction of the Library at Alexandria proved the destruction of Pergamon's library as well. Marc Antony, seeking to comfort Cleopatra after the the Library burned down during the Roman civil war, gave her the contents of Pergamon's Library. A new library at Alexandria used the Pergamon volumes as the core of its new collection. The loss would have been Pergamon's alone, except that after Alexandria's fall to the Arabs in 642, Caliph Omar ordered the contents of the library destroyed, eliminating in a single blow the accumulated knowledge of millenia.*

The great **Red Basilica**, in the center of town, provides an arresting sight, a vast stone wreck looming above an otherwise typical-looking

Turkish city. The basilica is built atop the **Selinus River**, with arched passageways in the foundation for the river to pass through. The peculiar situation of the basilica owes to the fact that it was not built as a basilica at all, but as a great temple, probably to the Egyptian god **Serapis**. The building was clearly built as a center for worship, and the river's course underground was probably integral. The round towers alongside the main building served related religious functions and had pools within. The Pergamenes completed the complex, originally clad in marble, in the second century A.D. under Emperor Hadrian. Serapis worship flared up in the second and third centuries, only to be extinguished by Christianity. Christianity staked its claim to the site after the Edict of Theodosius in 392, and a church was built here. Today there is a mosque on the site.

The **Pergamon Archaeology Museum** has an admirable collection of ruins, but they are not arranged to inform. The museum has inscriptions, altars, and statues galore inside the building and on the grounds, and the pieces succeed in breathing some life into the ruin. Of particular value are depictions of great pieces looted by the Germans. There is also a statue of Nike, pre-swoosh.

## BEHRAMKALE (ASSOS)

Winding around the **Gulf of Edremit** you are often within sight of a great island off to the west; this is the Greek island **Lesbos**, accessible from Ayvalık, not Ayvacık. The green, beautiful hills surrounding the gulf have, locals insist, uncommonly pure air. Everyone here is convinced that the region is an "oxygen tent," whose curative and invigorating properties are second to none. There is supposedly a scientific study that deemed the local air the second finest in the world, owing to upwelling in the deep, crystal clear waters of the Aegean. We haven't found evidence of such a study, but based on our own non-scientific study the air sure is nice. The road on the northern side of the gulf can be harrowing, but take it slow and you'll be fine.

**Behramkale**, ancient **Assos**, offers a wonderful combination of ruins, charming accommodations, sparkling blue sea, and the aforementioned air.

## ARRIVALS & DEPARTURES
### By Bus

Behramkale is 12 miles south of **Ayvacık**, the regional transportation hub on the main E87 road from Izmir to Çanakkale. Once in Ayvacık's otogar, find a dolmuş heading south to Behramkale, better yet the Behramkale/Iskele harbor, if that's where you are headed. In summer dolmuş depart hourly, but they are only occasional in the winter. If the dolmuş leaves you at the intersection, it is a 1.5 mile walk down the hill to the Iskele, although taxis will take you for $2.50. In the off season private drivers heading into Ayvacık will take you for the going dolmuş fare.

Dolmuş serve the beaches to the east and the towns to the west, stopping at the town's main intersection as they head out along the coast road. **Küçükkuyu** is on the E87 route, and dolmuş run from here to the beaches in the direction of Assos, covering major hotels.

### By Car

Follow the signs one mile off the main highway to Ayvacık. Entering the city from the southeast, Assos Caddesi is just beyond the central otogar (garaj) on the left. Should you be stuck in Ayvacık, stay at the Hotel Belediye (Municipal Hotel), also on Assos Caddesi. The road to Behramkale is plagued by fast drivers and broken shoulders. Lay on the horn in those blind turns.

A coast road runs from Behramkale to Küçükkuyu, with spurs down to various beaches. In Küçükkuyu, the turnoff for Çetmi Han (a great inn) is two miles west of town on the main Çanakkale highway. The Çetmi Han has signs posted, and is up the road one quarter of a mile toward Yeşilyurt.

## ORIENTATION

The modern town of Behramkale is divided in two parts – an **upper area** around the northwest side of the ruined Acropolis, and the **Iskele** in a tiny, cramped section at the bottom of the steep cliff face. A sharply winding, one mile road separates the two. The upper section of town is an interesting warren of houses and shops built with stones that people have been gathering at this site for thousands of years, and cobbled with more of the same. The stone town climbs toward the acropolis, where it is built up against great boulders jutting out of the hillside. The soaring acropolis, topped by the Doric **Temple of Athena**, was considered classic in the classic age, and remains beautiful even in its fallen state.

The town's lower section, the Iskele, is also constructed out of recycled stone, and is almost entirely given over to a handful of guest houses and restaurants. A few ships continue to fish out of the small harbor (which is not, as everyone says, the same harbor used in ancient times – the original harbor was further around the bluff to the east).

These ruins, sprawling down from the crest of the bluff, are not worthy of a long trip out of your way, but are a must-see if you stay in the neighborhood. The setting is marvelous, with a view of Lesbos six miles offshore.

## WHERE TO STAY

A collection of charming, rusticated old inns line the water along Behramkale's Iskele (lower town), which is exactly a stone's throw long. Another inn is located in Küçükkuyu 22 miles away. Resort hotels are also appearing along the coast to the east of Behramkale. Reservations at the Iskele hotels are imperative between June and early September. Most hotels in the area close in winter.

**BEHRAM HOTEL**, *İskele Mevkii, Behramkale, Ayvacık, Çanakkale, Tel. 286 721 7016, Fax 286 721 7044. Rooms: 17. Double: $50, half board. Restaurant.*

Smaller than the other three hotels along the Iskele waterfront, the Behram has its own charm. The public spaces are heavily decorated with plants and oversized art, and the rooms are cozy. There are eight waterfront rooms, with the upper level (rooms 302-305) in nice attic spaces, so long as you don't mind low ceilings. Unlike the other hotels, there is no large central public area so it stays quieter. Like the others, there is a patio restaurant. Ayhan at the front desk is knowledgeable and friendly.

**NAZLİHAN HOTEL**, *Iskele Mevkii, Behramkale, Ayvacık, Çanakkale, Tel. 286 721 7064, Fax 286 721 7387. Rooms: 35. Double: $65, half board. Restaurant.*

The Nazlıhan occupies a solidly constructed wood storehouse originally built in the 1890s. Some of the room detailing is "heavily-lacquered chess piece," but the bones of the place are good, from the stone walls and solid beds to the attractive tilework and Iznik-patterned sinks. The best rooms here have a sea view, of course, and some offer fireplaces and spacious balconies. Even the rooms in the back are rather pleasant. The rooms from 300 up are in a quieter second building, also on the water (beware those rooms facing the Fenerlihan bar to the west). Both sections have a courtyard, but the latter courtyard is a small garden, not a restaurant and social area.

**HOTEL ASSOS**, *Iskele Mevkii, Behramkale, Ayvacık, Çanakkale, Tel. 286 721 7017, Fax 286 721 7249. Rooms: 36. Double: $60, half board. Restaurant.*

In the same mold as the Nazlıhan. Family-run operation, with a building restored in 1989. Satellite TV, nice rooms, patio restaurant.

Also: Other good hotels in Behramkale's iskele area include the **HOTEL ASSOS KERVANSARAY**, *Tel. 286 721 7093, Fax 286 721 7200,* also along the water, and the **HOTEL YILDIZ SARAY**, *Tel. 286 721 7169, Fax 286 721 7025,* on the upper slope of the Iskele. Budget accommodations are available in Behramkale proper, atop the hill near where you first enter town.

**Near Küçükkuyu**

**ASSOS EDEN GARDENS,** *Behramkale Sahil Yolu, Kozlu Köyü Altı, Küçükkuyu, Tel. 286 762 9870, Fax 286 762 9404. Rooms: 102. Double: $72. Restaurant, nightclub.*

Luxury hotels begin dotting the landscape east of Behramkale, each with a long list of amenities – tennis, satellite TV, jacuzzi, pools, barber, bars, paddleboats. The Eden Gardens has all of this, together with the area's popular Eden Bar and Disco (outer space motif) across the road. Happy hedonistic captives of this isolated beach retreat will find the accommodations a shade ragged, but the staff is helpful and the place is fun. Minibuses serve the hotel from Küçükkale 17 kilometers east and, on rare occasions, from Behramkale, but public transportation is a serious problem. Closed in the off season.

**ÇETMİ HAN,** *Yeşilyurt Köyü, Küçükkuyu, Tel. 286 752 6169, Fax 286 752 6170. Rooms: 10. Double: $60, half board. Restaurant.*

Well-run Turkish inns have a lot in common with ranch-style inns in the American west – the rooms are comfortable and spare, the service is attentive, and the food is plentiful. Canadians and Americans fond of that atmosphere, and of long evenings in the public area by a fire, will love the Çetmi Han. You can't retire to your room to flip back and forth pointlessly between CNN and MTV – the only TV is in the small bar downstairs. You must socialize, with strangers or each other. If you will not socialize, you must read.

This pretty hillside hotel is built with blocks of pudding stone carved square with torches. The building is not a restoration, but a faithful rendering of traditional buildings true to owner Fahir İskit's imagination; simple and traditional, but there are wine nooks along the wall. İskit bought the land perched high above the Aegean in 1990 because he loved it and, retiring from a career with companies ranging from Sheraton to Citibank, commenced building in 1993. The hotel opened in 1995, introducing a new pit stop for those who appreciate Prokofiev over breakfast and true isolation.

The Çetmi Han connects to Ayvacık by a high, slightly harrowing 22 kilometer section of the E-87 highway. Another coast road connects Küçükkuyu to Behramkale/Assos, and dolmuş serve both routes. A taxi from Küçükkuyu costs about $5, although you get dropped off by dolmuş at the Yeşilyurt turnoff on the highway and walk one-quarter mile uphill.

## WHERE TO EAT

All four waterfront hotels have good fish restaurants, and the docks are lined with their tables in the summer. Breakfast and dinner are on your room bill in the high season, but be sure to drop in at the Fenerlihan.

**FENERLİHAN**, *İskele Mevkii, Behramkale, Ayvacık, Tel. 286 721 7385.*
On the western side of the İskele, big wood doors with black metal hinges open into the interior of a beautifully restored stone building. The long wood bar, heavily beamed wooden roof, and the small tables ringing the open upper level are all classic. Prices are slightly heavier than elsewhere, but the food is good. Watch the sun set from here – beer or rakı cost less than $1. The Fenerlihan pulses a little on summer nights.

## SEEING THE SIGHTS

### The Ruins of Assos

Behramkale's obvious site is **Assos**, a former Aeolian city with a glorious setting. This was the occasional home of Aristotle, who, later in life, would judge that a smallish, cosmopolitan city like Assos is ideal.

Assos was settled by colonists from Lesbos in 1000 B.C., chosen for its position atop a 900 foot granite bluff that rises abruptly out of the Aegean. In the ensuing centuries the settlement developed some permanent characteristics with a walled acropolis atop the peak and an artificial harbor in the sea below. Commerce thrived as the city began attracting regional trade, probably trade that had once been funneled through Troy, now in serious decline since the catastrophe of the Trojan War.

Assos' success caught the Lydian King Croesus' eye during his successful campaigns along the Aegean coast, and Croesus seized Assos by 555 B.C. The Lydian Empire was defeated by the Persians under Cyrus just ten years later, and the Persians went on to gain control of most mainland Aegean cities, Assos included. It was during these confused times that the **Temple of Athena** was founded (signs at the site say 530 B.C., but that's a little specific). When the Persian Emperor Xerxes' army and navy were defeated in Greece (479 B.C.), Assos was among the cities that broke free and joined the Athenian Sea League.

Assos' golden age dawned in the fourth century B.C. under **King Hermias**, a student of Plato. Hermias had studied alongside Aristotle and, realizing his friend's gifts, invited the great philospher to Assos. **Aristotle** founded his first school of philosophy in Assos in 348 B.C., a school that continued to thrive for centuries and established Assos as a place of higher learning. Soon after, Alexander the Great, Aristotle's pupil, passed unhindered through the region (334 B.C.) after giving the Persian army its first thorough beating at the River Granicus to the northeast. The Kingdom of Pergamon annexed the city toward the end of the third century B.C., and in 133 B.C. the Pergamene King bequeathed his kingdom to the Romans upon his death.

As the Romans tended to do, they brought a period of stability to Assos. St. Paul and St. Luke passed this way during their ecclesiastic journeys, and Assos became a center of Christianity as Roman power shifted to Constantinople. Alas, it was the wrong kind of Christianity for Byzantine Emperor Theodosius I, an ardent foe of "heretical" Christian sects. His edict resulted in the destruction of the town's principal temples around 382 A.D., just one of many scorched earth measures that led his Christian allies to bestow upon him the honorific "The Great." It was the same Theodosius who ended the Olympics and caused the destruction of temples throughout Asia Minor. Assos was thereafter a relatively minor city, passing back and forth between various kingdoms until annexation by the Ottomans in 1330.

The ruins at Assos are not well signed and no longer offer anything unique (to witness the wonders of the Temple of Athena you will have to visit museums in Boston, Paris, Berlin, and the Archaeological Museum in İstanbul). Still, Assos is filled with still-mighty old walls and tumbled buildings that are fun to spend a morning wandering in, and restoration work on the theater facing the sea is well underway.

The site of the **Temple of Athena** atop the hill is well marked, and has an exceptional setting. Some genuine capitals and column sections remain, but a lame restoration effort has left the temple littered with large concrete cylinders intended as faux-marble columns. The lions that once adorned the temple have been shuttled off to the aforementioned museums, along with long, beautiful reliefs and the rest of the most interesting things.

Near the upper entrance, the large stone buildings above the mosque are Byzantine towers, built on the foundations of earlier Greek structures, and the base of a Byzantine wall makes a circuit of the entire hilltop. Lower, near the road to the iskele, are the old marketplace and gymnasium, confined within a line of walls that run down toward the iskele and date back to Assos' thriving Roman period. Sections of this huge circuit of walls remain in very good condition. Note: local picture book guides to Assos are uniquely worthless.

On the way to the ruins you pass the **Murat Hudavendigar Cami**, a mosque that is especially boxlike and uninteresting. Sultan Murat I (1359-1389) was the second proper Ottoman sultan, whose 30 year reign brought great tracts of land under Ottoman sway.

## SPORTS & RECREATION
### Beaches
If you're staying at the Iskele, you can jump in the water to the east side of the harbor, but for a proper beach you must head back up to Behramkale and make your way a few miles east to **Kadirga** or one of the other beaches between here and Küçükkuyu. Kadirga beach is less than

three miles from Behramkale along the Küçükkuyu road. Dolmuş and share-taxis run from the Iskele to the nearby beaches during the high season, neglecting them in winter and in the off-season.

In high season boat trips are available to nearby beaches and for fishing – ask at any of the hotels in town.

## EXCURSIONS & DAY TRIPS

Other nearby places of interest include the **Ottoman fortress** at Babakale to the west and the **Ethnography Museum** in Tahtakuşlar village one mile off of the E87 highway east of Küçükkuyu.

The museum has a collection of artifacts from the eastern nomadic tribes that came west and eventually formed the Ottoman Empire, and the collection is all the more intriguing with its odd similarities to Native American art and tools (psst...ancient Bering Straits land bridge). Another diversion is in the curative waters of the **Kestanbolu springs**, located near Küçükkuyu.

## BOZCAADA

**Bozcaada Island** is a little-known gem tucked just southwest of the mouth of the Dardanelles. Because it scarcely makes its way onto maps and into guidebooks, it is not famed for its beaches, wine, sandy cleanliness, soaring Venetian fortress, or atmosphere of relaxed calm. It should be. The hot summer season is relatively short, from June to late September, but the island's quiet times have their advantages.

### History

If the wine and beaches are not enough for you, if you need some historic underpinning to justify spending a few nights on the vineyard-covered island, Bozcaada has that as well. Bozcaada, once known as **Tenedos**, was where the Greeks retired during the Trojan War to lull the Trojans into thinking the war was over. It is also home to a magnificent fortress that was occupied by the Byzantine empire, the rival Venetian and Genoese mercantile navies, and the Ottomans.

The name Tenedos comes from the island's first king, Thenes. Thenes' father, King Kynikus of Kolonus, was turned against the boy by Thenes' wicked stepmother. As seemed to be the habit at that time, Kynikus put the boy in a chest and cast him into the sea. Sure enough, Thenes washed up on a small island and became a mighty king in his own right. Years later, when his father learned of his wife's deceit he sailed out to find his son and beg his forgiveness. Alas, Thenes saw the old man approach and rushed to the docks, bitterly slashing his mooring lines. The end; the moral is wrapped up in there somewhere.

The best time to visit is between May and September, and the island is at its most beautiful toward the end of this period when the vineyards that cover the island are nearing harvest.

## ARRIVALS & DEPARTURES

### By Ferry

A ferry runs from Geyikli's Yeni Iskele to Bozcaada twice daily, at 10 a.m. and 4:30 a.m., and back again at 7:30 a.m. and 3 p.m. During the high season it runs more often, and on winter Mondays it runs only once. You can get the morning ferry, visit Troy, and make a leisurely way back to Geyikli even using public transportation. To get to Geyikli from the north, leave the main highway at Taştepe, a few miles after the Troy entrance, and follow the signs. From the south, turn off of the main highway at Ezine and continue to Geyikli. Once in Geyikli follow the signs to "Bozcaada" or "Yeni Iskele."

While waiting at the docks on the way to Bozcaada, stop off in the small restaurant just down the shore, Geyikli Sehayat Dinlenme Tesisleri, and get a bite to eat (go ahead and try the "tost," a compressed half-loaf of bread with ketchup and pastrami). Note that transporting a car across on summer weekends (especially Fridays and Sundays) can be a distinct problem as people pour in from İstanbul.

## WHERE TO STAY

Accommodations are basic, clean and usually quite appealing. The waterfront is lined with good fish restaurants.

**GÜRKOL PANSIYON**, *Bozcaada, Tel. 286 697 8011. Rooms:22. Double: $29.*

In a town packed with small pensions, the Gürkol pensions are the best. Try to arrange for a room with its own stove and bathroom, although all rooms in the two distinct old buildings have access to a stove. Pick up some fresh seafood on the docks and cook for yourself. The owner, Halit, is one of the island's few English speakers, ever helpful and knowledgeable.

**THENES OTEL**, *Bozcaada, Tel. 286 697 8888, Fax: Tel. 286 697 8367. Rooms: 35. Double: $45. Restaurant.*

Simple, spacious, and in a cove to the south of town, the Thenes is Bozcaada's most ambitious hotel. It fails to mar the landscape or disrupt Bozcaada's peace, however. The Thenes has wonderful sea views and a small cove almost to itself. The hotel's biggest drawback is its inconvenience to Bozcaada town, but transportation options abound.

**STAR OTEL**, *Bozcaada, Çanakkale, Tel. 286 697 8037. Rooms: 18. Double: $32.*

With the Thenes, this hotel is considered the island's premier lodging.

**HOTEL EGE BOZCAADA**, *Kale Arkası, Bozcaada, Tel. 286 697 8189, Fax 286 697 8389. Rooms: 36. Double: $35.*

Another of the town's smallish hotels, this one is located in the city center.

**Budget Pensions**

There are many small house pensions in Bozcaada as well, and you will probably be met at or even on the ferry by someone interested in taking you to their pension. Almost 100 percent certainly a good idea to have a look if you need accommodation, just don't be afraid to say no if you want to say no.

## WHERE TO EAT

**ZORBA RESTAURANT**, *Bozcaada, Çanakkale, Tel. 286 697 8616. Moderate.*

Quality seafood and other Turkish staples in a friendly atmosphere.

**YAKAMOZ BALIK RESTAURANT**, *Bozcaada, Çanakkale, Tel. 286 697 8616. Moderate.*

Hectic, but good food. The terrace bar upstairs is excellent on a hot afternoon.

## SEEING THE SIGHTS

The **Venetian fortress** is the first thing that will seize your attention upon arrival. The giant structure commands the Bozcaada harbor, and was always valued for its strategic location just across from the mouth of the Dardanelles. The Phoenicians and Greeks occupied the area, but the original fortress was Byzantine era. During the Byzantine Empire's decline the fortress became increasingly important to the great mercantile navies of the Venetians and Genoese, and the two fought and negotiated bitterly to control the island, eventually bringing the matter to arbitration in 1382, where it was decided to raze the fortress entirely. This the Venetians, who occupied the fortress, were loathe to do, and did slowly.

Still, by the time the island was ceded to the Ottomans in 1480, the fortress was a great ruin and the island virtually deserted. Under Sultan Mehmet II the Conqueror, the fortress was rebuilt, and settlers on the island were offered years of freedom from taxes. Later improvements were undertaken by Süleyman the Magnificent and Mahmud II, and, most recently, the Ministry of Culture and Tourism restored the site in 1970.

In the end, the fortress was almost too indomitable. No great battles were fought here because it was such a dominating fortification, although the Venetian and Genoese mercantile empires fought over it elsewhere. The fortress is ringed by a 30 foot wide moat and is entered from the land side by a single bridge spanning the moat – which today is used as a parking lot. The large enclosed area is fairly hilly, rising in the west to take advantage of the natural cliff face, and on the exterior grounds you find ammunition depots and wells. Within the middle ring of defenses åre several structures; from north to south are the barracks and toilets, the gate house for the central keep, a mosque, an infirmary, and, on the lowest level, a garden.

Entering the keep, there is an arsenal to your right, the main storehouse in the center and, straight ahead, the commander's tower. This place is a sprawling marvel that children, photographers, and immature adults will love.

## SPORTS & RECREATION
**Beaches**

The best beaches on the island are in the south, conveniently shielded from the summertime north winds. The southern beaches are all about four miles away over low rolling hills, and you can get there by dolmuş, share taxis, car, or rental bikes. For bike rentals, camping information, or most other needs, contact **Ada Turism**, *Tel. 286 697 8795*, near the city center.

**Ayazma** is the most popular beach, with a few small cafes along the bottom of the ridge behind it and an old Greek Orthodox monastery higher up. **Sulubahçe** and **Habbele**, further west, are also good beaches, but less isolated than Ayazma. None of these beaches are likely to be crowded in the Antalya sense, however, and the company is generally much more pleasant. If you want a section of coastline all to yourself, head to the northern side of the island and take one of the many small roads that jog one-quarter mile down to the water.

## SHOPPING
**Wine**

The island's three major wineries offer a variety of different table wines, all of them quite cheap and sassy. None of these wines are likely to put France out of business, but there are some decent ones in the bunch. Those who claim to know say the whites are especially good.

For the price of a few $2 bottles of wine you can make the rounds of all of the wineries and try sample glassfuls at each place. There's none of the studied elegance of wineries in North America; you'll often be served directly from the pumping hose in the warehouse.

The wineries are packed close to one another; **Talay** is behind and to the left of the Belediye (Municipality) building, while **Rağbet** is a few blocks deeper in that direction. **Ataol Fabrikasi** is closer to the sea, also over on the south side of the harbor.

## WINES AVAILABLE AT TALAY FABRIKASI

*The following is an example of one of the winery's offerings:*

| | | | |
|---|---|---|---|
| Ada Yıldızı | Red/white | 2 years | $1 |
| Trova | Red/white | 3 years | $1 |
| Halikarnas | Rose | 2 years | 70¢ |
| Assos | Red/white | 5 years | $1 |
| Talay | Red/white | 2 years | 50¢ |
| Tenedos | Red/white | 8 years | $2.50 |
| Talay Üzümlu | Red | 5 years | $1 |

# ÇANAKKALE

Çanakkale is not alluring, but it is practical. Situated between Gallipoli and Troy in the northwest corner of Turkey, Çanakkale is at the south side of the Eceabat-Çanakkale ferry crossing on the major E-87 highway route. Whether coming from İstanbul at the beginning of a loop out to the Aegean or heading back at the end of a trip, it makes sense to see both **Troy** and the poignant **Gallipoli** battlefields with a night somewhere in the region.

The declaration on the hill opposite Çanakkale on the northern side of the Dardanelles commemorates the Ottoman victory at Gallipoli and reads: "Stop ye passersby! The land you stand on is where an era sank. Listen! Put your ear to the ground. There beats the heart of a nation."

### History

Two of Turkey's most famed sites are located in the Dardanelles. The **Gallipoli** war memorial, a place of pilgrimage for Australians and New Zealanders on the European shore, is fascinating and touching. An altogether different sort of fascination transfixed the world in 1871, when Heinrich Schliemann announced that he had discovered the site of ancient **Troy** at the mouth of the Dardanelles. Thirteen distinct towns have been unearthed by archaeologists at Troy since Schliemann made his discovery, layered one on top of the other. And as Schliemann theorized, the ancient Troy, the Troy of Priam and Hector that passed into legend, is, indeed, in this cake of cities.

While wandering through the stark landscape of Gallipoli and hunting through Troy, you will appreciate the beauty of the **Dardanelles** – or **Hellespont** – as a backdrop. The Gallipoli peninsula and the Hellespont have been a beautiful lure for thousands of years, and skeptics say it was the control of these straits, not Helen, that the Greeks coveted in the 13th century B.C. Whatever the truth, myth and reality are wonderfully intertwined in this region.

The name "Hellespont" derived from the mythical princess Helle who, with her brother, was kept imprisoned by her stepmother. Fortunately, a winged ram came along and rescued them, but, alas, young Helle fell from the soaring ram, drowning in the straits. Her brother, Phrixus, wisely waited until landing, then slew the flying ram and put the ram's golden fleece in a tree protected by a dragon, where it hung until its discovery by Jason and the Argonauts. The strait's current name, the Dardanelles, refers to Dardanos, the second king of Troy (and, they say, one of Zeus' many bastard sons).

A last, fairly pointless piece of guidebook mythology is the story of **Hero and Leander**. Leander, a native of Abydos on the Asian side of the strait, fell deeply in love with the beautiful Hero, a priestess at the Temple of Aphrodite on the European side. Every night he would brave the Hellespont and swim to her, returning in the morning. One stormy night the young Hero waited in vain; Leander never came. Knowing him drowned, Hero leapt into the sea and drowned herself. An interesting note: experts say that the only way to swim the strait is from Sestos to Abydos, not in reverse. Lord Byron swam the straits in 1810 as an experiment, concluding that the young Leander could have made the crossing, but that he would have been too exhausted by the ordeal to consider romance.

Not everyone here was mythical; real people populated the area, too. With the help of hundreds of ships, **Xerxes** bridged the section of the Dardanelles near Çanakkale. His engineers used braided cords of papyrus and flax strung from shore to shore and twisted taut with wooden windlasses. Dirt, logs, and brushwood were laid over this. The effort failed initially, but was eventually successful. Xerxes mighty army – not as mighty as Herodotus' estimate of 5 million men – passed over the straits, but was stalled by the Spartans and eventually defeated at sea at the Battle of Salamis and on land at the Battle of Plataea by the united Greeks. The Persians fled back over the strait piecemeal. Note that the Serpent Column in the Hippodrome in Sultanahmet, İstanbul, was built in Greece to commemorate the Greek land victory at Plataea in 479 B.C.

Some 150 years later, Alexander the Great bridged the strait in reverse, crossed into Asia, and within two years shattered the Persian Empire. Mastery of the straits assured control of the heavy

## PERSIAN MANAGERIAL TECHNIQUES

*Herodotus tells of Xerxes' famous crossing in 480 B.C. As a prelude to his invasion of Greece, the Persian King assembled hundreds of ships to draw cables across the sea and form bridges for his vast army.*

*"But when the strait had been bridged there came a great storm upon it and smashed it and broke it all to pieces. On learning this Xerxes was furious and bade his men lay three hundred lashes on the Hellespont and lower into the sea a yoke of fetters. Indeed, I have heard that he sent also branders to brand the Hellespont. He told those who laid on the lashes to say these words, of violent arrogance, worthy of a barbarian: "You bitter water, our master lays this punishment on you because you have wronged him, though he never did you any wrong. King Xerxes will cross you, whether you will or not; it is with justice that no one sacrifices to you, who are a muddy and briny river." So he commanded that the sea be punished, and he ordered the beheading of the supervisors of the building of the bridge."*

*In **The Innocents Abroad**, Mark Twain mulled over this last detail: "The King, thinking that to publicly rebuke the contractors might have a good effect on the next set, called them out before the army and had them beheaded. In the next ten minutes he let a new contract on the bridge. It has been observed by ancient writers that the second bridge was a very good bridge. If our government today would rebuke some of our shoddy contractors occasionally, it might work much good."*

commerce between Europe and Asia, and was critical to the later success of the Romans, Byzantines, and Ottomans.

## ARRIVALS & DEPARTURES

### By Bus

Bus travel is easy in all directions, with its hub at the otogar on Atatürk Caddesi several blocks inland of the ferry terminal – although most buses drop you off and pick you up at the ferry terminal. If you arrive by bus, it is best to travel to Çanakkale, unload your baggage at a local hotel, and then venture out to see the sights.

If you are traveling lightly and heading south you may want to pack your things along with you to Troy and afterwards get a ride to the main highway where you can grab one of the frequent southbound dolmuş (Ezine or Ayvacık) on the highway and travel onward to Assos/ Behramkale or Geyikli/Bozcaada. Çanakkale buses to both İstanbul and Izmir should cost about $10 and take 5 hours.

**By Car**

Çanakkale is at the intersection of two major highways: the E-90 heading out to Bursa via Bandirma, and the E-87, the north-south road that runs along the entire Aegean coast, crosses from Çanakkale to Eceabat by ferry, and continues up the Gallipoli peninsula to Edirne. The northern, E87, route has the better roads, but both are two lane highways maintained in acceptable condition – but be wary of broken down shoulders and buses passing on blind turns.

If you are interested in both Troy and Gallipoli, visit Gallipoli on the way into the area. You can stay in Çanakkale, although a better option is the Tusan Hotel to the west, and, better still, Assos or Bozcaada. Ferries run hourly from Eceabat on the European shore to Çanakkale between 6 a.m. and midnight and cost about $6 for a car carrying four people.

**By Ferry**

No ferries stop in Çanakkale anymore, but you should consider the five hour ferry from İstanbul to Bandirma (departures at 9 a.m. on Tuesday, Thursday, Friday and Saturday). Buses between Bandirma and Çanakkale are frequent. The mini-cruise costs only $7 per person and leaves you with a mostly painless 168 kilometer drive between Bandirma and Çanakkale. See Erdek and İstanbul sections.

## WHERE TO STAY

The hotel selection is lackluster, with nothing at the top end, a few decent mid-range hotels, and fiercely competitive pensions at the bottom end. The adventurous can get a ferry from Kabatepe on the European side of the straits for **Gökçaada**, an island with several peaceful little towns and pensions.

If you arrive the third week in March, you will run headlong into the week-long commemoration of Gallipoli; someone will offer to shoehorn you in to their hotel, but it will be a hassle.

**HOTEL AKOL**, *Kordon, Çanakkale, Tel. 286 217 9456, Fax 286 217 2897. Rooms: 138. Double: $75. Restaurant.*

The best Çanakkale has to offer, earning four stars from the Tourism Ministry. The Akol isn't especially charming or meticulous, but it has remarkably good food. The Akol is clean, with nice views on the waterfront side, satellite TV, a great terrace, and a pool.

**HOTEL ANAFARTLAR**, *İskele Meydanı, Çanakkale, Tel. 286 217 4454, Fax 286 217 4457. Rooms: 70. Double: $45. Restaurant.*

A solid hotel, directly alongside the ferry terminal. It shows its 13 years, but it is clean, nicely managed, has satellite TV, and has its own local guide company, Sudular.

## In Güzelyalı

**THE TUSAN HOTEL**, *Güzelyalı, Tel. 286 232 8210, Fax 286 232 8226. Rooms: 64. Double: $45. Restaurant.*

An excellent alternative to staying in lackluster Çanakkale. The Tusan is nestled in a pine forest at the water's edge, 20 minutes west of Çanakkale. The hotel has pleasant grounds, satellite television, and a quick 13 mile drive to Troy. The Tusan is closed between November and May.

## Budget Pensions

The pension business in Çanakkale is competitive, even cutthroat. Young Australians come here in droves on their way to Gallipoli, fostering booming business. We recommend these pensions despite cold in the off season and warn you about enjoyable chaos in the summer.

The current top dog is the **YELLOW ROSE PENSION**, *Tel/Fax 286 217 3343*, with its fierce competitor the **ANZAC HOUSE**, *Tel. 286 217 0156*, close behind. Both are clean, recently remodeled, and at rates of $9 a double that include showings of the Mel Gibson movie *Gallipoli* and a documentary about the battle, you can hardly do better. The Yellow Rose even has a patio garden. Both hotels are a one minute walk inland of the ferry terminal and a pack of youths are always on hand to show you the way.

## WHERE TO EAT

There is little to distinguish most of the restaurants in town. The Hotel Akol's buffet dinner is quite good at a cost of $11.

**YALOVA LİMAN**, *Kayserlı Ahmet Paşa Caddesi, Çanakkale, Tel. 286 217 1045.*

Our favorite, with a good view over the strait from its terrace. The food's the same as most other places, but it goes down better with a view like this. Besides, the beer is cheap.

**ŞEHİR LOKANTA**, *Iskele, Çanakkale, Tel. 286 217 1148.*

Another fairly nice restaurant with a good selection of mezes and grills. The Şehir is located just behind the Kilitbahir ferry terminal and has patio dining in the summer.

**AUSTRALIA NEW ZEALAND RESTAURANT**, *Yalı Caddesi No. 32, Çanakkale, Tel. 286 212 1722.*

The Australia New Zealand obviously targets the superabundance of kids from Down Under making their pilgrimage to Gallipoli, but its food tends toward standard Turkish grills. You'll see some familiar names on the menu, however, and it's cheap. In the neighborhood behind the clock tower.

## SEEING THE SIGHTS

If you have some spare time, you should have a look around Çanakkale's **Military Museum** (closed Monday and Wednesday, closed lunch, 50¢). You can't miss it; it's housed alongside the old **Çimenlik fortress** on the shore. The fortress was one of two built at this section of the strait by the industrious Sultan Mehmet II, in preparation for his conquest of İstanbul. Together with the Kilitbahir ("Lock of the Sea") fortress on the European side, Çimenlik (whose name translates into the less menacing "Meadow Plain") formed the tightest bottleneck in a long gauntlet of Dardanelles fortresses.

The Çimenlik fortress houses a smattering of old artillery pieces and the **Piri Reis Gallery** of maps and books within the arsenal. Piri Reis (1470-1551) was a Gelibolu native, the foremost sailor among a people famed for their skill at sea: Gelibolu's children natives "grow up in water like alligators, their cradles are the boats, they are rocked to sleep with the lullaby of the sea" wrote one Ottoman historian. Reis demonstrated just such an affinity for sailing, and combined it with cartographic genius to create navigation books, current atlases, and even two ambitious maps of the world relying only on scattered charts and accounts.

Reis had the good fortune to be a sailor in the Ottoman fleet at its zenith under Barbarrosa, and rose to the rank of admiral of Ottoman naval forces in Egypt. His luck ran out, however, when Sultan Süleyman sent him against the Portuguese in the Gulf of Oman. After several initial successes, Reis was unable to dislodge the Portuguese from their key fortress on the Straits of Hormuz and lost his fleet in the Persian Gulf. The elderly Reis escaped, but upon his return to Cairo he was beheaded for his failure.

The maps, weapons, and munitions at Çimenlik are all interesting, but the highlights may be the two gargantuan holes poked in the fortress by the *HMS Queen Elizabeth*, one of which penetrated a deeply buried magazine. Incredibly, both shells were fired 15 miles over the Gelibolu peninsula from the open sea.

Inside the house near the entrance is a collection of models, photos, and paraphernalia that helps explain the campaign, and an entire floor devoted to pleasant charcoals and watercolors of the various battlefields by Mehmet Ali Ağa, a soldier at the time. The ship in front of the castle is a recreation of the *Nusrat*, a mine layer that helped doom the Allied naval assault.

The **Archaeology Museum** (closed Mondays, 50¢) in the west of town is highly recommended if you are heading out to Troy and south down the Aegean coast. Besides having, predictably, lots of pottery and other discoveries from the nearby Troy ruins, the museum has artifacts and historical information on other sites in the region. Many of the Iron and Bronze Age pieces are from the Frank Calvert Collection, named after a U.S. Consulate officer who did some digging of his own at Hisarlık and owned much of the land there before Schliemann showed up. Across the straits is **Kilitbahir Fortress** ($1), whose rounded walls give it a remarkably pretty appearance. Together with Çimenlik, Sultan Mehmet II built Kilitbahir to prevent assistance from reaching Constantinople during his siege, and, likewise, to challenge anyone seeking to evacuate. It is interesting to tramp around, but pretty bare.

## NIGHTLIFE & ENTERTAINMENT

There are two fine hamams in Çanakkale, the **Tarihi Yali Hamamı** two blocks inland of the waterfront near Çimenlik fortress, *on Çarşı Caddesi*, and the **Büyük Hamam**, further inland at *Namik Kemal Mahallesi No. 31*, across from the Kurşunlu Mosque. Both are open from 6:30 to midnight ($2 plus massage, rub).

## EXCURSIONS & DAY TRIPS

You've probably come out to the northeastern tip of Turkey to see **Troy**, perhaps **Gallipoli** as well. Unlike Ephesus or others of Turkey's great ruins, Troy does not speak for itself; to appreciate this badly scattered site you need a refresher in the Iliad legend. Similarly, Gallipoli is more immediately meaningful for another great battle, not so different in character than the Trojan War, that happened earlier this century.

Both sites should be seen as day trips from Çanakkale, and both are treated differently than other excursions in this book, as sites worthy of their own separate sections.

## TROY

**Troy's** ragged appearance belies its incredible past. The past 3,200 years have not been kind to Ilium, lasting evidence of the Greeks' great success. Trade routes probably began shifting at the time of the Trojan War, and Troy remained a small town until 400 A.D., after which it slipped out of sight. People continued to inhabit the site, but the town was eventually abandoned in the 1300s as the Ottoman Empire began consolidating power in the region. More than a century of digging has recovered considerable cut stone and marble, but Troy does not have the sheer sprawling mass of the great ruins to the south. Moreover, with its nine layers and multiple sublayers, Troy can be quite confusing.

What distinguishes Troy is its marvelous history. Heroes walked the earth here, Hector and Achilles, Paris and Ajax. There is something defiantly magical about this place of myth and childhood fairy tales.

## History

One of the greatest, most enduring legends in western civilization is the **Trojan War**. The tale of the Trojan War was scrabbled together from the accounts of Greek soldiers and lords – and a few Trojan survivors – who sailed home after the long, successful siege. Thereafter, the tale was passed from generation to generation as oral history, assuming different variations and new dramatic elements through the centuries. By the time Homer committed *The Iliad* to writing, the story had acquired sea serpents, a magical apple, and a cast of meddlesome gods.

By the 19th century, 3,100 years after the actual battle, most good historians were extremely skeptical of the tale, and thought the real Trojan War likely bore little resemblance to Homer's epic. Archaeologists made some desultory attempts to locate Troy, which had fallen off the map since its 12th century B.C. heyday, but most efforts were concentrated near Ballidağ south of the actual site. In 1870, an eccentric tycoon named **Heinrich Schliemann** showed up at a mound known as **Hisarlık**, convinced that the experts were wrong. Troy was here, he said, it had to be.

Schliemann had used *The Iliad* as his guide, and the story was very clear in some of its particulars: Troy was a close march from the sea; Troy was near two springs; the city was small enough, and the terrain smooth enough, that Hector could race around it, and later be dragged around it by Achilles' horse. Using these and other clues, Schliemann hunted through the region, finally concluding that Troy was at Hisarlık. Years of sifting through the increasingly ancient layers proved Schliemann correct.

How correct Homer was is still the subject of debate. How much of Homer's story was fabricated, and how much based in fact? For those of you desiring more information, we offer three more detailed historical sections below: *The Iliad; The Historians;* and *The Layers of Troy*.

## ARRIVALS & DEPARTURES

### By Bus

From Çanakkale, there are dolmuş to Troy every 30 minutes during summer, leaving from the station across from the marketplace. Go straight inland from the ferry terminal on Demircioğlu Caddesi, turn right on the main Izmir-Bandirma road (Atatürk Caddesi), go three blocks until you are about to cross the bridge. The dolmuş stop is on your right. From the central otogar continue four blocks west along Atatürk Caddesi.

There are no major bus lines serving Troy directly from the south, but you can get a dolmuş from Ezine to Tevfikiye or from the highway to Tevfikiye, although dolmuş run infrequently in the winter.

## By Car

From Çanakkale in the east take the E87 past Intepe, staying on E87-D550 by turning left at the Kumkale-Taştepe fork. The Troy turn off is five kilometers along the E87 on the right hand side, posted with customary yellow road signs, and the ruins are four kilometers further on just past Tevfikiye.

From the south the main coast road, E87, takes you north past Ayvacık and Ezine. The Troy turn off is to the left about 8 kilometers after Taştepe.

## By Tour

A guided tour is quite helpful at Troy, although a run through the Archaeology Museum in Çanakkale and this book are a fine substitute. It is easy to lose your bearings among the layers and the confused terrain. There are plenty of tour guides around the area, including **Troy-Anzacs Tours**, *Tel. 286 217 5847, Fax 286 217 0196*, and **Anatur**, *Tel. 286 217 0156*. Both are located on the main road in Çanakkale by the ferryboat landing.

Another good option is Mustafa Aşkın, a guide who occasionally works for Çanakkale tour companies and also runs a gift shop in town. He has written a book on the site based on his years of guiding and chatting up the archaeologists who descend on the site each summer, including teams from the University of Cincinnati and Bryn Mawr.

## THE ILIAD

The **Trojan War** began innocently enough, with a wedding. The goddess of discord, not invited, chose to liven up the proceedings by lobbing a golden apple into the crowd labeled "To the Fairest." The goddesses Hera, Athena, and Aphrodite all claimed that the apple was theirs, and called upon Zeus to decide. Zeus neatly sidestepped the request, electing the naive young Trojan prince **Paris** instead. The goddesses each offered the young prince a bribe. Hera offered wealth and rule of Asia, Athena enticed him with wisdom and martial success, and Aphrodite promised the most beautiful woman in the world for his bride. Paris gave Aphrodite the apple, winning the beautiful **Helen** as a prize and the eternal loathing of Hera and Athena.

Helen, unfortunately, was married to **Menelaus**, king of Sparta. When Paris sailed off with his bride the enraged Menelaus formed a league against Troy with the help of his brother, the great king **Agamemnon**. After long preparation, a force of 1,184 ships from throughout the Mediterranean set sail against Troy, seeking to force Helen's return. The attackers built siege fortifications around **Ilium** (ancient Troy), but did not risk an outright assault against the massive city walls.

For nine years the war continued, with pressure mounting on both sides – the Greeks eager to return home and the Trojans suffering from the long siege.

*The Iliad* is an account of the last months of the siege. The Greek camp is in disarray owing to the unwillingness of its champion, **Achilles**, to fight. Achilles and his soldiers remain at the rear of the Greek camp throughout the siege, embittered by an insult from Agamemnon. Determined to put an end to the long standoff, and emboldened by Achilles' absence, the Trojans begin increasing their pressure on the Greek army. With losses mounting, the Greeks beg Achilles to return to battle. He refuses, even when the Trojan champion **Hector** leads an attack that leaves Greek ships burning. The fortunes of the Greeks continue to deteriorate, and finally Achilles' best friend, **Patroclos**, urges Achilles to fight. Achilles refuses yet again, but sends Patroclos into battle in his armor.

As Patroclos had predicted, the Trojans fall back at the mere sight of Achilles' armor. Finally, driven across the plain to the city walls, Hector turns to challenge the Greek champion. As he courageously fights Patroclos, thinking him the indomitable Achilles, Hector delivers a powerful blow that knocks off Patroclos' helmet. The relieved Hector sees that his opponent is not Achilles at all and kills Patroclos. As the Greeks flee the field Hector takes Achilles' armor.

This victory is the Trojans' undoing. When Achilles hears of his friend's death he is tormented and enraged, and at last vows to return to battle. With Achilles leading them the Greeks are irresistible, forcing the Trojans back into their city. Once again, Hector stands forth as the Trojan champion, challenging Achilles outside the city walls. However, at Achilles' approach Hector is seized with fear and tries to escape, running three times around the walls of Troy, with Achilles on his heels. Hector, resigning himself to his fate, finally turns and fights, but is overpowered by the Greek champion and killed on the spot. Achilles drags Hector's lifeless body around the besieged city on horseback, repaying the Trojans for his grief over Patroclos. In time he returns Hector's body to his father the King, and *The Iliad* ends with Hector burning on a funeral pyre.

As told elsewhere, Achilles died soon after, struck in the **heel** – his only vulnerable spot – by Paris' arrow. The Greeks, now thoroughly exhausted, resolved to try one more trick, then go home. They abandoned the field and pretended to sail away, leaving behind a **great wooden horse**. The Trojans found a lone Greek remaining, a man who claimed to have escaped becoming a human sacrifice. The man, an agent of the Greeks, said that the horse was an offering to Athena, and that if the Trojans wheeled the horse into their city they would have the blessings of Athena all to themselves. The Trojans guilelessly brought the horse within the walls and celebrated. In the dead of night, however, Greek soldiers secreted in the horse stole out and opened the gates for the Greek army, which had crept back to Troy under cover of darkness. In the ensuing carnage, the Greeks slaughtered or enslaved the entire population (except Aeneas, whose family escaped to the south and set sail to found Rome), and Troy was looted, burned, and destroyed.

## THE HISTORIANS

There is indeed evidence to suggest the Trojan War occurred. A likely scenario is this: Troy had accumulated immense wealth because of its location at the mouth of the Dardanelles. Merchants, unwilling or unable to battle the great north wind that blows down the Hellespont nine months of the year, stopped at the mouth of the strait and did business in the marketplaces of Troy. The Trojans encouraged this with a naval force that could close the strait or demand payment for safe passage. Thus Troy profited from all of the trade between east and west and became the marketplace of interior Asia and Europe. Centuries of such commerce made the city prosperous.

Troy's success was coming at the expense of Greek colonists and merchants, however. The Greeks wanted unrestricted access to the interior markets and were tired of paying the Trojan duties and taxes. Compounding this, Herodotus reports that the Trojans had invaded Europe and seized a great expanse of lands extending toward Greece. The threat and the market restrictions were probably at the heart of the real conflict, although the kidnapping of Helen could certainly have been used as a pretext. The Greeks, under Mycenean control, assembled an army and landed at Troy – perhaps to the west at Beşik Cove – investing the city with siege walls rather than attacking it. Housing within Troy VIIa, the level thought to correspond with the Trojan War, is extremely cramped, and storage containers for food and water suddenly appear in this period, which would make sense if the Trojans and their goods were forced within the city walls for security reasons.

In the end, the city was defeated, looted, and burned in the 13th century B.C. How that was accomplished is unknown, but one theory is that the earthquake that struck Troy in this period coincided with the siege, and the Greeks poured through the breaches. In the aftermath, the Greeks erected a horse as a tribute to the gods. The earthquake could have predated the siege, however, and the Trojans may have been defeated by sheer force of arms – or trickery.

Defeat finally befell the Trojans, and at least one historian puts an ironic twist on the ten year war. No less an authority than **Herodotus** writes that Helen was never in Troy, having been seized, along with Menelaus' loot, in Memphis by the Pharoah Proteus. Proteus was appalled to learn that Paris had abducted Helen from her husband and stolen his treasure, and held Helen and the treasure until the wronged Greek Menelaus should come to claim them.

Herodotus says that Helen fit too tidily in Homer's epic poem to discard merely because she wasn't really there.

## THE LAYERS OF TROY

### I. Prior to 2500 B.C.

The first Troy was a standard town of the early Bronze Age, a collection of crude brick huts with roofs of wood and earth. As time went on houses began to assume more sophisticated designs, and defensive walls appeared around the entire citadel. Troy I was abruptly destroyed.

### II. 2500-2280 B.C.

This is the level that Schliemann picked as the Troy of legend, and "Priam's Treasure," largely collected here, demonstrated that it was a time of great wealth. The Trojans repeatedly expanded their city walls to accommodate an increasing population. Troy II was destroyed by fire.

### III, IV, and V. 2280-1800 B.C.

Schliemann's dig did the most damage to these layers, and he left inadequate records to reconstruct this period. The culture was unchanged from Troy II, and archaeologists believe that the town continued to prosper.

### VI. 1800-1270 B.C.

Evidence appears of a new culture, probably Greek, and pottery and art establish a link with the empire at Mycenae. The city walls rise to a new height, 12 feet wide at the base and 15 feet high. There is a distinct city plan, suggesting strong authority. An earthquake ravaged Troy VI.

### VII. 1270-1190 B.C.

Troy was rebuilt and its walls further strengthened, the period of wealth apparently continuing. However dwellings within the walls grew increasingly cramped, and a cataclysm befell the city around 1250 B.C. Fire raged through Troy, and there is evidence of slaughter – both of which suggest that this was indeed the unfortunate Troy of legend. As the period came to an end, people were rebuilding amid the ruins.

### VIIb-2. 1190-1100 B.C.

Troy is occupied by unknown people with relatively primitive artistic skills. The city is sacked at the end of the period, and is left unoccupied.

### VIII. and IX. 700 B.C.-330 A.D.

The Greeks appear again at Troy, this time establishing their own city, Ilium. *The Iliad* was already a famous piece of legend, and travelers came from afar to visit the city. Ilium never had the commercial success of ancient Troy, however, and in 85 B.C. the Roman general Gaius Flavius Fimbria sacked and burned the city, afterwards declaring that he had done in 11 days what it took the Greeks 10 years to do.

The city was again rebuilt, and it proved popular with the Romans, whose legendary ancestor Aeneas was supposed to have been an escaped Trojan warrior. Its success was so great that in 321 A.D. Constantine seriously considered founding his new Roman capitol here – laborers had started erecting great gates at the ancient city when a dream convinced Constantine to build at Byzantium instead. That fateful decision shifted the focus of trade to the east and into Europe, and Troy's fortunes declined steadily thereafter.

## SEEING THE SIGHTS

The site is open 8 a.m. to 8 p.m. in summer, 8 a.m. to 5 p.m. during the winter, with the museum, **The Excavation House**, maintaining the same hours ($1.50). The museum is at the entry to the site, and offers an important overview.

Making your way around the ruins is easy, but identifying what you are looking at is hard.

1. As you descend toward the East Gate the city wall beside you is Trojan War-era. Called **Cyclopean walls** for the massive pieces of stone used in their construction – only a giant Cyclops could have built using such stones – they are at the cutting edge of the period's engineering. The walls would have been topped by a breastwork for defenders. Note the tower built later than the walls using iron-cut stones was also Trojan War-era. The ground at the base of the walls was the real ground-level in Troy VII.

The entrance was built on a Hittite model, with the actual gate recessed back at the end of the curved path. This simple expedient was proof against battering rams.

2. A cluster of homes dating to Troy's heyday. These were apparently the residences of relatively affluent Trojans.

3. A cistern recessed into the wall, and a small well standing alone nearby.

4. Ascending, you pass the site where the **Temple of Athena** once was, atop a hill overlooking the Dardanelles. The temple here was similar to the one later built at Assos (whose foundation remains). Alexander the Great, Julius Caesar, and even the Persian King Xerxes made offerings

here, although offerings here did the Trojans very little good – Athena was one of the goddesses humiliated by Paris.

5. This was once the centerpiece of Troy, the **acropolis** and **royal palace**. Not only has the palace ground plan been scattered and unearthed, much of the hill it sat on has been removed. If Agamemnon laid a 3,000 year curse on Priam's palace it could not have gone better. It is a good vantage point from which to look into Schliemann's massive trench, which modern archaeologists have continued using with far greater delicacy. It is also a good vantage point to see how Troy stood above the surrounding plain. The Greek ships were drawn up at the coast, probably near the point of land near Kumkale to the northwest, and the sea was considerably nearer.

6. The foundations of the outer Troy II gates.

7. A Troy II ramp gate to the city. The ramp remains in excellent condition, and was once flanked by guard towers. It was probably used to access the palace in later eras.

8. This is the supposed site of Schliemann's great discovery. Although it was later established that he cobbled together "**Priam's Treasure**," he found *something* here. Why a great wealth of Troy II era rings and diadems and silverware would be hidden outside the Troy II city walls is never adequately explained.

9. One of the ongoing digs outside the gates of Troy. Archaeologists are becoming more interested in the area surrounding Troy, hoping to find evidence of Trojan life in the surrounding areas, as well as evidence of the Greek siege.

10. This Roman-era **odeon** sits with its back flush against the Troy VII walls. The immediate vicinity has become a storage area for chunks of stone and marble.

11. This is the **Scian Gate** through which the Trojans issued to attack the Greeks in the plain below. Atop the tower here King Priam and his wife Hekabe saw his son Hector killed by Achilles, his body dragged around the city: *"his mother tore out her hair, and threw the shining veil far from her and raised a great wail as she looked upon her son; and his father beloved groaned pitifully."*

### Driving Around The Ruins

After seeing the city ruins, we encourage those with a car to take a drive around the surrounding plains. The drive gives you a better perspective of Troy's eminence and lets you see dozens of burial mounds, some of which are thought to date back to the Trojan War. Caesars and kings have paid their often unusual respects to the fallen heroes here. According to Plutarch, Alexander the Great carried a single book with him on his campaigns, a copy of *The Iliad* with corrections by his tutor,

## SCHLIEMANN'S DREAM

Heinrich Schliemann was captivated by The Iliad as a boy, and vowed to his father that he would one day find Troy. In young adulthood, he demonstrated a unique gift for languages, and could read, write, and speak a language after only six weeks of intense shouting and ranting in the new tongue that drove his neighbors berserk. He also proved a cunning businessman: he had made a fortune by his thirtieth birthday exporting olive oil to Russia, multiplied his wealth by trading goods in the gold fields of Northern California, and eventually built a small trading empire. Then, with characteristic single-mindedness, Schliemann suddenly freed himself of his business responsibilities and dedicated his resources to pursuit of his childhood dream. He at last acquired the Greek language, which he had waited to learn lest he be seduced too early by the search for Troy. He set out on some preliminary digs at Mycenae – where he concluded that the site was, as suspected, the home of the Greek overlord Agamemnon.

Next Schliemann began scouring The Iliad for clues about Troy. After a thorough survey of the region he decided that the true site was near Hisarlık at the mouth of the Dardanelles. Because of his faith in The Iliad, he employed such simple expedients as trying to run around the Alexandria-Troas site that historians of the period agreed upon as Troy. Finding Hector's run impossible, Schliemann ruled out the site. At Hisarlık, he dug deep trenches through the layers and was able to amass an impressive collection – 8,700 pieces of gold that included rings, earrings, images, dishes, and a golden goblet weighing 600 grams. Schliemann smuggled the wealth out of the Ottoman Empire and home to Germany, stunning the world with "proof" that he had discovered Troy.

In addition to a gift for tongues, Schliemann had a knack for melodrama and carnival theatrics – he claimed that the wealth from the years of digging was all from King Priam's treasury, and he adorned his wife Sophia with a diadem and, famously, whispered "Helen!" Photos tell us that even in regal jewelry Sophia's face might only have launched a solidly built rowboat or two, but Schliemann captured the world's imagination.

Schliemann fabricated parts of his story and was wrong about which level was the Troy of The Iliad – his Troy II predated Homer's Troy by almost 1,000 years – but he was right about the site. Unfortunately, in his excavations of Troy II, Schliemann destroyed much of the evidence from the shallower levels, including Troy VIIa, which long study and increasingly precise dating has determined must be the Troy of legend. Furthermore, the treasure Schliemann unearthed at the site was scattered during World War II, disappearing in the wreck of Nazi Germany. In 1996, the treasure reappeared at Moscow's Pushkin Museum.

Aristotle. He considered this the definitive guide to military strategy, and himself, as Achilles' descendent, the man to continue the epic deeds of the book. Upon arriving on the Asian shore he emulated the Greeks, sinking a spear into the earth and claiming it as his own, and, finding Achilles' tomb he sprinkled it with oil, stripped naked, and ran around it sprinkling flowers.

Schliemann is among those who did some digging to determine whose barrow was whose, but the search was largely futile. If you want to pay homage to Achilles the way Alexander did, his is said to be one of the two tumuli just west of Kumkale, with the other barrow belonging to his friend Patroklos (vegetable oil and flowers at Kumkale market, $2 for one liter, 50¢ for assorted seasonal flowers). The giant warrior Ajax's tomb is more obvious, inland of Yeni Kumkale and marked by an arch erected for the Emperor Hadrian on his grand tour.

# GALLIPOLI

A spare peninsula juts into the sea on the northern side of the Dardanelles, and it is here that the Allies in World War I felt certain they could claim the high ground and force the famous straits. They failed, and the bloody campaign marked a startling change in nations around the world. This site is particularly moving for the British, French, Australians, New Zealanders and, of course, Turks, whose people died here, but there is plenty of sadness to go around.

## History

World War I had settled into a stalemate in the west, when a maverick British First Lord of the Admiralty named Winston Churchill helped conceive an attack that promised to bring the war to a sudden end. The British and French resolved to punch their way through the Dardanelles and assault İstanbul. In a single stroke this would cripple one of Germany's allies, threaten Germany's flank, and open the supply route between the allies and the tottering Russian monarchy. At a time when both sides were tired of "sending men to chew barbed wire" in Europe's trenches, the plan had appeal.

A mighty French and British fleet was ostentatiously assembled in the Aegean. Eighteen British and French battleships and a collection of support vessels steamed into the Dardanelles on March 18, 1915, ran afoul of several mines, plowed into the shelling crossfire between the gauntlet of Turkish fortresses, and sailed right back out again. The fleet commander, British Admiral Draybeck, lost his nerve when six battleships were knocked out – the Bouvet, Ocean, and Irresistible sank outright – even before reaching Çanakkale. Unknown to the allied fleet, the Ottoman defenses were exhausted and out of ammunition and the ships would have fared better had they continued up the straits.

The British did not know this, however, and became determined to clear a path through the straits with a land operation. One month after the naval setback, troops from British Commonwealth nations, including, famously, the **ANZACs** (Australian and New Zealand Army Corps), landed on the northern side of the long Gallipoli peninsula. The plan was for the forces to dig in, seize the high ground, then descend on the Dardanelles fortresses from behind. There was every reason to expect that the battle would end quickly. The British armada had control of the Aegean and offered protection to its troops along the coast, and the Ottoman military – routed in the 1912-1913 Balkan conflicts by Greek, Bulgarian, and Serbian armies – was expected to fold up in the face of a determined attack.

Ironically, the attackers were bedeviled by failures in the vaunted British officer corps. The British landed their troops at some of the steepest points in the Ottoman defensive line, relying on surprise and speed. However, when the ANZACs poured up the ridges on the first day they were left unsupported and the early opportunities provided by the colonial army were squandered – in some cases the ANZACs deepest penetration of the coming nine months was on the first day. The Ottoman Turks were soundly led by the German Marshall **Liman Von Sanders** and, critically, by an intelligent and courageous Lieutenant Colonel **Mustafa Kemal (Atatürk)**. Kemal, the pivotal figure in contemporary Turkish history, had an uncanny ability to anticipate Allied strategy. From the eve of the battle, when Kemal exceeded his orders by reinforcing the highlands near Anzac Cove, his forces were dug in and prepared every time the ANZACs came flooding over a ridge.

Kemal led the resistance despite being raddled with malaria and other illness. He was famously unconcerned for his own well-being, and in the early stages he coolly barked orders and surveyed the battle from atop ridges where the ANZACs could get off pot shots at him. On one fateful occasion his pocket watch stopped a piece of shrapnel from piercing his heart. He was also pitiless with his own troops, most of whom did not have pocket watches in the right places.

On the first day of the Allied attack, determined to control the critical ridge below Chunuk Bair, he barked this famous order: *"I am not ordering you to attack; I am ordering you to die. In the time it takes us to die, other troops and commanders will arrive to take our places. I cannot believe that there is anyone in the troops I command who would not rather die than suffer again the disgrace that fell on us in the Balkans."* The men of the regiment did, indeed, die, but they held out long enough for reinforcements to arrive.

Kemal lends a heroic element to what is otherwise a sad tale of mutual butchery. As was happening in Europe, military tactics had not caught up with technology, and neither entrenched side could sustain an attack against withering machine gun fire and high explosives. Both sides fought with great resolve, hurling themselves into almost certain death. The British commanders (and the ranking ANZACs eager to prove their countrymen's mettle) refused to relent, even after the situation was clearly hopeless, and continued upping the ante with mostly colonial ANZAC troops. By the time the British recognized the futility of further attacks and pulled out in January 1916, there were a total of 500,000 casualties and 100,000 dead, evenly divided between the attackers and defenders.

Almost 20 years later Atatürk, who reluctantly engineered so much of the Gallipoli bloodshed, returned to Anzac Cove and wrote a brief speech that cast the struggle in an appropriate light:

*"Those heroes that shed their blood and lost their lives are now lying in the soil of a friendly country, therefore rest in peace. There is no difference between the Johnnies and the Mehmets to us where they lie side by side here in this country of ours. You, the mothers who sent your sons from far away countries wipe away your tears. Your sons are now lying in our bosom and are in peace. After having lost their lives on this land they have become our sons as well."*

## ARRIVALS & DEPARTURES

### By Car

The Anzac Cove/Çunuk Bair area is just a few miles off the main E87 Izmir-Edirne highway. Turn inland just two miles north of Eceabat. Four miles along you can turn north (right) and wind through the cemeteries and memorials here. To reach the British and French landing areas and the massive Turkish memorial in the south, follow the same road inland and turn south at the signs to Kum Koyu/Morto Bay. Note that the town of **Gelibolu** (Gallipoli) is actually quite distant from the battle sites, on the opposite side of the peninsula.

### By Taxi

Taxis offer the only way to see the sights without a car or a tour, unless you are interested in a long, long walk.

### By Tour

Guided tours of the Gallipoli battle site are a better option if there aren't enough of you for a taxi. The major battle sites are narrated with signs posted by the British War Graves commission. The guides, however, do have some good tales to tell, and provide transportation to the area of the ANZACs attack. If you are using public transportation, get a guided tour in Çanakkale, where the price for a four hour guided tour begins at $7 per person.

Both the **Troy-Anzac Tour** company and **Anatur** have stood the test of time, and offer four hour group tours. Both, also, neglect the southern end of the peninsula where the French and British died in droves and where the Turks have built a great monument.

## SEEING THE SIGHTS

The greatest concentration of memorials begins about six miles from Eceabat – two miles north there is a well-signed road that cuts across the peninsula past the Kabatape Museum and arrives at Brighton Beach, just south of the Allied landing site. The ANZACs landed in the shadow of the steeper ridges just north of here, and if you drive along the coast you arrive at **Anzac Cove** and numerous cemeteries. Like military cemeteries at Normandy or elsewhere the uniformity of the grave markers, like the uniformity of the dead men's youth and fear, leave even the most boisterous visitors hushed.

Backtrack a little to the ridge road and turn inland. As you ascend you pass further cemeteries and monuments. The **Lone Pine monument** commanding a ridge marks, vaguely, the ANZACs side of the battlefield, and all of the terrain between here and Çunuk Bair was hotly contested. There remains a warren of trenches and even the mouths of tunnels – an ambitious idea that was never used with great success – on the ridgeline above Lone Pine. Shrapnel and bones still turn up among the pine needles.

The road winds along the ridge past more monuments, including a new Turkish monument to the 57th Infantry Regiment who received the order to attack and die. Further along is a spur of road that goes a short distance in the direction of the Aegean. This is **The Nek**, a piece of land that the ANZACs tried in vain to take in one of the campaign's decisive battles, and, incidentally, the area immortalized in the *Gallipoli* film. There is another cemetery here, and yet another atop the next hill, **Çunuk Bair**. In the height of summer the ANZACs scaled the surrounding hills despite steady fire and got a foothold here. The Turks mounted an attack of their own and pressed them back, and when the ANZACs effort was finally exhausted almost 30,000 men lay dead here, filling the trenches and soaking the earth. There is a massive Turkish memorial here, and a statue of Atatürk near where his pocketwatch stopped the shrapnel, as well as a collection of restored trenches winding through the trees.

Descend the direction you came from Çunuk Bair to the **Kabatepe Museum** (all days, 50¢). The museum is not particularly edifying, but it further emphasizes the awfulness of the whole affair. There is a collection of weapons, shell casings, ribbons, letters, and even some skulls from the battle.

If you head down the peninsula instead of back toward Eceabat, you arrive at another cluster of cemeteries and monuments on the southern tip of the peninsula. This is where the bulk of the French and British troops came ashore, with the expectation that the ANZACs assault in the center of the peninsula would cut the peninsula in two and trap the Ottoman defenders between the two forces. The troops here at **V Beach** and **Cape Hellas** were stopped and pinned down just like the ANZACs inland, however, and their progress was measured only in meters.

This region is dominated by the commanding **Martyrs' Memorial**, Çanakkale Şehitleri Abidesi, at **Morto Bay**. The 150 foot tall structure was erected in gratitude to the Turkish men who gave their lives here, in effect saving İstanbul from the guns of Allied warships and, ultimately, saving Turkey from collapse.

## SPORTS & RECREATION

There are swimming beaches at **Kum Koyu, Morto Bay,** and just south of **Kabatepe**. Car ferries depart from Kabatepe for **Gökçaada**, a pleasant, little visited island just outside the Dardanelle Straits.

# 22. OTHER POINTS OF INTEREST IN TURKEY

We have presumed to lead you through our favorite spots in Turkey, but Turkey is far too big to fit in any single guide book. Should you set out in another direction, here is some information that will help.

## ANTAKYA

**Antakya** (Antioch) is one of the great cities of antiquity, and even in its fallen state it makes an impression. Few people get out this far unless they're traveling to Syria, and those who do are rewarded with the fascinating ruins of **Seleucia** and its colossal drainage system, and by the remnants of Antioch's 18 mile circuit of **walls**.

The $75 per night status address is the 72 room **BÜYÜK ANTALYA HOTEL**, *Atatürk Cad. No. 8, Antakya, Tel. 326 213 5860, Fax 326 213 5869*, and a cheaper alternative is the **DIVAN OTEL**, *Istiklal Cad. No. 62, Antakya, Tel. 326 215 1518.*

## ALANYA

**Alanya** is one of the Mediterranean's truly beautiful cities. The city is commanded by a massive fortress spilling down from a peninsula hilltop, with great red ramparts suggesting the power of the Selçuks who once occupied the battlements. The catch is that Alanya is overrun by package tour groups and has long since stopped being pleasant. Even the mammoth hotels are less impressive than those to the west.

Among the beachfront giants, the best is the five star **GRAND KAPTAN HOTEL**, *Oba Göl Mevkii, 07400, Alanya, Tel. 242 514 0101, Fax 242 514 0092*. For a fraction of the price try the centrally located **EMEK OTEL**, *Iskele Cad. No. 12, Alanya, Tel. 242 512 1223.*

## AFYON

Cappadoccia doesn't have a monopoly on stone oddities; near **Afyon** you'll find several Phrygian rock cut tombs with impressive facades – echoes of the strangeness at Ünye. Afyon is Turkey's opium capital, but this is good opium, harvested before it turns narcotic.

Other things of interest are the delicious pans of cream that arrive each morning and **Afyonkarahisar**, the Black Fortress of Opium above town. The **ORUÇOĞLU HOTEL**, *Bankalar Cad. No. 3, Afyon, Tel. 272 212 0120*, offers decent accommodation.

## AYANCIK

This small Black Sea village's accommodations include the **BELEDIYE TESISLERI**, *Tel. 368 613 1003*, and the **Apart Hotel** (*contact Adem Tahtacı, Sinop, Tel. 368 261 7900*).

## AYVALIK

**Ayvalık** is, like Assos/Behramkale, a picturesque coastal village. There are several decent beaches, but the town is usually, and appropriately, a transit hub to Lesbos. The best local accommodation is the tiny **CHALET CHOPIN PENSION**, *Tel. 266 396 1044, Fax 266 396 0697*, but it has only four rooms, and they're much in demand.

The area's best luxury hotel is south of town, the **GRAND HOTEL TEMIZEL**, *Sarmisaklı Sahil Boyu, Ayvalık, Tel. 266 324 2002, Fax 266 324 1274*. Ayvalik's otogar is two kilometers north of town, and the Lesbos ferry departs from slightly south of town.

## BOLU

**KORU HOTEL**, *Ömerler Köyü, Bakirli Mevkii P.K. No. 10, Bolu, Tel. 374 215 2528, Fax 374 215 3850*, is on the main road, which, come the (potential) 1997 opening of the new superhighway, will be the old main road and more peaceful for the demotion. This is an appropriately alpine/Stratford on Avon looking hotel, excellent for spending a few days hiking in the forests and lakes nearby.

## ÇAVDARHISAR/AIZANOI

Few people make it to **Aizanoi**, where one of the best preserved temples in Asia Minor still stands. The Temple of Zeus here is as complete an Ionic Temple as you are likely to find. It is built above an underground shrine, which was appropriated by Zeus when the temple was built in the second century A.D. Cybele was originally worshipped here.

**Kütahya** is the nearest major town, 60 kilometers northeast, and if you get a dolmuş to the **Çavdarhisar intersection** the ruins are just a short hike. Dolmuş pass back and forth between Kütahya and Uşak occasionally throughout the day.

## ERZURUM

Erzurum has to be considered the official crossroads of east and west, the fortified site where western empires have fought off invasions and launched their own. Erzurum's elevation (6,300 feet) and location in the center of the Anatolian plain subject it to extreme cold in winter, but the town is a fascinating mishmash of beautiful mosques and old fortifications – especially impressive is the **Çifte Minare Medresse**.

Most lodging is near the train station. The **ORAL HOTEL**, *Terminal Caddesi No. 3, Erzurum, Tel.* 442 218 9740, *Fax 442 218 9749*, is a reliable three star hotel, and the area's best is the wintertime **PALANDÖKEN DEDEMAN**, *Palandöken Dagı PK 115, Erzurum, Tel.* 442 316 2414, *Fax 442 316 3607*, 15 kilometers out of town at the country's best ski mountain, **Palandöken**.

## GÖÇEK

Göçek is a popular marina at the head of a pretty bay. The town is small, supported largely by the people that stop in to stock up on food and drink. A relaxed town with a strange schizophrenic quality owing to the fact it is not a resort town, but yachties spend time here. The local class act is the newly opened **DENIZ HOTEL**, *Tel.* 252 645 1902, *Fax 252 645 1903*; $70, offering CNN, NBC, clean, well-appointed rooms, and a cafe out the back door that is on Göçek's pretty harbor.

On a budget? **SARIOĞLU PANSIYON**, *Iskele Mah., Tel.* 252 645 1875, is the best of the cheaper places.

## GERZE

Our notes remark that Gerze would be a "nice place to hide." Some good beaches, particularly the one on the west side of town. The **ERMIŞ OTEL**, *Tel.* 368 718 1540, in the middle of town is spacious and peaceful, with a largely Turkish crowd taking advantage of the local beaches.

## KASTAMONU

If you want to see how a man famed for sacking fortresses built them himself, you should take the time to look around Tamurlane's **Kastamonu fortress** (1403). Tamurlane razed the original structure (and slew those inside) and had a new structure built.

## KIZKALESI

The beautiful island castle is just offshore of the CLUB BARBAROSSA HOTEL, *Kızkalesi Erdemli, Kızkalesi, Tel. 324 523 2364, Fax 324 523 2090*, named for the great German conqueror who drowned in a stream nearby. The Barbarossa's satellite television, pool, and beach are yours for $80 for a double.

## LABRANDA

**Labranda** was the Carians' holy city, and the site of a **Temple of Zeus**. The city was once connected to **Milas**, 12 kilometers south, by a Sacred Way, but the current road is in bad shape. The temple terrace is cleared and pieces of columns suggest the outline of the former colonnade. The city looks out over the valley toward Milas below, and is the ideal place to get away from crowds.

The ruin is largely intact, with impressive sarcophagi still in place in the necropolis. From Milas follow the signs toward Labranda, near Türbe village, perhaps named for the burial chambers at the site.

## MERSIN

People come to **Mersin** to make the crossing to The Turkish Republic of Northern Cyprus; you didn't fly from North America to stay here. If you do, however, the best hotel in town is the **MERSIN HILTON SA**, *Adnan Menderes Bulv., Mersin, Tel. 324 326 5000, Fax 324 326 5050*, and a good, fairly cheap hotel is the **HOTEL GÖKHAN**, *Mersin, Tel. 324 231 6256*.

The **tourism information** office is in the city center, *Ismet Inönü Bulv. No. 5/2, Liman Girişi, Tel. 324 238 3270*. Ferries depart for Northern Cyprus at 10 p.m. on Mondays, Wednesdays and Fridays.

## MILAS

**Milas** was long the capital of the Caria, but its ruins are in poor condition. The most interesting site is the atop the original settlement, at **Peçin Kale** (Beçin), visible from the road just south of Milas. Peçin Kale is a flat topped mesa that was populated in archaic times owing to its natural defenses.

As Milas grew it shifted onto the valley floor, but Turkish tribes resettling the area again saw the advantages of Peçin Kale, building a fortress there. The mesa is reached from Milas, following the road toward Ören and the Ceramos ruins 48 kilometers distant on the Gökova Bay. Peçin Kale is just five kilometers from Milas.

# ORDU

The **BELDE HOTEL**, *Kirazlimanı Mah., Ordu, Tel. 452 214 3987, Fax 452 214 9338, Rooms: 64. Double: $50,* is one of the best full-service hotels on the Black Sea coast. Ordu is convenient to several beaches (**Çaka** and **Efirli**), but it is not especially close to any historical sights. The ancient name of the settlement is Cotyra, and one the city's distinctive feature is the beautifully restored Greek Orthodox cathedral just to the west of the town center. Xenophon's 10,000 considered stopping here and founding a city, they were so fond of the area.

# PEÇIN KALE

Just south of Milas, this is one of the most compelling ruin-sites in Turkey. **Peçin Kale** was built atop a tall, imposing mesa. In Herodotus' day there was a substantial Temple of Zeus located here – and he should know, having come from Helicarnas just on the coast.

# SAFRANBOLU

A pretty, quiet town frequented by people from Ankara eager to get away from it all. **Safronbolu** boasts several outstanding pensions and hotels, including the **TAHSIN BEY & PAŞA KONAKLARI,** *Çeşme Mah. Hükümet Sok. No. 50, Tel. 372 712 2014, Fax 372 712 6062,* and the **HAVUZLU KONAĞI,** *Tel. 372 721 2883, Fax 372 72 0530.* The latter is a beautiful Ottoman-era house, secure in its small walled compound. It has been beautifully restored by the Turkish Touring and Automobile Association.

# SAGALASSUS

Alexander passed through **Sagalassus**, too, welcomed by the war-like Pisidians as an ally against the Persians. Excavations by the Catholic University of Louvain have turned up some excellent mosaics and temples on the terraces of Sagalassus. This is one of Turkey's most beautiful ruins.

# SAMSUN

An unappealing transit hub on the Black Sea. This fairly large industrial center has several large hotels, including the four star **BÜYÜK SAMSUN OTEL,** *Atatürk Bulvarı No. 629, Samsun, Tel. 362 435 8018, Fax 362 431 0740,* and the cheaper **YAFEYA OTEL,** *Cumhuriet Meydanı, Tel. 362 431 1531, Fax 362 431 1135.* The otogar is to the east of town.

If you must spend time here, stop in at the museum. For more on Samsun, contact the **tourism information,** *Tel. 362 435 2887.*

## SIDE

Side's impressive ruins add a little cachet to what is otherwise an overburdened holiday town. The town winds out along the former citadel peninsula, and its residents have created a big open air market. In town you'll find good inexpensive accommodations at **PETTINO PANSIYON** just off the main road in town. Outside of town you'll love Emperyal's **SEVENSEAS RESORT & CASINO**, *Titreyengöl Mevkii, Manavgat, Tel. 242 456 9000, Fax 242 756 9007*, provided you can afford $140 per night.

Side's **tourism office**, *Tel. 242 753 1265*, is ridiculously far outside town and occasionally beset by an incredible stench, but you can always call them.

## TERME

Presumably near the ancient city of Themistikos on the Thermodon River. **Terme** has a single hotel just a block from the otogar, and is rarely visited. The city's greatest claim to fame is its association with the legendary city of the Amazons, of which there is today no trace. The **Thermodon** (now Terme Çayı) has completely choked the former site of Themistikos with soil, creating a beautiful, lush plain and several small lakes. Beneath one of these shallow lakes, Akgöl, local residents say buildings have been spotted.

## YALOVA

The healing powers of **Yalova/Termal's hot springs** are explained thusly in one of the hotel brochures "with its radioactivity, semi-dead cells are reactivated." If you can bear up to that, Termal is a fairly quick ferry ride from İstanbul, 15 kilometers from the Yalova ferry stop.

The **TURBAN YALOVA HOTEL**, *Yalova, Tel. 226 675 7400, Fax 226 675 7413; Double: $58*, is recommended, an old standby at the area, just uphill from the extensive thermal bath.

# 23. RECOMMENDED READING

If you're interested in Turkey's history and the many ruins dotting the landscape, you'll probably be interested in some of these books. This bibliography is supplemental to various books we've mentioned throughout the text.

Gibbon, Edward, *The Decline and Fall of the Roman Empire*. London, 1910

Gibbons, Herbert Adams, *The Foundation of the Ottoman Empire*. Oxford, 1916

Plutarch, *Selected Lives and Other Essays*. Roslyn, N.Y., 1951

Guillaume, Alfred, *Islam*.New York, 1967

Procopius, *The Secret History* (trans. G.A. Williamson). London, 1966

Joinville & Villehardouin,*Chronicles of the Crusades*.Baltimore, 1963

Sewell, Brian, *South From Ephesus*. London, 1988

Ostrogorsky, George, *History of the Byzantine State*. New Brunswick, New Jersey, 1969

Miller, John, (Ed.), *İstanbul, Tales of the City*. San Francisco, 1995

Vasiliev, A. A, *History of the Byzantine Empire* (two volumes). Madison, Wisconsin, 1952; Madison, Wisconsin, 1958

Melville, Herman,*A Visit to Europe and the Levant*. New York, 1857

Arrian, *The Campaigns of Alexander* (trans. Aubrey de Selincourt). Middlesex, 1958

Sumner-Boyd, Hilary, and Freely, John, *Strolling Through İstanbul, A Guide to the City*. London, 1972

Harrel, Betsy, *Mini Tours, Book II*. İstanbul, 1978

Durant, Will, *The Story of Civilization*. New York, 1935

Appollonius, *The Voyage of Argo* (trans. E.V. Rieu). Middlesex, 1971

Akurgal, Ekrem, *Ancient Civilizations and Ruins of Turkey*. Ankara, 1983

Stoneman, Richard, *A Traveler's History of Turkey*. New York, 1993

Şen, Ömer, *Sümela: Monastery in the Clouds.* Trabzon, 1994

Freely, John, *The Bosphorous.* İstanbul, 1993

Yazici, Nuri, *Terme Tarihi.* Samsun, 1982

Kranzler, Jerry and Kranzler, Carolyn, *On the Trail of Ulysses.* İstanbul, 1989

Erim, Kenan, *Aphrodisias, City of Venus Aphrodite.* London, 1986

Freely, John, *Classical Turkey.* London, 1990

Sunay, Melisa, *Executives Handbook Turkey Almanac 1996.* İstanbul, 1995

Straube, Hanne, *Türkei.* Hamburg, 1990

Bulutoğlu, Halim, *Hotel Guide 1996.* İstanbul, 1995

Spiro Kostof, *Caves of God.* Oxford Press

Guillaume de Jerphanion, *Une Nouvelle Province de l'Art Byzantin.*

# INDEX

## THINGS CHANGE!
*Phone numbers, prices, addresses, quality of food, etc, all change. If you come across any new information, we'd appreciate hearing from you. No item is too small! Write us at:*
**Turkey Guide**
*Open Road Publishing, P.O. Box 20226*
*Columbus Circle Station, New York, NY 10023*

# TRAVEL NOTES

# TRAVEL NOTES